CANALETTO *and* GUARDI

VIEWS OF VENICE AT THE WALLACE COLLECTION

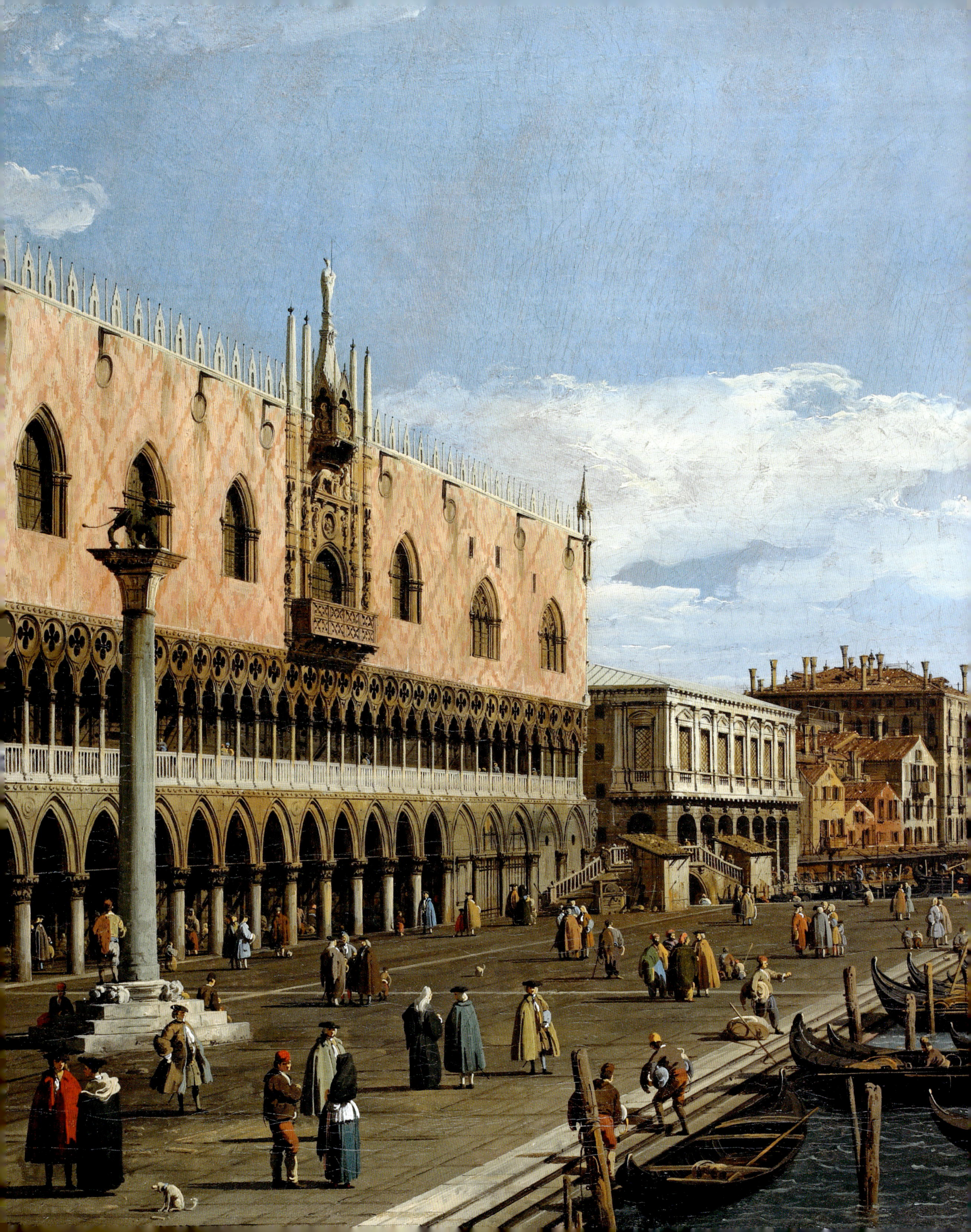

CANALETTO *and* GUARDI

VIEWS OF VENICE AT THE WALLACE COLLECTION

Lelia Packer
Charles Beddington

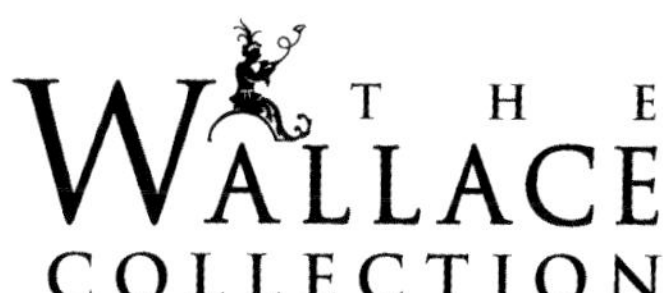

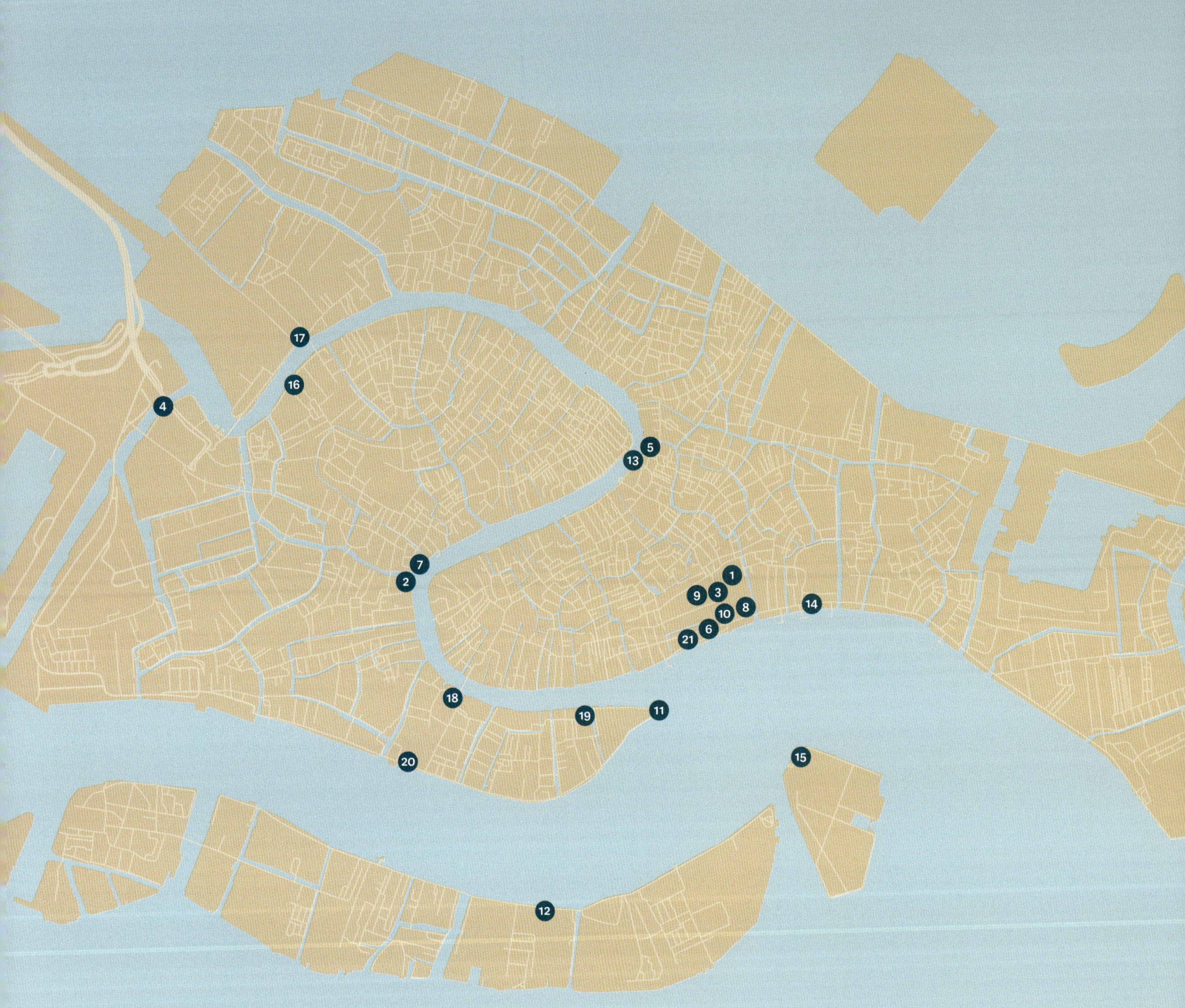

MAP OF VENICE WITH A KEY TO LOCATIONS

1. Basilica di San Marco
2. Ca' Foscari
3. Campanile di San Marco
4. Canale di Santa Chiara
5. Fondaco dei Tedeschi
6. Libreria Sansoviniana (Library of San Marco)
7. Palazzo Balbi
8. Palazzo Ducale (Doge's Palace)
9. Piazza San Marco
10. Piazzetta di San Marco
11. Punta della Dogana (Customs House Point)
12. Redentore
13. Rialto Bridge
14. Riva degli Schiavoni
15. San Giorgio Maggiore
16. San Simeone Piccolo
17. Santa Maria degli Scalzi
18. Santa Maria della Carità
19. Santa Maria della Salute
20. Zattere
21. Zecca (Mint)

CONTENTS

DIRECTOR'S FOREWORD

During his long and prolific career, Giovanni Antonio Canal, known as Canaletto, portrayed Venice's famous sites in his paintings so effectively and convincingly that he shaped the collective imagination of the city for decades to come. The works by Canaletto and his near-contemporary Francesco Guardi allow us to travel back to eighteenth-century Venice, immersing ourselves in this unique and special city that continues to draw countless visitors to this day. Venice was Canaletto's greatest preoccupation and constant source of inspiration to the extent that he created an entirely new artistic genre, the *veduta*, or topographical view, around it.

The Wallace Collection possesses one of the most renowned *vedute* collections in this country. Over the course of the twentieth century, this part of the collection was overlooked and the clear blue skies and aquamarine waters for which Canaletto is famed grew murky and yellowed. My judicious predecessor, Dr Christoph Vogtherr, embarked on a large-scale conservation and research project, in partnership with the Hamilton Kerr Institute (HKI), to restore the original beauty of these paintings. When I arrived at the Wallace Collection in late 2016, the project had recently begun. I want particularly to thank Dr Lucy Davis for spearheading it in its initial stages, and Dr Lelia Packer, who took over the project in 2017 and has since led it to its completion.

It has been a pleasure to work with distinguished Canaletto expert Charles Beddington. I thank him for his thoughtful contributions to this book, especially on the paintings by artists working in Canaletto's circle for which he has provided several exciting new attributions.

Over the past eight years, each one of our magnificent *vedute* has been restored along with its frame, and technical analysis has been undertaken to better understand the artists' working methods by our talented colleagues at the HKI, whom I sincerely thank.

Such an ambitious, multi-year project could not have been possible without a number of generous supporters to whom I am greatly indebted. The Bank of America Art Conservation Project was first to support us with a major grant, followed by individuals, trusts and organisations who adopted *vedute* to conserve over the years. This publication was made possible thanks to the generosity of David and Molly Lowell Borthwick, the Gladys Krieble Delmas Foundation, ARTscapades, the McCorquodale Charitable Trust and other enthusiastic art lovers.

In the late nineteenth century, Sir Richard Wallace hung the paintings together in what is today the Sixteenth-Century Gallery on the ground floor, transporting his visitors from foggy London to majestic Venice. This book, the first in-depth catalogue of the Wallace Collection *vedute*, may inspire you to travel to Venice to visit the beautiful and timeless sites portrayed in Canaletto's pictures. I hope it will also bring you (back) to the Wallace Collection to experience these magnificent paintings first-hand.

Dr Xavier Bray, Director, The Wallace Collection

SUPPORTERS

This publication was made possible thanks to the generosity of the following supporters:

David and Molly Lowell Borthwick
The Gladys Krieble Delmas Foundation
ARTscapades
McCorquodale Charitable Trust
Patrick K.F. Donlea
Excel Fund

We are grateful to all those who made the conservation project possible:

Bank of America Art Conservation Project
Gifts in honour of Sir António Horta-Osório
Charles Hayward Foundation
Cecilia Versteegh
Nick and Debbie Barton
Sir Bruce Bossom, Bt
Suzannah Jacobs in memory of her grandparents, Sandra and
    Malcolm Jacobs
Timothy and Ellen Schroder
The European Friends
Suzie and David Newman
McCorquodale Charitable Trust
The Radcliffe Trust
Paul Rivlin
Thomas and Elsebeth Gatacre
Jessica Pulay in memory of Juliet Garmoyle, Serena Prest and
    Kate Wiseman
The Clare McKeon Charitable Trust
Woodmansterne Art Conservation Awards 2019
The John S. Cohen Foundation
Excel Fund
The Circles of Art
Art Happens, Art Fund's supported crowdfunding platform

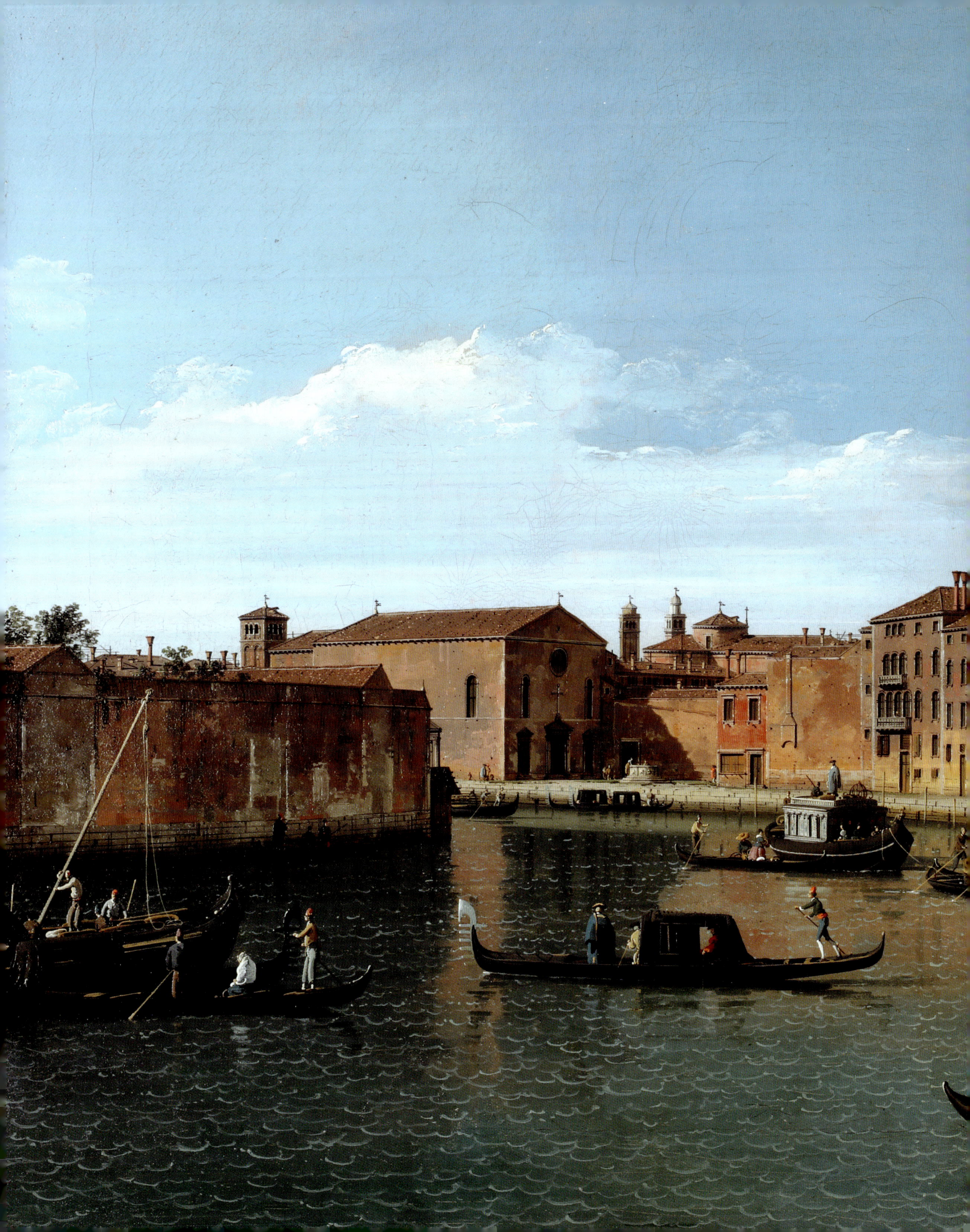

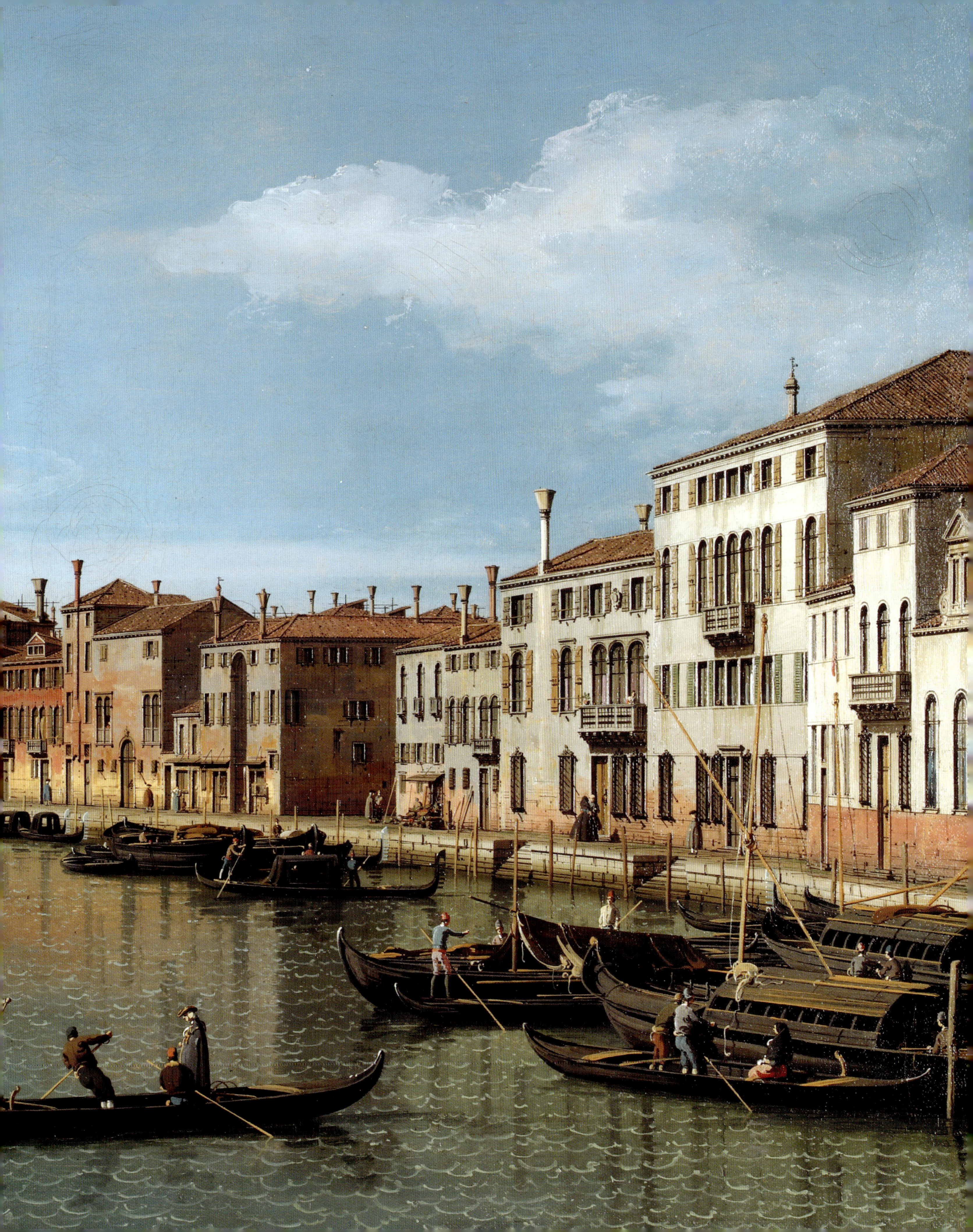

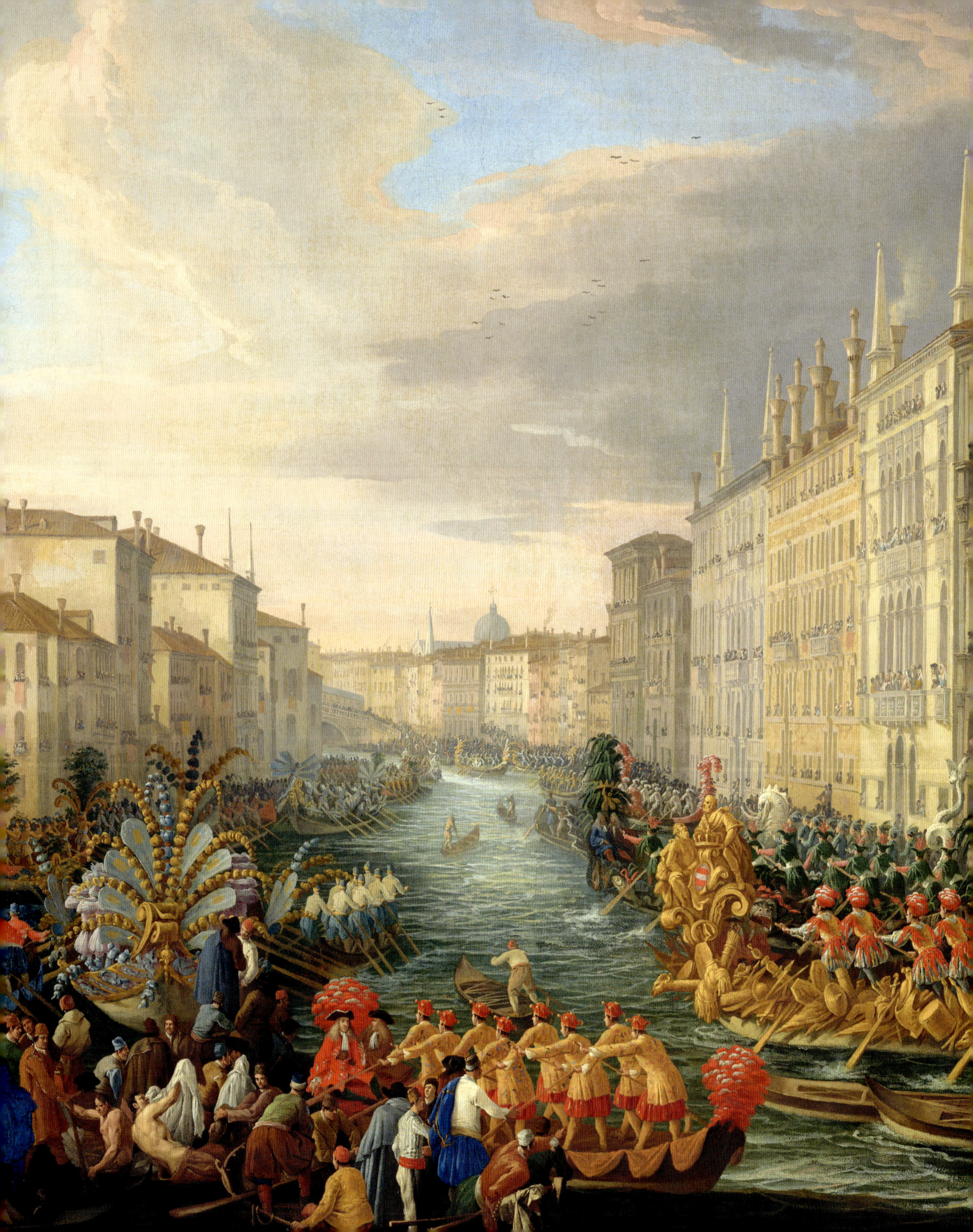

1 CANALETTO, GUARDI AND VENETIAN VIEW PAINTING IN THE EIGHTEENTH CENTURY

Lelia Packer

Topographical view paintings, or *vedute*, are most often associated with eighteenth-century Venice and with the painter Giovanni Antonio Canal (1697–1768), better known as Canaletto. During this period, the *veduta* became an artistic genre in its own right. Canaletto and his followers shaped the collective imagination of Venice for generations to come. Here, the unique set of circumstances that contributed to Venice becoming such an attractive subject of representation at this particular moment in time is explored. Canaletto and his circle, Francesco Guardi (1712–1793) and the public that enjoyed their art are also introduced.

The Rise and Fall of the Venetian Republic

Venice's unique history, government and setting were instrumental to its allure. Founded in 421 AD as the first republic of the new Christian era, Venice was initially subject to the authority of Byzantium, but, in time, asserted its independence. In 1177 the Venetian Doge Sebastiano Ziani mediated peace between Pope Alexander III and Holy Roman Emperor Frederick Barbarossa in what became known as the Peace of Venice (fig. 1). From then on, the Republic of Venice became a strong sovereign state, unconquered until it fell to Napoleon Bonaparte in 1797.

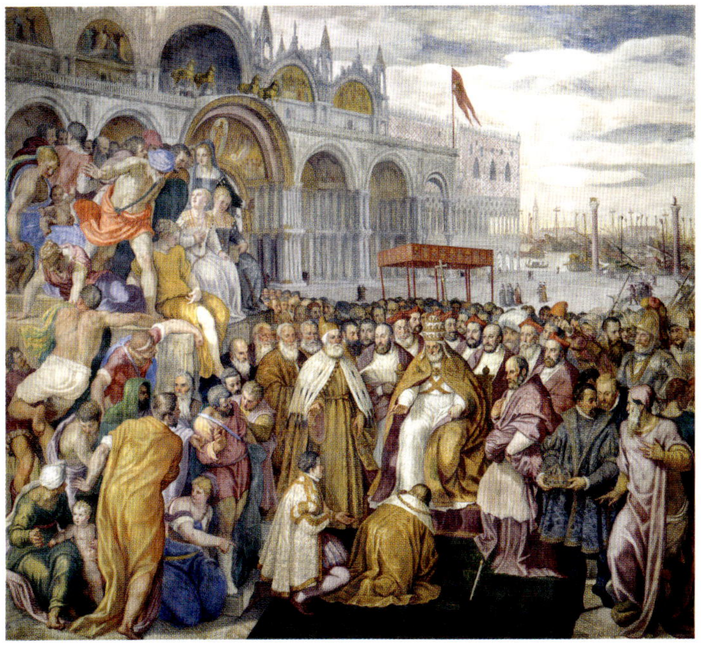

Fig. 1. Giuseppe Salviati (1520–1575), *Frederick Barbarossa Asking Forgiveness from Pope Alexander III*, c.1563, fresco, Sala Regia, Vatican Palace, Rome

OPPOSITE:
Detail of fig. 9

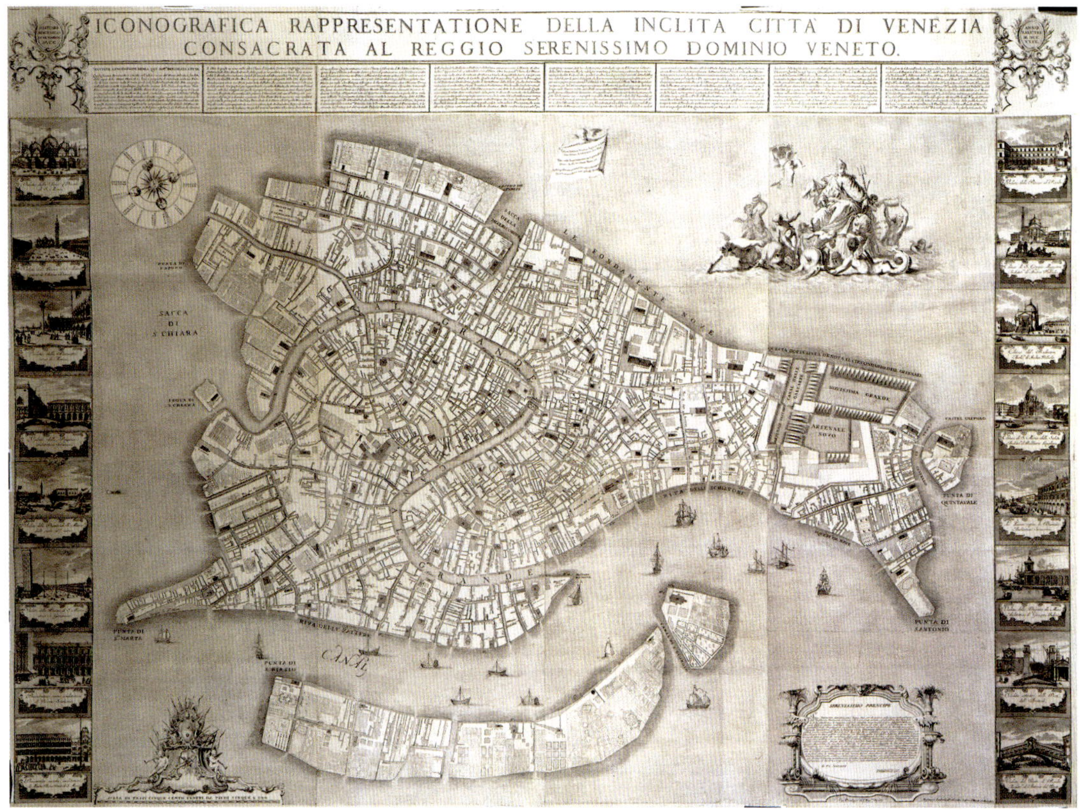

LEFT:
Fig. 2. Ludovico Ughi (active *c.*1700–50), *Iconografica rappresentatione della inclita città di Venezia*, 1729, engraving and etching, 148 × 203 cm

OPPOSITE, ABOVE:
Fig. 3. Marco Ricci (1676–1730), *Nicola Grimaldi and Lucia Facchinelli*, 1728, pen and brown ink over black lead, 18.2 × 24.4 cm, Royal Collection (RCIN 907288)

OPPOSITE, BELOW:
Fig. 4. Francesco Tironi (active in the last quarter of the eighteenth century), *The Bacino di San Marco on Ascension Day with the Bucintoro Departing for the Lido*, after *c.*1770, 52.8 × 81.3 cm, The Wallace Collection, London (P513)

Venice's unusual setting as a group of offshore islands assured its independence for centuries (fig. 2). It was governed by a small number of nobles through a tripartite system consisting of a Great Council, a Senate and a Doge. This harmonious, democratic, oligarchic and monarchic structure, institutionalised in an exemplary constitution, ensured the stability of power through a system of checks and balances. The Republic's exceptional government secured its sovereignty and made it a paragon of justice in the eyes of the world.[1] As early as 1364, the renowned Italian humanist and poet Petrarch described Venice as the 'home of liberty, peace and justice'.[2] By the eighteenth century, the British Whig nobility highly admired Venice's system of government.

With its strategic position between East and West, Venice was a centre of maritime trade. Centuries of mercantile trade in exotic Eastern goods such as velvet, silk and spices brought the city abundant prosperity. During the sixteenth century, Venice's great maritime power extended its empire from the northern Italian *terraferma* along the Adriatic coastline, to embrace Corfu, Crete and Cyprus.

For centuries, Venice was wealthy, powerful and cosmopolitan, and constituted an exemplar of the ideally formed, sovereign state governed by the rule of law. By the start of the eighteenth century, however, just as painters began to celebrate the beauty and splendour of the city in their art, the Venetian state was in decline and the Republic's economic powers were waning. Napoleon's occupation of Venice in 1797 brought the curtain down on the Republic, resulting in the abdication of the last Doge, Ludovico Manin (1725–1802), and Venice becoming an appendage of the Austro-Hungarian empire.

The Allure of Venice in the Eighteenth Century

During the eighteenth century, with its empire mostly lost and its political and commercial powers in decline, Venice – often called 'La Serenissima' (the most serene republic) – became the stage for a burgeoning tourist industry. The city's unique setting on the sea, ostensibly rising miraculously out of the waters of the lagoon, made it a spectacular sight to behold (as it still is today), especially upon first glimpse when arriving by boat: 'all the way we admired to see such a stately City lying as it were at Anchor, in the midst of the Sea; and standing still while everything else floats'.[3]

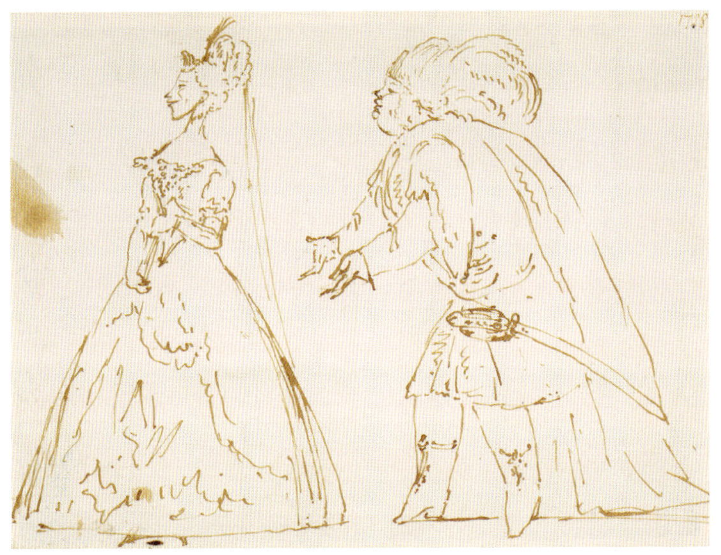

Visitors admired Venice's exceptional architecture – its impressive *palazzi*, magnificent churches, countless *campanili* (bell towers) and bridges – seemingly floating above the labyrinth of narrow canals. The city's numerous theatres, opera houses, concert halls and conservatories made it a centre of music and culture (fig. 3). Printmaking reached its apogee in the eighteenth century, with Venice becoming a publishing capital. Venice's rich Renaissance artistic heritage also held great allure, with paintings by Giovanni Bellini, Titian, Tintoretto and Veronese accessible throughout the city.

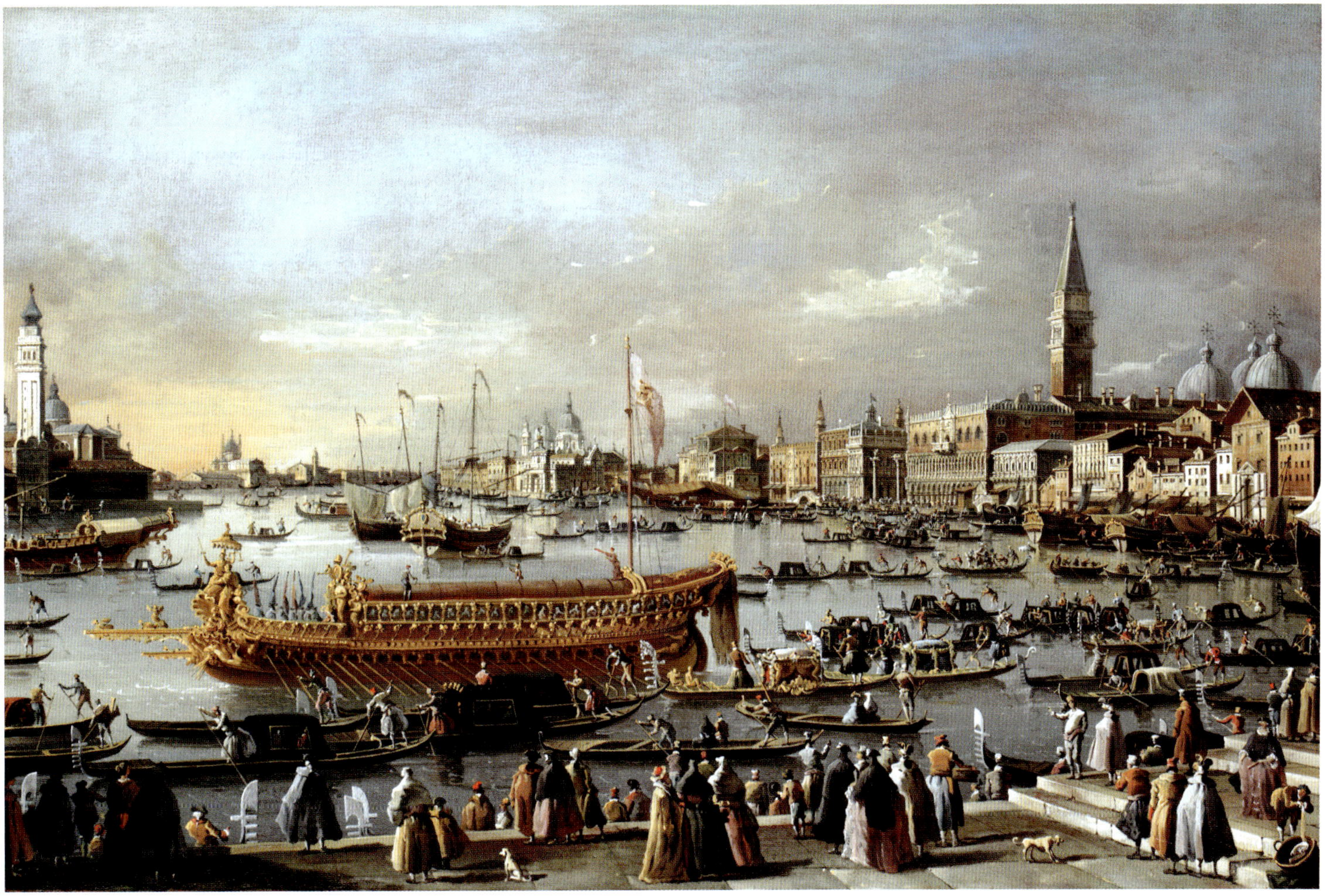

Furthermore, Venice's numerous public spectacles were enduringly fascinating for visitors. Among the annual festivals, the foremost was Ascension Day on 25 March, a magnificent celebration of Venice's symbolic marriage to the sea and its domination over the Adriatic (cat. 17). Grand ceremonies that took over the city for days were organised to honour foreign ambassadors and important visitors.[4] Thirty-six annual ducal processions meant that a parade took place, on average, three times per month. Carnival, which lasted from the Feast of Saint Stephen on 26 December to the start of Lent in spring, held immense appeal due to the countless pageants, masked balls, outdoor plays and *tableaux vivants* organised during this period. Visitors partook in Carnival alongside locals by dressing up in elaborate costumes as well as the traditional *bauta*, consisting of a white mask, veil and tricorn (fig. 5). Their anonymity added a sense of freedom to their experience abroad.

Venice was not only a spectacle for the eyes and ears, but engaged other senses as well. The Republic's tolerant leanings meant that in addition to its two hundred or so cafés and restaurants, it also boasted ample casinos and brothels. Gambling and prostitution, considered licentious behaviours elsewhere, were here commonplace, expected and accepted, as was homosexuality. Venice gained a reputation as the *città galante* (libertine city) where the pursuit of pleasure predominated. Despite this apparent libertinism, Venetian patricians were conservative and interacted little with foreign visitors. Some feared that state secrets would be betrayed if they did so.[5] More so than elsewhere, religious toleration was widely practised in Venice, with Jews, Muslims and Christians coexisting peacefully. For all this, and much more, visitors described Venice as 'one of the fairest cities in Europe', as indeed they still do.[6]

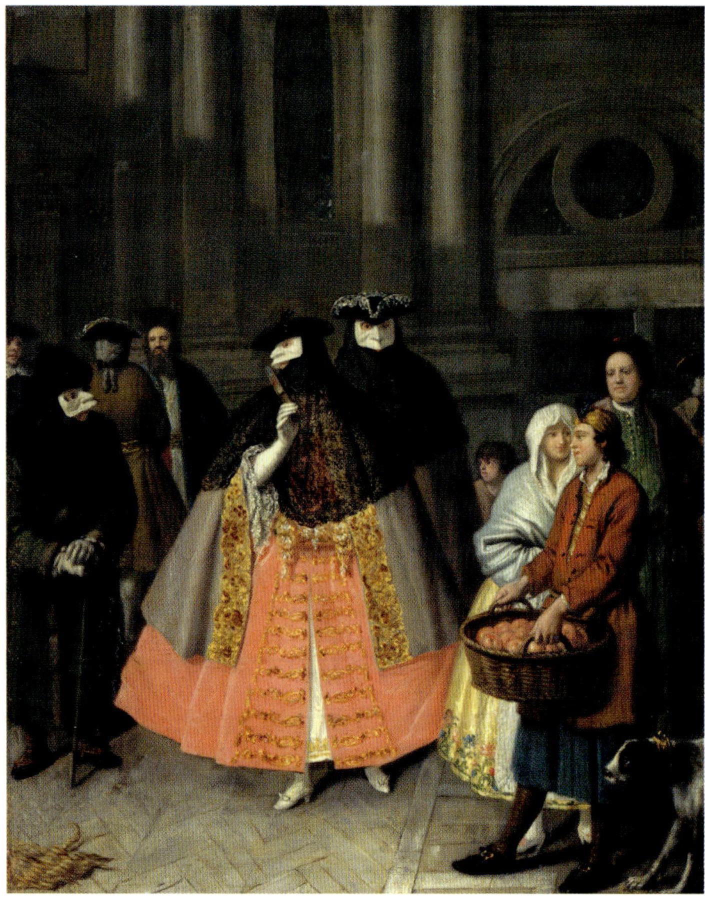

Fig. 5. Pietro Longhi (1701–1785), *Conversation with Masks*, *c.*1750–60, oil on canvas, 162 × 51 cm, Ca' Rezzonico, Venice (inv. 1313)

The Grand Tour

The majority of tourists travelling to Venice in the eighteenth century were undertaking the fashionable Grand Tour, a period of extensive European travel by upper-class young gentlemen as a means of completing their classical education.[7] Participants were mostly British, but also Irish, French, German and Scandinavian. The Grand Tour phenomenon lasted from about 1690 to 1820 and was cosmopolitan. The core of the Tour was in Italy, with stops in Florence, Venice, Naples and Rome, for the latter two due to the lure of antiquity. A visit to Rome was incomplete without a portrait by Pompeo Batoni (1708–1787), which tourists proudly brought home to hang in their town or country houses as symbols of their newly affirmed status and accomplishments (fig. 6).[8] Less grandiose alternatives were provided in Venice by the celebrated pastel portraitist Rosalba Carriera (1673–1757).

The Grand Tour was considered essential for the formation of the complete gentleman. This British patrician male rite of passage from boyhood to manhood was meant to strengthen the constitution and equip young men with independence, confidence and self-reliance, even though a tutor, or bear-leader, accompanied them throughout. Through exposure to different languages, cultures and customs, the young British gentleman would better appreciate his home and reaffirm his superior British identity.[9] As the eighteenth century progressed, travellers diversified to include women, older men and children.

Despite its merits, a general ambivalence pervaded the Tour due to the numerous temptations on offer. In Venice, young men learnt not only about politics, economics and art, but also about sexuality, which had the potential to corrupt. Contemporary accounts describe Venice's notorious courtesans, infamous for their beauty, skill and availability: '[they] dress in the gayest of colours, with their breasts open, and their faces all bedaubed with paint, standing by dozens at the doors and windows to invite their Customers'.[10] Some were anxious about

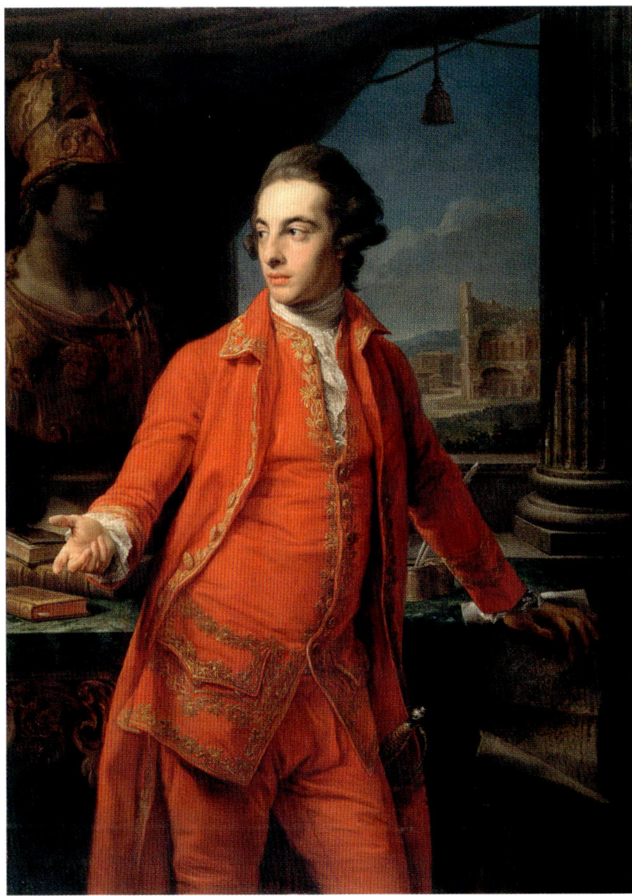

Fig. 6. Pompeo Batoni (1708–1787), *Sir Gregory Page-Turner*, 1768, oil on canvas, 134.5 × 99.5 cm, Manchester Art Gallery (inv. 1976.79)

importing venereal diseases into England from encounters with courtesans: 'Others desire to go to Italy, only because … there are fine courtesans in Venice … And thus by a false aiming of breeding abroad, they return with those diseases which hinder them from breeding at home.'[11]

These fears especially haunted mothers, such as the Countess of Chichester, who commented that her son, Thomas Pelham, could do without visiting Venice because the city could 'be well conceived from a good Canaletti'.[12] For the Countess, and others, a good *veduta* by Canaletto was a much safer option than an actual visit to Venice.

Venice offered curious and unsettling sights and experiences. Many were fascinated, but others felt uncomfortable and were eager to leave after only one or two weeks. In his *Voyage of Italy* (1670), Richard Lassels, a British Catholic priest living in Rome who apparently saw all of Venice in one month, asserted that Venice is 'a fine town for a fortnight but not to dwell in always'.[13]

Lassels described Venice's 'stinking channels' that emanated insufferable odours, and the 'scarcity of Earth even to bury the Dead in'.[14] Lassels's text both shaped and conditioned later reactions to the Grand Tour and, in turn, to Venice itself. Moreover, the term 'Grand Tour' was first used in the 1671 French translation of this text.

At the end of the eighteenth century, the traumas of the Napoleonic Wars contributed to the demise of the Grand Tour. The invention of steam travel and the development of package tourism for the middle classes meant that the Tour lost its exclusivity and therefore its *raison d'être*.[15]

The Rise of View Painting

For the wealthier tourist, no trip to Venice was complete without placing an order for one or more *vedute* as souvenirs. *Vedute* displayed the city's glorious sites and showed off one's travels. In fact, view paintings were produced for – mainly British – tourists or, in two notable cases, foreign residents.[16] With Venice on their doorstep, Venetians had no interest in view paintings, which explains their near absence from Venice today.[17]

Although *vedutismo* is a specifically eighteenth-century phenomenon, it is rooted in a longer tradition of topographical art in Venice. City maps and prints of Venetian edifices and costumes had been in circulation since the sixteenth century.[18] With the rise of the Grand Tour and the influx of visitors to Venice at the turn of the eighteenth century, a sophisticated market was cultivated for the painted *veduta*. Its production spanned the eighteenth century, with the earliest dated example being from 1697 and the latest from the 1790s.[19] Never before and, arguably, never again was a city the subject of such sustained artistic representation.

In the earliest painted representations of Venice, the city served as a subsidiary backdrop to other subject matter. The most famous example is Gentile Bellini's massive *Procession in the Piazza San Marco*, which illustrates the Feast of the Holy Cross on 25 April 1444 (fig. 7).[20] On that day, a merchant from Brescia, visible in the right foreground, knelt before the relic of the Holy Cross being processed through the Piazza and prayed that his dying son be saved. Bellini employed multiple viewpoints and adjusted the architecture for aesthetic effect. For example, he set the Campanile back in order to provide a view of the Doge's Palace, which would otherwise have been obscured. Bellini thus created a precedent for putting

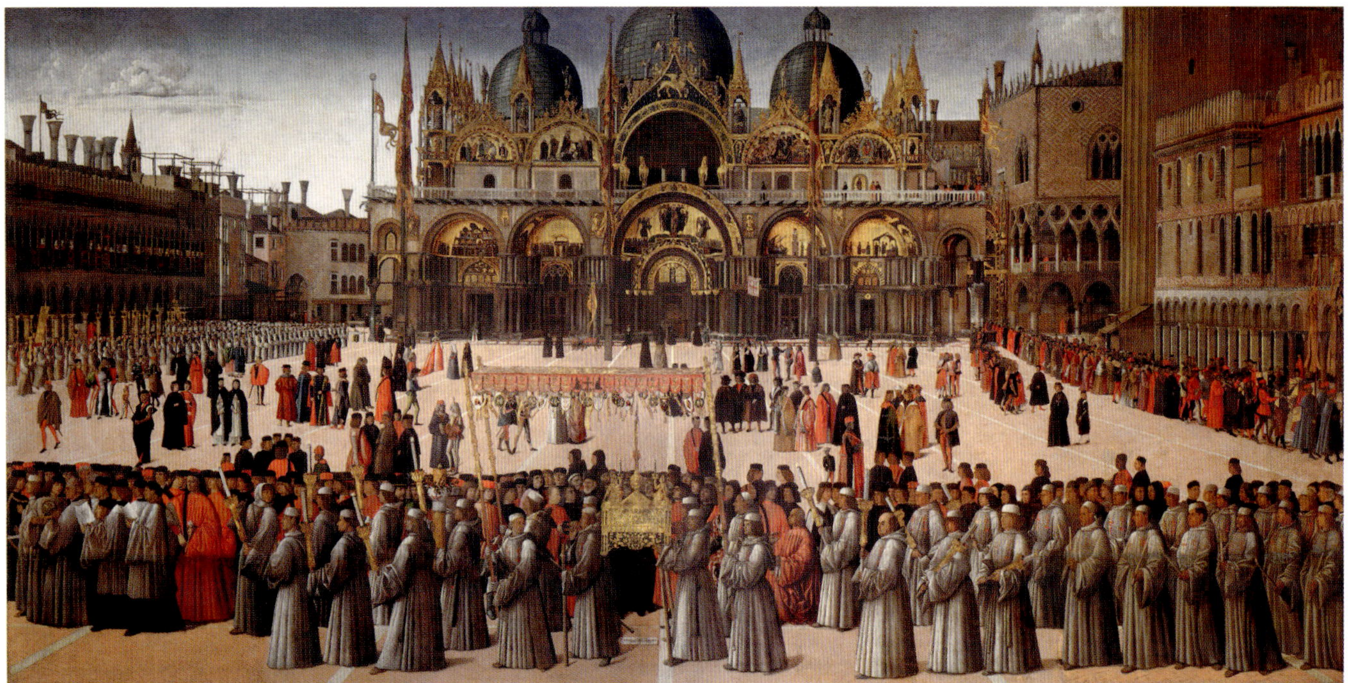

Fig. 7. Gentile Bellini (*c*.1435–1516),
Procession in the Piazza San Marco,
1496, oil on canvas, 367 × 745 cm,
Gallerie dell'Accademia, Venice (inv. 567)

composition before topographical accuracy, a key, recurring feature in the work of Canaletto and Guardi.

Apart from a few isolated earlier examples, view painting emerged as an independent genre during the eighteenth century, largely the creation of Gaspar van Wittel (1653–1736), known in Italy as Gaspare Vanvitelli.[21] Born and trained in the Netherlands, but based in Rome, Vanvitelli travelled to Venice in 1695. His trip resulted in about 40 views of the city, mainly of the Molo, the broad quay along the waterfront of the Piazzetta and the buildings flanking it (fig. 8). Taken from the Bacino di San Marco, Vanvitelli's view of the Molo became a standard prototype for views of that site, later adopted and replicated by Canaletto and his circle.[22] Like Bellini before him, and his successors after, Vanvitelli was not concerned with the exact representation of topography. Rather, his wide-angled, often panoramic views are characterised by their sharp focus throughout.

The major precursor to Canaletto among resident Venetians was Luca Carlevarijs (1663–1730). Originally from Udine, Carlevarijs was taken to Venice by his sister Cassandra in 1679. Lauded as 'the very founder of Venetian view painting', Carlevarijs excelled at depicting festivals and public ceremonies.[23] His most famous painting illustrates the *regatta*, or public rowing race,

organised to celebrate King Frederick IV of Denmark's visit to Venice in March 1709 (fig. 9). Another version of this work was widely disseminated in print and it became the standard composition for later *regatta* paintings.[24] Carlevarijs's depictions of official receptions and of the Piazza San Marco also became standard prototypes for later *vedutisti*.[25] In 1703 Carlevarijs published the first major set of engravings of Venetian buildings, *Le Fabriche, e vedute di Venetia*, with no fewer than 103 plates.

Canaletto (1697–1768)

Canaletto was the leading practitioner of the *veduta*, establishing view painting as a work of art. Building upon his predecessors, Canaletto popularised and transformed the *veduta* into something new and fresh, creating an enduring image of Venice for future generations. Canaletto was born on 28 October 1697 in Venice, in Corte Perin near the Rialto Bridge. The only certain likeness of him is a print showing him at the age of 38, inscribed 'Origine Civis Venetus' (fig. 10). Canaletto's family were *cittadini originari*, a class just below patrician, and he was evidently proud of his social standing.

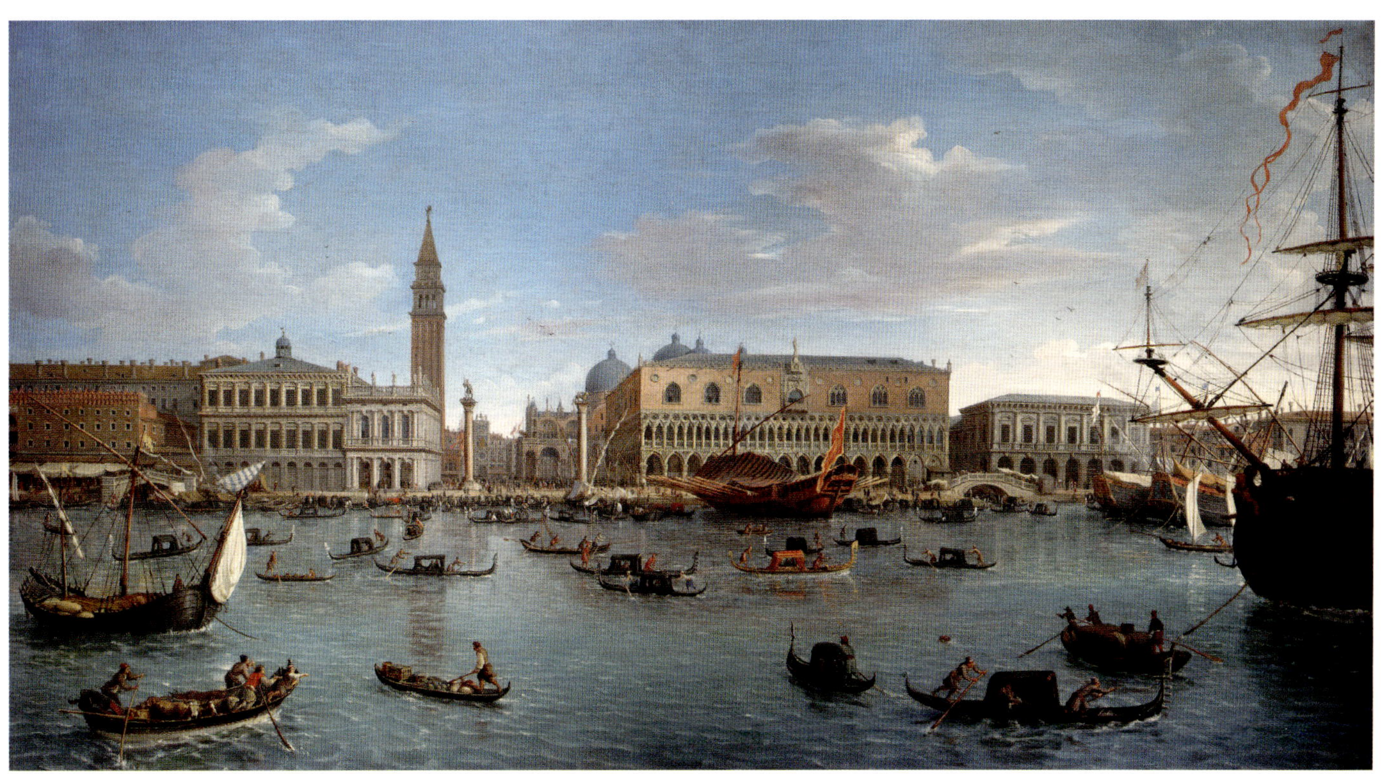

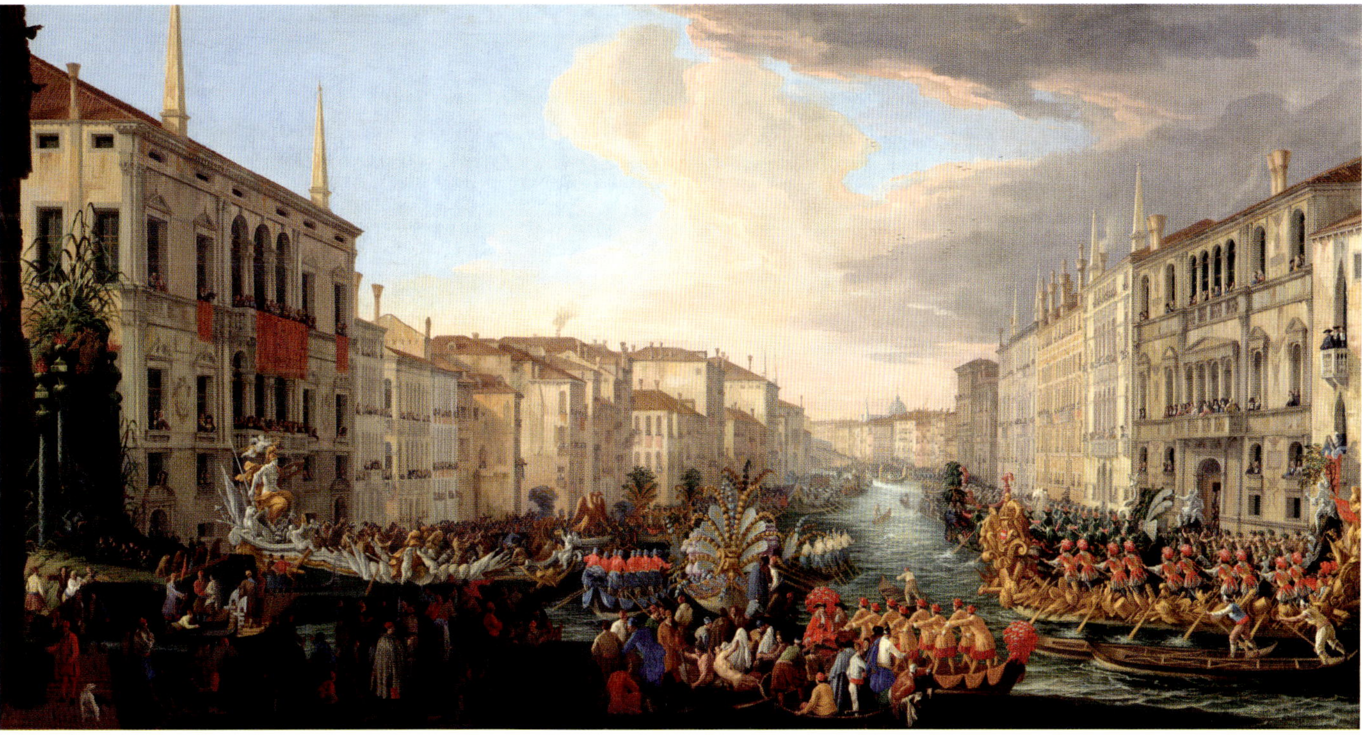

Fig. 8. Gaspare Vanvitelli (1653–1736),
View of Venice from the Island of San Giorgio,
1697, oil on canvas, 98 × 174 cm, Museo
Nacional del Prado, Madrid (inv. P000475)

Fig. 9. Luca Carlevarijs (1663–1730), *Regatta on
the Grand Canal in Honour of Frederick IV, King of
Denmark,* 1711, oil on canvas, 135.3 × 259.7 cm,
J. Paul Getty Museum, Los Angeles (inv. 86.PA.599)

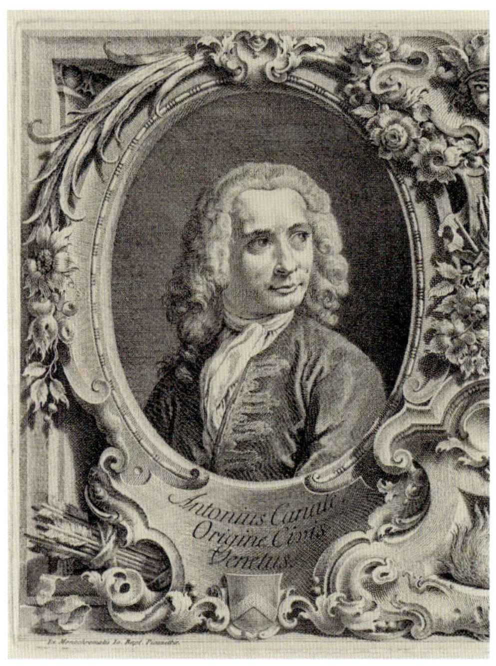

In one of the earliest biographies of the artist, the Parisian connoisseur Pierre-Jean Mariette (1694–1774) wrote that Canaletto first trained with his father, Bernardo Canal (1664?–1744), a theatrical-scene painter.[26] Mariette records that Canaletto accompanied his father to Rome in 1719 and, while there, turned to view painting. This sequence of events is corroborated by the historian Anton Maria Zanetti, who mentioned Canaletto's beautiful designs for the theatre from this period in his 1771 tome on Venetian painting.[27] Additionally, Canaletto and his father are credited as scene designers for two operas by Alessandro Scarlatti in a Roman libretto from 1720. Canaletto's early style is clearly indebted to his training in stage design.

Upon his return to Venice in 1720, Canaletto joined the Fraglia, or painters' guild, and began to sketch and paint his native city incessantly. Although he concentrated on central areas of touristic interest such as the Piazza San Marco,

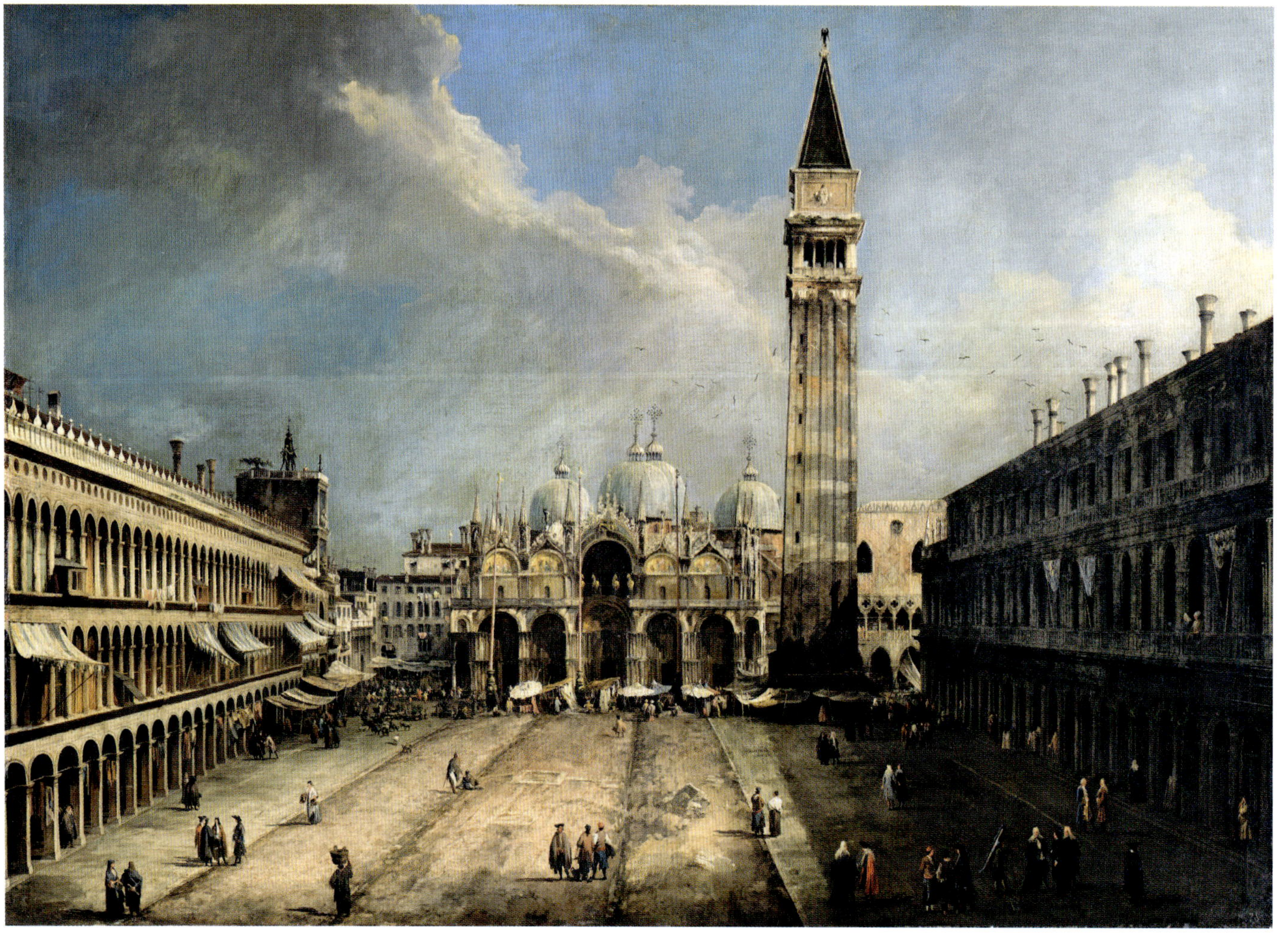

Venice's religious and civic centre, or the Rialto Bridge, the city's commercial hub, he also went further afield. Canaletto quickly surpassed Carlevarijs as Venice's foremost view painter. In 1725 the wealthy Lucchese textile merchant Stefano Conti was looking to expand his collection of Venetian paintings through his agent Alessandro Marchesini. In a now famous correspondence from July that year, Marchesini wrote to Conti that Canaletto's work was astounding all those in Venice who saw it and, although similar to Carlevarijs, 'you can see the sun shining in it!'[28] Canaletto's ability to capture natural effects of light – beyond anything achieved previously – had clearly caught the admiration of his contemporaries. In his early view of the Piazza San Marco, sunlight is intensely cast on the north side of the Piazza, with the south side set in strong shadow (fig. 11). In the same vein, Mariette considered Canaletto's work superior to that of Vanvitelli.[29]

By the late 1720s, Canaletto was successfully catering to a wealthy clientele. In a 1727 letter to Lord March, later 2nd Duke of Richmond, Owen McSwiney, an Irish impresario and art agent, wrote that Canaletto 'has more work than he can do, in any reasonable time'.[30] McSwiney criticised Canaletto and, in so doing, shed a rare glimpse on the latter's character: 'The fellow is whimsical and varies his prices every day: and he that has a mind that has any of his work, must not seem to be too fond of it, for he'll be ye worse treated for it, both in the price and the painting too.'[31] In a 1730 letter McSwiney further lamented on Canaletto's steep prices '[just] because he's in reputation people are glad to get anything at his own price'.[32]

Joseph Smith (c.1674–1770)

Joseph Smith, a merchant, dealer, collector, connoisseur and in the years 1744–60 British Consul in Venice, was in large part responsible for Canaletto's success.[33] Smith arrived in Venice around 1700 as a young man and remained there for the rest of his life. He met Canaletto in the early 1720s, soon after the latter began painting Venetian views, and was to become his greatest patron. Smith's imposing *palazzo* on the Grand Canal provided the perfect setting for his fast-growing *vedute* collection, which he could use as a showcase for potential clients. By 1730, Smith must have had some kind of exclusive agreement with Canaletto to market his work to Grand Tourists or directly to patrons in England where they were delivered by his brother, John Smith. In June 1783 Horace Walpole criticised Smith for engaging Canaletto to work for him for little pay and then selling his works at much higher prices.[34] Still, the relationship between Canaletto and Smith must have been mutually beneficial.

Smith was also instrumental in disseminating Canaletto's art via the print medium. An effective means of cataloguing and marketing view paintings, prints had the added bonuses of being more portable and economical than paintings and

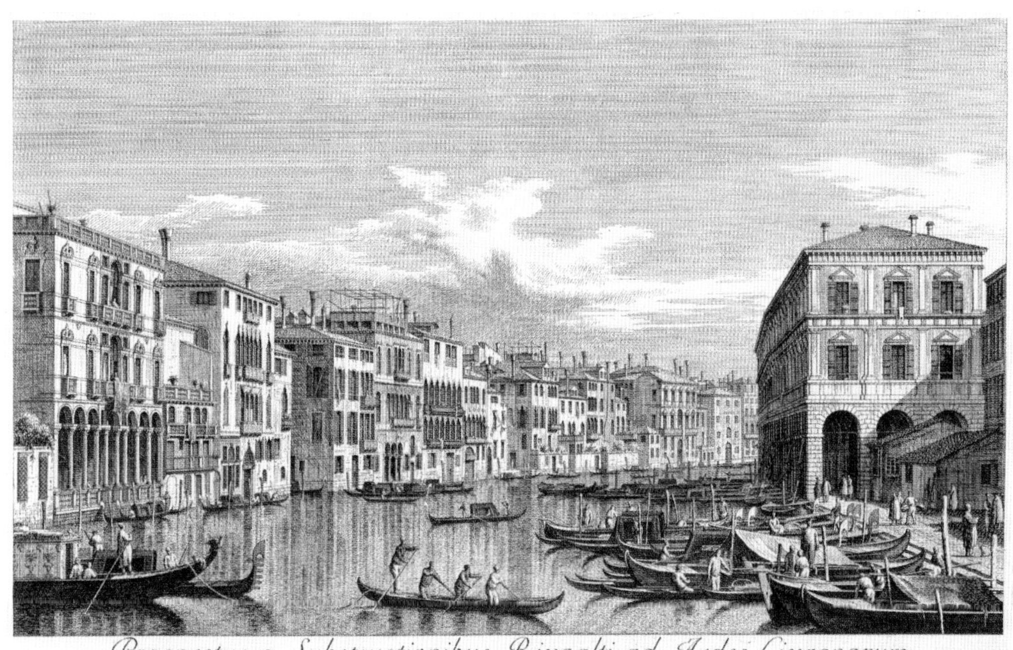

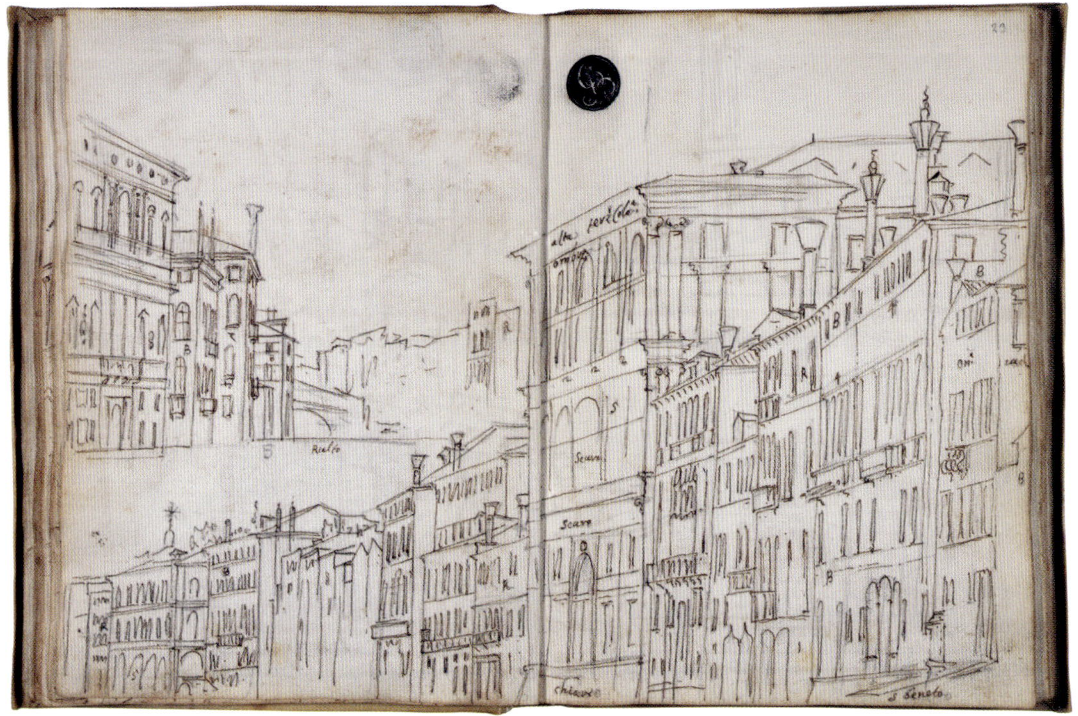

LEFT:
Fig. 13. Canaletto (1697–1768), *The Grand Canal from Palazzo Coccina Tiepolo to San Beneto* from the *Cagnola Sketchbook*, 1730s, pen and ink over black chalk, 23 × 17 cm (each folio), folios 22v–23r, Gallerie dell'Accademia, Venice

OPPOSITE:
Fig. 14. Michele Marieschi (1710–1743), *Grand Canal with Santa Maria della Salute, c.*1735–40, oil on canvas, 125 × 213 cm, Musée du Louvre, Paris (inv. 162)

therefore accessible to a wider public. Smith commissioned two editions of views after Canaletto in 1735 and 1742 (fig. 12).[35] Engraved by Antonio Visentini, both series were published by Smith at his Pasquali Press in Venice. In 1744 Canaletto etched a series of 31 views of the environs of Venice. He dedicated these to Smith, who probably also commissioned and financed the project. In 1762 Smith famously sold his collection and library to King George III for £20,000. This included 54 paintings and 142 drawings by Canaletto, today in the Royal Collection, the largest repository of Canaletto's work in the world.

Manipulating Views for Aesthetic Effect

The popularity of Canaletto's views meant that by mid-century many travellers to Venice already had some idea of the city's appearance. Some, like the surgeon Samuel Sharp, considered Venice's beauty superior to Canaletto's paintings.[36] Others preferred Canaletto's pictures over the real city. In 1770 the musician Charles Burney complained: 'particularly after seeing Canaletti … there was neither the symmetry nor the richness of materials I expected'.[37] In 1789 the English writer Arthur Young lamented that the city 'does not equal the idea I had formed of it from the pictures of Canaletti'.[38] In 1792 Lady Sheffield commented that Canaletto's views 'raise the Imagination to a Pitch which the Original does not fulfil'.[39]

The discrepancy between the real and the imaginary is a fascinating and persistent feature of Canaletto's art. Canaletto's patrons embraced his artfully constructed views of an ideal Venice based on thorough topographical knowledge. The artist masterfully filtered and interpreted what he saw first-hand, revising and rearranging elements for aesthetic effect. Paradoxically, Canaletto's views have for a long time been praised for their topographical accuracy. In the aforementioned 1727 letter to Lord March, McSwiney wrote that Canaletto's 'excellence lies in painting things which fall immediately under his eye'.[40] Moreover, both Zanetti and Mariette described Canaletto's works as truthful.[41] In reality, Canaletto often included edifices that were not visible from his chosen viewpoint, rearranged curves, widened or narrowed the Grand Canal, altered the perception of distance so that people, boats or buildings appeared closer or further away, simplified architecture or varied its proportions, and fused multiple, imaginary viewpoints.

Canaletto's Working Method

Canaletto often conceived his paintings in pairs or series, a tactic that enabled his patrons to see more of the city, but also one that assured the sale of multiple pictures to a client. Canaletto's extraordinarily detailed approach to painting everything in sharp focus gives the false impression of an eyewitness. One way that scholars have accounted for Canaletto's apparent topographical precision is to suggest that he employed a camera obscura, consisting of a dark box with a small hole through which an image is projected onto a piece of paper onto which its outlines can be traced. This idea originated with Canaletto's earliest biographers and has been the subject of great debate.[42] According to both Mariette and Zanetti, Canaletto painted views after nature but used the camera obscura to correct mistakes.[43] Canaletto may have employed a camera obscura in his drawn studies of the city, but the distortions and multiple viewpoints in his finished paintings were of his own creation.

Canaletto's drawings survive in a wide range of types.[44] His sole surviving sketchbook dating from the 1730s, today in the Accademia in Venice, is a testament to his direct observation and careful study of the urban landscape. The sketchbook is ripe with annotated jottings, such as notes about colours (fig. 13).[45] From these preliminary *in situ* studies

Canaletto devised final drawn compositions in the studio, which he then employed in the preparatory stages of his paintings. At the other end of the scale, Canaletto produced impressive, finished pen and wash drawings that functioned as independent works of art. These were carefully prepared with underdrawings in graphite.

Canaletto trained his nephew, Bernardo Bellotto (1722–1780), to work closely in his manner.[46] Bellotto left Venice in the 1740s, travelling around the Italian peninsula before moving to northern Europe in 1747. Canaletto's father also contributed to the studio.

The only painter that came close to rivalling Canaletto in Venice was Michele Marieschi (1710–1743) who, like Canaletto, had trained as a scene painter.[47] Marieschi turned to view painting in the mid-1730s when Canaletto was in his prime. His fresh and lively manner, and his use of highly distorted viewpoints, appealed to collectors, who often opted for his more affordable views over those of the more famous Canaletto (fig. 14). Sadly, Marieschi died prematurely at the age of 33, leaving the *veduta* market once again open to Canaletto.

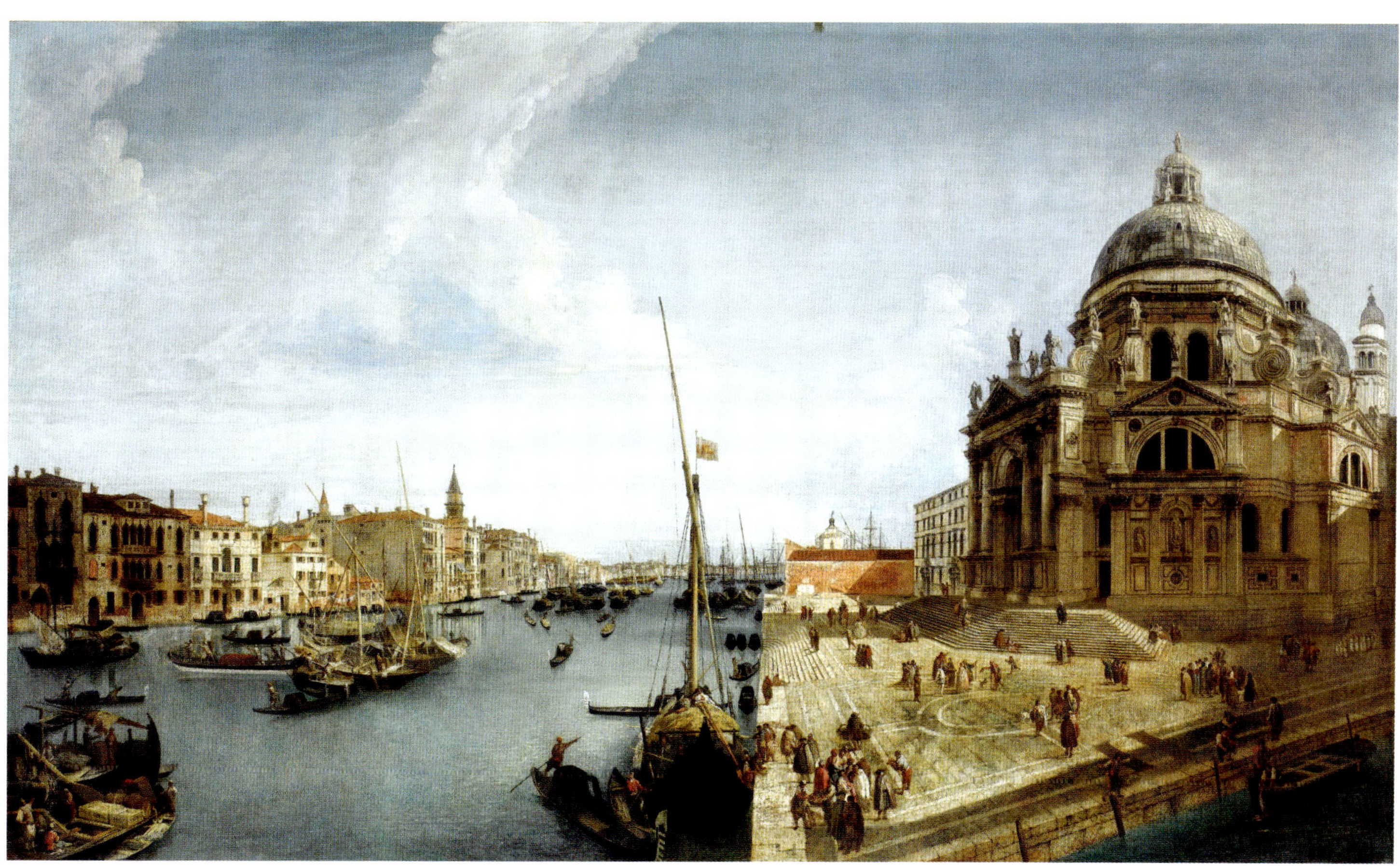

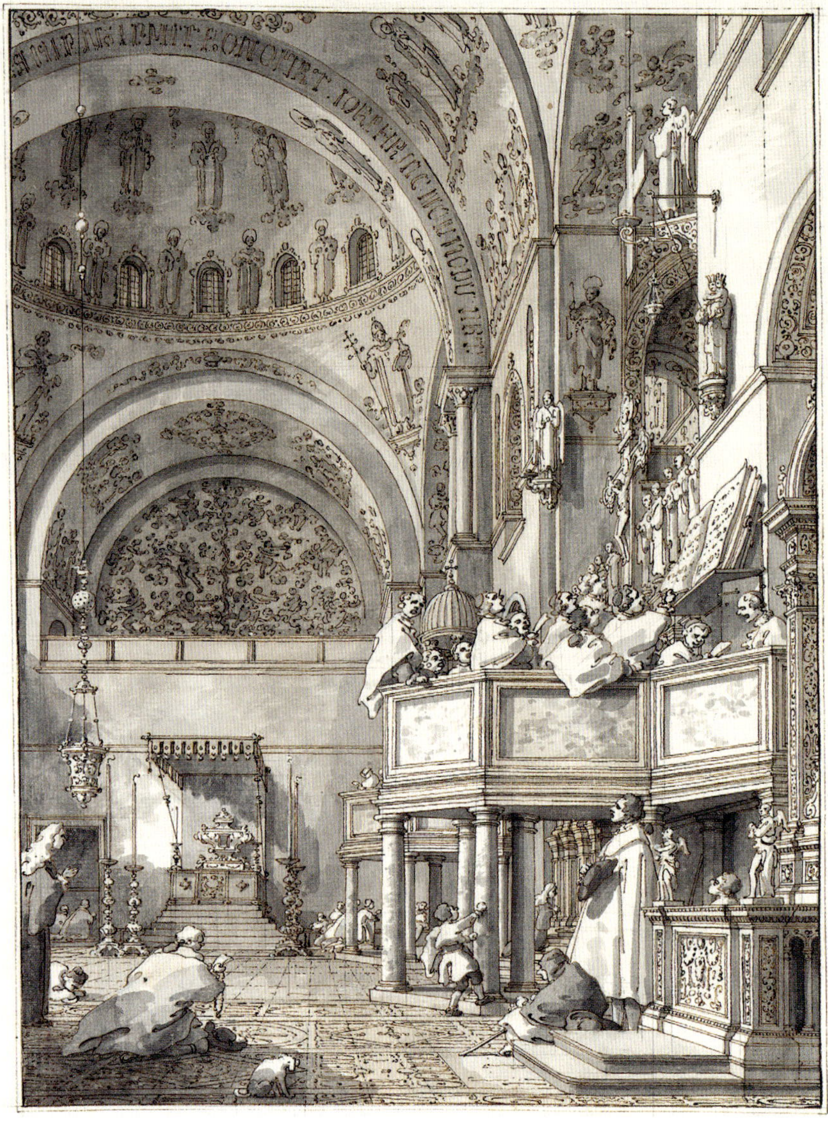

The Later Years

By the 1740s, the War of Austrian Succession had reduced the flow of tourists to Venice. In May 1746, equipped with letters of introduction from Smith, Canaletto decided to try his luck in England, where he remained for nine years, apart from a nine-month period back in Venice in 1750–51.[48] Soon after his arrival, the diarist and engraver George Vertue noted that although Canaletto had 'great merit and excellence … [and] … is much esteemed … many persons already have so many of his paintings' in England.[49]

Upon his return to Venice in 1755, Canaletto continued to actively produce novel views of Venice. The Revd John Hinchcliffe is said to have encountered Canaletto at age 63, sketching the Campanile.[50] Prejudices against view painting – long regarded as the lowest in the hierarchy of artistic genres – must have waned, as Canaletto was finally admitted to the Venetian Academy in 1763, at the age of 66. His reception piece was not a *veduta* but a *capriccio*, a work of the imagination, in which Canaletto showed off his ability at rendering perspective.[51] Canaletto proudly noted in an inscription on his last great drawing that he achieved the work without spectacles, a testament to his enduring eyesight (fig. 15). Canaletto died in April 1768, a poor man with meagre possessions despite a long and successful career.[52] He influenced many artists, both in Italy and abroad, including Joseph Mallord William Turner who paid homage to Canaletto by portraying him painting his native city (fig. 16).

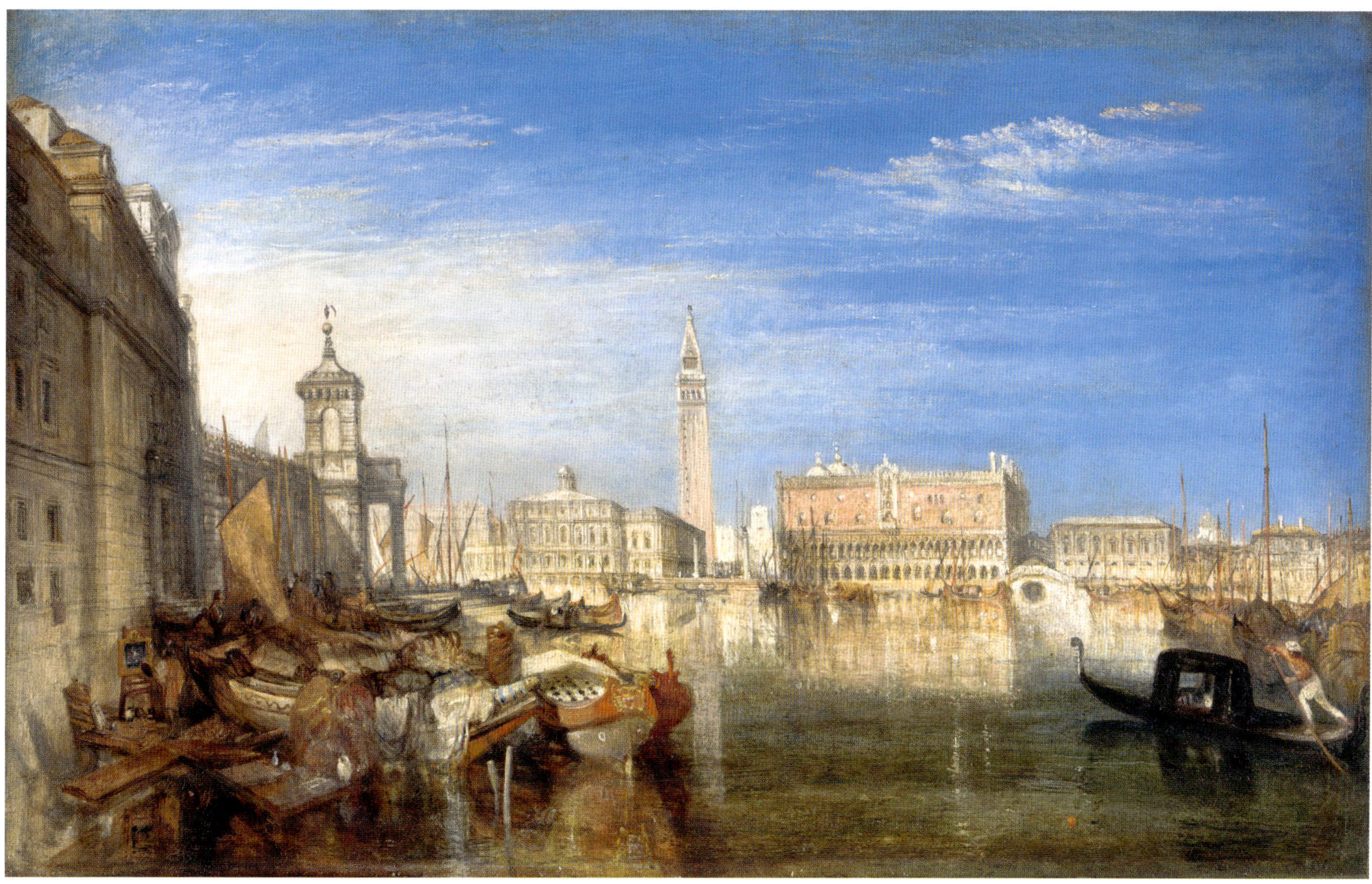

Francesco Guardi (1712–1793)

Francesco Guardi was Canaletto's most notable successor.[53] He was portrayed by a fellow Venetian artist, Pietro Longhi, at age 52 with his paintbrush and palette in hand (fig. 17). Although he employed many of the same compositions as Canaletto, Guardi transformed them into something entirely his own. Less famous and well remunerated than Canaletto in his own day and lost to posterity after his death, Guardi was rediscovered in the early twentieth century as the last major contributor to the *veduta* genre.[54]

Guardi was born in 1712 in Venice into a family of artists. His father, Domenico (1678–1716), whose family originated from Val di Sole in northern Italy, trained as a painter in Vienna before relocating to Venice in 1700. Domenico died when Francesco was a young boy; little is known about his meagre artistic output. Francesco's older brother, Giovanni Antonio (1699–1760), headed his father's studio after the latter's death. Francesco presumably learnt to paint from his older brother and assisted him from a young age. A third brother, Nicolò (1715–1786), was also a painter, but none of his works are known. In 1719 their sister Cecilia married the immensely successful painter Giovanni Battista Tiepolo (1696–1770). The earliest mention of Francesco as a painter is in a 1731 will, which lists copies 'by the Guardi brothers'.[55]

Francesco seems to have turned to view painting late in his career, around the middle of the eighteenth century, after decades of painting copies after figurative works.[56] In 1764 the Venetian diarist Pietro Gradenigo referred to Guardi as 'a good pupil of the celebrated Canaletto'.[57] More plausible is Francesco turning to view painting while Canaletto was in England in order to fulfil the demand for views in Venice, while simultaneously continuing his activities as a figure painter. Guardi probably began by executing copies after Canaletto's compositions, employing prints by or after Canaletto as his models, but quickly proved to be much more than a mere

copyist. As John Strange, the British resident in Venice, put
it, 'though he has taken Canaletto's department, he has still
followed a particular manner, which is spirited and quite his
own'.[58] Perhaps Guardi saw Canaletti in Smith's collection,
still in Venice in the 1750s.[59] His marriage in 1757, and the
birth of his two sons in 1760 and 1764 respectively, may have
also contributed to Guardi's turn to *vedute*, which were more
lucrative than his figural work. Moreover, the death of Giovanni
Antonio in 1760 provided freedom and impetus to work in a
new genre.

According to Gradenigo, Guardi was well received as a
vedutista. When two of his paintings were on public display
in the Procuratie Nove, they apparently received universal
approval.[60] Gradenigo attributed Guardi's success to the
camera obscura. Guardi's preference for light and atmospheric
effects over topographical accuracy, however, would have been
difficult to achieve with this device. His paintings display an
increased emphasis on natural phenomena and a strong ability
to capture light effects on the water, sky and architecture (cats
19, 20, 21, 22). Guardi excelled at conveying fleeting impressions
of famous sites. His interest in transitory atmospheric effects
produced an entirely new type of *veduta*. Guardi's paintings
emphasise the beauty and vastness of Venice's skies and
waters. His ample use of distortions to modify the proportions
of architecture and to expand canals, and his invention of
lighting for expressive effect, infuse his works with a graceful
personal touch. Guardi's imaginative facility is particularly
evident in his numerous *capricci* (cat. 27). Moreover, his prolific
output of drawings is characterised by a nervous, fleeting line
that parallels the evanescence conveyed in his paintings (fig. 18).[61]
Guardi's unique approach catered to a distinct clientele, namely
middle-class Venetians and English visitors to Venice of more
modest means than Canaletto's patrons.[62]

Like Canaletto, Guardi was admitted into the Academy
late in life, in 1784, when he was 72 years old. Guardi's death
in 1793 marked the culmination of a magnificent century for
vedute in Venice. In 1804 the great sculptor Antonio Canova
wrote to Pietro Edwards, Inspector-General of Venetian public
collections, asking for some Venetian view paintings to be
bought and sent to him in Rome. The latter replied: 'What a
pity it is, even this branch of our tree of painting is drying up
in Venice. There are no more view painters of repute.'[63]

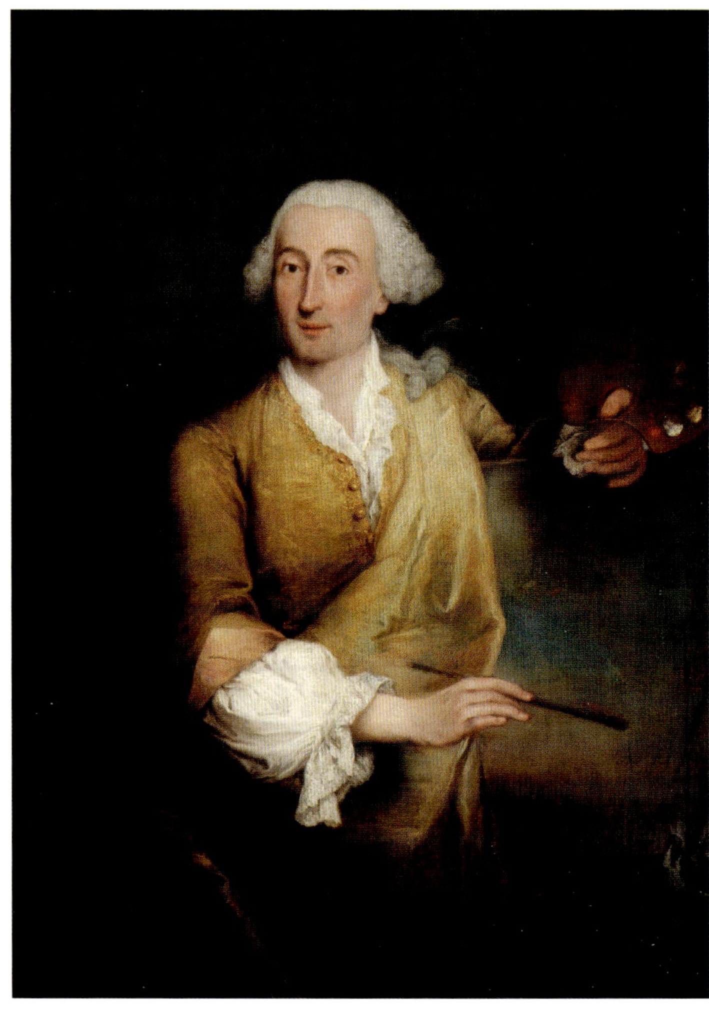

Fig. 17. Pietro Longhi (1701–1785), *Francesco Guardi*,
1764, oil on canvas, 132 × 100 cm, Ca' Rezzonico,
Venice (inv. 0761)

Fig. 18. Francesco Guardi (1712–1793), *The Staircase
of the Giants, Ducal Palace, Venice*, pen and brown
ink, brush and brown wash, over red chalk,
selectively pricked holes for the construction
of straight lines, 26.4 × 18.5 cm, Metropolitan
Museum of Art, New York (inv. 37.165.85)

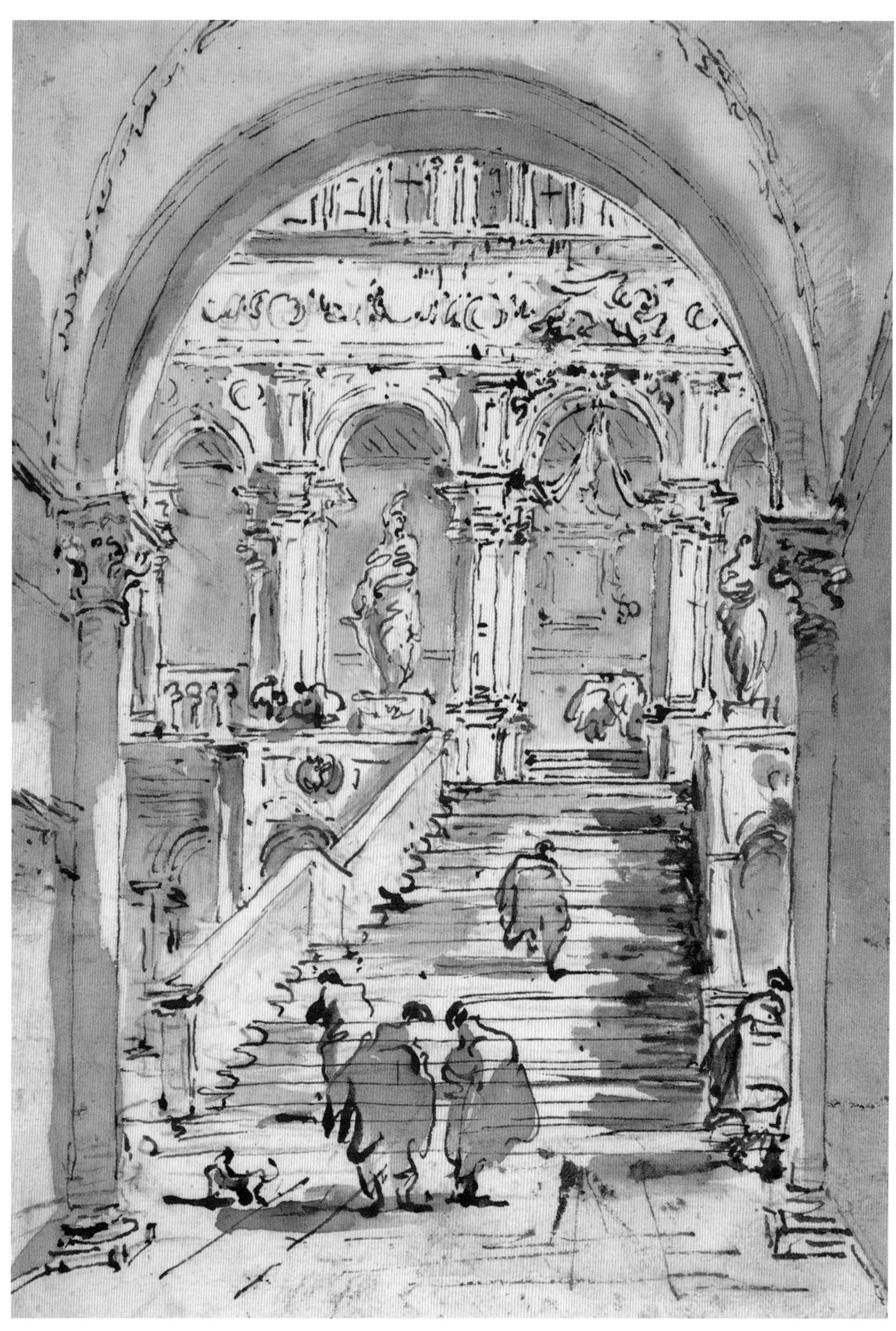

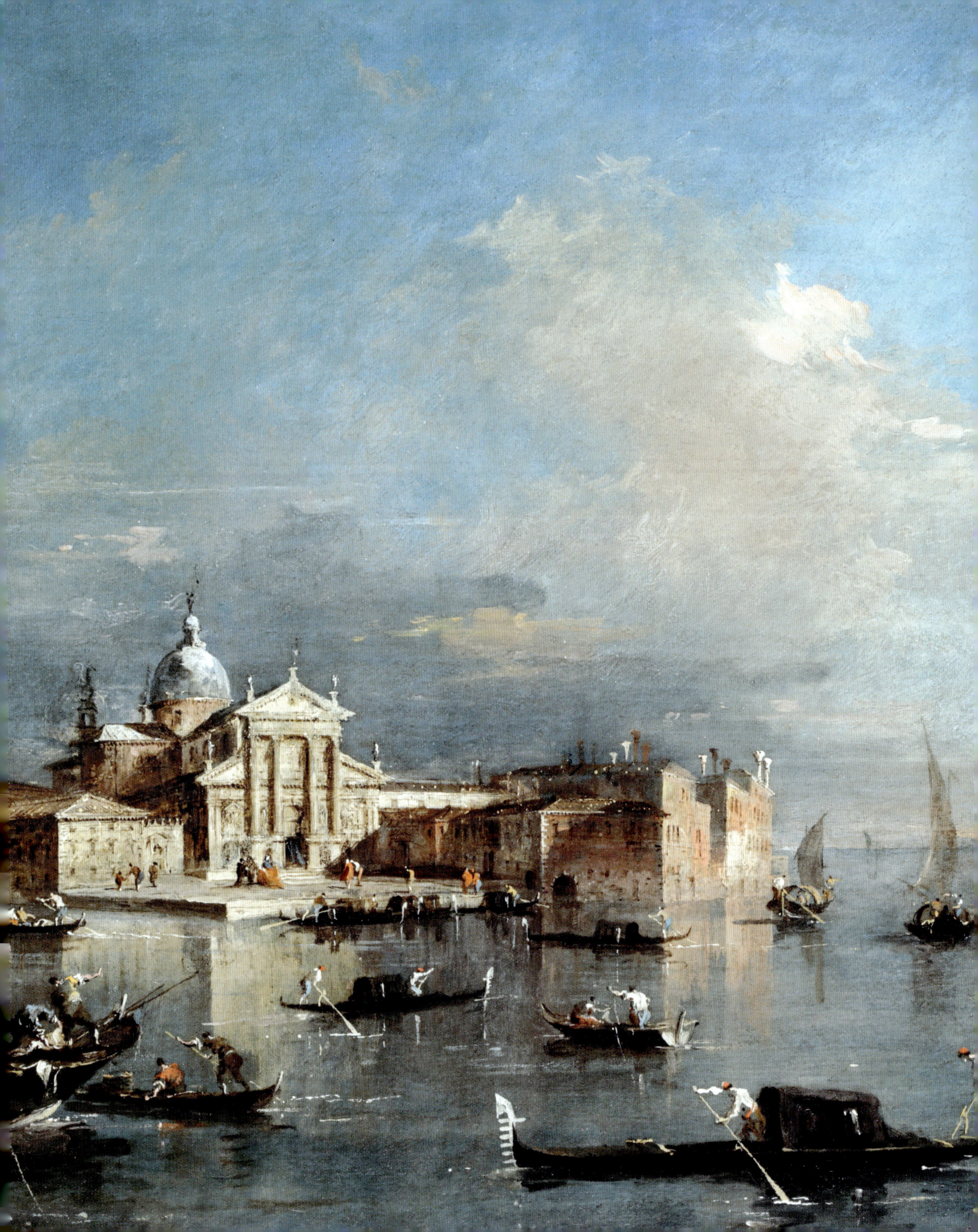

COLLECTING VENETIAN VIEWS AT THE WALLACE COLLECTION

Lelia Packer

'We are pretty rich in Canalettis,' proclaimed Richard Seymour-Conway, 4th Marquess of Hertford, in 1861.[1] 'The English collection richest in Guardi and Canaletto is that of Sir Richard Wallace,' wrote the art critic Charles Yriarte in 1878.[2] The French press in the late nineteenth century declared the Venetian views at Manchester House, now called Hertford House, as 'without rival'.[3] Indeed, the Wallace Collection holds an impressive group of 27 *vedute* by Canaletto and Guardi, and by artists working in Canaletto's circle. Since 1875, these paintings have been displayed together in a dedicated gallery at Hertford House. Exceptionally for the Wallace Collection, they were acquired by three generations of the Hertford family between the middle of the eighteenth century and the late nineteenth century. Francis Seymour-Conway, 1st Marquess of Hertford, purchased the first six Canaletti in the eighteenth century, including the most impressive pair of Bacino views. This core group was greatly expanded during the middle of the nineteenth century by his great-grandson, the 4th Marquess of Hertford, who acquired 20 additional paintings by Canaletto and Guardi.[4] During the late nineteenth century, Sir Richard Wallace, Lord Hertford's heir and probably his illegitimate son, completed the collection with one final view.[5] Here, the acquisition history of these pictures, and their subsequent display in various family properties, are traced for the first time. The unique character of the collection, rich in works by both Canaletto and Guardi, reflects the distinctive Anglo-French taste of the Wallace Collection's founders, compared to other *vedute* collections in Great Britain.

Francis Seymour-Conway (1719–1794), 1st Marquess of Hertford

The Hertford family's substantial fortune was built predominantly on Irish land ownership and expanded through financially advantageous marriages.[6] A contemporary of Canaletto, the 1st Marquess, who only gained his title in 1793, the year before his death, undertook the Grand Tour as a young man of 18 (fig. 19). He spent at least three years abroad, between March 1737 and March 1740.[7] He is recorded in Rheims, Geneva, Rome and Genoa, and most likely travelled to additional cities, such as Venice. For part of his travels, the 1st Marquess was accompanied by the Scottish tutor and antiquary Walter Bowman (1699–1782), who would also accompany his son, Francis Ingram Seymour-Conway, on his Grand Tour in 1765.[8]

A politician and courtier, the 1st Marquess was also exposed to Venetian art through the royal collections. Between 1766 and 1782 he served as Lord Chamberlain, a role that put him at the centre of courtly life. He was a friend to King George III and would have been familiar with the latter's substantial purchase of Consul Joseph Smith's Canaletti in 1762.[9]

The 1st Marquess acquired three *vedute* pairs: the two large Bacino views (cats 1, 2), two views of the Grand Canal (cats 5, 6) and two festival scenes (cats 9, 10). His other contribution to the Wallace Collection was a group of family portraits by Sir Joshua Reynolds from the 1780s.[10] He also bought a few Dutch pictures no longer in the collection.[11] The 1st Marquess's preference for Canaletto, English portraits

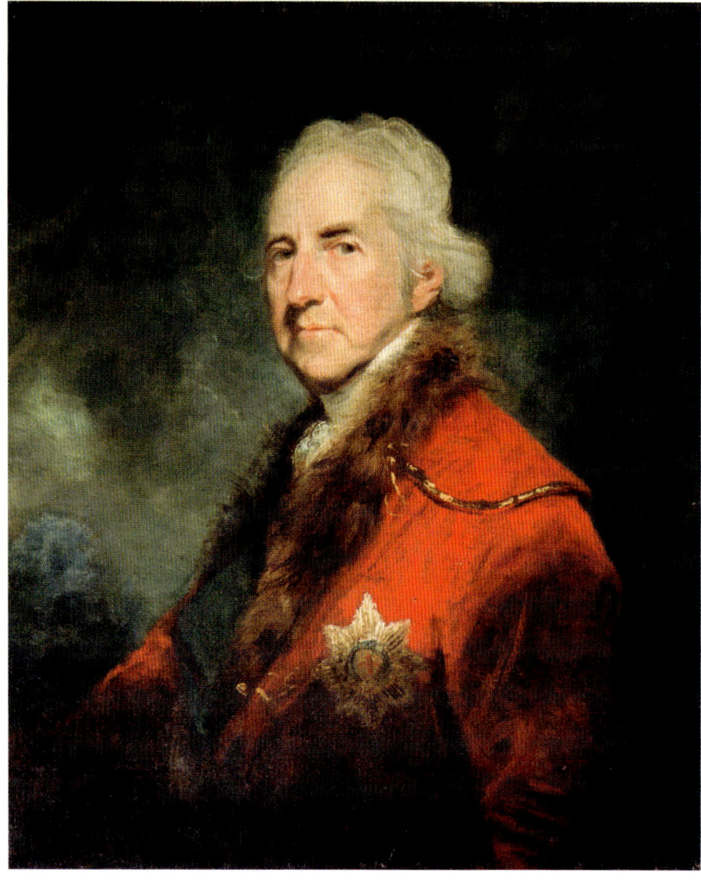

and Dutch painting was in line with eighteenth-century British aristocratic taste.

The 1st Marquess probably acquired, or at least commissioned, his *vedute* while on his Grand Tour. It was customary for young aristocrats to do this, as was the case with the Dukes of Bedford, Leeds, Buckingham and Carlisle. The Duke of Bedford was only 21 when he began commissioning his magnificent set of 24 Canaletti in 1731.[12] The presence of certain bell towers in the Bacino view taken from San Giorgio Maggiore (cat. 2), together with the confident and mature handling displayed across the pair, helps date that picture to c.1738, when the 1st Marquess was on his tour.[13] He is likely to have commissioned his *vedute* while in Venice, directly from Smith, and received them a few years later.

Apart from Canaletto, the only other eighteenth-century Venetian artist represented in the Hertford family collection early on was the pastellist Rosalba Carriera. A pair of allegorical figures representing *Spring* and *Autumn* is recorded in the 1834 inventory of Manchester House (figs 20, 21).[14] These may

well have been bought by the 1st Marquess to complement his *vedute*. They appear in subsequent Manchester House inventories and were part of the Hertford family entail that passed to the 5th Marquess who, in turn, sold them in 1875.[15]

Francis Ingram Seymour-Conway (1743–1822), 2nd Marquess of Hertford, and Francis Charles Seymour-Conway (1777–1842), 3rd Marquess of Hertford

Francis Ingram Seymour-Conway, 2nd Marquess of Hertford, undertook the Grand Tour between 1763 and 1765.[16] This period coincided with the last years of Canaletto's life during which his artistic production waned. The 2nd Marquess is recorded in Fontainebleau, Turin, Genoa, Florence, Milan and Paris. Although he expressed a desire to go to Venice, a city he would have known from his father's paintings and which he described as one of the 'towns of note', it remains uncertain whether he actually visited.[17]

A politician, the 2nd Marquess added a few British portraits to the family collection.[18] His most important acquisition, Thomas Gainsborough's portrait of Mrs Mary Robinson, was a gift from his friend the Prince of Wales (later King George IV), in 1818. After succeeding to the marquisate in 1794 and acquiring an annual income of £70,000, the 2nd Marquess took up residence at Manchester House in 1797, beginning the Hertford association with the property.

Francis Charles Seymour-Conway, 3rd Marquess of Hertford, was the first major art collector in his family. Although he spent a significant amount of time in Italy, he did not contribute to the *vedute* collection.[19] This is understandable as *vedute* had fallen out of fashion by this time and their availability on the art market had waned. The 3rd Marquess's taste was typical of early nineteenth-century aristocrats, with a penchant for highly finished Dutch seventeenth-century cabinet pictures, which he also acquired for the future King George IV.[20]

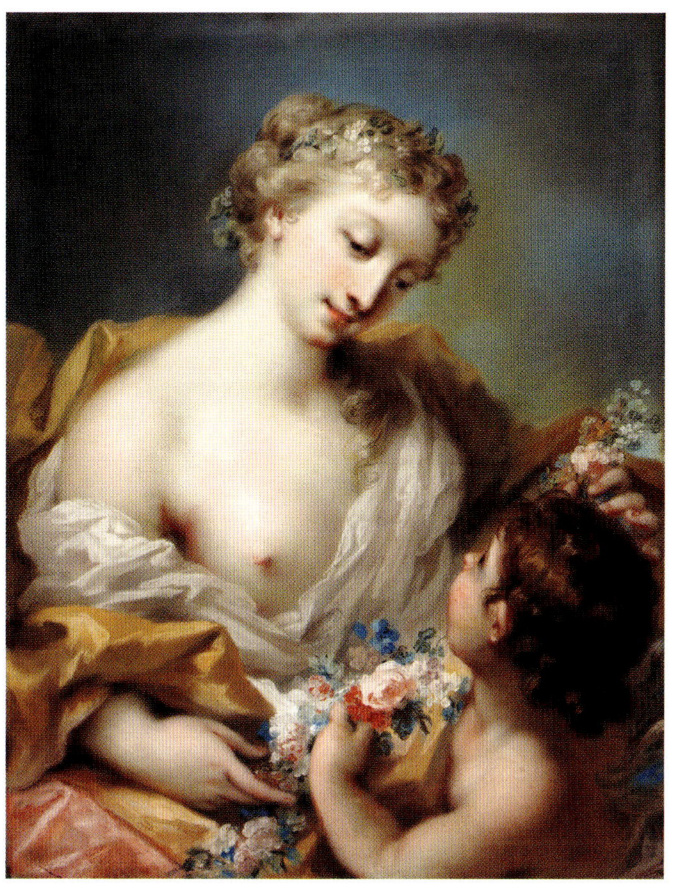

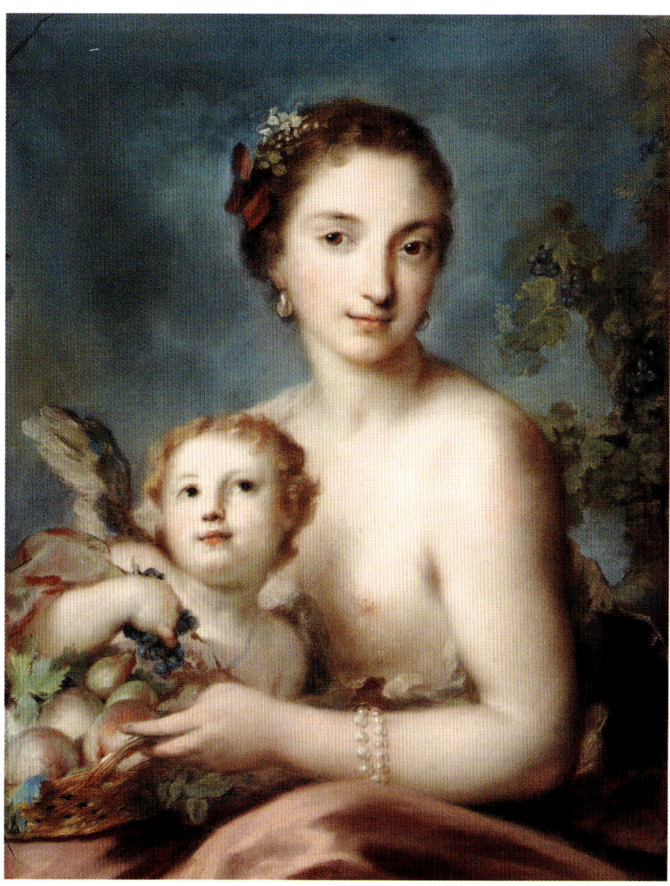

Richard Seymour-Conway, 4th Marquess of Hertford (1800–1870)

The man who contributed most to what is today the Wallace Collection was Richard Seymour-Conway, 4th Marquess of Hertford (fig. 22). Lord Hertford's avid collecting spanned about 35 years from around 1835 until his death in 1870. For the majority of his life Hertford lived on Paris's Right Bank in a luxurious residence at 2 rue Laffitte, perfectly situated near the best art dealers of the day. He also spent time at Bagatelle, his Louis XVI château in the Bois de Boulogne outside Paris. After succeeding to the marquisate in 1842, the 4th Marquess inherited an estate reputedly worth the enormous sum of two million pounds. He enjoyed an annual income of at least £250,000, which accorded him the greatest buying power on the European art market. He purchased 'at prices seldom given to Governments, still less [to] private individuals'.[21] Lord Hertford had high standards for his acquisitions and was attentive to quality, condition and provenance. This holds true for his *vedute* collection, which he expanded significantly with 20 pictures. By mid-century, the 4th Marquess was revered as the most renowned European art collector, and his collection

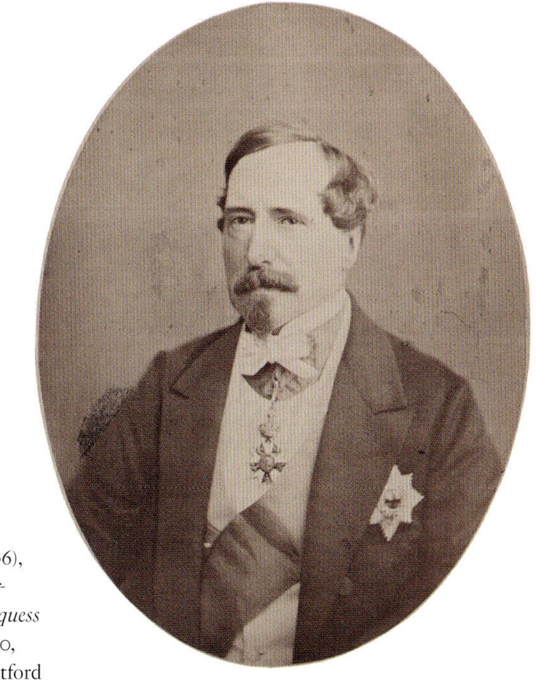

Fig. 22. Etienne Carjat (1828–1906), *Richard Seymour-Conway, 4th Marquess of Hertford*, c.1860, photograph, Hertford House Historic Collection, The Wallace Collection, London (inv. 2011.31)

was lauded as 'indubitably the most important of all the collections that have been formed'.[22]

Focusing his acquisitions on specific painters he admired, Lord Hertford 'only like[d] pleasing pictures' that lacked violence.[23] After inheriting six *vedute* from his great-grandfather, Hertford bought what were believed to be eleven Canaletti and nine paintings by Guardi. His affinity for *vedute* was in line with his general preference for pleasant pictures. Lord Hertford's regard for Guardi, an artist better appreciated on the Continent than in Britain in the middle of the nineteenth century, reflected the Anglo-French character of his collecting. Apart from *vedute*, Hertford had relatively little interest in Italian painting.

Lord Hertford may have visited Venice early in his life. In 1829 he served as attaché to the British Embassy in Constantinople (now Istanbul) for several months, a destination that he would have probably reached via Venice. He also travelled to Italy in 1838 and was in Rome in 1845. His interest in *vedute* may have been nurtured by these travels.

His extensive correspondence with his London-based art agent, Samuel Moses Mawson, sheds light on his *vedute* collecting.[24] On 29 March 1855 Hertford wrote to Mawson about a Canaletto painting that was part of a pair of views showing opposite reaches of the Grand Canal: 'They are very pretty & appear to me to be in a very good state. They are neither of them very good views of Venice but nevertheless I must say I should rather like to have one of them – n° 70. The other I have no fancy for.'[25] Lord Hertford owned at least eight paintings by Canaletto by 1855, including one view of the Grand Canal (cat. 14). In the end, Hertford bought the pair, describing the pictures as 'brothers' that he was reluctant to separate.[26] This is understandable since Lord Hertford referred to his paintings as his 'children' and to his collection as 'the result of [his] life'.[27] He never married and lived a reclusive life in Paris amid his art treasures.

A few months later, evidently eager to expand his *vedute* collection, Hertford enquired about 'two or three' more Canaletti that he had heard were coming up for sale in Paris.[28] He selectively chose *vedute* that appealed to him and that complemented his extant holdings. For example, in 1857 Hertford did not acquire two Canaletti showing the Piazza San Marco and Santa Maria della Salute with the Dogana, despite being very fond of them and describing them as 'beautiful'.[29] This was probably because he already owned one picture of the latter subject (cat. 15). Equally, Hertford did not purchase a 'Regatta on the Grand Canal' at the 1859 Lord Northwick sale,

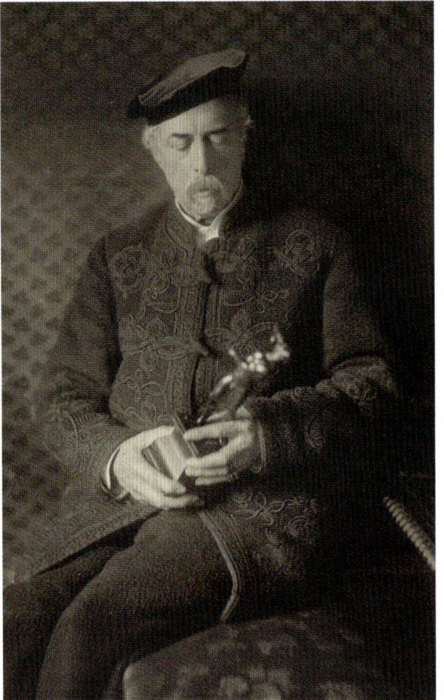

despite Mawson's praise of it as a 'superb', 'first rate' picture, since he owned a comparable regatta (cat. 9).[30] Hertford was also particular about the orientation of his *vedute*, preferring landscape over portrait formats. In 1861 he wrote to Mawson, 'the Canalettis you advise are upright & I do not much like that shape'.[31]

In 1857 Hertford's penchant for Guardi was underscored by his description of two pictures by the artist in the Earl of Shrewsbury's sale as 'pretty if good'.[32] Hertford did not acquire those pictures, however, probably because they represented a regatta, a subject he already possessed (cat. 9). Mawson was attuned to Hertford's predilection for Guardi and advised him about 'a fine little specimen by Guardi – wanted as a specimen of the artist' in the 1859 Lord Northwick sale.[33] Hertford ended up buying that picture, a *capriccio* showing the courtyard of the Doge's Palace (cat. 27).

Sir Richard Wallace (1818–1890)

Lord Hertford bequeathed his unentailed estate, with its magnificent art collection, to Richard Wallace, his likely, and at the time presumed, illegitimate son (fig. 23).[34] By bequeathing his collection to Wallace, Hertford separated the unentailed part of the collection from the Hertford title. With no legitimate direct heir, the Hertford title and entailed property went to Hertford's cousin, Francis George Hugh Seymour (1812–1884), who became the 5th Marquess of Hertford. This put into question the ownership of the six entailed Canaletti bought by the 1st Marquess, and a few other paintings by Reynolds and Gainsborough at Manchester House that Wallace was keen to retain with the rest of the collection.[35] Correspondence reveals that the 5th Marquess was eager to resolve the matter.[36] Wallace held his ground on the question of the said pictures, and the 5th Marquess eventually conceded.[37] Thanks to Wallace's determination, the six Canaletti acquired by the 1st Marquess remained together with the rest of the 4th Marquess's *vedute* and are in the Wallace Collection today.

After spending the majority of his life in Paris, Wallace relocated to London following Hertford's death in 1870. Wallace's move coincided with the siege of Paris and the Commune in 1870–71, which provided further impetus to leave the city. With 26 *vedute* in his collection, Wallace focused his collecting on less represented areas and media such as arms and armour. Nevertheless, soon after his arrival in London, he acquired what he believed to be two Canaletti, including the only English view in the collection (fig. 24).[38] Somewhat surprisingly perhaps, given the sheer number of *vedute* already in his possession, on 2 May 1884 Wallace wrote to his dealer, Charles Davis, asking him to secure two paintings by Canaletto in an upcoming sale the following day.[39] Wallace was so keen to buy the pictures that he told Davis he could increase the price from £120 to £150.[40] In the end, it does not appear that Wallace purchased the pictures. However, he was clearly looking to expand his Canaletto collection with non-Venetian views, as the pictures in the 1884 sale were either English, Roman or Florentine views.

Wallace had amassed his own art collection from around 1846 until 1857, when he was sadly forced to sell it due to financial difficulties. He owned at least two paintings by Guardi that he sold in 1857.[41] The art agent Ferdinand Laneuville, whom Hertford often employed to act on his behalf at auction, bought 21 paintings at Wallace's sale, six of which correspond to works of art in the Wallace Collection today.[42]

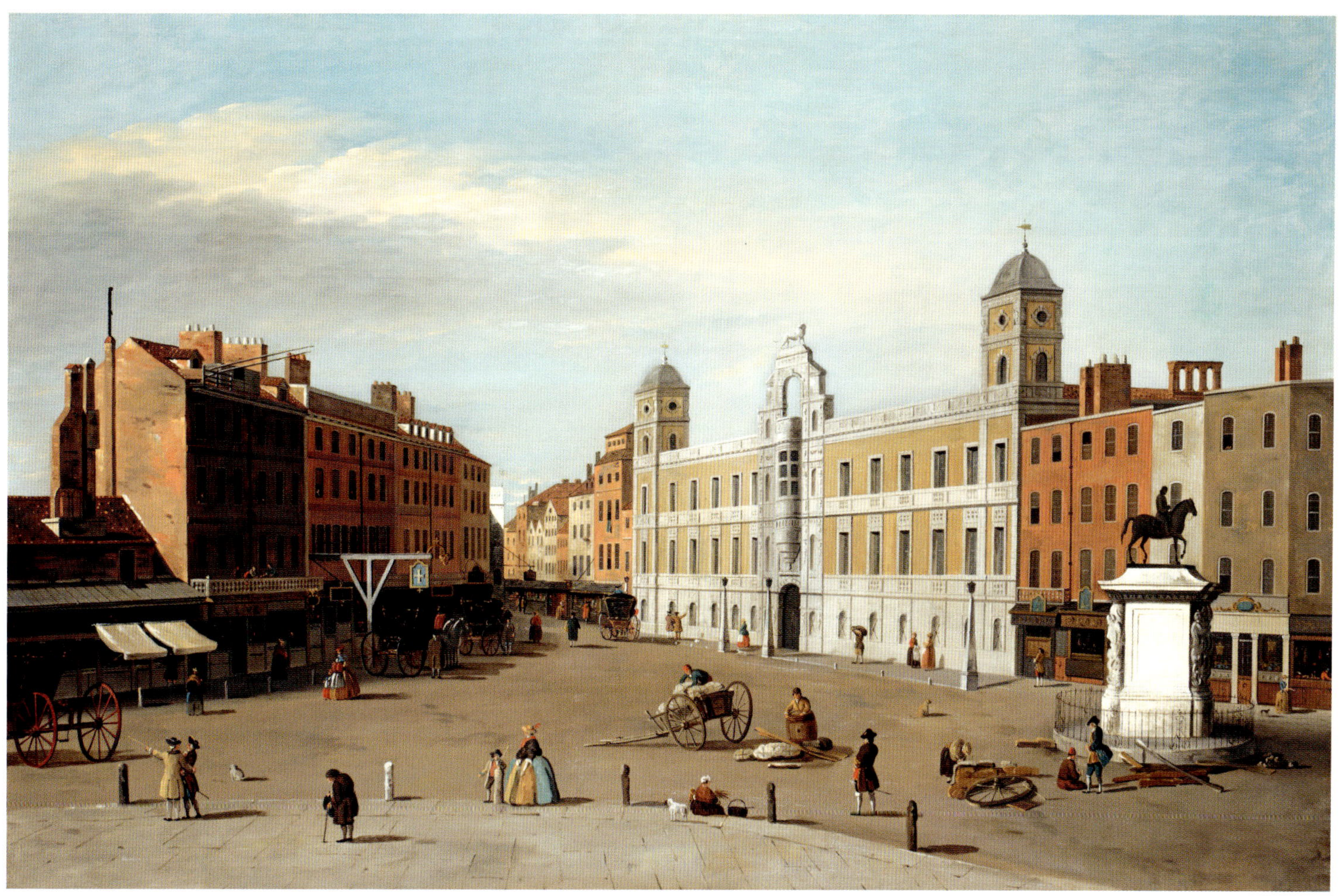

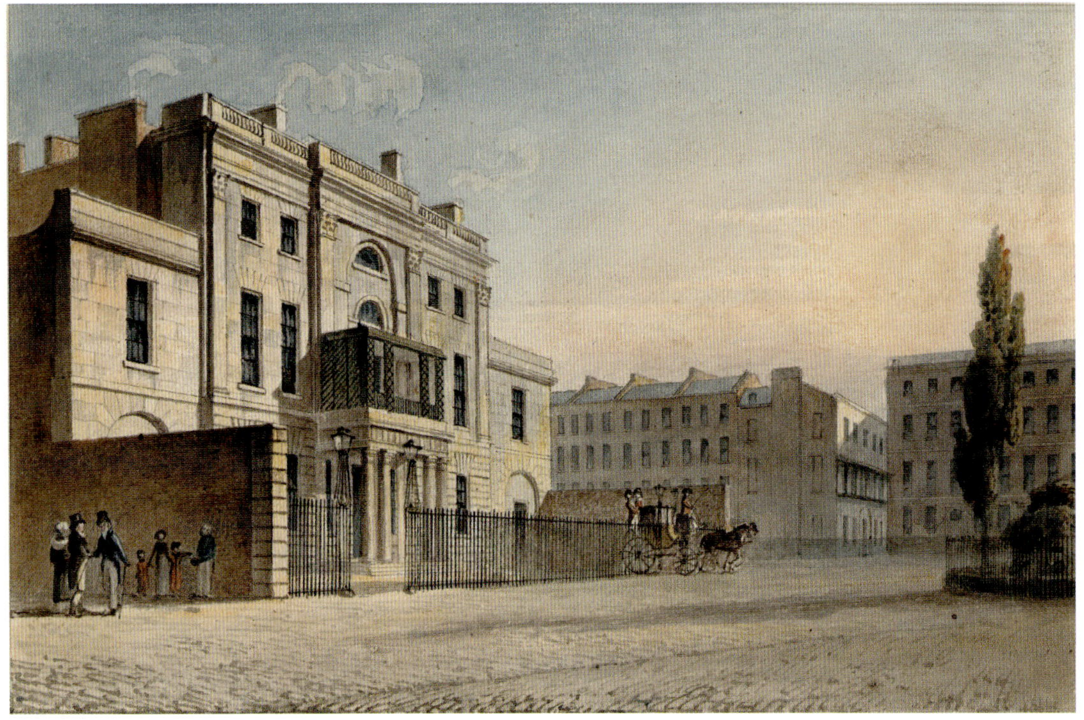

Although Laneuville also purchased the two Guardis from Wallace, it is uncertain whether they correspond to works in the Wallace Collection.[43] They may be the small Guardi pair showing the churches of San Giorgio Maggiore and Santa Maria della Salute (cats 23, 24), but this does not explain why one painting was described as a view of the Grand Canal in the sale catalogue, unless the auctioneer made a mistake. In either case, one wonders whether it was Wallace who directed Hertford's attention to Guardi.

Although he considered bequeathing the collection to the nation, Wallace did not manage to do so during his lifetime. When he died in 1890, he left his collection to his wife, Julie Amélie Charlotte Castelnau (1819–1897), better known as Lady Wallace. Upon her death in 1897, Lady Wallace bequeathed the works of art on the ground and first floors of Hertford House to the nation. The Wallace Collection opened its doors to the public three years later, on 25 June 1900. The national collections were greatly enriched with 27 superb *vedute* by Canaletto and Guardi. At this point, the National Gallery had only two paintings by Guardi.[44]

The residue of Lady Wallace's estate went to Sir John Murray Scott (1847–1912), the Wallaces' private secretary and Lady Wallace's residual legatee. An inventory taken of Scott's residence at 13 Connaught Place lists a pair of 'Canal Scenes'

by Guardi.[45] These were part of Scott's own collection, and do not appear in any Hertford inventories. Conversely, Wallace kept four paintings by Guardi in Paris, which passed to Murray Scott and were subsequently sold.[46]

Whereabouts and Display of the Vedute Collection

The earliest record of the Hertford *vedute* is a memorandum written by the 3rd Marquess on 21 July 1832:

> To please my Father ... I entailed the settled Estates on the Title ... Vide [see] my Grandfathers will ... Ergo [therefore] – all the glasses, pictures, plate, diamond China &c. removed from Grosvenor Street to Manchester house are now my property ... Exempli gratia: in Manchester House the Canalettis in the Blue room are mine[47]

This document confirms that the 1st Marquess acquired the initial six *vedute* and that these were displayed together at Manchester House, from at least 1832 but probably earlier, in a room known as the Blue Room (fig. 25). An inventory and valuation of the house taken two years later, upon the death of the 2nd Marchioness, helps identify these paintings as the two large Bacino views, the pair of Carnival scenes and the pair of

Grand Canal views acquired by the 1st Marquess.[48] This 1834 inventory records the Hertford collection prior to its dispersal to various family properties while Manchester House was leased to the French Embassy between 1835 and 1850. The 3rd Marquess lent 38 pictures (mostly portraits) to the Embassy as well as the two Carriera pastels (figs 20, 21) and a drawing.[49] Of the six *vedute*, the French borrowed the Grand Canal pair (cats 5, 6), perhaps as a nod to British taste.

In 1842 two 'splendid view[s] in Venice – large' are listed as hanging in the Dining Room at Dorchester House on Park Lane, the 3rd Marquess's residence at the time (now the Dorchester Hotel).[50] These must have been the two large Bacino views (cats 1, 2), which may have hung opposite each other on either side of the dining table. That same year, 'two Canaletti entailed pictures' were inventoried as hanging in St Dunstan's Villa in Regent's Park (demolished in 1937).[51] St Dunstan's was built by the 3rd Marquess in 1825 'regardless of expense, in a unique style' for his lavish entertainments.[52]

By a process of elimination, these were the two Carnival scenes, fitting for a party residence (cats 9, 10). Interestingly, in his plans for St Dunstan's from the early 1820s, the renowned architect Decimus Burton envisioned the two large Bacino views as hanging in the Tent Room (fig. 26) together with John Hoppner's portrait of George IV as Prince of Wales (P563). According to inventories from around that time, this arrangement never materialised. Following the 3rd Marquess's death in 1842, the six Canaletti were returned to Manchester House, still the French Embassy, after being separated for eight years.[53]

On 1 May 1846 the Countess of Saint Aulaire gave a magnificent ball at the French Embassy in Manchester Square to celebrate King Louis-Philippe's birthday. The entire ground floor of the house was open to guests, including the 'blue drawing room', which was used as 'the room of reception where the Countess and his Excellency welcomed their friends and visitors'.[54] As a reception room, the blue drawing room must have been one of the rooms near the main entrance to the

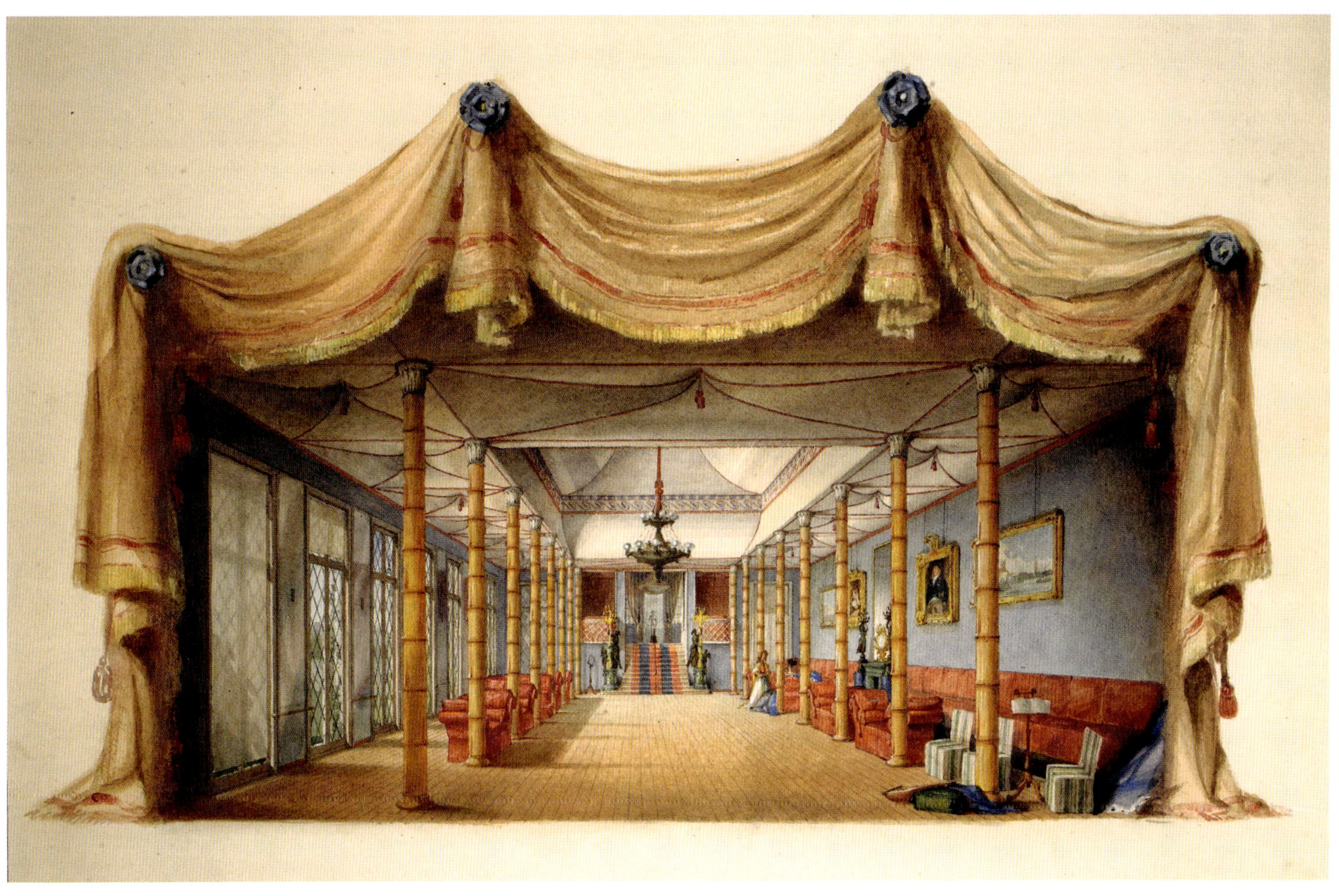

house. Furthermore, an 1868 account of the house reported that 'the first room you are shown into, contains seventeen Venetian scenes by Canaletti'.[55] By 1870 the *vedute* were confirmed as hanging in the Breakfast Room. The Blue Room cited by the 3rd Marquess in 1832, the blue drawing room reported in 1846 and the Breakfast Room cited in 1870 were one and the same, namely the first room west of the main entrance on the ground floor (today's Shop).

Between 1832 and 1859 the appellation of the room varied between 'Blue Room' and 'Canaletto Room'.[56] It may be that, with the growing number of paintings by Canaletto in the collection, it seemed fitting to rename the room after the artist. In late February 1850 it was reported that the French were about to leave Hertford House.[57] The 4th Marquess took over the lease and, by the following January, the house had 'undergone great improvements and considerable internal decoration'.[58] This work probably comprised the redecoration of the Blue Room at the front of the house, perhaps to a different wall colour. Other great Canaletto rooms in England include those at Woburn Abbey, Castle Howard and Langley Park.

Hertford was simultaneously rebuilding 105 Piccadilly, a grand mansion overlooking Green Park, formerly the Pulteney Hotel. The published plans show a sizeable picture gallery with a glass ceiling for natural light (fig. 27).[59] Of the possible paintings intended to hang there, a 'Canal, Venice by Canaletti' was suggested.[60] The Canaletti may thus have been intended for 105 Piccadilly at one time.

Dr Gustav Waagen (1794–1868), the German art historian, connoisseur and first Director of the Berlin Gemäldegalerie, mentioned Lord Hertford's *vedute* in his description of the collection. Waagen was frustrated not to be able to access a large part of Hertford's London collection in 1850–51, 'one of the chief inducements for [his] journey to England'.[61] He complained that 'the bulk of the collection was lying, well packed, in the Pantechnicon', a storage facility on Motcomb Street.[62] From 1851 to 1852, Hertford sent any remaining works from his collection to the Pantechnicon while the house was being refurbished. Even so, Waagen wrote of Lord Hertford's masterpieces, which he had seen in previous collections. He listed 'four very admirable pictures inherited from the late Marquis' by Antonio Canale.[63] Although he got the number wrong, Waagen substantiated that (part) of Hertford's Canaletti collection had passed down to him through family lineage.

By May 1852 Lord Hertford's pictures were back at Manchester House. When Waagen returned to England in 1854

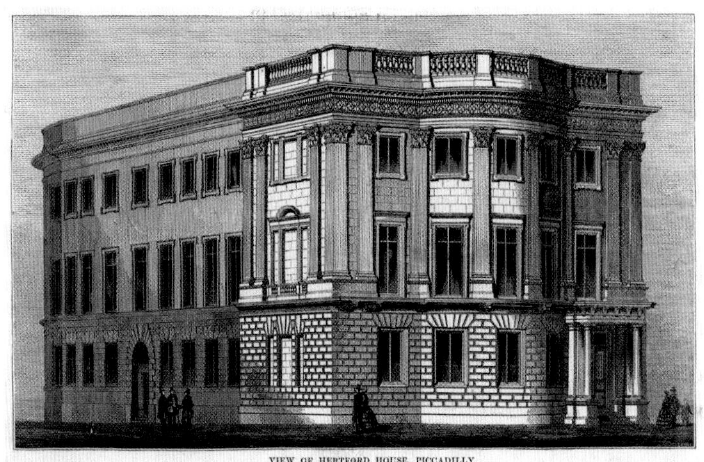

and 1856, he was finally able to see the collection *in situ*.[64] In his 1857 supplement, Waagen erroneously listed eight instead of 13 Canaletti, although he rightly considered the large Bacino views *chefs-d'oeuvre*.[65]

Lord Hertford did not lend any of his 13 *vedute* to the 1857 Manchester *Treasures of Art* exhibition to which he sent 44 pictures 'of rare beauty'.[66] Hertford was praised as 'the most generous' lender, and his collection hung in a dedicated 'Hertford Gallery' likened to the Louvre's Salon Carré.[67] The absence of *vedute* might be explained by Hertford's predilection for Old Masters and the *ancien régime*.[68]

Hertford took an avid interest in the care, display and preservation of his collection. An 1859 frame invoice informs us that eight *vedute* were reframed that year, along with 67 other pictures.[69] Mawson commissioned the firm W.P. Evans for this work, whom he also tasked to clean, refresh and varnish 28 pictures, including one of the large Bacino views (cat. 2).[70]

During his lifetime, Lord Hertford's collection was split between his London and Paris residences. This division is reflected in his *vedute*, with the Canaletti kept in London and the Guardis in Paris. In 1867 the famous French art critic Théophile Thoré (1807–1869), better known by his pseudonym William Bürger, described Hertford's magnificent Parisian collection in his guide to the city's art. Of Hertford's 250, mainly French, paintings, Bürger noted that the Italian School was represented by Guardi and Sassoferrato, thus confirming the absence of Hertford's Canaletti from Paris.[71] Contemporaries distinguished between Hertford's art collections in Paris and London. It was reported that Hertford kept objects that were more personal to him in Paris, such as his paintings by Guardi.[72]

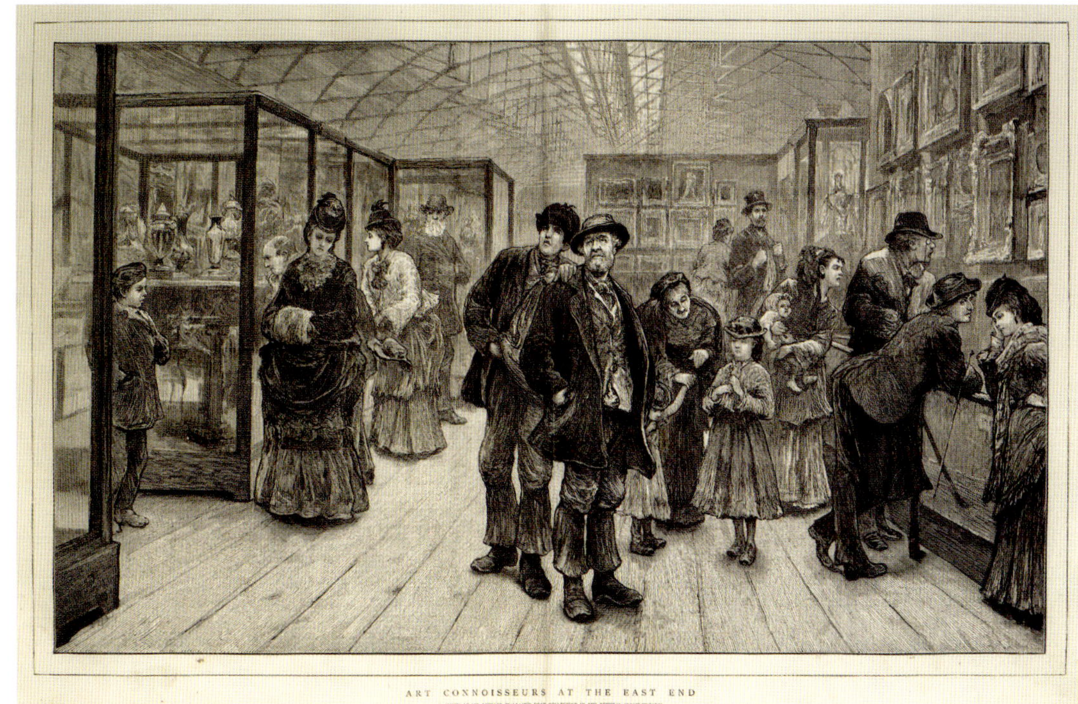

When Hertford died in 1870, lists were drawn up of the entailed and unentailed property at Manchester House.[73] All 17 of his Canaletti were at Manchester House that year. Hertford acquired Canaletti on the English art market and naturally kept them together with the six he inherited, which had been at Manchester House at least since 1832. In 1870 the Canaletti hung together in the Breakfast Room on the ground floor (today's Shop), previously the Blue Room.[74] An anonymous view of Malta (P493), then misidentified as 'A panoramic view of Venice including the Doge's Palace' by Canaletto, was also displayed there.

No paintings by Guardi appear in the 1870 Manchester House inventory, confirming that these were kept in Paris. Although he bought at least one of his nine Guardis on the English art market (cat. 27), Hertford probably sent it to Paris to be united with the rest of his Guardis that he acquired there. However, only five works by Guardi appear in the 1871 inventory of 2 rue Laffitte. These were 'A View of Italy' in the Great Gallery and four Guardis described as pendants hanging in a small room.[75] The latter are the set of four Guardis acquired at the duc de Morny sale in Paris (cats 12, 20, 21, 22). The Italian view could be cat. 27, the only picture without a pendant in the collection. In addition, 'two views of Venice' by an unidentified master hung in a bedroom. Perhaps these were cat. 23 and cat. 24? An unidentified painting of the Piazza San Marco 'attributed' to Guardi is listed in the nearby family property at 1–3 rue Taitbout.[76] Guardi's two small oval *capricci* (cats 25, 26) seem to have been overlooked.

After Hertford's death, Wallace brought the majority of the works he had inherited from Paris to London. He took over the remaining lease on Manchester House – soon to be renamed Hertford House – in April 1872, and between 1872 and 1875 refurbished and extended the house to accommodate his growing collection. While the house was being refurbished, Wallace exhibited more than 2,000 of his works of art in the new branch of the South Kensington Museum at Bethnal Green (fig. 28).[77] For Victorian art lovers, this exhibition represented a unique opportunity to see one of Europe's finest art collections for the first time. Wallace brought all nine paintings by Guardi from Paris for the opening of the exhibition on 24 June 1872. For the first time, the Guardis and Canaletti were displayed together.[78] Contemporaries hailed Wallace's *vedute* as being the best in private hands: 'Antonio Canaletto is represented with a fulness which no private collection in the world could equal; there are no fewer than seventeen panoramic views of Venice from the master's hand, and ten by another Venetian painter contemporary with him, and scarcely inferior – Guardi.'[79] Others commented on Wallace's

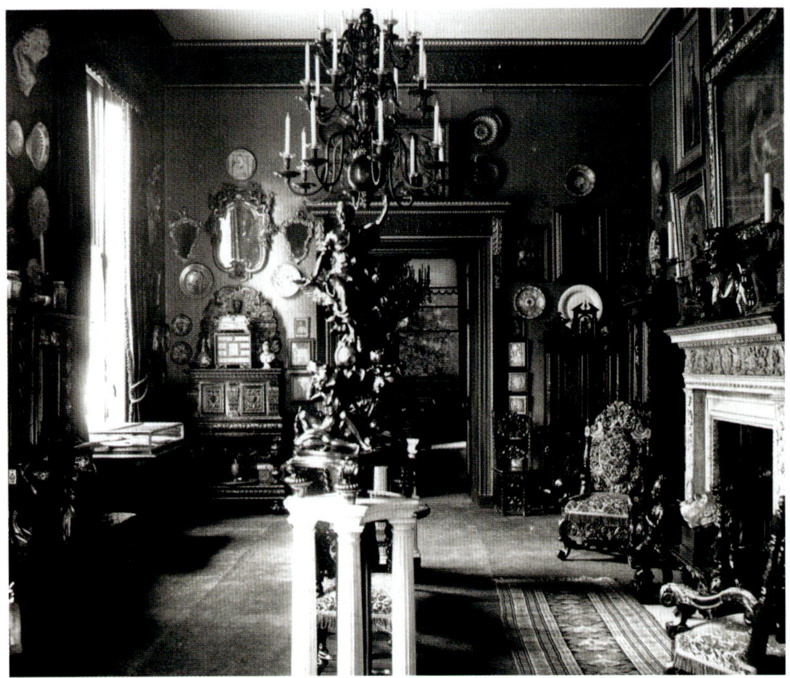 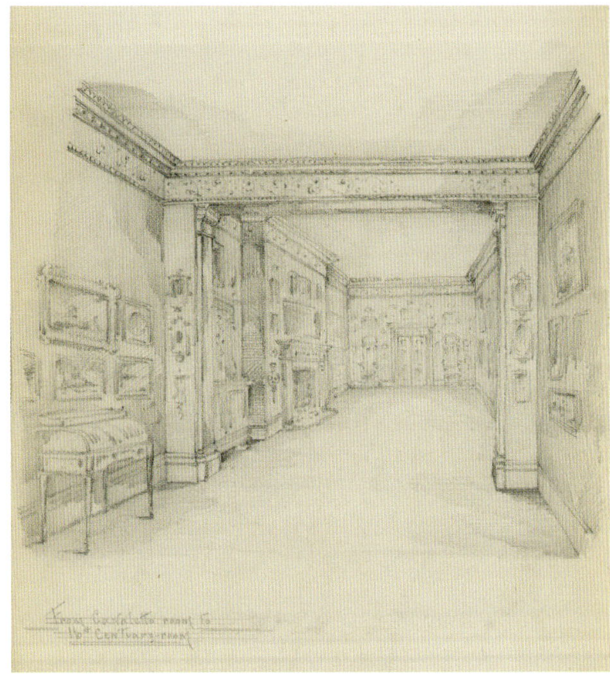

much richer selection of Venetian views than those at the National Gallery: 'We think much of the two or three Canaletto's in the National Gallery. Well here are 17 views of Venice by Canaletto.'[80] Nearly three decades before the Wallace Collection opened to the public as a national museum, Wallace's *vedute* were enjoyed by more than two million visitors from all walks of life.[81]

In 1875, once building works were complete, Wallace reinstalled the collection at Hertford House according to his taste. The earliest record of the collection following Wallace's redisplay was compiled by the German art historian Jean Paul Richter (1847–1937) between 1880 and 1881 for King Ludwig II of Bavaria.[82] Richter visited Hertford House in April 1879, together with art historians Wilhelm von Bode and Gustavo Frizzoni. Despite hanging the majority of his pictures upstairs on the first floor, Wallace kept the *vedute* on the ground floor where they had been since at least 1832. From Richter we know that Wallace moved the *vedute* from the Breakfast Room to what is today the Sixteenth-Century Gallery, which at that time consisted of two rooms: the Sixteenth-Century Room in the northern half and the Canaletto Room in the southern half. Sadly, there is no visual record of the Canaletto Room from Wallace's time; a photograph of the adjacent Sixteenth-Century Room sheds light on how Wallace displayed his collection (fig. 29). From inventories we know that Wallace hung his *vedute* alongside furniture and sumptuous decorative art

objects such as Sèvres porcelain. Interested mainly in the furnishings, Richter briefly noted the Venetian views. His account, erroneous in terms of attribution and number of pictures, is valuable as it confirms that Wallace continued to hang the *vedute* together in a dedicated gallery and that he changed their location within the ground floor.

During Wallace's time, the Canaletto Room was adjacent to the Reception Room (the Front State Room today) and functioned as a second reception. In 1897 Wallace's friend, the art critic Charles Yriarte, referred to the Canaletto Room as the parlour:

> In the parlour on the left are forty canvases of Canaletto and De Guardi, showing all the sights and monuments of Venice, of Brenta, the Laguna of the Campi and the Stradine. The four paintings over the door are probably the best of the masters', and came from the Duc de Morny's sale.[83]

The four large Guardis were rightly considered highlights of the collection. The inventory taken in 1898 after Lady Wallace's death the previous year still listed the view of Malta (P493) among the *vedute*; the small *capriccio* by Guardi (cat. 27) was relegated to the Billiard Room, probably because Wallace had been short of wall space.[84]

Two months after Lady Wallace's death on 16 February 1897, the government appointed a committee to consider the best location for the Wallace Collection as a museum. Members considered the visibility of the *vedute* on the ground floor and discussed the possibility of moving them to a top-lit gallery upstairs.[85] In the end, they decided to leave them in place for the time being.

That same year, the Wallace Collection's first board of trustees was formed. On 9 August 1897 the trustees proposed that 'the Canaletto Room and the Renaissance Room should be thrown together so as to make a single gallery'.[86] This proposal was agreed by 12 January 1898:

> In the gallery which will be formed by throwing into one the present Canaletto and Italian rooms we propose to concentrate the medieval and renaissance collections … It will be desirable however in subsequent arrangements to keep together as far as possible the great series of pictures by Canaletto and Guardi.[87]

The trustees clearly prized the *vedute* collection and wished wholeheartedly to continue to display it together as it had been for most of the nineteenth century.

A drawing from the late 1890s illustrates a draft of this proposal (fig. 30). It shows the north end of the Canaletto Room leading into the Sixteenth-Century Room.[88] In 1898–99 the partition wall dividing these two rooms was removed as part of building works undertaken from 1897 to 1900 to convert Hertford House into a museum.[89] Visitors were now able to move freely between what had been the Canaletto and Sixteenth-Century Rooms.

In the end, for the opening of the museum in 1900 the *vedute* were moved upstairs to the first floor. This was probably for better lighting and to be closer to the rest of the paintings collection. The *vedute* were hung in Gallery XII, which also featured French furniture and decorative art objects in cases (fig. 31).[90] They stayed there at least until the 1930s, and remain on the first floor to this day. The two large Bacino views now hang in the Great Gallery, while the rest of the *vedute* are in West Gallery I together with sculpture and furniture produced in Venice during the eighteenth century.

When the Wallace Collection first opened in 1900, the *vedute* were hailed as a highlight of the collection, as they still are today. Contemporary press celebrated the 'important series' of Venetian views by Canaletto and Guardi.[91] Writing in 1901, Mr Claude Phillips, the Wallace Collection's first Keeper, underscored how the *vedute* had always been 'one of the boasts of Hertford House'.[92] There was also an element of national pride: 'in this collection alone there are as many good "Canalettos" as in the whole of France'![93]

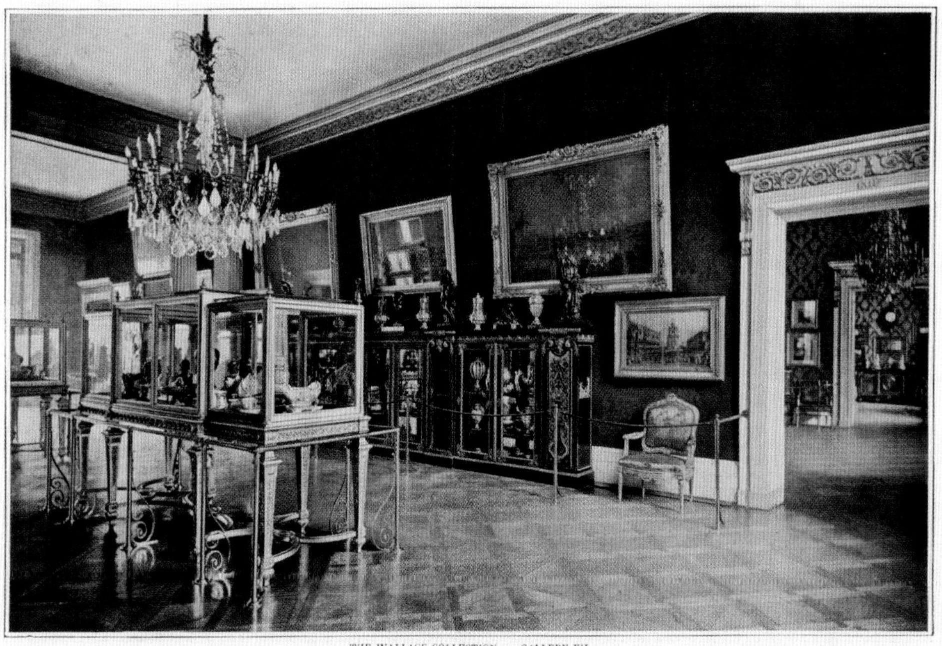

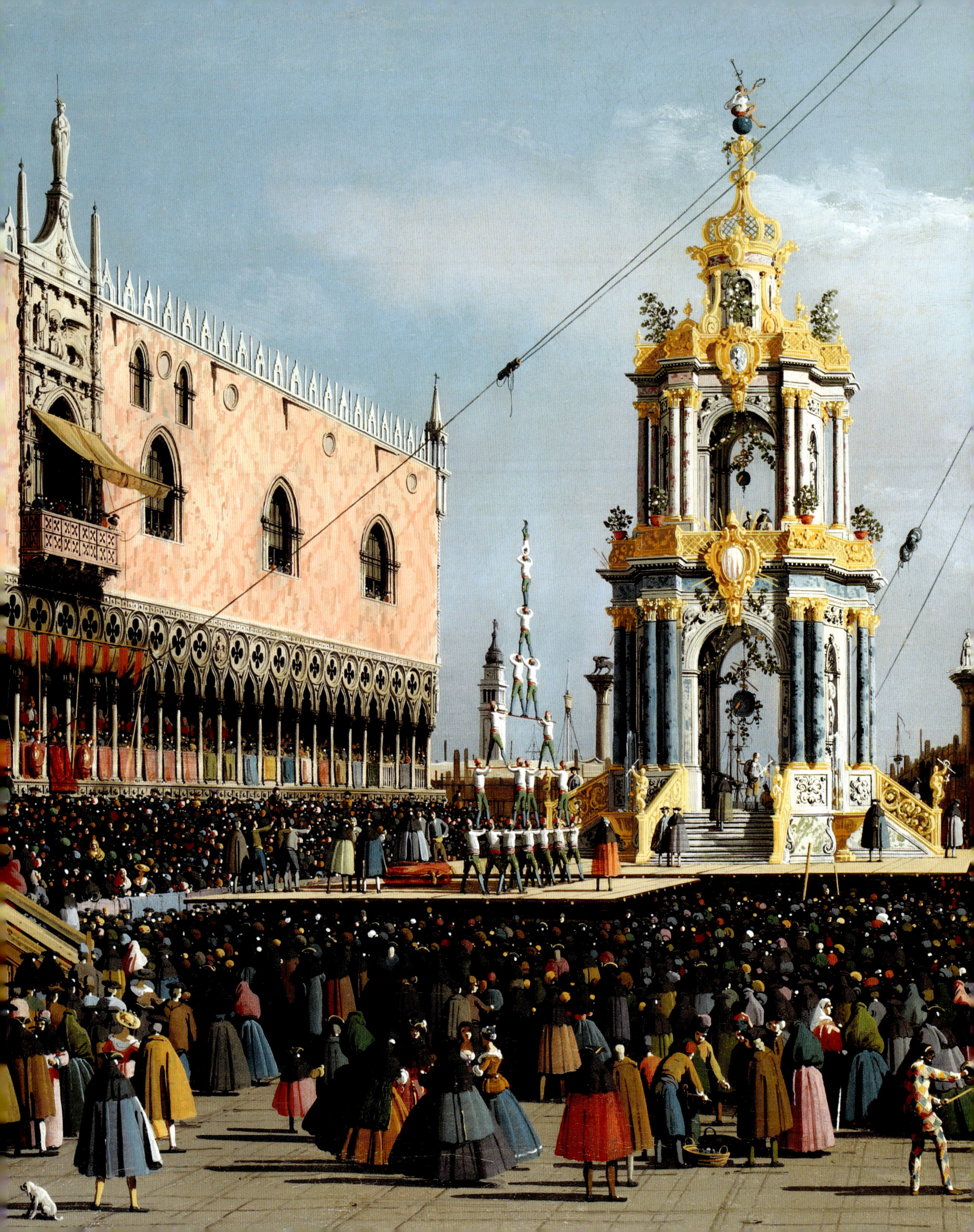

3 VENETIAN VIEWS BY PAINTERS IN CANALETTO'S CIRCLE

Charles Beddington

The demand from visitors to Venice for views of the city as a record of their trip grew exponentially in the first decades of the eighteenth century. Those unable to afford works by leading artists could have their appetite for souvenirs sated by paintings of a wide spectrum of quality and presumably cost. As well as the exceptional works by Canaletto, the Wallace Collection has a particularly interesting and instructive group of paintings from the artist's studio and close circle. Many of these raise attributional issues. Almost all of the paintings by Canaletto and his circle were catalogued as 'school' works in 1928,[1] and have been misunderstood consistently since. Their recent cleaning has facilitated a reassessment.

The first Venetian views to enter the collection were those acquired by its initiator, Francis, 2nd Baron Conway, later 1st Earl and 1st Marquess of Hertford (1719–1794). These included two pairs of paintings fundamentally accepted as Canaletto's work by the great Canaletto scholar W.G. Constable in his monographic catalogue of 1962, but with some disparaging remarks that he might have omitted if he had been aware of the early provenance. Any reservations about the level of quality have been dispelled by the recent cleaning.[2] Regrettably, it is not known exactly when Conway was in Venice on his Grand Tour, but it was probably in 1738 or 1739.[3] The style of Conway's acquisitions and what we know of Canaletto's normal modus operandi leave no doubt that the paintings were commissioned by the patron in Venice and delivered as soon as the artist could fulfil the order. It is curious that the paintings seem to have never been linked to Conway's Grand Tour and he is not even mentioned by the Canaletto specialist J.G. Links in his book on Canaletto's patrons.[4]

Several patrons of Canaletto around this date received groups of paintings surprisingly disparate in quality, size, style and authenticity, notably Henry Howard, 4th Earl of Carlisle, who was in Venice in November 1738 for a few months, and Henry Fiennes Clinton, 9th Earl of Lincoln, later 2nd Duke of Newcastle, who was in Venice from 5 June to 12 July 1741. Conway was no exception, receiving two other paintings, *A Regatta on the Grand Canal* (fig. 32) and *The Festival of Giovedì Grasso in the Piazzetta* (fig. 35), which, although of similar size, do not work well as a pair. The first of these has tended not to be highly regarded and appreciation of it is not helped by its overbearing nineteenth-century frame. It is, however, an original composition, varying significantly from the known versions by Canaletto of this subject dating from the 1730s: the one executed for Joseph Smith in *c.*1733–34 and now in the Royal Collection (fig. 34) and that painted in *c.*1735 for John Russell, 4th Duke of Bedford, and now at Woburn Abbey (fig. 33).[5] This should alert us immediately to the probability that Canaletto was more closely involved with it than has generally been recognised. It is much the smallest version of the subject (the only other 'small' variant, that in the Royal Collection, measures 77 × 125.7 cm) and Canaletto's highly distinctive touch is evident throughout, in the figures, the ornamental details of the *bissone* (Venetian ceremonial

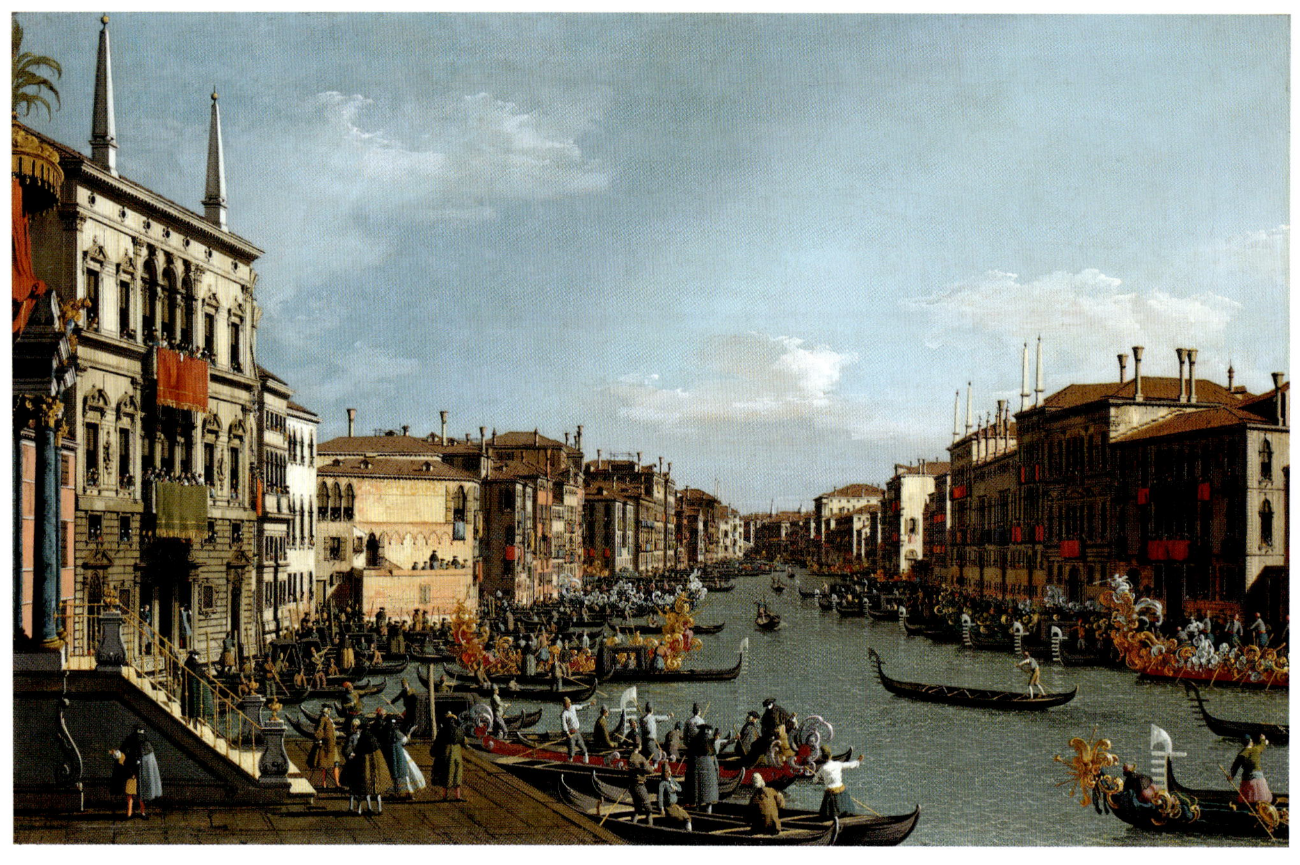

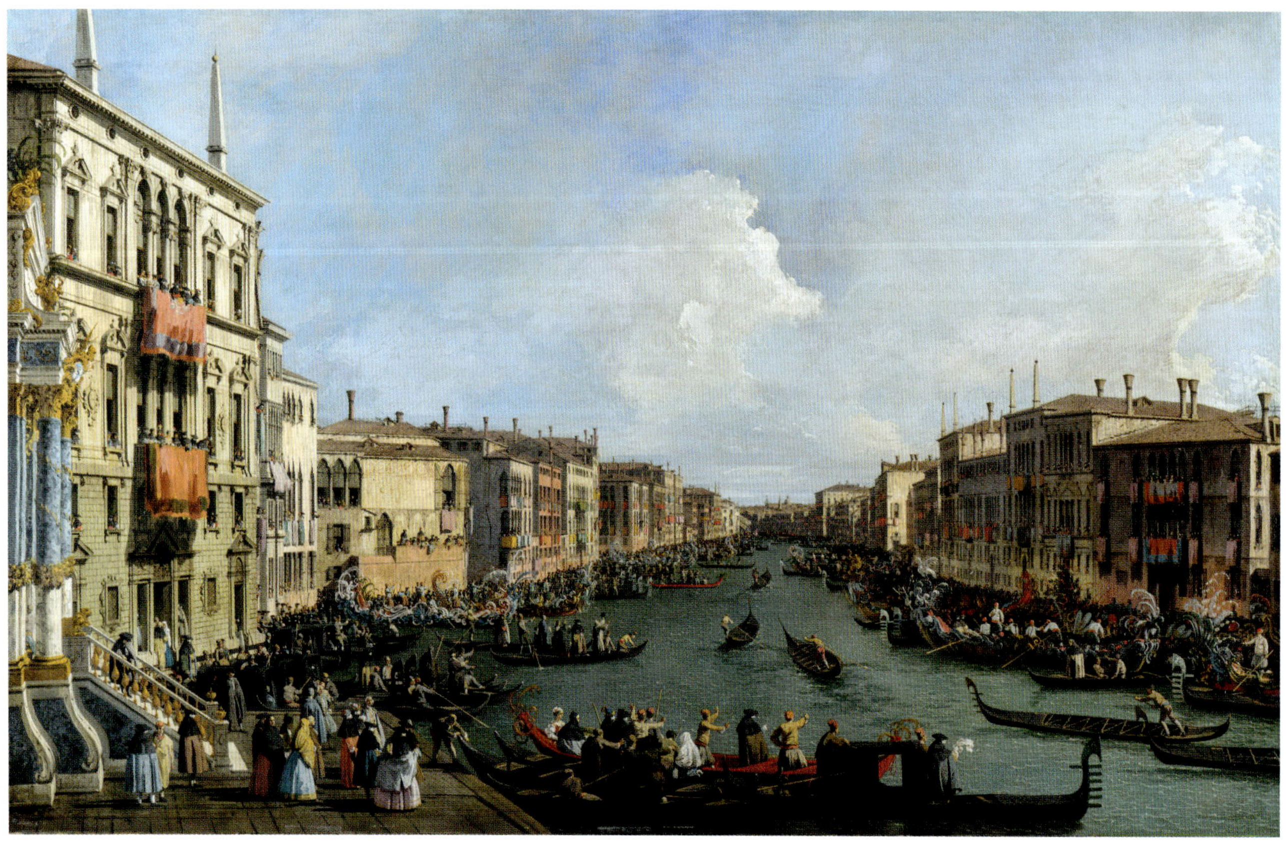

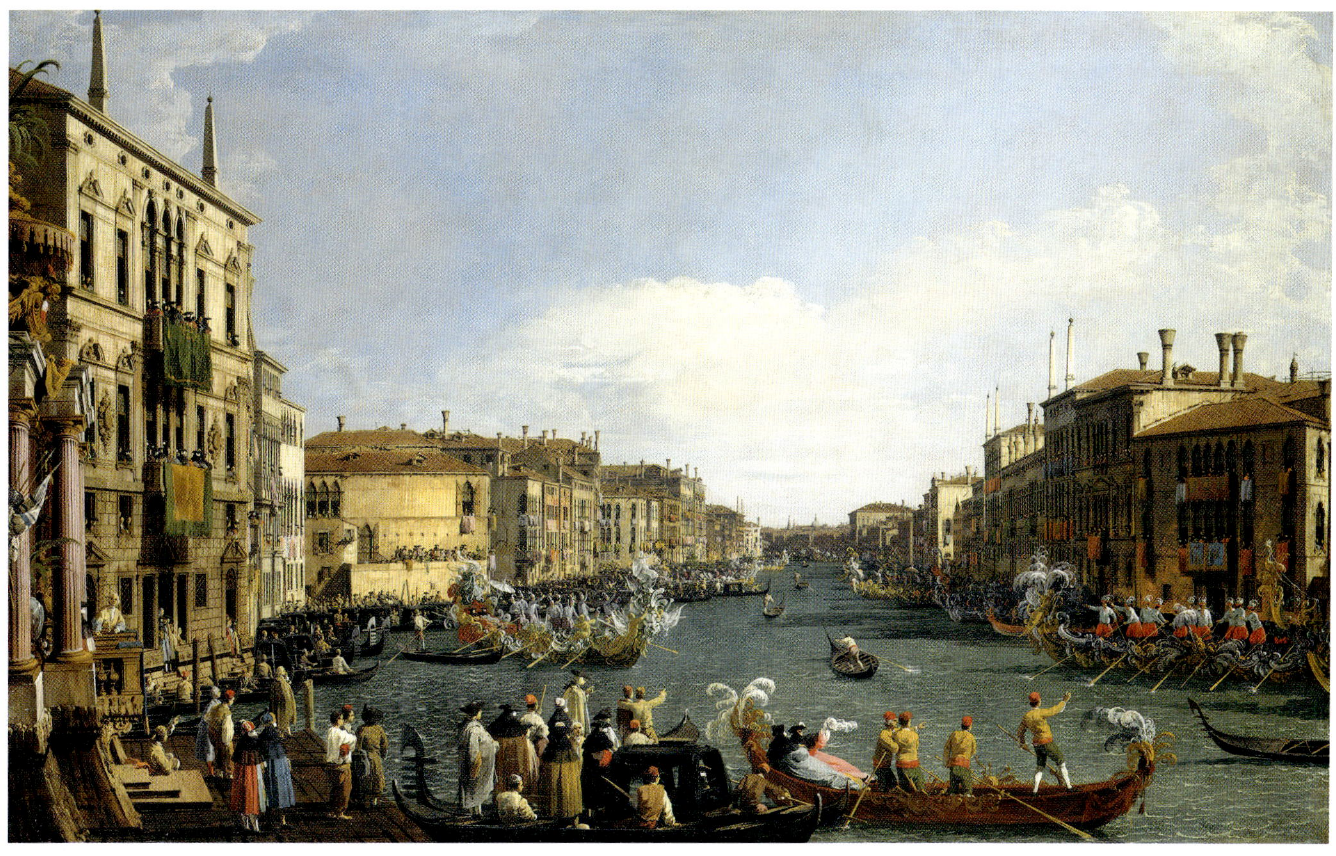

gondole) and the clouds. The painting was, indeed, the only one of the Wallace Venetian views described unequivocally as the work of Canaletto in the 1958 catalogue of the collection by its Director Sir Francis Watson, no mean connoisseur.

Opinions have differed on the relevance of coats of arms in Canaletto paintings. The painter does indeed often demonstrate a disregard for topographical accuracy, but also can be remarkably precise when he wants to be. The coat of arms on the *macchina* (temporary structure) on the far left is that of Alvise Pisani, who, having been elected in January 1735, was Doge when Conway was in Venice and remained so until his death on 17 June 1741 (fig. 36). On stylistic grounds there is no reason to doubt that the painting was executed during Pisani's reign.

The Festival of Giovedi Grasso in the Piazzetta (fig. 35) makes an awkward pendant to *A Regatta on the Grand Canal* (fig. 32), but is closely related to it in size, bright colouring and the subject being another of the city's more significant annual festivals. Here, the Pisani arms feature again, on the upper part of the temporary *macchina*, but are accompanied by the

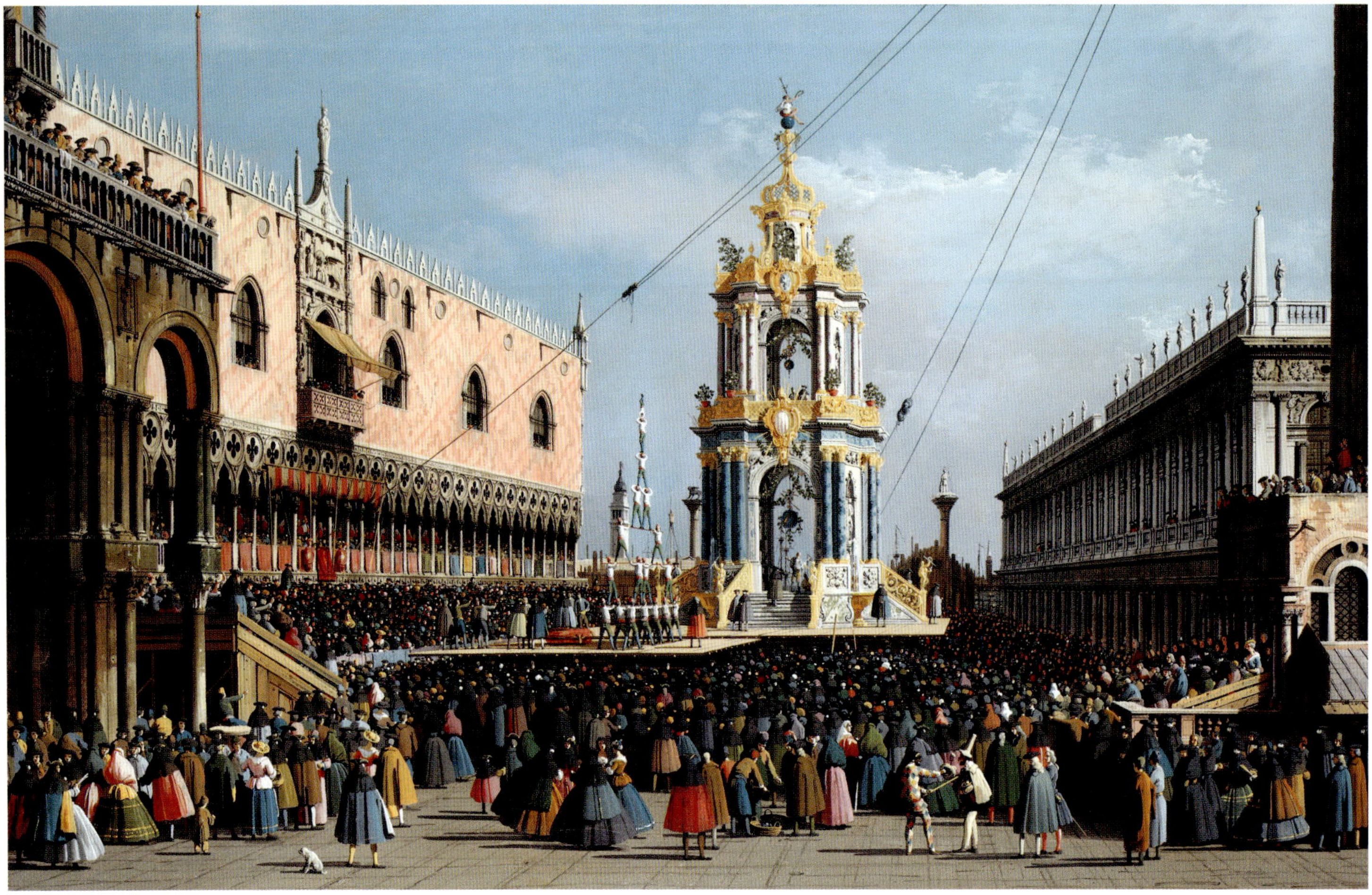

ABOVE:
Fig. 35. Studio of Canaletto (1697–1768), *The Festival of Giovedì Grasso in the Piazzetta*, *c.*1741/42, oil on canvas, 58.5 × 92.7 cm, The Wallace Collection, London (P500)

OPPOSITE:
Fig. 39. Canaletto (1697–1768), *The Festival of Giovedì Grasso in the Piazzetta*, *c.*1765/66, pen and brown ink with grey wash over traces of graphite, tip of the brush with black wash, heightened with touches of white gouache, sheet 38.7 × 55.5 cm, National Gallery of Art, Washington, DC (inv. 2007.111.55)

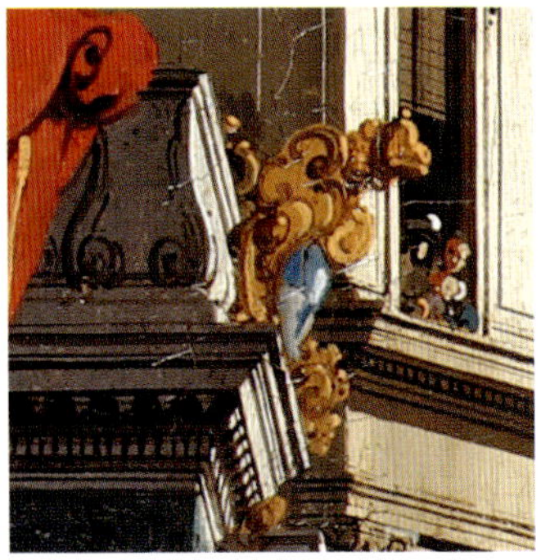

Fig. 36. Detail of fig. 32

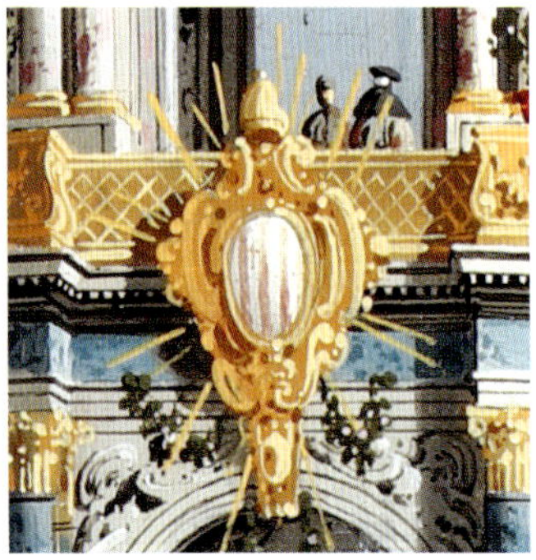

Fig. 37. Detail of fig. 35

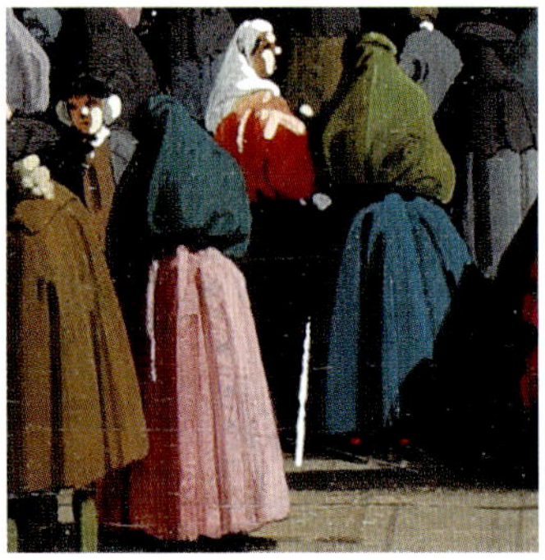

Fig. 38. Detail of fig. 35

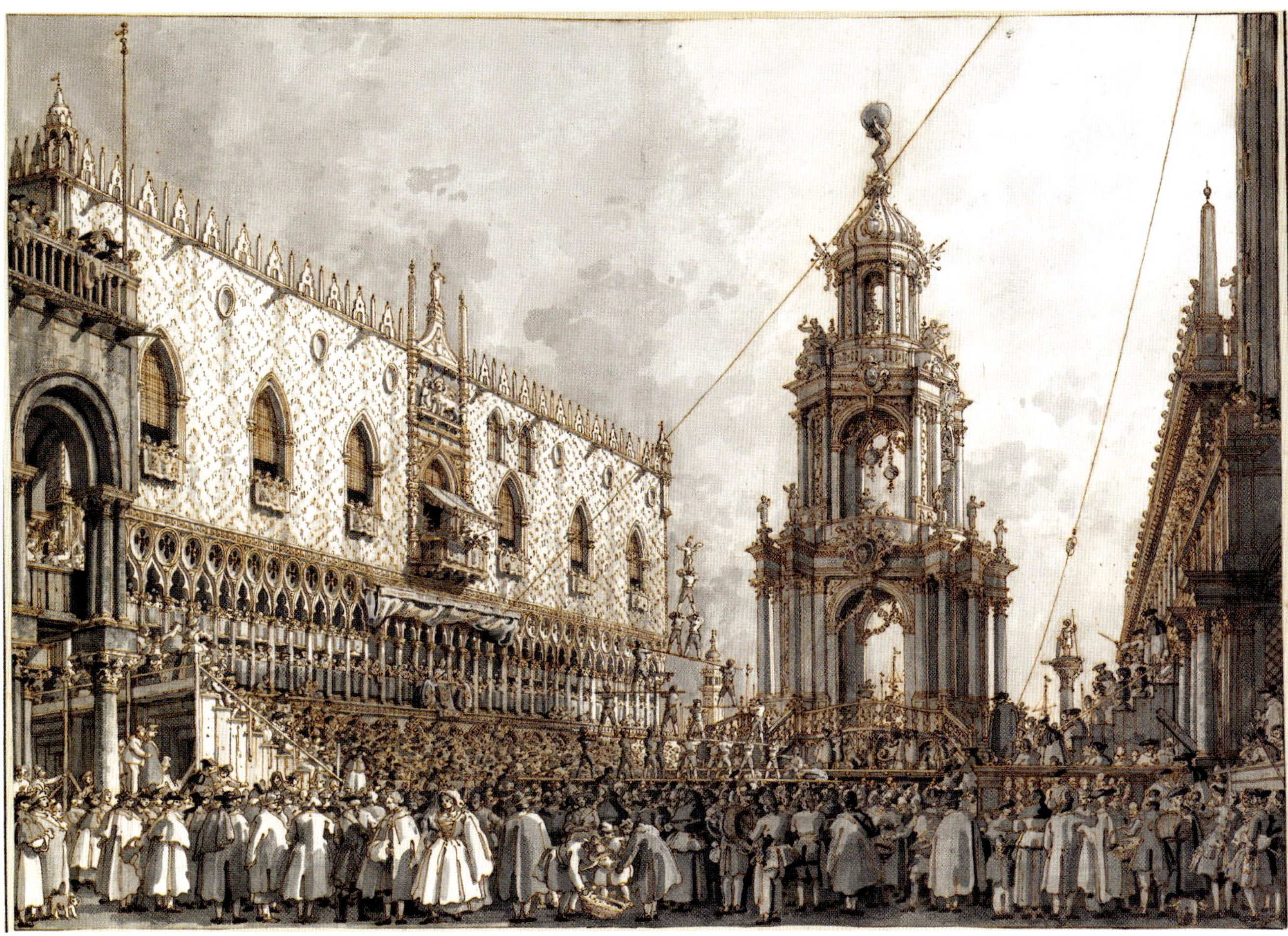

larger arms of the Grimani family (fig. 37). A *terminus ante quem* ('date before which') would seem to be provided by the absence of Antonio Gai's bronze gates to the forecourt of the Loggetta on the right, which were installed in 1742, and there is no reason to think that this painting is not of similar date to the other components of the group. It is thus all the more difficult to explain why the handling is so distinct from that of Canaletto. The quality of the painting is unquestionable.[6] It is executed with skill, spontaneity and even apparent haste, since the artist has, very surprisingly, left a long white vertical drip to the right of the pink skirt in the foreground just right of centre (fig. 38).[7]

Furthermore, there can be no question that Canaletto was responsible for the composition, not least because similarities with a drawing by him of the subject cannot be coincidental (fig. 39).[8] The drawing dates from late in Canaletto's career and was made as the model for a print, one of a set of 12 *Feste Ducali* by Giovanni Battista Brustolon (1712–1796). All of the other compositions are entirely original, but the drawing now in Washington is a self-conscious updating of the composition of this painting. The viewpoint has been lowered, pulled back and moved to the right, and the *macchina* is different, but the resemblances include men bending over a basket or baskets in the centre foreground, a solitary gentleman in a *bauta* (Venetian mask, veil and tricorn) and a dark cloak directly in front of the right edge of the *macchina*, and the way that the tips of ships' masts poke up in gaps in the background. To those details may be added the treatment of most of the central bay of the façade of the Doge's Palace, above the Doge, including the figures on the balcony. The figures and faces are entirely Canaletto types and painted very much in his manner – also the dog – but there is a flatness and stiffness in the dresses and cloaks and there are obvious weaknesses, notably the legs of the Pulchinello. Most significantly, Canaletto's characteristic handwriting and unique ability to render texture and form are nowhere apparent and it must be presumed

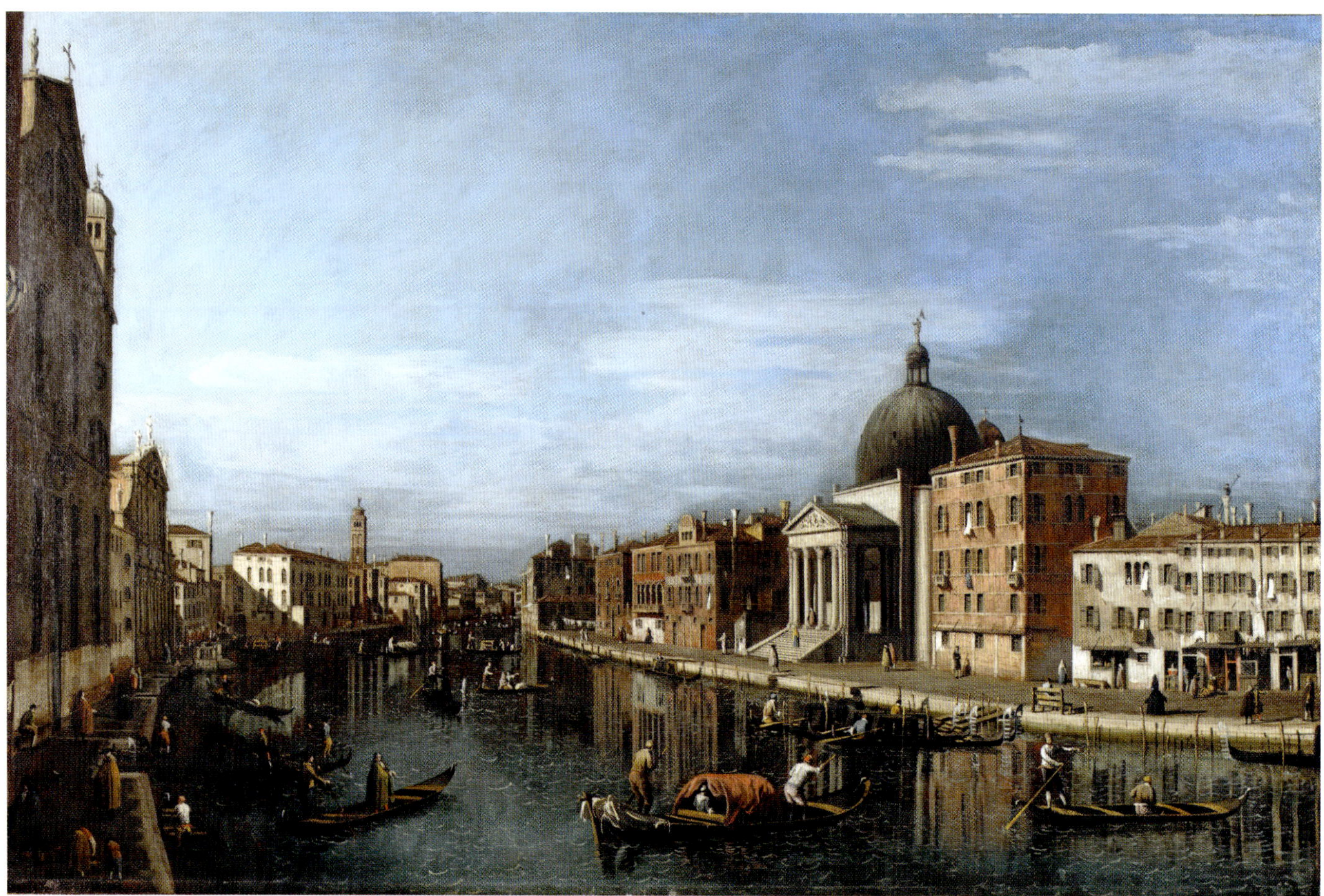

Fig. 40. Bernardo Bellotto (1722–1780), *The Grand Canal, Looking East, with the Church of San Simeone Piccolo*, *c*.1737, oil on canvas, 96.4 × 148 cm, The Wallace Collection, London (P498)

that the execution of this sixth component of the group of paintings for Conway was delegated to a highly proficient studio assistant. The studio was particularly well stocked with assistants in the years around 1740 and their contributions to Canaletto's work are yet to be properly investigated, let alone established.[9]

The larger painting of *The Grand Canal, Looking East, with the Church of San Simeone Piccolo* (fig. 40) must date from the same period, around the time of the completion of the church of San Simeone Piccolo, which was consecrated on 27 April 1738.[10] It was bought in 1859 as 'a very important and capital work' by 'Canaletti',[11] and in 1900 was considered by Claude Phillips, the first Keeper of the Wallace Collection, as the most authentic of its Canaletti. Its very variable quality has resulted in much discussion in recent decades of its possible authorship, but in general it has been considered probably

the furthest from Canaletto of the paintings in the collection. Much the weakest elements are some of the foreground figures, which are crudely painted and disproportionately tall in relation to their far more elegant smaller neighbours. On the other hand, the composition is a remarkable achievement. Showing the view in the opposite direction to Canaletto's masterpiece of *c*.1740 (fig. 41),[12] it is unique, and the care with which it was worked out is shown by *pentimenti* (changes), notably in the width of the quay on the left, whose edge initially ran through the left side of the bending woman. The stretch of buildings on the far right, and the quay and figures in front of them, are particularly Canalettesque and especially beautifully painted. Constable noted, 'Definitely not [Canaletto]. Has smudgy touch … But very beautiful sense of tone, & finely dramatic lighting.'[13] In fact, much about the painting is consistent with the work of Canaletto's

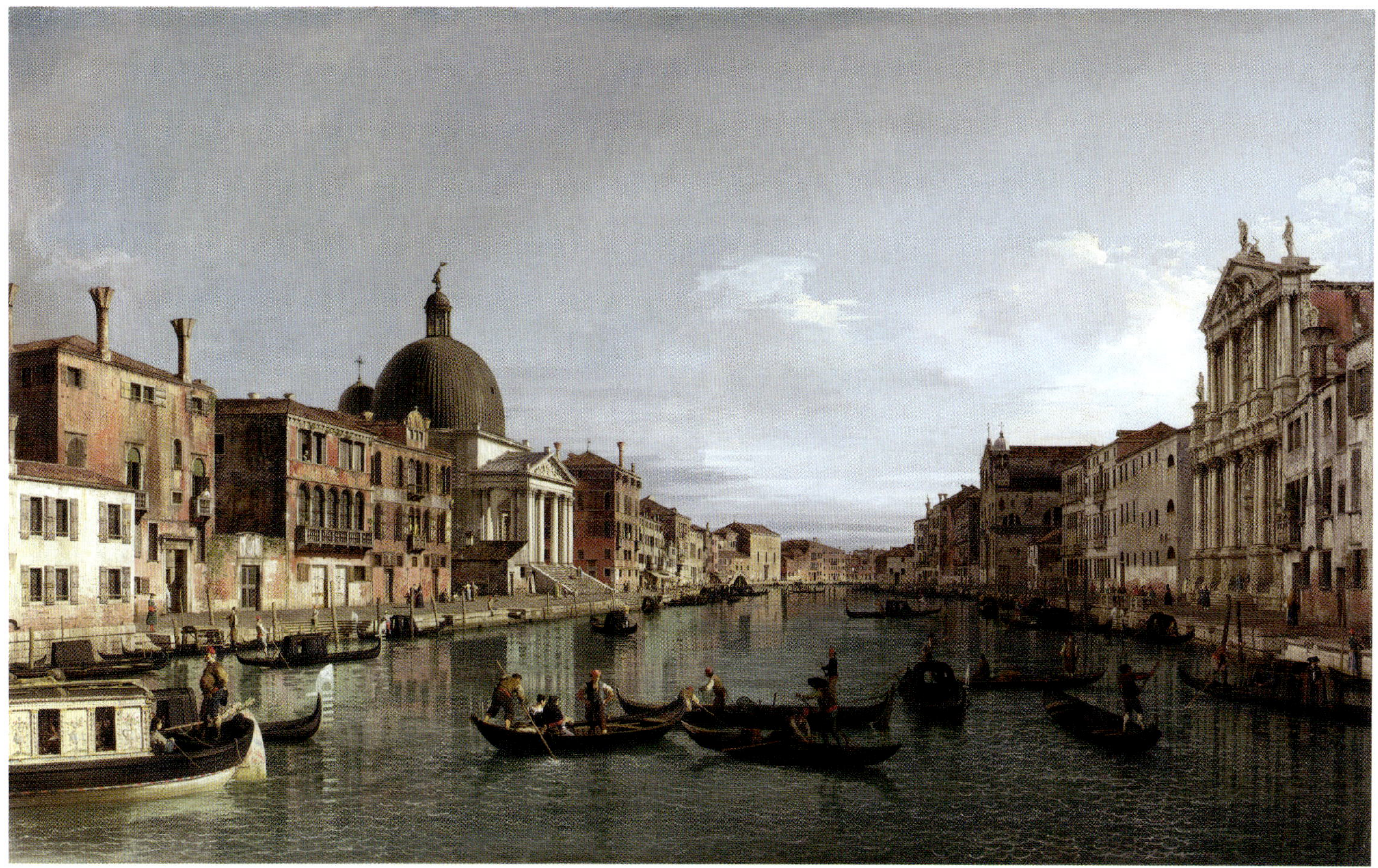

unquestionably most talented studio assistant in the years around 1740, his nephew and pupil Bernardo Bellotto. His authorship was proposed, apparently for the first time, by Bożena Anna Kowalczyk in 1996, but did not find wider agreement at that point.[14] Characteristic of his work are the cold light, much of the colouring, the application of the sky diagonally towards the lower left, the treatment of reflections of buildings, the way that boats tend to sit on rather than in the water, the formula for the water and many of the figure types. A number of the more prominent figures look away from the viewer, so that the artist did not have to paint their faces. The clumsy large figures have parallels in such paintings as *The Bacino di San Marco on Ascension Day* of *c.*1739 at Castle Howard (fig. 42).[15] Bellotto was astonishingly precocious and was inscribed in the Venetian painters' guild in 1738, when he was only 16 years old. This painting might well be of an even

earlier date; the consecration of the church in 1738 does not provide help because its exterior was already substantially complete ten years earlier, as a painting by Canaletto in the Royal Collection demonstrates.[16]

All of the other Venetian views in the Wallace Collection are, at least to a large degree, copies of compositions by Canaletto. Copies were fundamentally of two types, differing widely in quality. They could easily be made from prints, from the 1730s onwards notably the etchings by Antonio Visentini published in 1735 as the *Prospectus Magni Canalis Venetiarum*. These were after a series of 14 Canaletto views, all but one of the Grand Canal, in the collection of Canaletto's agent and foremost patron Joseph Smith (often known as Consul Smith from his role as British Consul, 1744–60). A second edition of 1742 with a further 24 plates after paintings that had been commissioned through Smith helped to expand the copyists' repertoire.

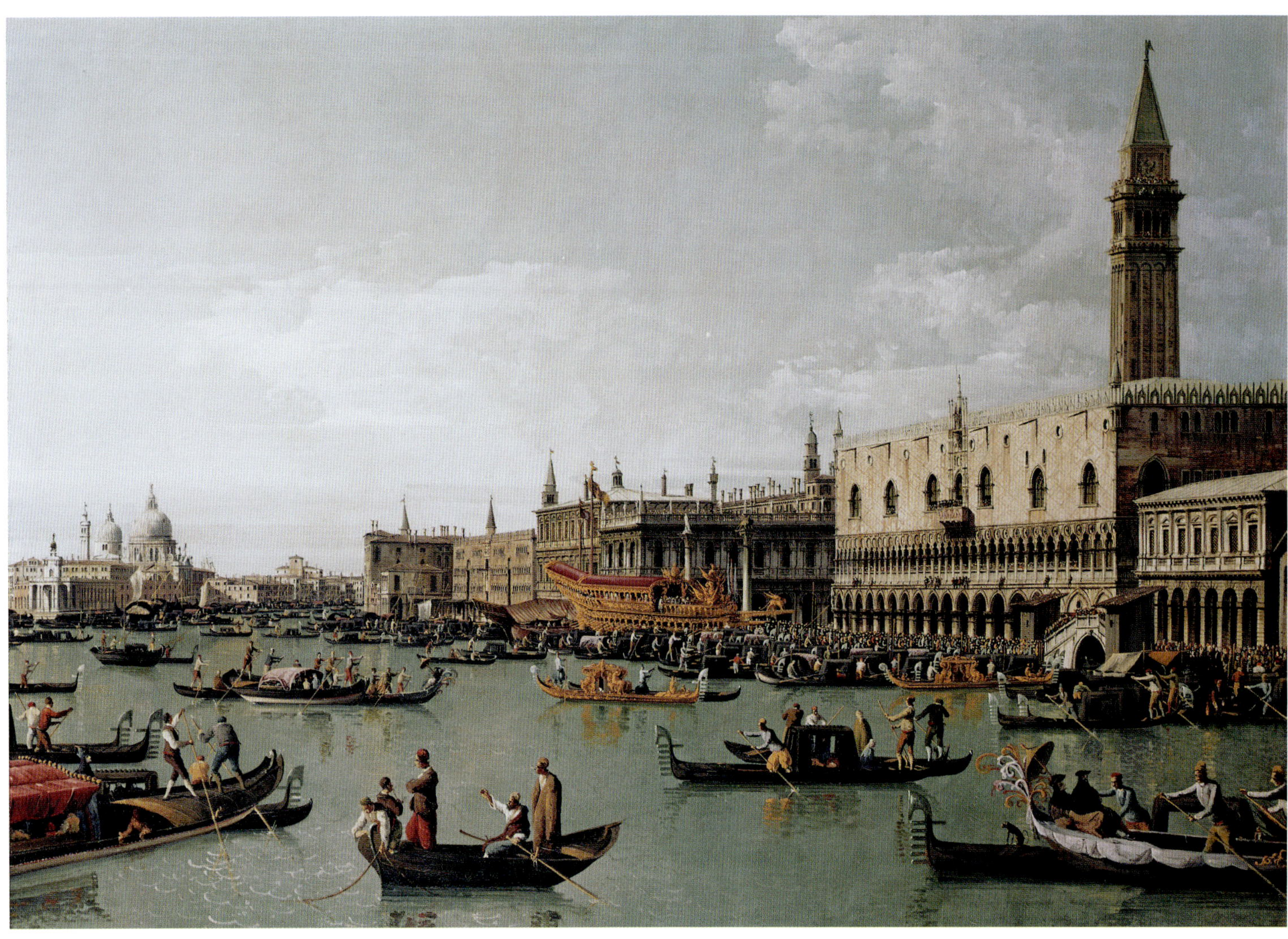

Even Bellotto seems to have had to depend on Visentini's prints when he came to do his own versions of the compositions of his uncle's views in Smith's collection. Bellotto aside, copies by painters who had direct access to Canaletto's paintings were of significantly higher quality. Almost all of the better copies are clearly by Venetian painters, and correspondence of colour may usually be taken as evidence that they are coeval with the prototypes, since Canaletto's paintings would have been sent off as quickly as possible to the clients who had commissioned them. Most of the examples in the Wallace Collection are of this type.

Four of the Wallace views are interesting exceptions. Evidently by the same hand, they might be mistaken for a set, but they came into the collection as two pairs, *The Grand Canal from the Palazzi Foscari and Moro-Lin to Santa Maria della Carità* (fig. 43) with *The Entrance to the Grand Canal, Looking East, with the Church of Santa Maria della Salute* (fig. 44) and *The Grand Canal from the Campo San Vio* (fig. 45) with *The Dogana and Santa Maria della Salute from the Molo* (fig. 46). They differ from other early copies of Canaletto paintings in several significant respects. All are based not on pictures commissioned through Smith for dispatch to Britain or Ireland, but on works in his personal collection at his house on the Grand Canal, where they remained until most of the collection was sold to King George III in 1762, since when they have been in the British Royal Collection. While the prototypes date

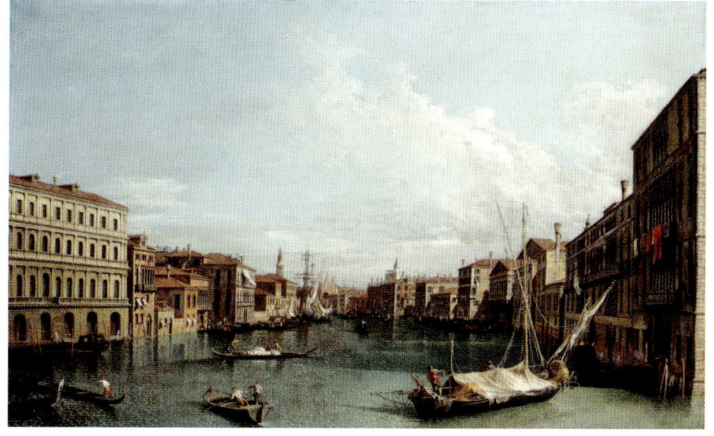

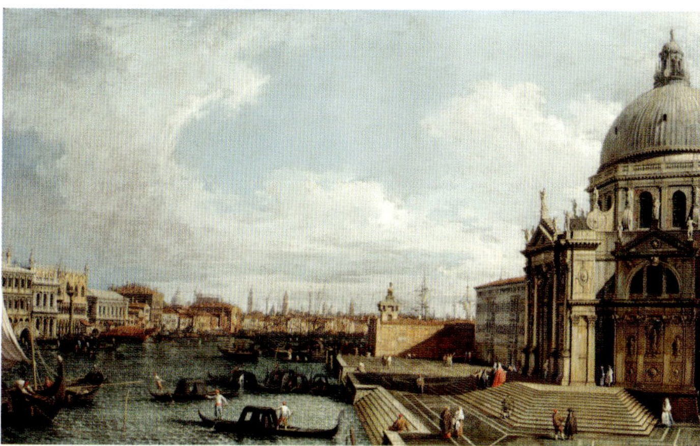

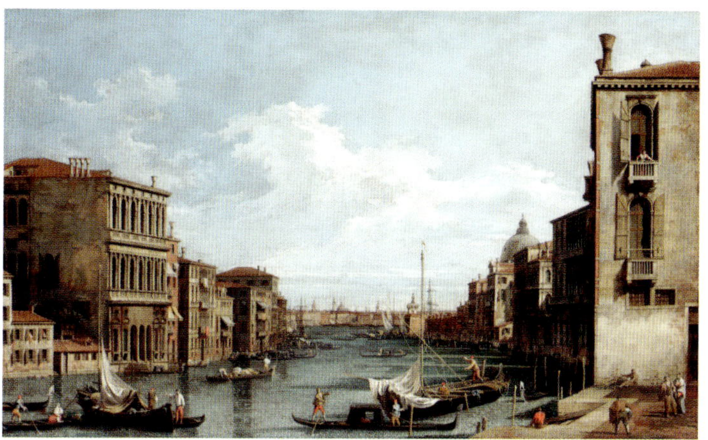

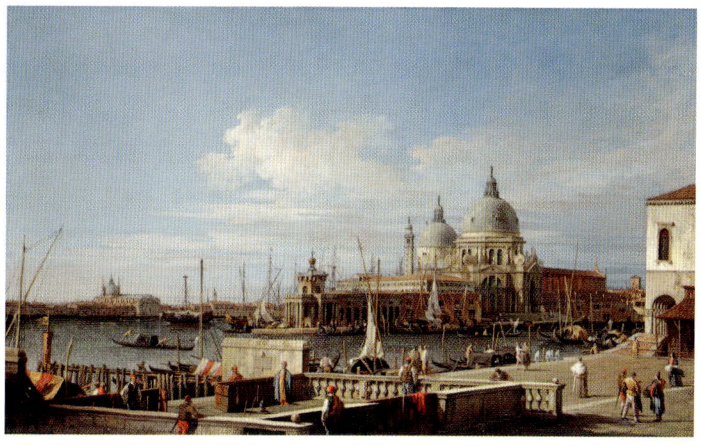

Fig. 43. Antonio Visentini (1688–1782), *The Grand Canal from the Palazzi Foscari and Moro-Lin to Santa Maria della Carità*, c.1750s, oil on canvas, 47 × 78.5 cm, The Wallace Collection, London (P492)

Fig. 44. Antonio Visentini (1688–1782), *The Entrance to the Grand Canal, Looking East, with the Church of Santa Maria della Salute*, c.1750s, oil on canvas, 47 × 78.3 cm, The Wallace Collection, London (P495)

Fig. 45. Antonio Visentini (1688–1782), *The Grand Canal from the Campo San Vio*, c.1750s, oil on canvas, 47 × 78.5 cm, The Wallace Collection, London (P512)

Fig. 46. Antonio Visentini (1688–1782), *The Dogana and Santa Maria della Salute from the Molo*, c.1750s, oil on canvas, 48.5 × 79.5 cm, The Wallace Collection, London (P515)

from the late 1720s and early 1730s, the copies are not coeval but must be of the 1750s. They must therefore be by a painter (unique among copyists) given access to Smith's house. While all are of similar size to the prototypes, the painter did not feel bound to slavishly copy them and in *The Grand Canal from the Campo San Vio* (fig. 45) he has 'improved' the composition by including four new figures.

The present writer has identified 18 other copies (with or without variations) of Venetian views by Canaletto as the work of the same hand and has recently identified him as Antonio Visentini.[17] Visentini had a working relationship with Smith from 1717 until the latter's death in 1770, serving him as etcher, architect (including notably of the façade of Smith's palazzo

on the Grand Canal, unveiled in October 1751), draughtsman and librarian, as well as the painter, in 1746 in collaboration with Francesco Zuccarelli, of 11 *capricci* overdoors (probably for Smith's country villa at Mogliano). He subsequently served as Professor of Architectural Perspective at the Venetian Accademia di Belle Arti and his most exceptional paintings are a set of eight huge *capricci* of imaginary palatial villas, a dock and a country convent in the portico of the Palazzo Contarini Fasan, Venice, which form one of the great decorative ensembles of eighteenth-century Venice (fig. 47). He is most widely known today for his series of etchings after Venetian views by Canaletto (fig. 48), 44 exquisite drawings for which are in an album that belonged to Smith (fig. 49).

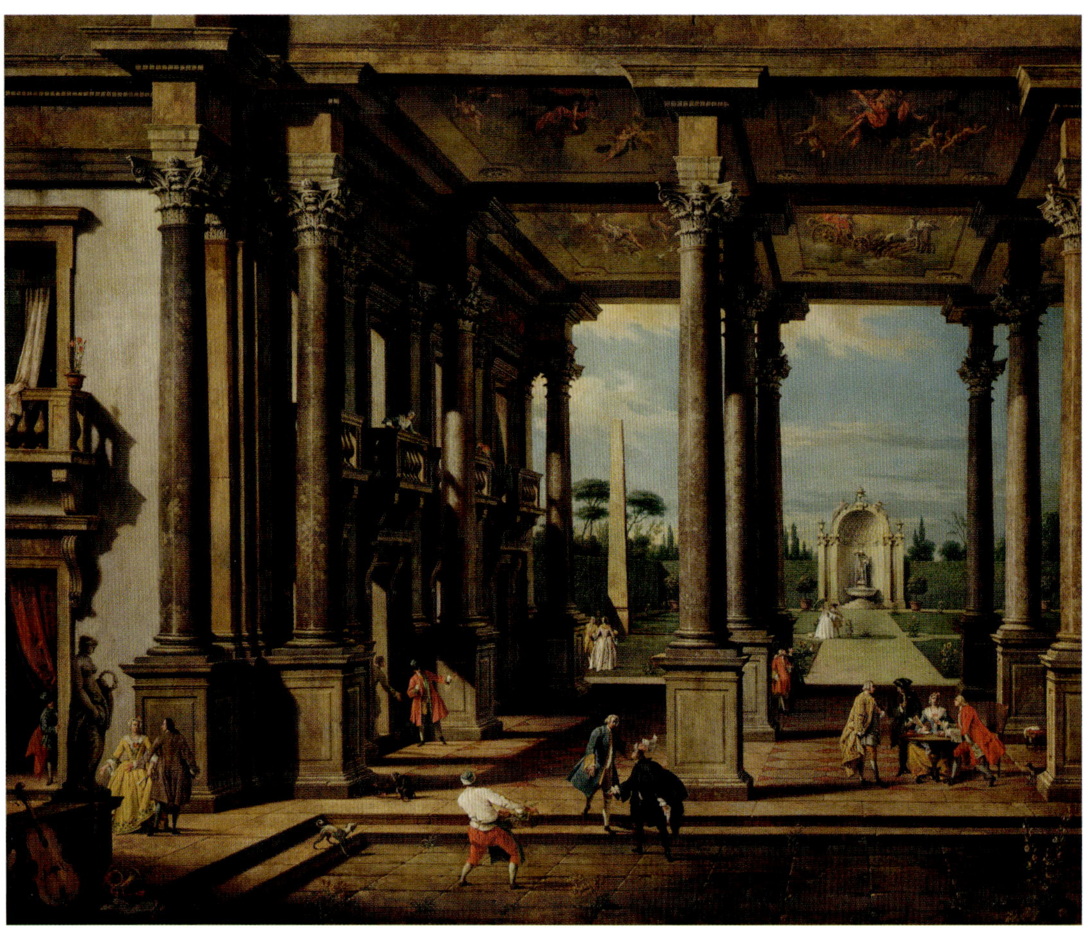

Fig. 47. Antonio Visentini (1688–1782),
*An Imaginary Palatial Villa with
a Reading of Tarot Cards*, c.1740,
oil on canvas, 207 × 252 cm,
Palazzo Contarini Fasan, Venice

Visentini's highly distinctive, finicky formula for water owes
more to his engraver's mentality than it does to the models for
his prints. There is every reason to believe that Smith was in
need of painters of Venetian views while Canaletto was absent
in London (1746–55) and that at some point around 1750 he
persuaded Visentini to help out by adding view painting to his
repertoire for probably the first time.

The Molo from the Bacino di San Marco (fig. 50) is by one
of the first copyists to make high-quality copies of Venetian
views by Canaletto after the artist's career took off at the
beginning of the 1730s. That had much to do with Canaletto's
business arrangement with Smith, probably agreed in 1730,
and it was no doubt Smith who had the idea of employing
very able local painters to cater to a less affluent clientele by
having copies made before the originals were shipped off to
the British and Irish gentlemen who had commissioned them.
Whether Canaletto was aware that his work was being copied
we may never know. This painter, who we may call 'the Wallace
Master', set out to produce same-size, stroke-for-stroke replicas

of works by Canaletto, in this case one of a pair unrecorded
before their sale in London in 1928 and their acquisition
for the Pinacoteca di Brera, Milan (fig. 51).[18] The result is
convincing enough that Constable described it as 'a studio
repetition, probably in part by Canaletto',[19] and indeed another
version, sold at auction in London in 1998 as 'Attributed to
Canaletto and Studio', was repeatedly, through the following
decade, exhibited and published as the work of Canaletto and
eventually sold as such to a private collector.[20] A copy by the
same hand of the Pinacoteca di Brera pendant showing *The
Grand Canal from the Campo San Vio* was bequeathed in 2001
to the Ashmolean Museum, Oxford (fig. 52); it may originally
have been the pendant to one or other of the Molo views.[21]
Another copy of *The Grand Canal from the Campo San Vio* in
an English private collection has as a pendant a copy of *The
Entrance to the Grand Canal, Looking East* from a different pair
by Canaletto.[22] This is interesting, as it shows that the painter
must have had access to both pairs of prototypes more or
less simultaneously, and the pairing demonstrates a degree of

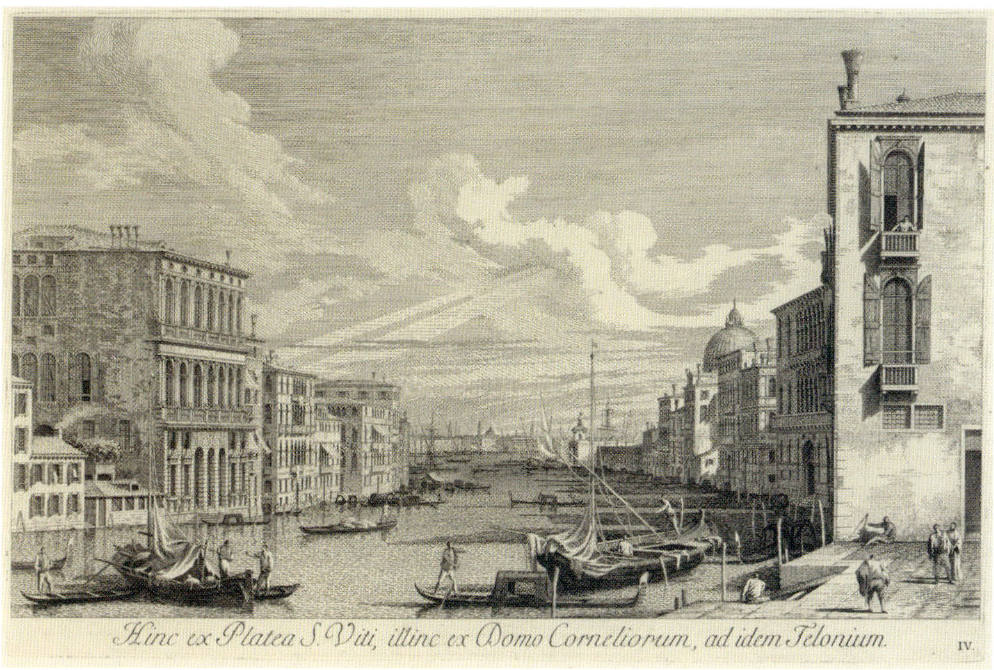

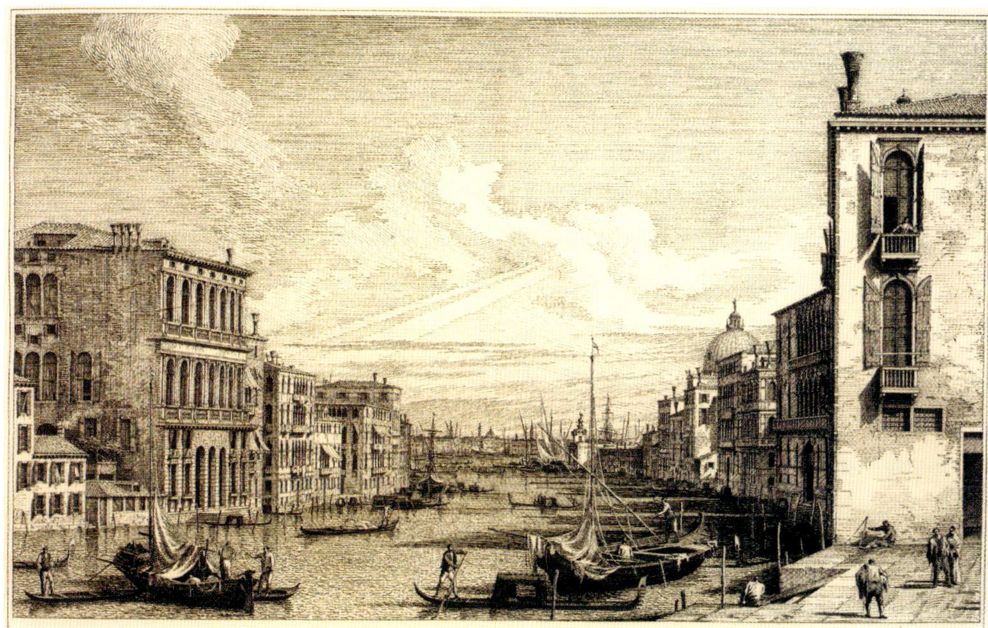

Fig. 48. Antonio Visentini (1688–1782) after Canaletto (1697–1768), *The Grand Canal from the Campo San Vio*, 1735, etching, 25.2 × 42 cm, plate 4 from *Prospectus Magni Canalis Venetiarum*

Fig. 49. Antonio Visentini (1688–1782) after Canaletto (1697–1768), *The Grand Canal from the Campo San Vio*, early 1730s, pen and brown ink, 25.5 × 42.7 cm, British Museum, London (inv. 1948,0704.7)

invention usually absent from the copies themselves. A view of *The Quay of the Dogana and the Giudecca Canal* sold at auction in 1999 is unusual in including a notable variation from the prototype in the Kunsthistorisches Museum, Vienna; a figure in a gondola at the lower left has been replaced by two quite different figures.[23] In a copy in an Italian private collection of the Vienna *Riva degli Schiavoni, Looking West*, there are some differences in the colours of the clothing, generally making

them brighter.[24] Elsewhere, this copyist's work is notable for the precision with which he aims to replicate every stroke, but he fails to emulate the differentiation of textures in the prototypes and his surfaces are uniformly smoother.

The Bacino di San Marco on Ascension Day with the Bucintoro Departing for the Lido (fig. 54) is clearly based on Giovanni Battista Brustolon's etching after Canaletto of *c.*1766 (fig. 55), from the same series of *Feste Ducali* as *The Festival of Giovedì*

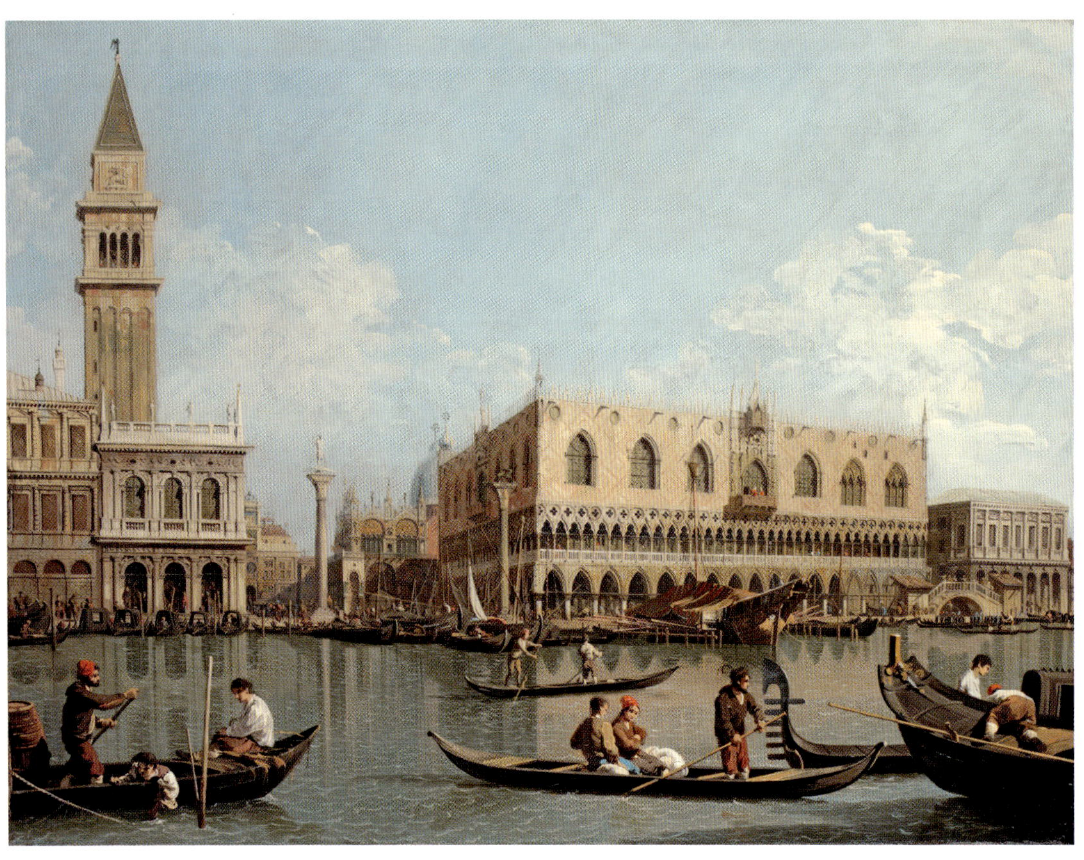

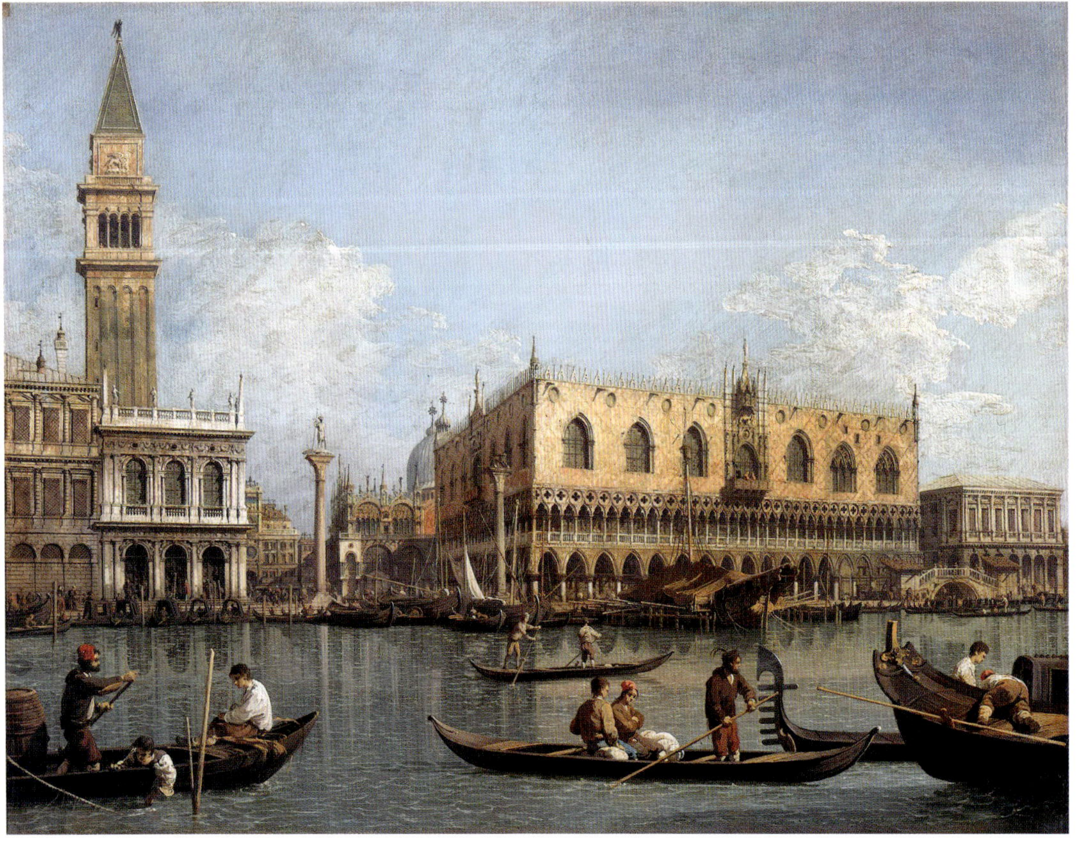

ABOVE:
Fig. 50. The Wallace Master (active in the 1730s), *The Molo from the Bacino di San Marco*, *c.*1734, oil on canvas 53.8 × 70 cm, The Wallace Collection, London (P514)

BELOW:
Fig. 51. Canaletto (1697–1768), *The Molo from the Bacino di San Marco*, *c.*1734, oil on canvas, 53 × 70 cm, Pinacoteca di Brera, Milan (inv. 2236)

OPPOSITE:
Fig. 52. The Wallace Master (active in the 1730s), *The Grand Canal from the Campo San Vio*, early 1730s, oil on canvas, 52.4 × 70.5 cm, Ashmolean Museum, Oxford (inv. WA 2001.183)

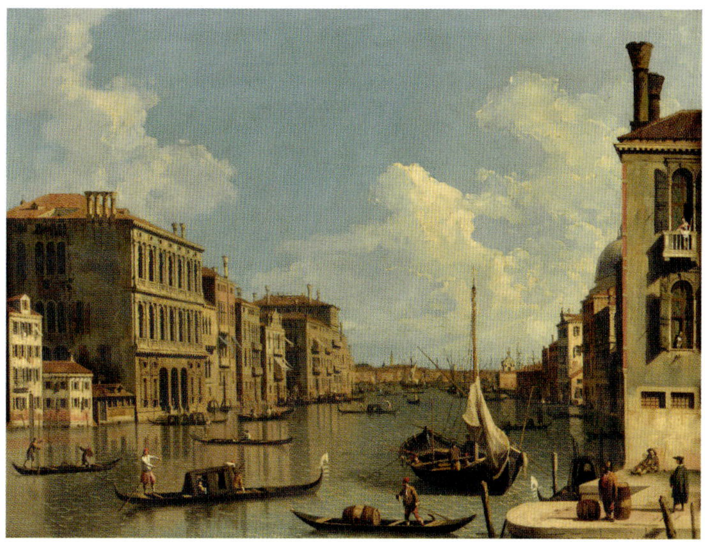

Grasso in the Piazzetta mentioned above (fig. 39). It adheres so loosely to the composition, however, that it would be inappropriate to describe it as a copy. This is particularly evident in the figures, which in their colouring and in their agitated forms are closer in style to Francesco Guardi than to Canaletto. This blend of the styles of Canaletto and Guardi is characteristic of the work of Francesco Tironi. Surprisingly little is known about Tironi's life; in fact, all that we know for certain is that in 1806 he had 'died too young a few years ago'.[25] He has been identified with a priest of that name who died on 28 February 1797 at the age of about 52, but that was hardly 'young' by Venetian standards of the day and there is no evidence that this priest was also an artist. Another candidate is a Francesco Spiridione Tironi (1757–1791), but his stated business was running a shop that sold account books and white paper. There is, however, a substantial body of drawings that are certainly by Tironi, many of them for etchings by Antonio Sandi (1733–1817), including a set entitled *Twenty-Four Views of Islands in the Venetian Lagoon*, published by Ludovico Furlanetto in Venice at some point after 1779.[26] There are also quite a few paintings signed with the initials 'F T' that are clearly by the same hand, and a very large quantity in the same style but varying too widely in quality to be the work of the same artist.

The Piazza San Marco, Looking West (fig. 56) is the exception to the rule and, in this context, of particular interest in being so, as it is a copy or variant of significant quality that is demonstrably not by a Venetian painter nor painted in Venice. During recent cleaning it was found to have a typically English warm grey ground.[27] Furthermore, that the artist

was unfamiliar with Venice has become highly obvious due to him having been asked to extend the composition on the sides, to make a wider, overdoor shape. In the prototype, then at Bedford House in Bloomsbury Square, London, and now at Woburn Abbey, the composition is cut on the left through the keystone of the arch over the doorway of the Loggetta (fig. 57).[28] Beyond that point this painter has got everything wrong, with the Loggetta curiously abbreviated to one bay. The size has been scaled up from the prototype, roughly in the ratio 3:2, and a scaling-up grid in the centre foreground, revealed by infrared light but just visible to the naked eye, would seem to be unique in a painting of this kind (fig. 53). It is annotated 'Cop' and 'Ori', which offers no proof of the nationality of the painter. The handling and colouration make an English hand highly probable. His skill as a copyist and ability to provide three additional convincingly Canalettesque large figures, two gentlemen on the left and a lady on the right, very unusual in English Canaletto copies, suggest that he may become identifiable. The Duke of Bedford presumably allowed him access to the original at Bedford House (although the possibility that he copied another copy cannot be excluded). In the 1870 Hertford House inventory the painting was described as 'Beckford's'. William Beckford (1709–1770), who inherited Fonthill, Wiltshire, in 1737 and who became an alderman of London in 1752, happens to have been both a political associate of the Duke of Bedford and a patron of the view painter Antonio Joli (1700–1777).

Thus, the large group of Venetian views at the Wallace Collection is unequalled in its representation of the work of Canaletto and his imitators in the 1730s and 1740s. The only significant copyists in this period whose oeuvre it has been possible to define (to date) and who are not represented in the collection are the two who provided Venetian views for William, 1st Viscount Bateman (c.1695–1744).[29]

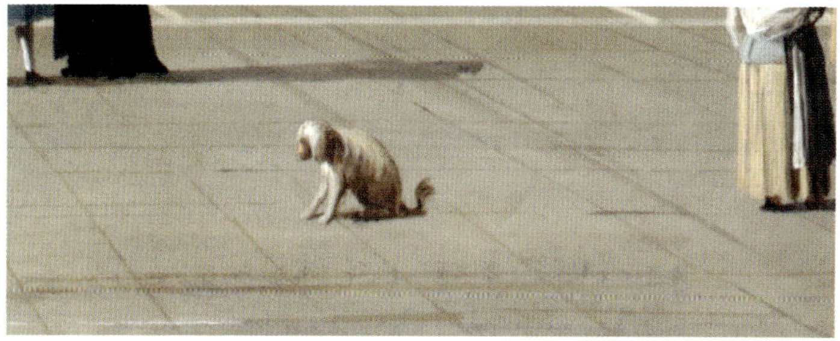

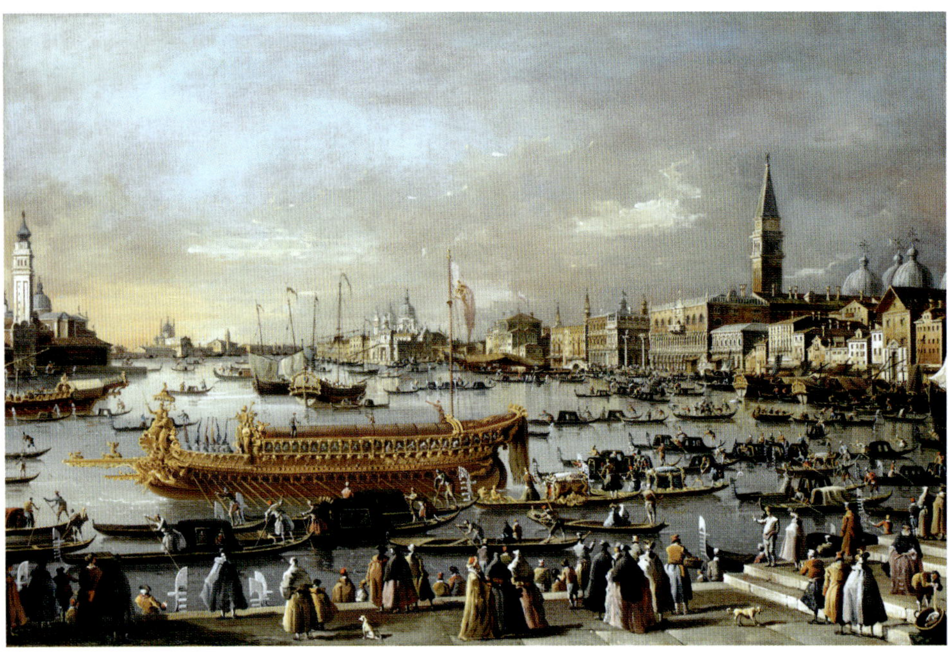

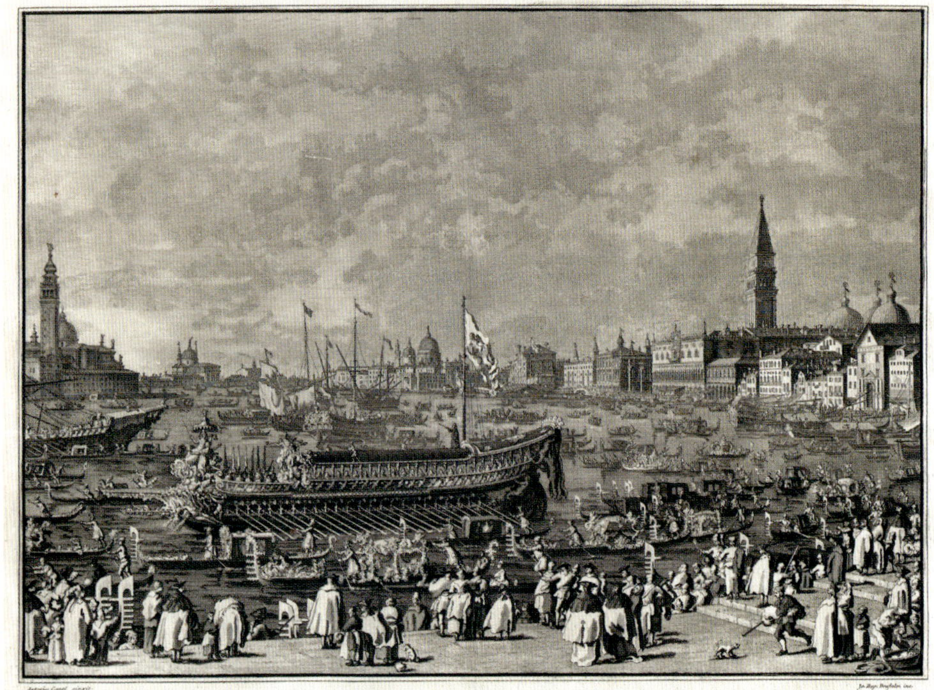

ABOVE:

Fig. 54. Francesco Tironi (active in the last quarter of the eighteenth century), *The Bacino di San Marco on Ascension Day with the Bucintoro Departing for the Lido*, after *c.*1770, oil on canvas, 52.8 × 81.3 cm, The Wallace Collection, London (P513)

BELOW:

Fig. 55. Giovanni Battista Brustolon (1712–1796) after Canaletto (1697–1768), *The Doge in the Bucintoro Departing for the Porto di Lido on Ascension Day*, *c.*1766, etching, 45.1 × 56.9 cm, plate 5 from *Le Feste Ducali*

OPPOSITE ABOVE:

Fig. 56. English School (mid-eighteenth century), *The Piazza San Marco, Looking West from South of the Central Line*, *c.*1750?, oil on canvas, 58.2 × 126 cm, The Wallace Collection, London (P505)

OPPOSITE BELOW:

Fig. 57. Canaletto (1697–1768), *The Piazza San Marco, Looking West from South of the Central Line*, *c.*1732, oil on canvas, 47 × 80 cm, Collection of the Duke of Bedford, Woburn Abbey

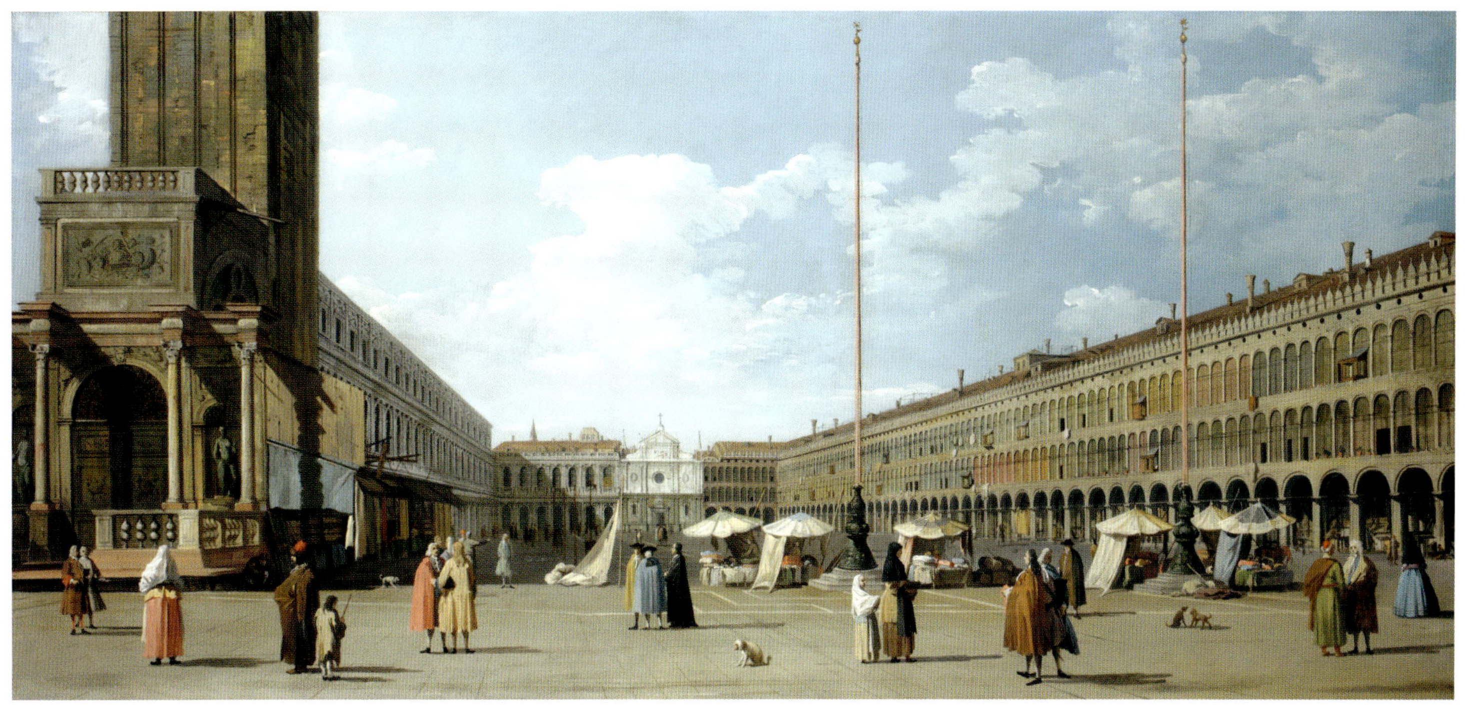

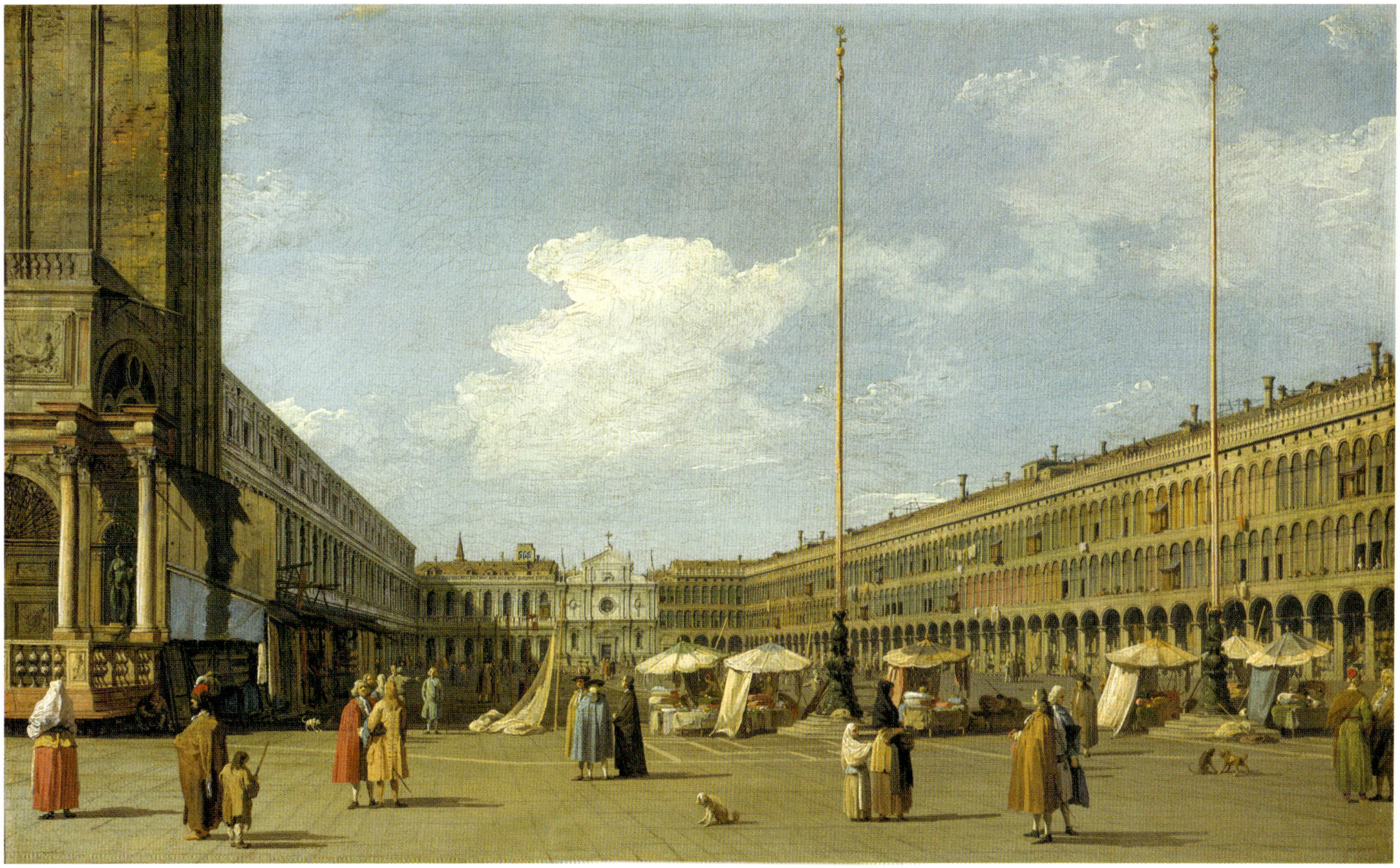

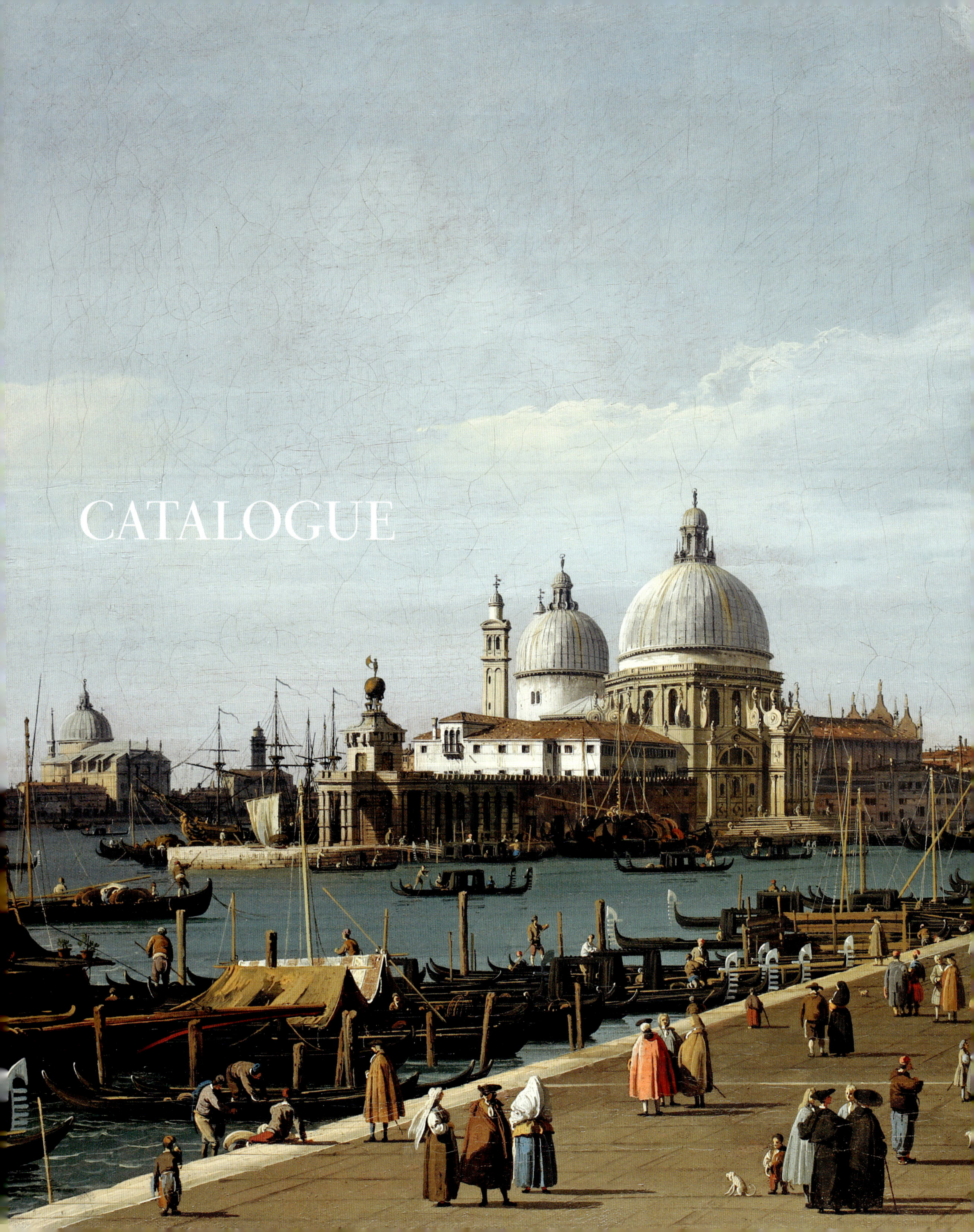
CATALOGUE

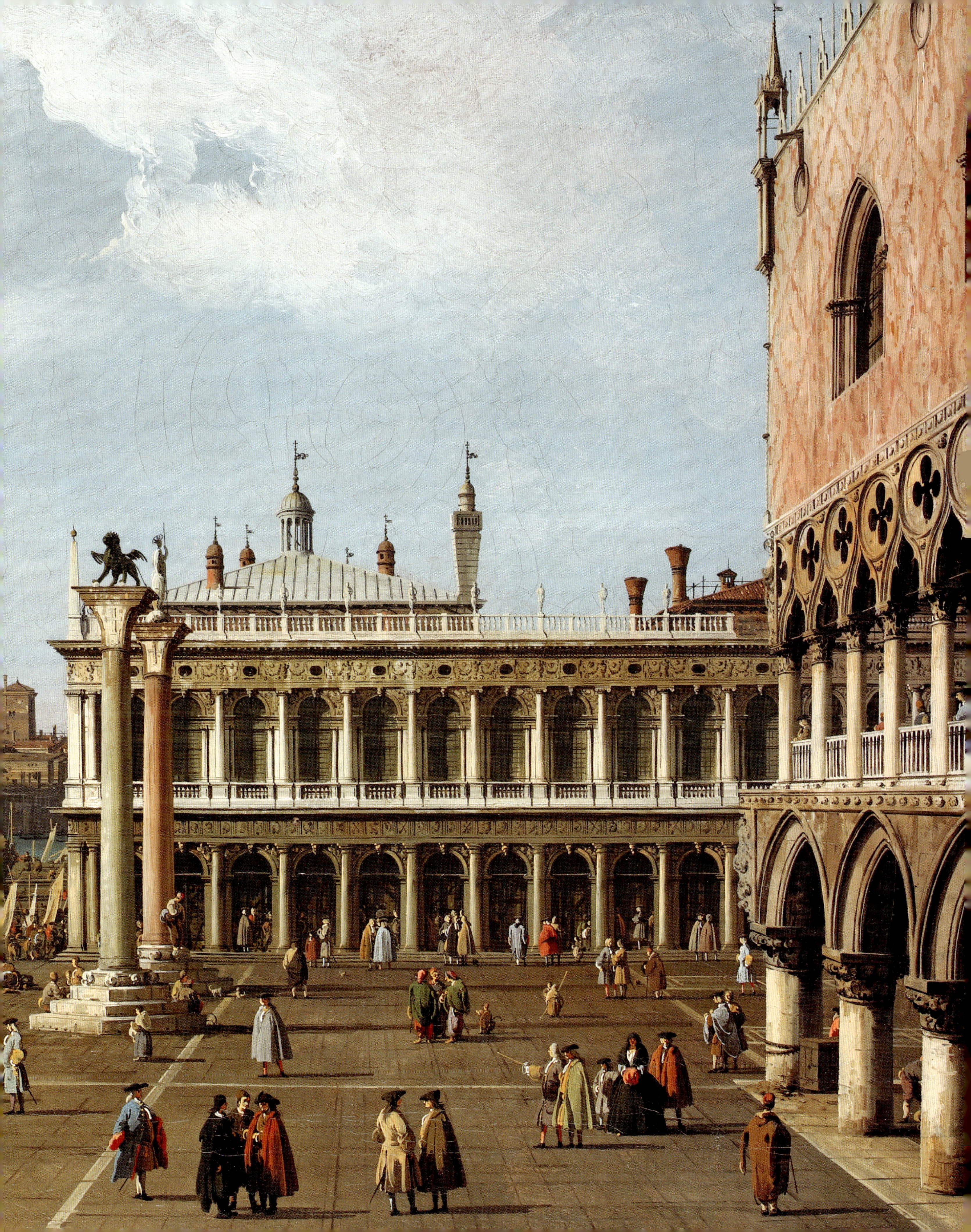

GIOVANNI ANTONIO CANAL, IL CANALETTO (Venice 1697–1768)

The Bacino di San Marco from the Canale della Giudecca

*c.*1738
oil on canvas
130.2 × 190.8 cm
P499

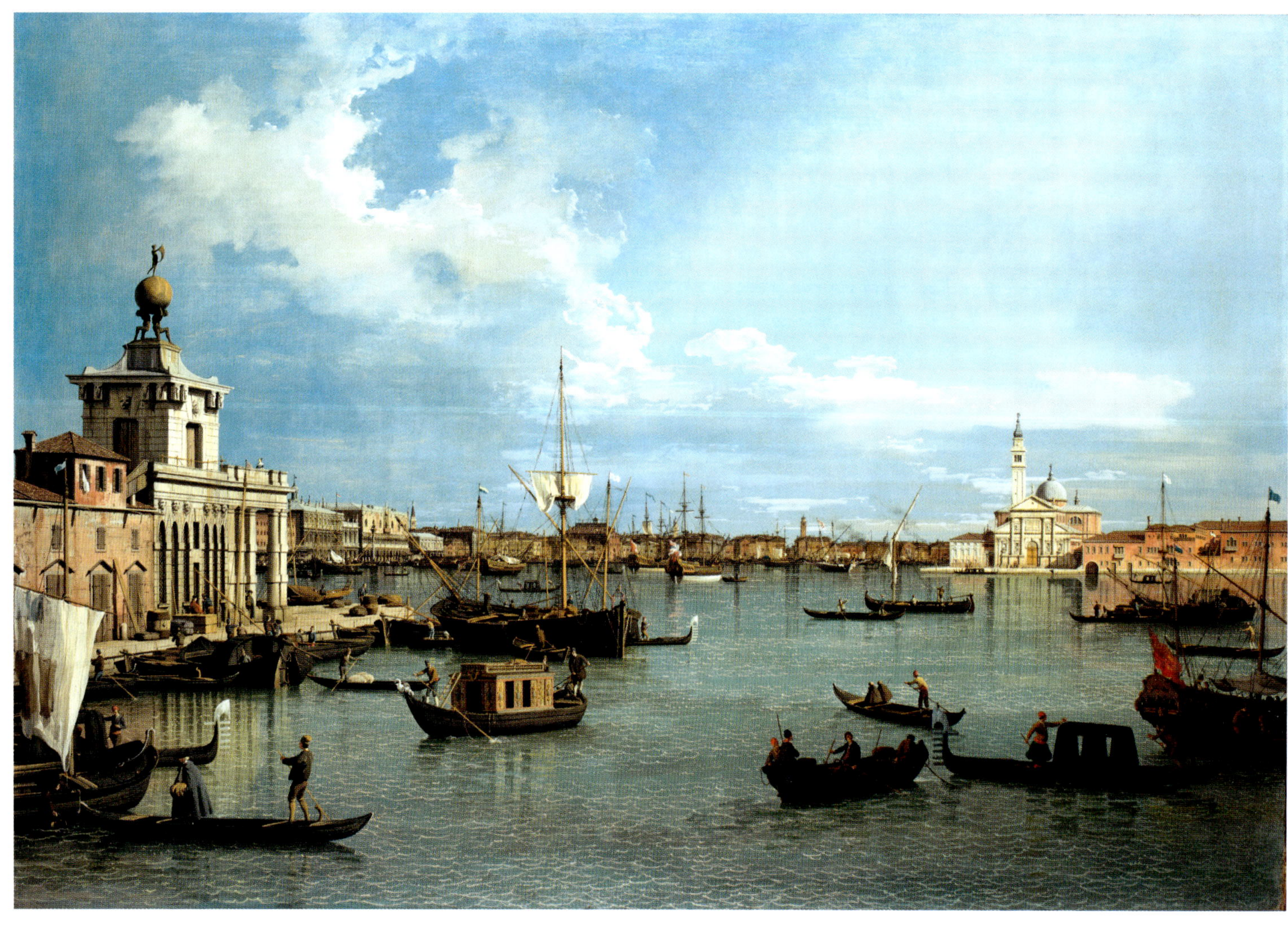

2. GIOVANNI ANTONIO CANAL,
IL CANALETTO (Venice 1697–1768)

*The Bacino di San Marco from
San Giorgio Maggiore*

*c.*1738
oil on canvas
129.2 × 188.9 cm
P497

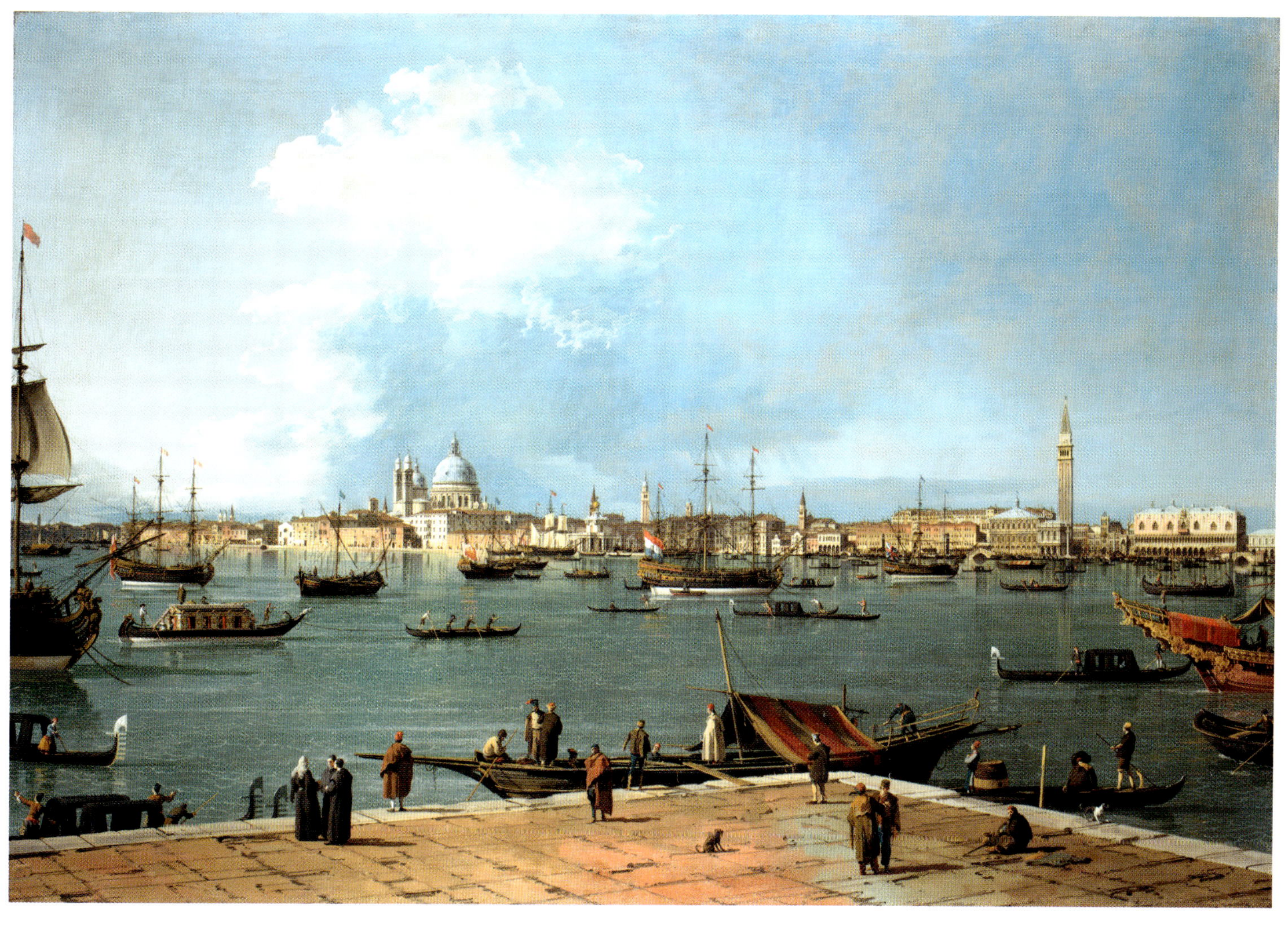

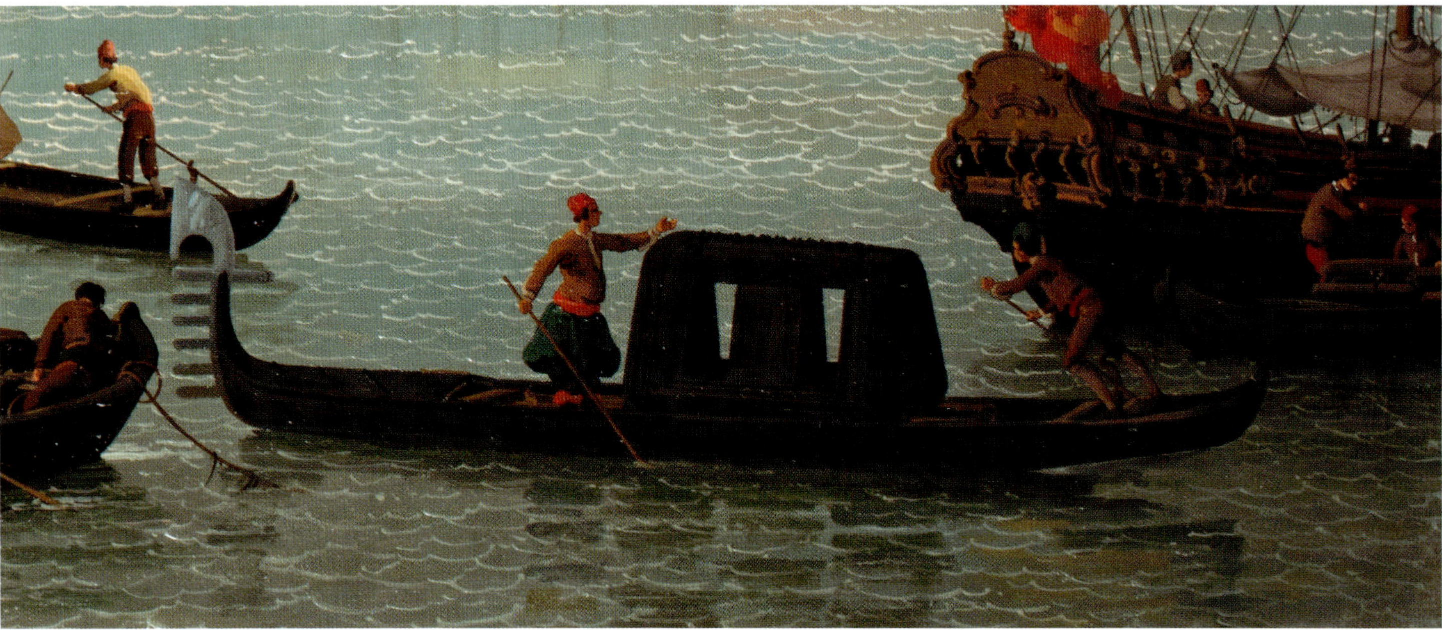

Fig. 58. Detail of cat. 1

These unusually large views of the Bacino di San Marco – Venice's irregularly shaped inner harbour – from opposite vantage points were painted at the height of Canaletto's career in the early 1740s. The high quality of execution, fine state of preservation, imposing format and unique pairing make them a highlight of Canaletto's career. When the great connoisseur Gustav Waagen saw them in the 1850s he rightly pointed out that they 'belong for choice of subject and admirable keeping to his [Canaletto's] chefs-d'oeuvre'.[1]

The Bacino was the impressive point of arrival for visitors to Venice in the eighteenth century. Venice's most important buildings lined the Bacino, such as the Mint, Library, Doge's Palace and Prison, as well as numerous imposing churches. This breathtaking civic and religious heart of the city especially appealed to Grand Tourists seeking *vedute*. In the Wallace Collection pair, vast expanses of sky and water surround buildings positioned along a continuous horizon line. The city's most famous sites are clearly identifiable and calculated to appeal to the tourist.

The panoramic view in cat. 1 is taken from an elevated point above the mouth of the Giudecca Canal. Palladio's imposing Benedictine church of San Giorgio Maggiore with its onion-shaped steeple completed in 1611 is prominently positioned in the distance. The Dogana, or customs house, frames the composition on the left, with its golden globe surmounted by the figure of Fortune. Beyond are the Molo (the broad stone quay along the waterfront of the Piazzetta) and the Riva degli Schiavoni (the quayside abutting the Molo) in the centre of the painting. Further on is the *campanile* of the Basilica of San Pietro di Castello followed by the dome of San Nicolò di Bari by the convent on Sant Antonio, both demolished in 1807.

The complementary panoramic view in cat. 2 is taken from an elevated point across the Bacino above the entrance to San Giorgio Maggiore. The view takes in the Canale della Giudecca on the left and the buildings on the Zattere facing it, such as the Jesuit church of Santo Spirito with its white façade and central round window. The impressive church of Santa Maria della Salute with its soaring domes, the Dogana and the entrance to the Grand Canal occupy the centre of the composition. To the right are the Campanile, the Doge's Palace and the Molo, as well as a partial view of the prisons on the extreme right, the most feared lock-up in Europe at the time. The Torre dell'Orologio is visible between the Campanile and Doge's Palace. A technical and engineering feat, this large astronomical clock was a great tourist attraction in the eighteenth century.

The paintings complement each other in numerous ways. They are lit from opposite sides, cat. 2 from the left and cat. 1 from the right.[2] Their continuous horizon lines are predominantly punctuated by rigging in cat. 1 and by *campanile* in cat. 2. A variety of vessels are cut off by the edges of both paintings, giving the impression that these are snapshot views that extend further beyond. One sizeable vessel with partially open sails set against the sky is included in both paintings. The considerable quantity of boats reinforces the vitality of the maritime enterprise of the Serenissima.

Ships flying the Dutch, British and Venetian flags dot the calm blue waters in both works. In the centre of cat. 2 a large ship flies the Dutch red, white and blue flag. To the right, a ship flies the British flag and to the left another flies the red and white Venetian flag, recognisable by the golden lion of Saint Mark, the patron saint of Venice. In the foreground, a *burchiello*, or passenger barge with decorated cabins that transported people between Venice and Padua, is being towed by a *barca*,

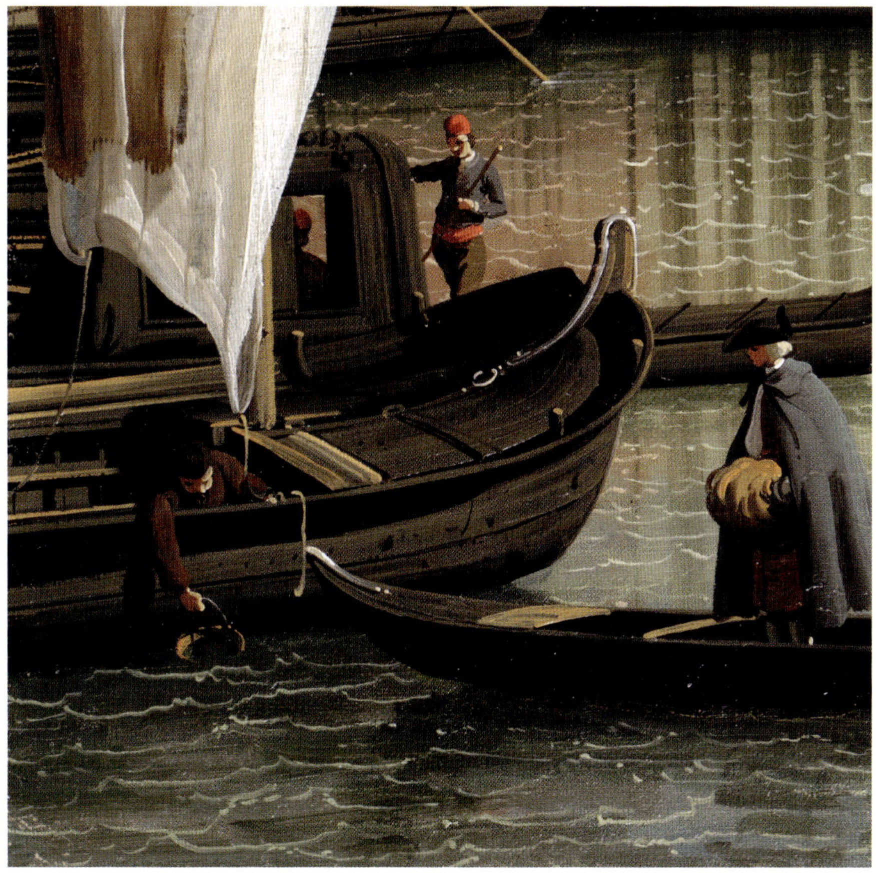

which appears to enter the scene from the left as if on a stage. Several gondolas occupy both paintings, with their characteristic *felze*, or cabins, that gave protection from intemperate weather and provided privacy and discretion for those who sought them. The numerous gondoliers driving the 20,000 or so gondolas in Venice were famous for their musical prowess. Contemporary accounts praise gondoliers' music over that in the opera houses.[3] The red-capped gondolier with his left arm outstretched in the right foreground of cat. 1 seems to be in the middle of an aria (fig. 58). One has to imagine the rich aural component of both scenes.

The paintings are enlivened by comparatively large figures engaged in a variety of activities. In the left foreground of cat. 1 a man leans out of his boat to fill a bucket with water (fig. 59). On the Dogana quay above, a man peeks out from behind a column, while further up on the Dogana terrace, a solitary woman looks upwards (fig. 60). Canaletto illustrated the diverse strata of Venetian society and its rich international appeal in the foreground of cat. 2. Three figures wearing ecclesiastical and lawyers' dress chat on the left, Ottoman merchants occupy the centre and a seated beggar is seen on the right. Two lively dogs add a sense of spontaneity and observed reality to the scene.

As was customary for Canaletto, he took liberties to achieve these composite views, which are otherwise impossible from any point on land or water. In reality, the view from the Ponte de l'Umiltá just before reaching the Dogana takes in buildings past the Doge's Palace on the Riva degli Schiavoni. The closer one gets to the Dogana itself, the more buildings disappear from view, with the Doge's Palace, for example, only visible from the tip of the Dogana (fig. 61). In cat. 1 Canaletto altered the perspective to include the Doge's Palace and other iconic buildings; he also made the Library and Doge's Palace

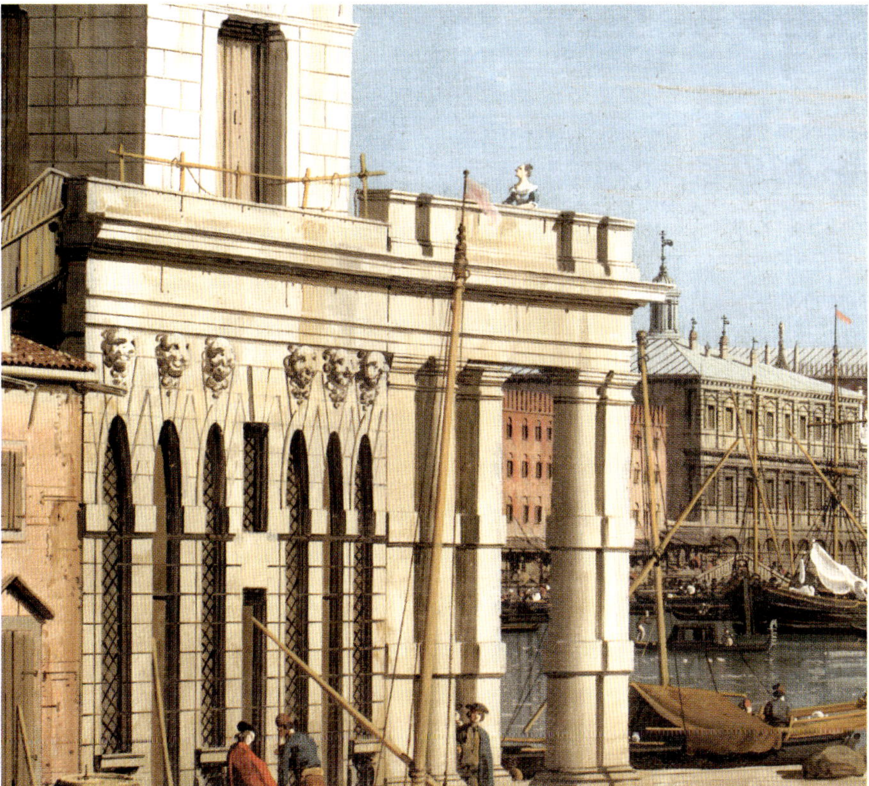

Fig. 59. Detail of cat. 1

Fig. 60. Detail of cat. 1

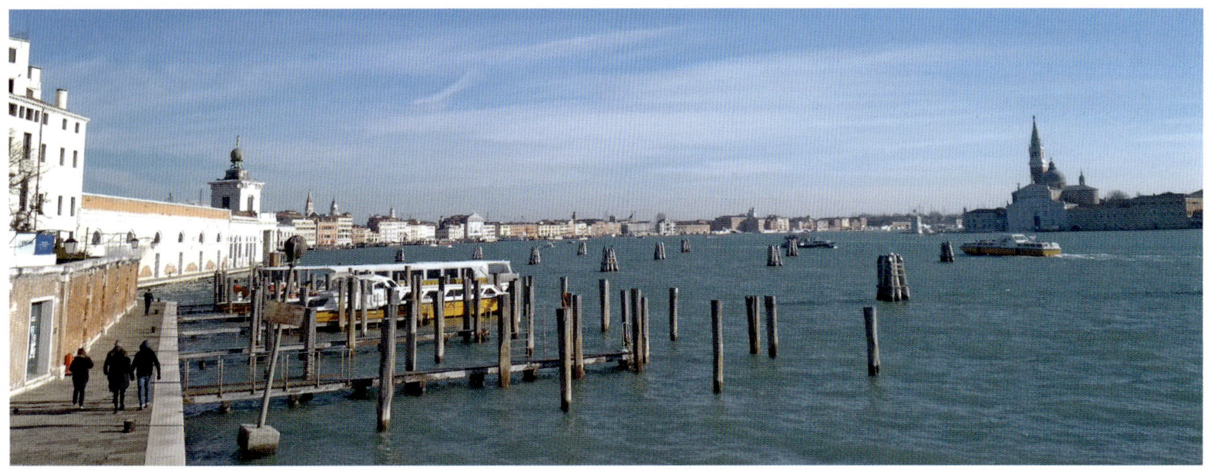

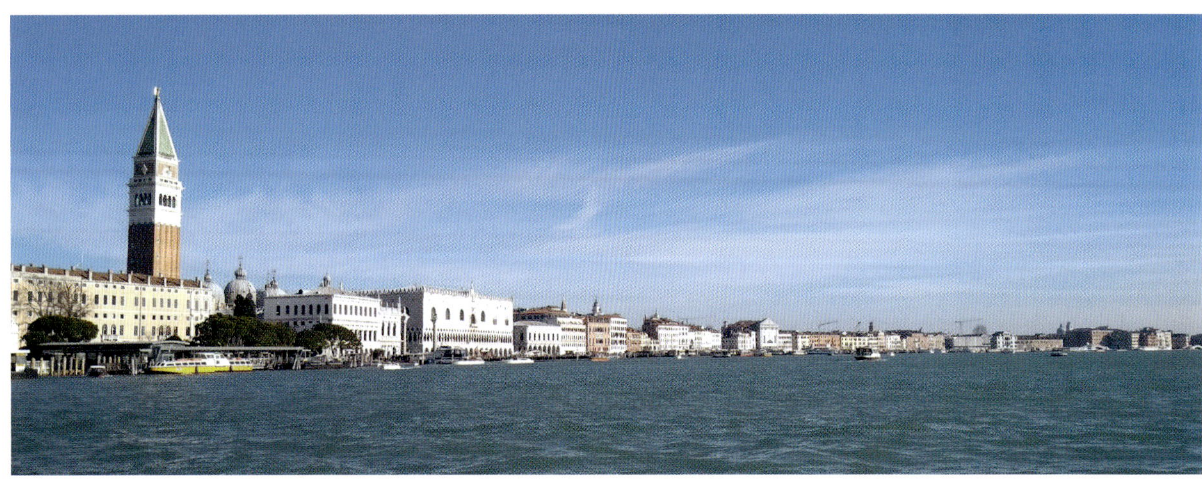

Fig. 61. Photographs of the Bacino di San Marco and the Canale of the Giudecca, February 2019

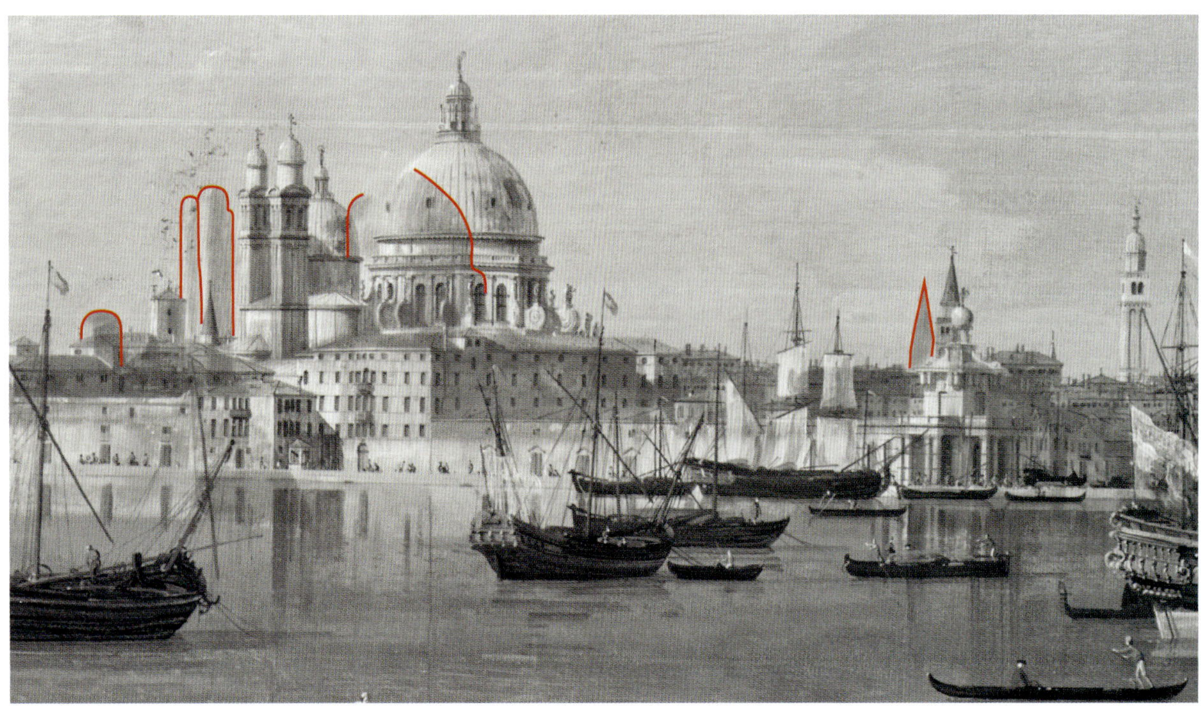

Fig. 62. Detail of IRR of cat. 2 showing changes to the composition marked in red

appear closer together, all for aesthetic effect. Canaletto omitted the column of San Tòdaro and the Campanile from cat. 1, but afforded them prominence in cat. 2. Similarly, the buildings across the Bacino in cat. 2 are actually closer than they appear in the painting, while the Campanile is shorter and stouter. Furthermore, all the flags on the boats in cat. 1 fly rightward while the smoke from the chimney tops blows leftward. Canaletto thus asserted his artistic prowess as active creator of these superb compositions. Finally, Canaletto mixed up the architectural detailing on the Prison windows by including first triangular then segmental pediments, rather than the other way around. It is not clear whether this was intentional.

Recent conservation of the paintings revealed the subtlety of the true colour harmonies and the descriptive texture of the paint. No carbon-containing underdrawing medium was detected in either painting through infrared reflectography (IRR). Furthermore, X-radiographs of both paintings did not reveal any notable compositional changes. The IRR and X-rays suggest that the layouts were carefully planned prior to painting, probably on a separate support. There is one notable exception in cat. 2 where IRR revealed *pentimenti* in the architecture of and around the church of Santa Maria della Salute. Canaletto enlarged the main dome of the church and shifted it to the right (fig. 62). He also moved its two bell towers and a smaller tower nearby rightward. Additionally, he moved the *campanile* of the church of Santa Maria della Carità up and to the right, positioning it behind the golden globe of the Dogana.

The order of painting in both works is consistent with other works by the artist. The sky and water were laid in first, followed by the general outlines of the architecture. The vessels and figures were painted on top. The figures were rendered with fine, detailed brushstrokes, their relatively abstract forms composed with cursive dashes and dots of paint.

Numerous incisions in the wet upper paint layer were revealed in cat. 1, but not in cat. 2. These incisions were used predominantly in the architecture of San Giorgio Maggiore;

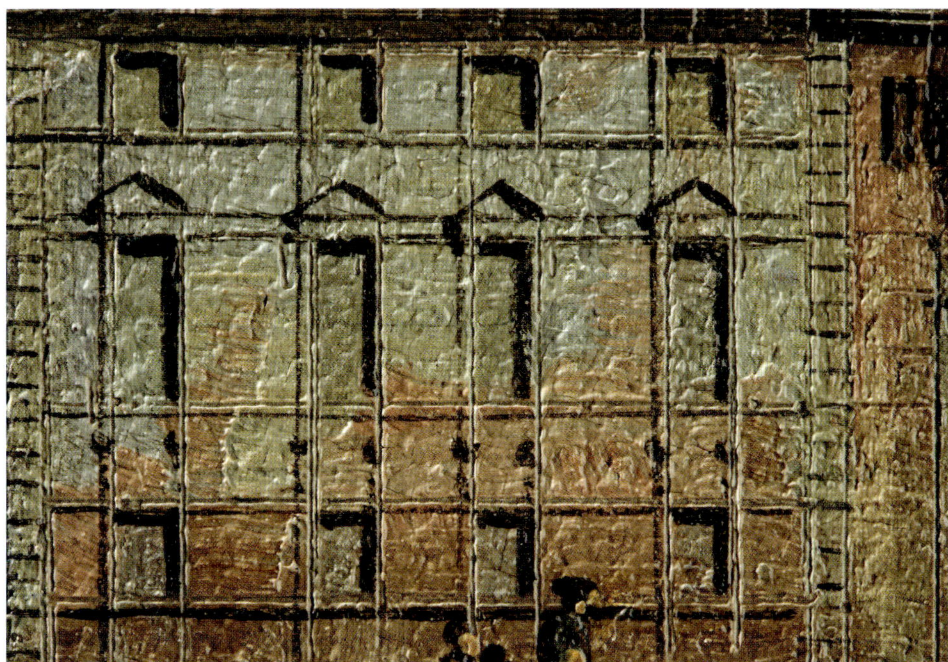

Fig. 63. Detail macro photograph of cat. 1 showing incisions after varnish removal

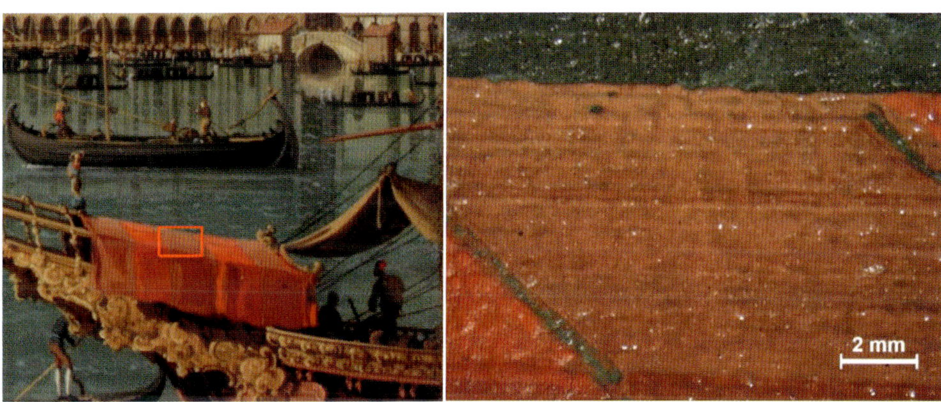

Fig. 64. Detail photograph (left) and photomicrograph (right, × 7.5 magnification) of cat. 2 showing Canaletto's use of the underlying turquoise paint to create an outline for the pink fabric

they were made while the paint was still wet with a fine implement, such as a compass point or stylus-like tool (fig. 63). The incisions had previously been covered up by dirt and thick, old, discoloured varnish that, when removed, made them read as light rather than dark lines. The incisions served to map out the architecture, add texture and a sense of three-dimensionality to the buildings and provide a subtle colouristic value. Canaletto subsequently painted thin, black lines to delineate architectural details, such as window or door frames, or to indicate cast shadows.

By contrast, scraping of paint probably with the butt of the brush was found in cat. 2, but not in cat. 1. For example, Canaletto scraped away red paint from the fabric cover on the ornate vessel partially visible on the right, exposing the turquoise paint of the water underneath (fig. 64). This enabled him to outline the forms on the fabric without painting additional lines.

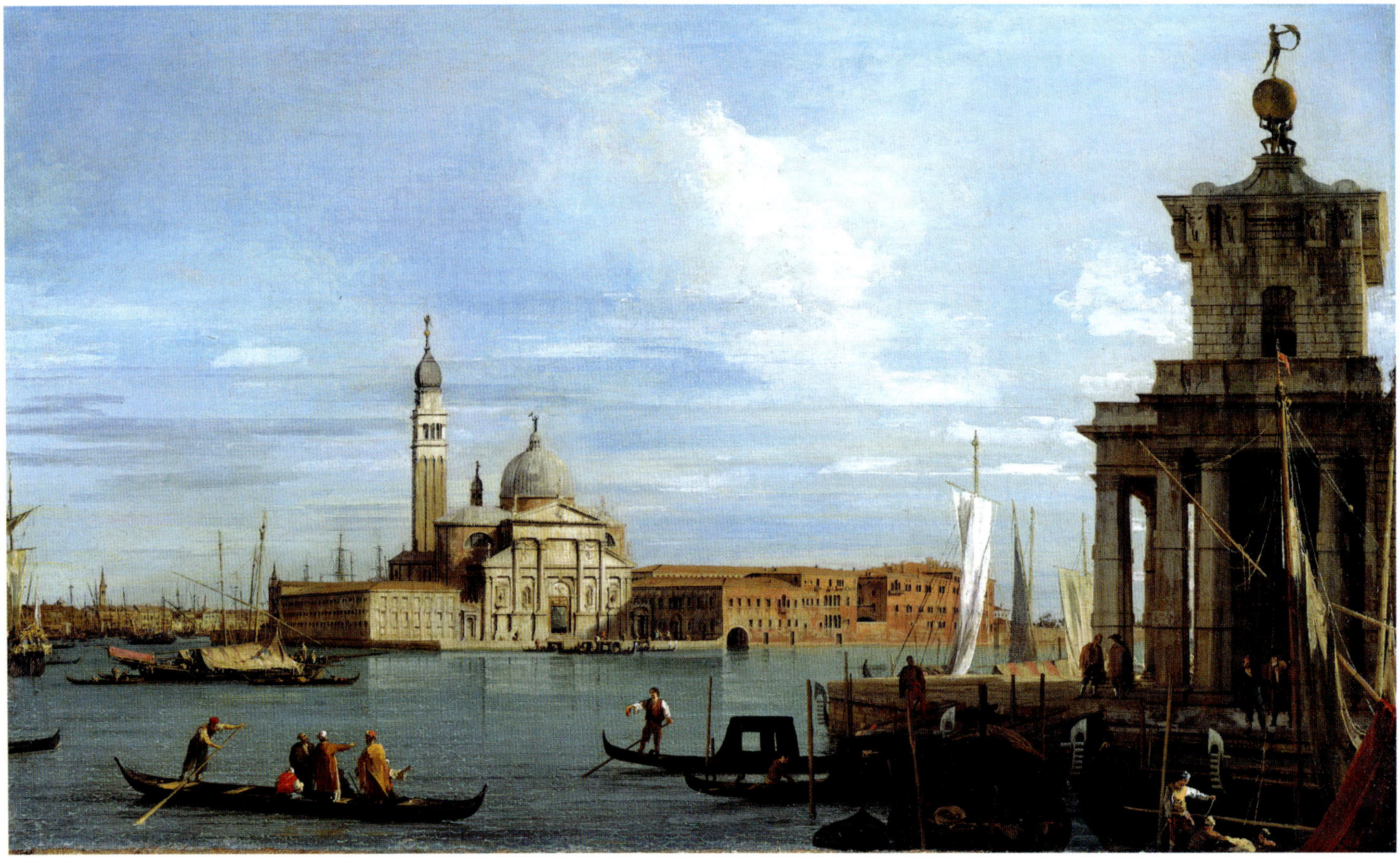

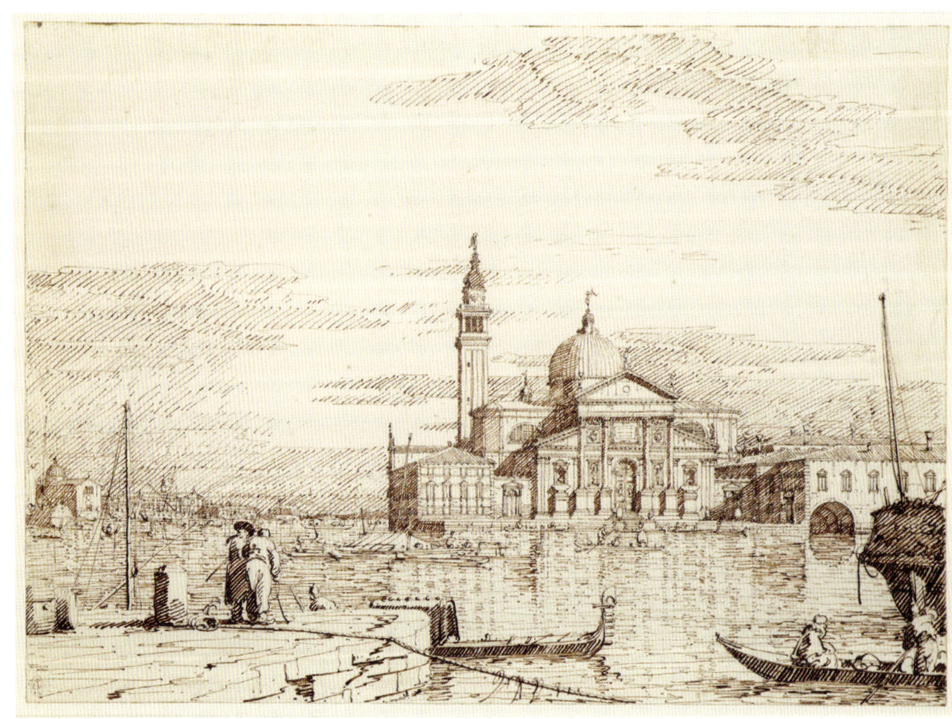

Fig. 65. Canaletto (1697–1768), *Venice: The Punta della Dogana and S. Giorgio Maggiore*, c.1727–30, oil on canvas, 47 × 78.9 cm, Royal Collection (RCIN 400971)

Fig. 66. Canaletto (1697–1768), *Venice: San Giorgio Maggiore*, c.1735–40, pen and ink, over a little ruled and free pencil and pinpointing, 26.8 × 37.7 cm, Royal Collection (RCIN 907482)

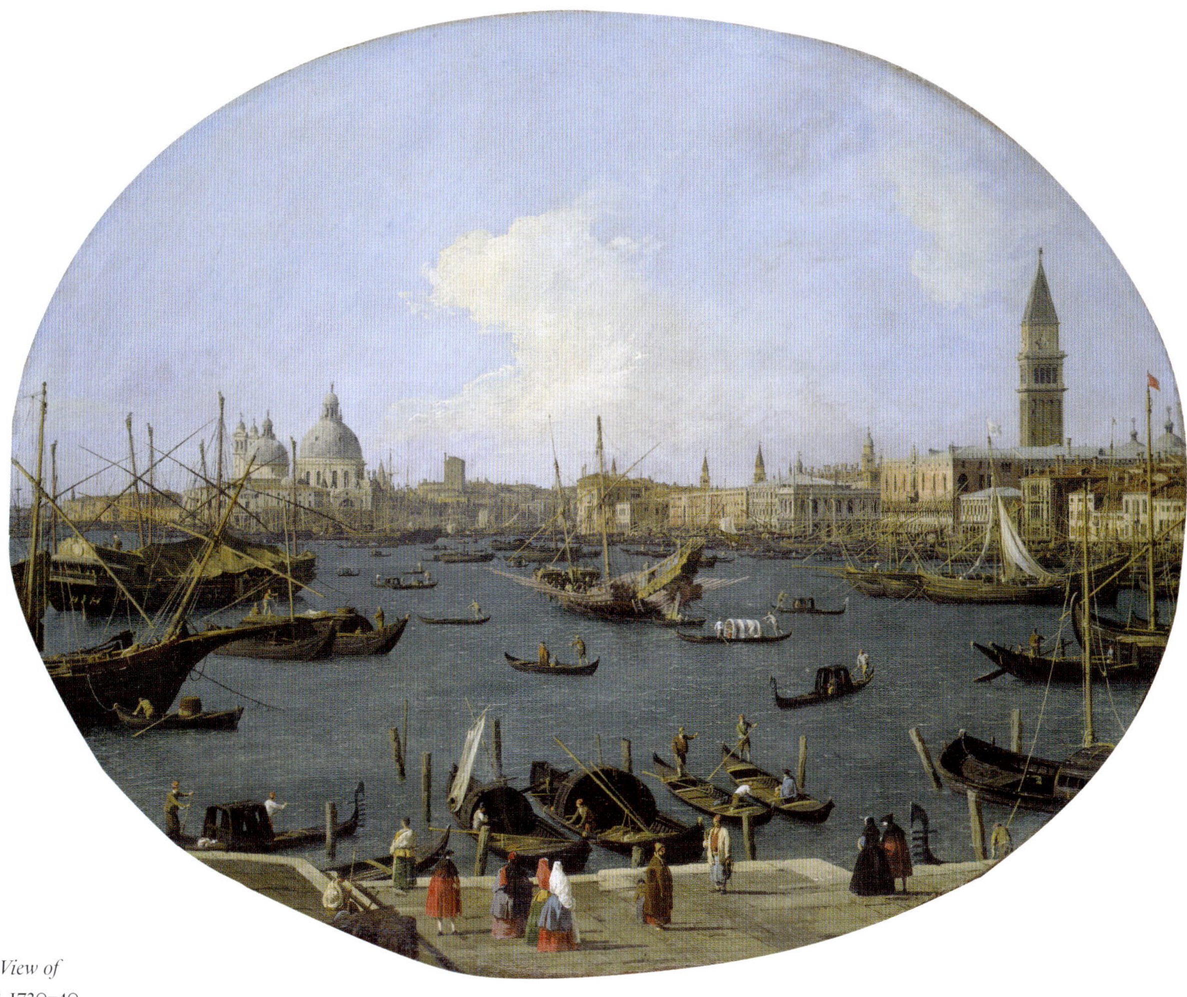

Both paintings are original compositions that do not repeat any of the works commissioned by Consul Joseph Smith. Canaletto had painted a smaller view of San Giorgio Maggiore a decade earlier for Smith (fig. 65). This view was taken from the Grand Canal side of the Dogana and was probably based on a composition by Luca Carlevarijs from *c.*1709.[4] There are at least three smaller derivative versions of cat. 1 (see below), but cat. 2 appears to be unique. A drawing of San Giorgio executed around the same time as the present pair reflects Canaletto's profound interest in and understanding of the church's architecture (fig. 66). Canaletto painted a similar view to cat. 2, on a smaller scale and from the

Riva degli Schiavoni, in a painting today in Frankfurt, where the buildings along the Molo are closer and at a sharper right angle (fig. 67). The Frankfurt view, with its uncharacteristic tondo format, is taken from even higher up.

Such large panoramic views of the lagoon are rare. The Bacino most often appears in scenes representing Ascension Day or in views of the Molo. A fine, slightly earlier comparison to cat. 1, similar in its vast scale, is now in Boston (fig. 68). This view, taken from an even more elevated position slightly to the left, omits the Dogana.

Despite the quality of the paintings, there was some doubt cast as to the full authorship of Canaletto. In 1968 William Constable suggested to Sir Francis Watson, the then

Director of the Wallace Collection, that Canaletto executed the pair with the help of studio assistants, and reiterated the same opinion (about cat. 1 only) in his monograph reprinted a few years later.[5] Recent technical analysis has revealed the high quality of both paintings, which are today considered to be entirely by Canaletto.

Given their unusually large scale, these paintings were clearly an important commission. Francis Seymour-Conway began his Grand Tour in 1737 at age 18 and returned home three years later in 1740.[6] He is likely to have travelled to Venice and visited Smith's *palazzo* on the Grand Canal, as did many British Grand Tourists passing through the city. As such, he would have commissioned

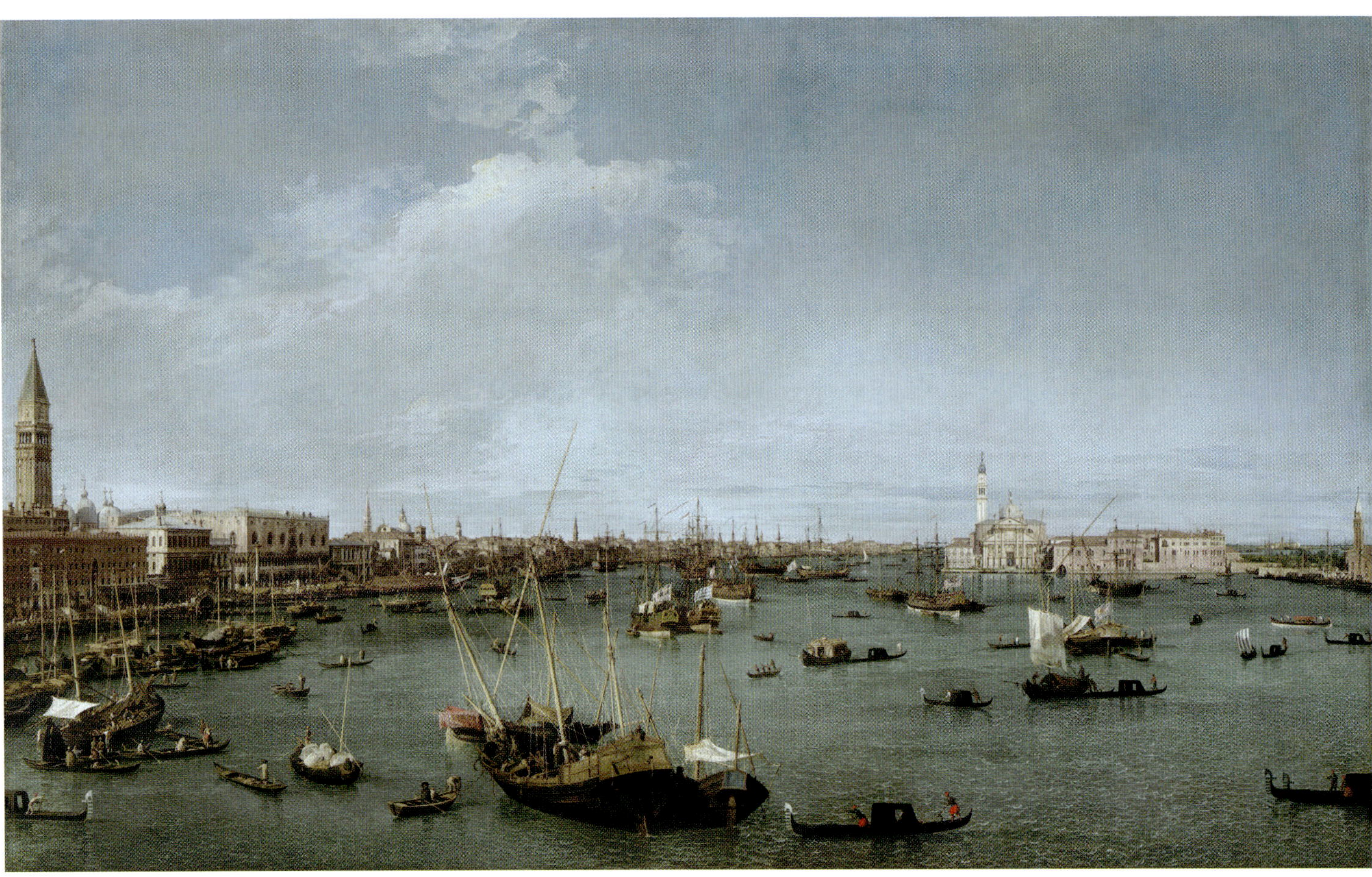

these pictures directly from Smith and had
them delivered to London after his return.
The most recent dating has been based on the
presence of certain bell towers on the skyline.[7]
The twin bell towers on the horizon to the
left of centre provide the earliest possible
date for that painting. The towers have been
variously identified as those of the church
of Angelo Raffaele or of the church of Santa
Maria del Rosario, built and consecrated
respectively in 1735 and 1736.[8] The bell tower
of the church of Santa Maria della Carità,
visible behind the golden dome on top of the
Dogana, collapsed in 1744 and may suggest
the latest possible date of execution (fig. 69).
Canaletto often embellished his compositions
with towers or edifices that had been altered
or destroyed, which means one cannot solely
rely on the city's topography for dating his
works. Stylistically, the pictures correspond
to Canaletto's output from around 1740 and
are comparable to a pair in Washington dated
to 1742/44, painted for the Earl of Carlisle's
residence at Castle Howard.[9] The earliest
surviving specific mention of the paintings
within the Hertford Collection is from the
1834 inventory of Hertford House, where they
are listed as:

> A Panoramic View of Venice, embracing
> the Doge's Palace, St Mark's Place,
> Custom House, & the other principal
> buildings from the opposite side of the
> Adriatic, enlivened by numerous vessels
> & figures – Canaletti (cat. 2)

> A View of ditto taken from the Custom
> House, the companion to the preceding
> (cat. 1)

When the pair was exhibited at Bethnal
Green with the rest of Sir Richard Wallace's
collection, cat. 2 was singled out as 'perhaps
the most wonderful'.[10]

Fig. 68. Canaletto (1697–1768), *Bacino di San
Marco, Venice*, about 1738, oil on canvas, 124.5
× 204.5 cm, Museum of Fine Arts, Boston.
Abbott Lawrence Fund, Seth K. Sweetser Fund,
and Charles Edward French Fund (inv. 39.290)

Fig. 69. Detail of cat. 2

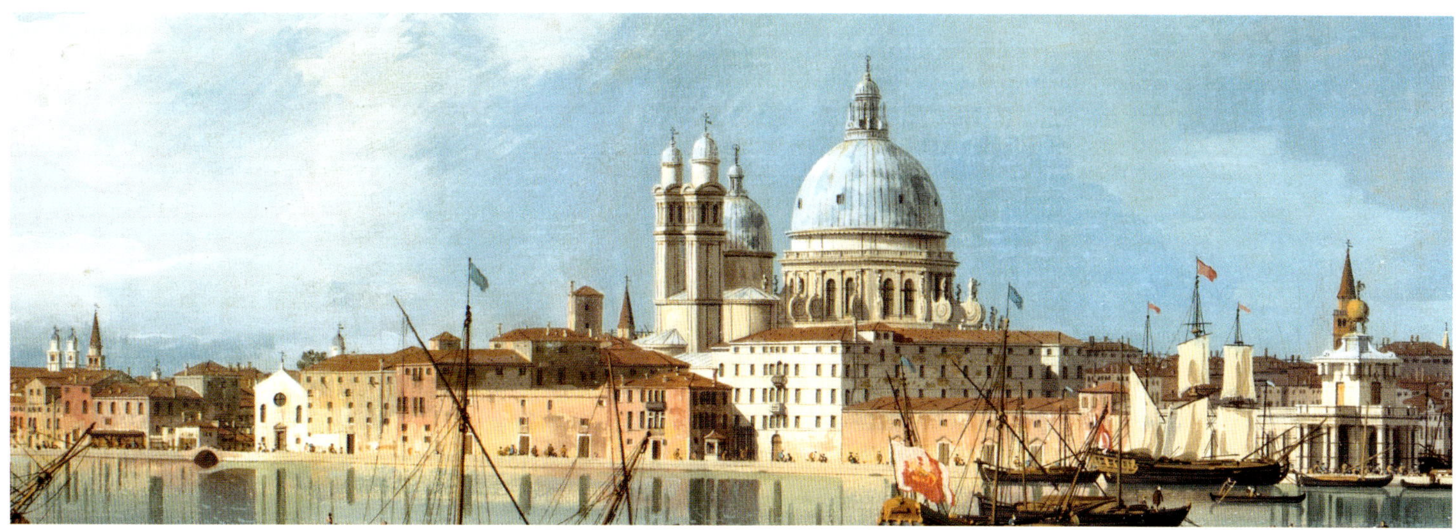

PROVENANCE
Presumably commissioned by Francis Seymour-
Conway, 1st Marquess of Hertford (1719–1794) on his
Grand Tour between 1737 and 1740; by descent to
Francis Ingram Seymour-Conway, 2nd Marquess of
Hertford (1743–1822); by descent to Francis Charles
Seymour-Conway, 3rd Marquess of Hertford (1777–
1842);[11] by descent to Richard Seymour-Conway, 4th
Marquess of Hertford (1800–1870); by descent to Sir
Richard Wallace, 1st Baronet (1818–1890); by descent
to his wife, Lady Wallace (Julie Amélie Charlotte
Castelnau, 1819–1897); by whom bequeathed with
the rest of the Wallace Collection to the British
nation, 1897.

EXHIBITION
1872–75: 'Paintings, Porcelain, Bronzes, Decorative
Furniture and other Works of Art lent by Sir Richard
Wallace to the Bethnal Green Branch of the South
Kensington Museum'.[12]

RELATED WORKS
There are no other full-size versions of these
pictures and neither view was reproduced in print.
There are a few smaller versions of cat. 1:

Canaletto, *The Bacino di San Marco: Looking
East*, oil on canvas, 75.5 × 105.5 cm, Milton Park,
Peterborough (C132)

Canaletto, *The Bacino di San Marco: Looking East*,
oil on canvas, 58.4 × 92.7 cm, Private Collection
(C/L133*)

Bernardo Bellotto, *The Bacino di San Marco:
Looking East*, oil on canvas, 61.5 × 96.5, Private
Collection, Spain (C133)

Bernardo Bellotto, *The Bacino di San Marco
from the Canale della Giudecca, Venice*, 1738, oil on
canvas, 121.3 × 218.5 cm, Private Collection

TECHNICAL NOTES
Both paintings have a medium-weight, plain-weave
linen canvas. The original canvases have been cut
down (most likely during a lining treatment) and
no longer have their original tacking margins.
The original canvas of cat. 2 sustained significant
damage at an early date, resulting in an inverted
L-shaped tear on the lower right side and a circular
patch of damage in the lower right quadrant of the
sky. Both paintings have a double-layered ground,
with a lower red-brown layer. The upper layers vary
slightly. Cat. 1 has a beige upper layer composed of
red earth and lead white, while cat. 2 has a light pink
upper layer composed of umber, bone black and
lead white.

The paintings were last relined with a glue-paste
lining and stretched onto their current stretchers
in the late nineteenth century. They were cleaned
in June 1948 by William Vallance, who frequently
worked for the Wallace Collection.[13] In February
1998 cat. 2 was surface cleaned by Anna Sanden.
Both paintings were cleaned and analysed at
the Hamilton Kerr Institute in 2017. Technical
investigation comprising X-radiography, infrared
reflectography and SEM-EDX paint sample analysis
was also undertaken at this point.

LITERATURE
Constable 1962, C134 (cat. 1), C137 (cat. 2)
Watson 1968, pp. 52–53
Puppi 1970, p. 105, nos 163 (cat. 1),
      164 (cat. 2)
Links 1981, p. 50, nos 143, 144
Ingamells 1985, pp. 225–29
Duffy and Hedley 2004, pp. 62–63

LP

3. **GIOVANNI ANTONIO CANAL, IL CANALETTO** (Venice 1697–1768)

The Grand Canal from the Palazzo Flangini to San Marcuola

c.1733–34
oil on canvas
46.5 × 77.5 cm
P506

Inscribed on the reverse: *490C. Lady Bernard.*

4. **GIOVANNI ANTONIO CANAL, IL CANALETTO** (Venice 1697–1768)

The Grand Canal from the Palazzo Foscari to the Carità

c.1739
oil on canvas
46.2 × 77.3 cm
P510

Inscribed on the reverse: *490C. Lady Bernard.*

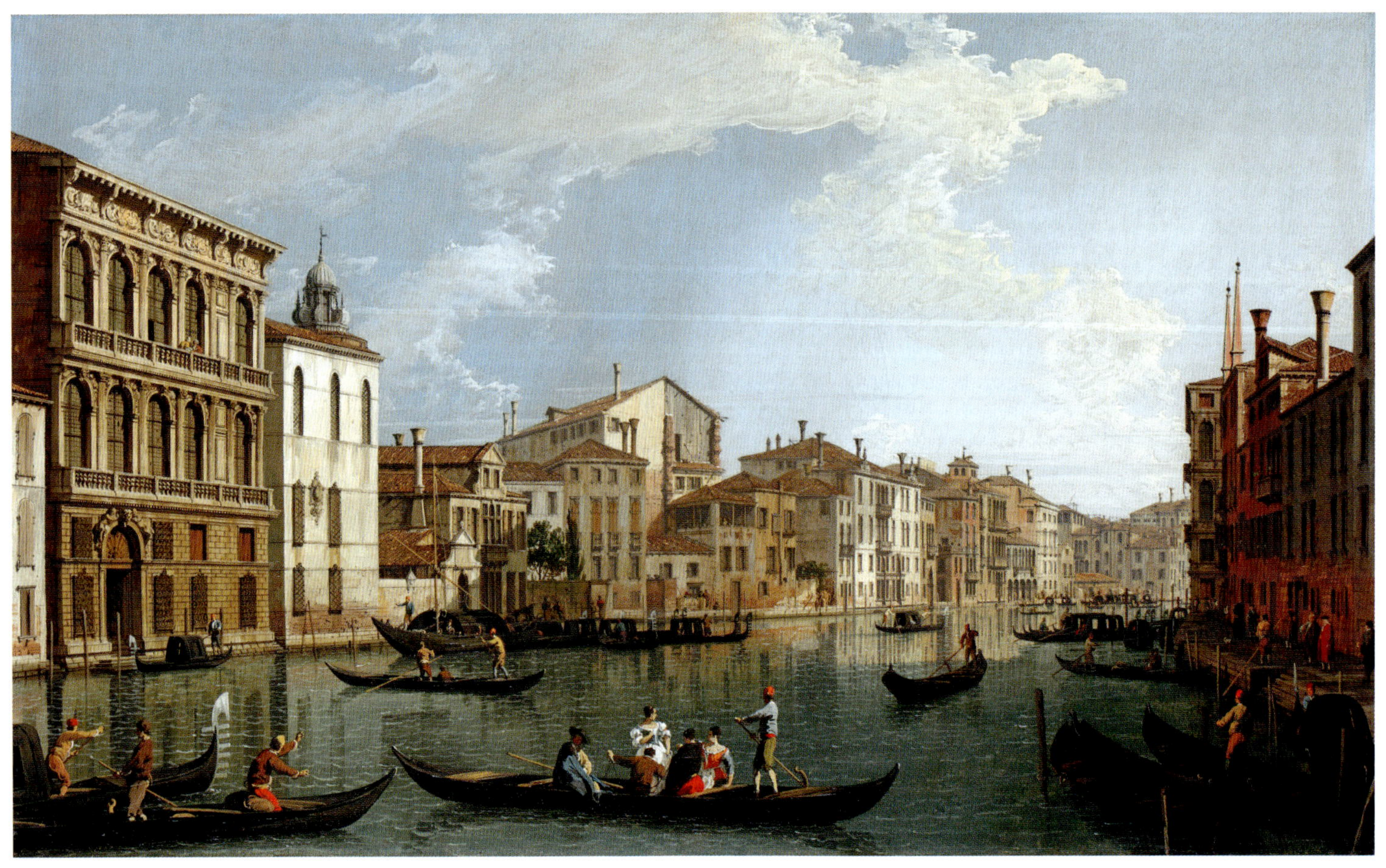

The Grand Canal was, and still is, Venice's principal artery and main thoroughfare. It winds in a reverse S-shape from the Bacino di San Marco in the south-east to today's railway station, the Stazione di Santa Lucia, in the north-west. The Grand Canal was, and is, a key tourist attraction due to the numerous sumptuous palaces and notable churches alongside it. As such, many Grand Tourists concentrated their visits on the Grand Canal without exploring much beyond it.[1] This accomplished pair of views illustrates two opposing reaches of the Grand Canal in the north and south. Canaletto skilfully rendered the sun-drenched palaces, fastidiously recording every window, door and chimney, and masterfully captured their brilliant reflections on the shimmering water.

Cat. 3 illustrates the upper reaches of the canal looking east. Today, one can see this approximate vista from the train station, although several of the buildings, particularly on the right bank, have since been demolished. The seventeenth-century Palazzo Flangini, designed by Giuseppe Sardi (1624–1699), is prominently positioned on the left. Next to it is the Scuola dei Morti, or School of the Dead, which belonged to the religious congregation known as the Santissima Madonna del Suffragio dei Morti. The building was seriously damaged during the Austrian bombardment in 1849 when the entire area suffered greatly, and was subsequently rebuilt in a different form. Above it is the voluted cupola of the church of San Geremia, consecrated in 1760 and

completed in the nineteenth century. The *canonica* (priest's house) of that church is the small building beyond the garden wall to the right. Further down is the low garden wall of the Palazzo Labia above which trees are visible. Canaletto almost concealed the mouth of the Cannaregio Canal, one of the main waterways in Venice that connects the Grand Canal with the northern lagoon. Its entrance is shown from an unfamiliar angle and can be easily missed to the right of the aforementioned trees. Beyond the mouth of the Cannaregio there seems to be a spacious warehouse behind the site of Palazzo Querini, completed in 1828. In front of it, on the canal side, is a house with a large loggia. A couple of houses down is the cream, stucco, seventeenth-century Palazzo

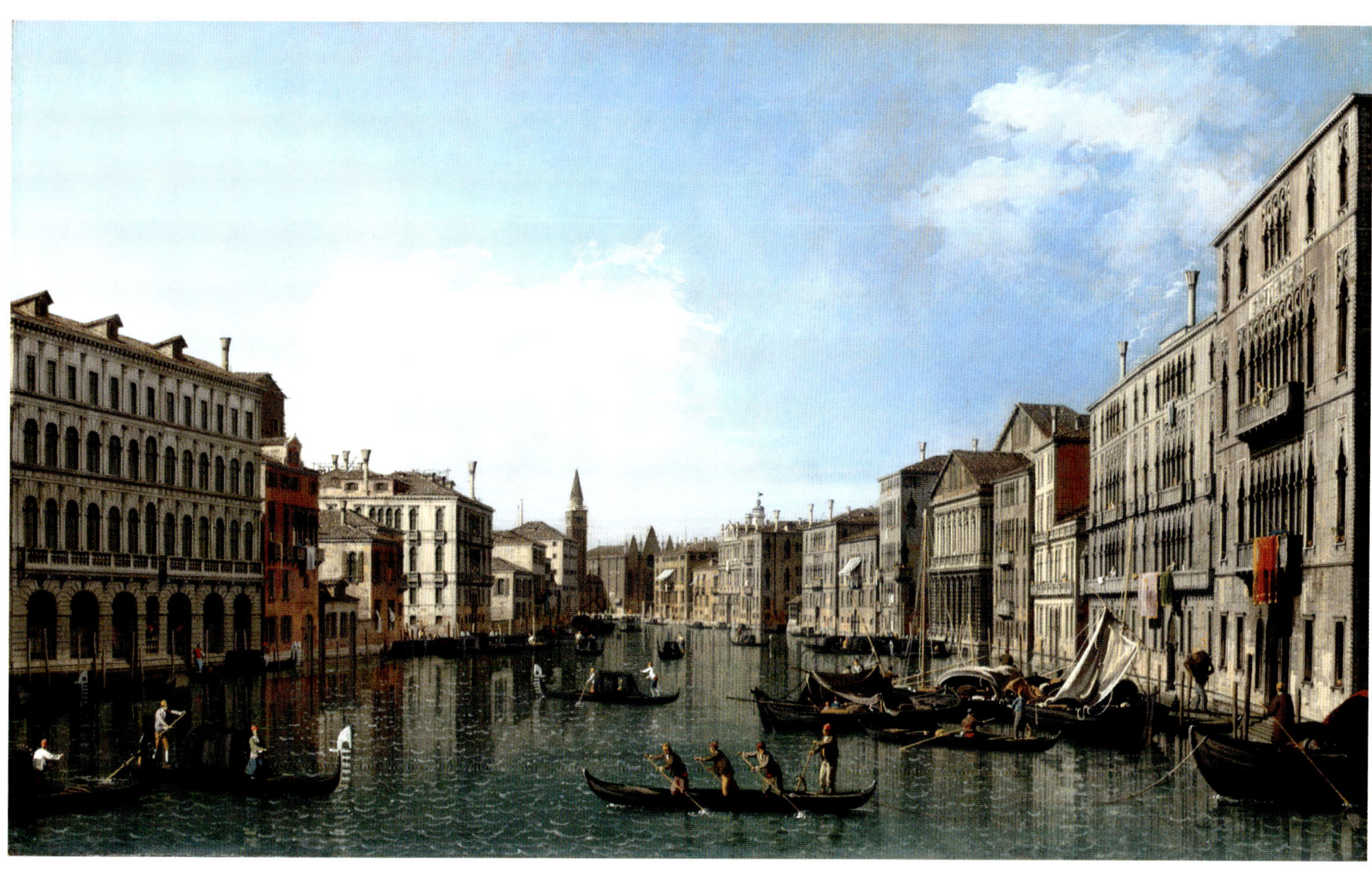

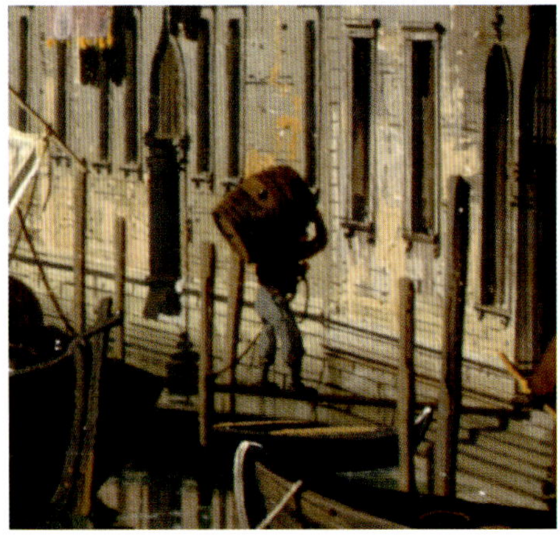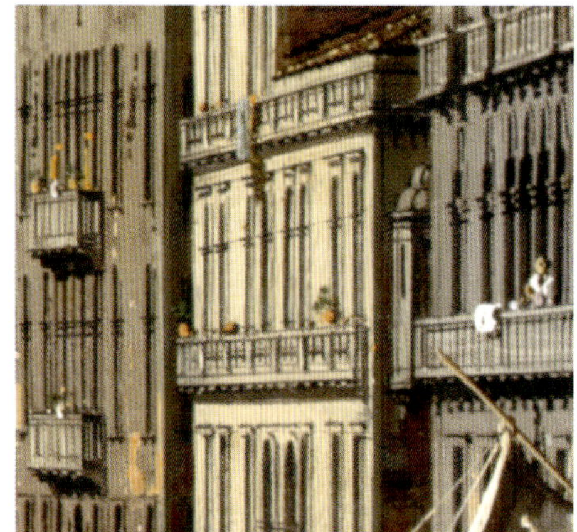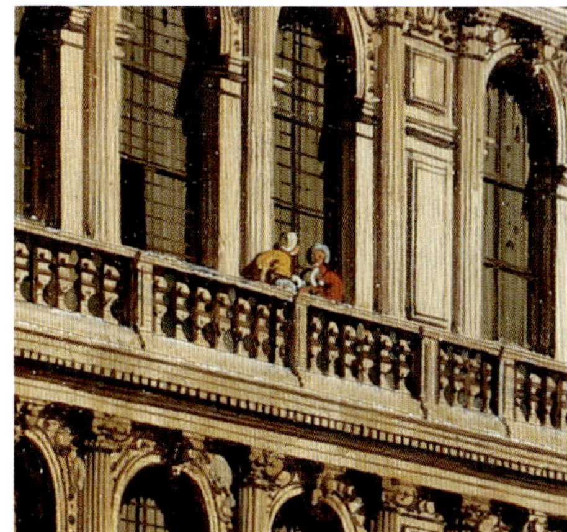

Fig. 70. Details of cats 4 (left and centre) and 3 (right)

Correr Contarini Zorzi, the façade of which survives to this day. The distant low buildings mark the site of Campo San Marcuola, including the low brick building with a door facing the canal.

On the opposite side of the canal is the Riva di Biasio, named after the murderous butcher Biagio Cargnico, who resided there. Legend has it that a child's finger was found in Biagio's famous *squazzetto* (meat stew). The sixteenth-century Palazzi Corner and Gritti, both greatly altered today, are visible. Further along, the Palazzo Zen (later Donà Balbi) is identifiable by its twin obelisks, destroyed in 1849 during the Austrian bombing. The projecting side of the sixteenth-century Palazzo Bembo is just beyond, prior to its enlargement with two *piani nobili*. The House of Bembo Valier died out later in the century and the palace was subsequently demolished.

Cat. 4 looks south down the Grand Canal from the Volta del Canal (the turn in the canal) towards the gabled façade and bell tower of the church of Santa Maria della Carità in the distance. This is the opposite view to most Regatta paintings, which follow the Grand Canal north-east from the same point (see cat. 9). In the left foreground is the unusually wide Palazzo Moro-Lin with its austere Tuscan-style façade, better known as *dalle tredici finestre* for its 13 windows on each storey. The *palazzo*, built between 1671 and 1673, was designed by the Florentine architect

Sebastiano Mazzoni (*c.*1611–1678) for the painter Pietro Liberi (1605–1687). Beyond it are more modest palaces in the Campo San Samuele, which were taken down when the massive Palazzo Grassi was begun for that family in 1749.[2] Further on is the elegant seventeenth-century Palazzo Malipiero, home to the influential Venetian senator Alvise Gasparo Malipiero who played a major role in Giacomo Casanova's life. The latter lived in the palace during his adolescence between 1740 and 1742, and took part in the numerous dinner parties held there that were attended by countless ladies of fashion. Anchoring the composition just left of centre is the prominent *campanile* of Santa Maria della Carità, which collapsed in 1744. Since 1807 the church and convent have housed the Gallerie dell'Accademia. To the left of the *campanile* are the twin obelisks of the Baroque Palazzo Giustinian Lolin, an early design by Baldassare Longhena (1598–1682), the same architect responsible for the great church of Santa Maria della Salute.

On the right, the painting is framed by the fifteenth-century Palazzo (or Ca') Foscari. This fine Gothic residence was built when Venice was at the height of its prosperity for Francesco Foscari, who was elected Doge in 1423. Beyond Ca' Foscari are the elegant fifteenth-century Palazzi Giustinian and Nani. Next is the imposing two-storey Ca' Rezzonico, also designed by Longhena for the Bon family

in 1667. Canaletto painted the building with its temporary wooden roof above the *piano nobile*. The building was acquired by the Rezzonico family in 1750 after which the top storey was completed between 1752 and 1756. Today, it houses the Museo del Settecento Veneziano, the only museum that specialises in eighteenth-century Venetian art. Further down are the Palazzi Contarini Corfù and Contarini dagli Scrigni. The latter with its gable window and white observatory tower was begun in 1609 to the designs of Vincenzo Scamozzi (1548–1616) in order to double the size of the powerful Contarini family's extant Gothic Palazzo Corfù.

The paintings are lit from opposite directions, with cat. 3 lit from the right casting the left bank in warm sunlight and cat. 4 from the left casting the façades of the buildings on the right bank in warm light. Canaletto employed pronounced contrasts of light and dark in cat. 3 in order to account for the sharper bend in the canal. Small waves on the surface of the water in both works flicker in the sunlight. Various gondolas and *sandaletti* (flat-bottomed 5- to 10-metre rowing boats) are being rowed or are moored. In cat. 4 a group of small sailing ships is moored at the right. In the centre foreground of both paintings, a *sandolo* is being rowed. In cat. 3 this vessel is occupied by two rowers, a party of three ladies conversing and a seated gentleman wearing a blue cloak and black hat who looks away

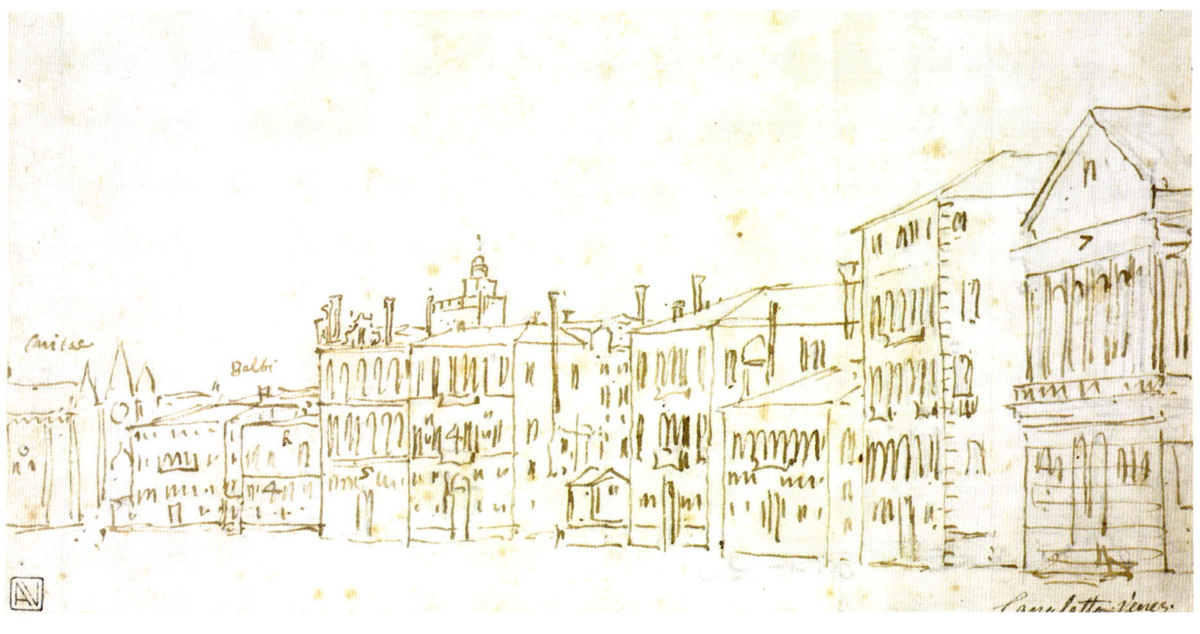

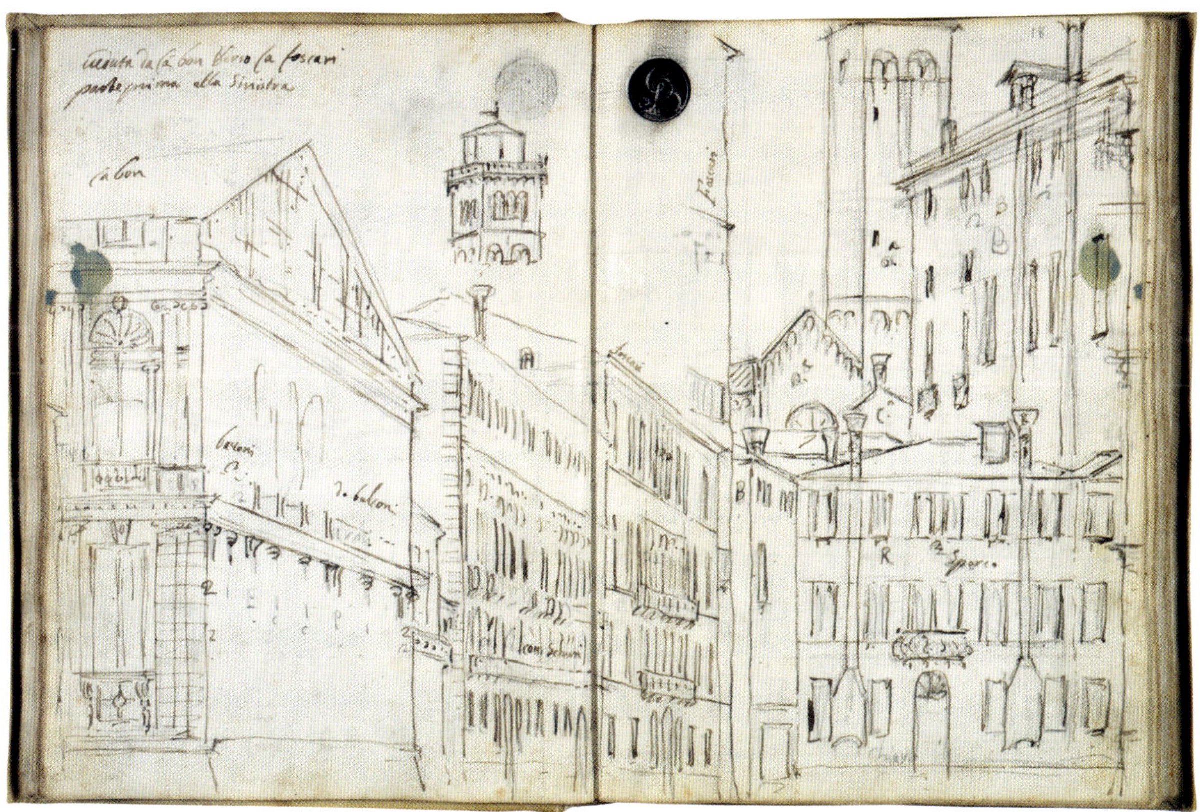

ABOVE:

Fig. 71. Canaletto (1697–1768), *The Grand Canal: Looking South from the Palazzo Rezzonico to Sta Maria della Carità*, pen and brown ink on paper, 11 × 22.4 cm, Galleria Nazionale d'Arte Antica, Trieste (inv. 298, recto)

BELOW:

Fig. 72. Canaletto (1697–1768), *From the Palazzo Rezzonico to the Palazzo Balbi* from the *Cagnola Sketchbook*, 1730s, pen and ink over black chalk, 23 × 17 cm (each folio), folios 17v–18r, Gallerie dell'Accademia, Venice

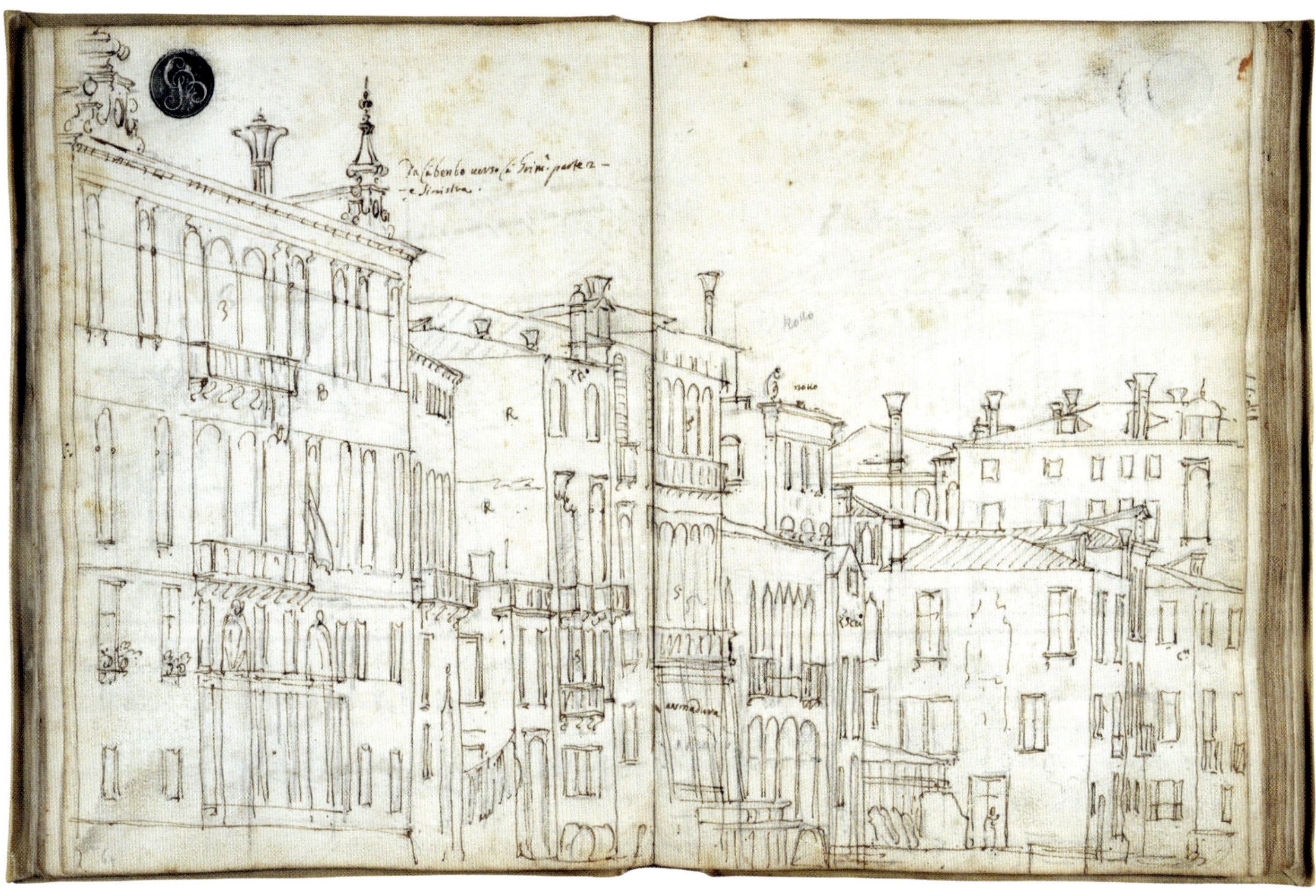

from them towards the viewer. By contrast, the *sandolo* in cat. 4 is populated by four men towing a bigger boat behind them. The figures in the foreground of cat. 3 are larger and appear closer to the beholder, while those in cat. 4 are smaller and further away. Canaletto widened the bend in the canal in cat. 4 and positioned the view from slightly higher up.

Canaletto skilfully captured Venice's quintessential charm through the inclusion of wonderful quotidian details, with figures populating the buildings, quays and waterway. In cat. 4 a man carries a barrel on his back into Ca' Foscari and potted plants adorn windows and balconies on the right bank; in cat. 3 two figures engaged in conversation on the second-storey balcony of Palazzo Flangini animate the scene (fig. 70).

A corresponding sketch of the buildings from Ca' Rezzonico to the Carità probably served as part of Canaletto's reference material for the composition in cat. 4 (fig. 71).[3] This cursory sketch made *in situ* marks the buildings and their layout, as well as their proportion in relation to one another. An opening in the *Cagnola Sketchbook*, which Canaletto used to record *in situ* outline drawings of buildings along the Grand Canal, shows his careful, up-close study of Ca' Rezzonico in the opposite direction (fig. 72). Canaletto wrote notes for himself such as 'balconi' for the balconies on the *piano nobile* and jottings in shorthand such as capital 'P's for the pilasters on the ground-floor façade. Working from the low viewpoint of a boat in the water, he adjusted the sketch as he moved down the canal by redrawing the edge of Ca' Foscari on a larger scale as the next sequence of buildings came closer into view. Other drawings in the same sketchbook correspond with buildings on the left side of cat. 3, such as a spread showing the Palazzo Correr Contarini Zorzi followed by the Palazzo Gritti and the Campo San Marcuola with a shack and a few pieces of marble before it (fig. 73). The next folio follows the buildings to the left of the Palazzo Correr Contarini Zorzi, the most prominent of which is a building with a spacious open loggia, which corresponds to that shown in cat. 3 (fig. 74 and fig. 78).

In his paintings of the Grand Canal, Canaletto often combined viewpoints, straightened curves in order to discern more buildings or brought distant architecture closer to the viewer. He took such liberties with the present pair by opening up the perspective in both works. He broadened the left bank in cat. 3 and widened the canal and straightened the left bank in cat. 4, which

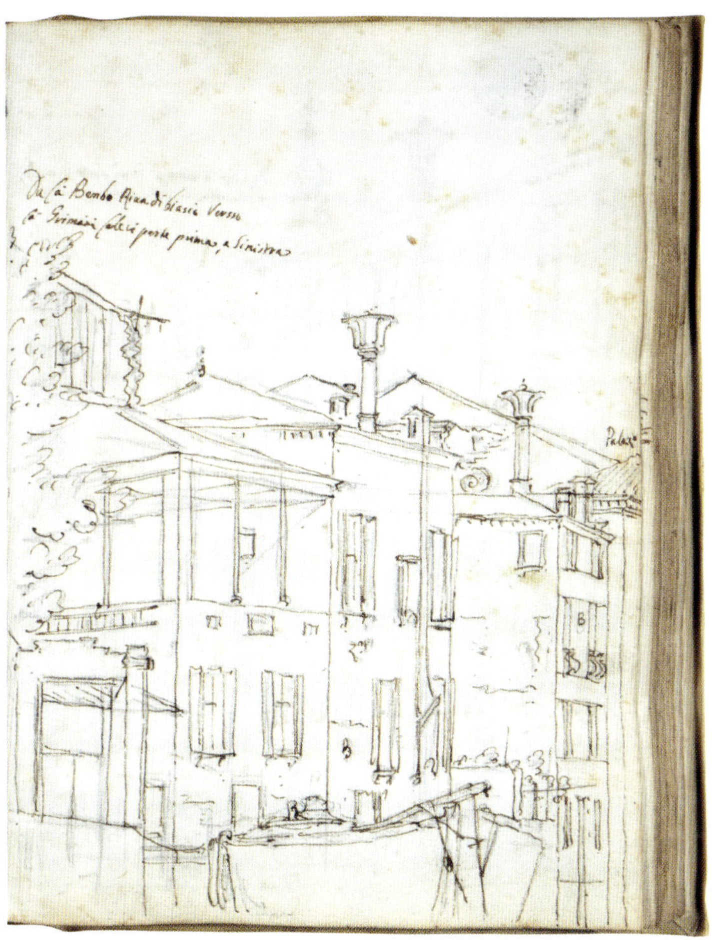

enabled him to include more buildings than would be visible from a single viewpoint.

Recent conservation and technical analysis did not detect any preparatory underdrawings beneath the paint layers. Yet the artist constructed both compositions in carefully conceived stages. As in other works, Canaletto painted the skies first after which he laid in the buildings and water with broad areas of variegated colour. X-rays reveal how he subsequently articulated the architecture with incisions in the wet paint in order to create details and relief (fig. 75). He then added in the waves with pale calligraphic strokes and, finally, the figures and boats on top of the architecture and water.

Both views were popular and exist in a number of versions by Canaletto and his followers. Cat. 3 is probably the prime version of the Cannaregio views. A close variant painted a few years later is at the Getty Museum, which is almost identical in size to cat. 3 but differs from it in compositional details, palette and lighting (fig. 76). The mouth of the Cannaregio Canal is easy to miss in cat. 3, whereas gondolas are seen going

Fig. 73. Canaletto (1697–1768), *From the Palazzo Correr-Contarini to the Palazzo Vendramin-Calergi* from the *Cagnola Sketchbook*, 1730s, pen and ink over black chalk, 23 × 17 cm (each folio), folios 48v–49r, Gallerie dell'Accademia, Venice

Fig. 74. Canaletto (1697–1768), *From the Rio di Cannaregio to the Palazzo Correr-Contarini* from the *Cagnola Sketchbook*, 1730s, pen and ink over black chalk, 23 × 17 cm, folio 49v, Gallerie dell'Accademia, Venice

Fig. 75. Detail of X-ray of cat. 4

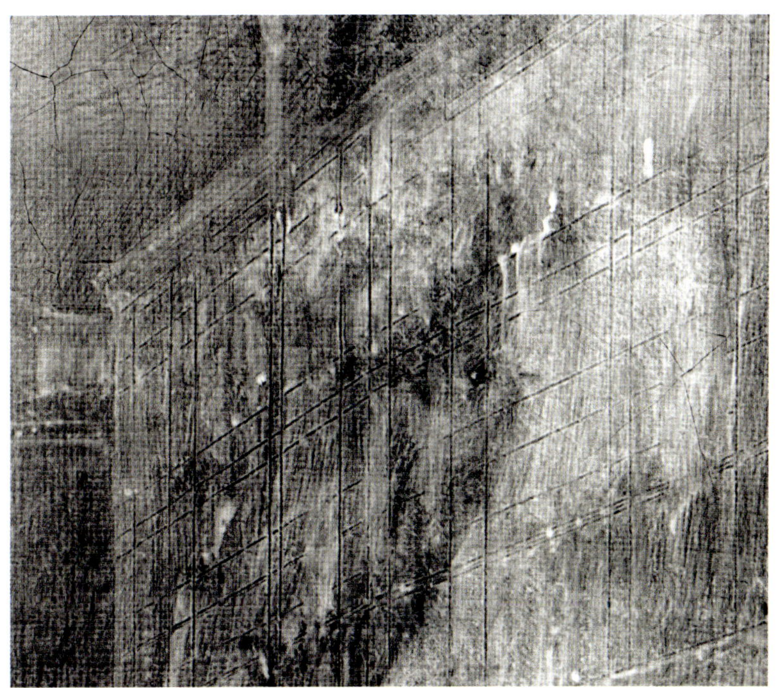

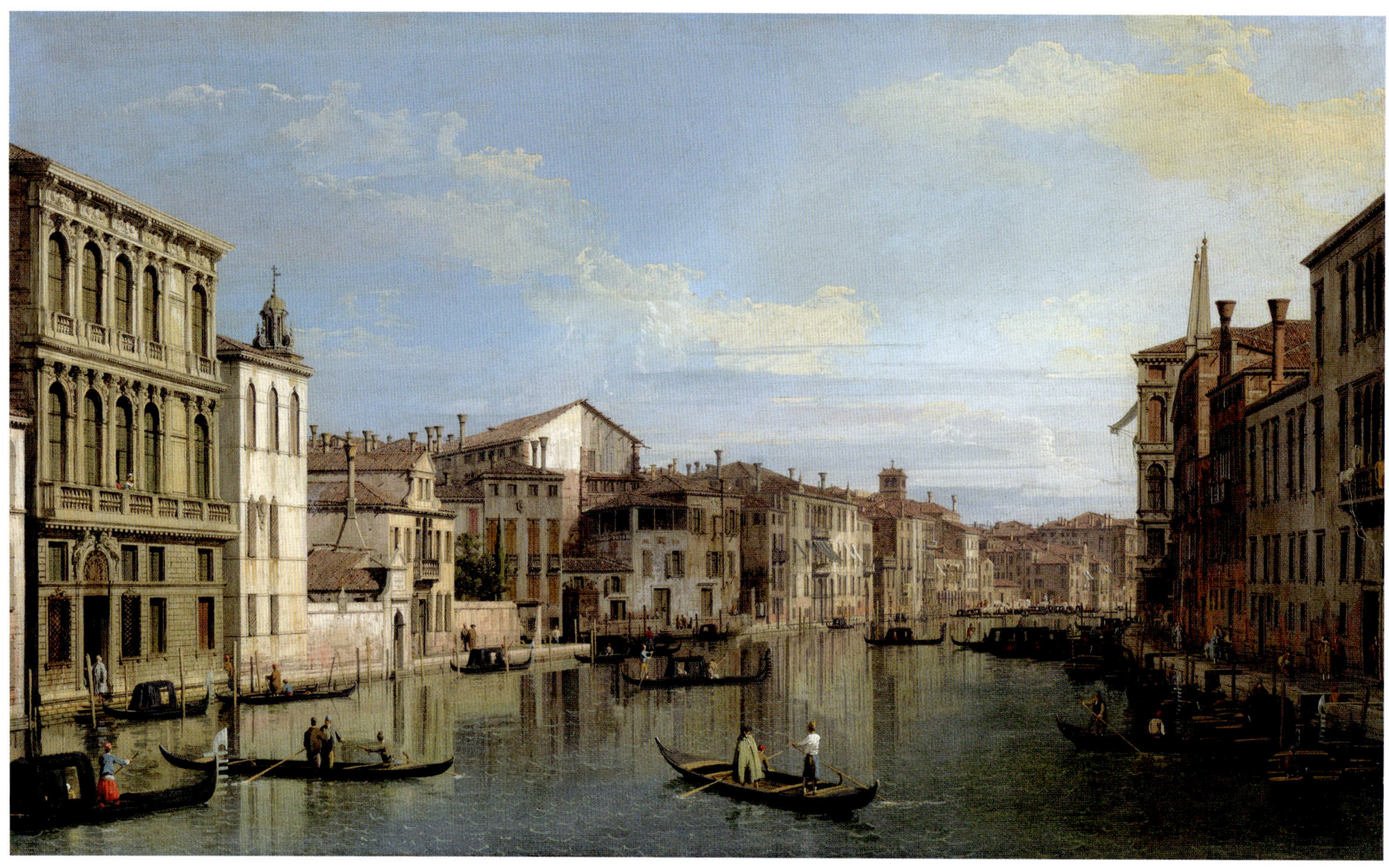

Fig. 76. Canaletto (1697–1768), *The Grand Canal in Venice from the Palazzo Flangini to the Campo San Marcuola*, c.1738, oil on canvas, 47 × 77.8 cm, J. Paul Getty Museum, Los Angeles (inv. 2013.22)

into it in the Getty picture. The view in cat. 3 is taken from lower down, closer to the level of the water, and thus appears closer to the beholder. Moreover, the pronounced contrast of light and dark in cat. 3 diverges from the more subdued, warm purplish-grey tonality of the Getty version. This is particularly discernible in the Riva di Biasio, fully cast in shadow on the left bank of cat. 3. There are also small alterations in the number and placement of chimneys, rooftops and windows. For example, in cat. 3 Canaletto omitted several rooftops and chimneys visible in the Getty painting to the right of the Scuola dei Morti behind the priest's house, but included

a prominent chimney on the large warehouse, absent from the Getty picture (fig. 77). There are fewer windows depicted in the building just above the house with the loggia at the mouth of the Cannaregio in cat. 3 compared to the Getty version (fig. 78). Moreover, the awnings on the left bank and on the Palazzo Bembo in the Getty picture are omitted from cat. 3. Lastly, in the left foreground of cat. 3 the two balustrades on the façade of the Palazzo Flangini are identical as they are today, unlike in the Getty version where they differ. It may be that the upper balustrade was modified between the creation of cat. 3 and the Getty painting, or that Canaletto purposefully

took liberties and made alterations between versions for aesthetic and distinctive effect.

The young Bernardo Bellotto, while still under his uncle's influence, painted two larger versions of the composition in which he varied details and staffage and employed a slightly cooler palette, both identified as Bellotto's work by Charles Beddington (fig. 79).[4] The composition also circulated in a print by Antonio Visentini, who probably based his etching on the Getty picture.[5]

The party in the *sandolo* in the foreground of cat. 3 is similar to the group of figures in a comparable, slightly earlier view painted for the Duke of Bedford around 1732 (fig. 80).

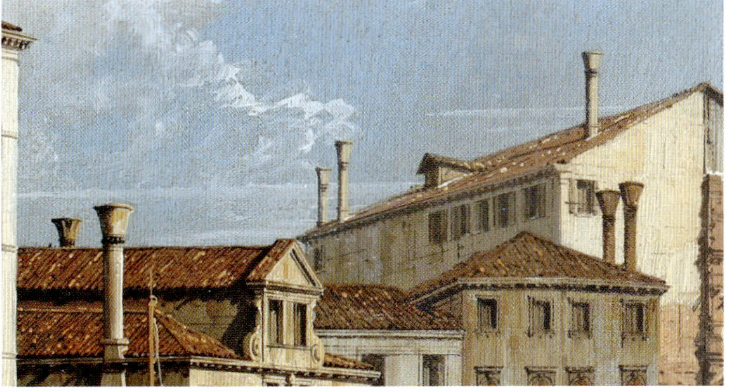 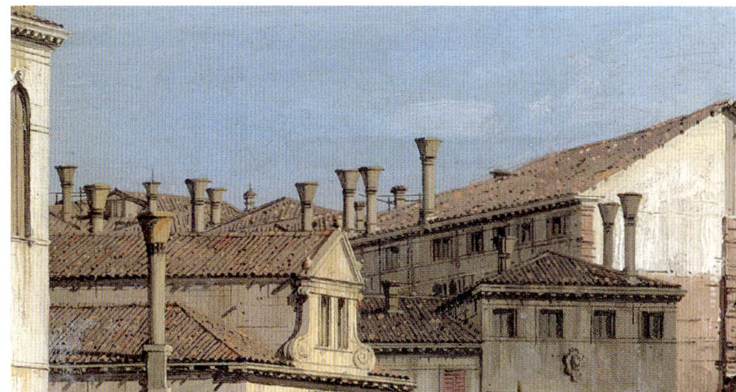

Fig. 77. Details of cat. 3 (left) and fig. 76 (right)

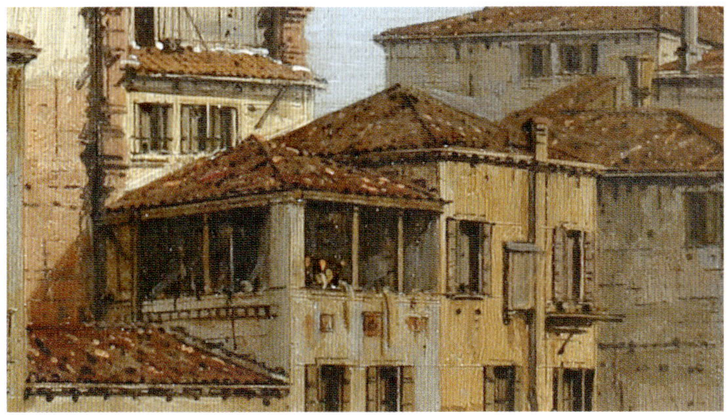 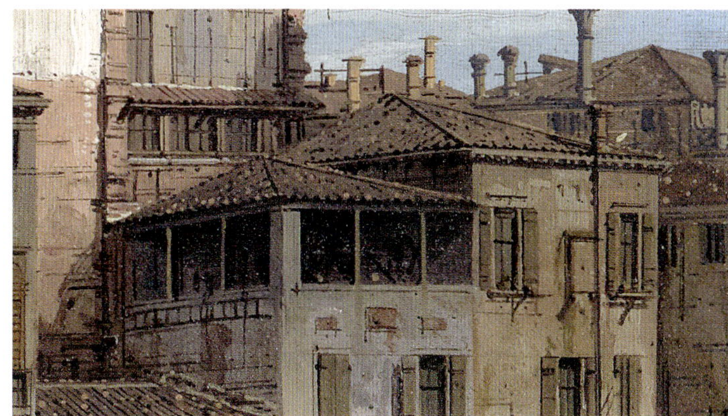

Fig. 78. Details of cat. 3 (left) and fig. 76 (right)

The latter view is taken from further left and east, closer to the entrance to the Cannaregio Canal. Both parties consist of three finely dressed women, two facing towards and one away from the viewer, as well as one standing and one seated rower.[6] In cat. 3 Canaletto included an additional gentleman, a means of ensuring the uniqueness of the picture.

Cat. 4 derives from a prototype to which it is similar but distinct. Canaletto first painted the composition around 1730 as part of a series of 12 views of the Grand Canal for Consul Smith, today in the Royal Collection (fig. 81). That work served as the basis for Visentini's print after it, published in 1735.[7]

The Wallace Collection possesses another version of this composition, which is a direct repetition in size and details of the painting in the Royal Collection picture (cat. 12). The distribution of both views via the print medium is likely to have contributed to their popularity and probably accounts for the multitude of versions of each composition.

Canaletto painted cat. 4 to scale, but made alterations in the details in order to create a unique work. He lowered the viewpoint so as to appear closer to the level of the water, while the Royal Collection view is taken from higher up. Moreover, Canaletto lit cat. 4 from the left rather than the right, probably to complement

its pendant. The lower half of the *campanile* of the Carità and the two obelisks of Palazzo Giustinian Lolin nearby are additions absent from the prototype. Nearby, to the right, the Palazzo Contarini dagli Scrigni is shown with its gable, but less of its white observatory is visible in cat. 4. Furthermore, the boats in cat. 4 differ in character and arrangement and there are more of them, creating a more bustling waterway. Small sailing ships replace the sizeable vessel with a cover at the lower right of the Royal Collection picture. The large, masted vessel prominently positioned in front of the Carità in the distance is absent from cat. 4.

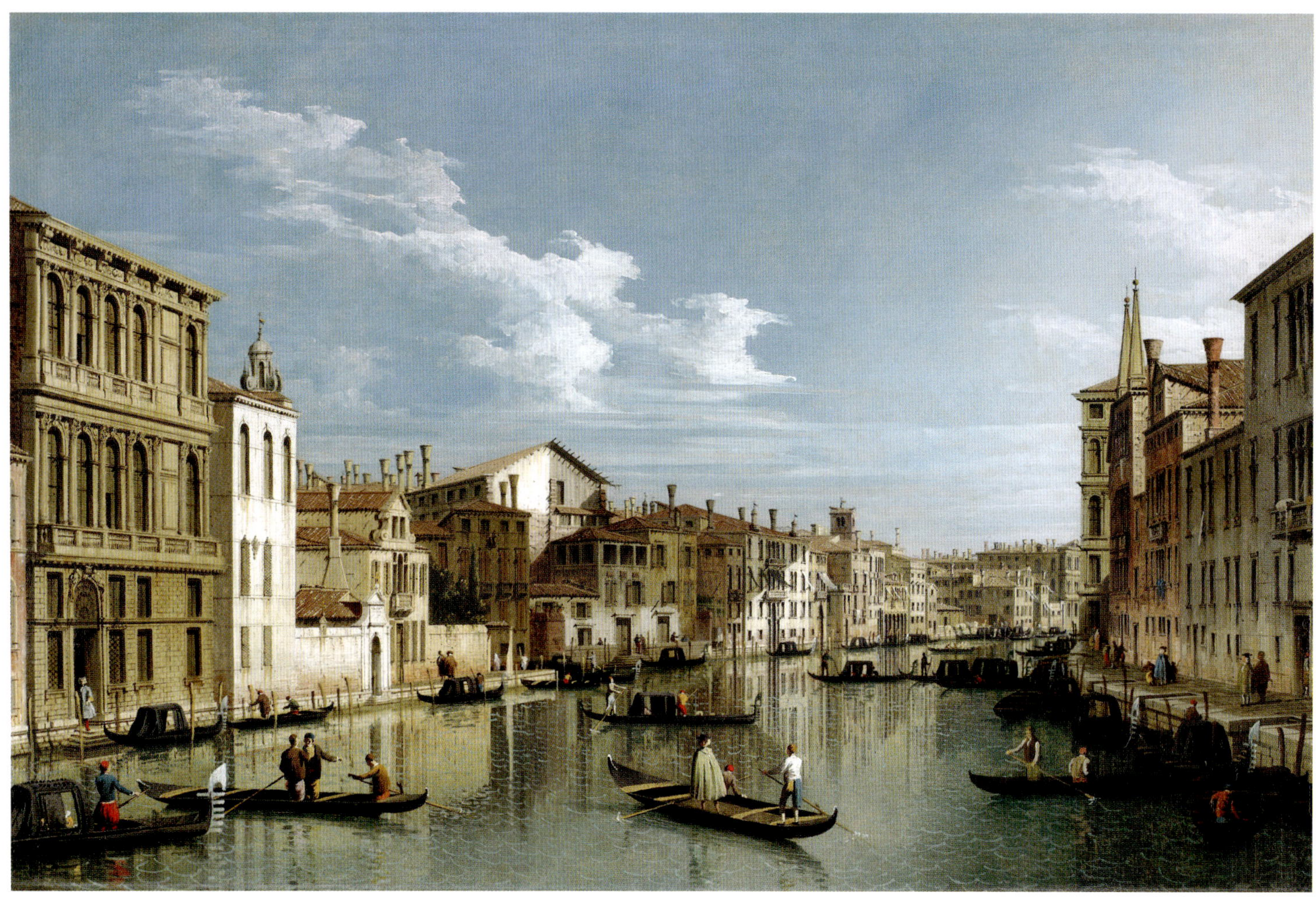

Fig. 79. Bernardo Bellotto (1722–1780), *The Grand Canal in Venice from Palazzo Flangini to Campo San Marcuola*, *c.*1740, oil on canvas, 61.3 × 92.4 cm, Minneapolis Institute of Art, Bequest of Miss Tessie Jones in memory of Herschel V. Jones (inv. 68.41.11)

Canaletto straightened the left bank in the prototype, but retained more of the bend in the canal in cat. 4. He adjusted the view of the Palazzo Moro-Lin to include all 13 windows for which the palace was renowned, rather than the ten shown in the painting for Smith, enabling him to include an additional dormer window. As with cat. 3, the positions and number of chimneys and awnings have been altered. Canaletto also added balconies on the *piano nobile* of the Palazzo Giustinian and the two-storey building next to it on the right bank. As with the Palazzo Flangini in cat. 3, Canaletto was either guided by real

architectural developments or added such details for aesthetic and distinctive effect.

Of the 11 Canaletti bought by Lord Hertford only four are still attributed to the artist today, including the present pair. However, the latter has not been spared attributional questions. In the first half of the twentieth century, both paintings were attributed to Bellotto. In 1968 they were given to Canaletto's studio, and by 1976 they were fully attributed to Canaletto.[8] The high quality of handling and numerous distinctive details make it likely that they were painted by Canaletto.

In terms of dating, pigments analysed from both paintings correspond with those observed in other works by Canaletto from around the mid-1730s onwards.[9] The quay on the left bank in cat. 3 near the entrance to the Cannaregio Canal is shown without the balustrade and statue of Saint John Nepomuk by Giovanni Marchiori erected in 1742. The statue is also missing from the Getty version, which is dated to about 1738. Canaletto was attentive to this detail and added it years later in his painting of *San Geremia and the Entrance to the Cannaregio* (*c.*1726–27), at Smith's request.[10] Moreover, the *campanile* of

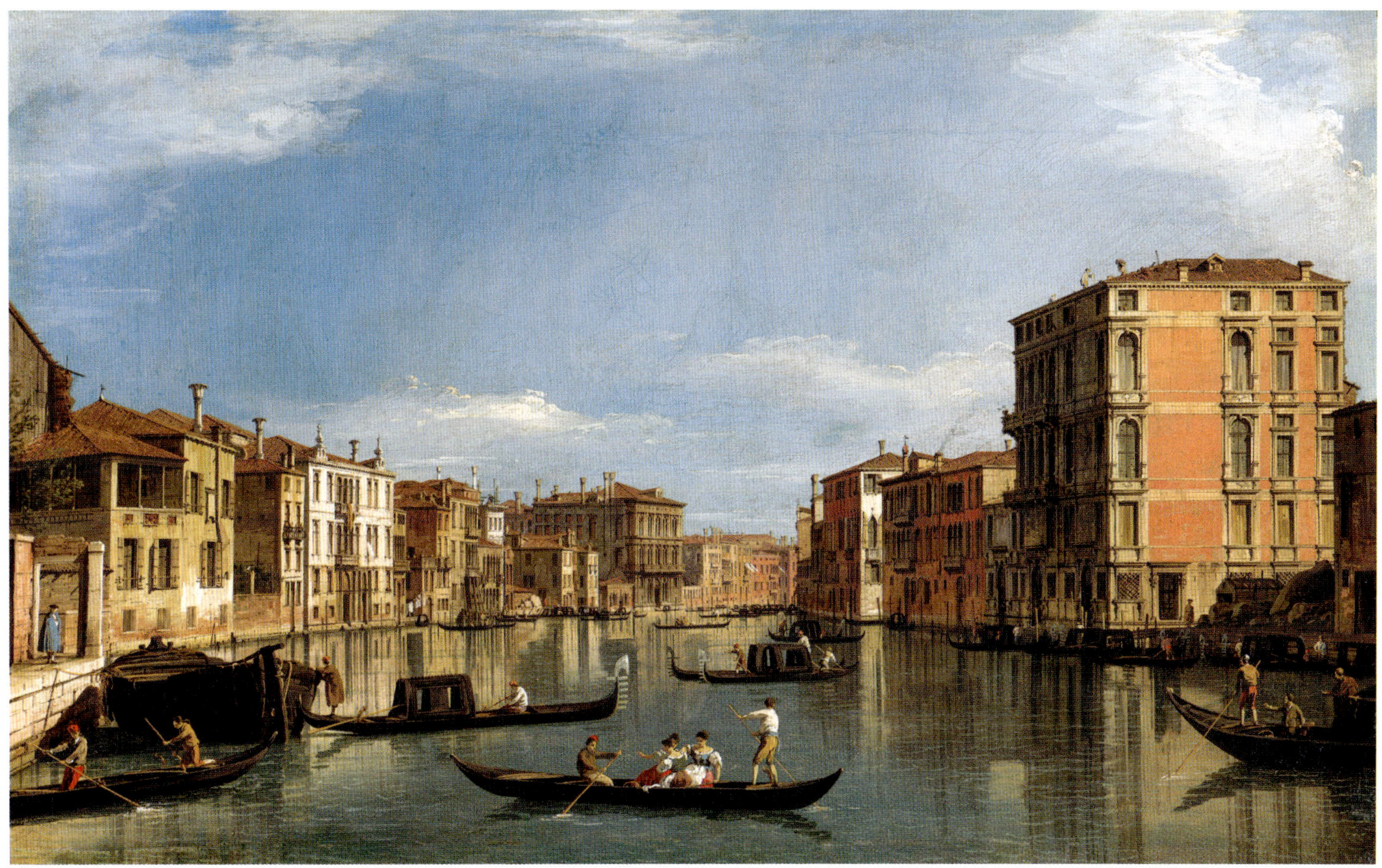

Fig. 80. Canaletto (1697–1768), *The Grand Canal Looking East from the Palazzo Bembo and the Entrance to the Cannaregio to the Palazzo Vendramin-Calergi,* early 1730s, oil on canvas, 47 × 80 cm, Collection of the Duke of Bedford, Woburn Abbey

the Carità in cat. 4 collapsed in 1741. The pair was thus painted prior to these dates.

The present pair may have been part of a set of four commissioned by Elizabeth Capell, Countess of Essex (1704–1784), the Duke of Bedford's sister, around May 1733 when she is recorded in Venice, although this remains uncertain.[11] Lady Essex lived in Italy together with her husband, William Capell, 3rd Earl of Essex (1697–1743), who was appointed ambassador at Turin in 1732. The couple may have met Canaletto while in Venice and certainly knew of the Duke of Bedford's substantial commission of 24

vedute from Canaletto, which are comparable in dimensions to the present works. In September 1734 Smith confirmed shipment of four pictures to Lord and Lady Essex.[12] Two of these have recently been identified at auction.[13] The latter replicate compositions in the Duke of Bedford's collection, while the present pair does not, making it less likely that together they formed the as-yet-unidentified set of four Essex pictures.[14] The Essexes' collection was dispersed at auction in 1777 when ten paintings were given to Canaletto, but the authorship of six of them remains uncertain.[15] It is tempting to think

that Sir Thomas Bernard bought the pictures at the Essex sale, but no buyers by that name were recorded.[16]

Lord Hertford favoured cat. 4 and was prepared to pay £250 to £300 for it. Two days before their sale, Hertford went to see the pictures at Christie's in London. His impressions are recorded in a letter to his agent Samuel Mawson:

Thanks too for mentioning the two Canalettis. I had seen them. They are very pretty & appear to me to be in a very good state. They are neither of

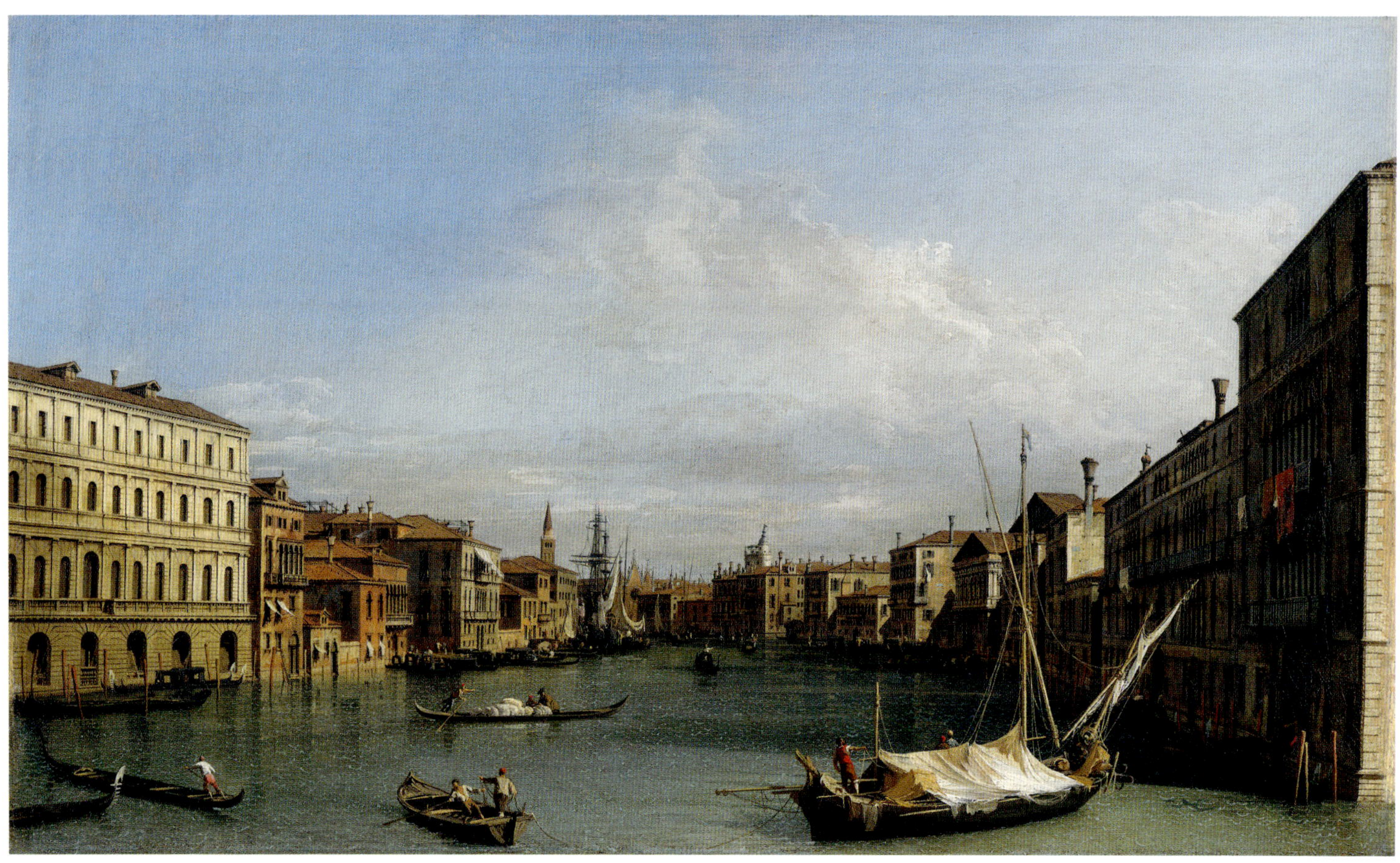

them very good views of Venice but
nevertheless I must say I should rather
like to have one of them – n° 70 [cat. 4].
The other I have no fancy for. I wonder
what you value them at? As n° 69 [cat. 3]
is of course sold before its brother 70,
the person who buys the first will
naturally wish to have its companion &
may for that reason be tempted to give
more than if a single Picture was sold.
I should think 250 to 300 at most for
n° 70, certainly the best of the two, would
be a good price.[17]

In the end, Hertford paid less than he was
prepared to for cat. 4 (£194.50), but bought
both pictures, probably because he was
reluctant to separate the 'brothers'.

At a late stage of the production of this
volume, Charles Beddington noted that the
two paintings are very different in style and
thus date, and cannot have been intended to
hang as a pair. This might make it more likely
that they were acquired by the Bernards at the
Essex sale since the ten Canaletti in that sale
may well have been delivered to the Essexes
over an extended period of time.

PROVENANCE
Sir Thomas Bernard (1750–1818);[18] by descent to
his wife Charlotte Matilda Bernard (1765–1846);
Sir Thomas Bernard sale, Christie's, 31 March 1855
(L.22337), lots 69 (cat. 3)[19] and 70 (cat. 4);[20] bought by
Edwards (cat. 3) for £194.50 (equivalent to 185 guineas)
and by King[21] (cat. 4) for £204.15 (equivalent to 195
guineas) for Richard Seymour-Conway, 4th Marquess
of Hertford (1800–1870); by descent to Sir Richard
Wallace, 1st Baronet (1818–1890); by descent to his
wife, Lady Wallace (Julie Amélie Charlotte Castelnau,
1819–1897); by whom bequeathed with the rest of the
Wallace Collection to the British nation, 1897.

EXHIBITION
1872–75: 'Paintings, Porcelain, Bronzes, Decorative
Furniture and other Works of Art lent by Sir Richard
Wallace to the Bethnal Green Branch of the South
Kensington Museum'.[22]

RELATED WORKS
To cat. 3:

Canaletto, *The Grand Canal in Venice from the
Palazzo Flangini to the Campo San Marcuola*,
c.1738, oil on canvas, 47 × 77.8 cm, J. Paul Getty
Museum, Los Angeles (inv. 2013.22) (C257d)

Bernardo Bellotto, *The Grand Canal in Venice
from Palazzo Flangini to Campo San Marcuola*,
c.1740, oil on canvas, 61.3 × 92.4 cm, Minneapolis
Institute of Art (inv. 68.41.11) (C257a)

Canaletto, *The Grand Canal in Venice from
Palazzo Flangini to Campo San Marcuola*, oil
on canvas, 61 × 91.5 cm, Private Collection, USA
(C257b)

Canaletto, *The Grand Canal in Venice from
Palazzo Flangini to Campo San Marcuola*, oil on
canvas, 38 × 62 cm, Private Collection (C257c)

To cat. 4:

Canaletto, *The Grand Canal Looking South from
Ca' Foscari to the Carità*, *c*.1726–27, oil on canvas,
49.9 × 80.3 cm, Royal Collection (RCIN 401404)
(C203)

Antonio Visentini, *Venice: The Grand Canal from
the Palazzo Foscari to the Carità*, *c*.1746–62, oil
on canvas, 47 × 78.5 cm, The Wallace Collection,
London (cat. 12) (C203a)

Bernardo Bellotto, *Venice, a View of the Grand
Canal Looking South from the Palazzo Foscari and
Palazzo Moro-Lin towards the Church of Santa
Maria della Carità*, oil on canvas, 59.7 × 89.5 cm,
Private Collection

Bernardo Bellotto, *View of the Grand Canal with
the Palazzi Foscari and Moro Lin*, oil on canvas,
101 × 162 cm, Nationalmuseum Stockholm
(inv. 49) (C204)

TECHNICAL NOTES
Both paintings have a fine, plain-weave, medium-
weight linen canvas. Exceptionally, the original
canvases have retained their four tacking margins.
Pronounced cusping apparent on all four sides
in the X-radiographs of both works confirms that
both compositions are complete and that no loss of
canvas or image has occurred. Both paintings have a
double ground consisting of a red-brown lower layer,
the standard Venetian ground which was most likely
commercially prepared. The upper layer is a pink or
peach colour and was probably applied in the studio.
This is consistent with Canaletto's practice from the
1730s onwards and can be found in other *vedute* at
the Wallace Collection such as cats 5 and 6.

In cat. 3 the impasto in the brushwork in areas
such as the clouds, figures and parts of buildings is
well preserved and not flattened from lining. This,
together with the retention of the tacking margins at
the time of lining, indicates that the operation was
carried out with sensitivity and care, possibly early
in the nineteenth century. Cat. 4 was cleaned and
relined by William Vallance in 1961. Both paintings
were cleaned and analysed at the Hamilton Kerr
Institute in 2021. Technical investigation comprising
X-radiography, infrared reflectography, ultraviolet
light photography, surface micrography and SEM-
EDX paint sample analysis was also undertaken at
this point.

LITERATURE
Constable 1962, C205 (cat. 4), C257 (cat. 3)
Watson 1968, p. 54 (cat. 3); p. 55 (cat. 4)
Puppi 1970, pp. 97–98, no. 83A (cat. 3);
     p. 96, no. 71B (cat. 4)
Links 1981, p. 32, no. 84 (cat. 3); p. 24, no. 51 (cat. 4)
Ingamells 1985, pp. 230–31 (cat. 3);
     pp. 236–37 (cat. 4)
Duffy and Hedley 2004, pp. 64–65

LP

5. GIOVANNI ANTONIO CANAL,
IL CANALETTO (Venice 1697–1768)

*The Grand Canal from the Palazzo
Dolfin-Manin to the Rialto Bridge*

*c.*1738
oil on canvas
58.5 × 93 cm
P511

6. GIOVANNI ANTONIO CANAL,
IL CANALETTO (Venice 1697–1768)

*The Grand Canal, Looking South-East along
the Fondamenta di Santa Chiara*

*c.*1738
oil on canvas
58.7 × 93 cm
P507

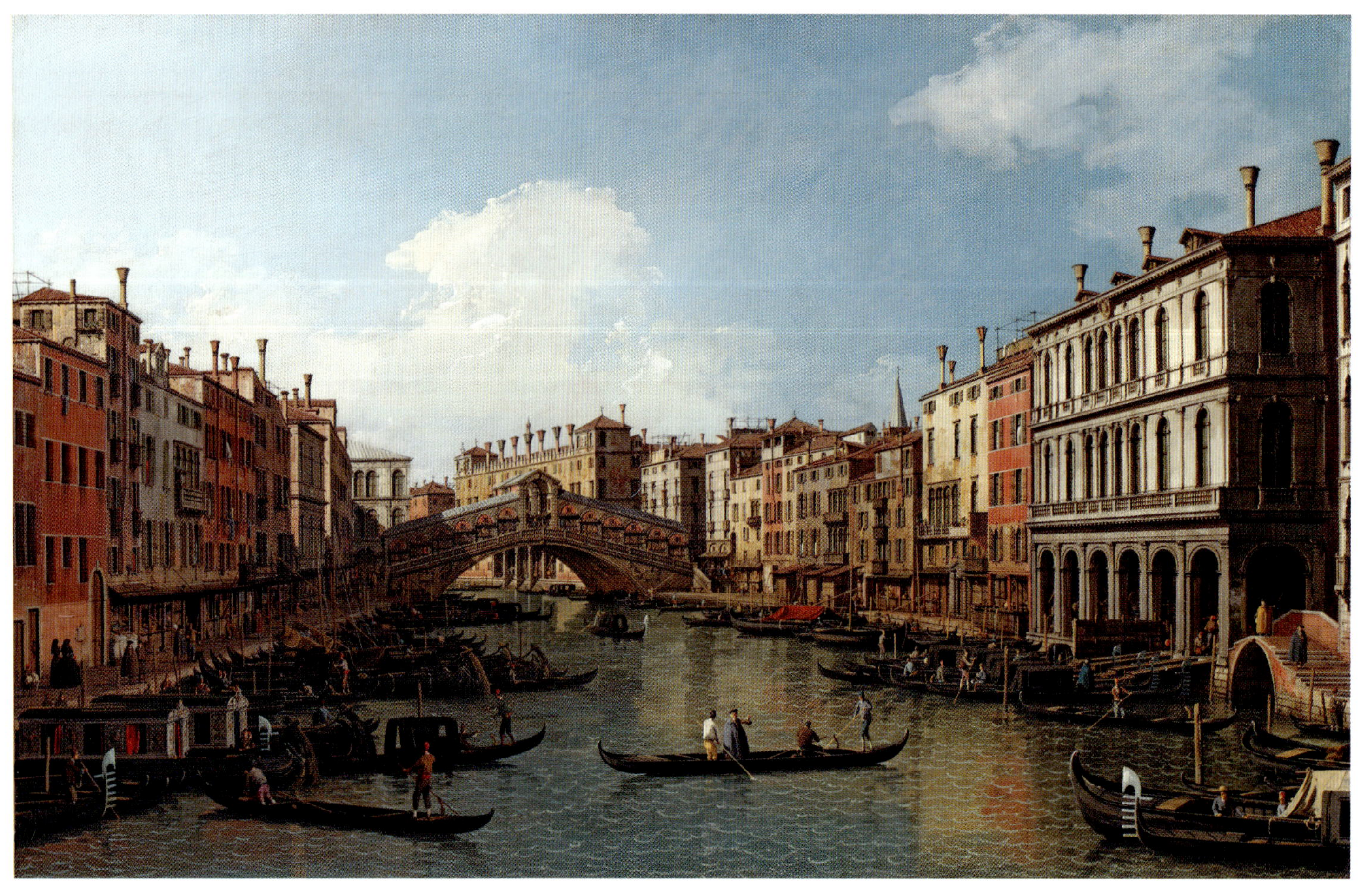

This pair of views illustrates two points along the Grand Canal. Cat. 5 depicts the famous and centrally located Rialto Bridge. This busy area was the commercial heart of Venice where all routes converged at the Canal's narrowest point, making it a natural place for a bridge. Cat. 6 depicts the Canal's quieter uppermost reaches just south of the Canale di Santa Chiara. The latter is a small canal that joins the Grand Canal in the north-west after the Grand Canal's final bend and prior to its effluence into the lagoon.

The view in cat. 5 looks north towards the Rialto Bridge. On the left is the Fondamenta del Vin, lined with shops. *Fondamentas*, or pedestrian streets that run along Venetian canals, facilitated the loading and unloading of boats. In the right foreground is a stepped bridge over the Rio di San Salvatore, the route by which goods were taken from the Rialto markets to as near the Piazza San Marco as a water vessel could travel. The bridge has only one parapet, a common feature of old Venetian bridges, many of which had no parapets at all. Beyond the bridge is Jacopo Sansovino's Palazzo Dolfin-Manin, built between 1536 and 1545 for the Dolfin family by merging two pre-existing medieval buildings. In 1787 the palace became the residence of the noble Manin family who possessed one of Venice's most important libraries. They commissioned the architect Giannantonio Selva (1751–1819) to make important modifications to the palace, such as eliminating the inner courtyard and replacing the entry staircase with a sumptuous neoclassical one. Ludovico Manin became Venice's last Doge in 1797. That same year he surrendered to the French army, abdicated and lived his last five years segregated in the palace. Today, the building houses Venice's branch of the Bank of Italy.

Beyond is the Fondamenta del Ferro, lined with shops and three free-standing stalls. Further on, the Rialto Bridge can be accessed by steps on both sides of the canal. During the seventeenth century, the bridge was described as 'one of the finest bridges in Europe, because of the one arch only, and of the vast wideness and height of that arch'.[1] There had long been a crossing point at this location, gradually assuming more permanent structures. In 1264 a wooden bridge was constructed that was twice destroyed, in 1310 and 1444. Those bridges were lined with shops and had a central section that could be raised to allow taller ships to pass, as can be seen in a painting by Vittore Carpaccio (fig. 82).

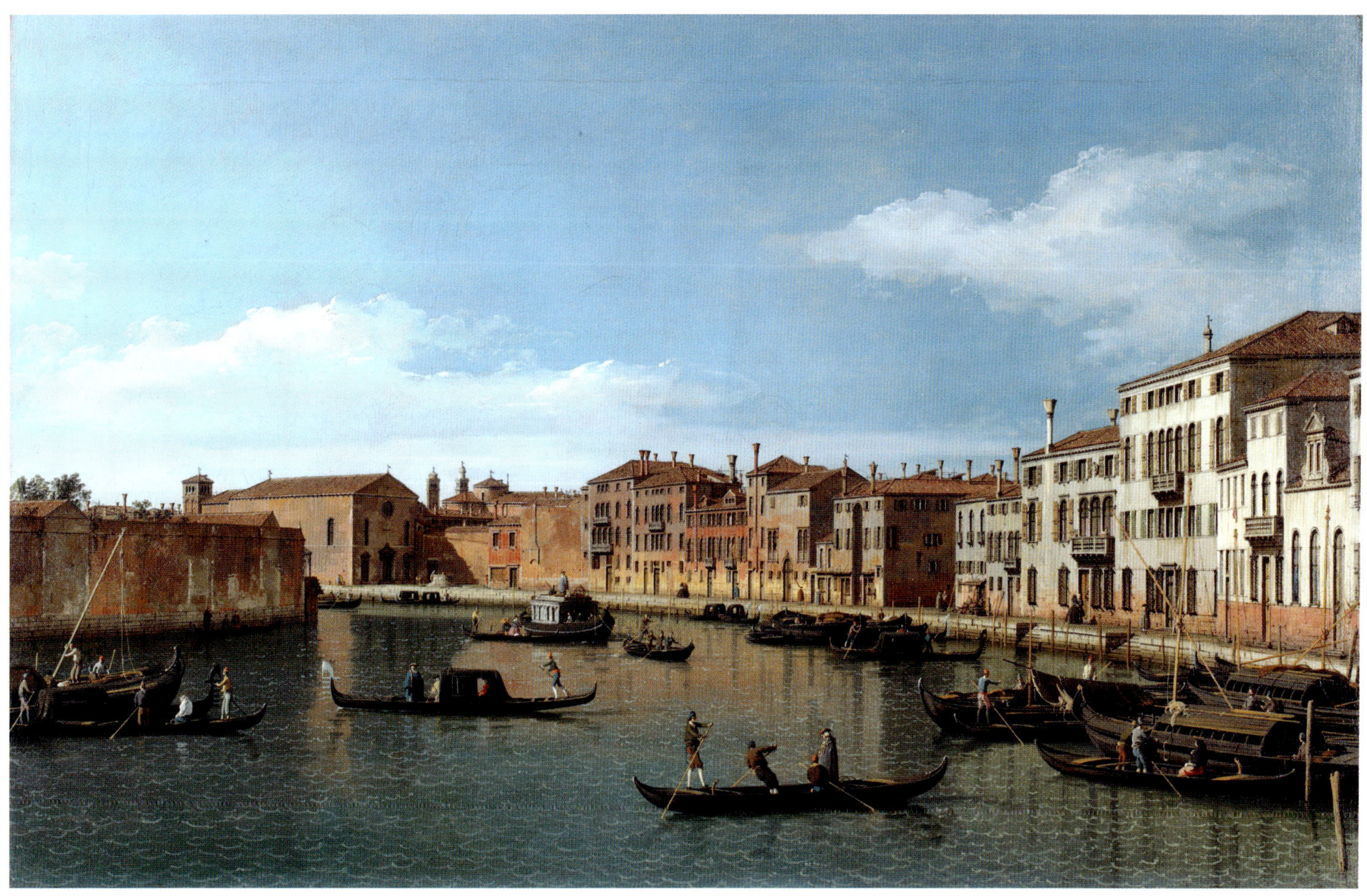

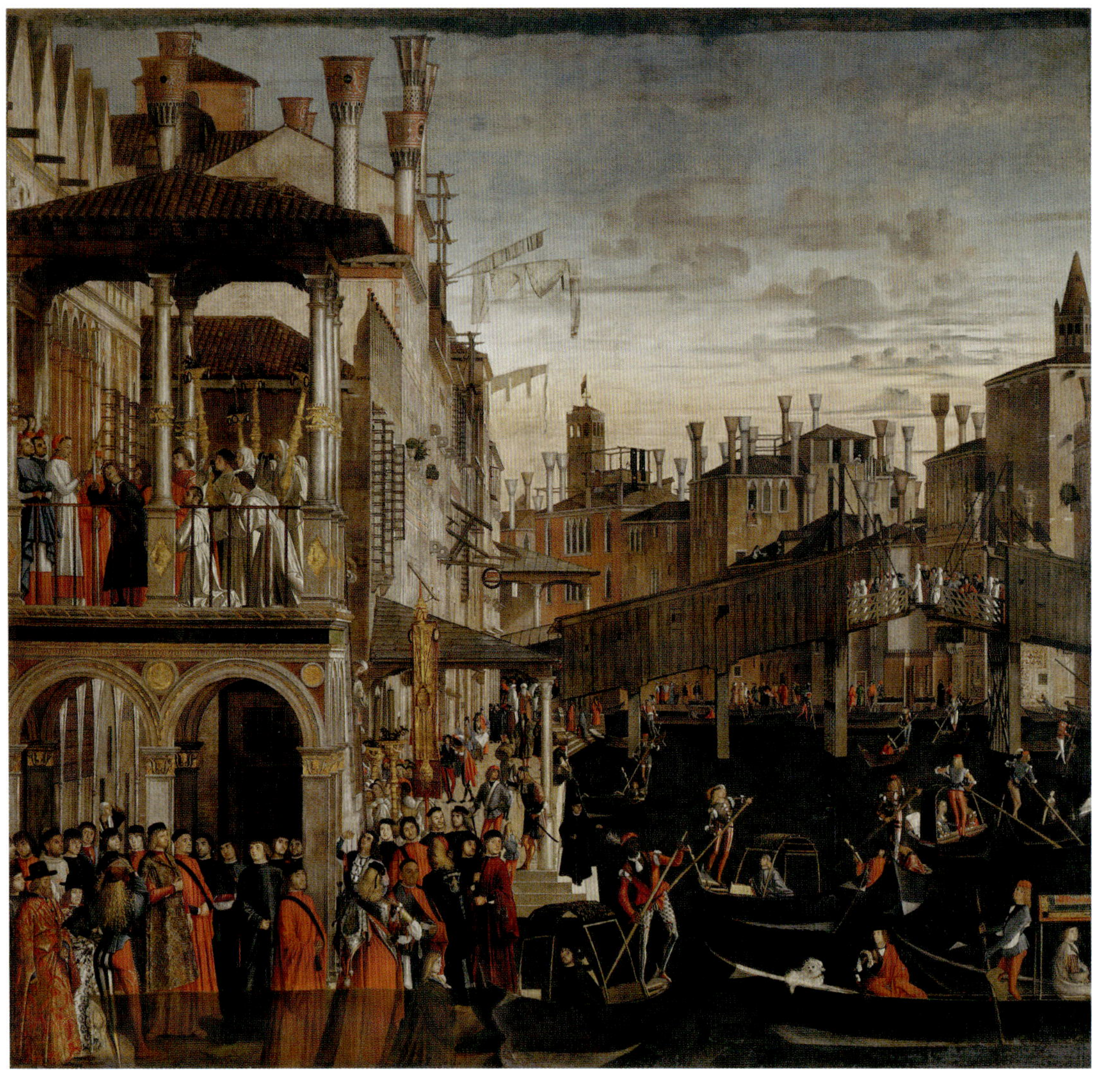

Fig. 82. Vittore Carpaccio (1465–1525), *Miracle of the Relic of the Holy Cross at the Rialto Bridge*, c.1496, oil on canvas, 371 × 392 cm, Gallerie dell'Accademia, Venice (inv. 566)

The bridge in Canaletto's painting, which still stands today, was designed and built between 1588 and 1591, fittingly, by Antonio da Ponte (1512–1595) and his nephew Antonio Contin (c.1566–1600). Other illustrious candidates contending for the role were Jacopo Sansovino (1486–1570) and Andrea Palladio (1508–1580), who submitted designs for a bridge with three arches (fig. 83). Canaletto must have been taken with Palladio's design in which full-length sculptures adorned the bridge, as he made a *capriccio* after it (fig. 84).[2] In 1570 Palladio described the site as follows: 'in the middle of the city, ... one of the greatest and most noble in Italy ... and there is an enormous amount of trade ... and the bridge came to be exactly ... where the merchants gathered to do business'.[3] Dal Ponte's single arch was ultimately chosen, resulting in a bridge that supports two rows of shops flanked by two walkways from which to look out onto the canal. On the left and right of the arch, reliefs depicting the Annunciation allude to the Republic of Venice's mythical 'birthday' on 25 March 421 on the Feast of the Annunciation. Reliefs representing Venice's patron saints Theodore and Mark adorn the opposite, northern side. Together these sculptures allude to Venice's heritage and divine perfection. They cost 250,000 ducats, a fortune at the time.

Immediately, the Rialto Bridge became a sensation and was considered one of the wonders of the world. William Shakespeare employed it as a meeting point in his *Merchant of Venice*. The bridge was admired both as a superb piece of architecture and as an engineering feat. Yet some visitors were disappointed to find that the bridge was obscured by shops, which at the time specialised in gold and jewels.[4] For many years, until the Accademia Bridge was erected in 1854, the Rialto was the only bridge across the Grand Canal, which was otherwise crossed on *traghetti*, or ferries. Prior to Canaletto, Luca Carlevarijs had depicted the Rialto Bridge twice in print and three times in painting, a modest number considering its importance. Canaletto developed the possibilities of the subject, painting the bridge from both sides and from closer up.

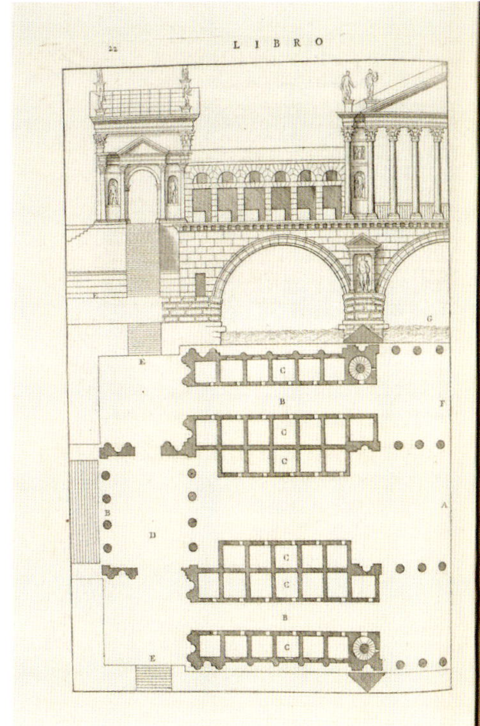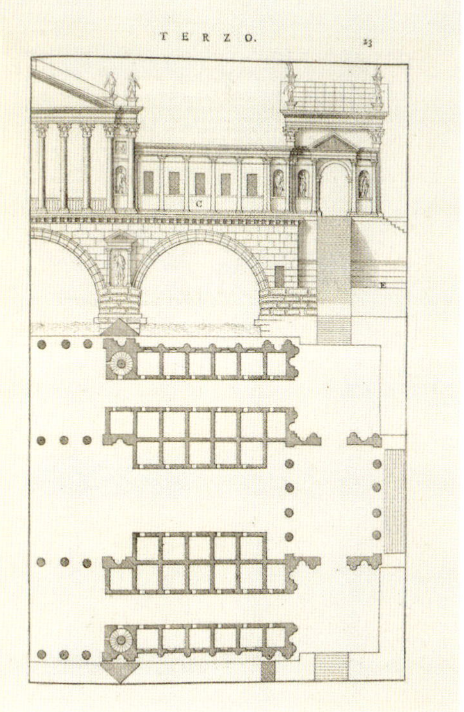

Fig. 83. Andrea Palladio (1508–1580), pages 22–23 from *I Quattro Libri dell'Architettura*, 1570, printed on paper, full leather bound in red goatskin, with gold-tooled border and spine decoration, 34.8 × 26.1 × 3.4 cm, Royal Collection (RCIN 1079104)

Fig. 84. Canaletto (1697–1768), *Capriccio View with Palladio's Design for the Rialto Bridge*, 1742, oil on canvas, 90.5 × 130 cm, Royal Collection (RCIN 404029)

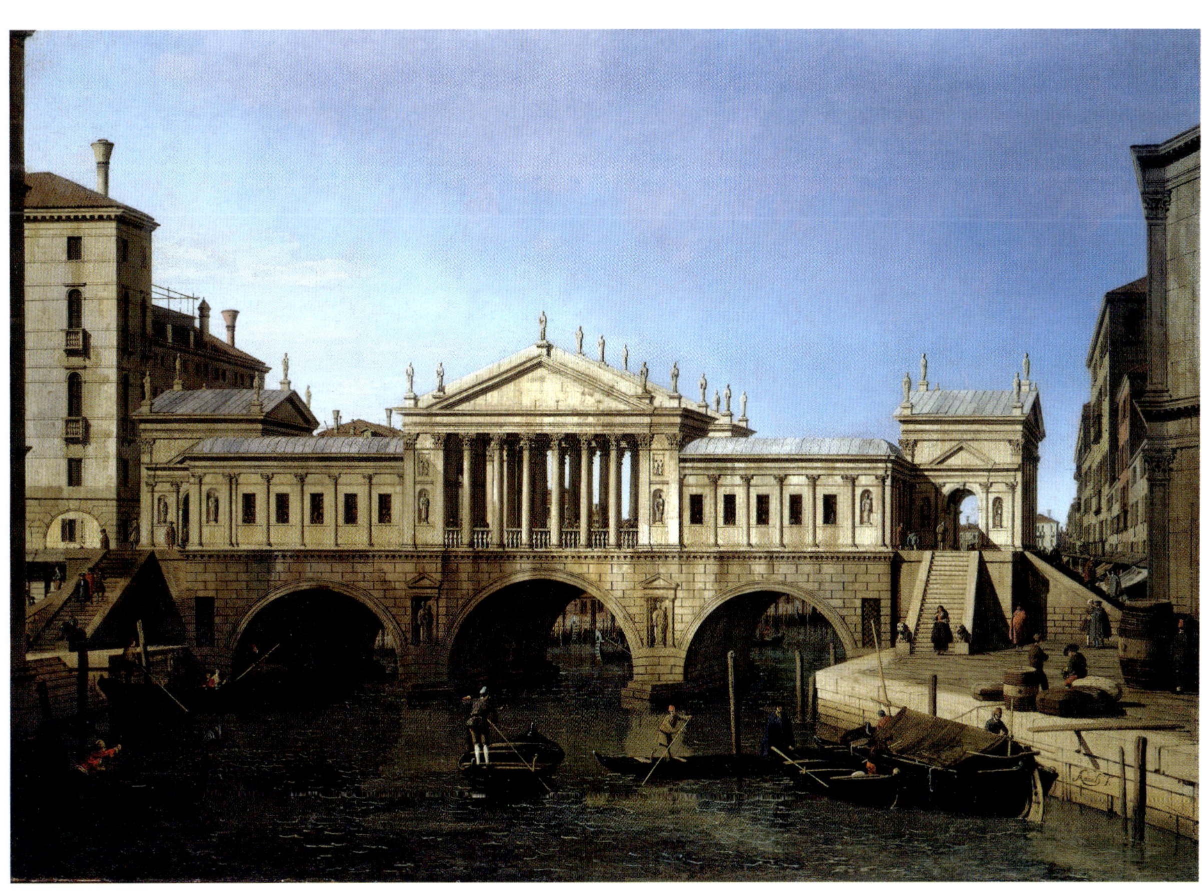

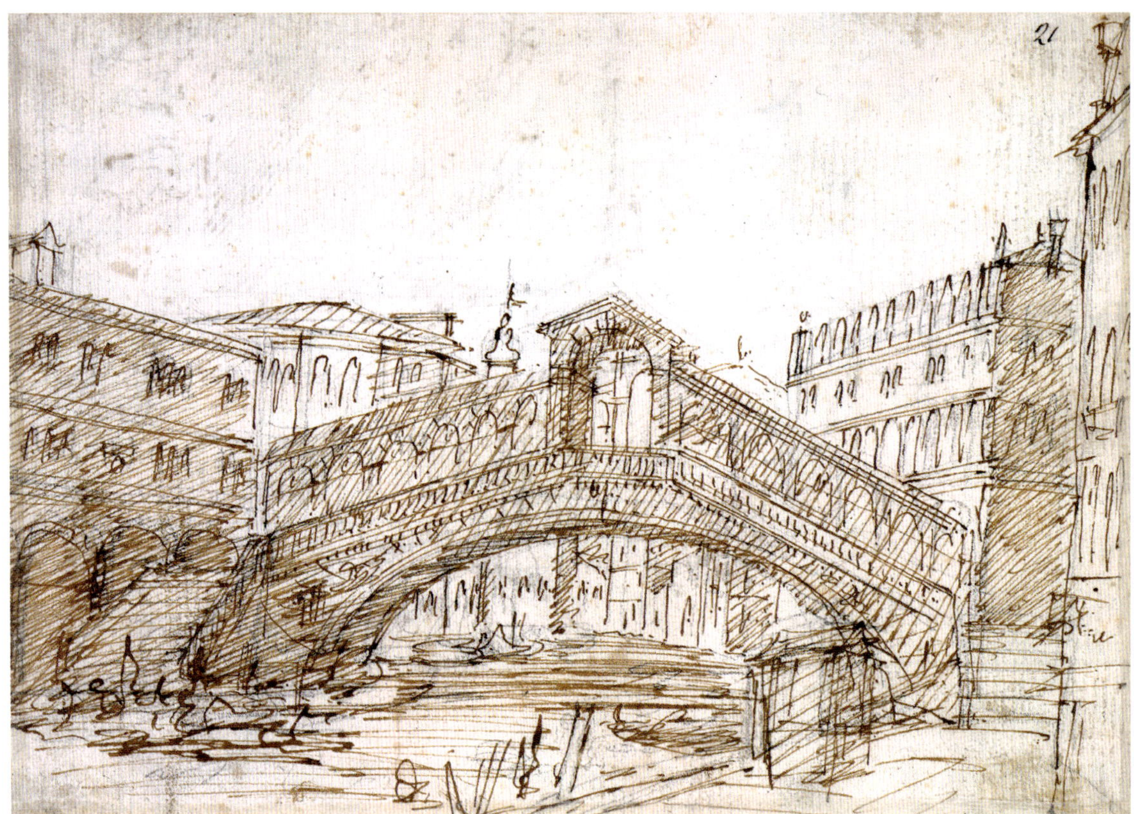

Fig. 85. Canaletto (1697–1768), *The Grand Canal with the Rialto Bridge from the South* (verso), *c.*1727–29, pen and ink over traces of graphite on paper, 20.3 × 14.2 cm, Metropolitan Museum of Art, New York (inv. 1975.1.292)

Beyond the bridge, in the centre of the painting, is the Fondaco dei Tedeschi where German traders had their offices, lodgings and warehouses. After a fire at the beginning of the sixteenth century, the Fondaco (derived from the Arabic word for 'storehouse') was rebuilt in 1508 in a traditional style. The façade facing the canal was famously decorated with frescoes by the 30-year-old Giorgione (1477–1510), while the southern side of the building towards today's Calle del Fontego (formerly the Calle del Buso) was frescoed by the 20-year-old Titian (active *c.*1506; died 1576). Although faintly visible in Canaletto's painting, the frescoes were so damaged that there is sadly no trace of them today.[5] When unveiled, the frescoes became the talk of the town, solidifying the painters' reputations. Later, the building was significantly altered. The original stone towers were removed and the central courtyard was covered with glass in the nineteenth century. In the 1930s it was almost entirely reconstructed in concrete. The purpose of the building also expanded with

time. It was used as a customs house under Napoleon Bonaparte and as a post office under Benito Mussolini. After a major refurbishment between 2009 and 2016, it now houses a contemporary urban department store.

To the left of the Fondaco is the large, white, three-storied Palazzo dei Camerlenghi. Completed in 1488 and subsequently enlarged in the mid-1520s, it served as the headquarters for several financial magistrates including the Camerlenghi di Comun, from whom it takes its name, who were senior fiscal officials of the Republic of Venice. The palazzo has an unusual pentagonal floor plan that follows the shoreline of the Grand Canal. There was a jail on the ground floor for those who defaulted on their debts, a warning to people passing by. The building currently houses the regional main offices of the Italian Comptroller and Auditor General. Just left of the bridge is another administrative building, the Palazzo dei Dieci Savi with its arched openings on the ground floor. Designed by Antonio Abbondi (1465–1549) and rebuilt in 1521 after a fire

seven years earlier, this building was the seat of the Dieci Savi alle Decime (Ten Wise Men at the Tithes) until 1797, a group of Venetian finance magistrates. The city's water officers occupied the building until 2014.

The view in cat. 6 faces south-east past the entry to the Canale di Santa Chiara. Today, this much transformed area is near the Piazzale Roma vaporetto stop. The long, plain wall on the left is the Convent of Corpus Domini, a house of Dominican nuns consecrated in 1394. After a fire, the original church was replaced by a larger building between 1440 and 1444. Like many other religious buildings, the convent was suppressed by Napoleon in 1810 and, within five years, most of the monastery complex and church were demolished. Part of today's railway station occupies the site.

Just opposite is the façade and side of the church of Santa Croce, one of Venice's oldest foundations, possibly dating from 568. Santa Croce was rebuilt in 1111 and reconsecrated in 1342. The church and monastery were also

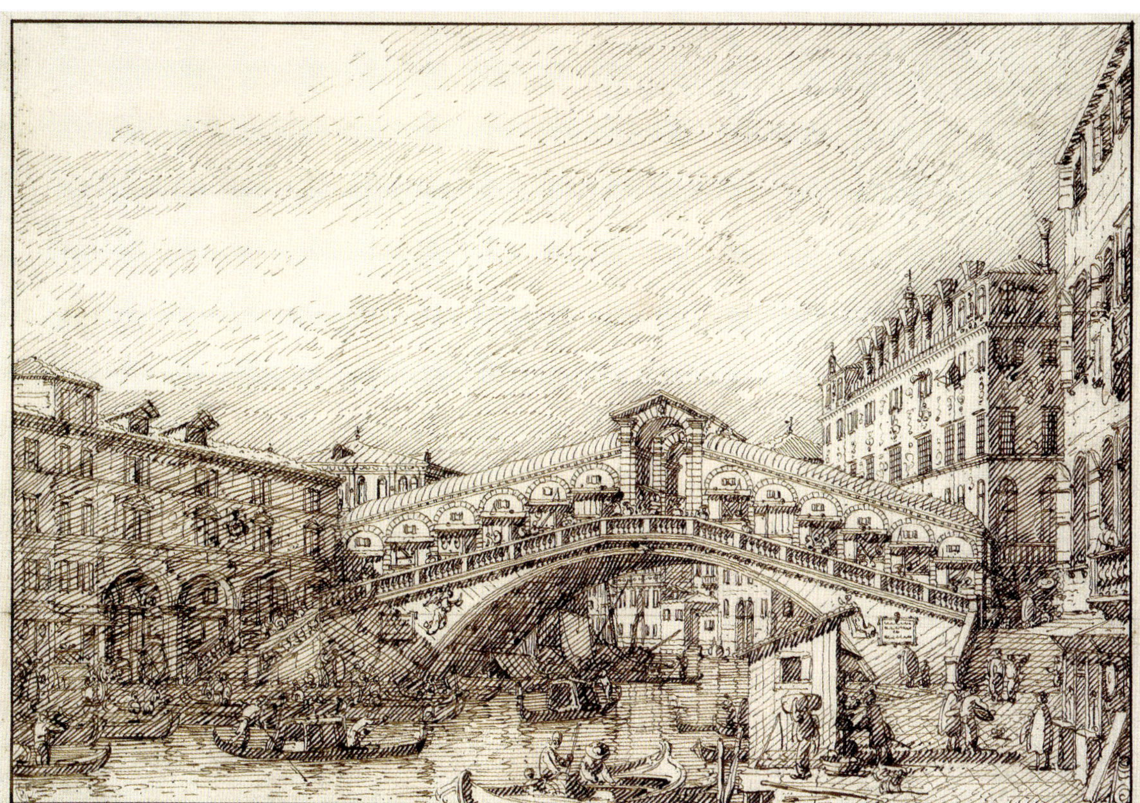

Fig. 86. Canaletto (1697–1768), *Venice: The Rialto Bridge from the South-West*, c.1740–45, pen and ink on paper, 26.6 × 36.7 cm, Royal Collection (RCIN 907466)

suppressed by Napoleon and subsequently demolished. In Canaletto's painting the façade opens onto a small square with a fountain in the middle. Today, the site is occupied by the Giardini Papadopoli, or public gardens. Left of the church of Santa Croce is its *campanile*.[6] To the right of the church is the *campanile* of the Frari, the largest church in Venice, located in the heart of the city in the Frari district. Further right are the *campanile* and cupola of the church of San Niccolò da Tolentino, which was designed by Vincenzo Scamozzi and built between 1590 and 1671. The cupola was taken down in the later eighteenth century.

The Fondamenta di Santa Chiara is lined with well-to-do residences, a few with shops and stalls on the ground floor. Among them, near the right foreground, is the house of the British Secretary-Resident, which still stands today. The house is identifiable by its large first-floor balcony, the armorial cartouche between the top-floor windows and the two women standing in front of the doorway. At the time, the post of Secretary-Resident, which

was superior to that of Consul, was held by Colonel Elizeus Burges, who was described by one contemporary as 'the most immoral man in the world'.[7] Burges served in the role between 1719 and 1722 and from December 1728 until his death in November 1736.[8] He was fond of the theatre and music and is believed to have entertained George Frideric Handel on at least one occasion, probably at this house. Burges may have been a patron of Canaletto and is probably the figure gesturing in the left foreground of the artist's early view of this area looking northward, in the opposite direction to cat. 6.[9]

The populated, bustling area around the Rialto Bridge complements the calmer northern reaches along the Fondamenta di Santa Chiara. Both paintings are lit from the left, with the left banks cast in shadow, more dramatically so in cat. 5. Cat. 6 is more evenly lit, with the muted terracotta shades of the buildings subtly reflected in the water. As was customary for Canaletto, several boats occupy both works with, understandably, a greater

concentration near the Rialto Bridge. Two *burchielli*, or large boats with decorated cabins that transported people between Venice and Padua, are moored in the left foreground of cat. 5, the terminus for this passenger service. A *burchiello* towed by a *barca* on its way out of Venice is also prominently positioned in the middle distance of cat. 6.

Canaletto studied both areas first-hand. In an *in situ* drawing from the late 1720s Canaletto sketched the bridge close up from the Fondamenta del Ferro (fig. 85).[10] His open, free penwork suggests that he produced the drawing on-site after first-hand observation of the bridge and of the buildings in its immediate vicinity. He would have probably referred to such a drawing in the planning stages of cat. 5. By contrast, a later, finished drawing, also taken from the Fondamenta del Ferro and complete with boats, people and a drawn decorative border, would have served as a stock composition in the studio (fig. 86).[11]

Canaletto also investigated the buildings to the right of Santa Croce in a series of

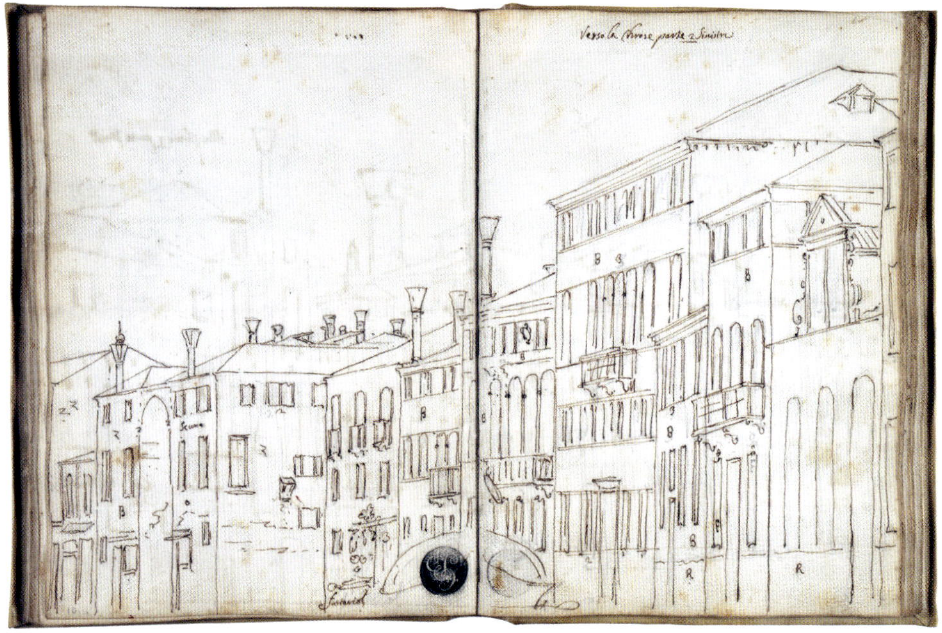

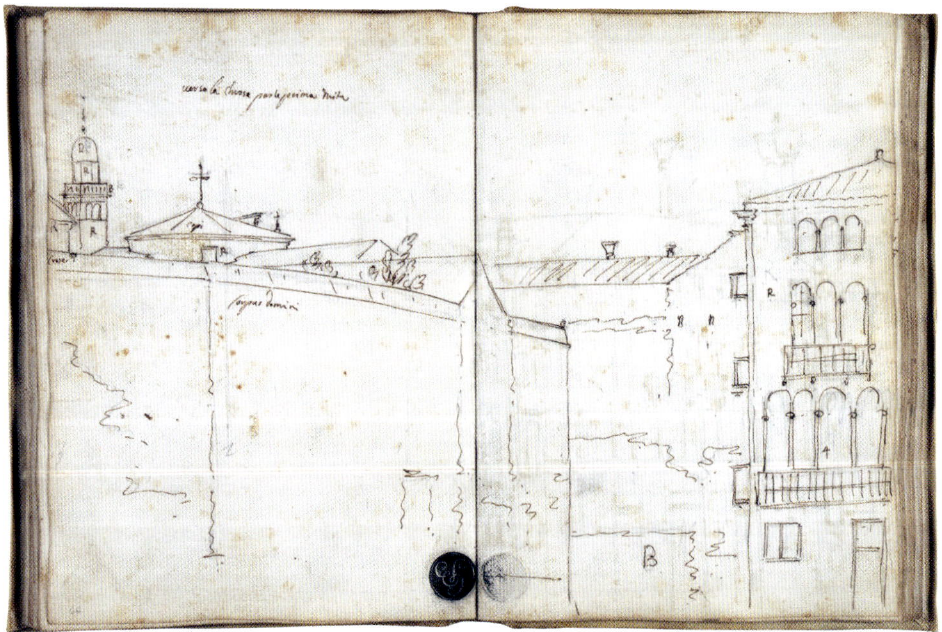

Fig. 87. Canaletto (1697–1768), *The Fondamenta di Santa Lucia* from the *Cagnola Sketchbook*, 1730s, pen and ink over black chalk, 23 × 17 cm (each folio), folios 30v–31r, Gallerie dell'Accademia, Venice

Fig. 88. Canaletto (1697–1768), *The Walls of the Convento del Corpus Domini and of the Convento della Croce and of a House on the Fondamenta di Santa Chiara* from the *Cagnola Sketchbook*, 1730s, pen and ink over black chalk, 23 × 17 cm (each folio), folios 32v–33r, Gallerie dell'Accademia, Venice

in situ sketches in the *Cagnola Sketchbook*.[12] In the centre of a spread is the residence of the British Secretary-Resident, which Canaletto annotated with a 'B' for *bianco* (white) in order to remember the colour of the building (fig. 87). He also added similar, single-letter colour annotations to buildings nearby. Canaletto wrote 'frutorial' (fruit seller) below a building two doors to the left of the Secretary-Resident's house. This was to remind him to include a projecting wooden fruit and vegetable stand in that spot in his painting.[13] Two further spreads of sketches depict the buildings that follow, culminating in the long wall of the convent of Corpus Domini, which Canaletto marked by name for his reference (fig. 88). Above he wrote the word 'copi', or roof tiles, on the cupola of San Niccolò da Tolentino as a reminder to include these later. He annotated the *campanile* of San Niccolò with the letters 'P' (for *pietra*: stone), 'R' (for *rosso*: red), 'B' (for *bianco*: white) and 'R' again on the lowest visible part of the tower. Canaletto left the tower's lantern white in cat. 6 rather than paint it as stone at the top and red lower down as he had indicated in his sketch.[14]

A pen-and-ink sketch dated on the verso 16 July 1734 further reveals Canaletto's close study of this area (fig. 89).[15] In this drawing, there is a plain wall on the right bank between Santa Croce and the nearby residence, which is replaced in cat. 6 with the side walls of two buildings flanking a smaller building seen from the front. The latter view appears in another, more finished drawing where a cartouche hangs over the British Secretary's door (fig. 90), a detail that is omitted from cat. 6 and from the dated sketch.[16]

Recent infrared reflectography and X-rays of both paintings did not detect any preparatory underdrawings. Incisions were employed for compositional planning in both works, albeit those in cat. 6 do not seem to have penetrated as deeply as those in cat. 5, or those in other *vedute* at the Wallace Collection for that matter. This might be explained by the fact that the buildings were executed wet-in-wet in cat. 6. By contrast, incised lines were used to mark the position of the buildings and the bridge and its archways in cat. 5 (fig. 91).

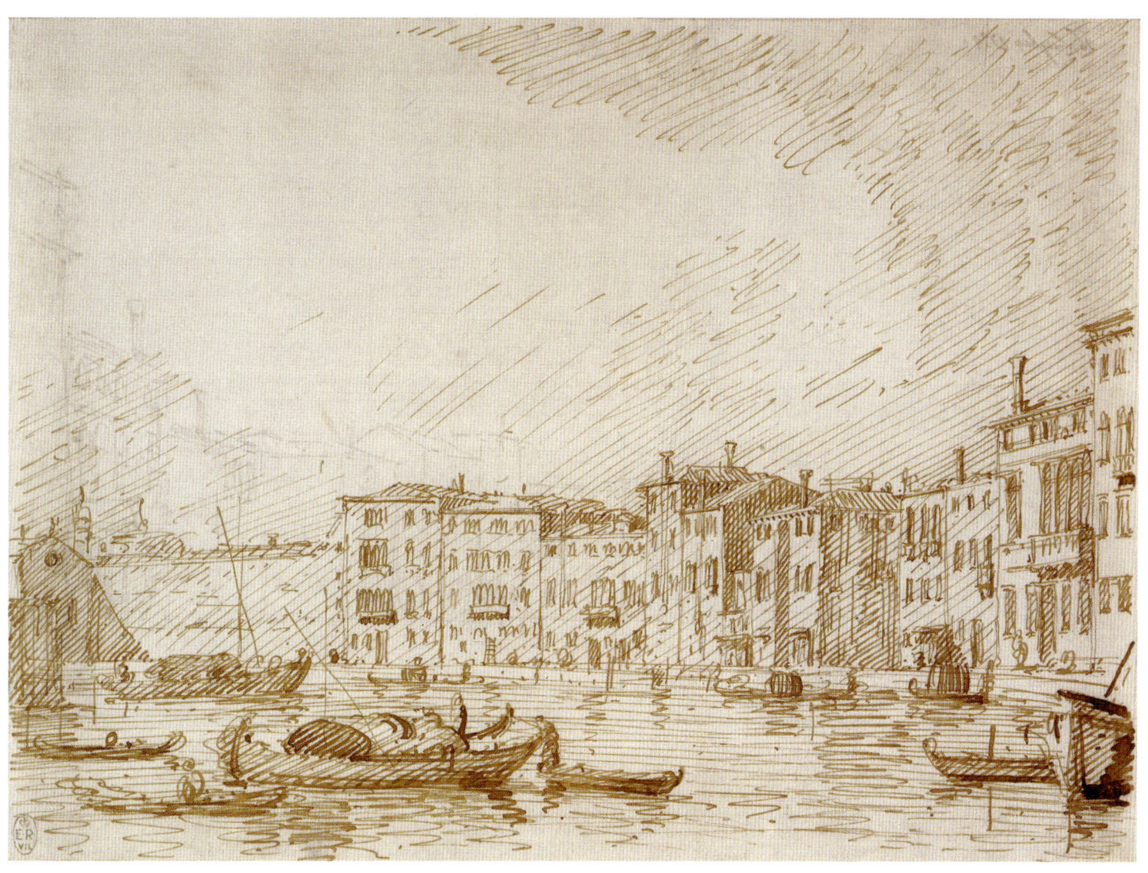

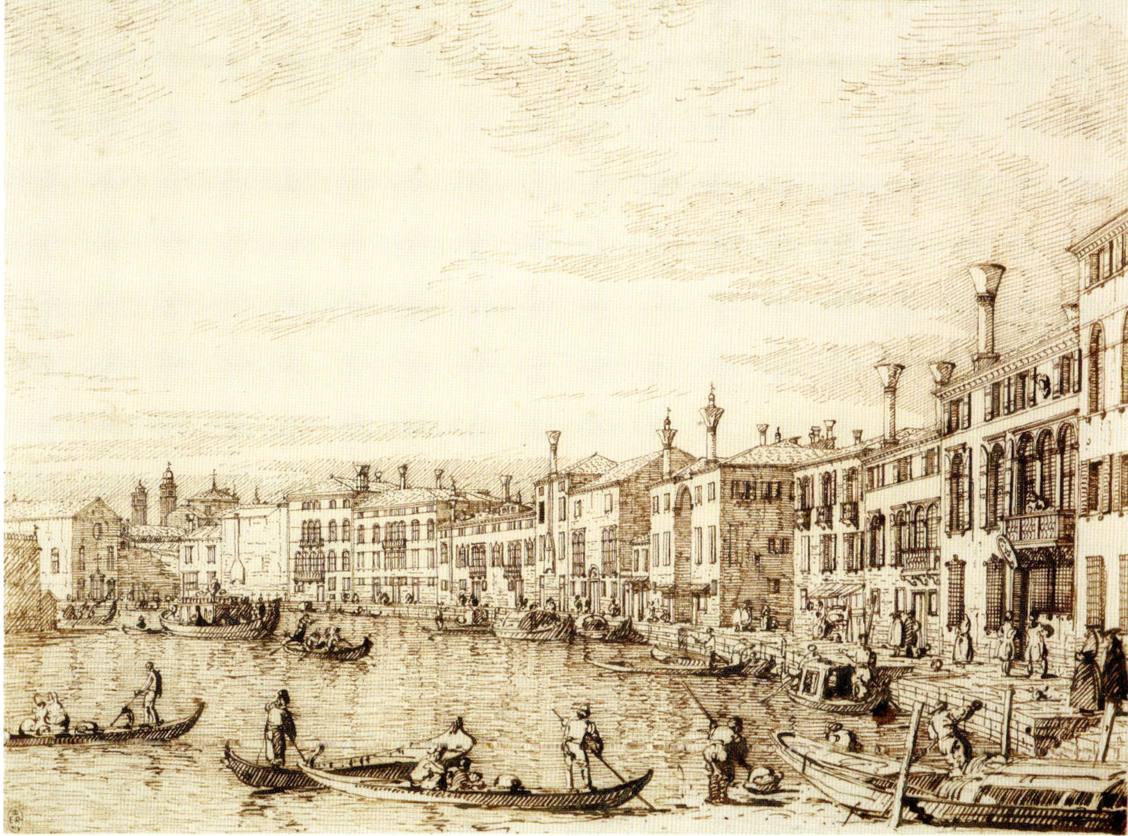

Fig. 89. Canaletto (1697–1768), *Venice: Upper Reaches of the Grand Canal, Looking South* (recto), 1734, pen and ink on paper, 17.5 × 24.2 cm, Royal Collection (RCIN 907489)

Fig. 90. Canaletto (1697–1768), *The Upper Reach of the Grand Canal Looking South*, c.1734, pen and ink on paper, 27 × 37.8 cm, Royal Collection (RCIN 907473)

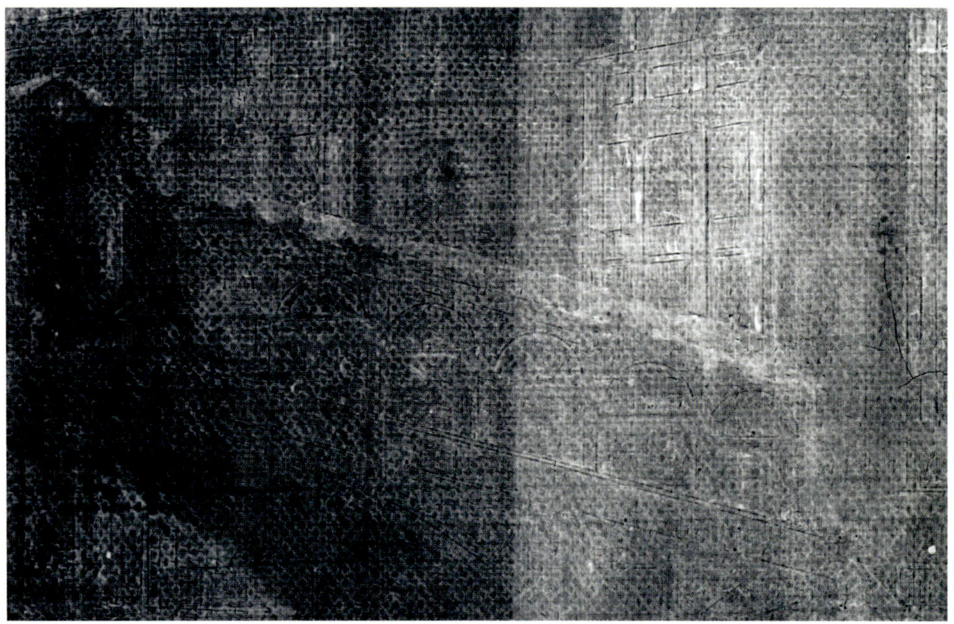

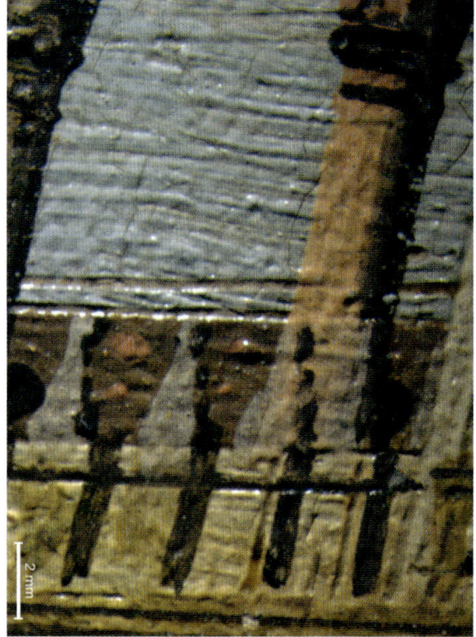

As with other works by Canaletto, the sky was painted first in cat. 5, followed by the buildings, while the figures, boats and rigging were painted last. Canaletto's careful planning and execution mean that *pentimenti* are relatively rare in his work, although they do occur occasionally. Notably, the position of the roof of the Fondaco dei Tedeschi in cat. 5 was slightly lowered so that the final painted line does not meet the incised planning line (fig. 92).

Both views were popular and exist in multiple versions, although the Rialto was, arguably, the more iconic of the two. Visentini included engravings of the two compositions in his 1742 second edition of the *Prospectus Magni Canalis Venetiarum*, for which they constituted novel views (figs 93, 94).[17] Comparable paintings to cat. 5 are in Rome and Paris (figs 95, 96). These are taken from a similar angle, but Canaletto altered the boats and figures in order to distinguish each picture. In the Rome and Paris versions as well as in Visentini's print, the second building on the left bank has a protruding bell hanging from the upper storey, which is omitted from cat. 5. Perhaps the bell was added after cat. 5 was painted. In his version, Bellotto also included the bell and further animated the

scene by adding more boats and figures (fig. 97). Other views of the Rialto position the viewer closer to the bridge on the Fondamenta de Ferro, as in a painting at Woburn Abbey that corresponds to Canaletto's study of the bridge cited above (fig. 85).[18] The subject's popularity continued later in the century with Francesco Guardi, who shifted the perspective slightly to the right (cat. 21).

Canaletto originally painted the Fondamenta di Santa Chiara in the early 1720s from the opposite direction, the first in his series of Grand Canal views for Joseph Smith.[19] A comparable version to cat. 6 is at the Musée Cognacq-Jay in Paris where the view is zoomed in and shifted slightly to the right (fig. 98).[20] In this work more people gather before the Secretary-Resident's house and the *campanili* of Santa Croce and of the Frari have been omitted. Visentini based his 1742 print on this painting apart from the featureless high wall to the right of Santa Croce, which corresponds to the buildings in fig. 93. Visentini included the plain wall in his preparatory drawing for the print.[21] Ultimately, however, he departed from his painted model and from his own design for the print, preferring instead the area as it appeared around 1738 when Canaletto painted cat. 6.

ABOVE LEFT:
Fig. 91. Detail of X-ray of cat. 5 showing incisions

ABOVE RIGHT:
Fig. 92. Micrograph of cat. 5 showing incised lines above roofs in raking light

OPPOSITE, ABOVE:
Fig. 93. Antonio Visentini (1688–1782) after Canaletto (1697–1768), *Prospectus in Magnum Canalem e Regione S. Clarae ad Aedem S. Crucis*, 1742, etching, 26.9 × 42.6 cm, from *Urbis Venetiarum prospectus celebriores ex Antonii Canal tabulis XL aere expressi ab Antonio Visentini*, II

OPPOSITE, BELOW:
Fig. 94. Antonio Visentini (1688–1782) after Canaletto (1697–1768), *Pons Rivoalti ad Orientem*, 1742, etching, 27.5 × 43.2 cm, plate 8 from *Prospectus Magni Canalis Venetiarum*, II

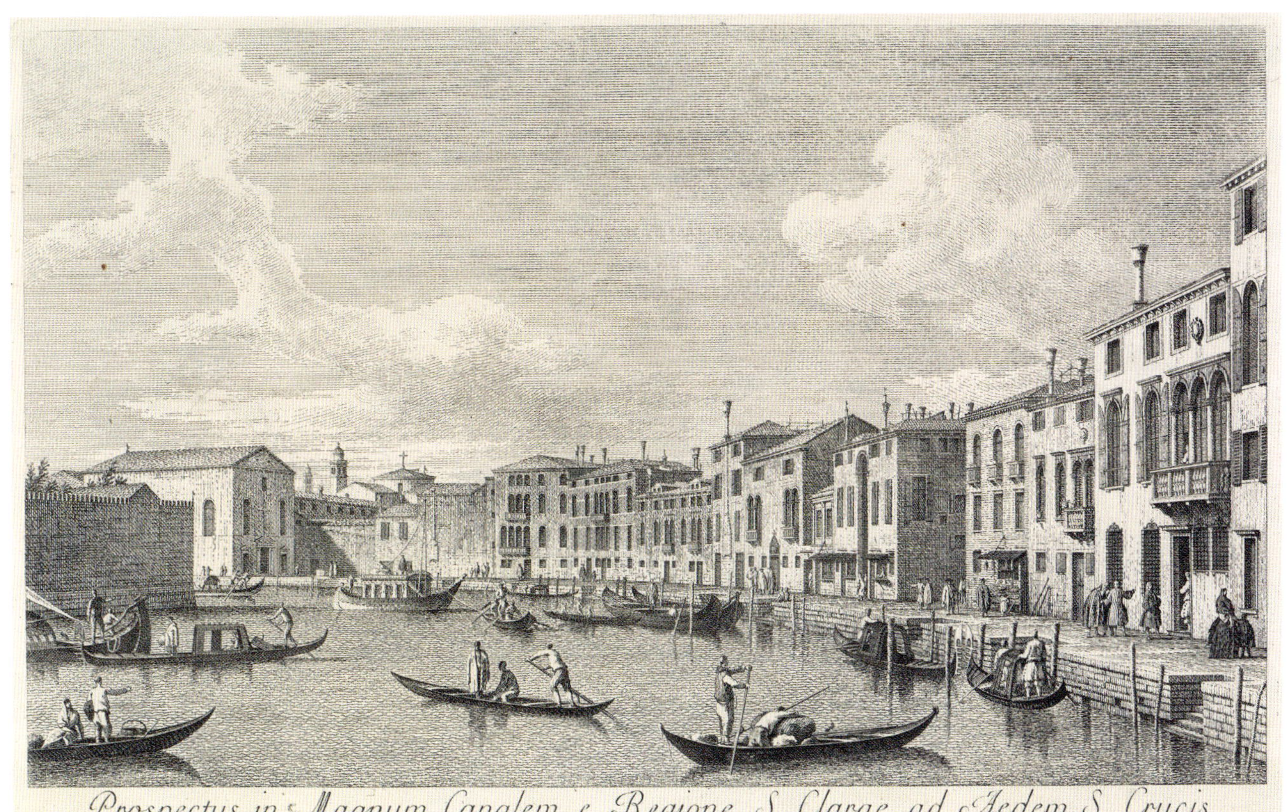
Prospectus in Magnum Canalem e Regione S. Clarae ad Aedem S. Crucis

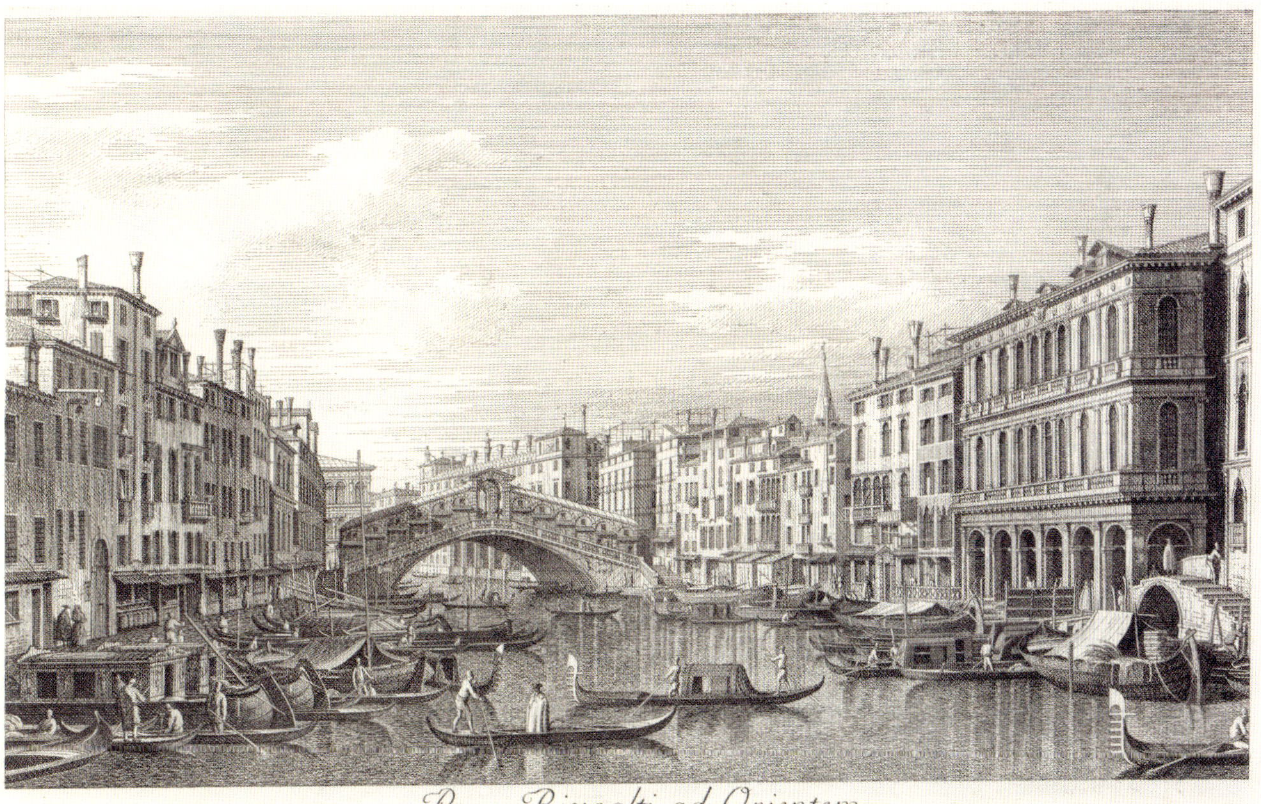
Pons Rivoalti ad Orientem.

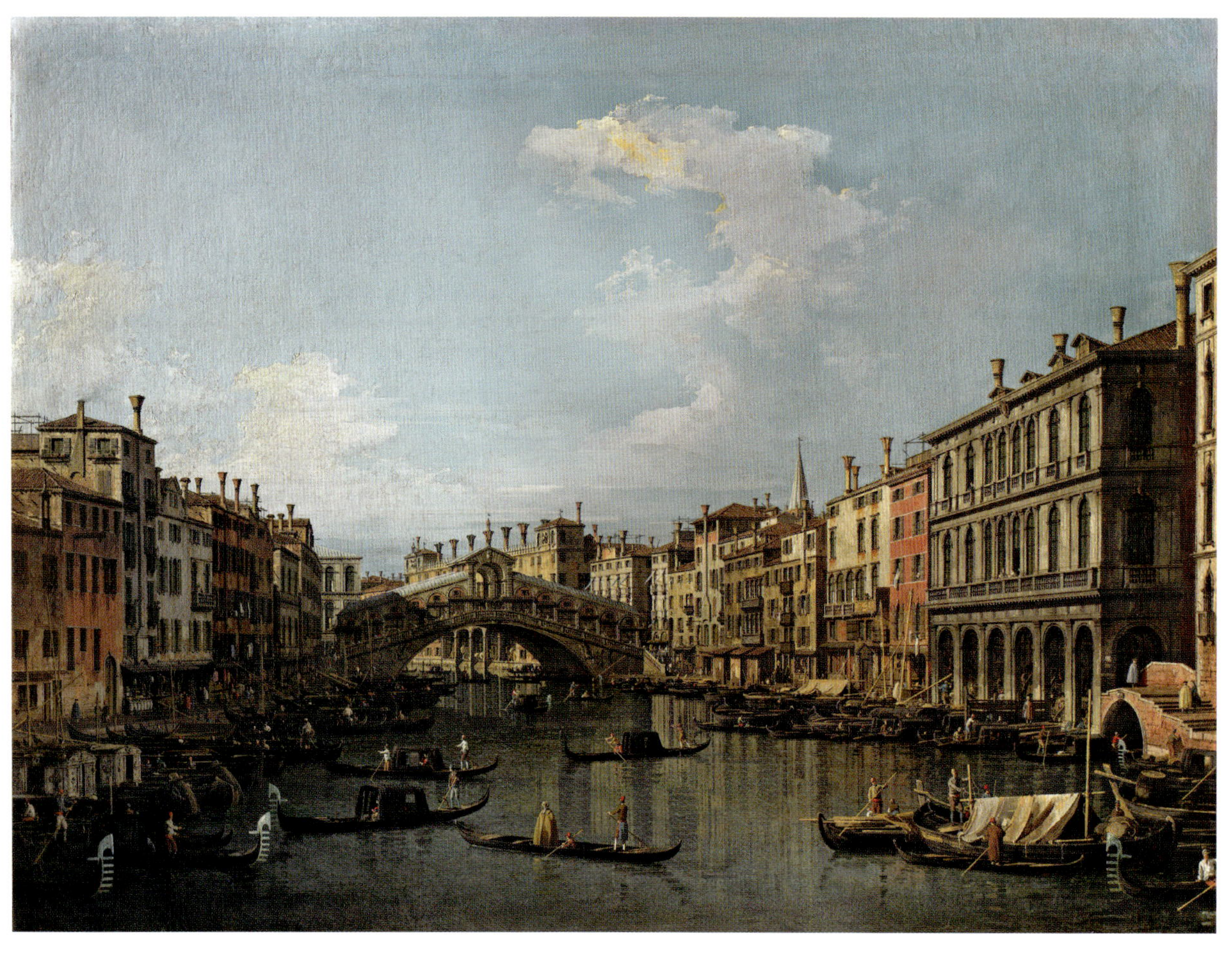

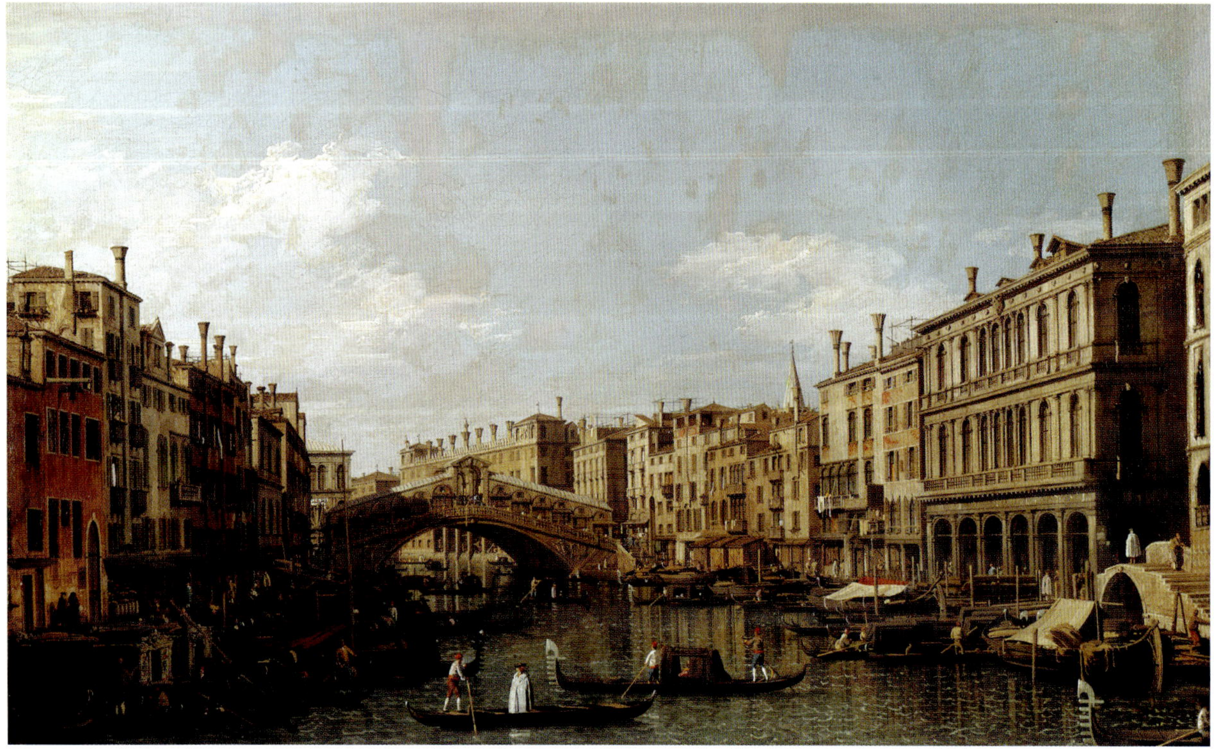

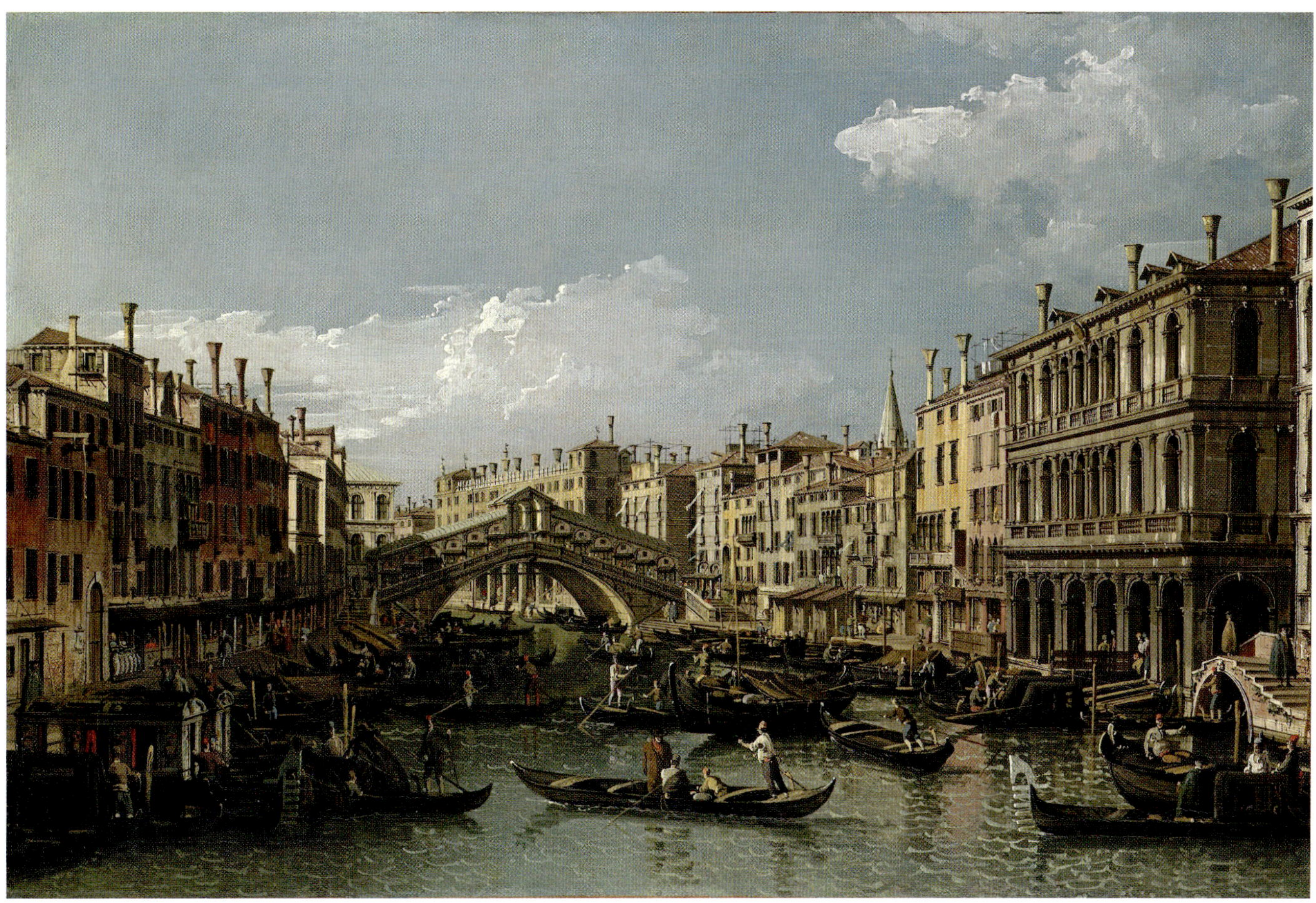

Perhaps a plain wall was erected after this point or maybe Canaletto preferred a plain wall for the painting in Paris.[22] In an earlier depiction of this area at Woburn Abbey painted sometime between 1732 and early 1736 the view is taken from further away, enabling a partial view of the Convent of Santa Chiara and of the entrance to the Santa Chiara Canal on the extreme right (fig. 99).[23] Unfortunately, the area to the right of Santa Croce is difficult to make out. In this version the viewpoint is lowered to the level of the water.

The Wallace Collection pair probably dates to the late 1730s, perhaps c.1738. The 1st Marquess is likely to have commissioned the paintings while on his Grand Tour.

There is no cartouche over Burges's door in cat. 6, which may mean that the picture was painted after Burges's death in November 1736. Although not always topographically accurate, Canaletto seems to have paid attention to this particular detail, which he included in the picture at Woburn Abbey that was painted during Burges's tenure. The earliest confirmed mention of the pictures is in the 1834 inventory of Manchester House where 'A View of the Rialto ditto ditto' is listed under paintings by Canaletto.[24] Cat. 6 follows as 'Another View of the Grand Canal ditto'. They were both valued at £60 at the time, which equates to £5,566 today.

OPPOSITE, ABOVE:

Fig. 95. Canaletto (1697–1768), *The Rialto Bridge from the South*, c.1738, oil on canvas, 68.5 × 92 cm, Galleria Nazionale d'Arte Antica, Palazzo Corsini, Rome

OPPOSITE, BELOW:

Fig. 96. Canaletto (1697–1768), *The Rialto Bridge*, c.1738, oil on canvas, 45 × 76 cm, Musée Jacquemart-André, Paris

ABOVE:

Fig. 97. Bernardo Bellotto (1722–1780), *Grand Canal Looking North-East to the Rialto Bridge*, c.1738, oil on canvas, 61 × 92.2 cm, National Gallery of Victoria, Melbourne. Felton Bequest, 1919 (inv. 965-3)

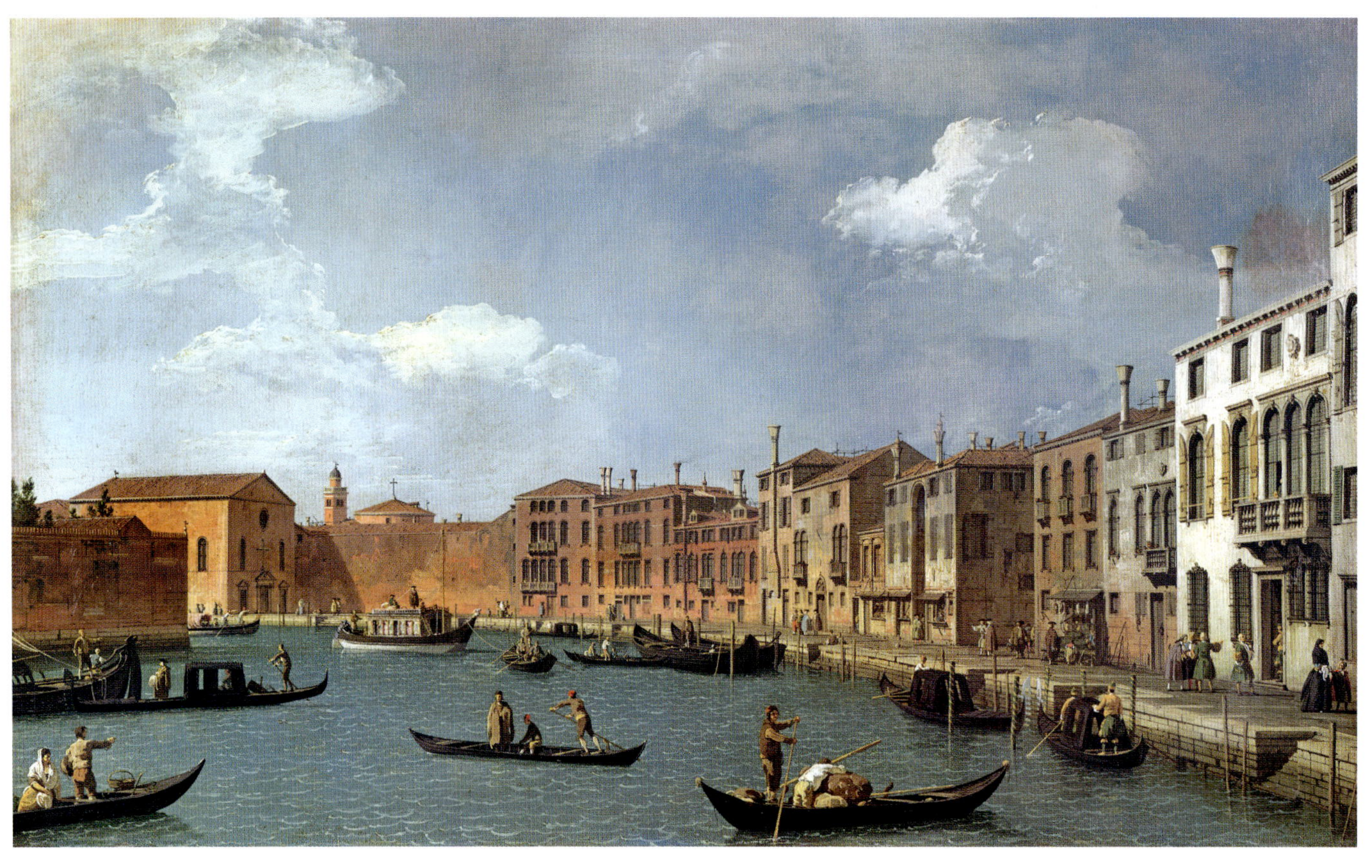

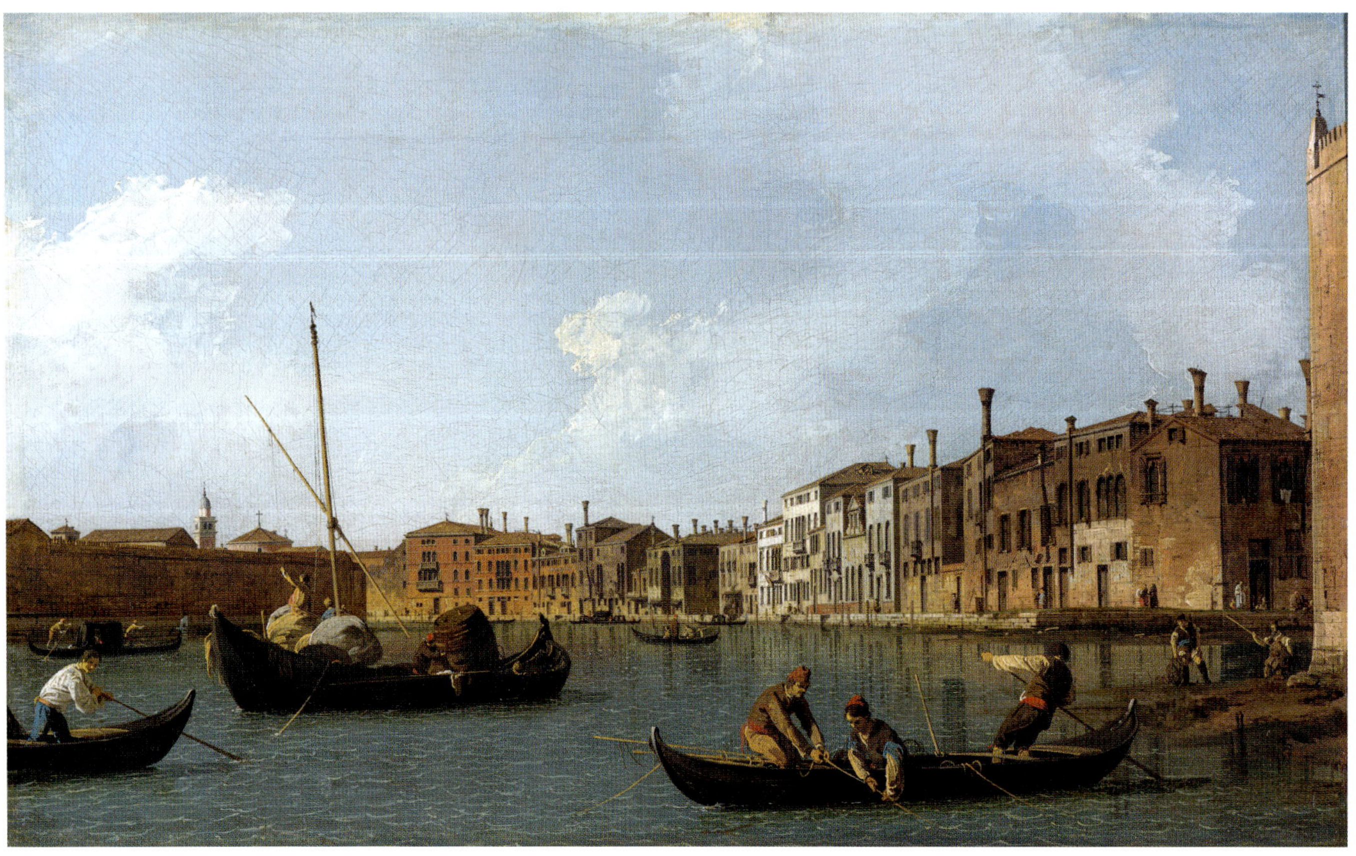

Presumably commissioned by Francis Seymour-Conway, 1st Marquess of Hertford (1719–1794) on his Grand Tour between 1737 and 1740; by descent to Francis Ingram Seymour-Conway, 2nd Marquess of Hertford (1743–1822); by descent to Francis Charles Seymour-Conway, 3rd Marquess of Hertford (1777–1842); by descent to Richard Seymour-Conway, 4th Marquess of Hertford (1800–1870); by descent to Sir Richard Wallace, 1st Baronet (1818–1890); by descent to his wife, Lady Wallace (Julie Amélie Charlotte Castelnau, 1819–1897); by whom bequeathed with the rest of the Wallace Collection to the British nation, 1897.

EXHIBITION
1872–75: 'Paintings, Porcelain, Bronzes, Decorative Furniture and other Works of Art lent by Sir Richard Wallace to the Bethnal Green Branch of the South Kensington Museum'.[25]

RELATED WORKS
To cat. 5:

Canaletto, *The Rialto Bridge from the South*, c.1735, oil on canvas, 68.5 × 92 cm, Galleria Nazionale d'Arte Antica, Palazzo Corsini, Rome (inv. 1033) (C228[a]4)

Canaletto, *The Rialto Bridge*, 45 × 76 cm, oil on canvas, Musée Jacquemart-André, Paris (C228[a]1)

Canaletto, *Grand Canal: The Rialto Bridge from the South*, oil on canvas, 47.5 × 77.5 cm, Périgord Museum, Périgueux (C228)

Canaletto, *Grand Canal: The Rialto Bridge from the South*, oil on canvas, 46 × 76 cm, Private Collection (C228[a]3)

Bernardo Bellotto, *Grand Canal Looking North-East to the Rialto Bridge*, c.1738, oil on canvas, 61 × 92.2 cm, National Gallery of Victoria, Melbourne (inv. 965-3)

Bernardo Bellotto, *The Grand Canal: The Rialto Bridge from the South*, c.1740–45, oil on canvas, 85.7 × 134.5 cm, Private Collection

To cat. 6:

Canaletto, *The Grand Canal, Looking South-East along the Fondamenta di Santa Chiara, at the Entrance to the Canale di Santa Chiara*, oil on canvas, 47 × 80 cm, Duke of Bedford, Woburn Abbey (C266)

Canaletto, *View of the Santa Chiara Canal, Venice*, c.1730–35, oil on canvas, 48.5 × 79 cm, Musée Cognacq-Jay, Paris (under C268)

Canaletto, *The Grand Canal, Looking South-East along the Fondamenta di Santa Chiara*, c.1736, oil on canvas, 47 × 77.7 cm, Private Collection, London (C267)

TECHNICAL NOTES
Both works are painted on a plain-weave canvas that is glue-paste lined onto another plain-weave canvas. Cusping visible along the edges in the X-rays of both works confirms that the compositions are intact, although the tacking margins were removed during lining. Both paintings have a double ground consisting of a red-brown first layer that is likely to have been commercially prepared, followed by a pale, warm pinkish-grey upper layer, probably applied in the studio as an *imprimatura* layer. This corresponds with grounds found in cat. 3 and cat. 15. 'I-PEEL / LINER' is stamped on the stretcher of cat. 6, one of several paintings at the Wallace Collection with this stamp.[26] This is the stamp of John Peel (c.1785–1858), who was lining pictures in London from 1820.[27] The painting's stretcher may date to Peel's relining. There is also a bill for framing cat. 6 dated 15 February 1859.[28] Both paintings were cleaned and analysed at the Hamilton Kerr Institute in 2021. Technical investigation comprising X-radiography, infrared reflectography, ultraviolet light photography, surface micrography and SEM-EDX paint sample analysis was undertaken at this point.

LITERATURE
Constable 1962, C228(a)2 (cat. 5), C268 (cat. 6)
Watson 1968, p. 55 (cat. 6); p. 56 (cat. 5)
Puppi 1970, p. 99, nos 99B (cat. 6), 94B (cat. 5)
Links 1981, p. 36, no. 103 (cat. 6); p. 22, no. 43 (cat. 5)
Ingamells 1985, pp. 232–33 (cat. 6); pp. 238–39 (cat. 5)
Duffy and Hedley 2004, pp. 66–67

LP

OPPOSITE, ABOVE:
Fig. 98. Canaletto (1697–1768), *View of the Santa Chiara Canal*, Venice, c.1730–35, oil on canvas, 48.5 × 79 cm, Musée Cognacq-Jay, Paris

OPPOSITE, BELOW:
Fig. 99. Canaletto (1697–1768), *The Grand Canal, Looking South-East along the Fondamenta di Santa Chiara, at the Entrance to the Canale di Santa Chiara*, 1732–36, oil on canvas, 47 × 80 cm, Collection of the Duke of Bedford, Woburn Abbey

7. **GIOVANNI ANTONIO CANAL, IL CANALETTO** (Venice 1697–1768)

The Molo and the Riva degli Schiavoni, Looking East

c.1739
oil on canvas
58.2 × 93.5 cm
P509

8. **GIOVANNI ANTONIO CANAL, IL CANALETTO** (Venice 1697–1768)

The Molo with Santa Maria della Salute

c.1739
oil on canvas
57.7 × 93.5 cm
P516

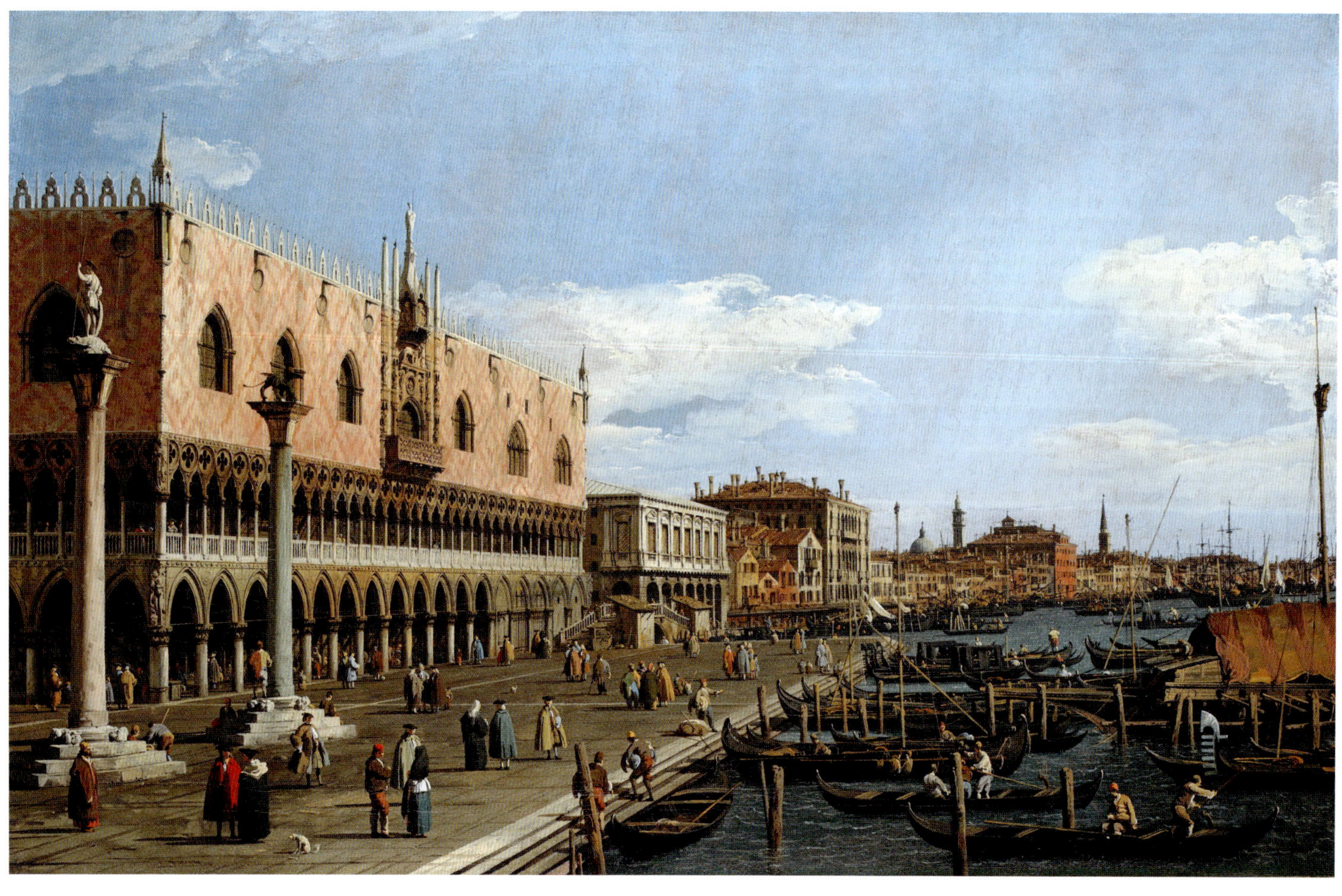

This superb pendant pair depicts the Molo, the broad stone quay along the waterfront of the Piazzetta, from opposite directions. Cat. 7 looks east to the Riva degli Schiavoni, the quayside abutting the Molo that stretches about half a kilometre along the northern rim of the Bacino. Cat. 8 faces west towards the Piazzetta and the mouth of the Grand Canal. In the eighteenth century the Molo was of high touristic interest as it served as the gateway into Venice, with most visitors arriving by boat. The public buildings around the Molo held huge symbolic and architectural significance, and constituted the archetypal image of Venice. As such, these are among Canaletto's most iconic views that were in great demand with Grand Tourists.

The left half of cat. 7 is dominated by the imposing Palazzo Ducale, or Doge's Palace.

A perfect blend of Roman, Lombard and Arab styles, it was described by John Ruskin as 'the central building of the world'.[1] This supreme Gothic edifice is the most significant piece of secular architecture in Venice. The site was probably established early in the ninth century by Doge Agnello Partecipazio (r. 811–27), who transferred the ducal seat from Malamocco on the Lido to its present location.[2] The edifice was begun in the 1340s and completed in 1484. Unfortified, it served as the Doge's residence, the Palace of Justice and the Town Hall. The arcades and courtyard were open to the public, a symbolic gesture that reflected the moral rectitude of the oligarchic Venetian state. The building's unique character, with arcades at street level, balconies fronted by delicate filigree tracery on the *piano nobile* and flat walls articulated by lozenge patterns

in pink Verona marble above, makes it stand out, even in Venice. Tourists appreciated the distinct quality of the rose-coloured marble, the impressive dimensions and the fact that the palace housed the Venetian Senate.[3] Conversely, they also remarked on the stench and waste surrounding the premises, an inevitable consequence of its location in a highly populated area. Canaletto included the entire southern side of the building, carefully rendering details such as the quatrefoils and relief sculptures. The furthest five bays of the arcade were boarded up following a fire in 1574.[4]

The Molo in front of the palace was used as a landing stage for ceremonies and visitors. In the foreground, two men carrying a load have just arrived and climb the steps of the Molo (fig. 100). Another man standing with

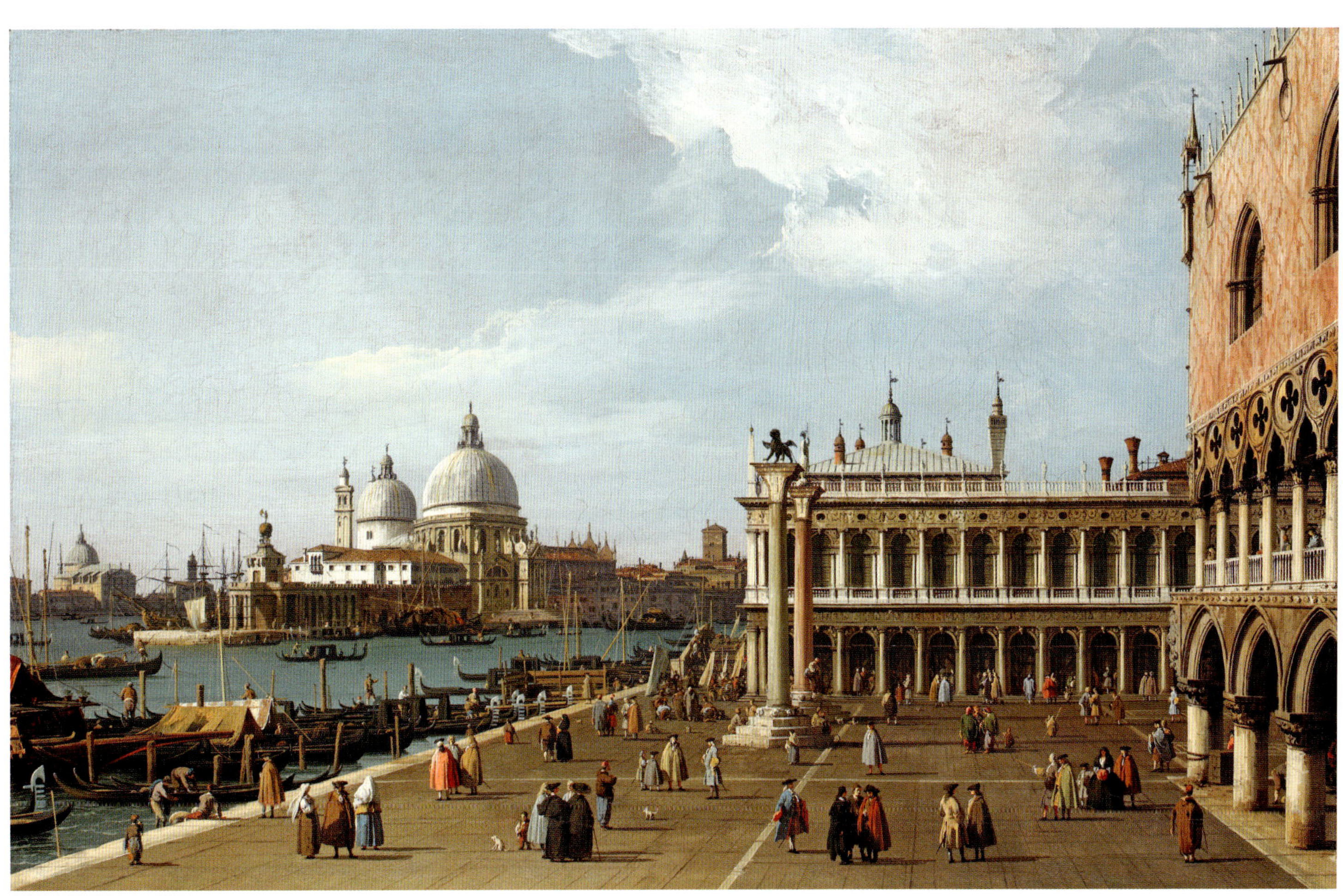

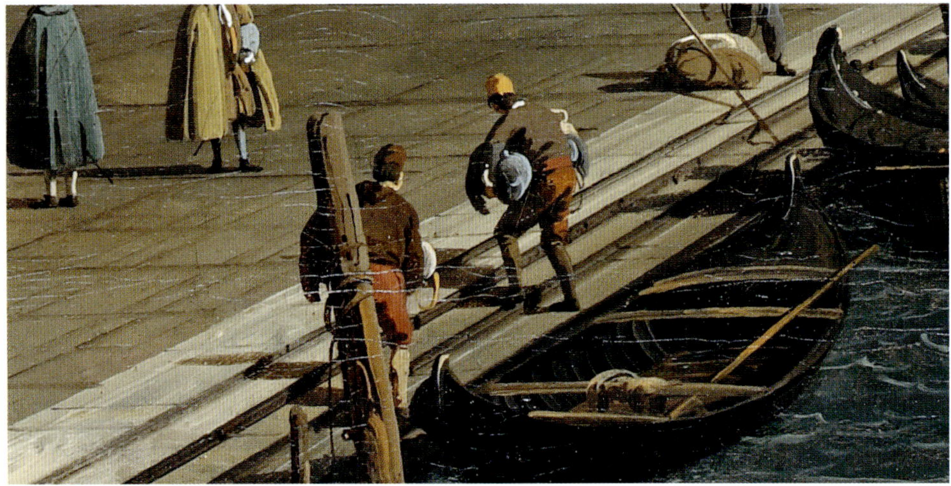

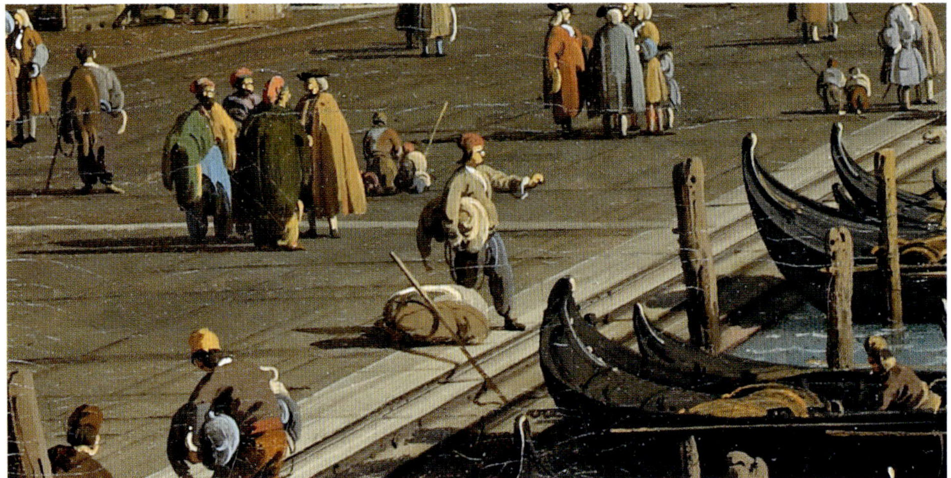

baggage at the top of the steps has his arm
outstretched as if hailing a ride out of town
(fig. 101). For Canaletto, the Molo provided
plenty of opportunity to showcase Venice's
diverse population of merchants, foreign
visitors, government officials in black robes,
locals, women, children and, of course,
charming dogs.

Flanking the south-western corner of
the palace are the celebrated twin columns
surmounted by statues of Venice's patron
saints, Theodore and Mark. Erected in 1172,
these major landmarks frame the city's gateway.
Saint Mark the Evangelist, traditionally
represented by the characteristic winged lion,
here takes the form of a bronze chimera, or
fire-breathing female monster with a lion's
head, goat's body and serpent's tail. The
sculpture might derive from the Sassanid

kingdom in Persia; it made its way to Venice
at an undetermined point, when wings were
added to it. San Tòdaro, the Byzantine Saint
Theodore of Amasea, became a martyr after
being killed for burning down a pagan temple.
He was Mark's predecessor as tutelary saint of
Venice. Theodore's statue was amassed from
pieces of fourth-century classical sculpture.
He stands on a crocodile, symbolising his
conquest over evil. The marble and granite
columns (originally three, but one was lost at
sea) were spoils from an eastern outpost in
Greece or Egypt. Public executions took place
between the columns for several hundred
years, with the condemned facing the city with
their backs to the lagoon.[5] As a result, even to
this day, superstitious Venetians will not pass
between what became known as the 'Columns
of Justice'.

In the right foreground, *sandolos* and
gondolas bob on the water. The *fusta*, the Doge's
galleon with a striped red and orange awning
partially visible on the right, was permanently
moored at the Molo and used for the temporary
confinement of prisoners after trial. The Ponte
della Paglia, so named for the boats mooring
nearby to offload straw (*paglia*), connects the
Molo to the Riva degli Schiavoni and the
Doge's Palace to the Prison. Today, this is one
of Venice's most popular bridges, in large part
because it provides a perfect view over the Rio
del Palazzo of the more famous Bridge of Sighs
nearby. Two wooden huts flank either side of the
bridge. Just beyond, the Prison, recognisable by
the gratings on the windows, was built around
1600. Originally located inside the Doge's Palace,
the Prison was moved because of poor hygiene
and insufficient space into a separate building

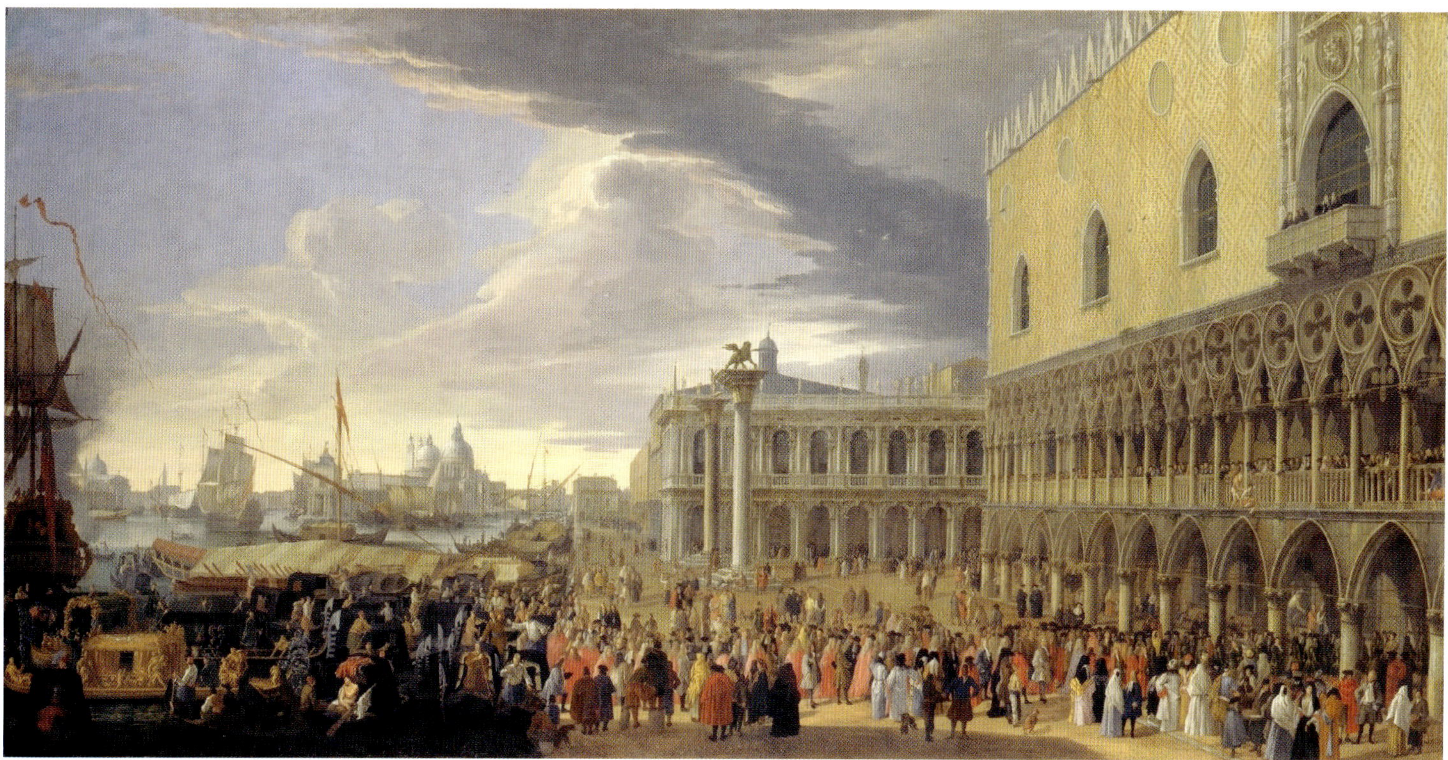

in order to improve the conditions. The new building accommodated up to 400 prisoners. Canaletto mixed up the architectural detailing above the Prison windows.[6]

The Riva degli Schiavoni begins at the Prison and can be seen almost in its entirety.[7] Its name derives from the Dalmatian (present-day Croatia) sailors who anchored there, known in the West as Schiavoni. What originally began as a narrow quay was gradually widened beginning in the 1780s into today's promenade. Large sailing boats with their masts lowered are moored along the Riva. Between the Prison and the Palazzo Dandolo (today the renowned Hotel Danieli), with its numerous chimney pots, are four unassuming buildings of various heights with triangular roofs. No permanent stone structures could be built on this site between 1172, when Doge Vitale Michiel II was murdered, and 1948.[8]

Beyond is the dome of San Zaccaria and the *campanili* of San Giorgio dei Greci and San Francesco della Vigna.[9] Between these *campanili* is the red-brick Ospedale della Pietà (Hospital of Mercy), a charitable institution established in the fourteenth century by the Franciscan friar Petruccio d'Assisi to care for orphans. In time, music became an integral part of the Ospedale, with the famous composer Antonio Vivaldi serving as its master violinist between 1703 and 1740. Under Vivaldi's direction, the Figlie di Choro (Daughters of the Choir) orchestra of the Ospedale became famous. Their concerts were a major tourist attraction in Venice, as well as an important source of income for the institution.

Canaletto often paired a view of the Riva degli Schiavoni looking east with a view in the opposite direction. In cat. 8 he framed the composition on the right with the highly foreshortened south-west corner of the Doge's Palace. Canaletto characteristically included a variety of figures (and dogs) arranged in pairs or small groups along the Molo. To the left of the palace arcade are two well-dressed gentlemen, probably Grand Tourists, one of whom is looking at, and pointing to, the iconic twin columns with Venice's patron saints. To the left of the columns in the middle ground are several market traders.

The Piazzetta is flanked to the east by the Doge's Palace and to the west by Jacopo Sansovino's Library. Like its larger neighbour, the Piazza San Marco, the Piazzetta is trapezoid in shape, the narrower, southern end of which is visible in cat. 8. At the opposite, northern end, the Piazzetta opens to the south flank of the Basilica di San Marco. Although the Piazzetta was used for processional purposes and celebrations on occasion, such as the Giovedì Grasso festival (cat. 10), it was generally a gathering place to socialise and gossip as is apparent in cat. 8.

Canaletto gave prominence to the Library, the Biblioteca Nazionale Marciana, by including half of its eastern façade in the painting. Designed by the state architect Sansovino and originally named after him (the Libreria Sansoviniana), it was begun in 1537 to accommodate a large bequest of manuscripts from the Greek Cardinal Bessarion of Trebizond in 1468. The building is made of Istrian stone and boasts Doric columns on the ground level and Ionic ones on the *piano nobile*. The ground-floor arcade opened onto a row of shops. Even prior to Canaletto's day, the Library was famous for the quality and quantity of its books.[10] Together

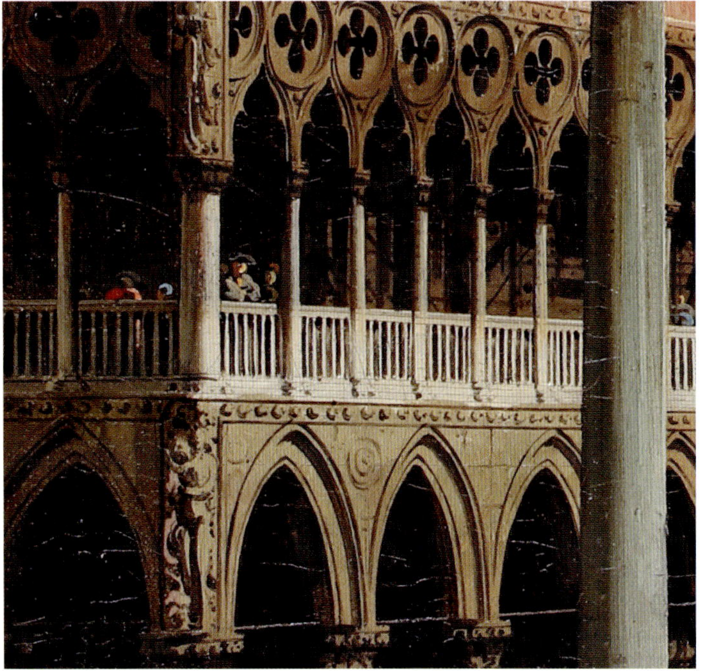

Fig. 103. Detail of cat. 7

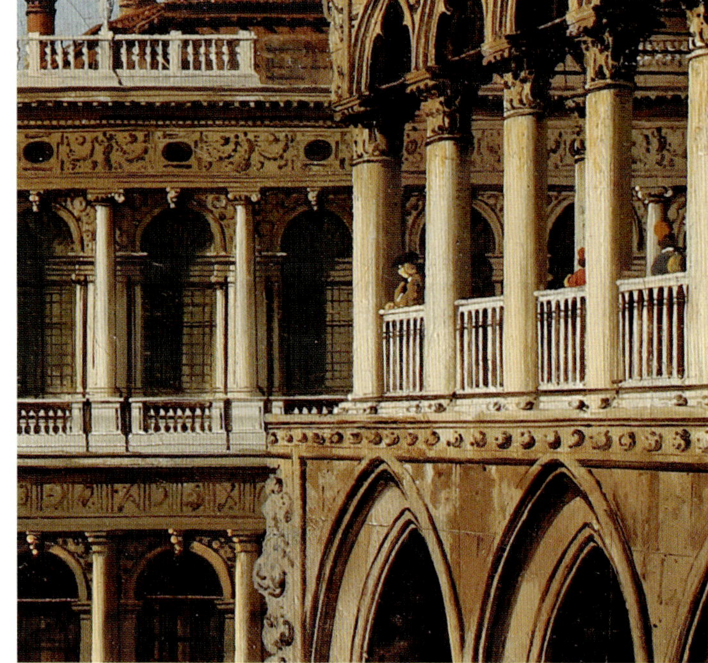

Fig. 104. Detail of cat. 8

with the Basilica di San Marco and the Doge's Palace nearby, these three buildings powerfully communicate the faith, justice and wisdom of the Venetian Republic.

The Library is flanked to the west by the Zecca, or Mint, the pointed roof of which is visible above the Library. It is here that the Republic's gold ducats, or *zecchini*, were coined. To the left is the tower of the Palazzo Venier dalle Torreselle, later demolished. Adjacent to the Library is the Ponte della Pescheria erected in 1339 and so named for the fish market that originally stood there. To the left is the mouth of the Grand Canal with the church of Santa Maria della Salute and the Dogana, or customs house, on the opposite bank. The Dogana was built by Giuseppe Benoni (1618–1684) in 1677. Its loggia is crowned by Bernardo Falcone's (*c.*1620–*c.*1696) two bronze Atlas figures supporting a golden globe surmounted by the figure of Fortune. After the devastating 1630–31 plague, the Senate commissioned the architect Baldassare Longhena to design a votive church dedicated to the Virgin Mary, protector of *la salute*, or health, resulting in the impressive Baroque edifice of Santa Maria della Salute.

Further to the left is the island of the Giudecca with the church of the Redentore, commissioned in 1577 by the Venetian Senate after one-third of the city's population perished in the devastating plague of 1575–77.[11] Designed by the famous architect Andrea Palladio, it was completed in 1593. Prior to taking on this commission, Palladio had finished the church of San Giorgio Maggiore between 1566 and 1576.[12] To the right of Il Redentore on the Giudecca is the church of Giacomo della Giudecca with its *campanile*, which was founded in 1338 but demolished in 1821.

Luca Carlevarijs painted this view prior to Canaletto, but widened the harbour in order to serve as a backdrop to colourful public ceremonies such as the arrival of foreign dignitaries like the British Ambassador Charles Montagu, 4th Earl of Manchester, in 1707 (fig. 102). Canaletto concentrated on the site itself, placing the architecture and its inhabitants at the forefront of his work.

The present pair provides a near 360-degree view of the Molo. The paintings complement each other well; both are framed by the Doge's Palace on opposite sides. Canaletto employed the edge of the Molo to create powerful diagonals that give a sense of space receding in the distance, and both paintings are taken from a slightly elevated viewpoint above the quayside and water. In cat. 7 the twin columns are silhouetted against the Doge's Palace while in cat. 8 they are set against the Library. Strong light entering from the right in cat. 7 and from the left in cat. 8 casts consistent shadows across the pair. A man wearing a black hat looks out onto the Piazzetta from the south-west corner of the *piano nobile* of the Doge's Palace in both paintings, as if modelling for the viewer how to enjoy the spectacle presented (figs 103, 104). Canaletto included wonderful quotidian details such as the two potted plants on the edge of the *fusta* in cat. 8 (fig. 105).

Canaletto made several drawings of the waterfront near the Piazzetta and the Doge's Palace, both *in situ* and back in the studio. This was among the first areas of Venice that he began to sketch. In fact, his earliest commission for Consul Joseph Smith from around 1723–24 was for a series of six large views of the Piazza San Marco and the Piazzetta for which Canaletto produced

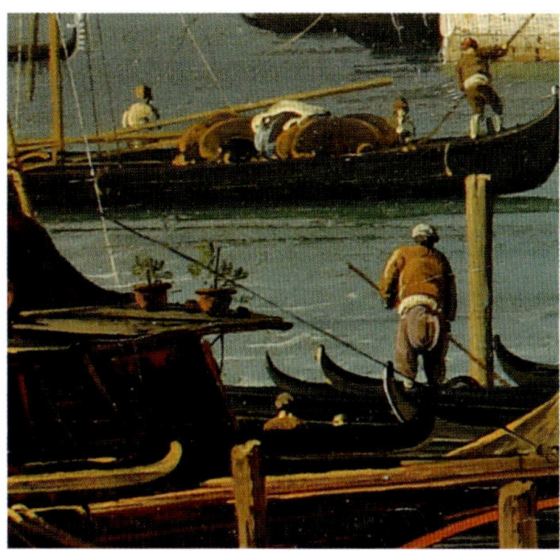

Fig. 105. Detail of cat. 8

Fig. 106. Canaletto (1697–1768), *Venice: The Molo and the Riva degli Schiavoni, Looking East*, 1729, pen and ink on paper, 19.6 × 30.6 cm, Royal Collection (RCIN 907452)

a number of studies.[13] No known drawing corresponds exactly to either painting in this pair. The closest sheet to cat. 7 is taken from a lower viewpoint, probably from a boat in the water, where Canaletto only included the column of Saint Mark as a framing device on the left (fig. 106).[14] He drew the column higher than in real life, or than in any other version of this view. There is a close drawing in Darmstadt, dated March 1729, in which the temporary hut next to the Ponte della Paglia is omitted.[15] Both sheets correspond to a painting at Tatton Park from 1730.[16] For cat. 8, Canaletto studied the eastern façade of the Library and the twin columns in a rough sketch with basic outlines in the *Cagnola Sketchbook* (fig. 107).[17] A more worked-up drawing taken from the Bacino, expanded to include the entire façade of the Doge's Palace and the Ponte della Paglia, reveals Canaletto's continued study of this area (fig. 108).

In 1872, when these paintings were exhibited at Bethnal Green with the rest of Sir Richard Wallace's collection, they were considered major highlights that faithfully transcribed the sites depicted. Canaletto, however, manipulated architectural elements to create these harmonious compositions. As with much of his work, the elevated perspective was implemented in the studio. Canaletto altered the position of the columns in both paintings to ensure their full visibility and that of buildings nearby. In cat. 7 he lowered the position of the statue of Saint Mark and brought the column of Saint Theodore closer to the south-west corner of the palace. In reality, the latter

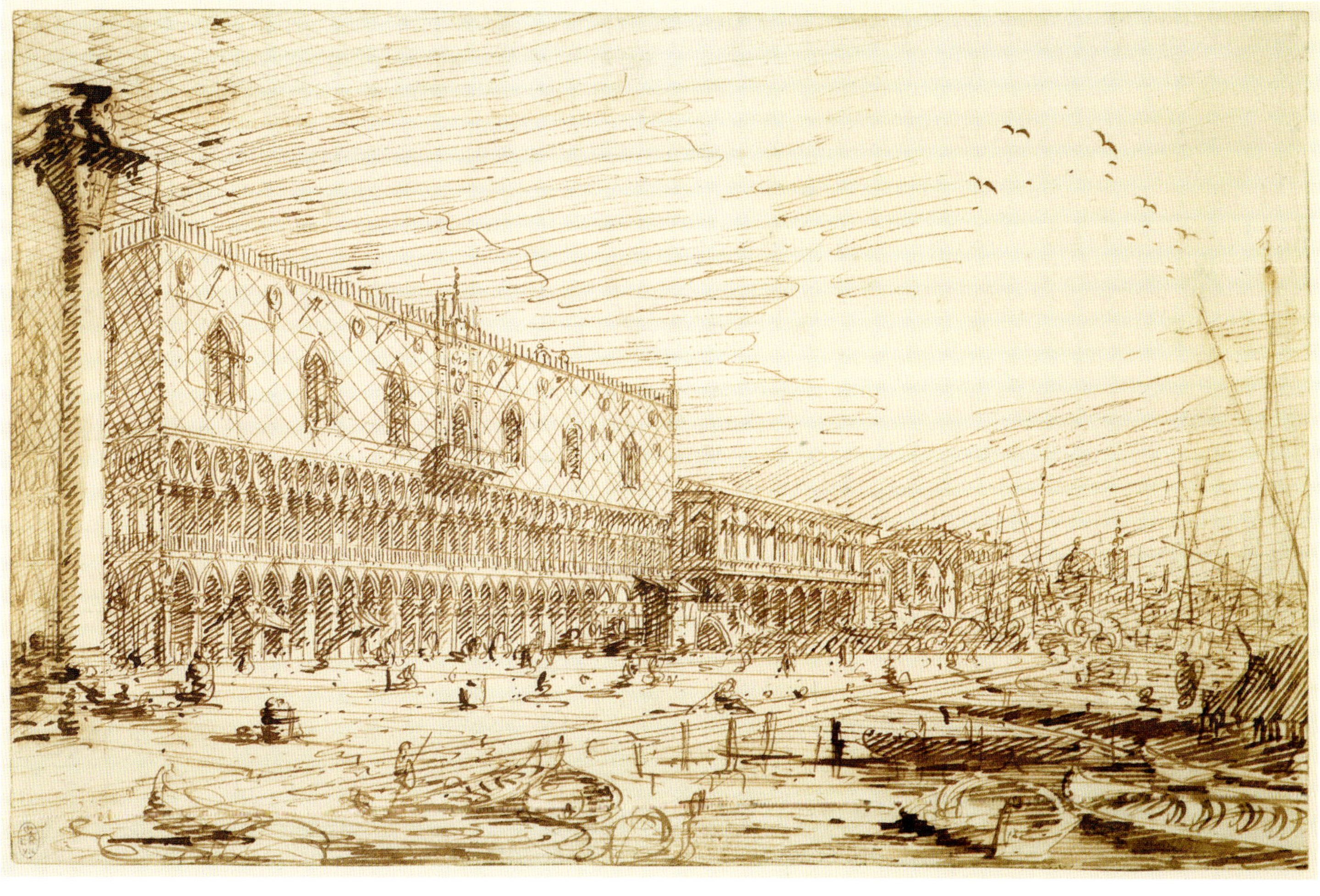

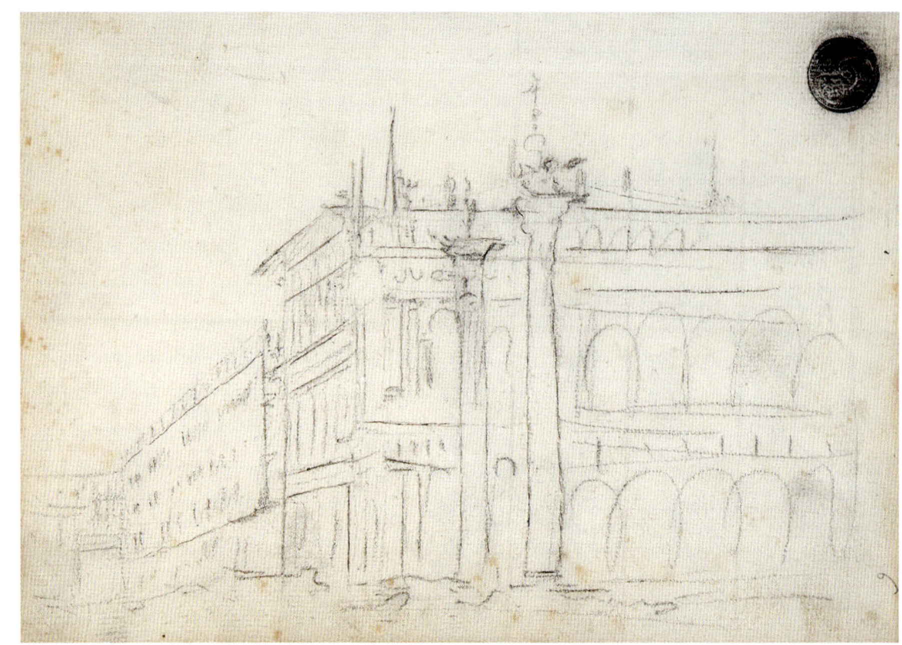

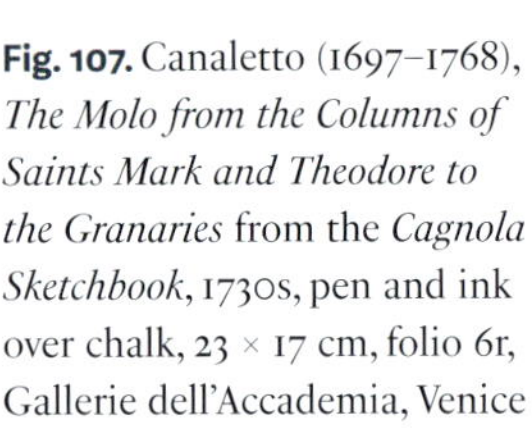

Fig. 107. Canaletto (1697–1768), *The Molo from the Columns of Saints Mark and Theodore to the Granaries* from the *Cagnola Sketchbook*, 1730s, pen and ink over chalk, 23 × 17 cm, folio 6r, Gallerie dell'Accademia, Venice

Fig. 108. Canaletto (1697–1768), *Venice: The Palazzo Ducale, Libreria and Molo*, *c*.1734, pen and ink over ruled and free pencil and a little pinpointing, 19.6 × 27.1 cm, Royal Collection (RCIN 907448)

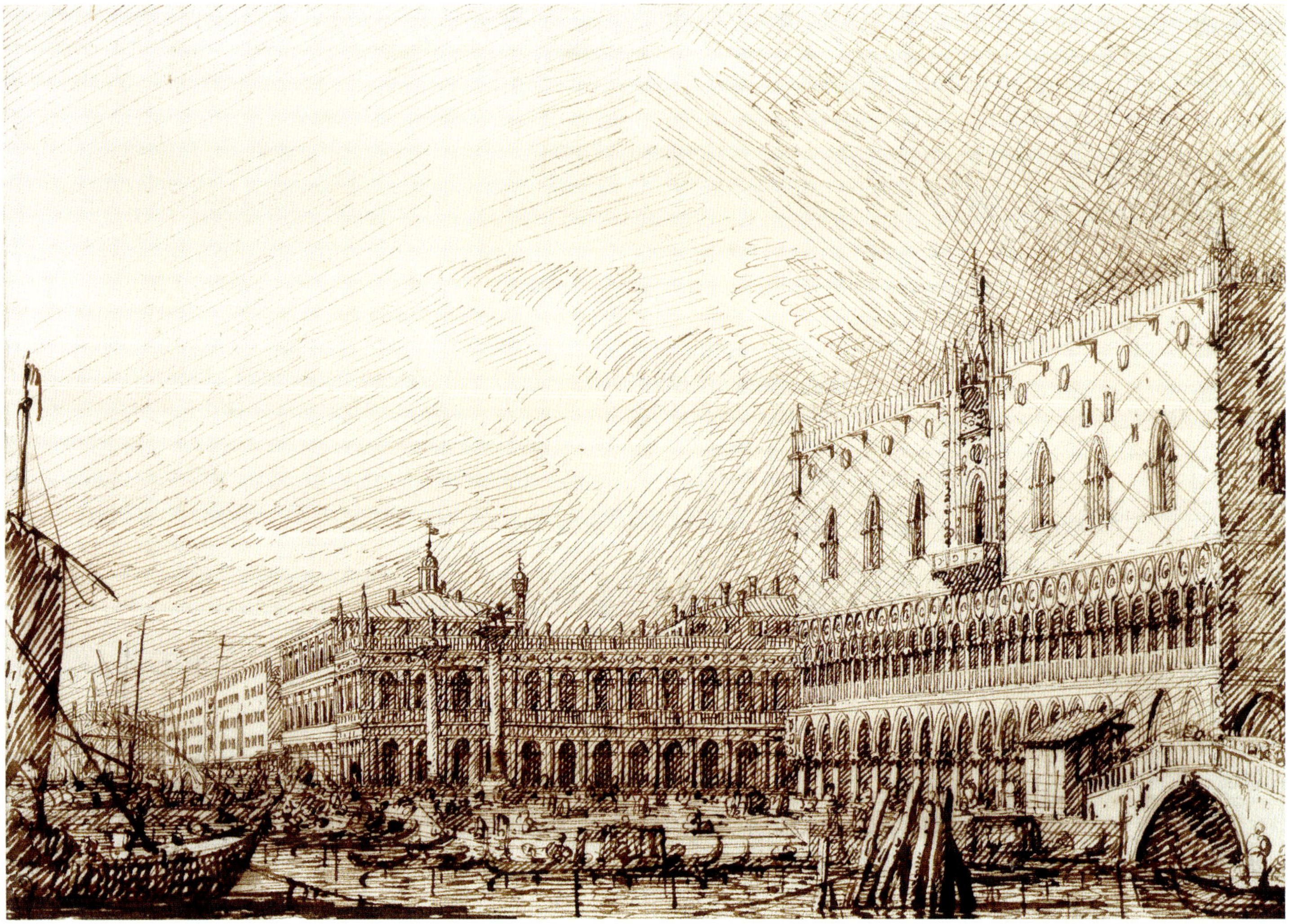

was further to the left of the window on the upper storey of the palace's western façade. Canaletto included the entire southern façade of the palace, a view that would only be possible from the water. From the present perspective, the façade should be at a much sharper angle. In cat. 8 Canaletto moved the churches of Santa Maria della Salute and Il Redentore closer to the Molo so that they are more visible.

Recent technical analysis did not detect any preparatory underdrawings or planning marks in the paintings. The infrared reflectogram of cat. 7 shows the western façade and roof of the Prison overlapping with the south-eastern corner of the Doge's Palace, suggesting that Canaletto worked out the position of the Prison in relation to the palace directly on the support (fig. 109). The order of painting in both works is consistent with that found more generally across Canaletto's oeuvre, with the sky painted first, followed by the quay and buildings, and the figures and boats painted last. Canaletto painted areas of the sky and architecture wet-in-wet in cat. 8.

Canaletto employed incisions in both paintings, but to different ends. Ruled incisions are detectable on the Doge's Palace in the X-ray of cat. 7. These register faintly and were probably used to articulate the surface decoration rather than lay in the composition. Incisions register more deeply in the X-ray of cat. 8, suggesting that they were used to lay in the architectural elements at an early stage in the painting process. Such incisions are particularly visible in the Library, where they define the arched tops of the windows on the *piano nobile*, the balustrade and the columns (fig. 110). Shallower incisions that do not penetrate to the ground layers on the façade of the Doge's Palace in cat. 8, comparable to those in the pendant, were similarly used to articulate the architecture. Dark, ruled, painted lines define elements on the façades of the buildings in both works (fig. 111). Despite relining, cat. 7 has retained areas of impasto in the clouds and on the *fusta*.

Canaletto began painting the Molo early in his career, at the end of the 1720s. Views of the Molo proved popular with his patrons, which explains the numerous known versions

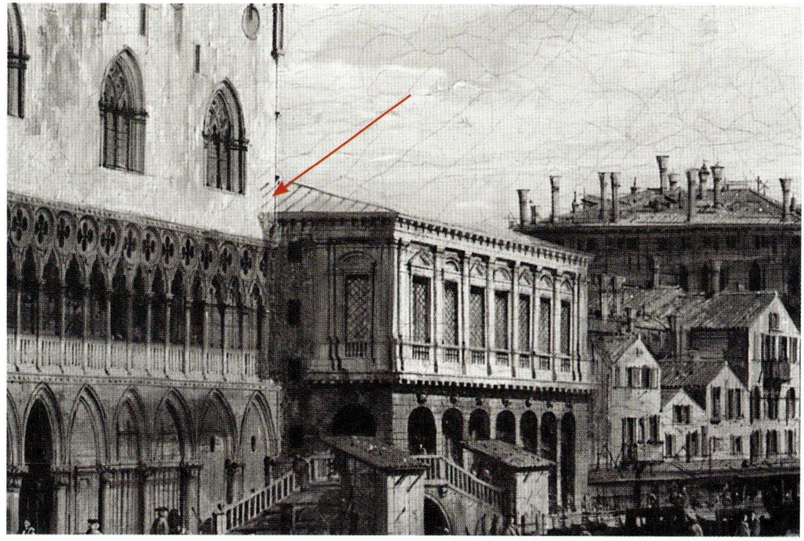

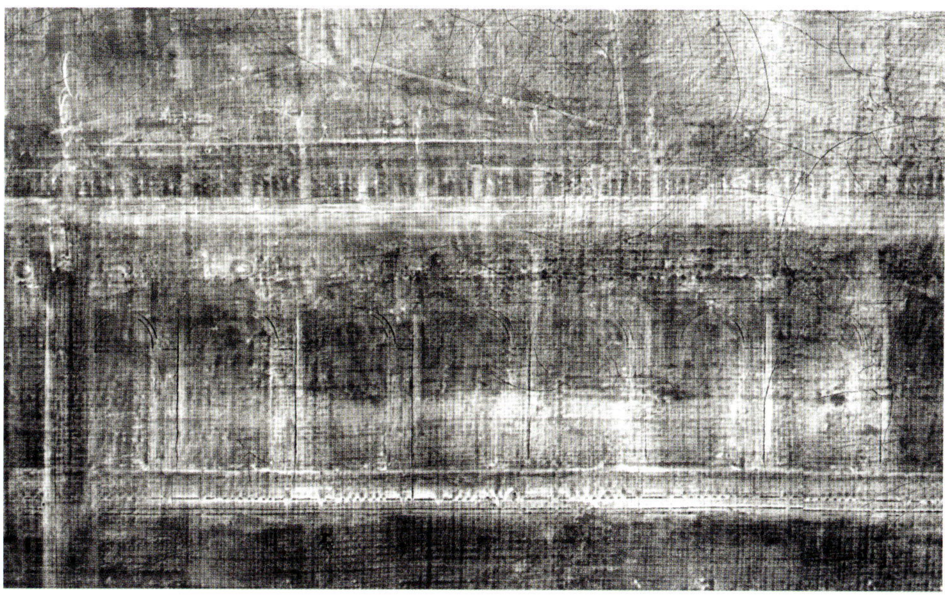

of the subject. The present pairing, however, is unique as there are no other known versions of cat. 8. In his views of the Molo looking west, Canaletto either zoomed out to include more of the Doge's Palace and the Molo or excluded the palace altogether to focus on the Molo itself (fig. 112). In the latter views, he only depicted the column of Saint Theodore, showed the Library from the south-west corner and integrated the Mint and Granaries. Comparable views to cat. 7 rarely include both columns (fig. 113).[18] The Molo is pristine in the Wallace Collection pair compared to the

Fig. 109. Detail of IRR of cat. 7 showing overlapping Prison and palace

Fig. 110. Detail of X-ray of cat. 8 showing incisions

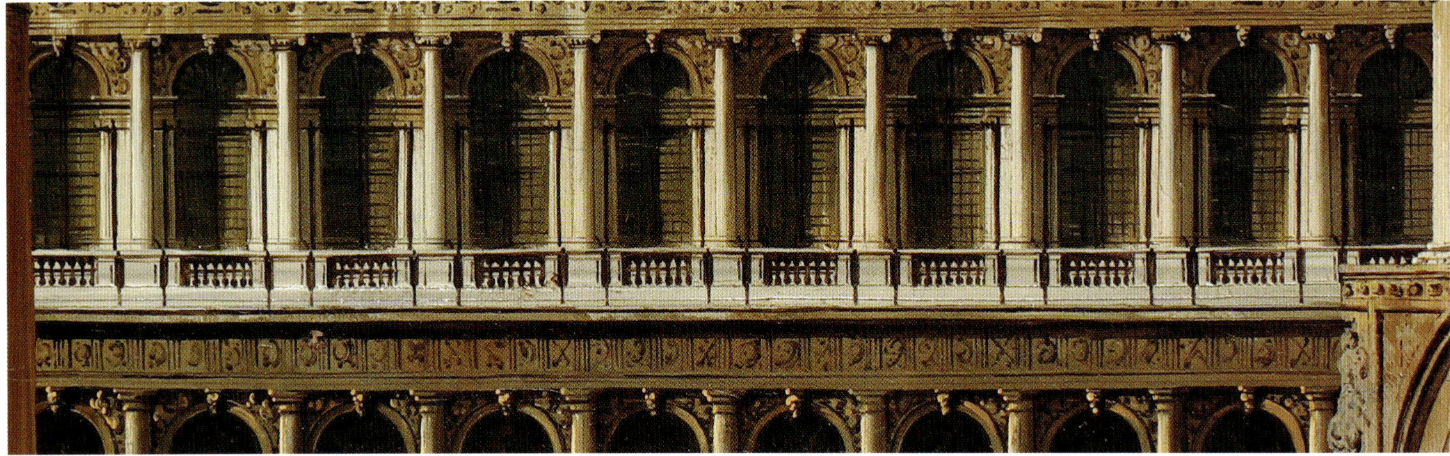

disrepair found in other versions with large stones on the quay and the steps dilapidated.

Given the subject's popularity it is surprising that Smith did not own a pair.[19] The pair was engraved by Antonio Visentini in 1742 in a modified form (figs 114, 115).[20] Cat. 7 differs from the print, which only includes the column of San Tòdaro and where the viewpoint is slightly further to the right. Visentini's print of the Molo looking west excludes the Ducal Palace and places the entrance to the Grand Canal and the Salute further back in the distance.

The pair had been dated to the early 1740s, prior to 1745 when the façade of the Pietà in cat. 7 was reconstructed.[21] Stylistically, the paintings are now dated to *c.*1739.[22] The smaller copperplate pair at Chatsworth serves as a useful precedent for the present pair.[23]

The pair of paintings belonged to William Wells of Redleaf, who acquired them sometime before 1838, when he lent them to the British Institution. In 1833 Wells's collection was described by the German artist and curator Johann David Passavant as 'very choice', in particular the Dutch masters.[24] Wells was 'a great patron of living artists' and had 'a large collection of modern landscapes and subject pictures'.[25] The Canaletti pair was on offer at Wells's May 1848 sale where Lord Hertford bought seven other pictures and where the present pair did not sell.[26] The paintings are listed in the 1870 Hertford House inventory; they were acquired by Hertford sometime between 1848 and 1870. Hertford was in London in May 1848 and may have acquired the paintings after Wells's sale via a dealer.[27]

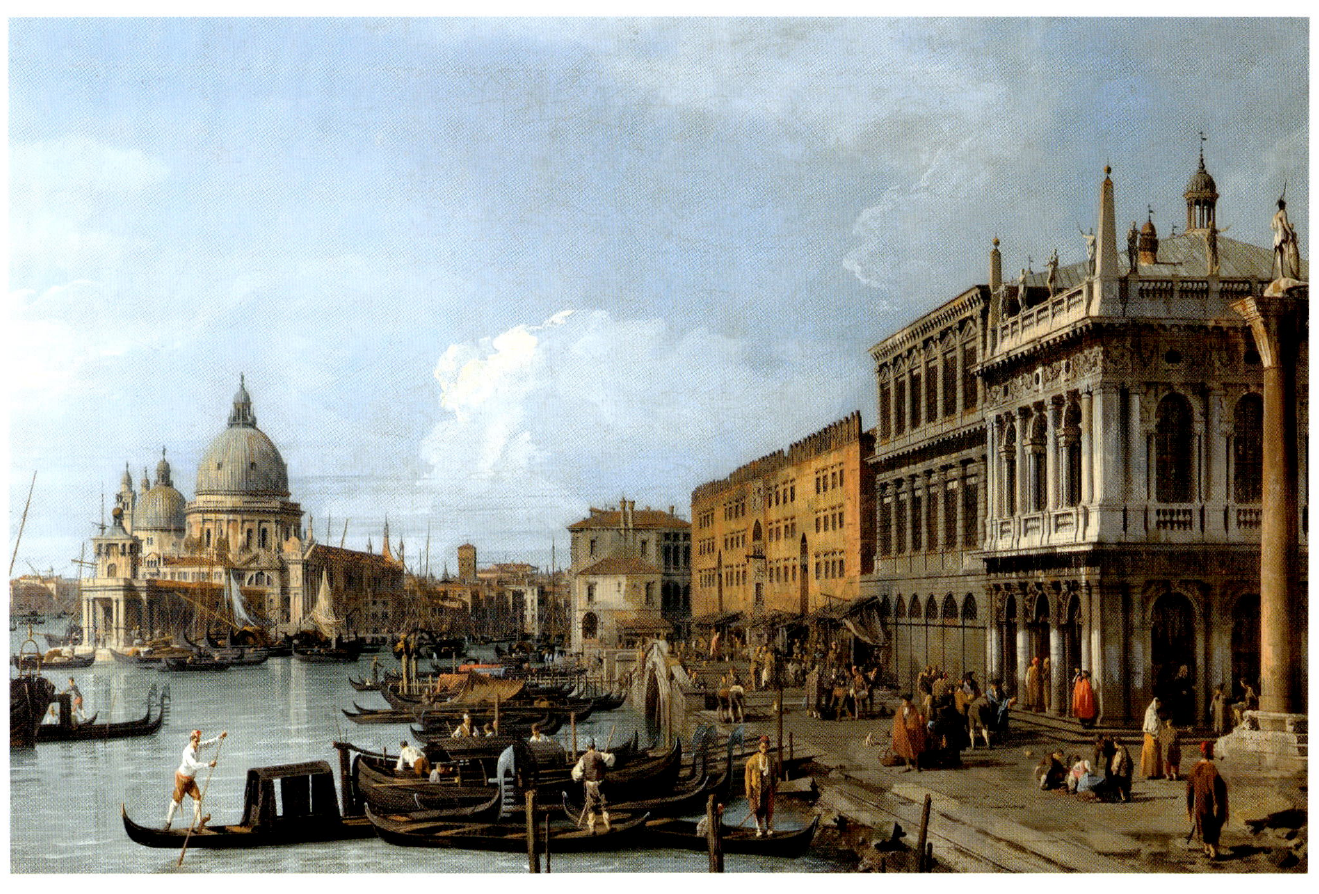

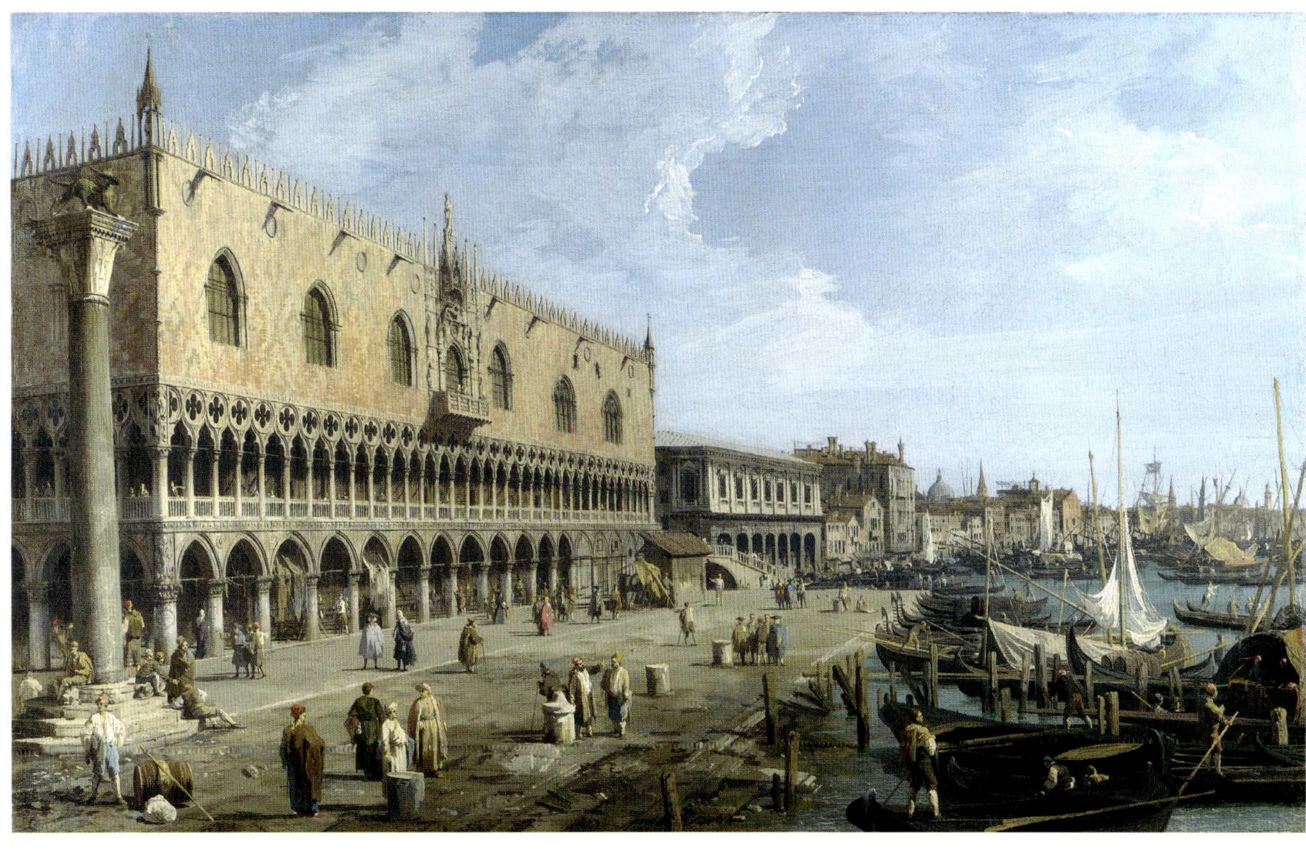

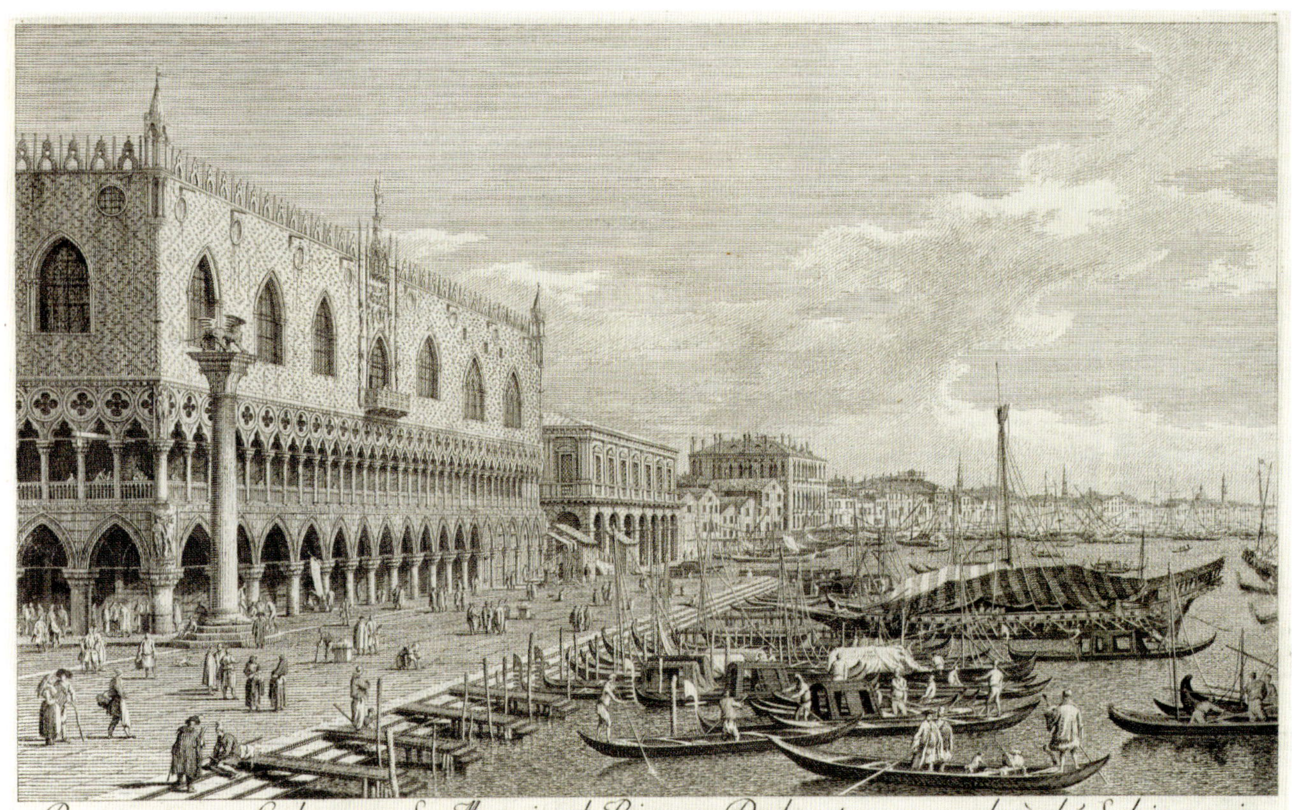

Prospectus a Columna S. Marci ad Ripam Dalmatarum vulgò de' Schiavoni.,,

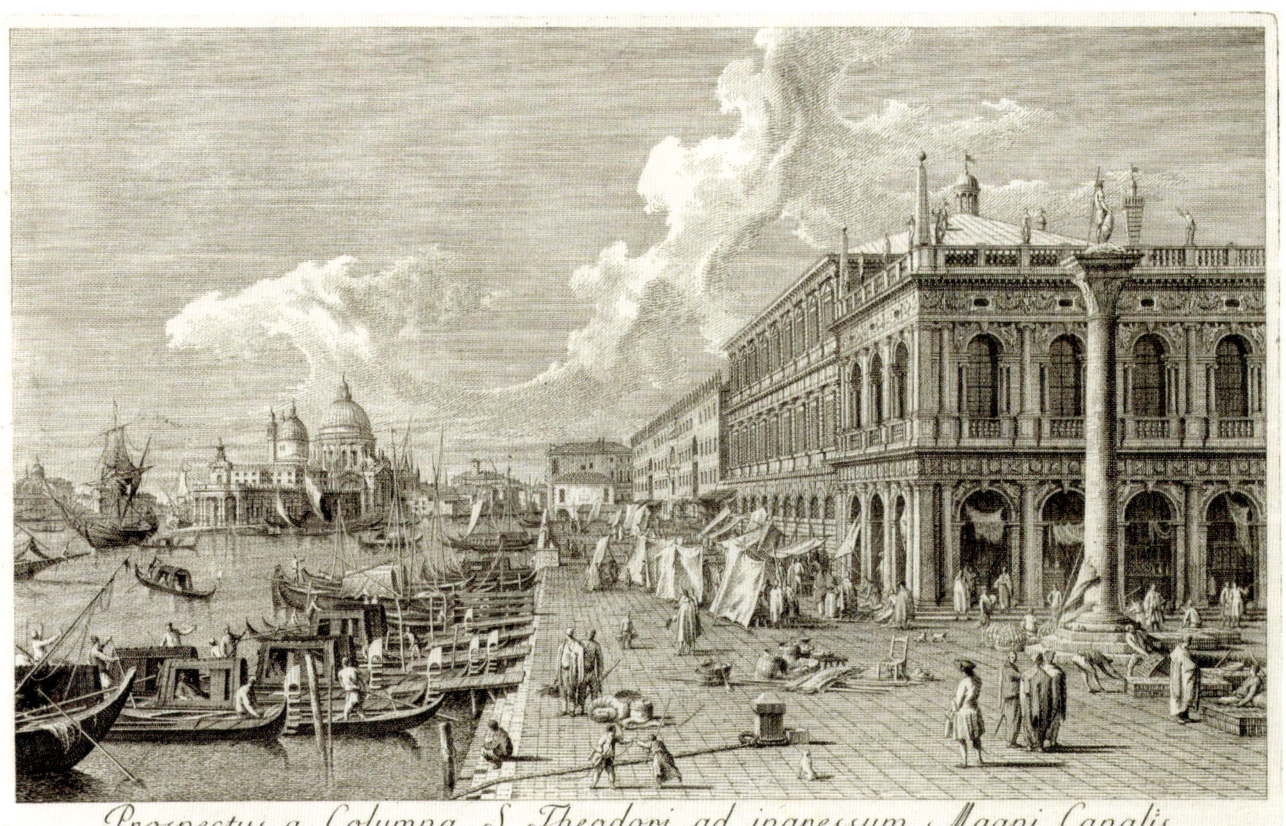

Prospectus a Columna S. Theodori ad ingressum Magni Canalis. 12.

William Wells (1768–1847),[28] of Redleaf, Penshurst, Kent, by 1838;[29] by inheritance to his grand-nephew, William Wells (1818–1889) of Redleaf; his grand-uncle's estate sale, Christie & Manson, London, 12–13 May 1848 (L.19021) (first day), lots 34 (cat. 7)[30] and 35 (cat. 8);[31] bought in by Wells for £178.10s (equivalent to 170 guineas) (cat. 7) and £173.6s (equivalent to 165 guineas) (cat. 8);[32] Richard Seymour-Conway, 4th Marquess of Hertford (1800–1870) before 1870; by descent to Sir Richard Wallace, 1st Baronet (1818–1890); by descent to his wife, Lady Wallace (Julie Amélie Charlotte Castelnau, 1819–1897); by whom bequeathed with the rest of the Wallace Collection to the British nation, 1897.

1872–75: 'Paintings, Porcelain, Bronzes, Decorative Furniture and other Works of Art lent by Sir Richard Wallace to the Bethnal Green Branch of the South Kensington Museum'.[33]

Although there are no other known versions of cat. 8, there are several versions of cat. 7:

Canaletto, *Riva degli Schiavoni, Looking East*, 57.2 × 92.7 cm, oil on canvas, Private Collection

Canaletto, *Venice: A View of the Doge's Palace and the Riva degli Schiavoni from the Piazzetta*, c.1729, 46.5 × 62 cm, oil on copper, The Duke of Devonshire and the Trustees of the Chatsworth Settlement (C 115)

The following versions show only the column of Saint Mark:

Canaletto, *Riva degli Schiavoni, Looking East*, 47.5 × 77.5 cm, oil on canvas, Bowes Museum, Barnard Castle (C 113a)

Canaletto, *Riva degli Schiavoni, Looking East*, 58 × 85 cm, oil on canvas, Private Collection, Belgium (C 111*)

Canaletto, *Riva degli Schiavoni, Looking East*, 46.5 × 62 cm, oil on canvas, Private Collection, Italy (C 115*)

Canaletto, *Riva degli Schiavoni, Looking East*, 73.5 × 104.5 cm, oil on canvas, Earl Fitzwilliam, Milton Park (C 114)

Canaletto, *Riva degli Schiavoni, Looking East*, 110.5 × 185.5 cm, oil on canvas, Collezioni Civiche d'Arte, Milan (C 113)

Canaletto, *Riva degli Schiavoni, Looking East*, 58.4 × 101.6 cm, oil on canvas, The National Trust, Tatton Park (C 111)

Canaletto, *Venice: The Doge's Palace and the Riva degli Schiavoni*, late 1730s, oil on canvas, 61.3 × 99.8 cm, National Gallery, London (NG940).

Both works are painted on a medium-weight plain-weave canvas that is glue-paste lined onto a finer plain-weave canvas. Cusping along all four edges in both paintings suggests that the original compositions are intact. Cat. 7 has an L-shaped tear in the upper centre of the sky that has caused paint loss. Cat. 7 has a standard double-layered ground with a red-brown initial layer followed by a pinkish-beige upper layer. This is consistent with many other paintings by Canaletto, but not with the pendant, where this ground structure is only apparent in the sky. Elsewhere, cat. 8 has a single ground consisting of the initial, lower red-brown layer, a rather unusual feature. Cat. 7 was cleaned more recently than its pendant, in 1961 by William Vallance, probably due to the tear.[34] Both paintings were cleaned and analysed at the Hamilton Kerr Institute in 2021. Technical investigation comprising X-radiography, infrared reflectography, ultraviolet light photography, surface micrography and SEM-EDX paint sample analysis was undertaken at this point.

LITERATURE

Constable 1962, C90 (cat. 8), C112 (cat. 7)
Watson 1968, p. 55 (cat. 7); p. 57 (cat. 8)
Puppi 1970, p. 112, nos 247A (cat. 7), 245B (cat. 8)
Links 1981, p. 26, no. 62 (cat. 7); p. 16, no. 20 (cat. 8)
Ingamells 1985, pp. 234–35 (cat. 7); pp. 240–41 (cat. 8)
Duffy and Hedley 2004, pp. 66–67

LP

Fig. 114. Antonio Visentini (1688–1782) after Canaletto (1697–1768), *Prospectus a Columna S. Marci ad Ripam Dalmatarum vulgò de' Schiavoni*, 1742, etching, 27.5 × 43.2 cm, plate 11 from *Prospectus Magni Canalis Venetiarum*, II

Fig. 115. Antonio Visentini (1688–1782) after Canaletto (1697–1768), *Prospectus a Columna S. Theodori ad ingressum Magni Canalis*, 1742, etching, 27.5 × 43.2 cm, plate 12 from *Prospectus Magni Canalis Venetiarum*, II

9. **GIOVANNI ANTONIO CANAL,
IL CANALETTO** (Venice 1697–1768)

A Regatta on the Grand Canal

*c.*1740
oil on canvas
58.7 × 93.3 cm
P496

The stretcher is stamped 'I·PEEL / LINER'
(presumably John Peel, *c.*1785–1858, active in
London as a picture liner by 1820).

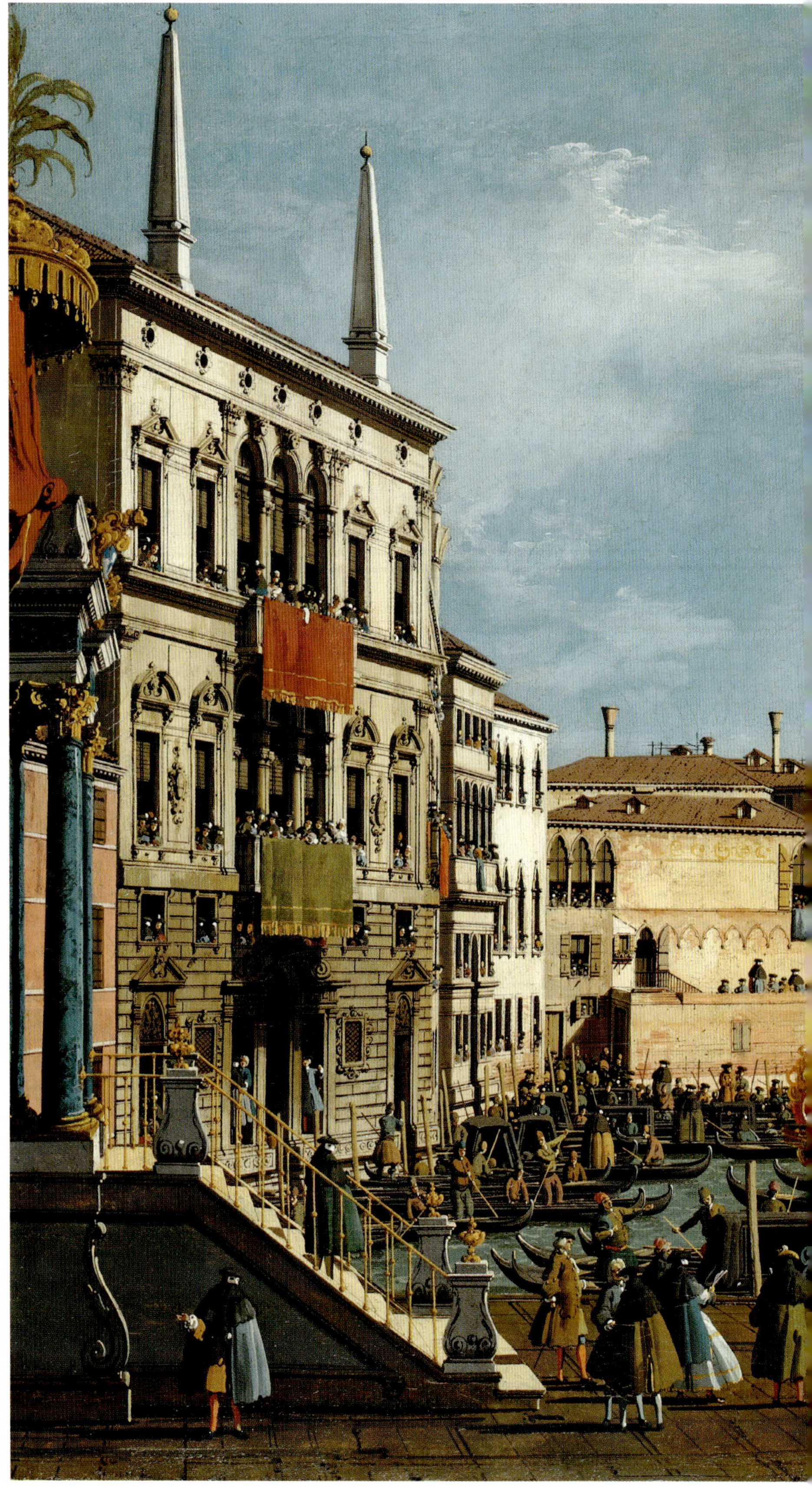

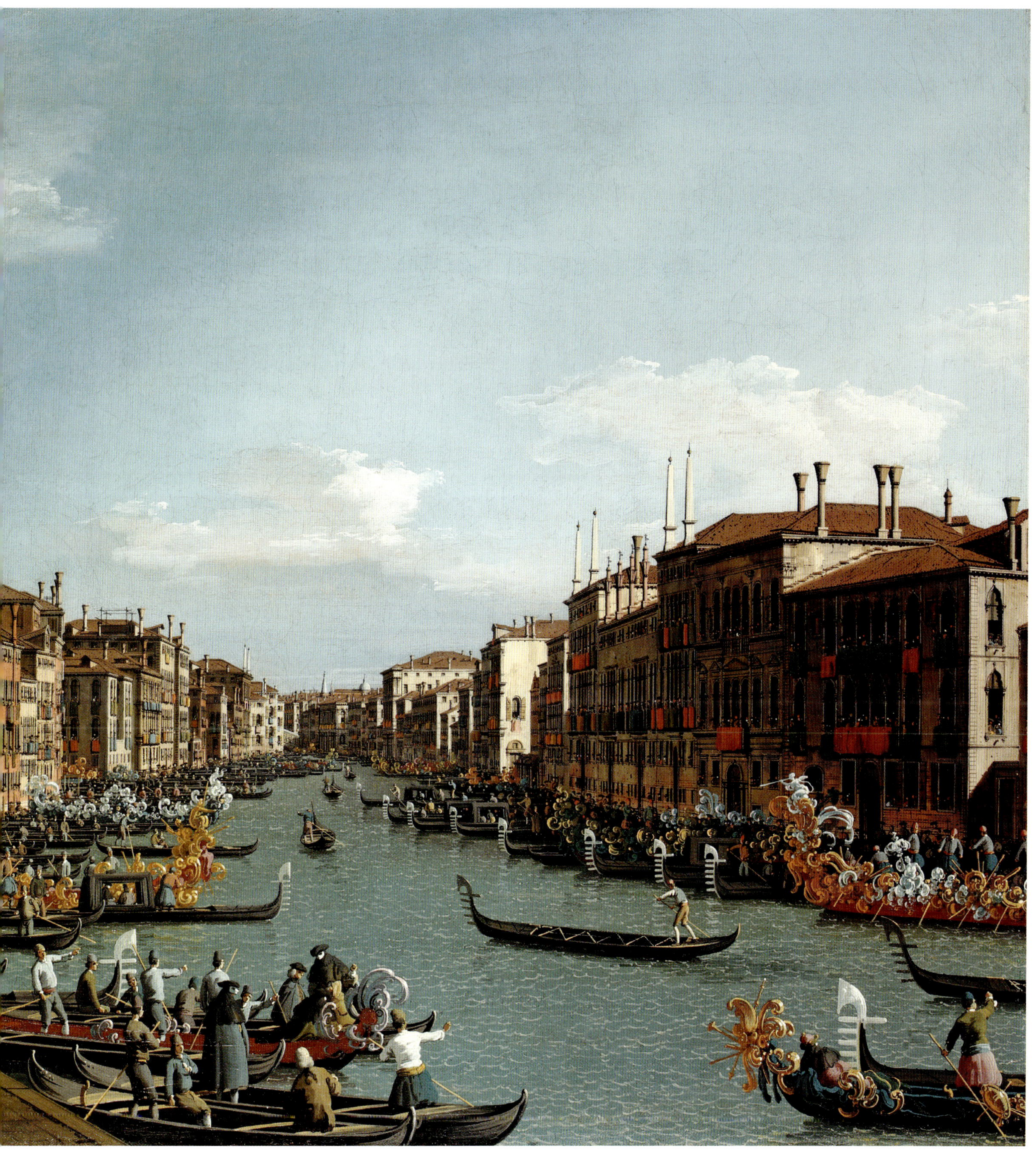

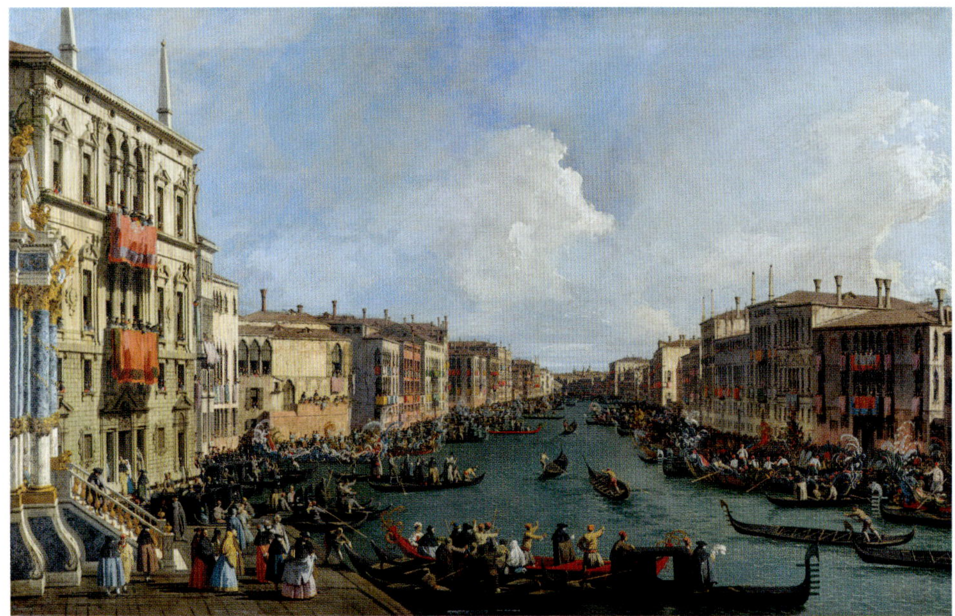

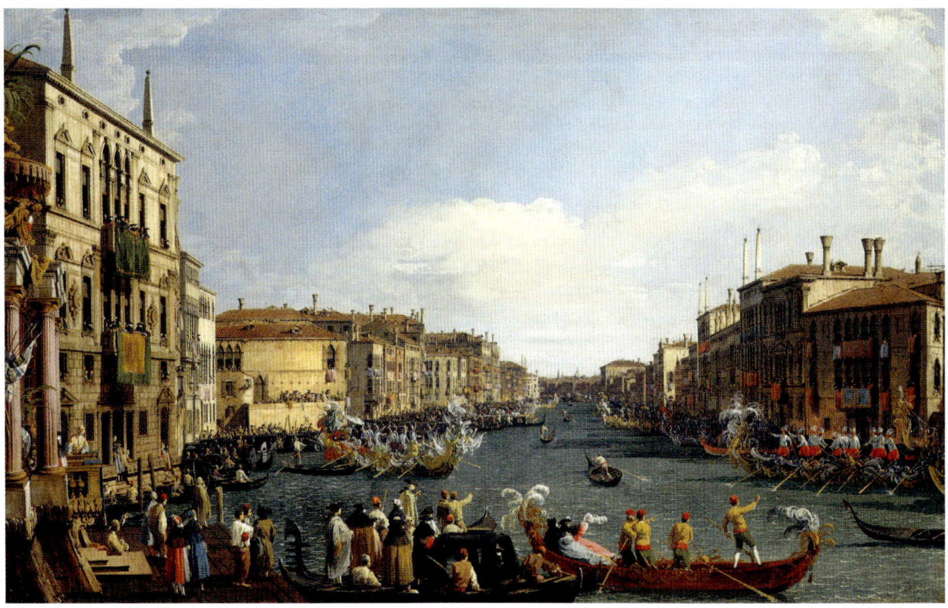

Fig. 116. Canaletto (1697–1768), *A Regatta on the Grand Canal*, c.1735, oil on canvas, 115.5 × 194 cm, Collection of the Duke of Bedford, Woburn Abbey

Fig. 117. Canaletto (1697–1768), *A Regatta on the Grand Canal*, c.1733–34, oil on canvas, 77 × 125.7 cm, Royal Collection (RCIN 404416)

The view is taken from the Palazzo Foscari, next to which a wooden *macchina*, shown on the left, which temporarily blocked the Rio di Ca' Foscari, marked the finishing line of regattas. Those were composed of gondola races of various types, and from the *macchina* the winners received their flags and prizes. The topography of Venice lends itself especially well to regattas, and, appropriately for a maritime Republic, the Venetian calendar was – and still is – peppered with boat races. They were held annually on 2 February and occasionally to honour particularly distinguished visitors to the city. The course ran from the Punta di Sant'Antonio at the south-east of the island, along the Riva degli Schiavoni and the Molo, up the Grand Canal to Santa Croce, then back to the Volta di Canal at Ca' Foscari.

Canaletto is generally credited with five variants of the composition. The first is the very large canvas in the Bowes Museum, Barnard Castle, the early history of which is unknown, but which is datable on stylistic grounds to around 1730.[1] In the version painted for Joseph Smith and now in the Royal Collection, the arms on the *macchina* on the left are those of Carlo Ruzzini, Doge from June 1732 to January 1735 (fig. 117).[2] Much smaller, it became the best known by far, mostly thanks to Antonio Visentini's engraving in the 1735 edition of his *Prospectus Magni Canalis Venetiarum*. In the large version at Woburn Abbey (and in all subsequent versions) the arms on the *macchina* are those of Alvise Pisani, Doge from January 1735 to June 1741 (fig. 116).[3] This would seem to indicate that the painting was among the last of the Duke of Bedford's paintings to be supplied, presumably within the years 1735–36. It was followed by two further large variants, one, in the National Gallery, London, with a pendant showing *The Bacino di San Marco on Ascension Day*, the two most glamorous components of a set of ten executed for Thomas Osborne, 4th Duke of Leeds (1713–1789), around 1738,[4] and a painting of *c.*1740 probably commissioned by John Montagu, 2nd Duke of Montagu (1690–1749), which remained in the collection of the Dukes of Buccleuch until 1952; untraced since its sale at Sotheby's, London, in 1967, it is thought to be in a German private collection.[5]

To these should be added the Wallace Collection painting, which has had a very mixed reception among scholars. Samuel J. Camp, while not accepting any of the Wallace Collection paintings as by Canaletto, did consider this to be 'probably by the same hand or hands as P509 and P516',[6] both certainly by Canaletto. It was the only Wallace painting endorsed as Canaletto's work without qualification by Sir Francis Watson. John Ingamells initially agreed, though described it, not unfairly, as 'mechanical',[7] but he changed his mind and the verdict since 1985 has been that it is a studio work. J.G. Links clearly intended to correct this, annotating a photograph in the Constable/Links Archive 'was school now mechanical but by Can',[8] but he never accorded it the status that is its due. While a certain degree of studio intervention must be assumed in a painting of *c.*1740, the quality is high and most areas reveal the touch of Canaletto himself. The composition is similar to that of the larger painting of the subject at Woburn Abbey, but with subtle variations in the lines of recession of the foreground buildings and entirely different figures and boats (although the gondolier with a raised right arm features in the foreground to the right of centre in both versions). It should take its place as the artist's sixth rendition of the subject, as both the last and the smallest depiction by the artist of the subject, significantly smaller than even the version executed for Smith now in the Royal Collection, which measures 77.1 × 125.7 cm. That painting may well have inspired Baron Conway's commission, as he must have been familiar with it in Smith's house on the Grand Canal.

PROVENANCE
Francis Seymour-Conway, 2nd Baron Conway, later 1st Earl and 1st Marquess of Hertford (1719–1794), by whom presumably commissioned in Venice in *c.*1739.

EXHIBITION
1872–75: 'Paintings, Porcelain, Bronzes, Decorative Furniture and other Works of Art lent by Sir Richard Wallace to the Bethnal Green Branch of the South Kensington Museum', no. 280.

RELATED WORKS
Canaletto, *A Regatta on the Grand Canal*, *c.*1735/36, oil on canvas, 115.5 × 194 cm, Collection of the Duke of Bedford, Woburn Abbey (C348; Beddington 2021, no. 24)

Other paintings by Canaletto of the same subject are in the Royal Collection (C347), the Bowes Museum, Barnard Castle (C349), the National Gallery, London (C350), and in an untraced private collection (C351).

TECHNICAL NOTES
The Hamilton Kerr Institute produced a technical report on the painting in 2019 after cleaning it, from which much of the following information derives. The support is a medium-weight plain-weave canvas, glue-paste lined, with cusping on all four sides. The ground comprises a pale buff layer over a dark red layer, consistent with Canaletto's usual practice. There is no sign of underdrawing or *pentimenti*. The painting was begun with the sky, which transitions from a subtly darker tone on the left over to a paler one on the right. The buildings and water were initially blocked in with flat colours and then the architectural features and boats were mapped out by scoring lines into the wet paint both freehand and with a straight edge. Architectural details, depicted in dark grey and black paint using a rigging brush, *gondole*, figures and smaller details such as the ripples on the water followed. Impasto was limited to faces and to accent highlights on the gilding of watercraft.

LITERATURE
Camp 1928, p. 47
Constable 1962, C352, as Attributed to Canaletto
Watson 1968, p. 51, as Canaletto
Ingamells 1979, p. 40, as a mechanical work by Canaletto
Ingamells 1985, pp. 242–43, as Studio of Canaletto
Duffy and Hedley 2004, p. 68, as Studio of Canaletto

CB

10. Studio of
GIOVANNI ANTONIO CANAL,
IL CANALETTO (Venice 1697–1768)

*The Festival of Giovedi Grasso
in the Piazzetta*

*c.*1741/42
oil on canvas
58.5 × 92.7 cm
P500

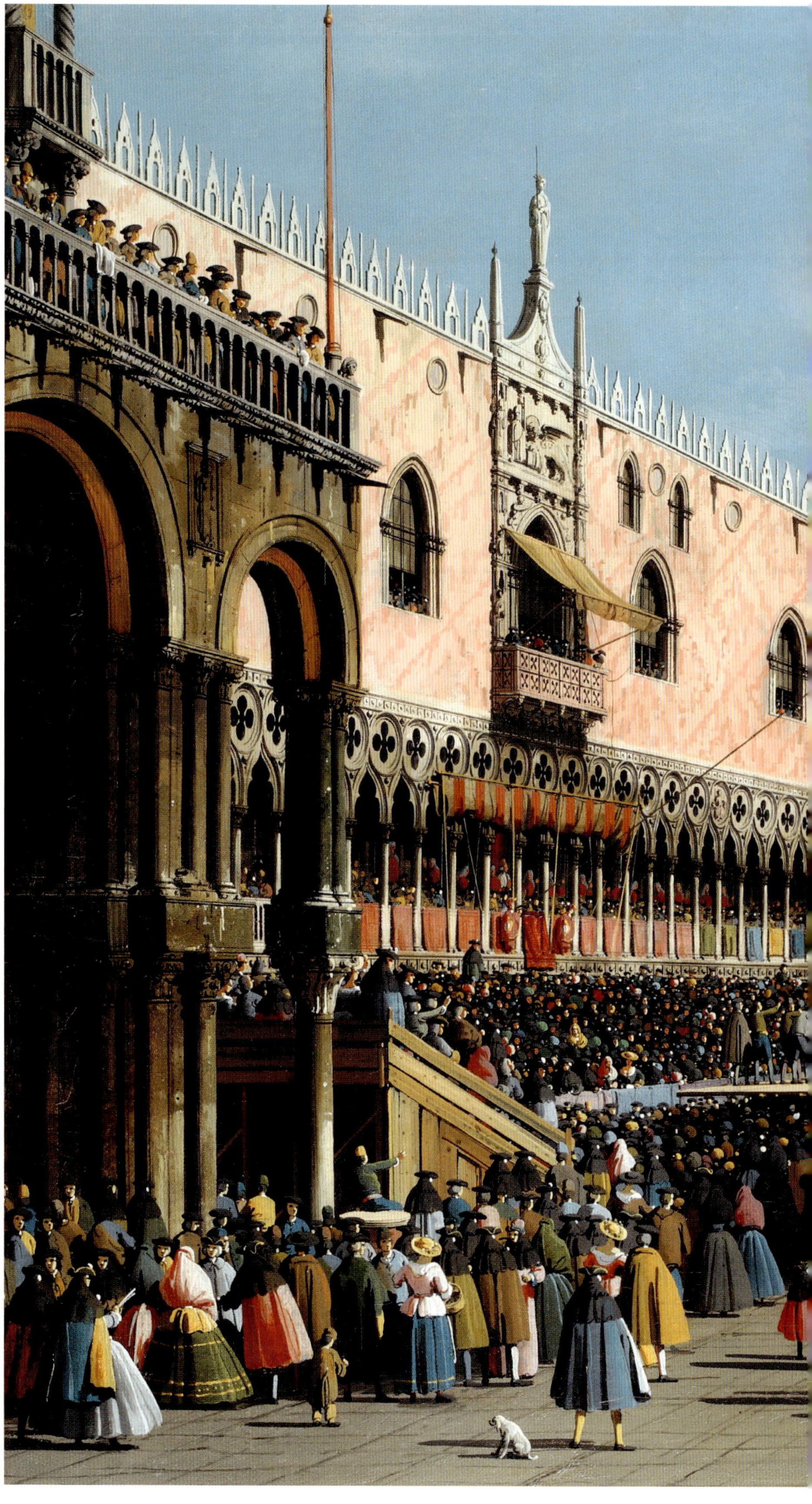

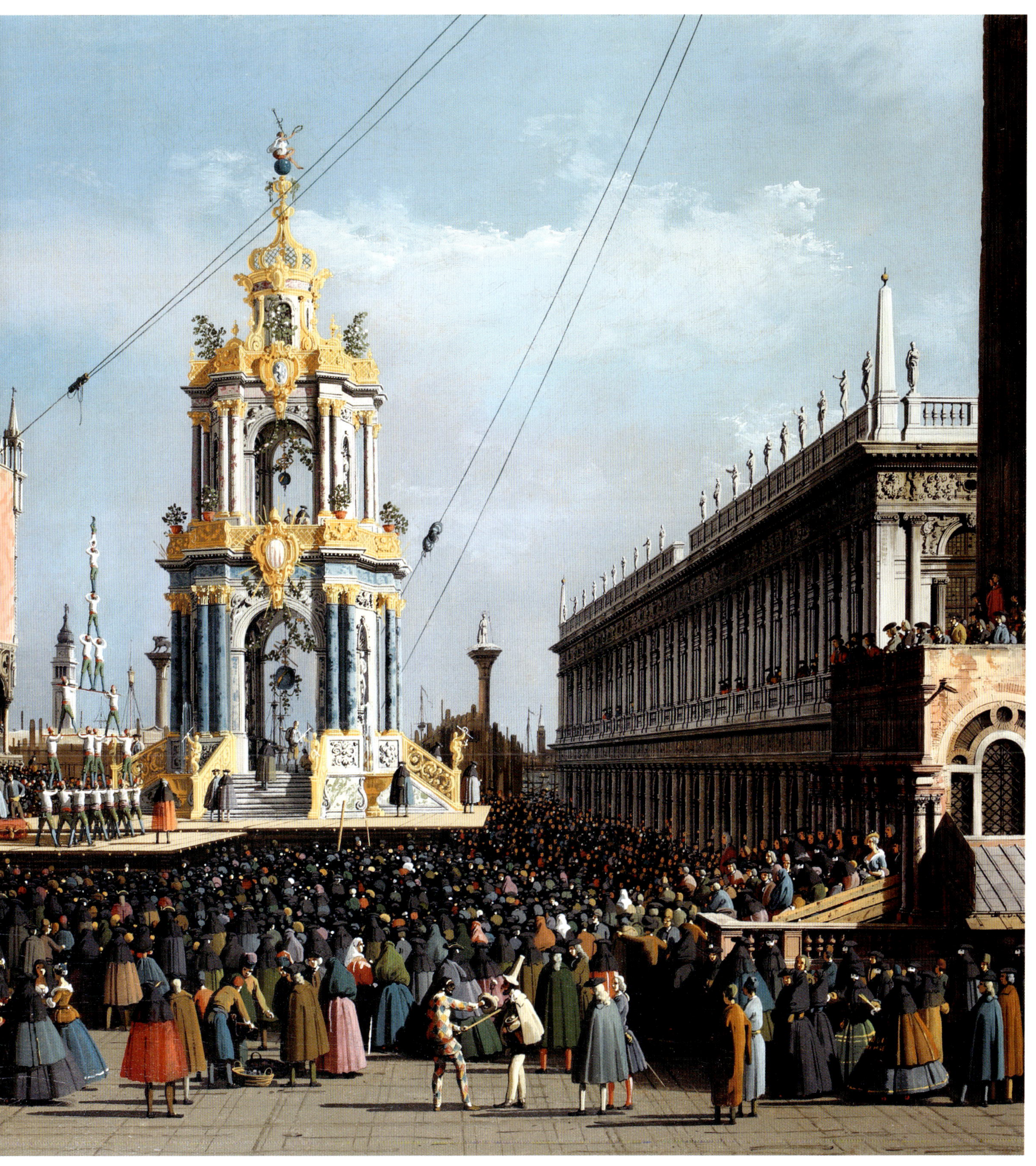

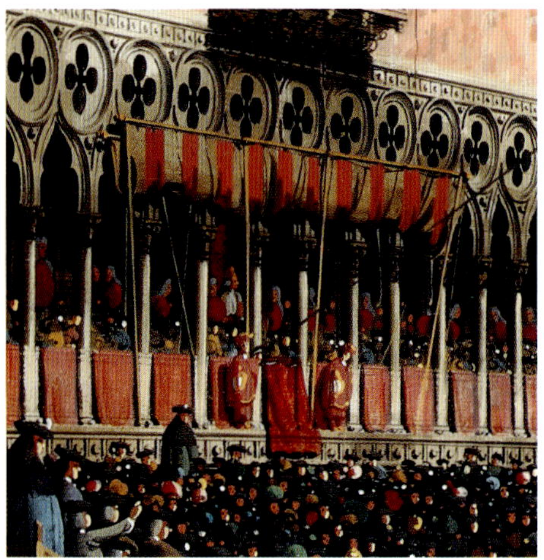

Fig. 118. Detail of cat. 10

Fig. 119. Canaletto (1697–1768), *The Festival of Giovedì Grasso in the Piazzetta*, c.1765/66, pen and brown ink with grey wash over traces of graphite, tip of the brush with black wash, heightened with touches of white gouache, sheet 38.7 × 55.5 cm, National Gallery of Art, Washington, DC (inv. 2007.111.55)

The festival of Giovedì Grasso, which marks the beginning of Lent, was initiated in 1162, as a consequence of the seizure of the Venetian vassal Grado by the German-born Patriarch Ulrich of Aquileia at the instigation of Frederick Barbarossa, Emperor of the West. Doge Vitale II Michiel immediately retaliated, recapturing the city on Maundy Thursday, destroying a number of Friulian castles and taking 700 prisoners, including Ulrich. The latter were released on condition that every year on the Wednesday before Lent the Patriarch of Aquileia would deliver to Venice a tribute of a bull, 12 pigs and 300 loaves of bread. The following day, the animals, which symbolised Ulrich and the 12 Friulian canons who had accompanied him, were formally condemned to death before being chased around the Piazzetta and decapitated there, in front of the Doge's Palace where public executions generally took place. By 1420, when the temporal domain of Aquileia was abolished, the spectacle had become so popular that the government found it necessary to continue it with animals provided from the public purse. Following a decree of 1525, the 12 pigs were spared but the beheading of the bull continued, accompanied by other, more decorous entertainments, until the fall of the Republic in 1797.

The Doge is shown watching from the centre of the loggia of the Doge's Palace (fig. 118). In the middle of the Piazzetta is the tall wooden structure used to launch fireworks, on a stage in front of which a gymnastic feat known as the *Forze d'Ercole* (Force of Hercules) is taking place. This was performed by members of the Castellani and Nicolotti factions, drawn from the parishes of San Pietro di Castello and San Nicolò dei Mendicoli, who competed to form pyramids. The wires running down from the Campanile were used in another spectacular element of the festivities, the *Volo dell'Angelo* (Flight of the Angel) or *Svolo del Turco* (Flight of the Turk), so named because in the sixteenth century Turkish daredevils were employed to perform it. In this a youth descended on a wire from the top of the Campanile to present the Doge with a bunch of flowers and complimentary verses. After being recompensed with a purse of money, he would then retrace his path back up the Campanile. Often there was more than one acrobat, the *Gazzetta Veneta* of 16 February 1760 recording that in that year there were no fewer than four.[1]

The painting has consistently been described as a studio work. Sir Francis Watson considered it 'perhaps partly by the artist himself, and painted at the very end of his life. Based on one of the twelve engravings made by G.B. Brustolon, after drawings by Canaletto, of the *Feste dogali*'.[2] W.G. Constable raised the possibility that the painting preceded the drawing but still considered it 'of a period after Canaletto's return from England'. It certainly shares compositional similarities, as well as some details, with the drawing by Canaletto of the mid-1760s now in the National Gallery of Art, Washington, for one of a series of etchings of *Feste Ducali* by Giovanni Battista Brustolon (fig. 119).[3] There is, however, no reason whatsoever to see it as of distinctly later date than the other five components of the group of paintings commissioned by Baron Conway. The absence from the balustrade of the Loggetta (at lower right) of Antonio Gai's gates installed in 1742 provides a probable latest date. The coats of arms on the *macchina*

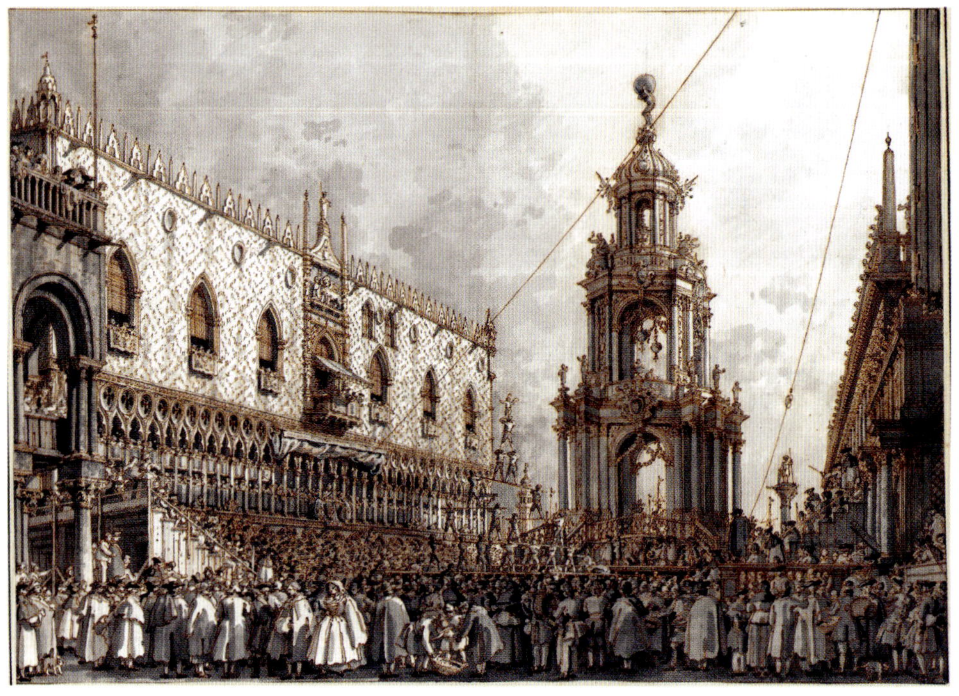

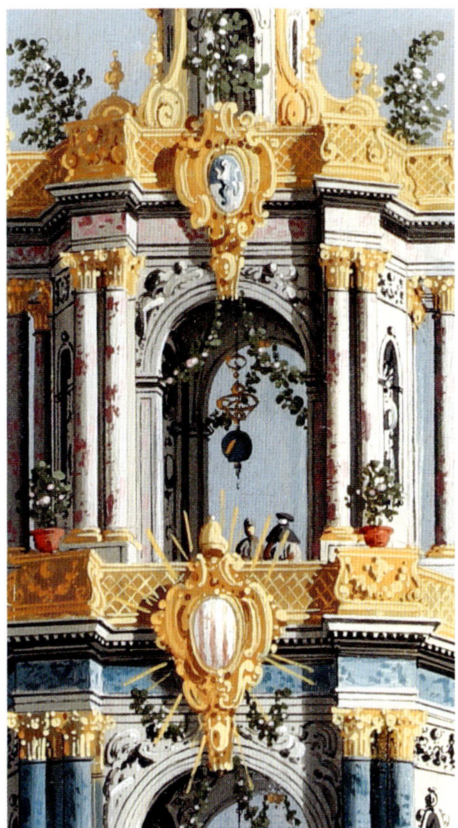

Fig. 120. Detail of cat. 10

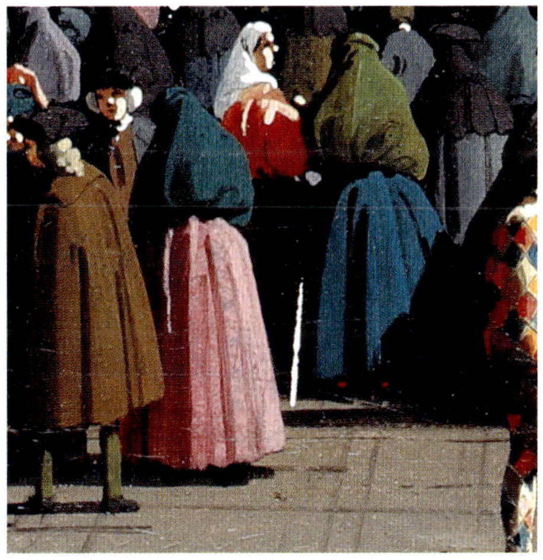

Fig. 121. Detail of cat. 10

happen to be those of the families who both provided doges in office in 1741 (fig. 120). The larger, lower one is of the Grimani family and Pietro Grimani (1677–1752) was Doge from 30 June 1741. The upper is of the Pisani family and Alvise Pisani (1664–17 June 1741) was Grimani's immediate predecessor. This may be coincidental, but the arms of Alvise Pisani also feature on the *Regatta* (cat. 9) for which this painting was presumably intended as an uncomfortable pendant.

The painting is intimately connected to the work of Canaletto in every way except execution, to which the artist does not seem to have contributed. His distinctive touch does not seem evident and there are some weaknesses that one would not expect in the work of Canaletto himself, but it is a painting of considerable quality. In this it is without parallel in the output of Canaletto's studio and it is the only studio painting illustrated in colour in J.G. Links's monograph of 1982, which is the best introduction to the artist's work in the English language. The way that an accidental drip of paint has been left on the canvas, in the foreground to the right of centre, is also highly unusual (fig. 121).

An eighteenth-century drawing of a vestibule in a country villa decorated with Venetian views includes one of similar composition (and size) to this, but showing the whole width of the Campanile and the *Volo dell'Angelo* in progress.[4]

PROVENANCE
Francis Seymour-Conway, 2nd Baron Conway, later 1st Earl and 1st Marquess of Hertford (1719–1794), by whom presumably commissioned in Venice in *c.*1739.

EXHIBITION
1872–75: 'Paintings, Porcelain, Bronzes, Decorative Furniture and other Works of Art lent by Sir Richard Wallace to the Bethnal Green Branch of the South Kensington Museum', no. 283.

RELATED WORKS
Canaletto, *The Festival of Giovedì Grasso in the Piazzetta, c.*1765/66, pen and brown ink with grey wash over traces of graphite, tip of the brush with black wash, heightened with touches of white gouache, 38.7 × 55.5 cm, National Gallery of Art, Washington, DC (inv. 2007.111.55) (C635)

Giovanni Battista Brustolon, *The Festival of Giovedì Grasso in the Piazzetta, c.*1770, etching

Derivations from Brustolon's etching include one by Francesco Guardi in the Musée du Louvre, Paris (Morassi 249), part of a complete set of the *Feste dogali*.[5]

TECHNICAL NOTES
The Hamilton Kerr Institute produced a technical report on the painting in 2019–20 during its cleaning, from which much of the following information derives. The support is fine plain-weave canvas, glue-paste lined, with cusping on all four sides. The ground consists of a dark red layer covered by two applications of a beige layer wet-in-wet. The artist began by laying-in the pale blue of the sky and the grey of the Piazzetta pavement. Then he painted the general outlines of the buildings along the horizons, blocking in the architecture using beige, pink and brown paint. Finally, the figures, for which no reserves had been left, were painted over the finished architecture. There are no obvious signs of underdrawing or *pentimenti* and there is some use of ruled incisions into the wet paint for architectural lines, all characteristics of Canaletto's painting practice. Much of the cloud is represented by leaving the off-white ground visible, with the highlights applied in pure lead white.

X-radiography reveals a diagonal line roughly bisecting the area of sky above the Libreria on the right. There is also an unexplained area of paint under the sky along the upper edge, to the left of the central *macchina*. Both of these details might suggest that the painting was originally started the other way up.

LITERATURE
Constable 1962, C330(VII.1) and C636(b)
Watson 1968, p. 53
Links 1982, pls 2, 4
Ingamells 1985, pp. 244–46
Duffy and Hedley 2004, p. 68, illustrated

CB

11.   BERNARDO BELLOTTO

(Venice 1722–1780 Warsaw)

*The Grand Canal, Looking East, with
the Church of San Simeone Piccolo*

*c.*1737
oil on canvas
96.4 × 148 cm
P498

The stretcher is stamped 'W. MORRILL / LINER'.
(William Morrill, London, 1838–1910).

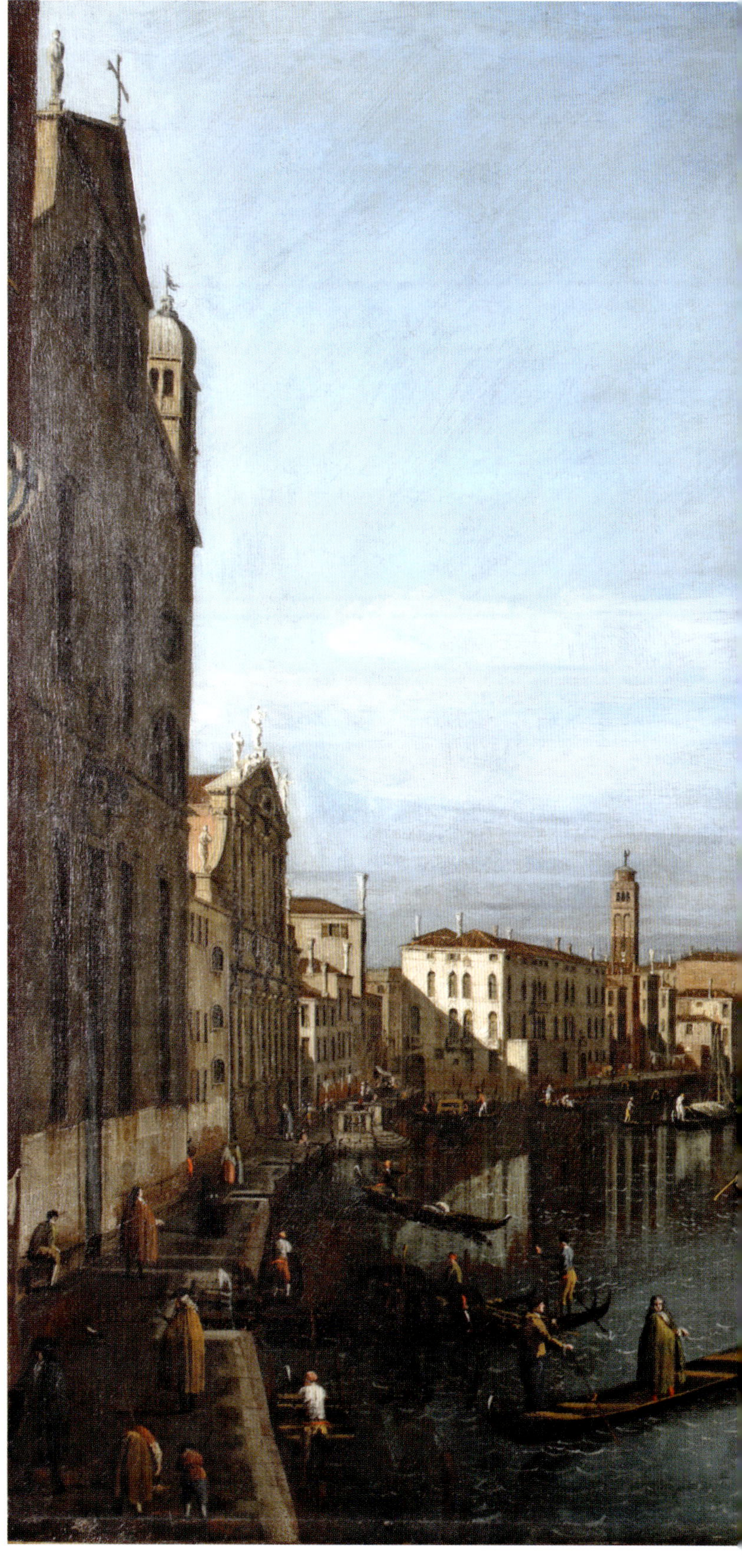

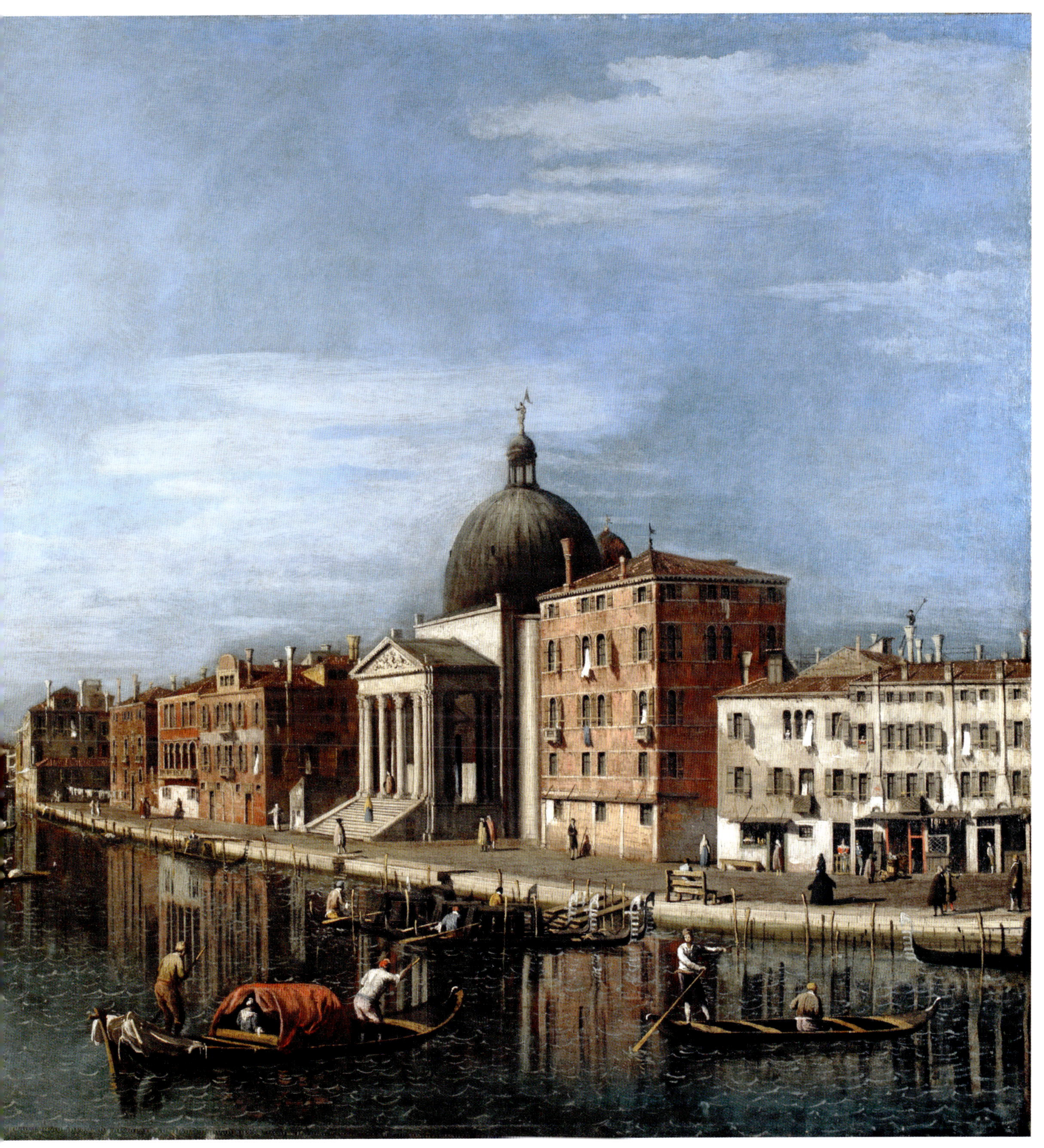

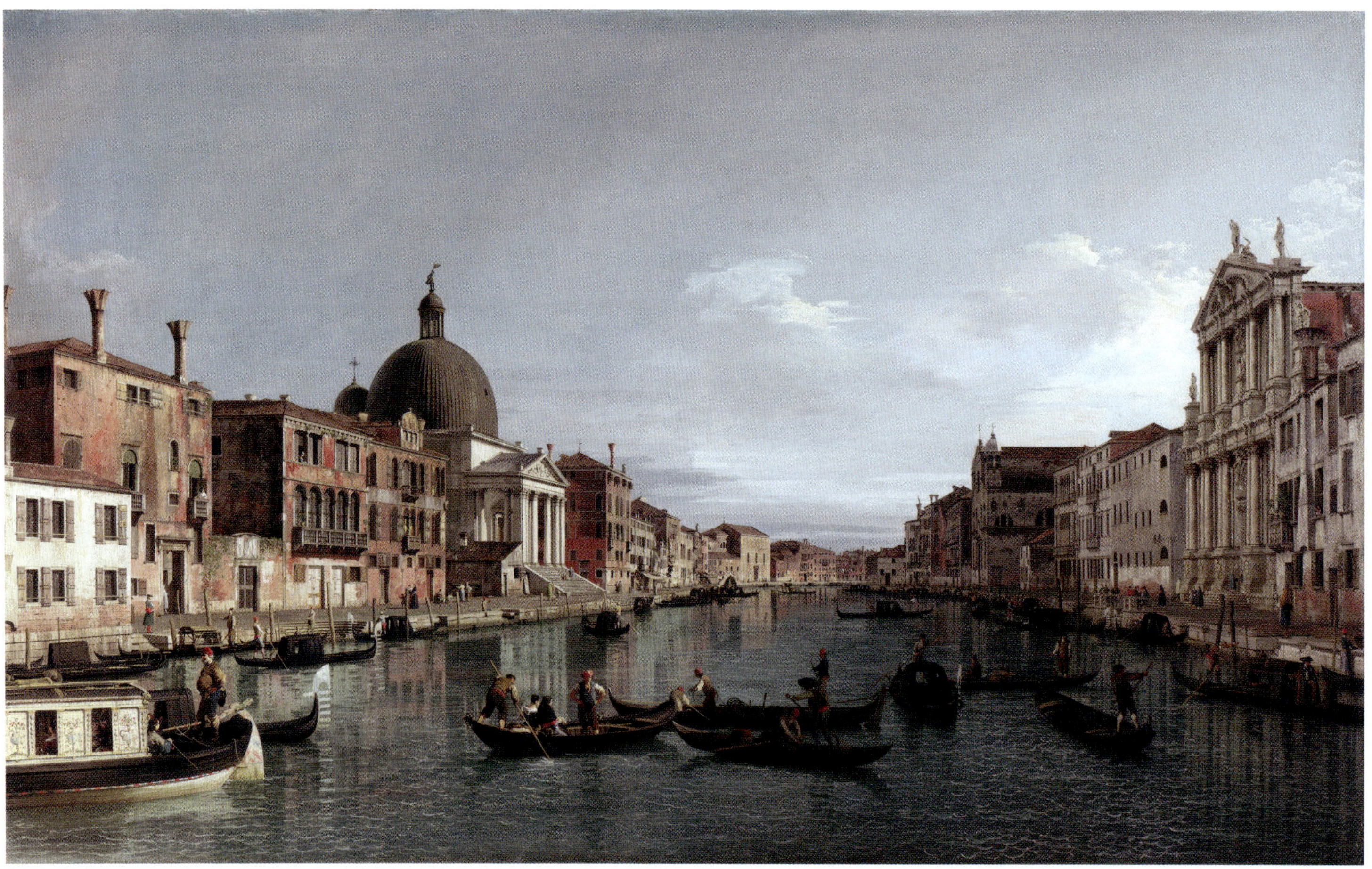

Fig. 122. Canaletto (1697–1768), *The Grand Canal with San Simeone Piccolo and the Scalzi*, *c.*1740, oil on canvas, 124.5 × 204.6 cm, National Gallery, London (NG163)

The composition of this imposing painting is unique and highly original, showing the view in the opposite direction to the very large canvas of *c.*1740 in the National Gallery, London, which is of one of Canaletto's greatest masterpieces (fig. 122).[1] It is taken from outside the church of Santa Lucia, its distinctive façade with a thermal window flanked by two *campanili* on the far left. The church was celebrated for housing, from 1280, the body of Saint Lucy, but was demolished in 1860 to make way for the Venice railway station named after it. The church of San Simeone Piccolo on the other side of the Grand Canal was consecrated in 1738 and both paintings include the shed against the east side of the flight of steps up to the church that was used by the builders. It is possible,

and indeed seems very probable, however, that this painting predates Canaletto's by several years, as the exterior of the church was already mostly complete ten years earlier, which a painting by Canaletto in the Royal Collection demonstrates.[2]

It might be felt that the idea and ambition shown by the composition are not matched by the execution, the differences in scale among the foreground figures being quite disturbing. The artist's process of working out the composition on the canvas is shown by the *pentimenti*, notably the shift in the line of the quay at lower left (fig. 123) and in the outline of the dome of the church of San Simeone Piccolo, and the quality is in general high. The painting was described by Sir Claude Phillips in 1900 as 'the most authentic of

[Canaletto's] art in the Wallace Collection', but its attribution has long presented a puzzle.[3] The quality led Lionello Puppi to revive the idea that it might be, at least in part, from the hand of Canaletto himself, despite its pronounced divergence from Canaletto's manner at this date. Samuel J. Camp was surely heading in the right direction when he wrote: 'By a painter of whom other examples are known. Characteristic are the uncertain architectural drawing and the horizontal brushwork in the sky; the dramatic emphasis and blackish shadows are similar to those in the later work of Bellotto.'[4] The painting does indeed display many of the characteristics of the work of Canaletto's nephew, and Bożena Anna Kowalczyk proposed it in 1996 as his work.[5] At the same time, she was also the first

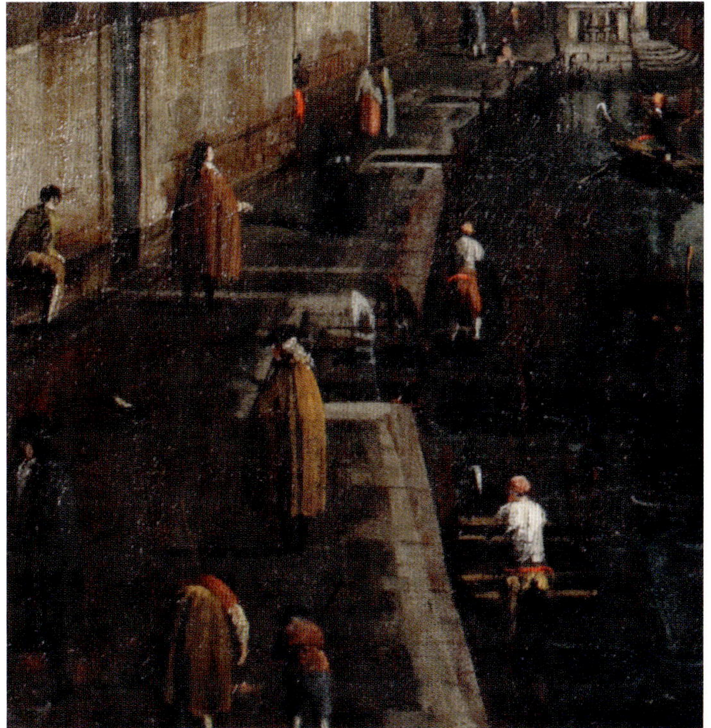

Fig. 123. Detail of cat. 11

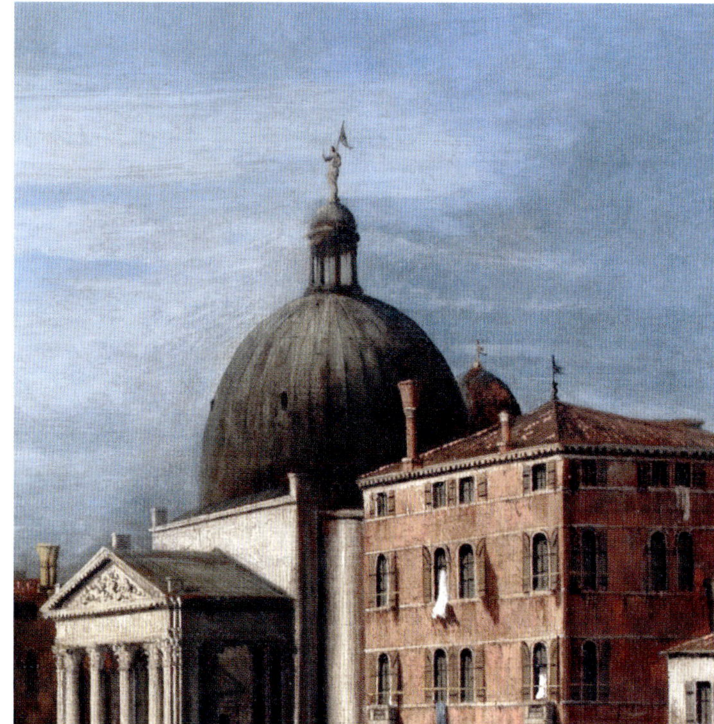

Fig. 124. Detail of cat. 11

to give serious consideration to Bellotto being the author of a larger *Bacino di San Marco from the Canale della Giudecca* then at Parham House, West Sussex. After extensive discussion she came to the conclusion that the Parham painting is less convincingly the work of Bellotto than the Wallace painting. Both pictures were obscured by old varnish, which has since been removed, and the Parham painting has turned out to be unquestionably from Bellotto's hand.[6] Jo Hedley argued against the attribution of the Wallace painting to Bellotto, finding all of its qualities uncharacteristic of Bellotto's style.[7] She does, however, agree with Kowalczyk in seeing reminiscences of the work of Bernardo Canal (1673–1744), Bellotto's grandfather. In fact, the curious discrepancy between the advanced composition and confident rendering of the buildings and the crudeness of the larger figures should be seen as exactly what one would expect of a very young Bellotto, at an age of no more than 16, and the painting may be considered a new stage in the development of the best-trained and most precocious of view painters.

PROVENANCE

Pryse Loveden Pryse, MP (1774–1849), Buscot Park; his sale, Christie's, London, 12 March 1859, lot 172, as 'Canaletti … A very important and capital work, in a very pure state' (262 guineas to Richard Seymour-Conway, 4th Marquess of Hertford).

EXHIBITION

1872–75: 'Paintings, Porcelain, Bronzes, Decorative Furniture and other Works of Art lent by Sir Richard Wallace to the Bethnal Green Branch of the South Kensington Museum', no. 267, as Canaletto.

RELATED WORKS

Views of the Grand Canal at San Simeone Piccolo from the same direction, of much smaller size, are known by members of the first generation of Venetian view painters, Johann Richter (1665–1745) and Bernardo Canal (1673–1744), father of Canaletto and grandfather of Bellotto.

TECHNICAL NOTES

The painting is on a medium-weight plain-weave canvas. The surface is rubbed, so that the russet ground is more evident than it should be, as are a number of *pentimenti*. The technique is entirely consistent with that learnt by Bellotto in Canaletto's studio, not least the sky, which is painted in Prussian blue and applied in diagonals descending towards the left, before the addition of the buildings. The figures and boats were painted last.

LITERATURE

Camp 1928, p. 48, as School of Canaletto
Constable 1962, C261, as School of Canaletto
Puppi 1968, no. 169, illustrated
Watson 1968, pp. 343–44, as Venetian School, XVIIIth Century
Ingamells 1979, p. 257, as Venetian School, 18th century
Ingamells 1985, pp. 256–57, as Manner of Canaletto
Kowalczyk 1996A, pp. 75–76, figs 5–6, as Bernardo Bellotto
Kowalczyk 1996B no. 2, illustrated
Links 1998, p. ix
Bomford and Finaldi 1998, p. 23, fig. 19, as Venetian School, eighteenth century
Hedley 2002, pp. 5, 7, figs 1, 3, 6–7, as Follower of Canaletto
Duffy and Hedley 2004, p. 69, as Follower of Canaletto
Beddington 2014, under no. 2, note 14

CB

 ANTONIO VISENTINI
(Venice 1688–1782)

*The Grand Canal from the Palazzi Foscari
and Moro-Lin to Santa Maria della Carità*

c.1750s
oil on canvas
47 × 78.5 cm
P492

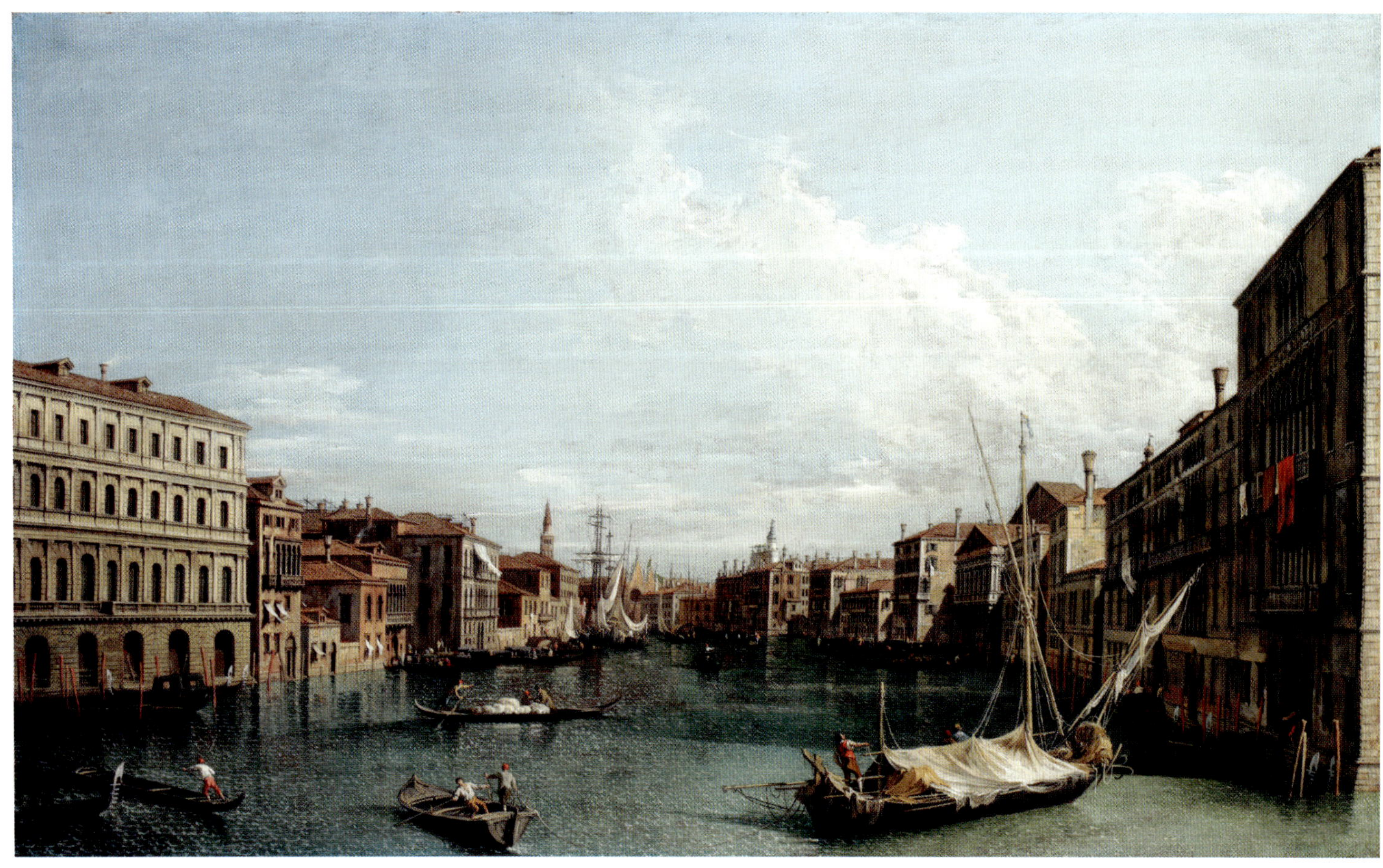

13. ANTONIO VISENTINI
(Venice 1688–1782)

The Entrance to the Grand Canal, Looking East, with the Church of Santa Maria della Salute

*c.*1750s
oil on canvas
47 × 78.3 cm
P495

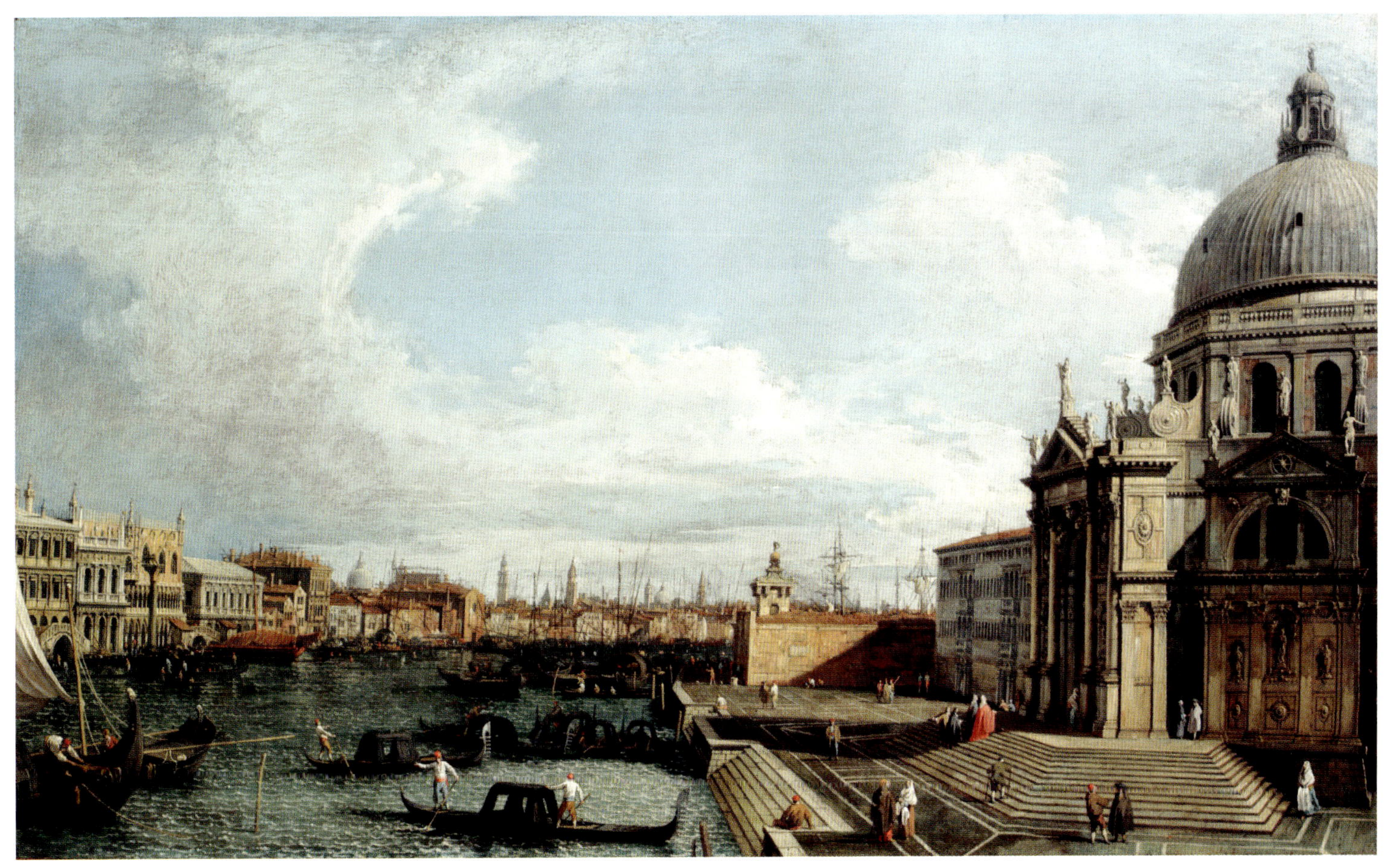

14. ANTONIO VISENTINI

(Venice 1688–1782)

The Grand Canal from the Campo San Vio

c.1750s
oil on canvas
47 × 78.5 cm
P512

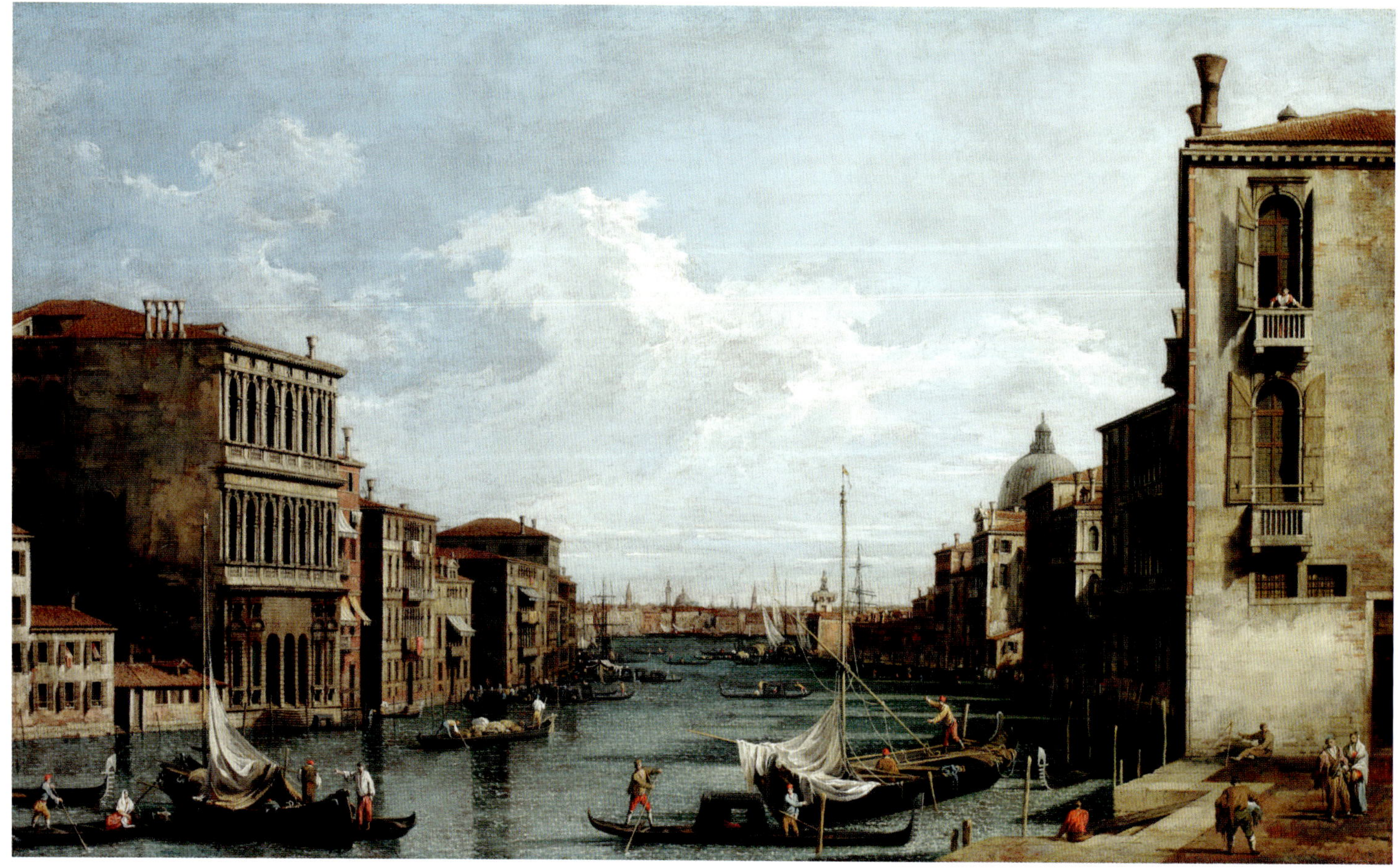

15. ANTONIO VISENTINI

(Venice 1688–1782)

The Dogana and Santa Maria della Salute from the Molo

c.1750s
oil on canvas
48.5 × 79.5 cm
P515

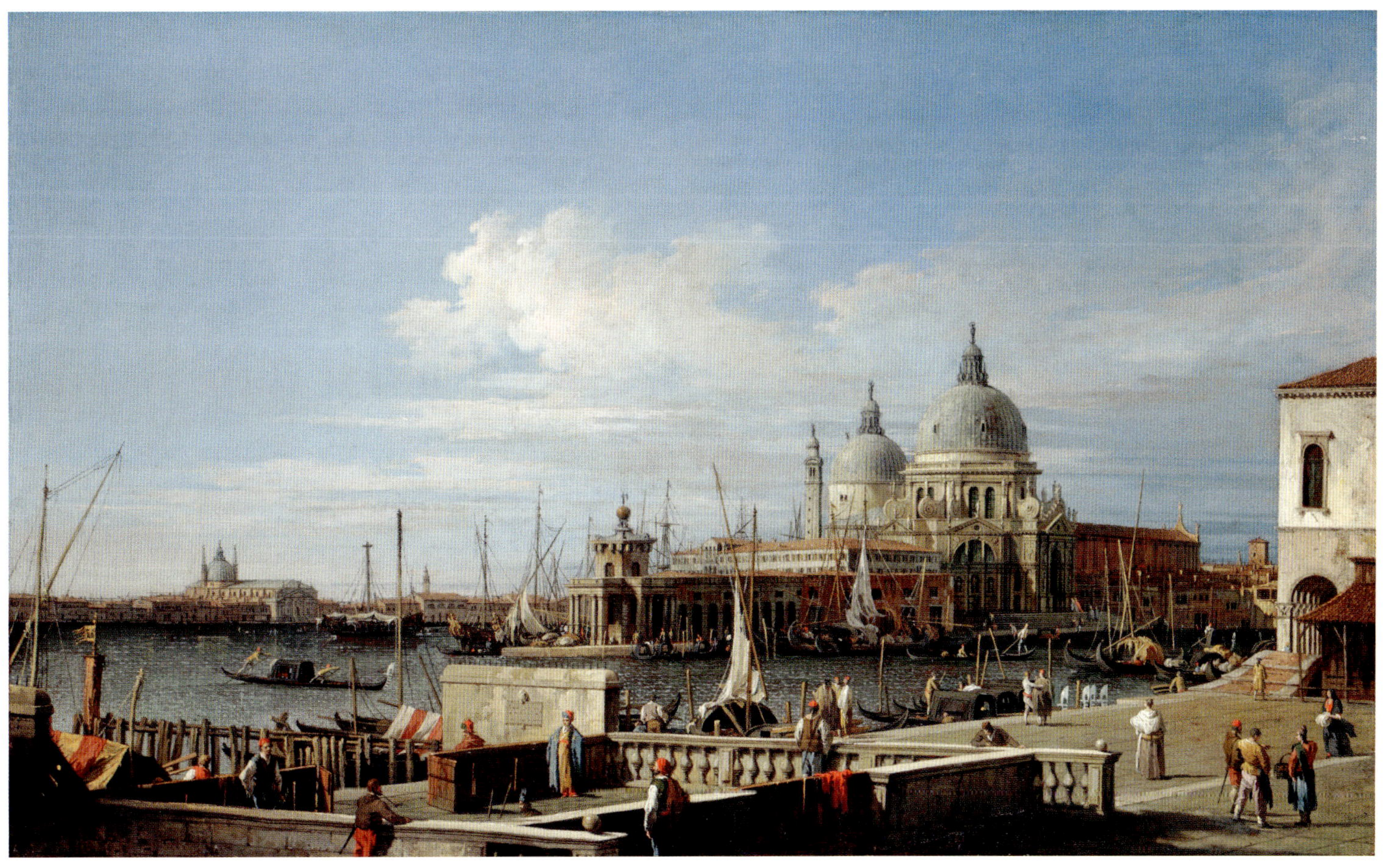

Although these paintings might seem at first glance to be a set of four, they are unquestionably two pairs, as the second pair was sold on its own in 1848. The first pair was framed by William and Philip Evans in 1859.[1] They were already recognised as by the same hand by Samuel J. Camp in 1928.[2] All are based on paintings by Canaletto in the Royal Collection that were acquired by King George III with most of the collection of Canaletto's agent Joseph Smith in 1762. Three follow the prototypes closely, including in size and colouring, the first two corresponding with components of the series of Grand Canal views, engravings of which by Antonio Visentini were published in 1735, the fourth with a separate painting of the early 1730s.[3] *The Grand Canal from the Campo San Vio* (cat. 14) differs, however, having four figures that do not feature in the prototype.[4] In the lower left corner the *sandolo* carries a seated woman with a basket not present in Canaletto's painting, and it is steered by a different gondolier. The gondolier towards the bow of the gondola in the centre foreground and the man in blue trousers bending over at the bow of the barge carrying bales in the middle distance are also absent from the prototype.

Eighteen other copies of Canaletto paintings by the same hand have been identified by the present writer, including closely corresponding versions of *The Entrance to the Grand Canal, Looking East, with the Church of Santa Maria della Salute* (cat. 13) at Uppark and in the collection of the Banca Intesa Sanpaolo, Cassa di Risparmio di Venezia, currently on long-term loan to the Fondazione Querini Stampalia.[5] *The Dogana and Santa Maria della Salute from the Molo* (cat. 15) is one of only two views by this painter that do not follow components of the Grand Canal series. Their author is unique among Canaletto copyists in only copying paintings retained by Smith in his personal collection and in clearly having access to those several decades after they were painted, when he updated the topography. He was also unusual in having no qualms about occasionally 'improving' the compositions by adding figures and boats. He has recently been identified by the present writer as Antonio Visentini, who was already known to have served Smith as etcher, architect, draughtsman and painter of *capricci*.

During the recent cleaning by the Hamilton Kerr Institute it was noted that while the first three paintings have a red ground throughout, that of *The Dogana and Santa Maria della Salute from the Molo* (cat. 15) is more complex, including an intermediary buff layer below the sky, making it appear a deeper and slightly cooler blue. Cleaning has, if anything, enhanced the quality of cat. 15, which was classified by W.G. Constable as 'Studio' of Canaletto, while the other three Wallace Collection paintings were called 'School'.

PROVENANCE

Acquired by Richard Seymour-Conway, 4th Marquess of Hertford (1800–1870), before 1859.

EXHIBITION

1872–75: 'Paintings, Porcelain, Bronzes, Decorative Furniture and other Works of Art lent by Sir Richard Wallace to the Bethnal Green Branch of the South Kensington Museum', no. 287 or 311 and no. 315.

LITERATURE

Camp 1928, pp. 46–47
Fritsche 1936, p. 108, no. VG38 (cat. 12)
Constable 1962, C203(a) and C170(c)1, as School versions
Watson 1968, pp. 50–51
Kozakiewicz 1972, vol. 2, pp. 419–20, and pp. 429 and 422, nos Z 166 and Z 139
Camesasca 1974, nos 273A and 276C
Ingamells 1985, pp. 248–50, 432
Duffy and Hedley 2004, p. 70, as After Canaletto
Beddington 2022, pp. 66–67, 85–86, nos 13–14, figs 4–5

CAT. 14 AND CAT. 15

PROVENANCE

Casimir Périer (1811–1876); Christie's, London, 5 May 1848, lot 24 (110 guineas to Richard Seymour-Conway, 4th Marquess of Hertford, 1800–1870) and lot 25 (156 guineas to Grisell).[6]

EXHIBITIONS

1872–75: 'Paintings, Porcelain, Bronzes, Decorative Furniture and other Works of Art lent by Sir Richard Wallace to the Bethnal Green Branch of the South Kensington Museum', no. 287 or 311 and no. 288.

LITERATURE

Camp 1928, p. 46. (cat. 14); p. 47 (cat. 15)
Constable 1962, C184(a), as a School version, and C153(a), as a Studio version
Watson 1968, pp. 56–57
Kozakiewicz 1972, vol. 2, pp. 428 and 419–20, nos Z 150 and Z 2112
Ingamells 1985, pp. 252, 255–56
Duffy and Hedley 2004, p. 71, as After Canaletto
Beddington 2022, pp. 66–67, 85–86, nos 15–16, figs 6–7

RELATED WORKS

To cat. 12:

Canaletto, *The Grand Canal from the Palazzi Foscari and Moro-Lin to Santa Maria della Carità*, c.1726/27, oil on canvas, 49.9 × 80.3 cm, Royal Collection (RCIN 401404) (C203; Razzall and Whitaker 65)

To cat. 13:

Canaletto, *The Entrance to the Grand Canal, Looking East, with the Church of Santa Maria della Salute*, c.1729/30, oil on canvas, 47.6 × 80 cm, Royal Collection (RCIN 400520) (C170; Razzall and Whitaker 68)

Antonio Visentini, *The Entrance to the Grand Canal, Looking East, with the Church of Santa Maria della Salute*, c.1752/53, oil on canvas, 47 × 78.7 cm, Private Collection, Uppark House, West Sussex (Beddington 2022, no. 6)

Antonio Visentini, *The Entrance to the Grand Canal, Looking East, with the Church of Santa Maria della Salute*, after 1742, oil on canvas, 47 × 77.4 cm, Banca Intesa Sanpaolo, Cassa di Risparmio di Venezia, on long-term loan at the Fondazione Querini Stampalia, Venice (C/L1976, no. 170(b)4; Beddington 2022, no. 12)

Antonio Visentini, *The Entrance to the Grand Canal, Looking East, with the Church of Santa Maria della Salute*, c.1750s, oil on canvas, 80 × 120 cm, Christie's, New York, 31 January 2024, lot 157, as Studio of Canaletto (Beddington 2022, no. 20)

To cat. 14:

Canaletto, *The Grand Canal from the Campo San Vio*, c.1727/28, oil on canvas, 47.8 × 79.5 cm, Royal Collection (RCIN 400518) (C184; Razzall and Whitaker 67)

Antonio Visentini, *The Grand Canal from the Campo San Vio*, c.1752/53, oil on canvas, 47 × 78.7 cm, formerly at Uppark House, West Sussex, destroyed by fire in 1989 (C184(b); Beddington 2022, no. 7)

To cat. 15:

Canaletto, *The Dogana and Santa Maria della Salute from the Molo*, c.1730, oil on canvas, 46.2 × 78.5 cm, Royal Collection (RCIN 400977) (C153)

TECHNICAL NOTES

The Hamilton Kerr Institute produced technical reports on the paintings before cleaning them in 2018, from which much of the following information derives. The paintings are on medium-weight plain-weave canvas, glue-paste lined. Cats 12, 13 and 14 have russet grounds characteristic of eighteenth-century Italian painting, while that of cat. 15 differs notably, having a thin buff-coloured second layer in the sky, resulting in it appearing a deeper and slightly cooler blue. Unsurprisingly, no *pentimenti* are evident. The technique in many ways resembles that of Canaletto: the way of depicting the texture and detail of the walls of the buildings, firstly laying-in broad areas of variegated colour, which were then articulated and defined with thin dark lines of paint around windows, columns and architraves; figures, boats and fine details such as masts and chimneys were added at the final stages; highlights such as the awnings of the larger boats are depicted using the thickness of the paint and impasto brushstrokes to heighten the sense of form and volume. There is no use of incising, however, and the technique differs markedly from Canaletto's in that reserves were left in the sky for the architecture and in the water for the boats, as one might expect of paintings which are to a large degree very careful copies.

CB

16

THE WALLACE MASTER

(active in Venice in the 1730s)

The Molo from the Bacino di San Marco

*c.*1734
oil on canvas
53.8 × 70 cm
P514

With inscriptions 'June 2 / 55' and '54' in chalk on the relining
canvas (the date and lot number from the 1855 sale, see below)
and '678C' painted on the stretcher (Christie's brush number
relating to that sale).

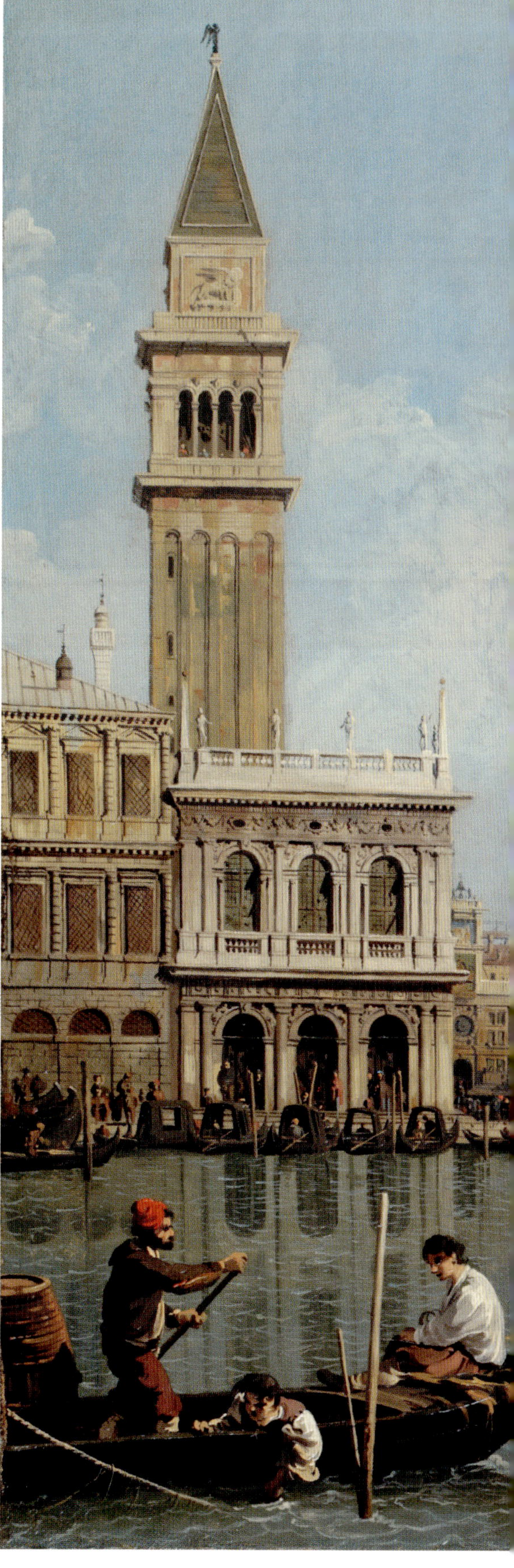

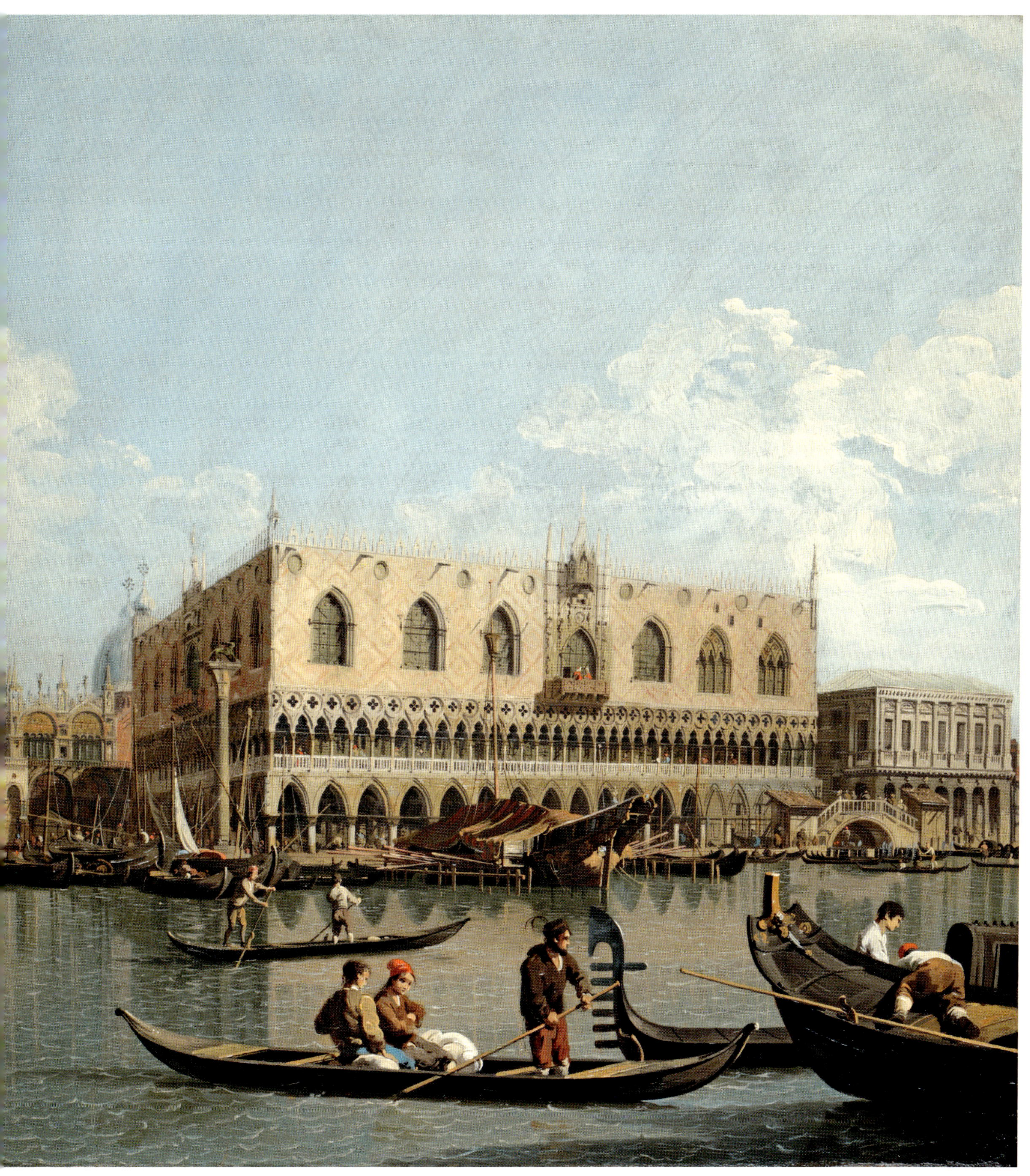

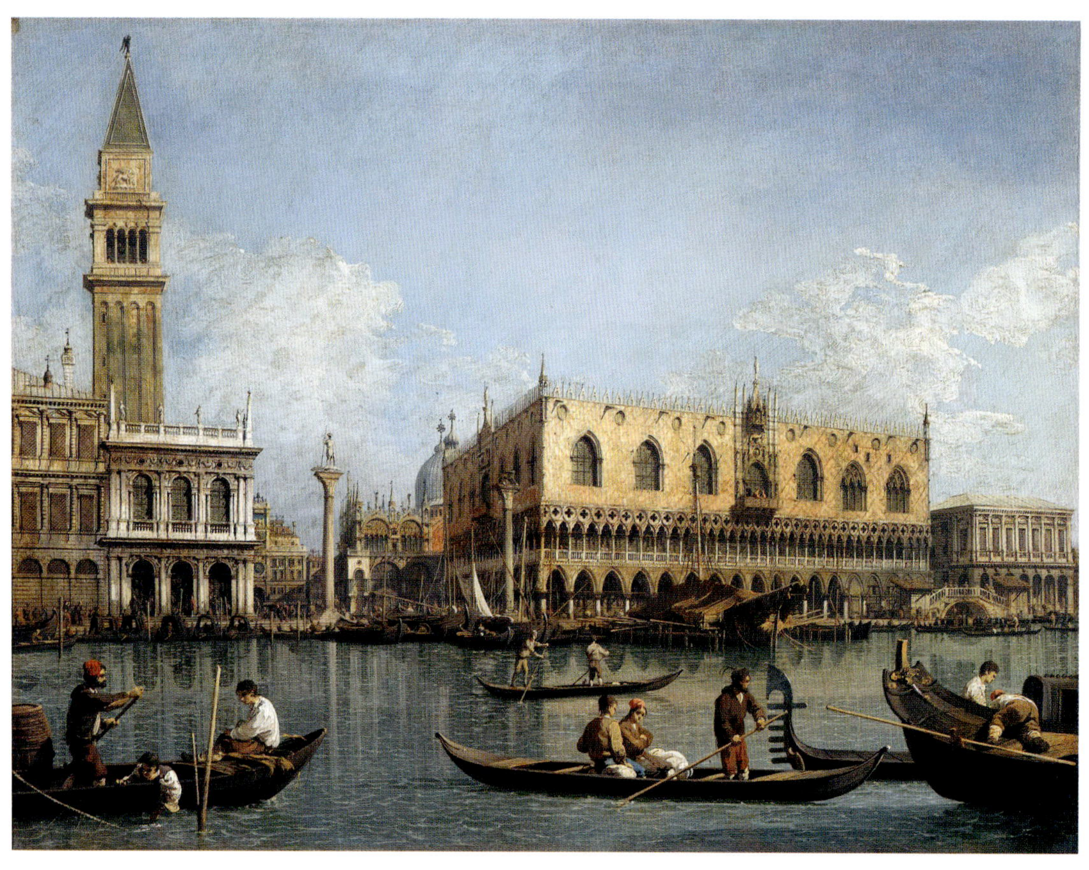

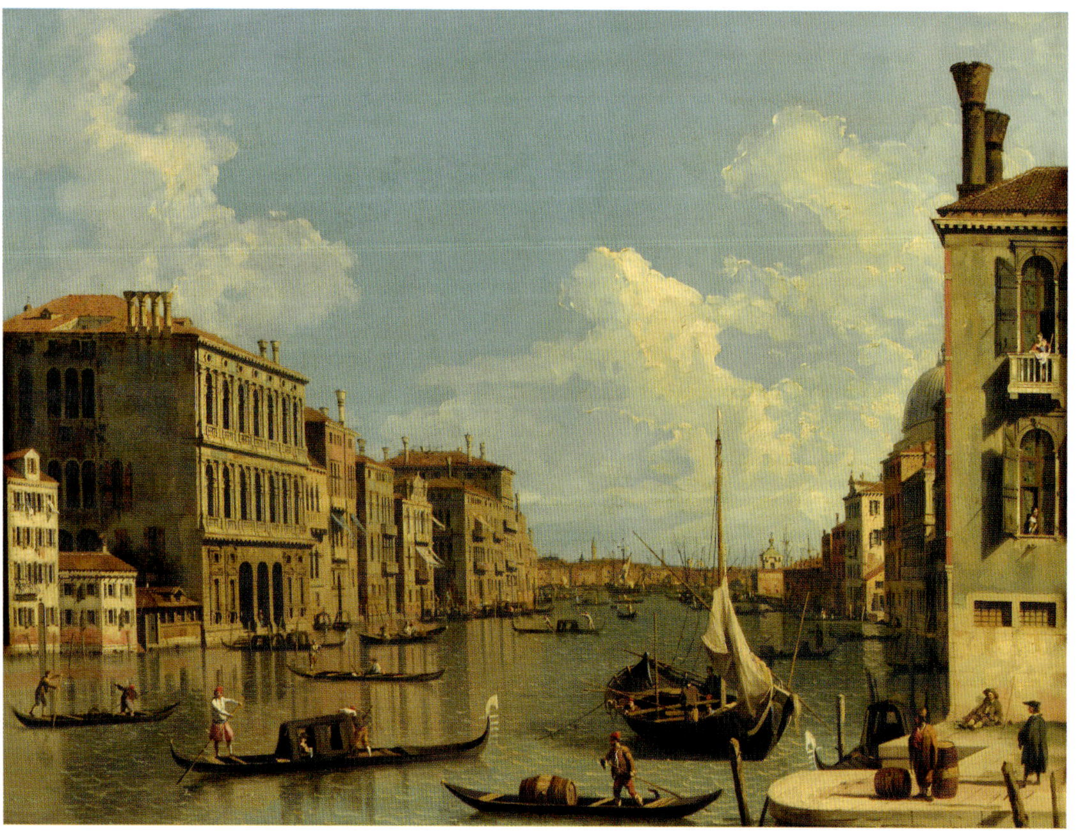

Fig. 125. Canaletto (1697–1768), *The Molo from the Bacino di San Marco*, c.1734, oil on canvas, 53 × 70 cm, Pinacoteca di Brera, Milan (inv. 2236)

Fig. 126. The Wallace Master (active in the 1730s), *The Grand Canal from the Campo San Vio*, early 1730s, oil on canvas, 52.4 × 70.5 cm, Ashmolean Museum, Oxford (inv. WA 2001.183)

Acquired by the 4th Marquess of Hertford in 1855 as 'a beautiful work of the very highest quality' by Canaletto, this painting was catalogued by W.G. Constable as 'a studio repetition, probably in part by Canaletto'.[1] Sir Francis Watson, who, as Director of the Wallace Collection, must have been much more familiar with it, was even less optimistic, describing it as 'from the studio of [Canaletto], possibly with some slight assistance from Canaletto himself'. Since then, it has been correctly seen as a particularly precise copy of a painting by Canaletto of the early 1730s in the Pinacoteca di Brera, Milan (fig. 125).[2] It is of similar size to the prototype and the painter has clearly intended to follow that almost stroke for stroke. Canaletto, an artist who, except on very rare and specific occasions, made every effort to avoid repetition, would never have involved himself in such an exercise. There can be no question, however, that the Wallace Collection painting is coeval with Canaletto's and it must have been executed in Venice before the prototype was shipped off to the patron who had commissioned it. Regrettably, nothing is known of the history of the Brera painting before its sale in London in 1928, but it is highly likely that it and its pendant had been in England from the time they were painted. The Wallace Collection painting is thus surely by an artist working in Venice, very probably for Joseph Smith, Canaletto's dealer, who may have embraced the business opportunity to sell copies as well as originals. It is an open question whether Canaletto would have been aware that copies such as this were being made of his newly finished work.

Watson was convinced that 'two hands at least' were involved in the execution of the Wallace painting, the depiction of the Biblioteca Marciana (Library of San Marco) being, in his opinion, 'markedly superior' to that of the adjacent Zecca (the Mint) on the far left. The handling, however, seems consistent throughout and is highly distinctive in the fluid application of the paint. That fails to emulate Canaletto's rendition of the textures of the various materials, his exceptional ability to differentiate marble, brick, tile, water and cloth. The copyist's colouring is paler than Canaletto's, the water having a green tinge, and he has also fallen short in his attempts to replicate the formula for ripples and in his depictions of reflections. Several other copies after Canaletto certainly by the same hand are known (see, for instance, fig. 126), all datable to the 1730s, and it seems appropriate to call him 'the Wallace Master'.

The view of the Molo from the Bacino di San Marco is arguably the greatest of all the great views of the city, the one that was intended to greet visitors on their arrival. It includes the buildings that formed the civic and religious heart of the city: the Zecca, the Biblioteca Marciana, the Campanile of San Marco, the Basilica of San Marco, the Doge's Palace and the Prisons. The Piazzetta is flanked by the twin columns of Saint Theodore and Saint Mark, symbolising the guardianship of the Eastern and Western churches. Paintings of the view were inevitably in demand and another painting by the Wallace Master of the same composition is in a private collection.[3]

PROVENANCE
Thomas Farrant, Montagu Street, London; his posthumous sale, Christie's, London, 2 June 1855, lot 54 (£104 to Richard Seymour-Conway, 4th Marquess of Hertford, 1800–1870).

EXHIBITION
1872–75: 'Paintings, Porcelain, Bronzes, Decorative Furniture and other Works of Art lent by Sir Richard Wallace to the Bethnal Green Branch of the South Kensington Museum', no. 312.

RELATED WORKS
Canaletto, *The Molo from the Bacino di San Marco*, c.1734, oil on canvas, 53 × 70 cm, Pinacoteca di Brera, Milan (inv. 2236) (C107)

The Wallace Master, *The Molo from the Bacino di San Marco*, c.1734, oil on canvas, 53.4 × 70.8 cm, Private Collection

Canaletto, *The Molo from the Bacino di San Marco on Ascension Day*, c.1733/34, oil on canvas, 76.8 × 125.4 cm, Royal Collection (RCIN 404417) (C335)

TECHNICAL NOTES
The Hamilton Kerr Institute produced a technical report on the painting in 2018 before cleaning it. All the following information derives from that. The painting is on a medium-weight, plain-weave canvas, lined in the mid-nineteenth century.[4] The ground is beige, consisting of lead white mixed with an iron-based red earth pigment, the same colour being applied in two distinct layers. An intermediate layer contains protein, which suggests that a medium such as animal glue may have been used. That would be typical of eighteenth-century English commercial grounds, as would the presence of natural chalk. It is noted, however, that in the absence of the original tacking margins it is difficult to ascertain whether the ground preparation is commercial or not, and the use of natural chalk is by no means exclusive to northern Europe. Furthermore, the technique – the use of incised lines, most notably in the façade of the Doge's Palace; the order of painting (the sky and water followed by the horizon line and the architectural features, and finally the figures and the finer details of the architecture); and the majority of the execution being in broad wet-in-wet brushstrokes, with the finer details applied with a smaller brush on top of dry paint – suggests that the copyist had a relatively thorough understanding of Canaletto's painting practice, perhaps within a workshop context or through direct access to the original painting. The pigments used are consistent with other works by Canaletto and contemporary Venetian artists of the period, with one notable difference, that the expensive vivid green earth pigment used in the Canaletto prototype (in the water) is not present here.

LITERATURE
Watson 1949, p. 14, note 61
Constable 1962, C107(a)
Watson 1968, p. 56
Ingamells 1985, pp. 254–55, as After Canaletto.
Duffy and Hedley 2004, p. 71, as After Canaletto

CB

FRANCESCO TIRONI

(active in Venice in the last quarter of the eighteenth century)

The Bacino di San Marco on Ascension Day with the Bucintoro Departing for the Lido

after *c*.1770
oil on canvas
52.8 × 81.3 cm
P513

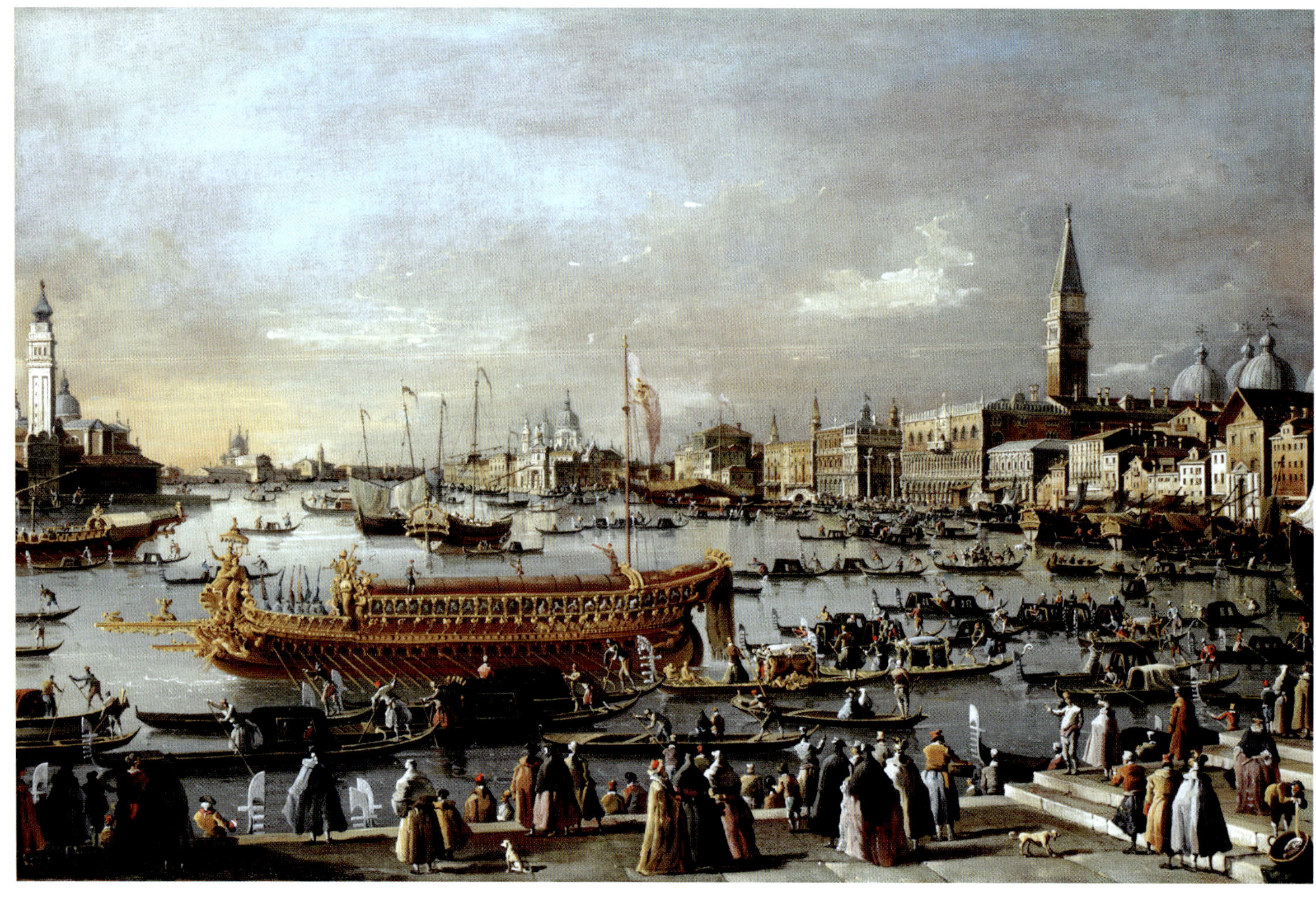

The Feast of the Ascension of Christ (the *Festa della Sensa*), celebrated on the 40th day after Easter, was the greatest of Venetian annual festivals, the only occasion when the ceremonial state galley, the *Bucintoro*, was brought out of the Arsenal. After a Mass celebrated by the Doge's chaplain in the Cappella di Collegio, the Doge and the Signoria embarked on it at the Molo. From there, they were transported to the Porto di Lido, where, with grandees of the Republic, foreign envoys and other onlookers, the Doge cast a golden ring into the sea in a symbolic marriage of the city with its greatest asset.

The procession by sea to the Porto di Lido originated in the year 1000 as an annual celebration of the triumph of the great Doge Pietro Orseolo over the Slav pirates of the Dalmatian coast. Ascension Day was chosen as it was the day on which the fleet had set sail from Venice. According to Venetian tradition, the ceremony of the Marriage with the Sea evolved when Pope Alexander III presented a ring to Doge Sebastiano Ziani in 1177, at the time of the Treaty of Venice between the Pope and Frederick I Barbarossa, the Holy Roman Emperor.

In the first quarter of the eighteenth century the *Bucintoro* first employed in 1606, and thought to be the third, was still in use. That shown here, which was to prove the last, was constructed to the designs of Michele Stefano Conti and inaugurated in 1729; certainly the most magnificent, it was described by the English visitor Richard Pococke in 1734 as 'without doubt ... the finest ship in the world'.[1] The Doge's throne and seats for the Signoria and other dignitaries were on the upper deck, with the 168 oarsmen, 4 on each of the 42 oars, out of sight on the lower deck, an arrangement that could be taken to reflect the pyramidal structure of Venetian government.

Already in 1702 the Marriage with the Sea ceremony had to be put off because of a French fleet operating in the Adriatic against the Austrians, an event that arguably 'symbolised the end of Venetian pretensions to control the operations of foreign warships in the Adriatic'.[2] That became increasingly true as the century progressed, and in 1781 John Moore could

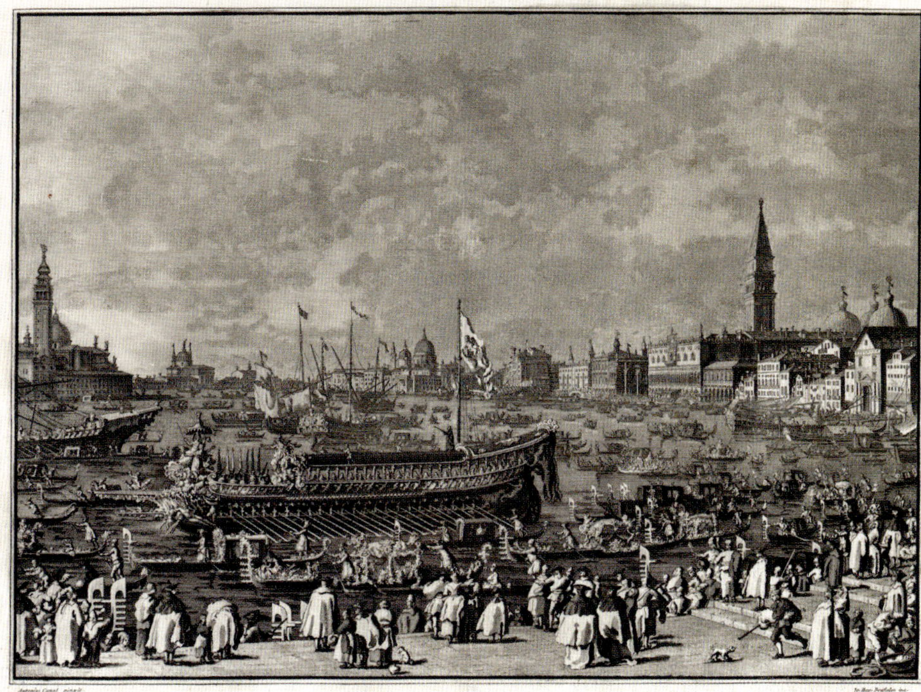

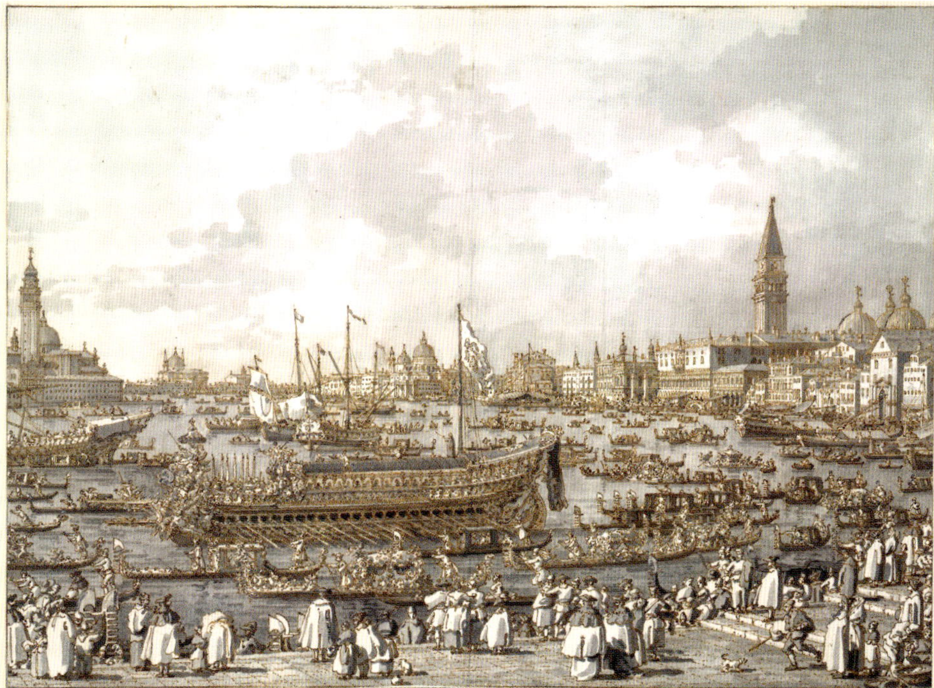

ABOVE:

Fig. 127. Giovanni Battista Brustolon (1712–1796) after Canaletto (1697–1768), *The Doge in the Bucintoro Departing for the Porto di Lido on Ascension Day*, c.1766, etching, 45.1 × 56.9 cm, plate 5 from *Le Feste Ducali*

BELOW:

Fig. 128. Canaletto (1697–1768), *The Doge Departing for the Lido in the Bucintoro on Ascension Day*, 1763–66, drawing, 39 × 55 cm, British Museum, London (inv. 1910,0212.19)

observe that 'the time has been, when the Doge had entire possession of, and dominion over, his spouse; but, for a considerable time past her favours have been shared by several other lovers'.[3] The *Festa della Sensa*, however, remained to the end an event of unrivalled splendour, and one that all gentlemen in Italy on the Grand Tour made every effort to attend. The ceremony perished, at least as a major public spectacle, along with the Republic itself, with the Napoleonic occupation in 1797, as did also the *Bucintoro*, which was burned by the French: a symbolic gesture but carried out only after removal of the gilding, said to have taken 400 mules to carry.

The composition is based on the fifth of a series of 12 etchings of *Feste Ducali* by Giovanni Battista Brustolon (fig. 127), after a drawing by Canaletto of the mid-1760s (fig. 128).[4] Unlike most of the numerous paintings based on the print, including that by Francesco Guardi in the collection of the Musée du Louvre, Paris, this varies widely. Sir Francis Watson astutely observed that its author is 'some independent Venetian view-painter',[5] and indeed the style is typical of that of Francesco Tironi. Surprisingly little is known about the painter's life; in fact, all that we know for certain is that in 1806 he had 'died too young a few years ago'.[6] Work by Tironi is rather more abundant. A set of engravings by Antonio Sandi (1733–1817) entitled *Twenty-Four Views of Islands in the Venetian Lagoon*, published by Ludovico Furlanetto in Venice at some point after 1779, follows drawings by Tironi, many of which survive and are his best-known works.[7] Of very fine quality, and a number of them formerly thought to be by Canaletto, many of these are now in the great drawings collections of the world: the Albertina, Vienna (6), the Robert Lehman Collection in the Metropolitan Museum of Art, New York (2),[8] the Whitworth Art Gallery, Manchester,[9] and the National Gallery of Art, Washington, DC. One is in the Former Collection of Franz Koenigs,[10] and six others are in private collections.[11] These have permitted the secure attribution of other drawings executed in the same distinctive and delicate style, similarly of compositions of the artist's own invention. Examples are in the Victoria and Albert Museum, London (6),[12] the Pierpont Morgan Library, New York (2),[13] the National Gallery of Art, Washington, and elsewhere (fig. 129).[14]

Attributions of paintings have in the past proved more complicated, Hermann Voss crediting Tironi in publications of 1928 and 1966 with some of the early views by Francesco Guardi,[15] while in more recent decades he has sometimes been identified as the author of work by the rather older 'Master of the Langmatt Foundation Views'.[16] A number of canvases signed with the initials 'F T' are now known, including *San Cristoforo, San Michele and Murano from the Sacca della*

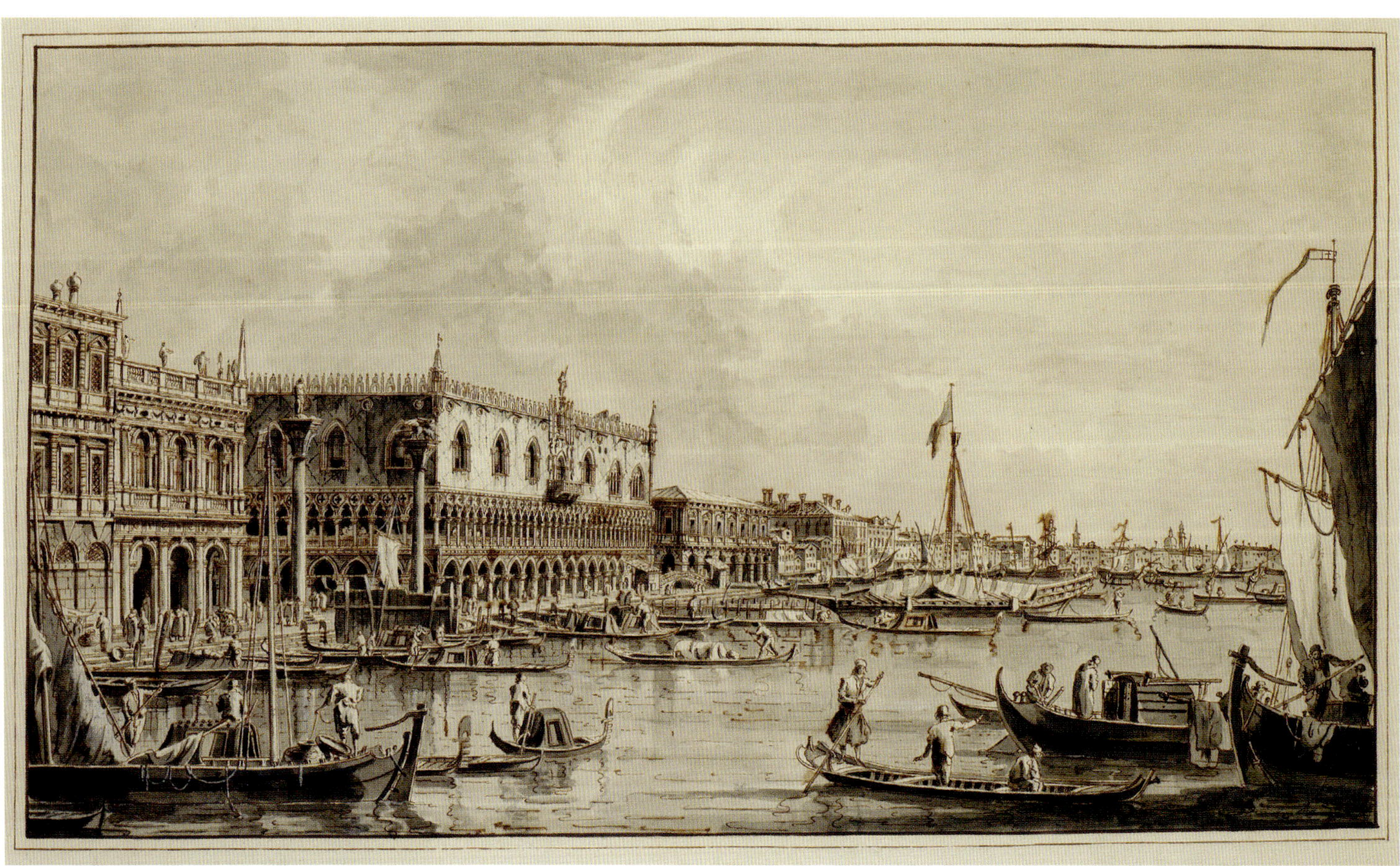

Misericordia (Staatliche Kunsthalle, Karlsruhe) and a pair showing *The Isola di San Giorgio Maggiore* and *The Molo Looking West*, which are both signed with initials,[17] and correspond precisely with descriptions of a pair offered for sale in Venice in 1785, the earliest known reference to paintings by Tironi.[18]

From the secure works a considerable group of paintings in the same distinctive style can be established, including views of the mainland such as *The Palazzo Recanati-Zucconi-Vendramin on the Brenta Canal*,[19] and a *capriccio* of the Doge's Palace and other prominent Venetian buildings set on a canal.[20] Tironi, as he can now be understood, is an original and interesting figure. While his drawing style and compositional structure recall Canaletto's methods such that it seems probable that he worked in Canaletto's studio, his mannered figures are closer to Francesco Guardi's mature types. His palette, dominated by greens and browns, and sombre often almost to the point of monochromaticity, finds parallels in much of the late work of both painters. While the drawings are mostly of a consistently high quality, the standard of the very large number of paintings in Tironi's style varies widely.

PROVENANCE
With C.J. Nieuwenhuys (1799–1883), from whom purchased by Sir Richard Wallace (1818–1890) in February 1872, as Francesco Guardi.

EXHIBITION
1872–75: 'Paintings, Porcelain, Bronzes, Decorative Furniture and other Works of Art lent by Sir Richard Wallace to the Bethnal Green Branch of the South Kensington Museum', no. 273, as Francesco Guardi.

RELATED WORKS
Canaletto, *The Bacino di San Marco on Ascension Day with the Bucintoro Departing for the Lido*, c.1765/66, pen and brown ink and grey wash, heightened with white, over black chalk, 39 × 55 cm, British Museum, London (inv. 1910,0212.19) (C634)

Giovanni Battista Brustolon after Canaletto, *The Bacino di San Marco on Ascension Day with the Bucintoro Departing for the Lido*, c.1766, etching, 45 × 57 cm, British Museum, London (inv. 1871,0812.3673)

Francesco Guardi, *The Bacino di San Marco on Ascension Day with the Bucintoro Departing for the Lido*, c.1775/80, oil on canvas, 66 × 101 cm, Musée du Louvre, Paris (inv. 20009) (Morassi 247; exhibited Musée Jacquemart-André, Paris, *Canaletto – Guardi, les deux maîtres de Venise*, 2012–13, no. 41)

TECHNICAL NOTES
The Hamilton Kerr Institute produced a technical report on the painting in 2018 before cleaning it, from which much of the following information derives. The support is canvas, with a weave that appears more textured, coarse and open than that of the lining canvas. The ground is a comparatively dark red, applied in two layers, possibly in swift succession. There is no sign of underdrawing, *pentimenti* or incising. Generally, the painting is executed in relatively cheap and widely available earth pigments. From the cross-sections of samples taken, it appears that there are never more than two layers of paint, the first used to block in, the second for detail and contrast shadowing. This has the effect of a high contrast between light and dark.

LITERATURE
Hertford House inventory, 1890, as Francesco Guardi
Constable 1962, C330.V.4(a), and C634(c), as School of Canaletto
Watson 1968, p. 344, as Venetian School, XVIIIth Century
Ingamells 1985, pp. 253–54, as After Canaletto
Duffy and Hedley 2004, p. 71, as After Canaletto

CB

Fig. 129. Francesco Tironi (active in the last quarter of the eighteenth century), *The Molo and the Riva degli Schiavoni, Looking East, from the Bacino di San Marco*, late eighteenth century, pen and ink and grey wash, 27.5 × 49 cm, Private Collection

18. ENGLISH SCHOOL (mid-eighteenth century)

The Piazza San Marco, Looking West from South of the Central Line

*c.*1750?
oil on canvas
58.2 × 126 cm
P505

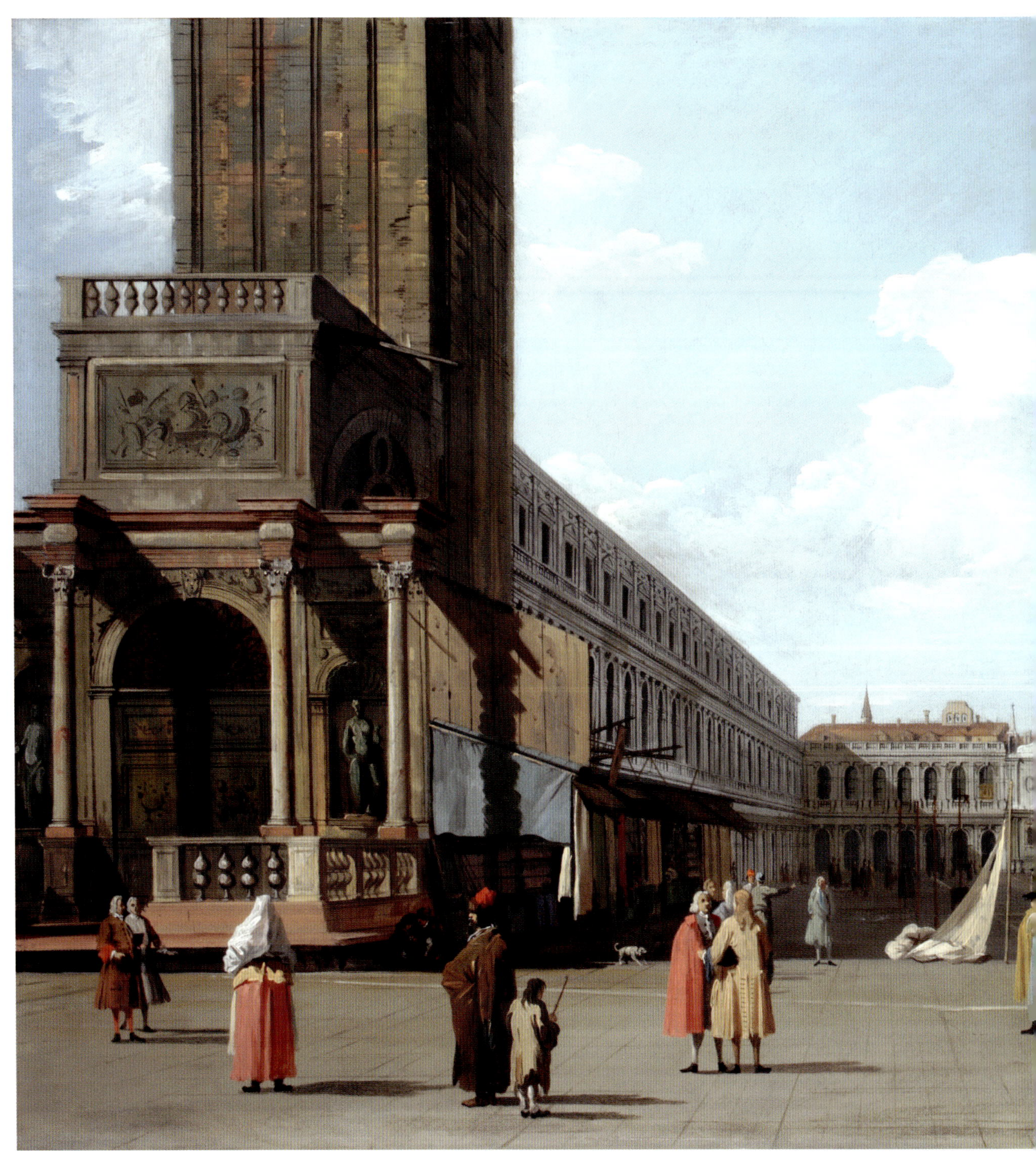

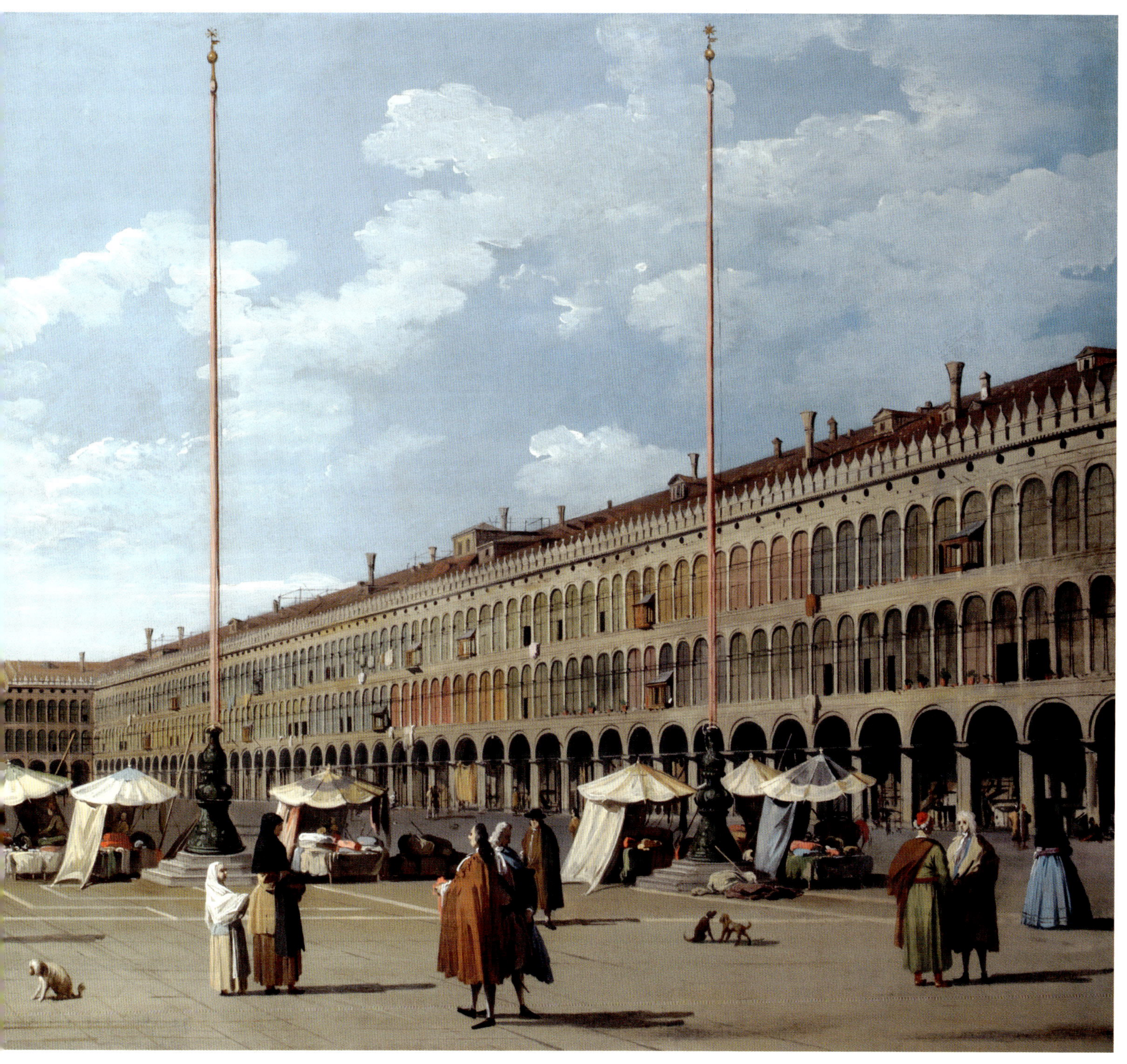

Accepted by W.G. Constable as the work of
Canaletto, this painting was considered by
Sir Francis Watson to be 'From the studio
of [Canaletto], but very largely by studio
assistants'.[1] He noted the topographical
error in the depiction of the Loggetta of the
Campanile on the left, but failed to draw
the appropriate conclusion. The painting is
obviously not of sufficient quality to be the
work of Canaletto and most of it is copied
directly from Canaletto's original, part of the
celebrated series of 24 views executed for John
Russell, 4th Duke of Bedford, in *c*.1732–35 and
still intact at Woburn Abbey (fig. 130).[2]

The suggestion of a Beckford provenance
provided by the annotation in the 1870
Hertford House inventory and the known
association of Alderman William Beckford
(1709–1770) with the Duke of Bedford, in
whose London dining room the prototype
hung, raises the intriguing possibility that
the painting might have been commissioned
by him. He is thought to have owned other
Venetian views and certainly employed
Antonio Joli (1700–1777) during the artist's
years in England.[3]

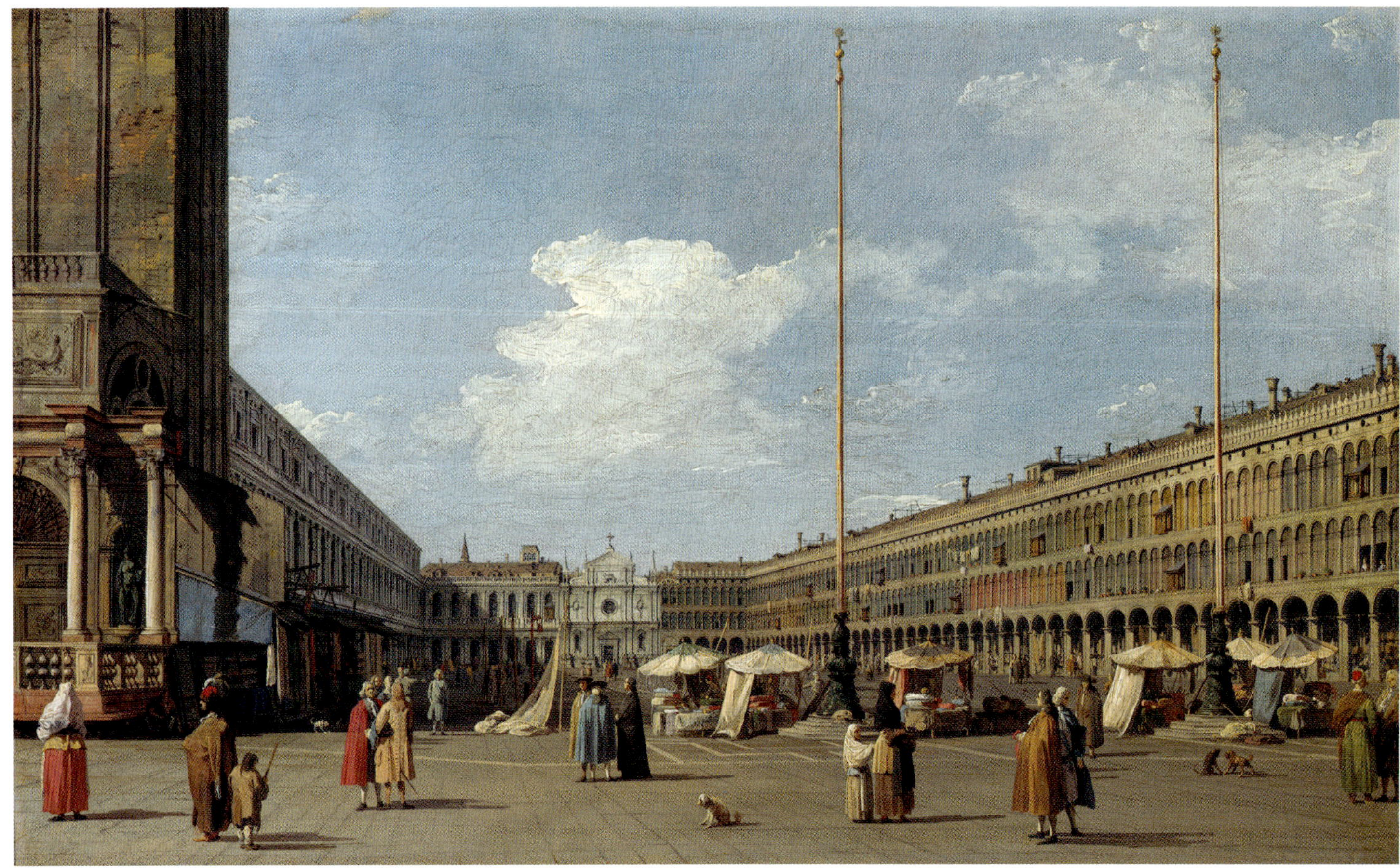

PROVENANCE
Described as 'Beckford's' in the 1870 Hertford House inventory but said to be untraceable in any Beckford sale; acquired by Richard Seymour-Conway, 4th Marquess of Hertford (1800–1870).

EXHIBITION
1872–75: 'Paintings, Porcelain, Bronzes, Decorative Furniture and other Works of Art lent by Sir Richard Wallace to the Bethnal Green Branch of the South Kensington Museum', no. 286.

RELATED WORKS
Canaletto, *The Piazza San Marco, Looking West from South of the Central Line*, c.1732?, oil on canvas, 47 × 80 cm, Collection of the Duke of Bedford, Woburn Abbey (C27; Beddington 2021, no. 4)

Other derivations from the painting by Canaletto at Woburn Abbey include:

By 'The Woburn Copyist', c.1732, oil on canvas, 47 × 80 cm, painted for William, 1st Viscount Bateman, and now in a UK private collection

Oil on canvas, 69.5 × 115.5 cm, Sotheby's, New York, 9 June 1983, lot 65, and 29 January 2009, lot 83; subsequently with the Lampronti Gallery

Oil on canvas, 68.5 × 114.5 cm, sold from a 'European Private Collection', Christie's, Paris, 23 June 2010, lot 46

Oil on canvas, 76 × 119.5 cm, acquired by Henry Fiennes Pelham Clinton, 9th Earl of Lincoln and later 2nd Duke of Newcastle-under-Lyme (1720–1794), who was only in Venice in 1741; sold at Christie's, London, 31 March 1939, lot 5, and 24 May 1991, lot 70, as by Canaletto (C28)

Oil on canvas, 64 × 129 cm; once in the collection of C.H. St J. Hornby and Michael Hornby, Faringdon, Berkshire; with Chaucer Fine Art, London, in 1991, and now in an Italian private collection. Considered by J.G. Links (in his editions of Constable, C27(a)) to be 'perhaps by the same hand or hands as [the Wallace Collection painting]'; Links 1998, p. 6, as 'Not a replica of [the Woburn painting]'

Oil on canvas, 72.4 × 113 cm, Sotheby's, New York, 29 January 2015, lot 382

Oil on canvas, 73 × 113.7 cm, Christie's, New York, 7 February 2006, lot 13, as 'English School, 19th Century, after Canaletto' (C under 27)

TECHNICAL NOTES
The painting was at the Hamilton Kerr Institute in 2017–19, when a technical report was produced, from which the following information derives. The support is a medium-weight, plain-weave canvas, coarser than the lining canvas. Cusping is evident on all four sides, indicating that the elongated horizontal shape is original and supporting the idea that the painting was intended as an overdoor. The ground is of two layers of a creamy greyish colour, which may place the painting as a copy done in England, but is (so far) unique in apparently lacking the glue inter-layer found in most eighteenth-century British paintings. Most of the sky and architectural elements are executed with soft transitions in colour and modelling. The work appears to have been painted swiftly, wet-in-wet. Highly raised impasto is used in the brightest parts of the clouds, and in localised areas where the artist applied dabs of paint to highlight the tops of individual tents and figures in the foreground. There are no *pentimenti* visible to the naked eye. Most of the sky appears to have been painted first without leaving obvious reserves for architectural elements. There are, however, some areas where the artist made a second localised application of the sky paint, going around the architecture. The architectural elements were painted first by blocking in the colours and then breaking them up into individual parts, with lines and added details. The artist used freehand and ruled incisions, in order to accurately set the perspective, as well as a guide for painting in further details, such as the repeating arches and windows in the buildings. The figures were clearly painted in at the final stage with swift and free paint strokes.

LITERATURE
Constable 1962, C30, as Canaletto
Puppi 1968, no. 136B
Watson 1968, p. 54
Ingamells 1985, pp. 246–47
Duffy and Hedley 2004, p. 68
Beddington 2021, p. 60

CB

19. FRANCESCO GUARDI

(Venice 1712–1793)

*San Giorgio Maggiore with
the Giudecca and Le Zitelle*

1770s–80s
oil on canvas
68.7 × 91.5 cm (enlarged to 70.5 × 93.5 cm in the
nineteenth century)
P491

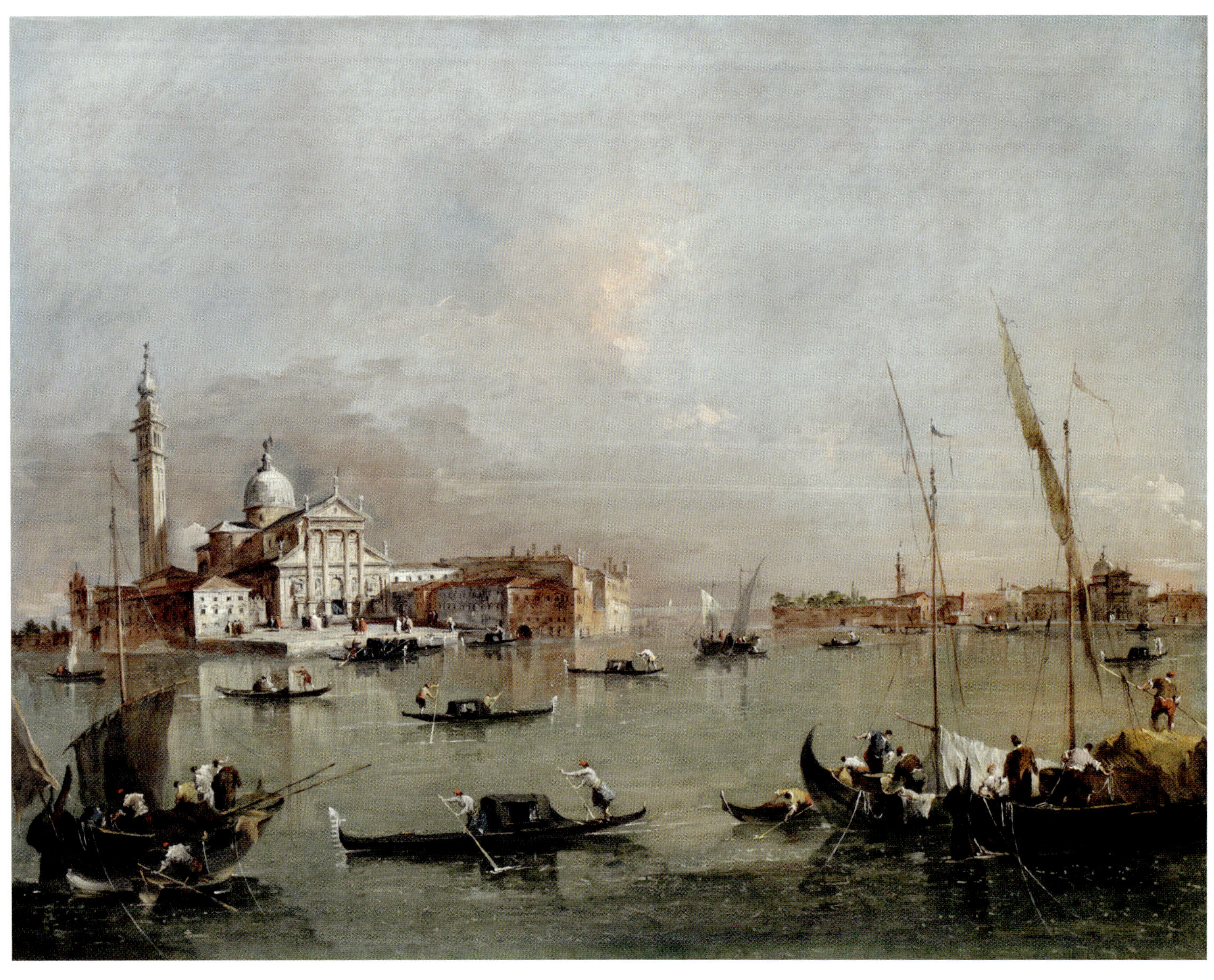

 # FRANCESCO GUARDI
(Venice 1712–1793)

Santa Maria della Salute and the Dogana

1770s–80s
oil on canvas
68.5 × 90.5 cm (enlarged to 70.5 × 93.5 cm in the
nineteenth century)
P503

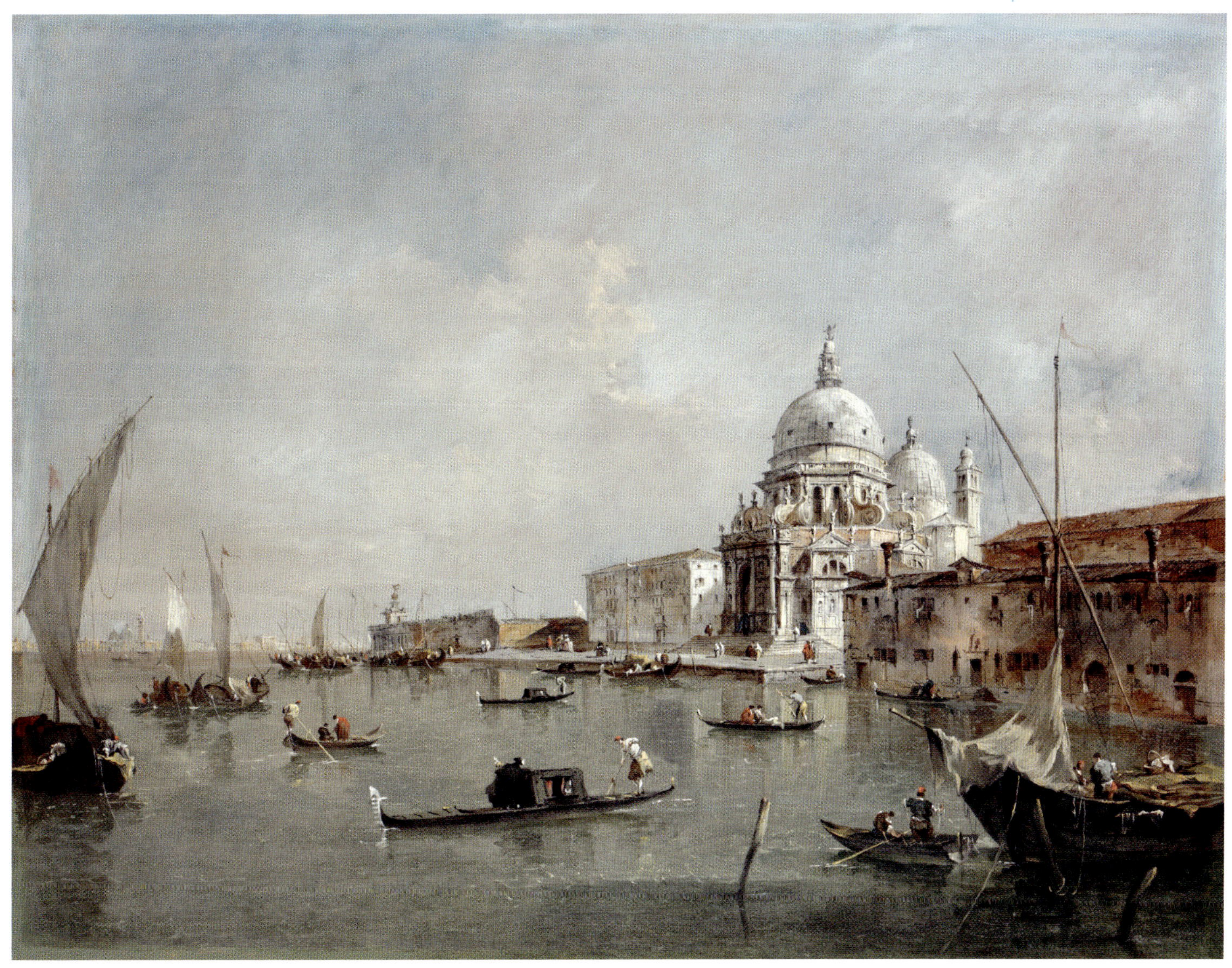

21. FRANCESCO GUARDI

(Venice 1712–1793)

The Grand Canal with the Rialto Bridge

1770s–80s
oil on canvas
68.5 × 91.5 cm (enlarged to 70.5 × 93.5 cm in the
nineteenth century)
P508

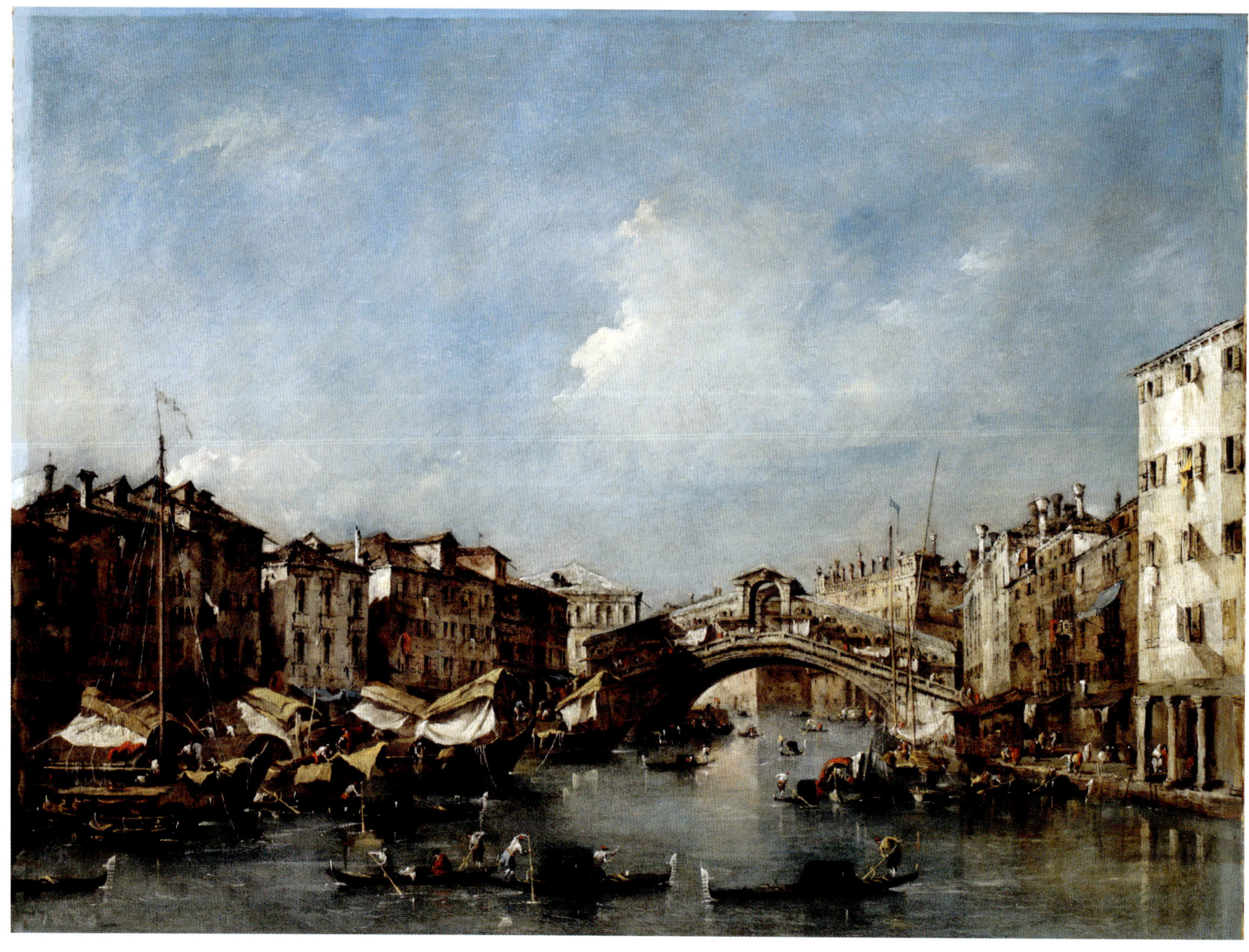

 FRANCESCO GUARDI
(Venice 1712–1793)

The Dogana with the Giudecca

1770s–80s
oil on canvas
68.2 × 91.3 cm (enlarged to 70.5 × 93.5 cm in the
nineteenth century)
P494

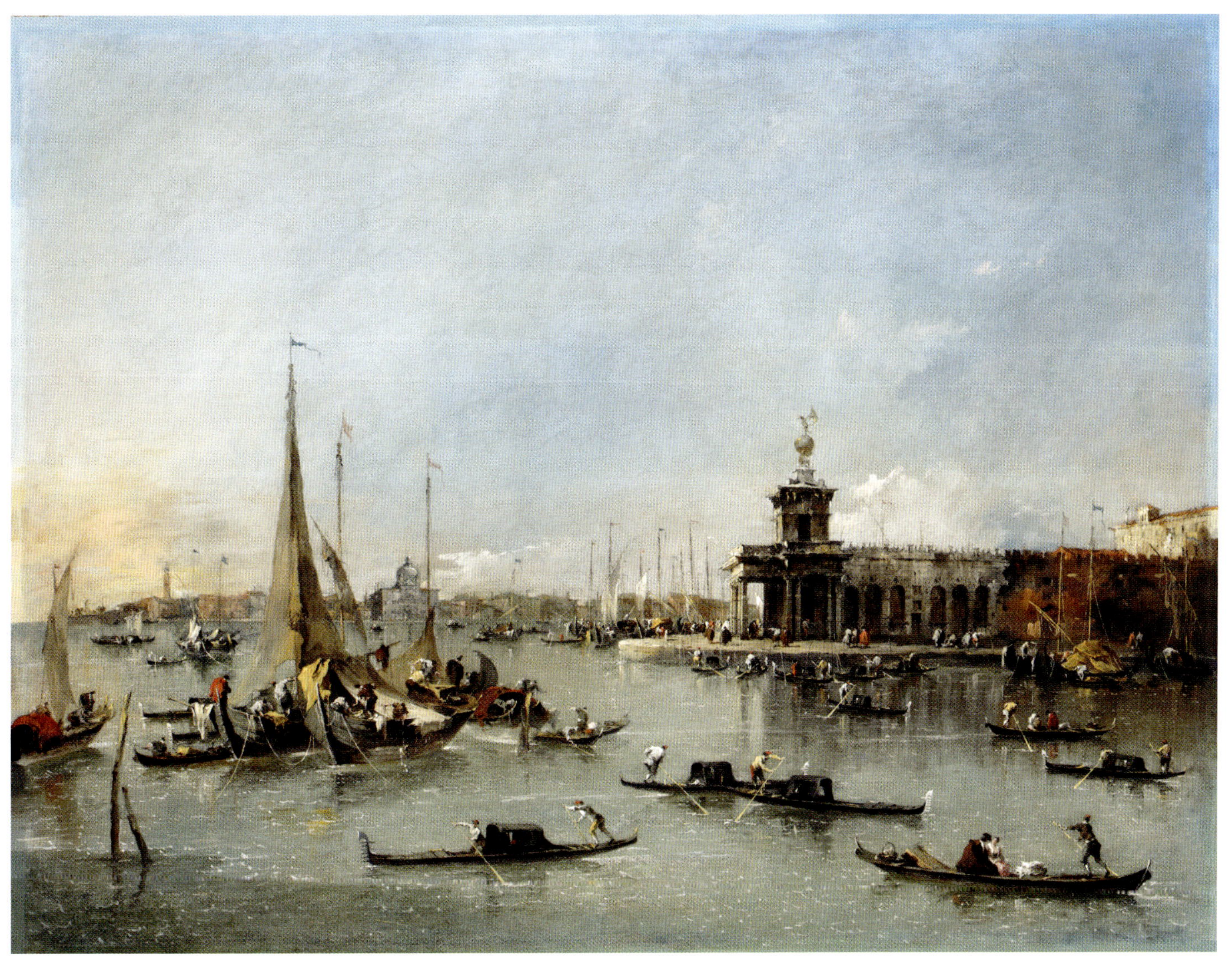

These paintings feature Venice's most impressive churches and sites and form the only set of topographical views by Guardi still together. Cat. 19 depicts the imposing Benedictine church of San Giorgio Maggiore situated on the island with that name. Cat. 20 shows the splendid Baroque edifice Santa Maria della Salute, located at the mouth of the Grand Canal. Cat. 21 and cat. 22 show the Rialto Bridge in the centre of the city and the Dogana in the south, by the entrance to the Grand Canal, respectively. The four sites were main tourist attractions in the eighteenth century and appear in countless *vedute* by Guardi, Canaletto and other *vedutisti*. The large scale and high quality of execution of these works make them major highlights in Guardi's oeuvre. In 1878 the art critic Charles Yriarte described the set as being among the finest that Guardi ever painted.[1] Guardi's lively brushwork and convincing atmospheric effects painted on a grand scale contribute to these impressions.

The view in cat. 19 is across the Bacino di San Marco towards the island of San Giorgio on the left. The church of San Giorgio was begun in 1566 by Andrea Palladio and completed a decade later, apart from the façade, which was realised between 1607 and 1611. This was the first church that Palladio designed from start to finish. It was described by the French philosopher Montesquieu as Palladio's 'ecclesiastical masterpiece' due to the superb combination of Benedictine and Venetian conventions with a classicising architectural language.[2] The *campanile* collapsed in 1774 and was rebuilt in 1791 by Fra Benadetto Buratti (1724–1804). To the right of the church is the Benedictine Monastery of San Giorgio, today the Giorgio Cini Foundation. The island has been the site of a church dedicated to Saint George since 790. In the eighteenth century, San Giorgio was one of the first sights visible to travellers approaching Venice by boat.

In the distance on the right, across the Canale della Grazia, is the island of the Giudecca, notable for the church of Santa Maria della Presentazione, or Le Zitelle, identifiable by its imposing dome.[3] Like San Giorgio, Le Zitelle was also designed by Palladio but built after his death between 1582 and 1586. On the eastern end of the Giudecca are the church and *campanile* of San Giovanni Battista (later demolished).

The view in cat. 20 faces westward towards the entrance to the Grand Canal. The pre-eminent church of Santa Maria della Salute was built in response to the 1630–31 plague that killed more than 46,000 people. It was designed by Baldassare Longhena following a Senate decree on 22 October 1630 in the hope that a church would help deliver Venice from the plague. This idea is reflected in the church's name 'Salute', meaning 'health' or 'salvation'. Completed in 1681, the church's towering domes are the focal point of Guardi's composition. The Salute is flanked on the left by the Seminario Patriarcale also built by Longhena, in 1669, to accommodate the cloister of the Somaschi Fathers, a charitable religious congregation of priests and brothers. Further on, at the mouth of the canal, is the Dogana. In the distance on the left are the Molo, the Riva degli Schiavoni, the domes of San Marco and the Campanile. To the right of the Salute is the Abbazia di San Gregorio, a Benedictine abbey, only a portion of which survives today.[4]

Cat. 21 depicts the Rialto Bridge from the south.[5] In the eighteenth century the bridge was lined with market stalls and shops, and was at the heart of Venice's commercial centre. On the left is the Riva del Vin, here obscured by large commercial barges draped in canvas canopies moored alongside it. This paved street runs from the church of San Silvestro to the Rialto Bridge. Along the Riva are the three-bay Palazzo Barbarigo and the Palazzo dei Dieci Savi, just left of the bridge. Beyond the bridge on the left is the Palazzo dei Camerlenghi across from the Fondaco dei Tedeschi. On the right bank is the Riva del Ferro with a free-standing stall alongside it. The arcaded building in the right foreground was later demolished to make way for the Via Giuseppe Mazzini.

The Rialto was a popular subject for *vedute* and was depicted by the likes of Canaletto, Marieschi and Guardi from the north and south. The present view was taken down the Grand Canal towards the right bank, offering

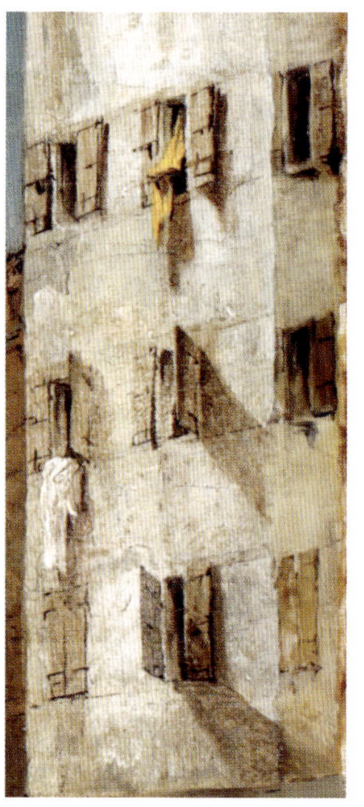
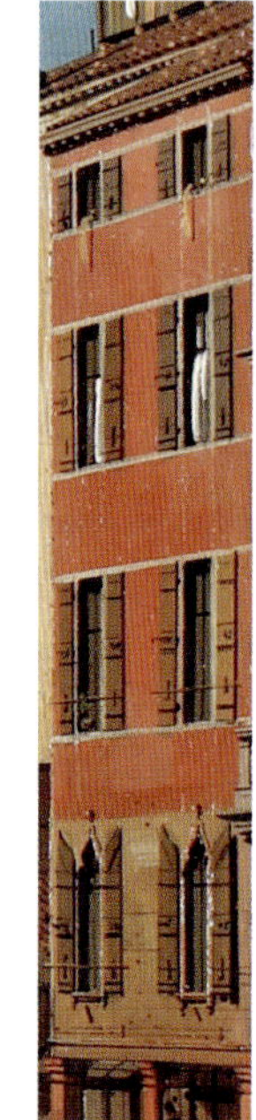

Fig. 131. Detail of cat. 21

Fig. 132. Detail of cat. 5

a wider view of the Riva del Vin and a more oblique one of the Riva del Ferro. Guardi effectively captured the hustle and bustle on a typical day in this area. On the left bank a smaller boat carrying four barrels is moored in the foreground. Shutters open at various angles lend a sense of informality and authenticity to the scene (fig. 131). By contrast, Canaletto's shutters in a painting of the same subject at the Wallace Collection lie perfectly flat against buildings (fig. 132). Untidy blue or white awnings adorn the Rialto and the properties nearby, while fluttering blue, white or red laundry injects accents of colour across the painting. Light entering from the left casts dramatic shadows on the bridge and on the buildings on the left bank.

Cat. 22 looks across the mouth of the Grand Canal to the Dogana in the middle distance and the island of the Giudecca further back along the horizon.[6] The domed church of Le Zitelle on the Giudecca was attached to a foundling hospital for girls (*zitella* is Italian for spinster). The ecclesiastical complex sought to assist young women without a dowry who were otherwise

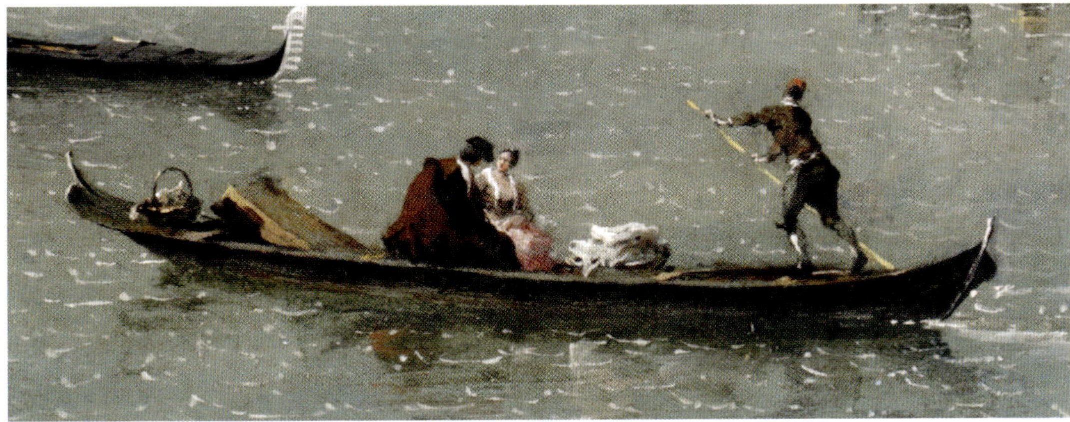

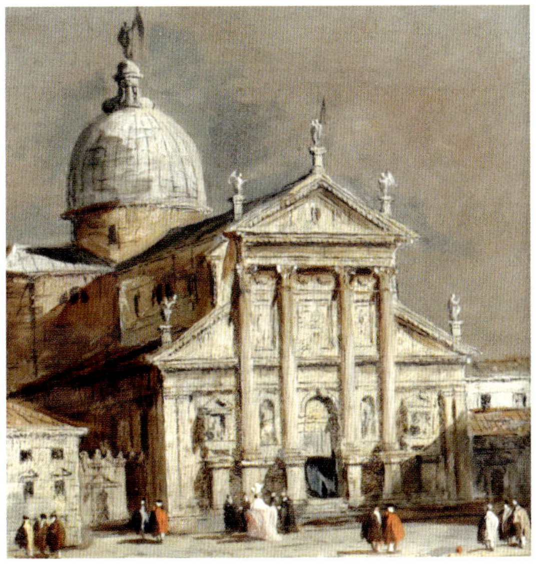

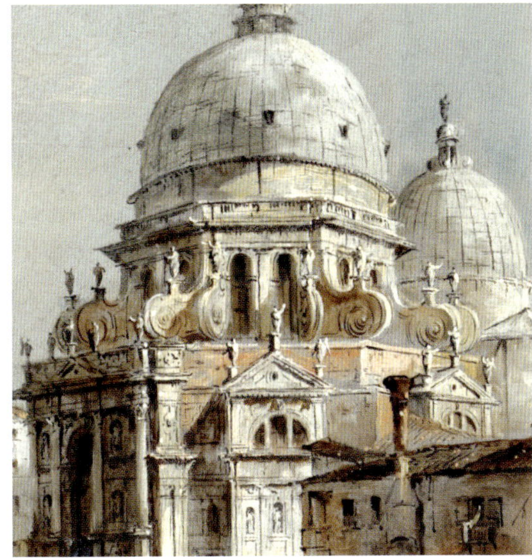

Fig. 133. Detail of cat. 22

Fig. 134. Details of cats 19 (left) and 20 (right)

destined for prostitution. Further to the left is the *campanile* of San Giovanni Battista, later demolished.

Guardi's main subject, however, is the Dogana, beautifully silhouetted on the horizon like a ship's bow seen in profile against the sky and water. Its golden globe with a weather vane in the shape of Fortune personifies Venice's supremacy over the Adriatic. Guardi had a particular interest in the Dogana and portrayed it on numerous occasions from varying viewpoints and distances, and on a variety of scales. As with the present view, he often concentrated on the Dogana itself, or paired it with the neighbouring – and arguably more famous – church of Santa Maria della Salute. In addition, Canaletto frequently incorporated the Dogana into wider views of the entrance

to the Grand Canal or of the Bacino.[8] On the furthest side of the Dogana boats arrive and sailors unload cargo before paying customs charges to enter the city's waterways. In the lower right foreground, a couple is out for a ride in a *sandolo*; the basket on the left-hand edge of their boat suggests they might be out for a picnic (fig. 133). Three large boats with their sails drawn on the left counterbalance the Dogana on the right.

The paintings work well as a set. Guardi depicted two contemporary churches designed by the same architect. He positioned them in mirror image across a watery expanse united by a continuous horizon line that is shared with cat. 22. A flurry of gondolas and sizeable barges inhabited by energetic figures populate all four paintings. Guardi inserted gondolas at a slight angle in the

central foreground of each work, and used larger vessels to frame the compositions on the left or right. He conveyed a sense of movement through animated brushwork. Hard-working merchants and fishermen are composed of skilful flicks of thickly applied paint. Guardi used thinner layers of paint to capture the effects of the changing light on the water. He constructed basic forms of buildings with mottled, layered blocks of translucent colour. Buildings, such as the façades and domes of San Giorgio and the Salute, masts, windows, shutters and stonework are articulated with the nervous, dark lines of a draughtsman (fig. 134). His loose, tremulous brushwork effectively captures the picturesque possibilities afforded by Venice's untidiness.

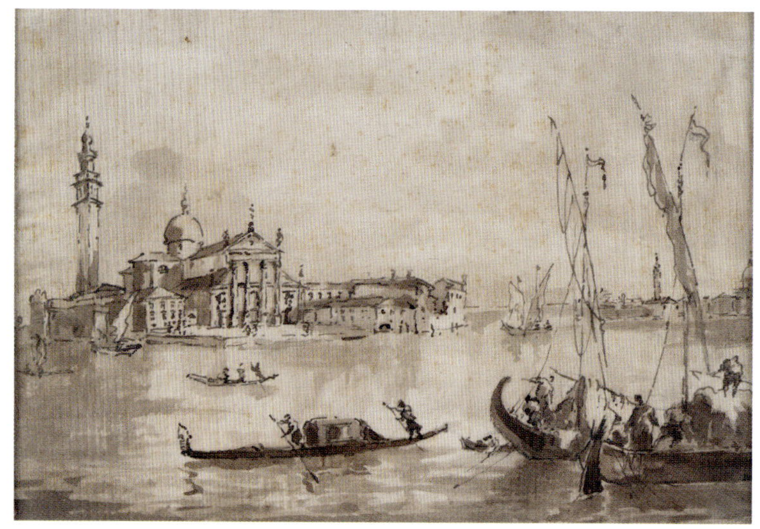

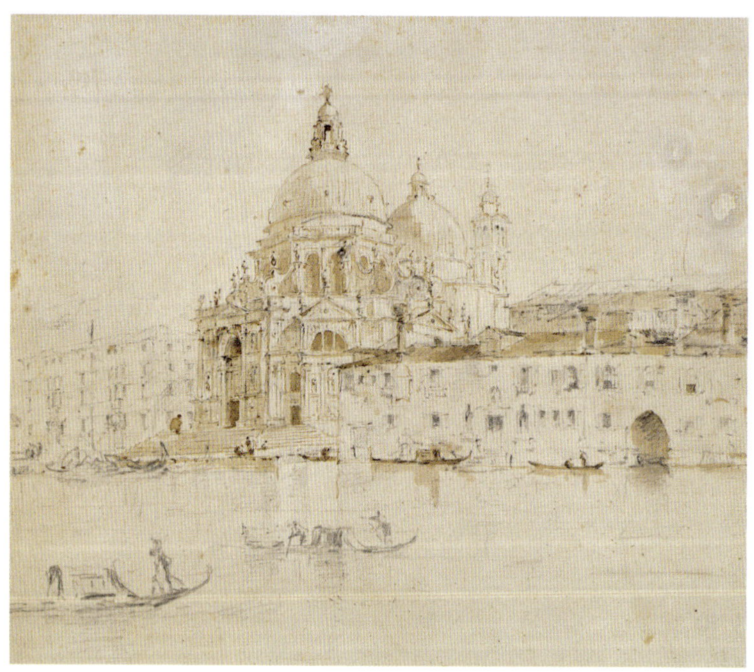

Fig. 135. Francesco Guardi (1712–1793), *View of the Island of San Giorgio Maggiore*, 1770–early 1780s, pen, ink and wash on paper, 16.7 × 21.9 cm, Borys Voznytskyi Lviv National Art Gallery, Ukraine (inv. Г-V-341)

Fig. 136. Francesco Guardi (1712–1793), *The Canal Grande with Santa Maria della Salute* (recto), *c.*1750–75. pencil, pen, ink and wash on paper, 24.2 × 28.3 cm, Collection Museum Boijmans Van Beuningen, Rotterdam (inv. I 434)

Drawings

A skilled draughtsman, Guardi studied all these sites first-hand. A drawing of San Giorgio taken from a similar perspective (albeit slightly closer up) and with a comparable configuration of boats and figures shows his investigation of what, for him, became a standard compositional type (fig. 135). A sheet in Rotterdam illustrates his close observation of the Salute and the buildings nearby from a similar angle (fig. 136). A sheet in Paris showing the Rialto Bridge from a comparable angle is the kind of reference material Guardi would have turned to in the planning stages of cat. 21 (fig. 137).[9] Likewise, his study of the Dogana in sheets such as that in Dresden would have informed cat. 22 (fig. 138).

Guardi employed a substantial degree of spatial distortion in these later works for aesthetic effect. In cat. 19 he brought the island of San Giorgio closer into view and positioned the Giudecca further away, ensuring the prominence of the church. He also exaggerated the distance between the islands. Similarly, he deliberately widened the mouth of the Grand Canal in cat. 20 to provide a more impressive watery base for the monumental building of the Salute. A drawing by Canaletto of the Salute from a comparable angle illustrates how much narrower the Grand Canal actually is (fig. 139). Moreover, the inclusion of the Molo and the buildings around it seems wilful according to the angle of the Salute. In cat. 21 Guardi widened the Grand Canal so that the

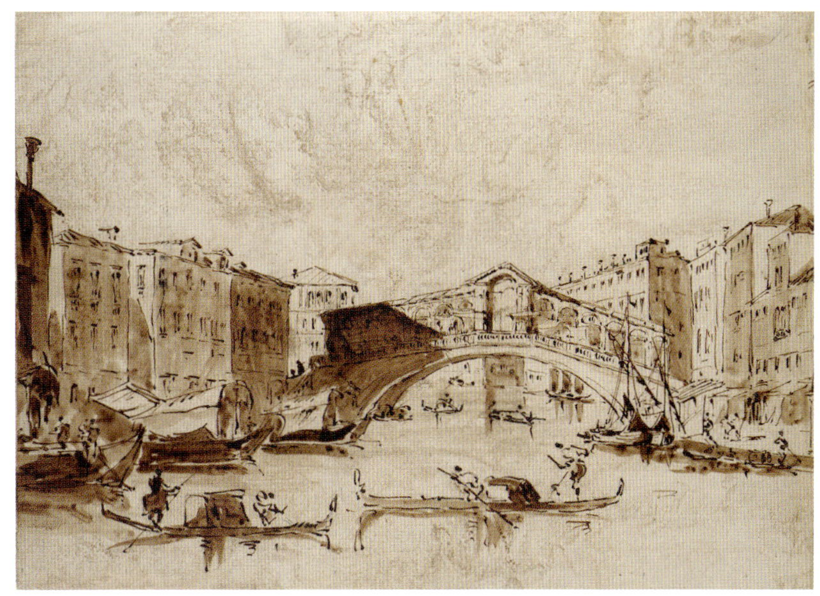

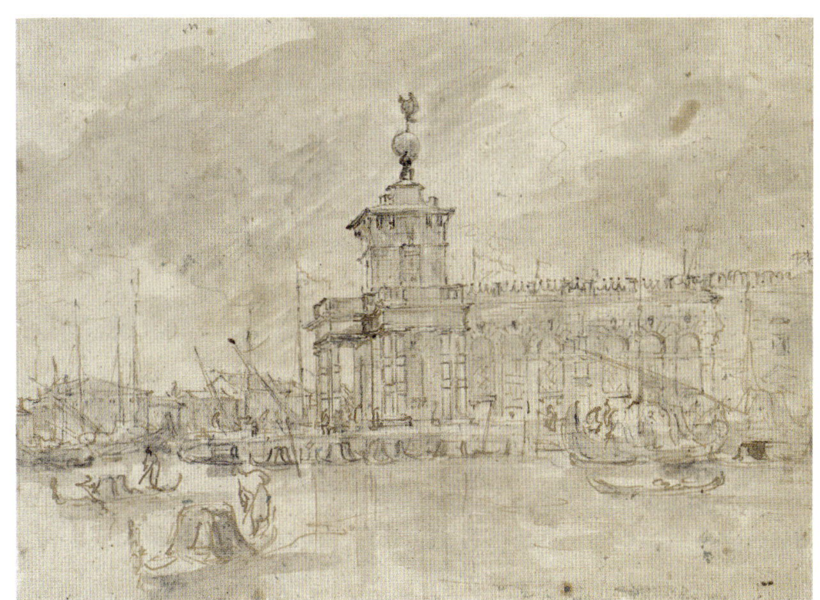

Fig. 137. Francesco Guardi (1712–1793), *View of the Grand Canal and the Rialto Bridge*, ink and wash on paper, 20 × 28.3 cm, Musée du Louvre, Paris (inv. RF 31177, recto)

Fig. 138. Francesco Guardi (1712–1793), *The Dogana*, pen and ink in grey-brown, washed grey-brown, over preliminary drawing with chalk, 28 × 39.5 cm, Kupferstich-Kabinett, Dresden (inv. C 1896-29)

buildings on both banks are visible and that the Rialto is the focal point of the picture. In cat. 22 he pushed the buildings on the Giudecca further back into the distance and shifted the position of Le Zitelle to the left so that the Dogana is prominent. All the views are taken from a high viewpoint above the water that would have been impossible to achieve in reality, but which enabled Guardi to present these sites at eye level.

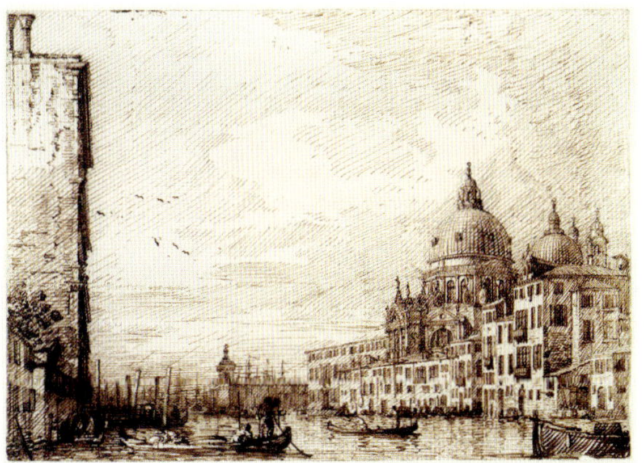

Fig. 139. Canaletto (1697–1768), *Venice: The Lower Reach of the Grand Canal, Looking East*, c.1734, pen, ink, wash and pencil on paper, 18.9 × 27.3 cm, Royal Collection (RCIN 907461)

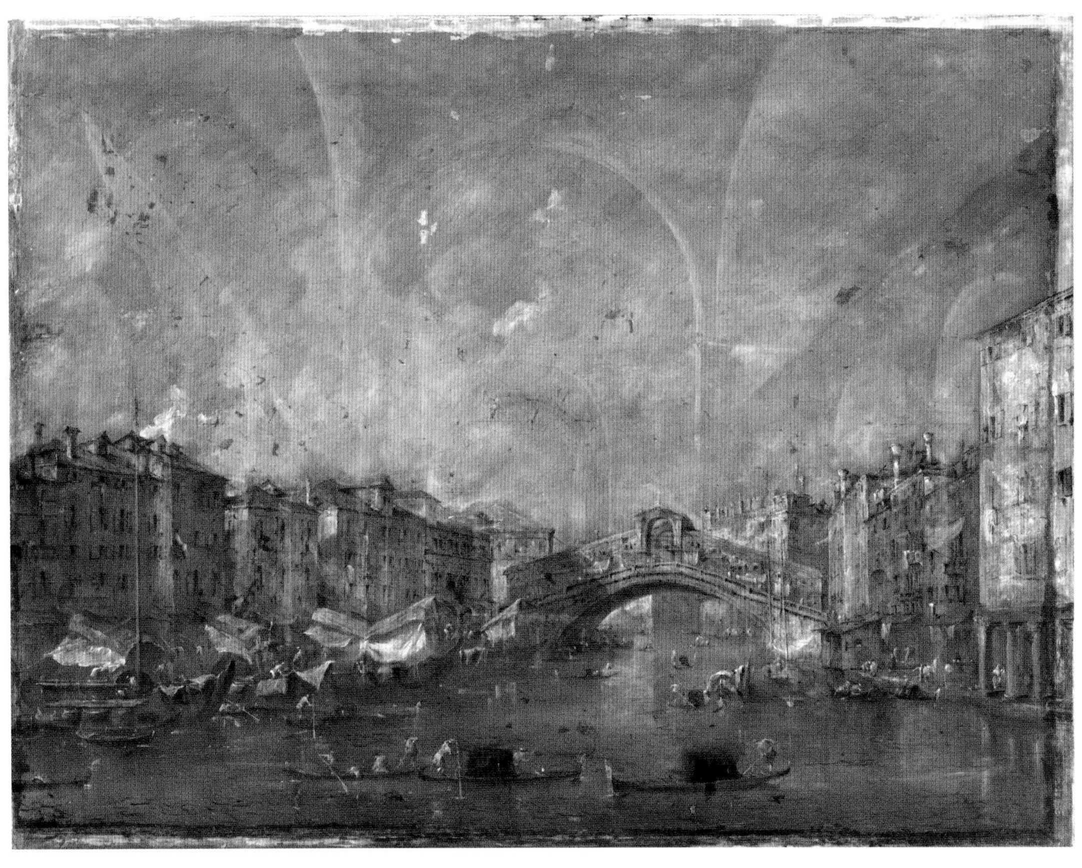

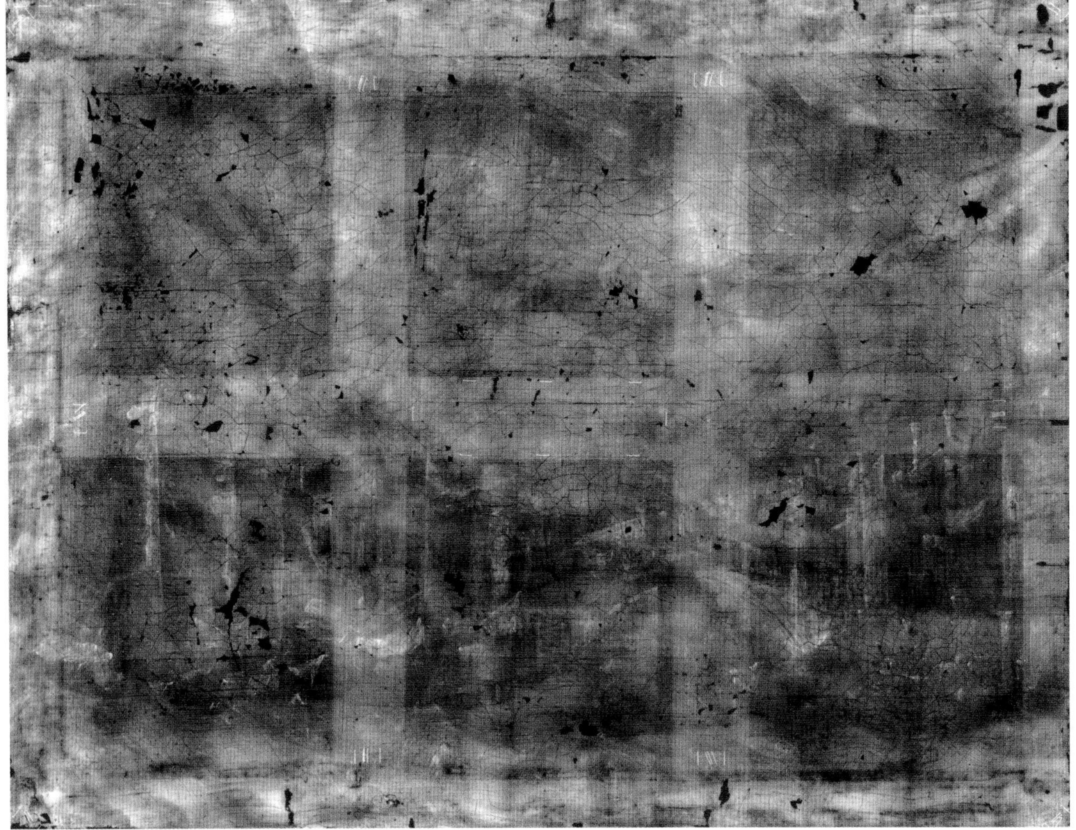

ABOVE:
Fig. 140. IRR of cat. 21

BELOW:
Fig. 141. X-ray of cat. 21

OPPOSITE:
Fig. 142. Francesco Guardi (1712–1793), *Doge Alvise IV Mocenigo Appears to the People in St Mark's Basilica in 1763*, 1775–77, oil on canvas, 67 × 100 cm, Royal Museums of Fine Arts of Belgium, Brussels (inv. 260)

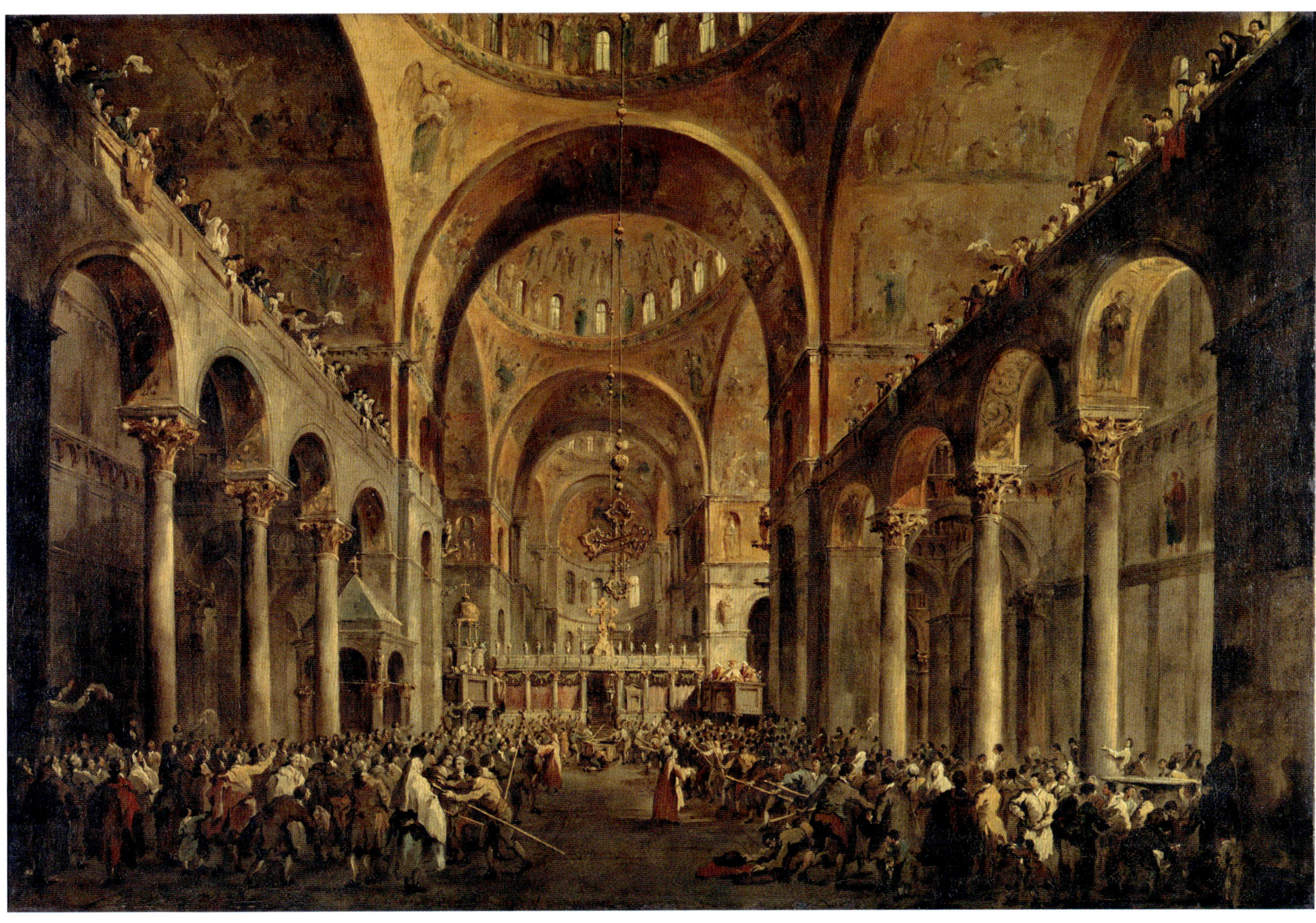

Guardi's Technique

Paint cross-sections reveal that cats 21 and 22 have a different ground structure from cats 19 and 20, namely a red-brown lower layer versus a yellow one.[10] Furthermore, cats 21 and 22 were executed on top of earlier compositions, while the other two were not. The infrared reflectogram of cat. 21 revealed a domed interior with a large central arch flanked by rows of smaller arches supported by columns (fig. 140). This initial composition barely shows up in the X-ray of cat. 21, probably due to the low proportion of lead white present (fig. 141).[11] The interior discernible in the infrared reflectogram relates to the Basilica di San Marco as seen in *Doge Alvise IV Mocenigo Appears to the People in St Mark's Basilica in 1763* in

Brussels (fig. 142). In that painting, the new Doge makes his first public appearance in the Basilica as crowds are being held back. This is the first in a series of 12 paintings by Guardi after the *Solennitá Dogali* print series by Giovanni Battista Brustolon produced between about 1763 and 1766. Brustolon's series commemorated the 12 ceremonies and festivals connected with the 1763 election of Doge Alvise Mocenigo IV, and was based on Canaletto's designs from around 1763. The composition represented in the Wallace Collection's painting of the Giovedì Grasso festival was also part of that series (cat. 10).

The infrared reflectogram of cat. 22 revealed a higher and distinct horizon line, which included the Campanile and

domes of San Marco on the right and the domes and tower of Santa Maria della Salute in the centre (fig. 143). This initial sketch relates to another scene from the *Solennitá Dogali* series, *The Departure of the Bucintoro to the Lido Venice*, of which there is a finished version by Guardi in Paris (fig. 145). There is also a version by Francesco Tironi at the Wallace Collection (cat. 17). The ceremony depicted is the *Sposalizio del Mare* (Marriage with the Sea) that took place annually on Ascension Day (see page 127 for more about this festival). Guardi used the fifth engraving in Brustolon's series as his model for the painting. That print was executed after a drawing by Canaletto now in the British Museum. The X-ray of cat. 22 picks up the outline of the Campanile faintly

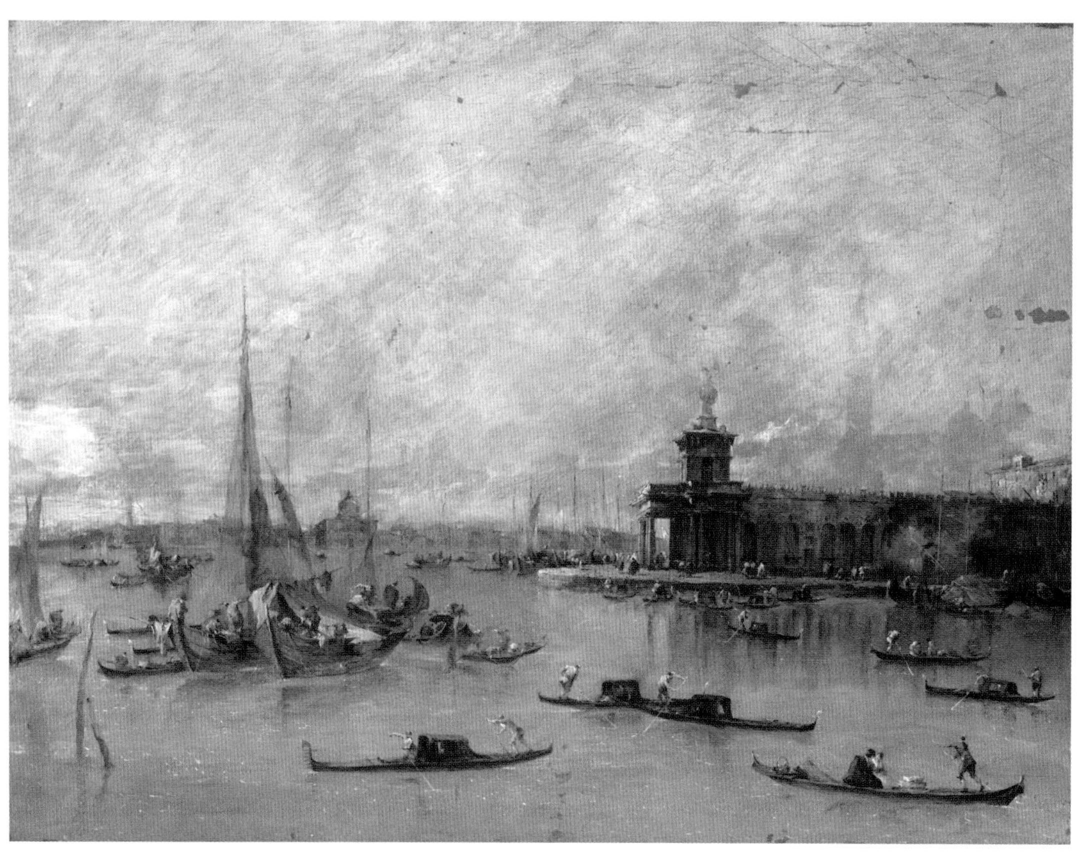

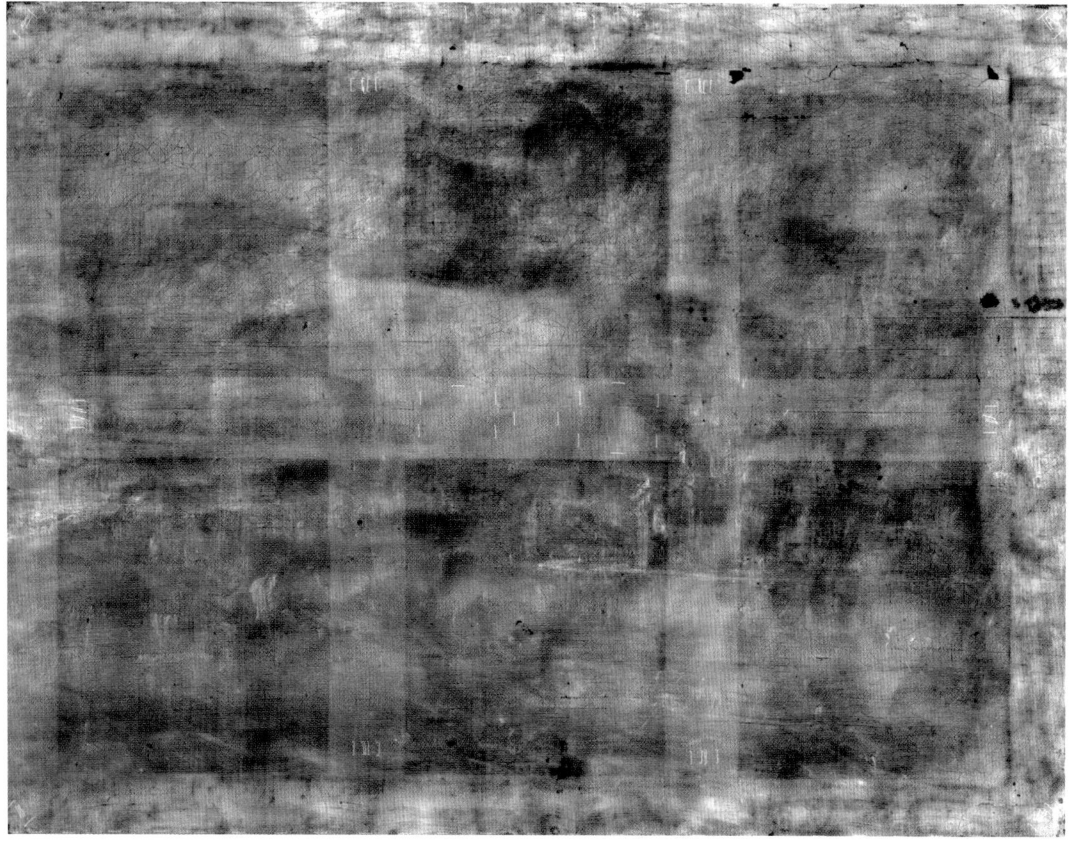

Fig. 143. IRR of cat. 22

Fig. 144. X-ray of cat. 22

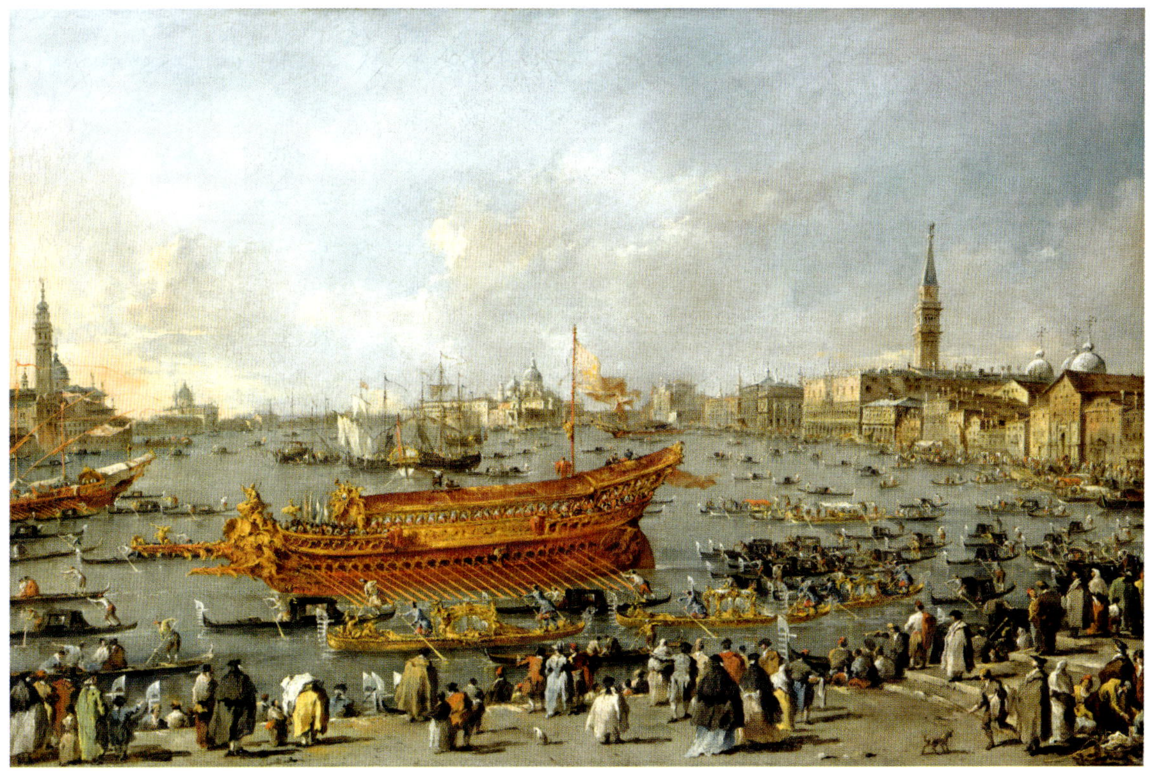

Fig. 145. Francesco Guardi (1712–1793), *The Departure of the Bucintoro to the Lido Venice*, 1770–80, oil on canvas, 66 × 80.6 cm, Musée du Louvre, Paris (inv. 20009)

but, as with the pendant, the lack of radio-opaque materials such as lead white prevents a clear reading of the initial sketch in the X-ray (fig. 144).

Cross-sections suggest that a reasonable amount of work had taken place in the depiction of the architecture and landscape in cats 21 and 22 before Guardi reused the canvases. However, as no figures were detected in the X-rays, it is safe to assume that the initial compositions were incomplete before Guardi abandoned them. This is not the only time that Guardi reused canvases.[12] It may be that he relinquished a pair of popular scenes from the *Solennitá Dogali* series in favour of a set of more generalised views. It has been suggested that Guardi gave up the earlier scenes in order to distance himself from Canaletto at a time when he was coming into his own.[13] Perhaps the final views of popular Venetian sites allowed Guardi more artistic scope for a personal touch.

Although cat. 20 is smaller by comparison, Guardi also made alterations to it before completing it. The infrared reflectogram shows bold passages of lead white paint in the sky to the left of the main dome of the Salute, which would normally indicate highlights (fig. 146). In the finished image, however, the focus of the highlights is altered, with the lightest passage in the central cloud shifted up and to the left. This suggests that Guardi modified the arrangement of the light in the final composition, suppressing the previous highlights with slightly darker paint.

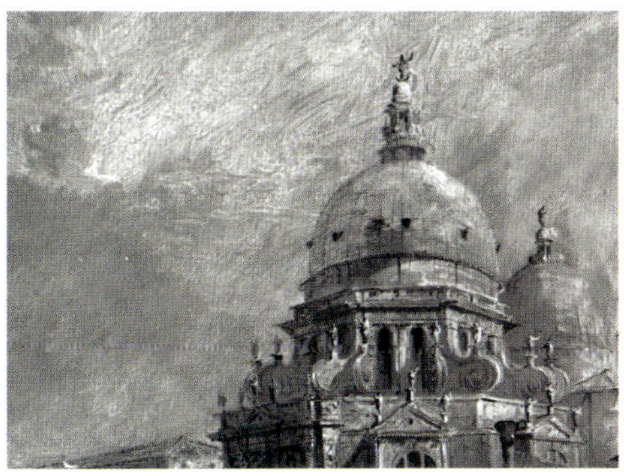 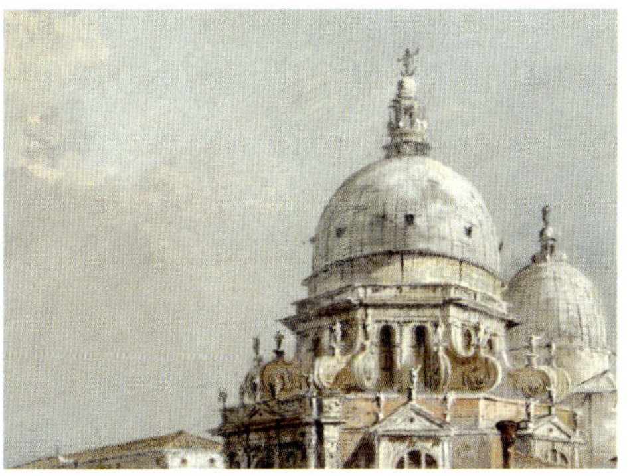

Fig. 146. Detail of IRR of cat. 20 (left) next to a detail of cat. 20 (right)

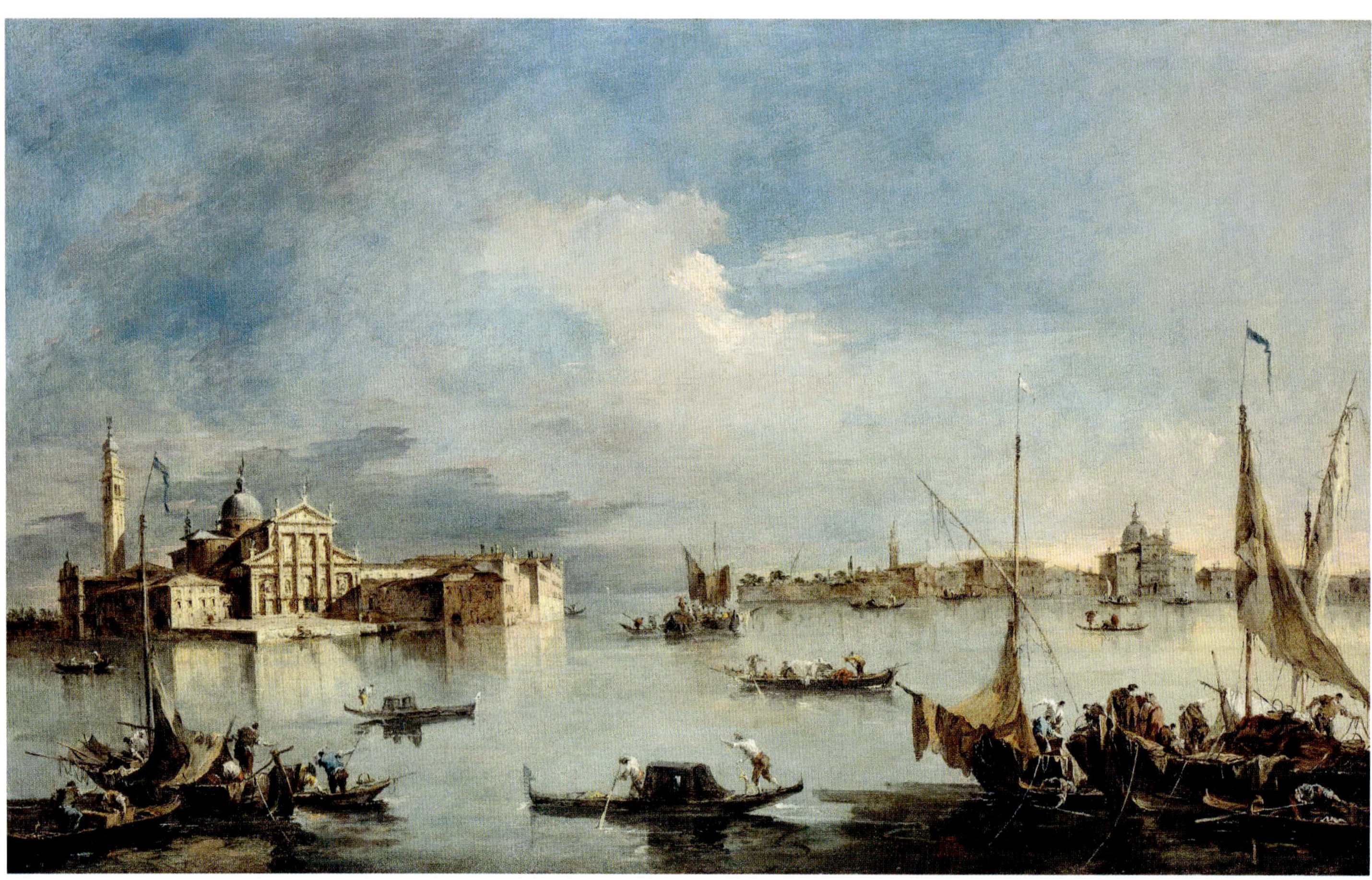

Fig. 147. Francesco Guardi (1712–1793), *San Giorgio Maggiore, Venice, c.*1790, oil on canvas, 46.5 × 76.3 cm, Toledo Museum of Art. Purchased with funds from the Libbey Endowment, Gift of Edward Drummond Libbey (inv. 1952.62)

A Set of Four or Two Distinct Pairs

The paintings were for a long time believed to form a set of four. Lord Hertford bought the pictures as a set at the duc de Morny sale in Paris in 1865.[14] They were described as four pendant views of Venice in the 1871 rue Lafitte inventory compiled after Lord Hertford's death.[15] Throughout the twentieth century this impression remained intact.[16] This idea was questioned during a conservation campaign in 2001, which concluded that the paintings were realised at two distinct stages of Guardi's career and that they constituted two pairs rather than a set of four.[17] More recent technical investigation at the Hamilton Kerr Institute in 2017 built upon these observations.[18] The main reason for this belief was that cats 19 and 20 lacked the compositional alterations evident in cats 22 and 21, which started out as different compositions. Additionally, cats 19 and 20 have a yellow rather than a red-brown lower ground layer, which contributed to the belief that they were not part of the same set.[19] Lastly, a stylistic view was taken whereby cats 19 and 20 were considered as representing Guardi's later style of the 1780s while cats 22 and 21 were believed to adhere to Guardi's manner from the previous decade.

During the first half of the nineteenth century, the paintings were together in Russia as a set and were bought from there as such by the duc de Morny in the middle of the century.[20] It is unlikely that they would have been assembled as a set from two pairs while there or, indeed, after leaving Guardi's studio. More probably, Guardi conceived the paintings as a set from the start.[21] The discrepancy in grounds may have to do with the overall effect he was intending to achieve. Moreover, that Guardi reused two of the canvases seems probable for a set of this scale. Lastly, Guardi's stylistic execution is consistent across the set.[22]

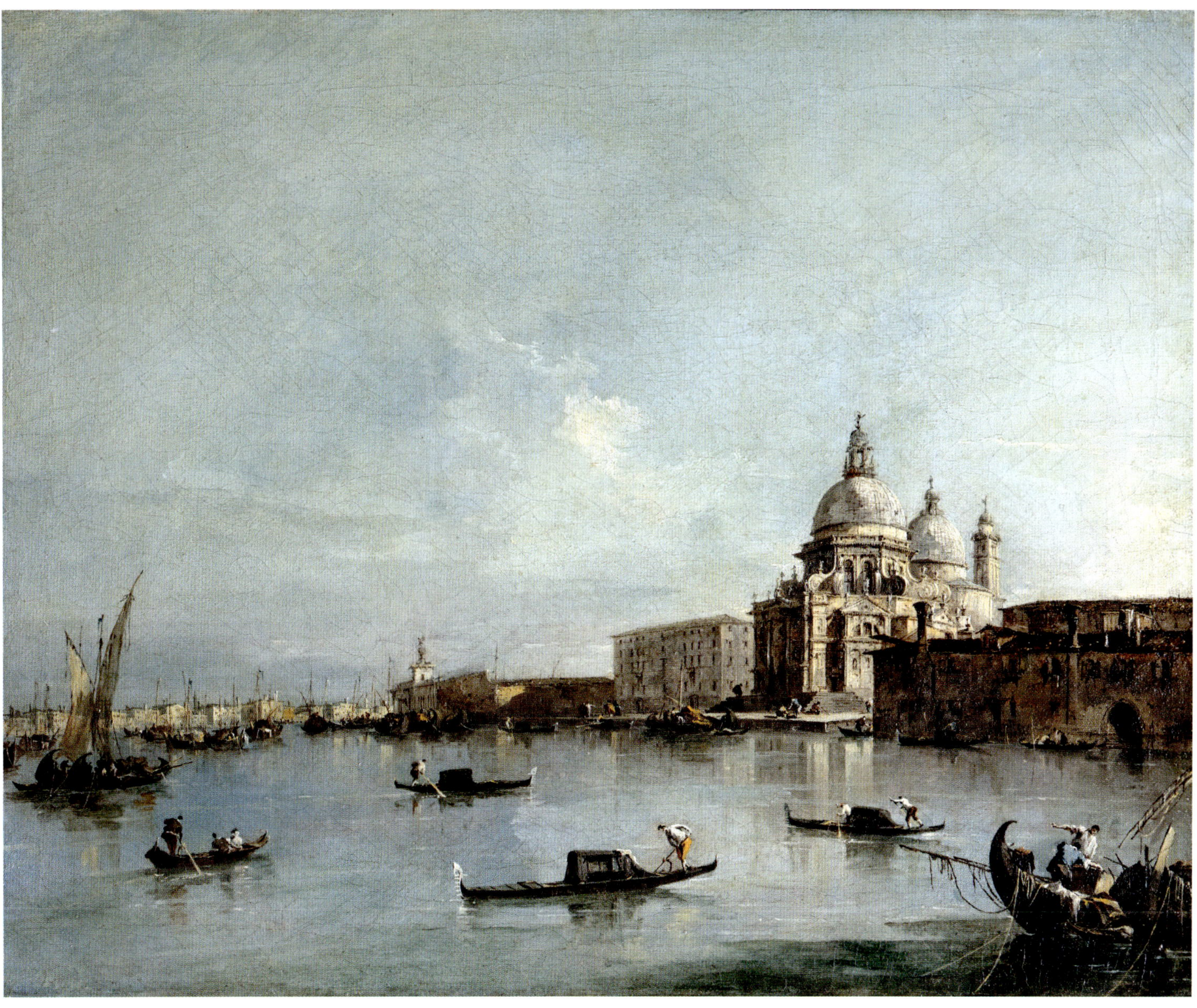

Other Versions

All four views exist in multiple versions with variations in the details of buildings, boats, figures, viewpoint and scale. The beauty and fame of these sites made them a popular subject for *vedute*. The view of San Giorgio is one of Guardi's most successful compositions, to which he returned repeatedly throughout his career with minor variations, such as the inclusion or not of Le Zitelle, or the alteration of the angle and field of view of San Giorgio. Antonio Morassi catalogued 19 versions, including a small picture without Le Zitelle at the Wallace Collection where the viewpoint is lowered and the Giudecca is brought closer into view (cat. 23).[23] Guardi added the small south-eastern turret of San Giorgio in the latter, which he omitted from cat. 19. Another comparable version is at the Toledo Museum of Art where Guardi included a similar configuration of boats in the foreground with a single gondola in the centre (fig. 147). He concentrated on the light reflecting off the façade of San Giorgio in the Toledo version and shifted the viewpoint to the left so that more of the Giudecca is visible.

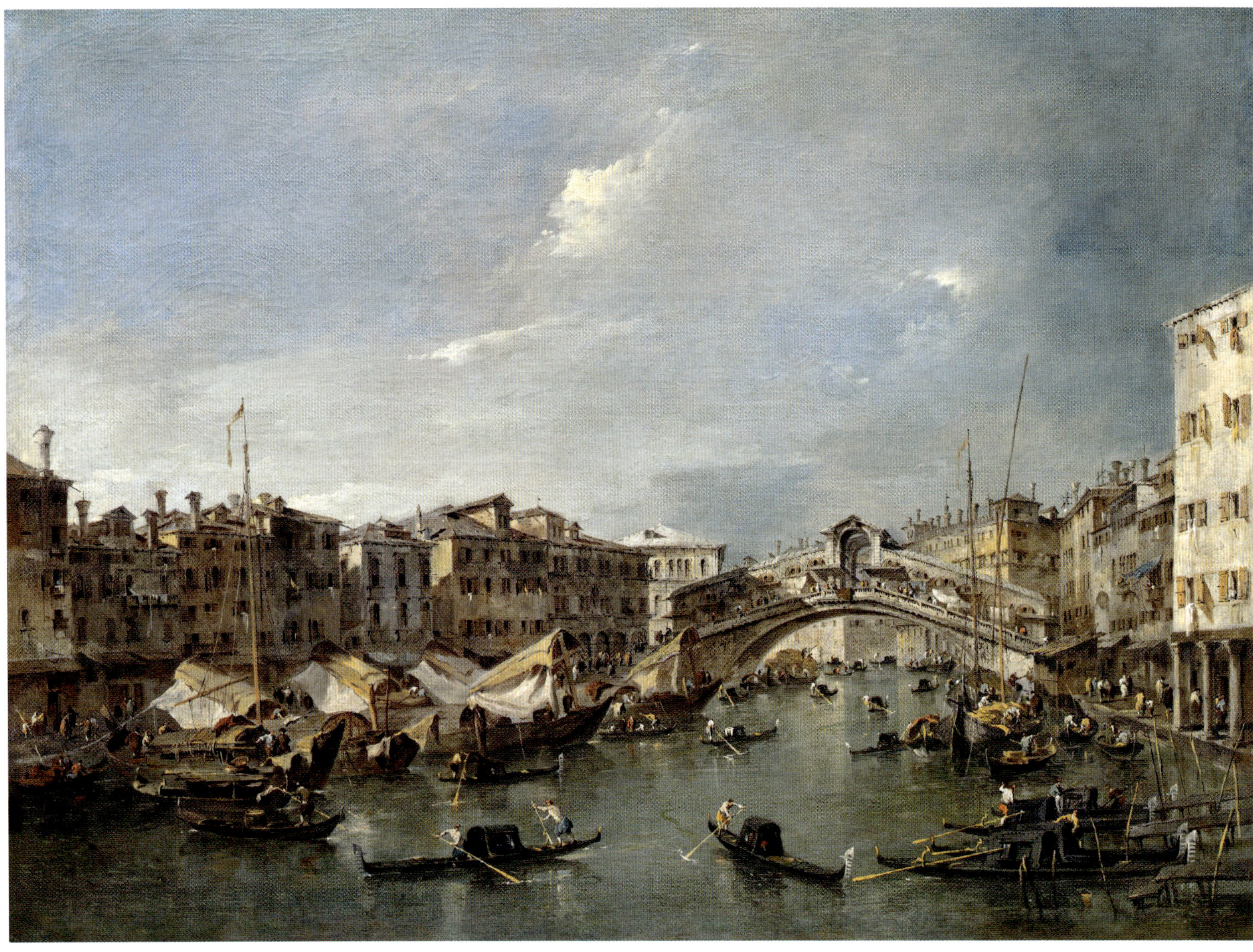

Fig. 149. Francesco Guardi (1712–1793), *Grand Canal with the Rialto Bridge, Venice*, c.1780, oil on canvas, 68.5 × 98.5 cm, National Gallery of Art, Washington, DC. Widener Collection (inv. 1942.9.27)

The popularity of this view is further attested by numerous prints that circulated after it.

The view of the Salute exists in fewer versions. Guardi most often depicted the church from the opposite side looking west, as in the pendant to the small view of San Giorgio, also at the Wallace Collection (cat. 24). A comparable view to the present painting is in the Norton Simon Museum where the vastness of the canal has been further exaggerated but the Molo and the Riva degli Schiavoni have been brought closer into view (fig. 148). When painted from this angle, however, the Salute was most often shown closer up from the right bank of the canal.[24]

Cat. 21 is close to a version of the composition in Washington (fig. 149). The latter has two additional buildings on the left bank as well as figures poking their heads out of windows to watch the spectacle of daily life. The configuration of boats is similar apart from the gondolas and docks in the right foreground of the Washington version that appear to have been added as a further variation from cat. 21, which may have been executed first.[25] Canaletto's comparable view of the Rialto at the Wallace Collection includes the Palazzo Dolfin-Manin in the right foreground, which Guardi omitted (cat. 5).

As with the Rialto, the Dogana held enormous appeal for Grand Tourists.

Therefore, Guardi depicted it often, with or without the adjacent church of Santa Maria della Salute, as in cat. 24.[26] In most versions, the portico of the Dogana is seen from a position slightly to the left, as in the present picture, but closer to the foreground. Guardi also painted variants of the Dogana from the front.[27] The popularity of both views is attested to by the numerous workshop versions on a modest scale perfectly suited for customers seeking a souvenir without the financial commitment of a large painting by Guardi himself.[28]

Dating

Throughout the twentieth century, the paintings were variably dated between 1760 and the 1780s.[29] The existence of the two earlier compositions underneath cats 21 and 22 from the *Solennitá Dogali* series means that the earliest the paintings could have been executed is around 1770, when Guardi is thought to have begun painting that series. The city's topography is not helpful in dating the pictures. Although San Giorgio's *campanile* collapsed in 1774, this does not necessarily furnish the latest possible date of execution for cat. 19 as Guardi often manipulated architectural elements for aesthetic effect. Equally, the woman standing on the *fondamenta* before San Giorgio dressed in a white and pink panniered dress and hair piled high up on her head characteristic of 1780s fashion does not necessarily assist in dating the picture (fig. 150).[30]

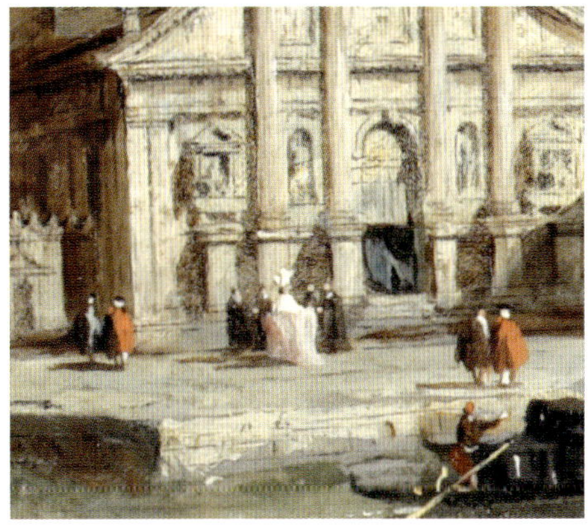

Fig. 150. Detail of cat. 19

Collecting History

The paintings were part of the illustrious collection of the duc de Morny, together with a fifth painting by Guardi of the Piazza San Marco.[31] The latter, previously considered lost, could be the painting in the Rothschild Collection, as it corresponds in size to the Wallace Collection picture.[32] The duc de Morny was a pivotal political and social figure during France's Second Empire. He was described by contemporaries as 'one of the most magnificent European art collectors of his day' with a collection 'worthy of being in the Louvre'.[33] Morny was a contemporary of the 4th Marquess of Hertford in Paris, collecting comparable works of art between 1840 and 1865.[34]

Morny's five paintings by Guardi were identical in size and presumably functioned as a set in his collection.[35] Two nineteenth-century sources corroborate their acquisition in Russia between 1856 and 1857 when the duc de Morny represented his half-brother, Emperor Napoleon III, at the coronation of Alexander II. The duc took his art expert, a 'Monsieur M.', with him to Russia to help him 'discover masterpieces either in Saint Petersburg or in Moscow'.[36] In 1857 Morny returned to Paris with his purchases and with a new wife, Princess Sophie Troubetskoï. An 1861 article on Morny's collection in *L'Artiste* confirmed that the Guardis were among the 'superb canvases' that the duc brought back to Paris from Russia; the author hailed two of the Guardis, in particular, as astonishing.[37] Two years later, an in-depth account of Morny's collection in the *Gazette des Beaux-Arts* began with a detailed description of the five Guardis. Clearly impressed, the author discussed paintings depicting the Rialto, the Salute, the Dogana and San Giorgio Maggiore, which correspond with the four large Guardi canvases at the Wallace Collection today.[38] The author also described a fifth painting of the Piazza San Marco and confirmed that all five canvases were acquired in Russia.[39]

It is uncertain how the Guardis came to be in Russia. One line of enquiry may be that they were brought from Venice in 1782 by Grand Duke Paul (Pavel) Petrovitch of Russia, later Tsar Paul I. The Grand Duke visited the city between 15 and 22 January that year with his second wife, Grand Duchess Maria Feodorovna, as part of a longer European tour with stops in Dresden, Paris and Vienna.[40] Travelling anonymously as the 'Count and Countess of the North', Russia's future Tsar and Tsarina arrived in Venice during Carnival season. Guardi was hired to record the events around their visit, which included a concert, a ball, dinners and a procession, resulting in six paintings and several drawings.[41] Incidentally, these paintings correspond in size to the five Guardis in Morny's collection.[42] During their stay, Paul and Maria visited Venice's famous sites and made a number of acquisitions of fine and decorative art objects for their palaces back in Russia. Nevertheless, it is unlikely that the four Guardis at the Wallace Collection were once in the Imperial Collection due to the lack of characteristic red seals on the stretchers or any traces of inventory numbers on the recto.[43]

There were otherwise a number of impressive private collections in St Petersburg and Moscow throughout the nineteenth century, with a thriving art market to boot in both cities. Most aristocratic collectors marked their paintings on the back with seals consisting of their coat of arms. Without these, it is difficult to trace the whereabouts of the four Wallace Collection Guardis in Russia.

Morny was among several aristocrats making important acquisitions in Russia during this period. Knowledgeable about the collections there, Hertford sent Sir Richard Wallace to St Petersburg in September 1867 to acquire works of art on his behalf. Returning in late October, Wallace acquired paintings, furniture and sculpture from the illustrious collection of Countess Koucheleff-Bezborodko.[44]

In the aforementioned 1863 article on Morny's collection, four of the five Guardis were hailed as being without rival.[45] These were presumably the four pictures at the Wallace Collection today that were each purchased for around four times as much as the view of the Piazza San Marco.[46] Hertford went on a shopping spree at the Morny sale, buying 15 pictures, including Jean-Honoré Fragonard's famous *Swing* (P430), for which he paid 30,200 francs.[47] Of the four Guardis, Hertford paid the most for the view of the Rialto Bridge, which speaks to the popularity of the site and the quality of the painting.[48] He also bought four lots of non-European arms and armour as well as sculpture and at least one snuffbox.[49] Although Hertford made some purchases in person at the sale, he also had others buying on his behalf, including Richard Wallace, who acquired some *objets d'art* for him. The four Guardis were bought by the sale expert Ferdinand Laneuville, who made numerous purchases for Hertford in Paris.[50]

Hertford installed his four Guardis together in a small room lit by a *croisée* (in the shape of a cross) window in his rue Laffitte apartment in Paris, corroborating the idea that he considered them a set.[51] Later, Wallace brought them to London and hung them as overdoors in the 'Canaletto Room' (today the southern half of the Sixteenth-Century Gallery) in 1875. According to the art critic Charles Yriarte, 'the four paintings over the door are probably the best of the masters, and came from the duc de Morny's sale.'[52] Yriarte favoured the four large Guardis over the rest of Wallace's *vedute* collection.

PROVENANCE

Acquired in Russia by Charles Auguste Louis Joseph, duc de Morny (1811–1865) between 1856 and 1857; his sale, Paris, 31 May 1865 (L.28564), lots 119 (cat. 19),[53] 117 (cat. 20),[54] 116 (cat. 21)[55] and 118 (cat. 22);[56] bought by Ferdinand Laneuville on behalf of Richard Seymour-Conway, 4th Marquess of Hertford (1800–1870) for 20,000 francs (cat. 19), 18,000 francs (cat. 20), 25,000 francs (cat. 21) and 20,000 francs (cat. 22); by descent to Sir Richard Wallace, 1st Baronet (1818–1890); by descent to his wife, Lady Wallace (Julie Amélie Charlotte Castelnau, 1819–1897); by whom bequeathed with the rest of the Wallace Collection to the British nation, 1897.

EXHIBITION

1872–75: 'Paintings, Porcelain, Bronzes, Decorative Furniture and other Works of Art lent by Sir Richard Wallace to the Bethnal Green Branch of the South Kensington Museum'.[57]

RELATED WORKS

To cat. 19:

Francesco Guardi, *The Bacino di San Marco with the Island of San Giorgio and the Giudecca*, before 1774, oil on canvas, 69 × 94 cm, Gallerie dell'Accademia, Venice (inv. 709)

Francesco Guardi, *San Giorgio Maggiore, Venice*, c.1790, oil on canvas, 46.5 × 76.3 cm, Toledo Museum of Art (inv. 1952.62)

Francesco Guardi, *San Giorgio Maggiore, Venice*, oil on canvas, 47.6 × 87.6 cm, Leeds Art Gallery

Francesco Guardi, *San Giorgio Maggiore with the Giudecca, Venice*, c.1770s, oil on canvas, 35.2 × 54.7 cm, Wallace Collection, London (cat. 23)

To cat. 20:

Francesco Guardi, *The Church of Santa Maria della Salute, Venice*, c.1770–90, oil on canvas, 71.1 × 94.9 cm, National Gallery of Canada, Ottawa (inv. 6188)

Francesco Guardi, *The Church of Santa Maria della Salute in Venice*, oil on canvas, 55 × 89 cm, Musée Toulouse-Lautrec, Albi

Francesco Guardi, *View of the Church of Santa Maria della Salute with the Dogana del Mare*, c.1770–80, oil on canvas, 40.9 × 51.2 cm, Norton Simon Museum, Pasadena (inv. F.1972.47.1.P)

Francesco Guardi, *The Entrance to the Grand Canal with Santa Maria della Salute*, c.1760–70, oil on canvas, 34 × 53 cm, Museum Boijmans Van Beuningen, Rotterdam (inv. 3147)

To cat. 21:

Similar in scale:

Francesco Guardi, *Grand Canal with the Rialto Bridge, Venice*, probably c.1780, oil on canvas, 68.5 × 91.5 cm, National Gallery of Art, Washington, DC (inv. 1942.9.27)

Francesco Guardi, *The Rialto Bridge in Venice*, after 1760, oil on canvas, 62 × 93 cm, Musée des Augustins, Toulouse

Francesco Guardi, *The Grand Canal with the Rialto Bridge from the South*, c.1775, oil on canvas, 54.6 × 85.1 cm, San Diego Museum of Art (inv. 1940.77)

Smaller versions, also by Guardi's Workshop:

Francesco Guardi, *View of the Rialto, Venice, from the Grand Canal Looking North*, c.1782, oil on canvas, 43.2 × 62.9 cm, Norton Simon Museum, Pasadena (inv. M.1966.10.05.P)

Francesco Guardi, *The Rialto Bridge*, c.1780, oil on canvas, 20.2 × 30.4 cm, Musée du Louvre, Paris (inv. RF 1961 44)

Workshop of Francesco Guardi, *Venice: The Rialto*, oil on wood, 18.1 × 32.1 cm, Metropolitan Museum of Art, New York (inv. 1982.60.15)

To cat. 22:

No comparable versions in size, scale or viewpoint (with the Dogana higher up in the composition). There are several smaller versions, such as:[58]

Francesco Guardi, *Venice: The Punta della Dogana*, 1780s, oil on canvas, 18.7 × 23.8 cm, National Gallery, London (NG6156)

Francesco Guardi, *View of the Punta della Dogana in Venice*, oil on canvas, 33 × 52 cm, Private Collection, Italy

Francesco Guardi, *The Punta della Dogana, Venice*, oil on copper, 13.2 × 16.2 cm, Christie's, London, 8 July 2016, lot 214

TECHNICAL NOTES

Cats 19 and 20 have a similar double-ground structure composed of a yellow lower layer and a fairly thick, off-white, upper layer. The off-white upper layer is composed of two layers. The upper of the two off-white layers was perhaps meant to contribute to the modelling of the architecture. Alternatively, Guardi may have used two layers of upper ground to obtain the tone and opacity he required. Cats 21 and 22 have a similar double-ground structure composed of a dark, red-brown lower layer and a fairly thick, off-white upper layer.[59] Across the set, Guardi first laid in the main architectural elements then added the figures and details at a later stage for decorative effect.

After the duc de Morny brought the pictures from Russia to Paris in 1857, he had them relined, probably around 1860. Cats 21 and 22 were transferred by having their original canvases removed and replaced with two layers of scrim (fine material) before being lined onto another canvas. This transfer process caused a distinct craquelure pattern, with the paint layers cracking across the surface of the pictures. Over time this led to serious flaking and blistering. In January 1904 the varnish was rising in several areas of cat. 22. As a result, the varnish was removed from points where it was rising, and the picture was revarnished by Frederick Haines & Sons.[60] Continued cracking led to more interventions to cat. 22 in July 1929, when the surface cracks and ridges were relaid with a hot iron by Frank Morrell and the varnish retouched by a Mr Dozer on both paintings.[61] Cats 19 and 20 were relined in the traditional way, with the original canvas kept intact. This, combined with the lack of earlier compositions underneath, resulted in cats 19 and 20 being in a better state of preservation than cats 21 and 22.

At the time of the nineteenth-century relining, the pictures were re-stretched onto larger stretchers and enlarged by approximately 2 cm on each edge. Those stretchers are still on the paintings today and bear the liner's label and stamp: 'MOMPER/A/PARIS'.[62] The pictures were enlarged in order to fit matching heavy nineteenth-century livery frames in which the duc de Morny habitually displayed his pictures. These frames were retained by Lord Hertford and still frame the pictures today.

In 2001 cats 21 and 22 were relined and re-stretched by Simon Bobak. At this point Bobak also consolidated paint in cats 19 and 20. All four paintings were cleaned and restored by Anna Sanden that same year.

LITERATURE

Watson 1968, pp. 140–41
Morassi 1973, vol. 1, p. 392, no. 432 (cat. 19);
     p. 402, no. 487 (cat. 20); p. 408, no. 528 (cat. 21);
     p. 404, no. 505 (cat. 22)
Rossi Bortolatto 1974, p. 104, no. 241 (cat. 19);
     p. 112, no. 377 (cat. 20); pp. 113–14, no. 405 (cat. 21);
     p. 98, no. 151 (cat. 22)
Ingamells 1985, pp. 285–86 (cat. 19); pp. 289–90
     (cat. 20); pp. 292–94 (cat. 21); pp. 287–88 (cat. 22)
Duffy and Hedley 2004, pp. 188–89

LP

23. **FRANCESCO GUARDI**
(Venice 1712–1793)

San Giorgio Maggiore with the Giudecca

c.1770s
oil on canvas
35.2 × 54.7 cm
P517

24. **FRANCESCO GUARDI**
(Venice 1712–1793)

The Dogana with Santa Maria della Salute

c.1770s
oil on canvas
35 × 54.7 cm
P518

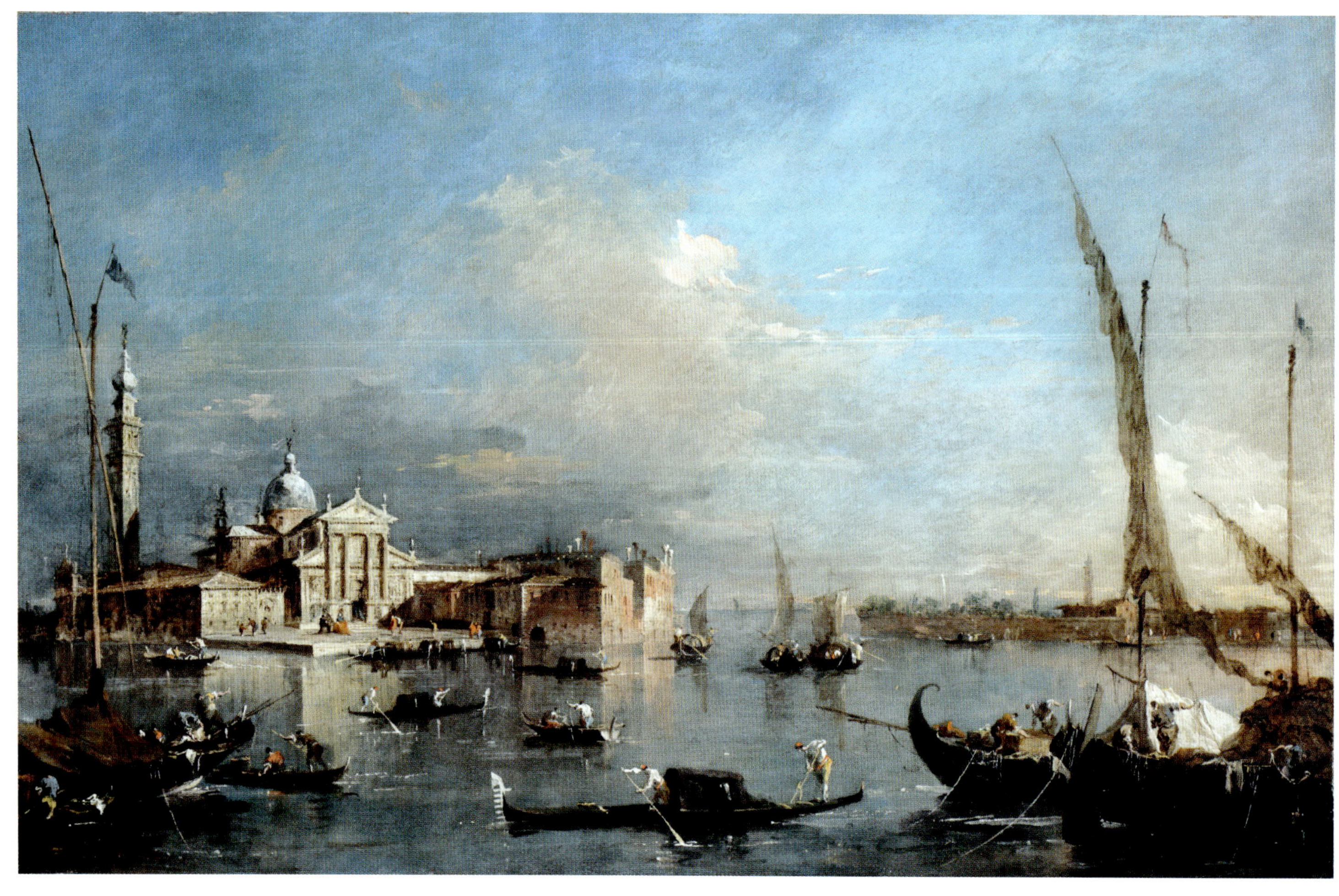

This delightful pair features two of Venice's most famous churches, San Giorgio Maggiore, situated on the island with the same name, and Santa Maria della Salute, located at the entrance to the Grand Canal. Guardi often paired these churches together, as attested by two other paintings at the Wallace Collection in which they appear that were part of the same series (cats 19, 20).[1] The views are taken from a similar vantage point on the quayside near the Piazzetta, looking east in the view of San Giorgio and west in that of the Salute. Painted on a relatively modest scale, this pendant pair was perfect for a client seeking a souvenir without the financial commitment of larger paintings by Guardi. Additionally, their modest scale made the pictures easy to transport, an added bonus for a Grand Tourist undertaking a long journey across Europe with multiple stops along the way.

The view in cat. 23 is taken from the Molo, just east of the Piazzetta before the Doge's Palace. Guardi featured the island of San Giorgio with its impressive church on the left and the island of the Giudecca with the church and *campanile* of San Giovanni Battista in the distance on the right. The picture repeats the composition in cat. 19, albeit on a smaller scale and with variations in the boats and figures.[2] Guardi also lowered the viewpoint in the present picture and omitted Le Zitelle from the Giudecca. As with cat. 19, Guardi included fishing boats with sails lowered to frame the composition on the left and right and a gondola positioned at an angle in the central foreground.

The view in cat. 24 is taken from slightly further along the mainland, at the far western edge of the Giardini Reali (Royal Gardens). It captures the mouth of the Grand Canal, the Dogana, the Seminario Patriarcale, the Salute and the Monastery of San Gregorio at the right. The Giudecca is visible in the left distance. The subject appears in two other paintings by Guardi at the Wallace Collection (cats 20, 22). The Dogana is represented from asimilar angle without the Salute in cat. 22 and the Salute is featured from the opposite side looking east in cat. 20.[3] The waterway is bustling with boats and figures and the quay before the Dogana is full of what are presumably merchants and sailors unloading cargo and paying customs charges. A beautifully curved, drawn sail frames the

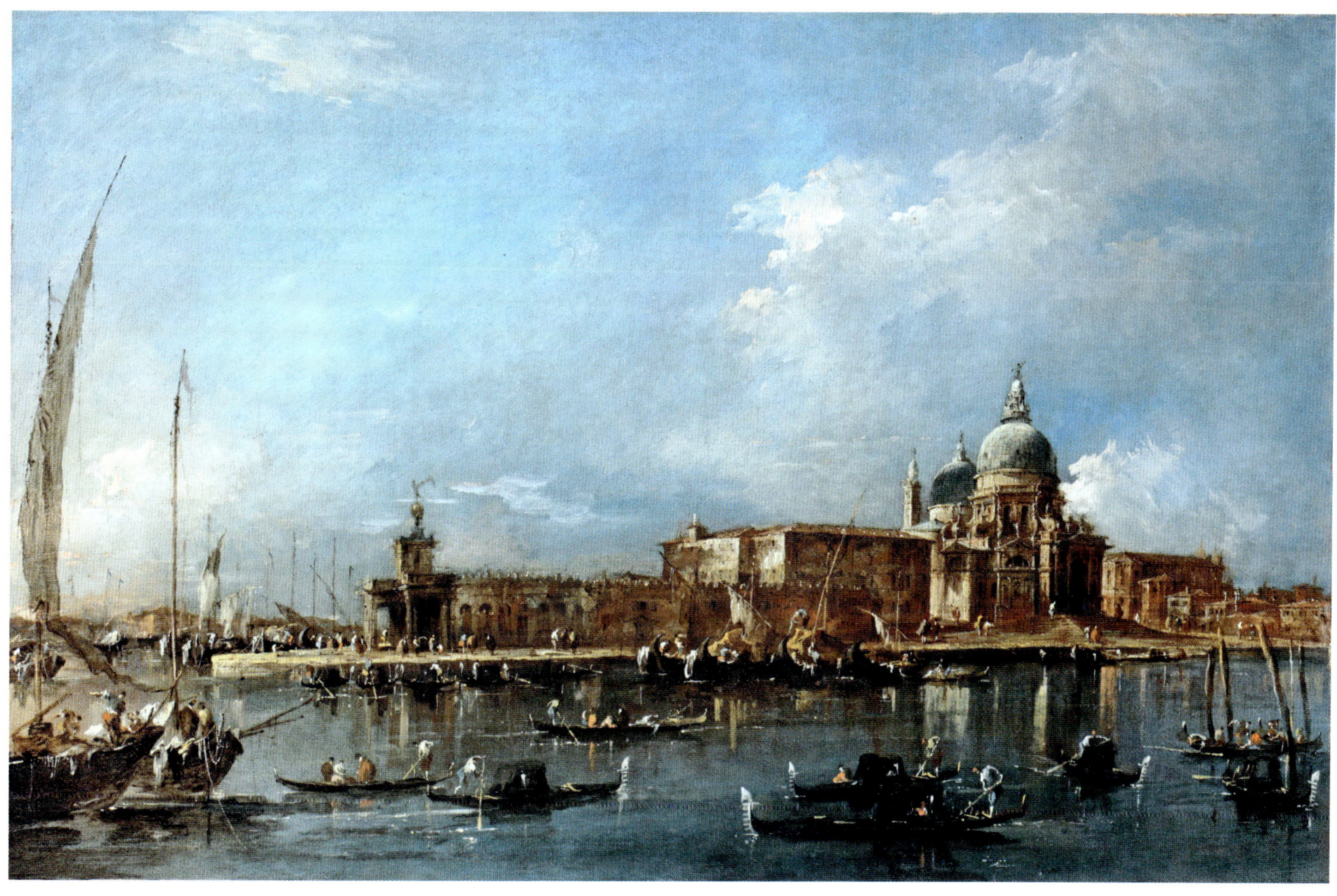

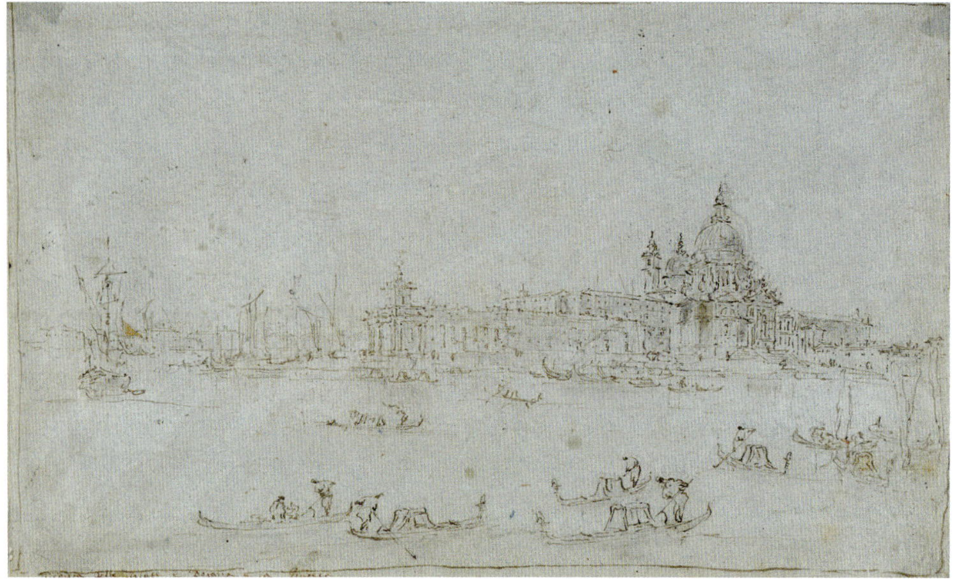

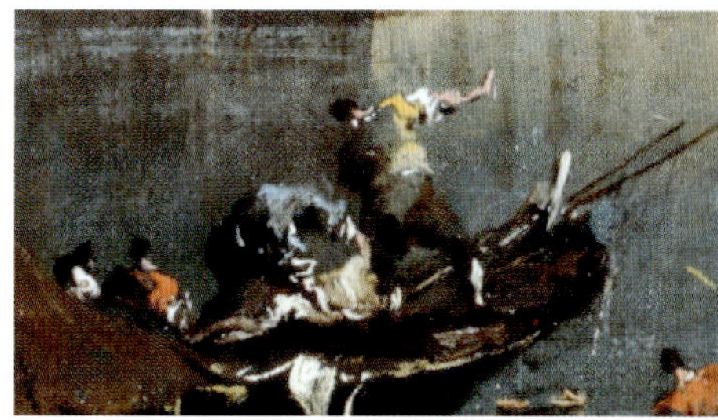

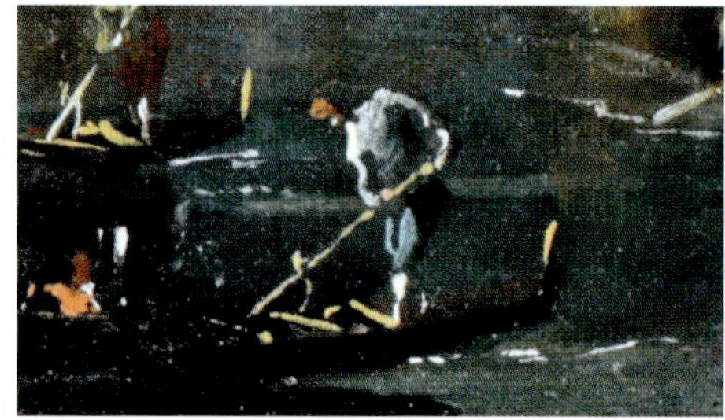

composition on the left and encourages the viewer to admire the famous sites depicted in the rest of the painting.

The pictures work well as a pair. When placed side by side, they present a 180-degree view across the Bacino. The horizon lines, Giudecca and cut-off boats create continuity across the pair. Moreover, bright morning light shining on the Salute balances the strong evening sun reflected on San Giorgio.

Both paintings were standard compositions that Guardi worked up in drawings. His close observation of the composition with San Giorgio has already been noted (see fig. 135).[4] A sheet at the Ashmolean, perhaps executed *in situ*, reflects Guardi's study of the Salute from the same angle as in the present view. He deliberated the position of the main dome directly on the sheet (fig. 151).

The paintings were built up quickly, with the sky and water painted first using a mainly wet-in-wet technique after which the buildings and figures were subsequently added. Guardi's shorthand and fluid painting of figures is

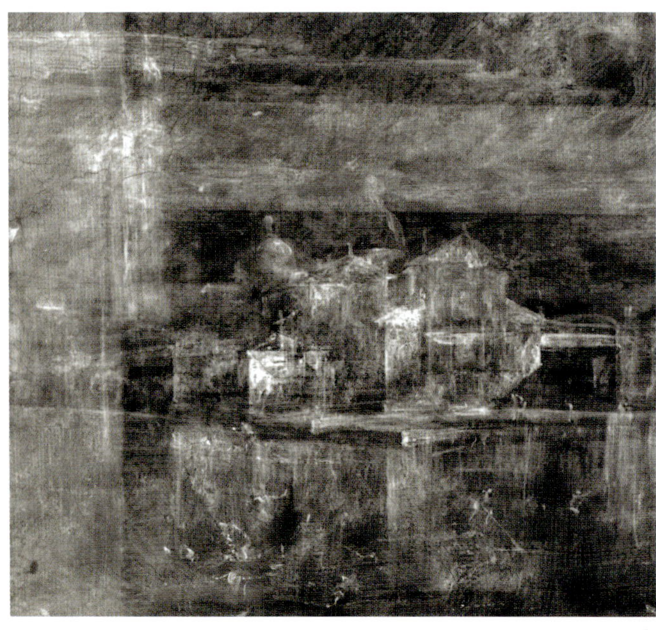

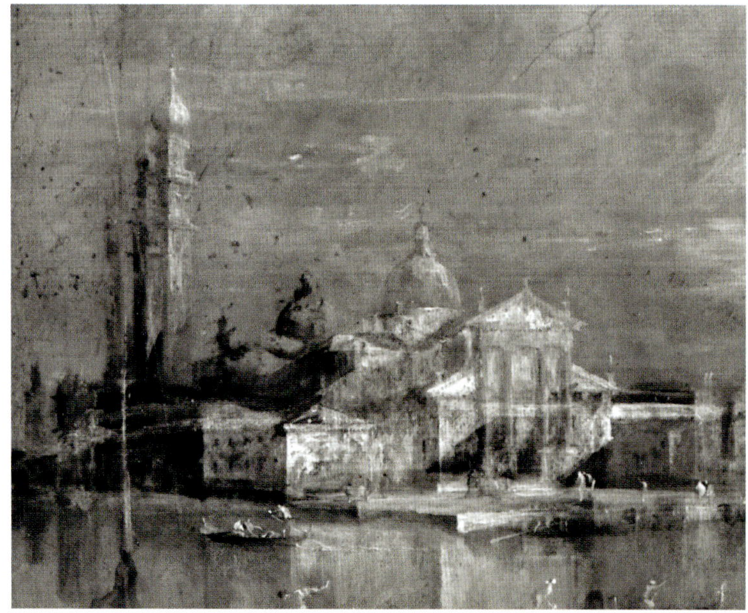

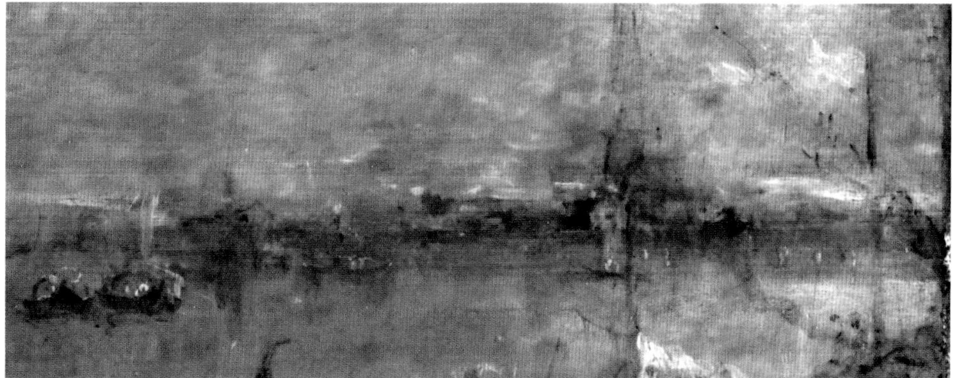

Fig. 154. Detail of IRR of cat. 23

apparent in both works. In cat. 23 he painted the standing figure with his right arm outstretched on the lower left using the blue background as the mid tone for the figure's back, and yellow and pink strokes for the garment, arm and neck (fig. 152). Similarly, in cat. 24 he rendered the standing gondolier in the right foreground using curvy, loose and quick brushstrokes of fluid paint on top of blue glazes for the water (fig. 153).

Pentimenti in both paintings suggest that Guardi worked out the final position of the architecture directly on the support. He initially placed San Giorgio and its *campanile* to the left and further back in the distance. X-ray and infrared reflectography reveal that

the initial church was well under way with the dome, façade, *campanile* and adjacent buildings blocked in with lead white before Guardi decided to shift the building to the right and bring it forward (figs 155, 156). Infrared reflectography also revealed that he initially positioned the church of San Giovanni Battista and its *campanile* further to the left on the Giudecca (fig. 154). He decided to shift the entire composition to the right in order to get a better (and closer) view of San Giorgio, his main subject. In the pendant, the X-ray reveals that Guardi enlarged the smaller of the two domes of the Salute, probably to make the church more prominent (fig. 157). Moreover, he elongated the Salute and

widened the quay before the Dogana with similar considerations in mind. Infrared reflectography did not reveal underdrawing in either picture and no incision lines or other marks were detected that could indicate drawing tools.

Study of the *pentimenti* coupled with technical analysis revealed Guardi's overarching concern with aesthetic effect over topographical accuracy. He probably originally conceived the pair as a single-viewpoint panorama. He began by painting San Giorgio as he saw it from the quay, smaller and further away. But in the final version the churches appear equidistant from the viewer. Guardi thus changed his mind and used different viewpoints for each scene in order to accord both landmarks equal prominence. As a result, the paintings balance each other out and are visually appealing as a coherent unit.

As already noted, both compositions exist in multiple versions with minor variations.[5] For example, in a comparable view of San Giorgio similar in scale, Guardi included more of the Giudecca so as to encompass Le Zitelle (fig. 158). Likewise, in a painting of the Dogana and Salute equivalent in size, he included fewer boats on the water (fig. 159).

The *campanile* of San Giorgio collapsed in 1774 and was rebuilt in 1791. However, this cannot be used to date the paintings as Guardi often manipulated topographical details for aesthetic effect. On stylistic grounds, the pictures adhere to the artist's manner from the 1770s.[6]

Although their exact date of acquisition remains unconfirmed, it is possible that the 4th Marquess purchased the paintings on one of two occasions. It may be that he bought them at the William Wells sale on 12 May 1848, where Lord Hertford also acquired his two views of the Doge's Palace by Canaletto (cats 7, 8) along with seven other pictures.[7] Two paintings by Guardi of the same subject were featured in Wells's sale and were bought by someone called 'White'.[8] As was customary for Hertford, he had multiple dealers buying on his behalf at that sale, including Mawson, Robertson and Theobald. It may be that White was among them. However, without further specification of the

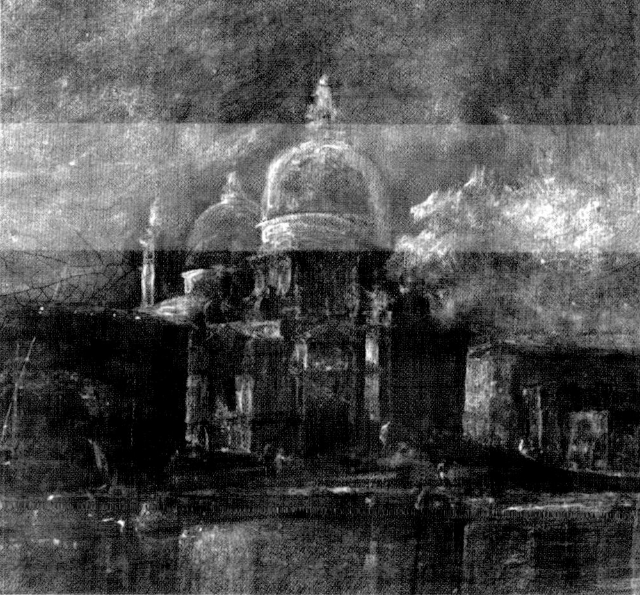

Fig. 155. Detail of X-ray of cat. 23

OPPOSITE, RIGHT:
Fig. 156. Detail of IRR of cat. 23

RIGHT:
Fig. 157. Detail of X-ray of cat. 24

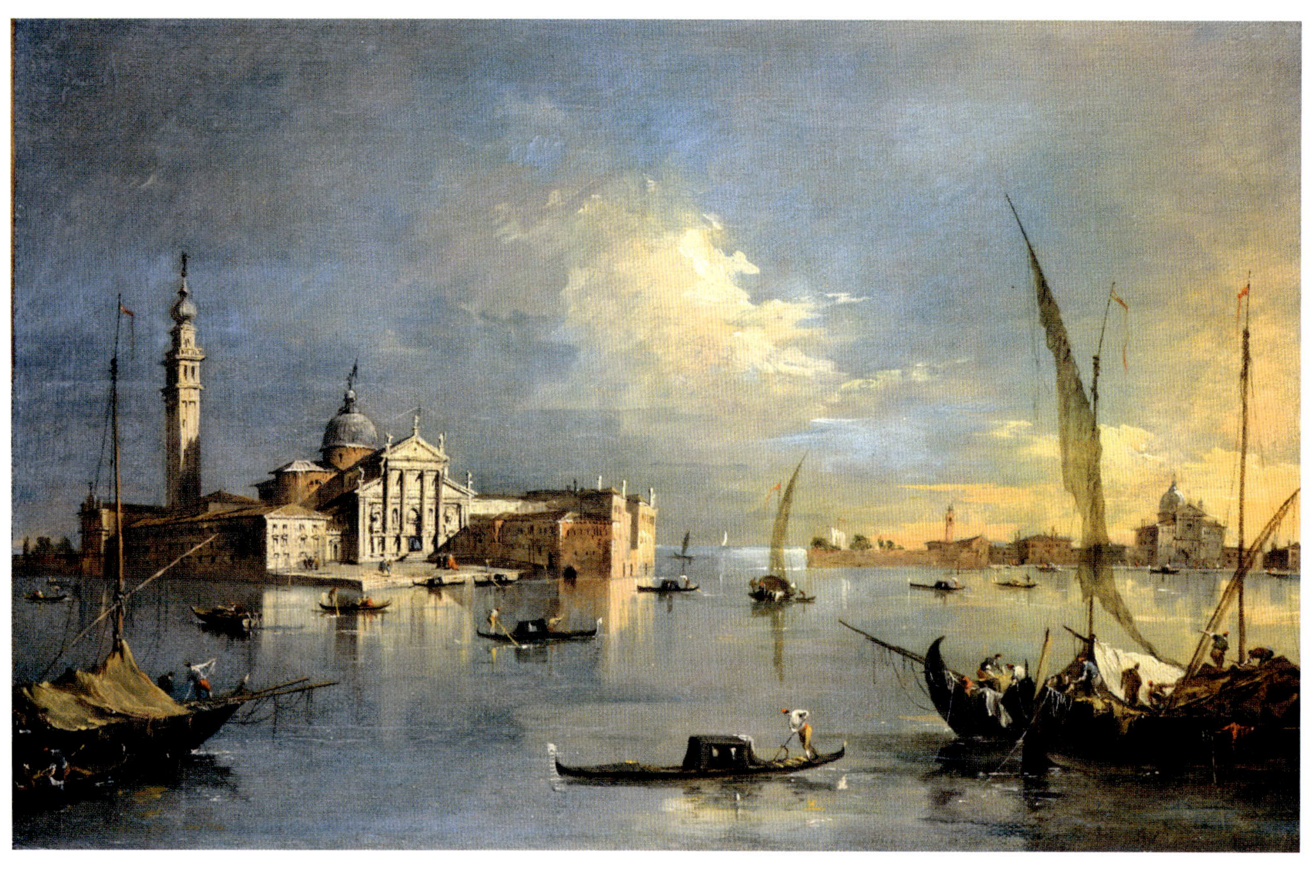

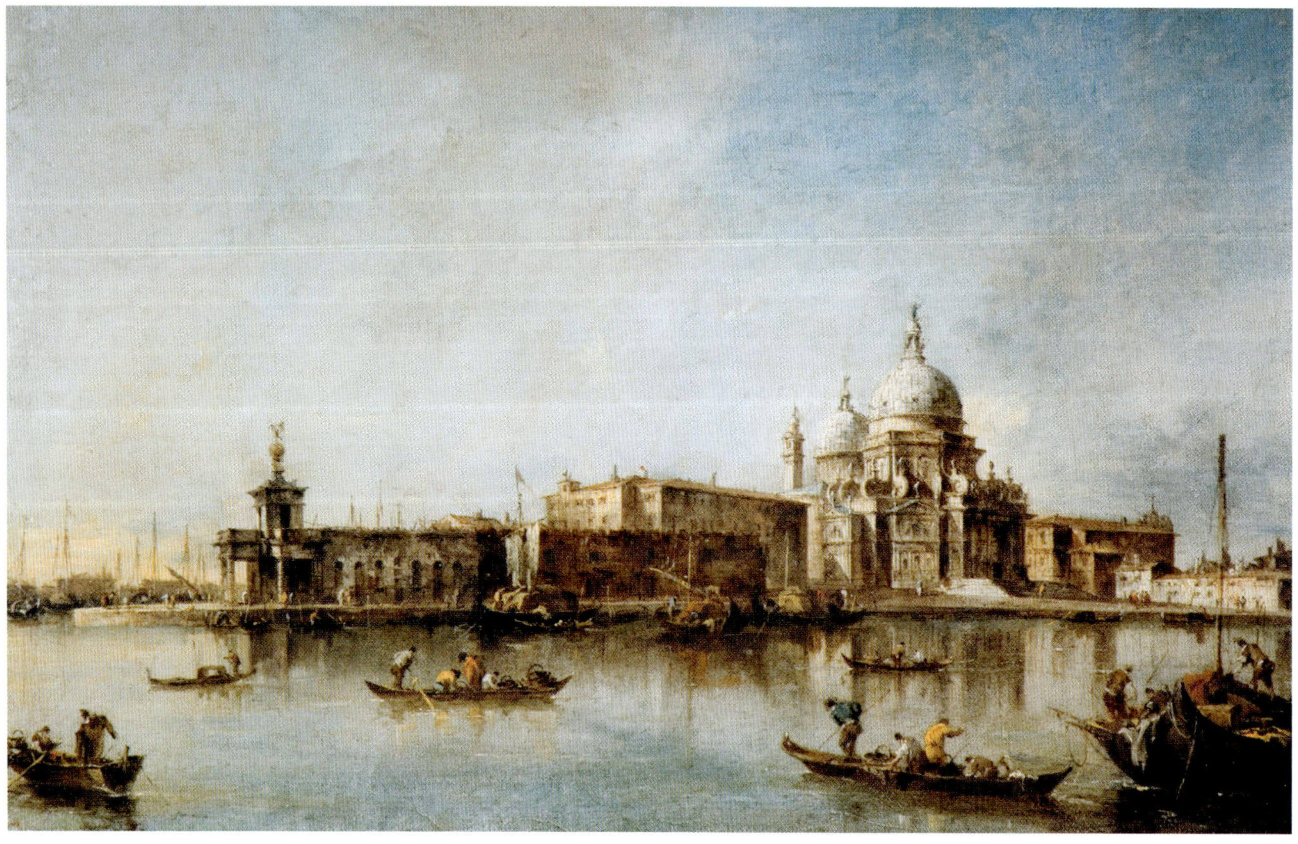

pictures' dimensions or confirmation that Hertford worked with a dealer by that name, it is difficult to know whether the present paintings were the ones sold in Wells's sale.

Alternatively, the pair was bought back by Hertford from Sir Richard Wallace at the latter's 1857 sale of his personal collection.[9] Wallace owned two paintings by Guardi described in the sale as a 'View of the Grand Canal' and a 'View of the Dogana'.[10] Perhaps the auctioneer made a mistake and described the view of San Giorgio as one of the Grand Canal. This was known to happen. The Guardi pair was bought by Ferdinand Laneuville, who purchased 19 other paintings at Wallace's sale, six of which correspond to works in the Wallace Collection today.[11] It may be that the present pair was among these.[12]

The pictures do not appear in the 1871 inventory of Hertford's Parisian residence at 2 rue Laffitte.[13] Moreover, there was no inventory taken of Hertford House upon the 4th Marquess's death in 1870. The pictures were in London by 1872 when they were exhibited with the rest of Wallace's collection at Bethnal Green.[14]

PROVENANCE

Acquired by Richard Seymour-Conway, 4th Marquess of Hertford (1800–1870); by descent to Sir Richard Wallace, 1st Baronet (1818–1890); by descent to his wife, Lady Wallace (Julie Amélie Charlotte Castelnau, 1819–1897); by whom bequeathed with the rest of the Wallace Collection to the British nation, 1897.

EXHIBITION

1872–75: 'Paintings, Porcelain, Bronzes, Decorative Furniture and other Works of Art lent by Sir Richard Wallace to the Bethnal Green Branch of the South Kensington Museum'.[15]

RELATED WORKS

To cat. 23:

Francesco Guardi, *San Giorgio Maggiore and the Giudecca*, c.1780, oil on canvas, 33 × 51.5 cm, Private Collection[16]

Francesco Guardi, *View of the Island of San Giorgio Maggiore*, 1765–75, oil on canvas, 43 × 61 cm, Hermitage Museum, St Petersburg

Francesco Guardi, *The Church of San Giorgio Maggiore in Venice*, c.1780, oil on canvas, 20.2 × 30 cm, Musée du Louvre, Paris, (inv. RF 1961 45)

Francesco Guardi, *San Giorgio Maggiore with the Giudecca and Le Zitelle, Venice*, 1770s–80s, oil on canvas, 70.5 × 93.5 cm, Wallace Collection, London (cat. 19)

To cat. 24:

Francesco Guardi, *Venice, Santa Maria della Salute and the Dogana*, 1790, oil on canvas, 32.5 × 52 cm, Birmingham Museum and Art Gallery (inv. 1947P74)

Francesco Guardi, *The Old Customs House and the Church of Santa Maria della Salute*, c.1785, oil on canvas, 48.3 × 66 cm, Legion of Honor, San Francisco (inv. 1940.55)

Francesco Guardi, *Santa Maria della Salute and the Dogana, Venice*, c.1783, oil on canvas, 49.8 × 89.9 cm, Museum of Fine Arts, Houston (inv. 44.562)

Francesco Guardi, *The Entrance to the Grand Canal*, oil on canvas, 24.1 × 35.6 cm, Private Collection[17]

Francesco Guardi, *The Entrance to the Grand Canal, Venice, Looking towards the Dogana and Santa Maria della Salute*, oil on canvas, 83.8 × 128.6 cm, Private Collection[18]

TECHNICAL NOTES

Both pictures were painted on a plain-weave canvas and were glue-paste lined onto a plain-weave canvas sometime in the nineteenth century. The tacking margins have been trimmed away in both works. The pictures have a similar double ground. The first layer consists of gypsum (calcium sulphate), some starch and a protein binder, most likely animal glue.[19] This is followed by a reddish-brown upper layer that has an oil medium as binder. Both paintings were cleaned by William Vallance in 1961.[20] They were then cleaned and analysed at the Hamilton Kerr Institute in 2021. Technical investigation comprising X-radiography, infrared reflectography, ultraviolet light photography, surface micrography and SEM-EDX paint sample analysis was undertaken at this point.

LITERATURE

Watson 1968, p. 142
Morassi 1973, vol. 1, pp. 391–92, no. 429 (cat. 23);
     p. 401, no. 481 (cat. 24)
Rossi Bortolatto 1974, p. 104, no. 249 (cat. 23);
     p. 107, no. 297 (cat. 24)
Ingamells 1985, pp. 295–96 (cat. 23);
     pp. 296–97 (cat. 24)
Duffy and Hedley 2004, pp. 190–91
Succi 2021, vol. 2, pp. 216–17

LP

OPPOSITE, ABOVE:
Fig. 158. Francesco Guardi (1712–1793), *San Giorgio Maggiore and the Giudecca*, c.1780, oil on canvas, 33 × 51.5 cm, Private Collection

OPPOSITE, BELOW:
Fig. 159. Francesco Guardi (1712–1793), *Venice, Santa Maria della Salute and the Dogana*, 1790, oil on canvas, 32.5 × 52 cm, Birmingham Museum and Art Gallery (inv. 1947P74)

25. FRANCESCO GUARDI

(Venice 1712–1793)

Capriccio with the Archway of the Torre dell'Orologio

late 1780s
oil on beech panel
27.6 × 22.1 cm (oval)
P502

Inscriptions and labels on reverse:
remnants of an undecipherable red wax
seal; a paper label with the number '444'
crossed through; dark brown paper backing.

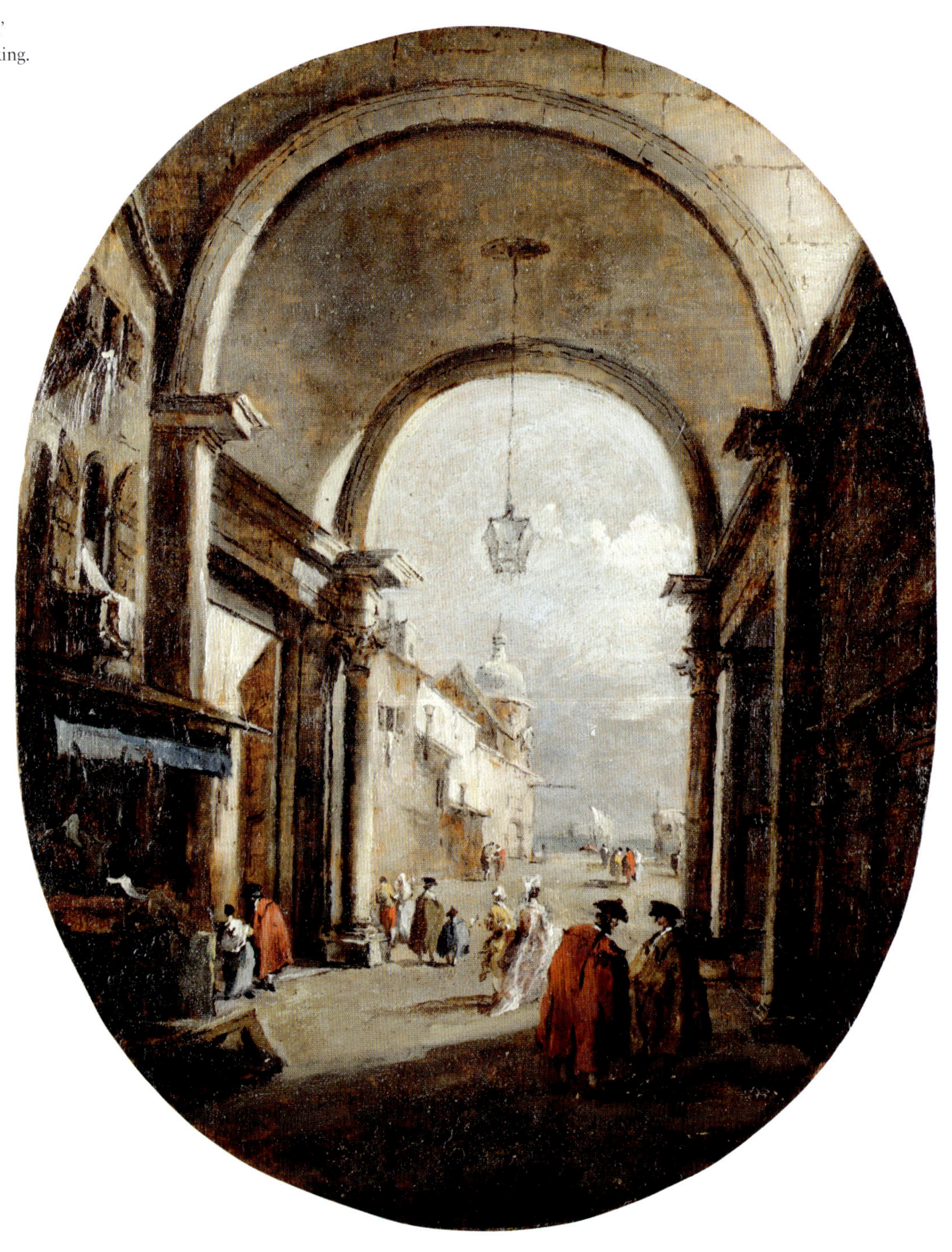

26. FRANCESCO GUARDI

(Venice 1712–1793)

*Capriccio with the Arcade of the Doge's Palace
and San Giorgio Maggiore*

late 1780s
oil on beech panel
27.6 × 22.1 cm (oval)
P504

Inscriptions and labels on reverse: remnants of
an undecipherable red wax seal; a paper label;
dark brown paper backing.

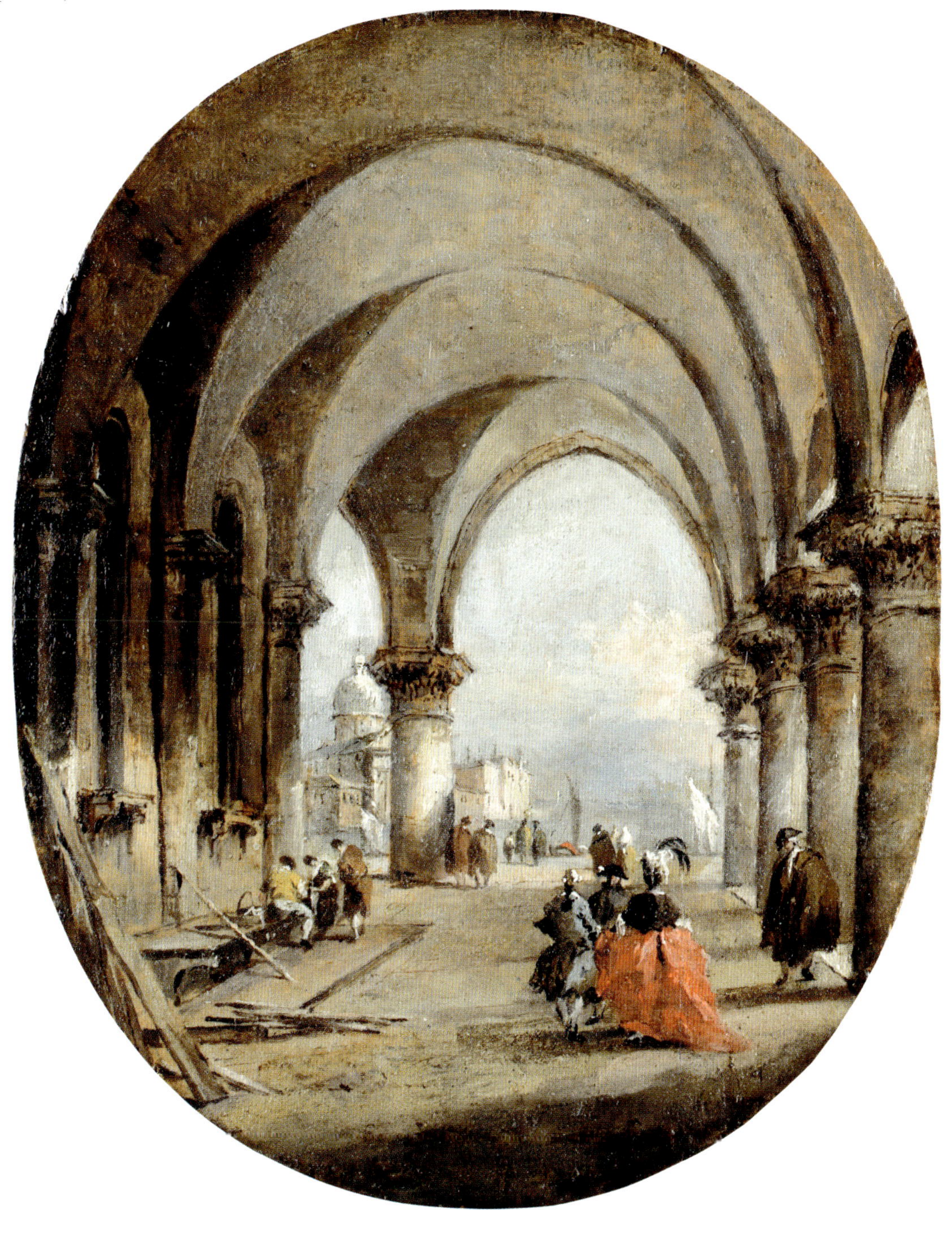

The *capriccio*, or architectural fantasy, developed into a popular independent genre during the early eighteenth century. The word derives from the Italian for the unexpected leaping of a young goat and describes a composition that combines imaginary and real architecture. Guardi excelled at the genre and produced a number of *capricci*. This whimsical pair of oval panels features recognisable Venetian archways with churches in the distance. Such views were used to conjure up images of Venice without the binds of topographical accuracy. They were highly popular with Grand Tourists, not least for their small size, which made them easy to transport on a long journey. *Capricci* were also collected by Venetians who enjoyed the playful rearrangement of familiar landmarks.

Both paintings feature archways in the foreground drawn from Venetian architecture. The archway in cat. 25 recalls that of the Torre dell'Orologio, the famous clock tower in Piazza San Marco.[1] A technical and engineering feat, the clock faces the square and was a great tourist attraction in the eighteenth century. Seen from the Merceria Orologio, the archway leads to an imaginary landscape inspired by the lagoon. In reality, this viewpoint looks out onto the Piazza San Marco with the Basilica on the left, the columns of San Tòdaro and San Marco in the Piazzetta and the church of San Giorgio Maggiore in the distance. Instead of the Basilica, Guardi included a single-domed church adjacent to a waterway, probably an allusion to the Bacino di San Marco. He painted a dilapidated shopfront in the left foreground, much like the shops that lined the Merceria. The hanging lantern is an extant feature, still used to illuminate the arcade to this day.

The archway in cat. 26 is that of the colonnade on the western side of the Doge's Palace.[2] The palace's arcade consists of a succession of arches supported by classical columns. Across the Bacino in the distance is a view of the church and monastery complex of San Giorgio Maggiore. Although mostly accurate, this view has some caprice elements. The buildings to the right of San Giorgio are brought closer to the church. On the left,

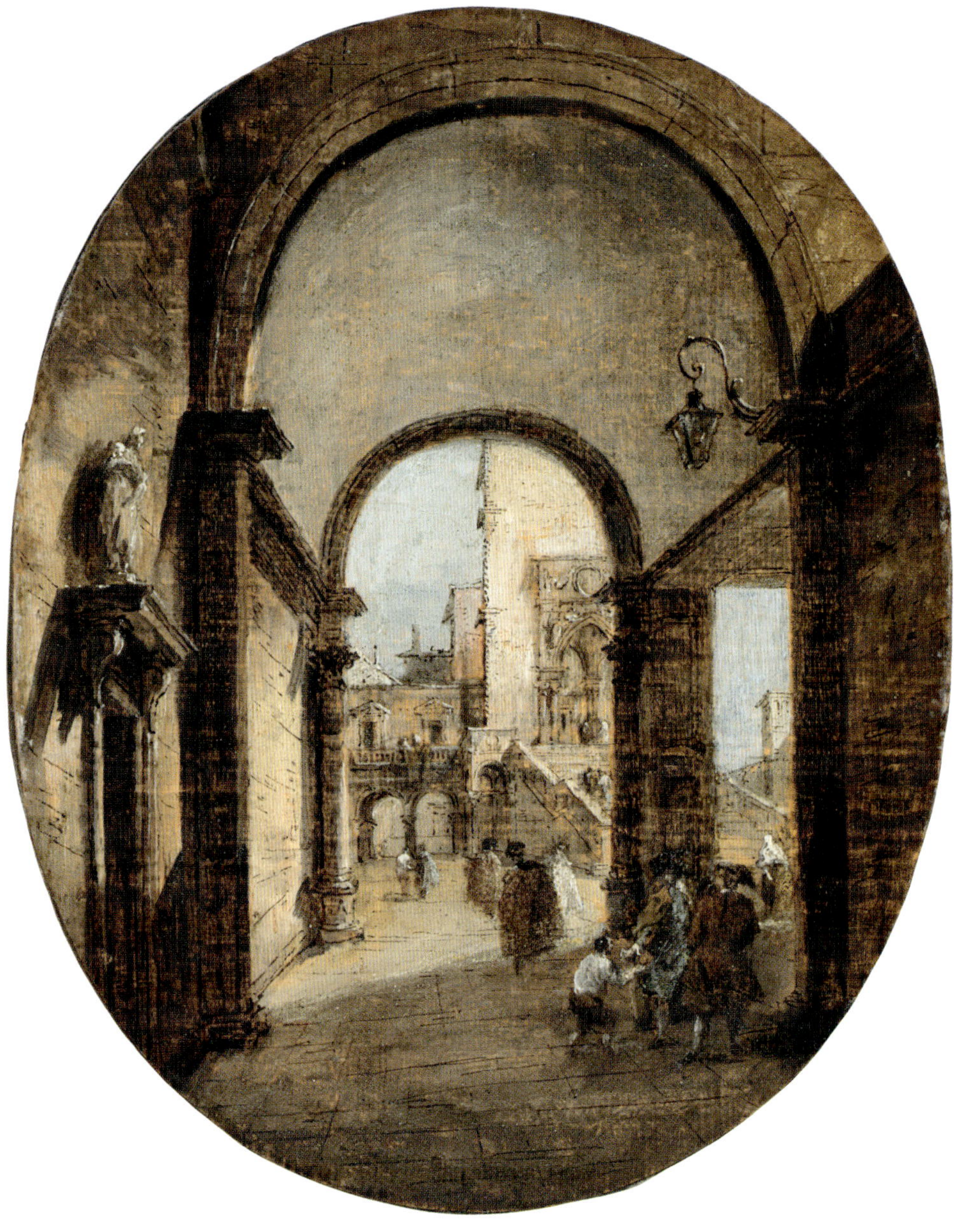

the wooden planks set against the wall and ground evoke a sense of dilapidated grandeur.

The pictures feature archways that frame the compositions and echo their oval support. The view in cat. 25 is taken from a slightly higher point and the waterway is further in the distance. In cat. 26 the viewpoint is lowered and the waterway is closer to the viewer. The pictorial rendering of light is particularly elaborate in these pictures, with vast areas bathed in sunlight and others cast in shadow. The views are populated by shimmering, evanescent figures, some of which

correspond across the pictures. For example, the figure wearing a brown cloak and black hat in the right foreground of cat. 26 resembles the man talking to another gentleman in red in the foreground of cat. 25. Moreover, the well-dressed couple seen from the back in the foreground of cat. 26 echo a comparable couple with their backs turned in the middle distance of cat. 25. The red dress of the elegant noblewoman in cat. 26 and the red cloaks worn by several figures in cat. 25 create accents of colour across the compositions. Open sails are seen in the distance of both pictures. The dome

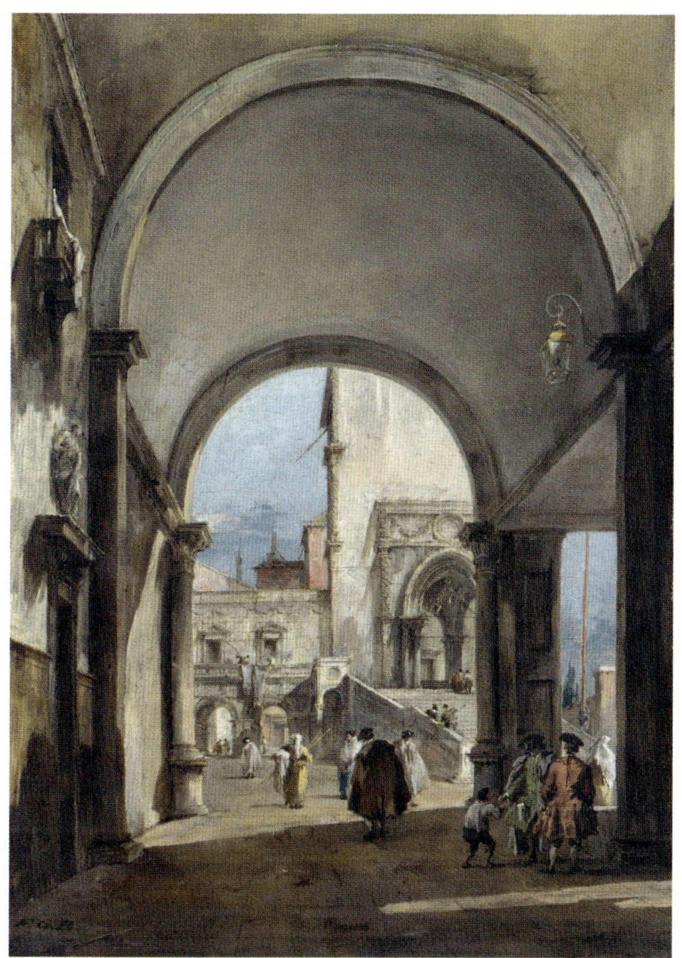

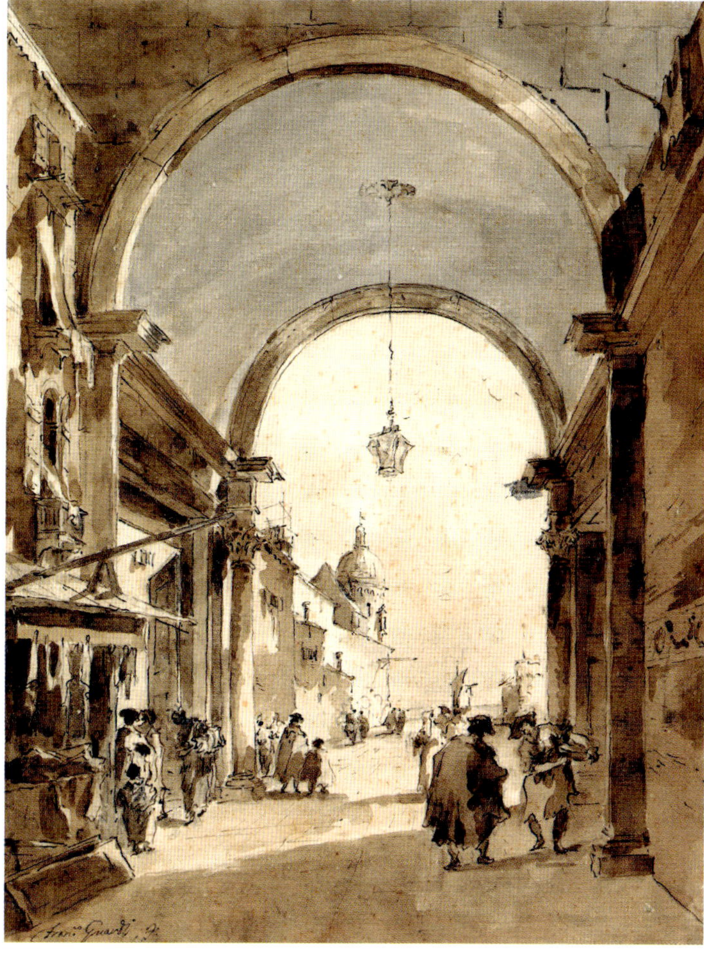

OPPOSITE:

Fig. 160. Francesco Guardi (1712–1793), *An Architectural Caprice*, 1780, oil on paper mounted on panel, 27.3 × 24 cm, Musée des Beaux-Arts de Lyon (inv. B-517)

ABOVE, LEFT:

Fig. 161. Francesco Guardi (1712–1793), *An Architectural Caprice*, 1770–80, oil on canvas, 54.2 × 36.2 cm, National Gallery, London (NG2523)

ABOVE, RIGHT:

Fig. 162. Francesco Guardi (1712–1793), *A View through an Arcade to a Church with Figures*, pen and brown ink, brown and grey wash over black chalk, 35 × 27 cm, British Museum, London (inv. 1861,0810.10)

of San Giorgio in cat. 26 is similar to that of the church shown in cat. 25. Guardi has taken delight in depicting certain details, such as the white cloth draped over a windowsill in cat. 25 or the planks of wood set against the wall in cat. 26 that cast shadows. He exaggerated the height of the arches in both paintings.

The pair was possibly part of a *terzetto*, or trio, together with an oval panel of comparable dimensions in Lyons (fig. 160).[3] The Lyons panel is closely conceived around the archway of the Torre dell' Orologio. The statue above the doorway at the left is of Guardi's invention. This view features a free adaptation of the inner courtyard of the Doge's Palace in the distance. Guardi painted the famous Scala dei Giganti (Giants' Staircase) but omitted the two marble sculptures of Neptune and Mars that adorn it. Two men in the foreground give a coin to a boy who is begging; they recall the two men

engaged in conversation in the foreground of cat. 25. The figure wearing a brown cloak and black hat in the centre recurs in both paintings at the Wallace Collection. The Lyons picture is an oval replica of a painting on a slightly larger scale and rectangular format at the National Gallery (fig. 161). The latter was also part of a trio together with two paintings of similar, rectangular dimensions previously in the collection of the Earl of Normanton.[4] These feature the same views as in the Wallace Collection paintings: the colonnade of the Doge's Palace and the arch of the Torre dell'Orologio.

The composition in cat. 25 exists in several drawings with slight variations. In a sheet in the British Museum, for example, the man in the right foreground is turned to face the viewer, is more plainly dressed and carries something (fig. 162). This sheet could have been a preparatory drawing for one of the paintings of this composition or a finished work in its own right based on such works.[5]

The paintings were executed using the same technique and materials and show similar paint handling and execution. The paint layers were thinly applied in both works. There are numerous passages where the pale colour of the support is probably intentionally visible as a warm mid tone. This is especially obvious in the architecture, such as the interior of the arches, although subsequent wear and increased transparency of the paint are likely to have made this effect more evident. *Pentimenti* on the arch on the right side of cat. 26 suggest that the height of the arch was slightly increased (fig. 163).

The order of painting is similar across the pair. The compositions were first defined with areas of semi-opaque brown and grey. The skies were painted after this initial laying-in, followed by the darker shadows and finer details of the architecture. The latter were painted using thin, broken and slightly undulating black or dark brown lines noticeable, for example, around the arch in cat. 25 (fig. 164). Details were subsequently added to define clouds and figures using more textured and viscous white and pale cream paint. X-rays did not show evidence of alteration to the composition, nor did infrared reflectography reveal any planning lines below the paint surface.

As with many of Guardi's works, other versions of the present pictures are known. Perhaps the closest composition to cat. 25 is a painting in Munich executed on a larger scale and in a rectangular format (fig. 165). In that work, Guardi included a charming dog, varied the figures and added a blue awning in the upper left and a figure leaning over a red drapery in the upper right. Comparable to cat. 26 is a painting in Lisbon in which the figures vary slightly and more wooden planks are featured in the foreground (fig. 166). The Wallace pair is datable to the late 1780s based on Guardi's execution and the fashions depicted.[6]

The 4th Marquess of Hertford bought the three *capricci* by Guardi in the collection, the present pair and cat. 27. In doing so he added a more Continental perspective of Venice to his *vedute* collection, as Guardi was popular on the French art market in the middle of the nineteenth century. Guardi's decorative finesse must have appealed to a man who liked pleasing pictures and who said 'with me fancy plays a big part'.[7]

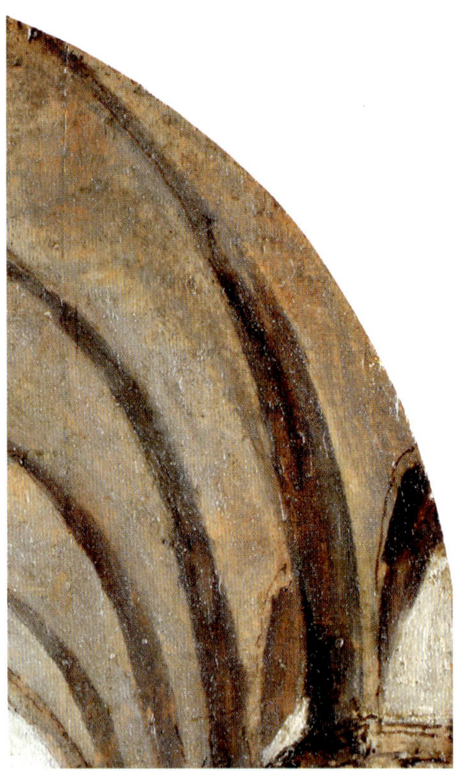

ABOVE:
Fig. 163. Detail of cat. 26

BELOW:
Fig. 164. Detail of cat. 25

OPPOSITE, LEFT:
Fig. 165. Francesco Guardi (1712–1793), *Archway View*, c.1750/85, oil on canvas, 60 × 43 cm, Alte Pinakothek, Munich (inv. HUW 10)

OPPOSITE, RIGHT:
Fig. 166. Francesco Guardi (1712–1793), *Arches of the Doge's Palace*, oil on panel, 24 × 17 cm, Museu Calouste Gulbenkian, Lisbon

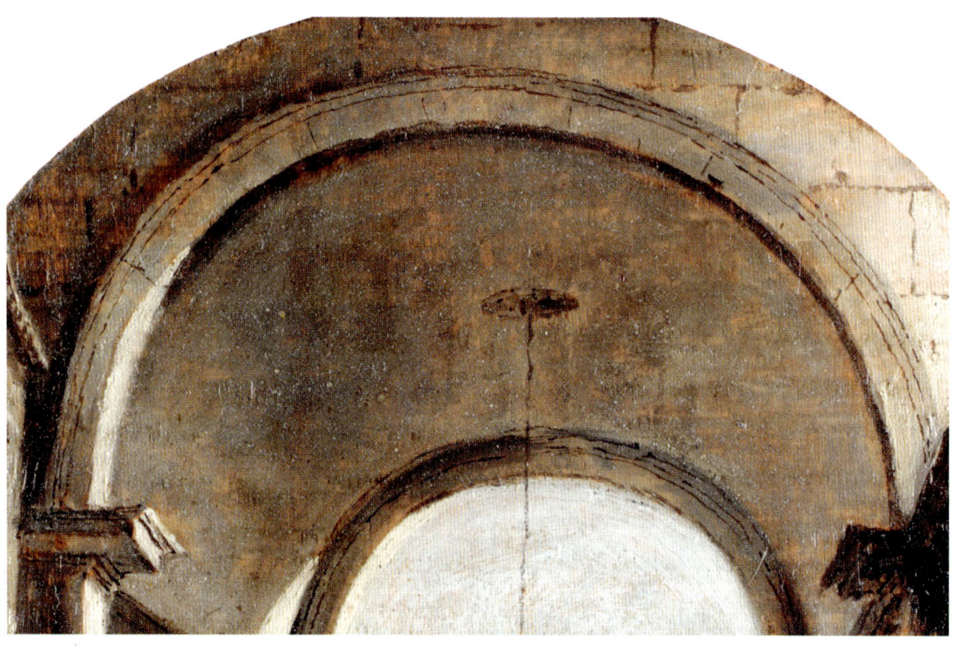

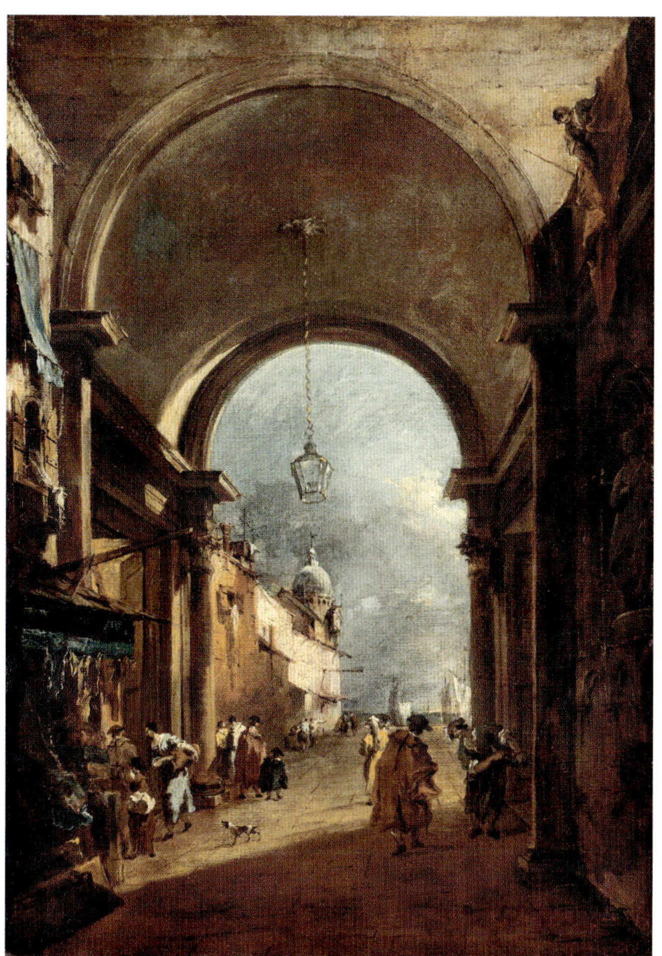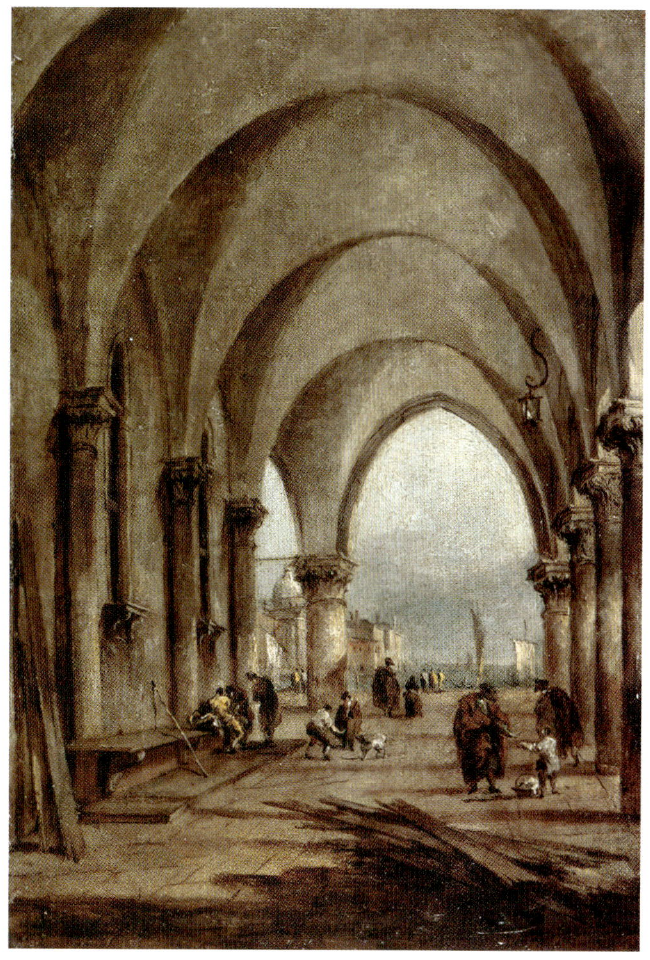

PROVENANCE
Acquired by Richard Seymour-Conway, 4th Marquess
of Hertford (1800–1870); by descent to Sir Richard
Wallace, 1st Baronet (1818–1890); by descent to his
wife, Lady Wallace (Julie Amélie Charlotte Castelnau,
1819–1897); by whom bequeathed with the rest of the
Wallace Collection to the British nation, 1897.

EXHIBITION
1872–75: 'Paintings, Porcelain, Bronzes, Decorative
Furniture and other Works of Art lent by Sir Richard
Wallace to the Bethnal Green Branch of the South
Kensington Museum'.[8]

RELATED WORKS
To cat. 25:

Francesco Guardi, *Archway View*, *c*.1750/85, oil on
canvas, 60 × 43 cm, Alte Pinakothek, Munich
(inv. HUW 10)

Francesco Guardi, *Capriccio with Archway
and Shops*, *c*.1780, 42 × 29 cm, oil on canvas,
Accademia Carrara, Bergamo (inv. 81LC 00091)

Francesco Guardi, *View of Venice*, oil on panel,
52 × 38.5 cm, Hermitage Museum, St Petersburg

Francesco Guardi, *Archway View*, oil on canvas,
49.5 × 36.5 cm, Private Collection

To cat. 26:

Francesco Guardi, *Arches of the Doge's Palace*,
oil on panel, 24 × 17 cm, Museu Calouste
Gulbenkian, Lisbon

Francesco Guardi, *Archway of the Doge's Palace*,
oil on canvas, 49.5 × 36.5 cm, Private Collection

TECHNICAL NOTES
Both paintings are executed on single pieces of very
thin beech wood panels without any joints. Cat. 26
has an irregular split running vertically to the
right of centre. The surfaces are roughly prepared,
in an inexact oval shape. The wood was not fully
smoothed, leaving irregular areas of grain texture.
There is no pigmented ground present in either
picture. Some preparation was probably applied
to the bare wood, such as an oil or resin coating to
seal the surface. Both paintings were cleaned and
analysed at the Hamilton Kerr Institute in 2018.
Technical investigation comprising x-radiography,
infrared reflectography, ultraviolet light photography,
surface micrography and SEM-EDX paint sample
analysis was undertaken at this point.

LITERATURE
Watson 1968, p. 141
Morassi 1973, vol. 1, p. 461, no. 814 (cat. 25);
    p. 455, no. 779 (cat. 26)
Rossi Bortolatto 1974, p. 121, no. 522 (cat. 25);
    p. 134, no. 749 (cat. 26)
Ingamells 1985, pp. 288–89 (cat. 25);
    pp. 291–92 (cat. 26)
Duffy and Hedley 2004, pp. 190–91

LP

27. FRANCESCO GUARDI
(Venice 1712–1793)

Capriccio with the Courtyard of the Doge's Palace

late 1770s
oil on canvas
38.6 × 28.9 cm
P647

Inscriptions and labels on reverse: '93' inscribed in white chalk on the back of the lining canvas;[1] there is a paper label on the horizontal crossbar of the stretcher that reads '647/606'.

This painting is a sound example of Guardi's *capricci*, as it shows a recognisable landmark in an inventive and imaginary light. The view depicts the courtyard of the Doge's Palace with the monumental Scala dei Giganti (Giants' Staircase) seen from the side. This impressive staircase was the principal entrance to the main floor and State Chambers of the Doge's Palace. It was designed by Antonio Rizzo (*c.*1430–1499), one of the most important fifteenth-century sculptors in Venice, between 1483 and 1485, and built in 1497. The staircase was a daring design with a half landing flanked by elegant balustrades. Its name derives from the two colossal statues that adorn it at the top, Jacopo Sansovino's Mars and Neptune, installed in 1567 as symbols of Venice's military and naval prowess. Guardi omitted those sculptures, opting instead for an imposing, gilded statue of Minerva. On the left is the Foscari Arch situated at the end of the Foscari Portico, which connects the Porta della Carità to the courtyard. The arch was built by Bartolomeo Bon (1407–1464) in collaboration with Antonio Bregno (active 1425–57) and Antonio Rizzo.

The view is taken from the waterfront in the south looking through an arcade. Guardi shows only part of the right-hand arch, evoking the sense of a snapshot of a larger scene beyond. The sun-drenched courtyard lies further on from the dark shadows of the arcade. Lively figures populate the scene, climb and descend the stairs and mingle in the square. A man offers money to a boy who is begging in the foreground. High above, two people drape a cloth over a balustrade.

Canaletto had previously used the double arch as a framing device in his *capricci* as a means of heightening their theatrical effect. In fact, he employed a comparable arch and a half in the foreground of a *capriccio* overdoor of the same subject painted for Consul Joseph Smith (fig. 167). The arch became a favoured framing device for Canaletto that he continued to use in his views of London, and it is probably from him that Guardi borrowed the conceit.

Guardi included a number of imaginative alterations designed to surprise and charm the viewer. He distorted the length of the courtyard and made it much shallower than in reality,

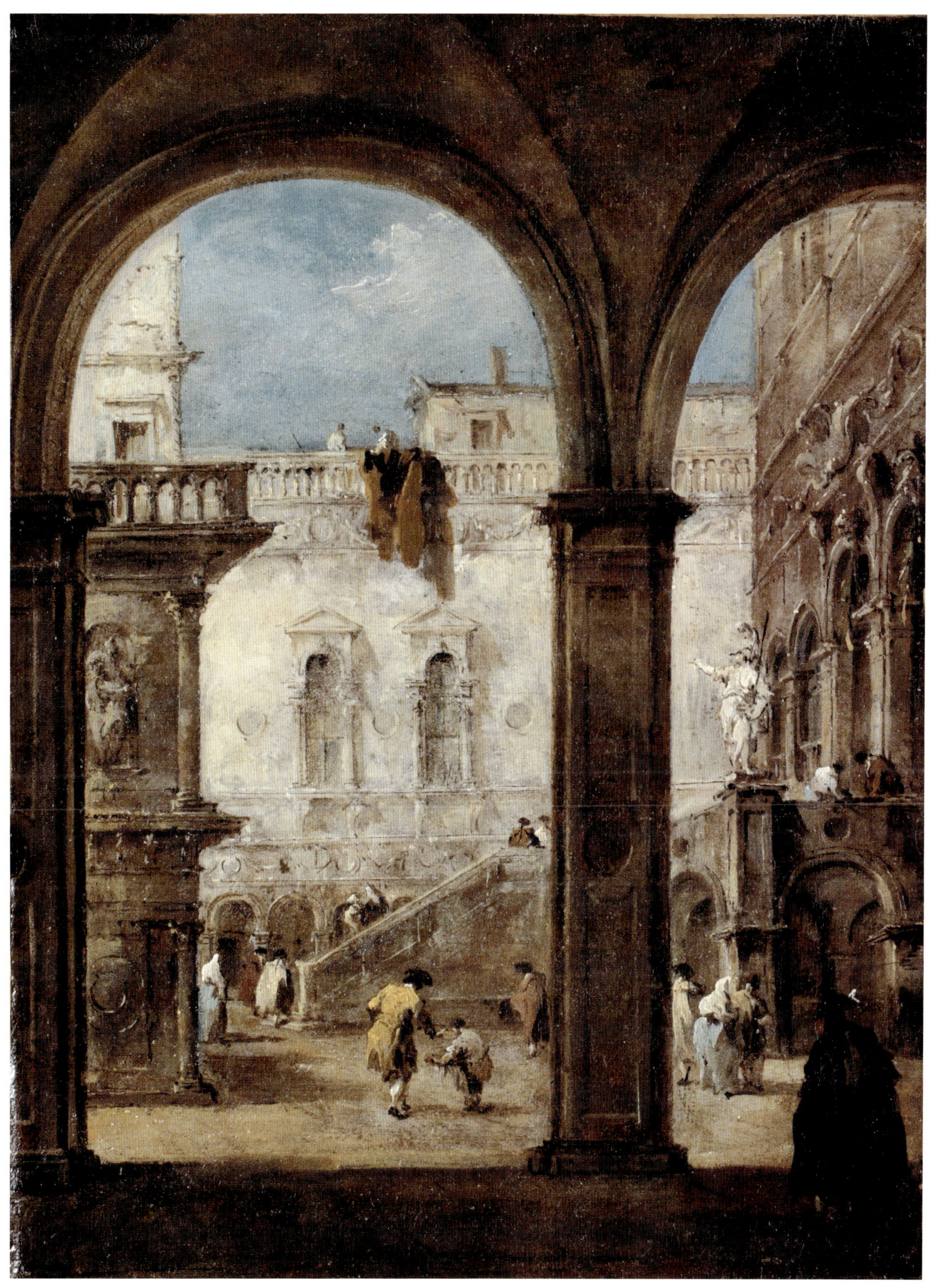

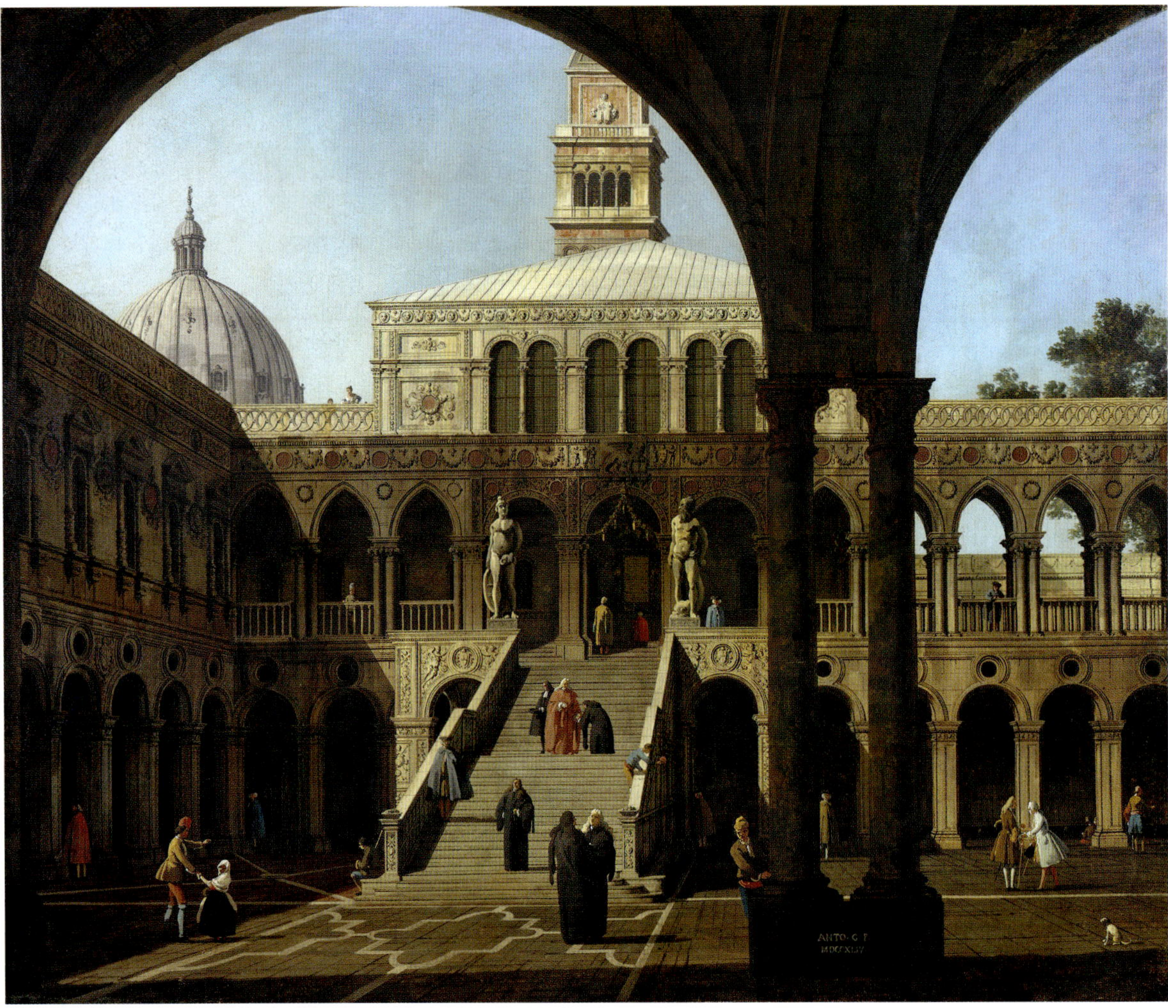

Fig. 167. Canaletto (1697–1768), *Capriccio View of the Courtyard of the Palazzo Ducale with the Scala dei Giganti*, signed and dated 1744, oil on canvas, 108.2 × 129.9 cm, Royal Collection (RCIN 406012)

creating a more intimate space. The fanciful façade beyond the staircase is of his invention.

The foreground arch also became a common motif in Guardi's *capricci*, functioning as a window onto another world. Here, the arch is disproportionately large compared with the row of arches on the right and across the square.

Guardi explored the subject in a beautiful pen and wash drawing where the arch is set at a slight angle to the picture plane (fig. 168). On the same sheet he also studied the position of the man giving alms to the boy begging beneath the arch rather than in the sun-drenched courtyard.[2]

Although he investigated the subject in related drawings, Guardi planned out the composition directly on the support. The infrared reflectogram shows traces of fine,

ruled and lightly incised planning lines in a few places in the architecture, notably on the right-hand side of the staircase and in the façade above (fig. 169). However, the use of incisions as a means of articulating building façades does not appear on the surface as in Canaletto's work. Moreover, most of the visible dark lines that Guardi used to articulate the architecture were applied freehand, unlike Canaletto who employed a ruler or compass.

Other versions of this composition are known with some variations. A comparable example, painted on a slightly smaller scale, is at the National Gallery, London (fig. 170). Here, there is no vaulting on the arcade in the foreground and Guardi has omitted a statue at the top of the stairs altogether. The figures also differ slightly, as does the colour of the

cloth hanging over the balustrade, in this case blue rather than brown.

Both the Wallace Collection and National Gallery paintings date from the 1770s. This type of picture-postcard view was extremely popular around this time. They were also a practical souvenir for Grand Tourists due to their manageable size, which made them easy to transport.

Cat. 27 was owned by John Rushout, 2nd Baron Northwick (1769–1859), one of the greatest nineteenth-century connoisseurs. From 1793 to 1800 he was in Italy as an attaché to the ambassador to the King of Naples, and it may be that he acquired the painting during those travels. In 1838 he purchased Thirlestaine House, a Greek Revival mansion in Cheltenham, to house

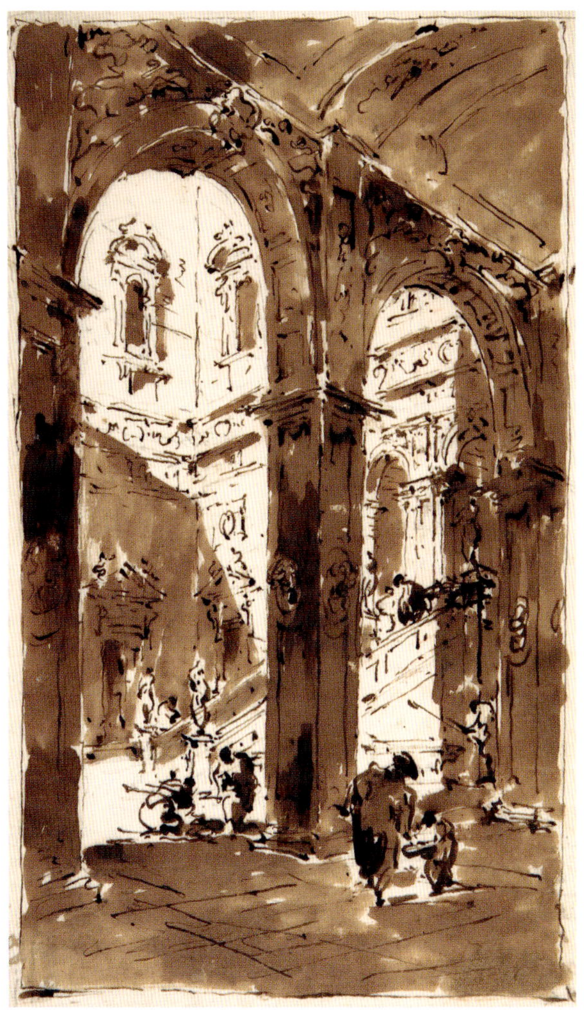

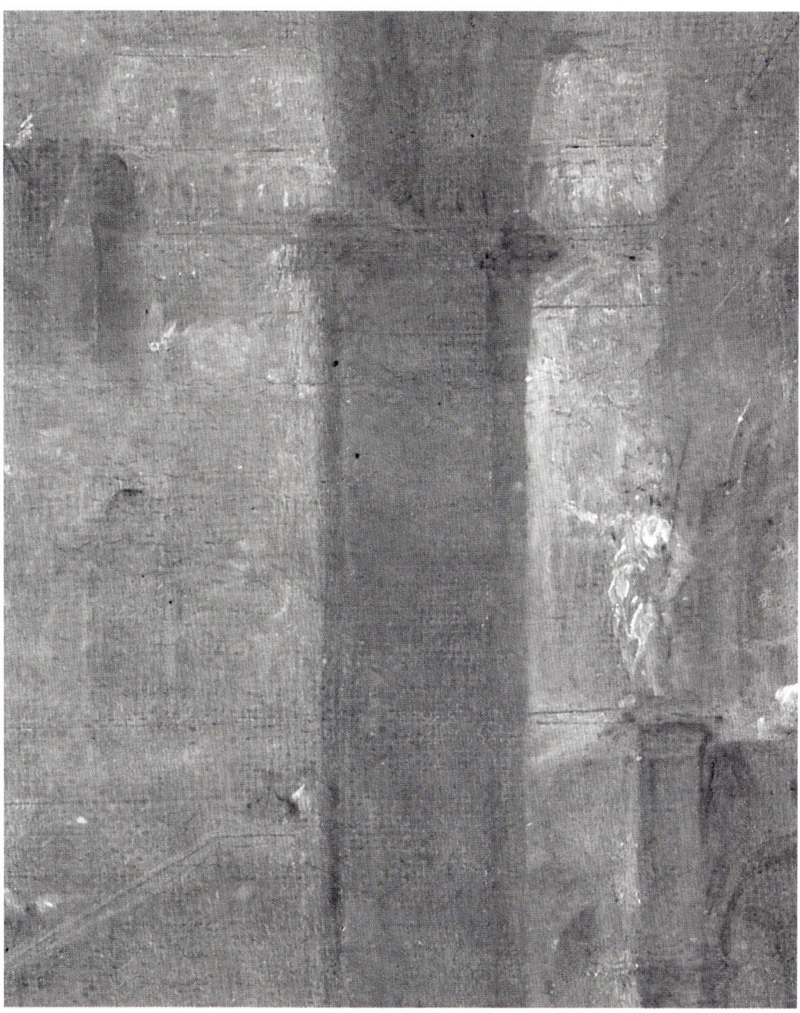

his exceptional collection of more than five hundred pictures at that point, which grew to around 1,400 by the time of his death. The Baron graciously opened his collection to the public free of charge every afternoon between one and three o'clock. The Guardi hung in his Dining Room together with many Old Masters, including paintings by Claude and Titian as seen in a painting from around 1846 (fig. 171).[3] Cat. 27 was described as 'a beautiful little architectural sketch, most admirably touched' in the 1846 catalogue of the Baron's paintings collection.[4] The Baron had a substantial collection of 13 Canaletti, six of which he housed in his Venetian Room.[5] Cat. 27 is the only work by Guardi that he owned. When Lord Northwick's pictures came up for sale in July 1859, Samuel Mawson,

Lord Hertford's trusted agent, advised his client to acquire the present work, referring to it as 'a fine little specimen by Guardi – wanted as a specimen of the artist'.[6] Interestingly, when he reinstalled the collection at Hertford House, Sir Richard Wallace chose to hang this picture in the Billiard Room apart from the rest of his *vedute*, which hung in the Canaletto Room, today the southern half of the Sixteenth-Century Gallery.[7]

ABOVE, LEFT:
Fig. 168. Francesco Guardi (1712–1793), *Architectural Capriccio: Courtyard of a Palace*, 1712–93, pen and brown ink, brush and brown wash, over graphite or lead or black chalk, framing lines in pen and brown ink, a few red chalk marks, 27.7 × 18.1 cm, Metropolitan Museum of Art, New York. Rogers Fund, 1937 (inv. 37.165.87)

ABOVE, RIGHT:
Fig. 169. Detail of IRR of cat. 27

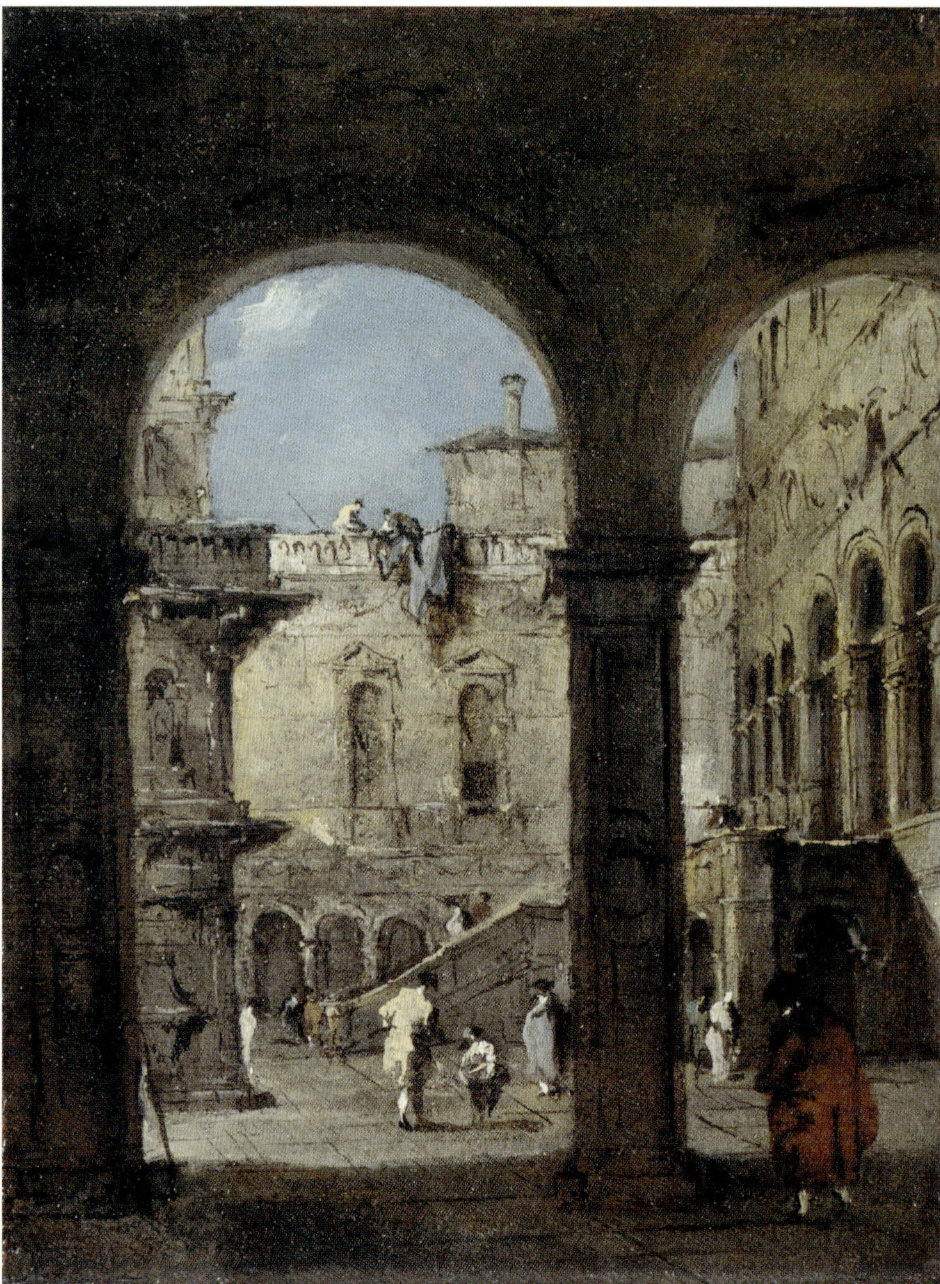

Fig. 170. Francesco Guardi (1712–1793),
An Architectural Caprice, probably 1770s,
oil on canvas, 22.1 × 17.2 cm, National Gallery,
London. Salting Bequest, 1910 (NG2519)

OPPOSITE:

Fig. 171. Robert Huskisson (1820–1861),
*Lord Northwick's Picture Gallery at Thirlestaine
House* [actually the Dining Room], 1846–47,
oil on canvas, 81.3 × 108.6 cm, Yale Center
for British Art, Paul Mellon Collection
(inv. B1981.25.213)

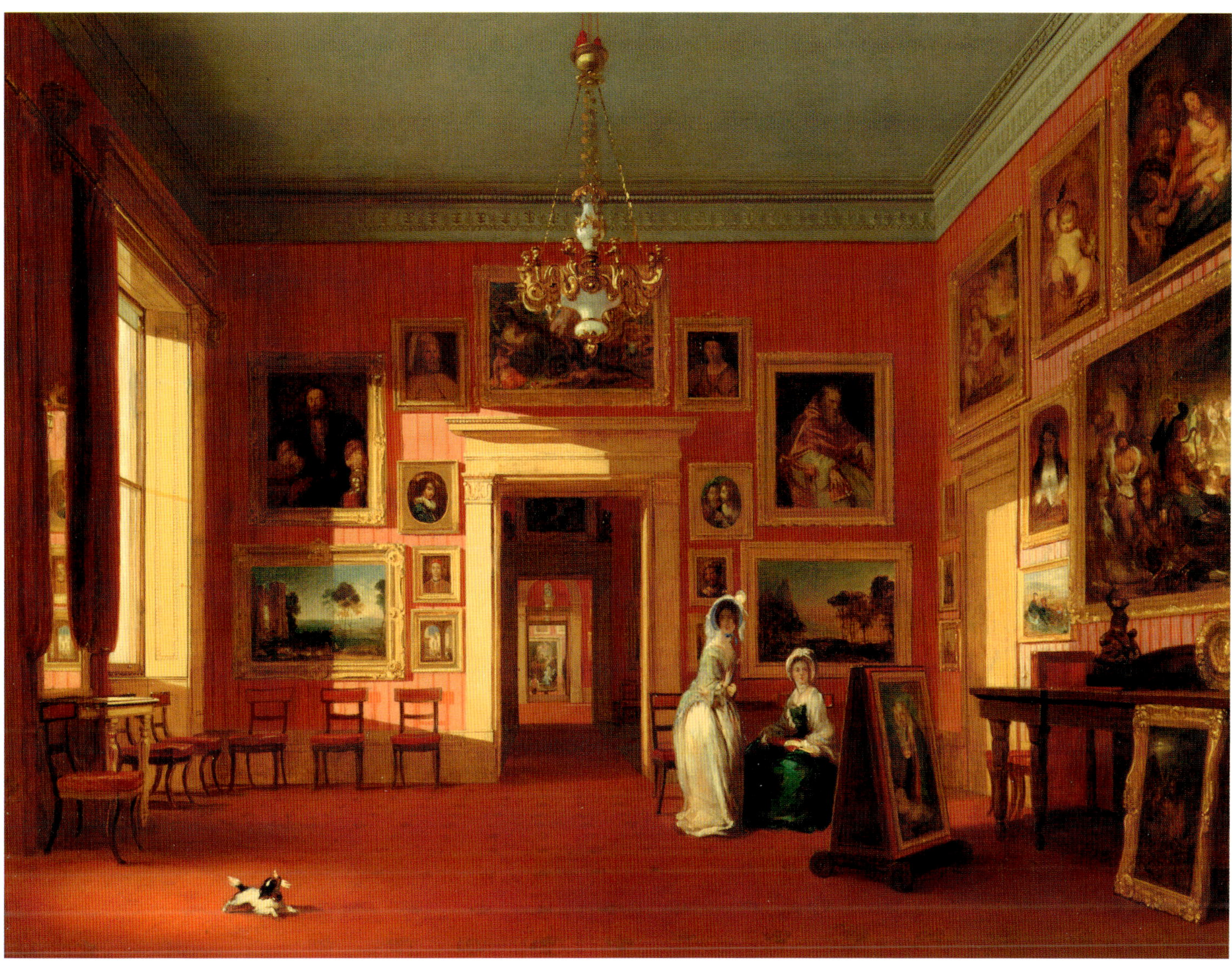

PROVENANCE

Acquired by the 2nd Baron of Northwick (1769–1859)
by 1846;[8] his sale, Thirlestaine House, Cheltenham,
Philips, 26 July–30 August 1859 (L.25025) [first day,
26 July], lot 93;[9] from where bought by Richard
Seymour-Conway, 4th Marquess of Hertford
(1800–1870) for £54; by descent to Sir Richard
Wallace, 1st Baronet (1818–1890); by descent to his
wife, Lady Wallace (Julie Amélie Charlotte Castelnau,
1819–1897); by whom bequeathed with the rest of the
Wallace Collection to the British nation, 1897.

EXHIBITION

1872–75: 'Paintings, Porcelain, Bronzes, Decorative
Furniture and other Works of Art lent by Sir Richard
Wallace to the Bethnal Green Branch of the South
Kensington Museum'.[10]

RELATED WORKS

Francesco Guardi, *An Architectural Caprice*, probably
1770s, oil on canvas, 22.1 × 17.2 cm, National Gallery,
London (NG2519)

The following versions show the arcade at an angle:

Francesco Guardi, *Palace Courtyard*, 1775–80, oil on
canvas, 45 × 32 cm, National Gallery, Prague

Francesco Guardi, *View of the Courtyard of Palazzo
Ducale and the Scala dei Giganti in Venice*, c.1780, oil
on canvas, 39 × 26 cm, Academia Carrara, Bergamo

TECHNICAL NOTES

The picture is painted on a fairly coarse, plain-weave
canvas. It was glue-paste lined on a plain-weave
canvas, probably in France around 1850.[11] There is
cusping on all four sides that corresponds to the
original stretching nails, which confirm that the
size of the composition was kept intact during
lining. A dark red ground is visible in areas
throughout the painting.

LITERATURE

Watson 1968, p. 142
Morassi 1973, vol. 1, pp. 456–57, no. 789
Rossi Bortolatto 1974, p. 117, no. 469
Ingamells 1985, pp. 298–99
Duffy and Hedley 2004, p. 192

LP

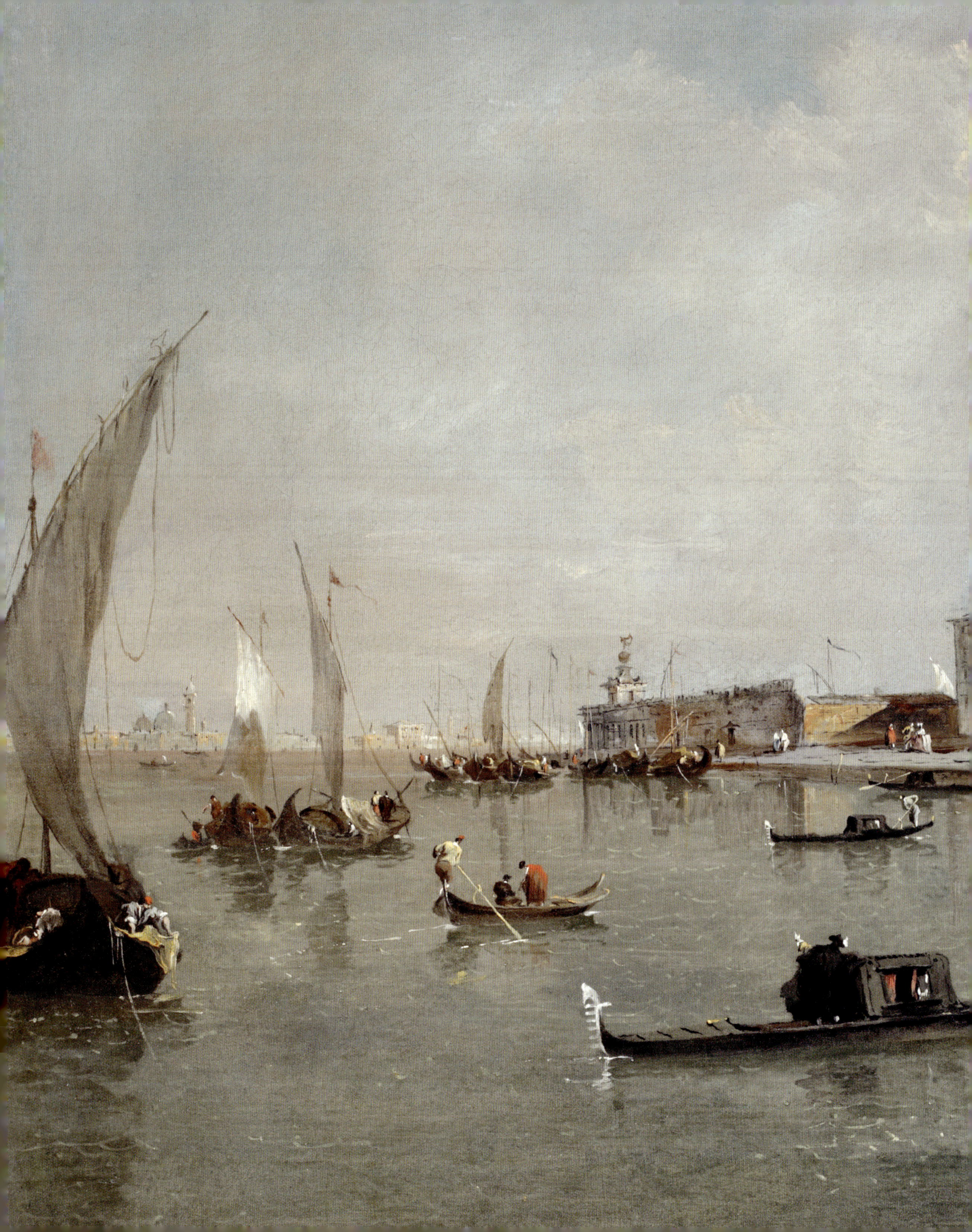

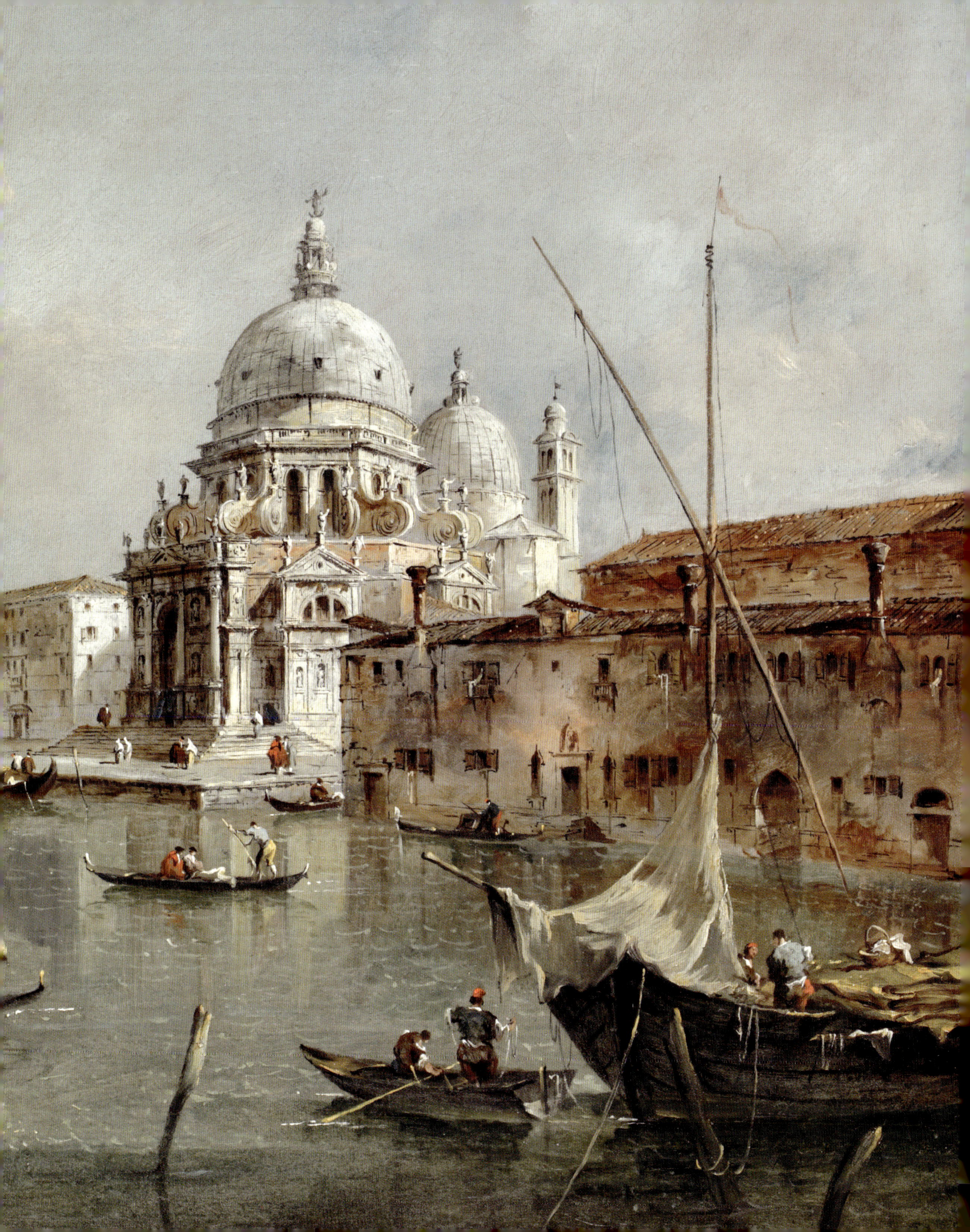

NOTES

1. CANALETTO, GUARDI AND
    VENETIAN VIEW PAINTING IN
    THE EIGHTEENTH CENTURY
    Lelia Packer

1. On the figuration of the ideal Venetian state, see Rosand 2001.
2. Petrarch, *Epistolae Seniles* IV, 3.
3. Lassels 1670, part II, pp. 362–63.
4. Kerber 2017 discusses view paintings that capture such contemporary events.
5. Apparently, Venetians did not let their wives visit the wives of foreign ambassadors 'for fear of being suspected of treason'. Lassels 1670, part II, p. 379.
6. Ibid., p. 365.
7. On the Grand Tour, see Redford 1996; Wilton and Bignamini 1996; Sweet 2012.
8. On Batoni, see Bowron and Kerber 2007; Bowron 2016. It was rare for Venice to appear as the backdrop in portraits, or for travellers to sit for full-length painted portraits in Venice. One exception is the portrait of Samuel Egerton (Bartolomeo Nazari, *Samuel Egerton*, 1732, oil on canvas, 218.4 × 158.5 cm, Tatton Park, National Trust, inv. 1298199), in which the sitter points to major sites such as the Dogana and the church of Le Zitelle in the background.
9. Italy was increasingly considered as a country of the past. By comparison, Britain defined modern civilisation. Black 1996.
10. Redford 1996, p. 57. Prostitution in Venice was a successful commercial operation coordinated by gondoliers who acted as pimps. See Sweet 2012, p. 223.
11. Lassels 1670, part II, Preface.
12. Countess of Chichester to Pelham, 13 June 1777, BL Add. MS 33127, fol. 261.

13. Lassels 1670, part II, p. 426.
14. Ibid.
15. Redford 1996, p. 14.
16. Joseph Smith (see pp. 19–20) and Marshal Johann Matthias von der Schulenburg (1661–1747), the German aristocrat and general who retired in Venice and became a great collector there.
17. One notable exception is Canaletto's reception piece for the Venetian Academy, *Capriccio: A Colonnade Opening onto the Courtyard of a Palace*, 1765, oil on canvas, 131 × 93 cm, Gallerie dell'Accademia, Venice.
18. See Wilson 2006.
19. The earliest view was painted by Gaspare Vanvitelli (fig. 8). The death of Francesco Guardi, the last great view painter, in 1793, and the fall of Venice in 1797, marked the end of view painting.
20. The painting was part of a series of nine large canvases representing the Miracles of the Cross, painted by the greatest Venetian artists of the day such as Pietro Perugino and Vittore Carpaccio, for the Confraternity of the Scuola Grande of San Giovanni Evangelista in Venice. The eight surviving canvases are preserved in the Gallerie dell'Accademia, Venice.
21. For a comprehensive survey of the evolution of *vedute*, see Beddington 2010, pp. 10–53.
22. See, for example, cat. 16.
23. Links 1977, p. 1.
24. See cat. 9.
25. See cat. 18.
26. Mariette 1851–53, p. 298. Mariette's account, apparently based on a document sent to him by Canaletto himself, was compiled during the eighteenth century, but was not published until the following century.

27. 'e fece bellissimi disegni per gli scenarii'. Zanetti 1771, Book V, p. 463.
28. On Conti's early commission of Canaletto's work, see Links 1977, pp. 12–19.
29. 'Il a travaillé dans la manière de Van Vytel; mais je le crois supérieur'. Mariette 1851–53, p. 298.
30. Constable 1989, p. 174.
31. Ibid.
32. Letter dated 27 September 1730 from McSwiney to John Conduitt. Links 1977, p. 28.
33. On Smith, see Razzall and Whitaker 2017, pp. 20–31; Haskell 1980, pp. 299–310; Vivian 1971.
34. Martineau and Robison 1994, p. 229.
35. The 1735 edition of the *Prospectus Magni Canalis Venetiarum* consisted of 14 prints after paintings still in Smith's personal collection. The second, expanded, 1742 edition included 24 additional views, ten of which were of the Grand Canal and ten of *campi*, or city squares, which had passed through Smith's hands.
36. Sweet 2012, p. 231.
37. Ibid.
38. Ibid.
39. Ibid.
40. Constable 1989, p. 174.
41. Zanetti 1771, Book V, p. 462; Mariette 1851–53, p. 298.
42. See, for example, Links 1977, p. 58–62; Beddington 2010, pp. 26–28; Bomford and Finaldi 1998, pp. 18–19; Beddington 2021, pp. 26–28. The camera obscura in the Museo Correr, Venice, inscribed 'A. CANAL' on the protective cover, has traditionally been thought to have belonged to Canaletto. This idea was recently refuted in Beddington 2021, p. 26.
43. 'il ne s'occupa plus qu'a peindre des vues d'après nature, faisant usage de la chamber noir, dont il savoit modérer le faux', Mariette 1851–53, p. 298;

'si diede a dipingere vedute dal naturale', 'I segno il Canal … il vero uso della camera ottica', Zanetti 1771, Book V, p. 463.

44. Baetjer and Links 1989, pp. 41–52; Razzall and Whitaker 2017, pp. 214–57.

45. On the sketchbook, including a facsimile, see Nepi Scirè 1997; Torrini 2012.

46. On Bellotto, see Kozakiewicz 1972; Bowron 2001; Schumacher 2014; Treves et al. 2021.

47. On Marieschi, see Succi 2016; Beddington 2010, pp. 30–35, 108–15.

48. On Canaletto in England, see Beddington 2006; Links 1977, pp. 63–72. There has been suggestion that Canaletto returned to Venice a second time, in 1753, based on a note by the Venetian diarist Pietro Gradenigo. See Watson 1948.

49. Links 1977, p. 64.

50. Hinchcliffe was in Venice as John Crewe's tutor, later the first Lord Crewe. The passage, written in 1856 by Revd Edward Hinchcliffe about his grandfather, is transcribed in Baetjer and Links 1989, p. 336.

51. See note 17 above.

52. For documents relating to Canaletto's estate at his death, listing his possessions, see Constable 1989, pp. 177–79.

53. On Guardi, see Craievich and Pedrocco 2012; Morassi 1973; *Problemi guardeschi* 1967.

54. Simonson 1904, the first monograph on Guardi, was instrumental in the artist's revival.

55. 1731 will of the wealthy Giovanni Benedetto Giovanelli of Noventa Padovana. Domenico Guardi had worked for Giovanelli and his brother from 1702. Martineau and Robison 1994, pp. 292–327; Watson 1966. On attribution questions, see Muraro 1960; Binion 1976.

56. On Guardi's turn to view painting, see Craievich and Pedrocco 2012, pp. 94–98; Mahon 1968.

57. Links 1977, p. 93.

58. Hedley 2002, p. 9.

59. Russell 1996, pp. 9–10, suggested an association between Smith and Guardi for the latter's earliest *vedute*.

60. Links 1977, p. 93.

61. On Guardi's drawings, see Shaw 1951.

62. On Guardi's patrons, see Bettagno 1993, pp. 15–26; Russell 1996.

63. 'Gran peccato! anche questo rame del nostro albero pittorico si va seccando in Venezia: non ci sono piu pittori vedutisti di buon nome'. An extract from this letter, dated 23 June 1804, is transcribed in Haskell 1960, p. 276.

2. COLLECTING VENETIAN VIEWS AT THE WALLACE COLLECTION
Lelia Packer

1. Ingamells 1981, p. 129.

2. 'La collection la plus riche en Guardi et en Canaletto est celle de Sir Richard Wallace.' Yriarte 1878, p. 178.

3. 'une collections sans rivale de *Vues de Venise* par Canaletto et Guardi'. *La Chronique des Arts*, 27 February 1897, p. 84.

4. Many attributions have since changed, the latest of which are elaborated in Chapter 3.

5. Wallace also bought an English view after Canaletto (fig. 24).

6. The Hertfords also had estates in Warwickshire and Suffolk. The 2nd Marquess's second wife, Isabella Anne Ingram Shepherd (1760–1834), inherited a significant fortune, as did the 3rd Marquess's wife, Maria Emily Fagnani (1771–1856). The latter was a great heiress due to the rival claims to her paternity by George Selwyn (1719–1791) and William Douglas, 4th Duke of Queensberry (1725–1810), who both left her their respective fortunes. On the Wallace Collection's founders, see Hughes 2014; Duffy and Hedley 2004, pp. xvii–xxxiv; Higgott 2019, pp. 20–27.

7. Ingamells 1997, p. 237.

8. Bowman returned to London from his travels abroad in April 1743. This supports the dating of the 1st Marquess's tour as being prior to this date. I thank Grant Lewis for his insights on Bowman.

9. See pp. 19–20.

10. These have since been dispersed, except for two portraits of the 1st Marquess's daughters, Lady Elizabeth Seymour-Conway (1754–1825) (P31) and Frances, Countess of Lincoln (1751–1820) (P33).

11. The 1st Marquess may have owned other works of art that were not part of the Wallace Collection bequest, such as Sèvres porcelain, for example; however, this remains uncertain.

12. See Beddington 2021.

13. See cat. 2 entry.

14. Wallace Collection Archives (henceforth WCA) HWF/INV/2. For a more legible copy of that inventory (produced around 1870), see HWF/INV/5. Listed as 'A pair of crayon drawings by Rosalba of Cupid & Flora framed and glazed'.

15. In the 1843 Manchester House inventory as 'Rosalba – A pair of crayon drawings of Cupid and Flora framed & glazed', WCA HWF/INV/12. In the 1870 list of entailed property at Manchester House as 'Rosalba – 2 Crayon drawings, Cupid & Flora', WCA HWF/INV/16. Sold at Christie's, London, 1 May 1875, lot 94 (mistakenly as by Guercino, and as Venus and Cupid rather than Venus and Flora). The pastels entered the Royal Collection in 1923. Razzall and Whitaker 2017, pp. 318–19.

16. Ingamells 1997, p. 63.

17. Ibid.

18. These include portraits by John Downman (*The 3rd Marquess of Hertford as a Boy*, 1781, P752; *Isabella, 2nd Marchioness of Hertford, as Lady Beauchamp*, 1781, P754), George Romney (*Mrs Mary Robinson*, 1780–81, P37) and Joshua Reynolds (*Miss Nelly O'Brien*, c.1762–64, P38).

19. He was in Rome, Naples and Milan at various points between 1829 and 1841. Raikes 1858, vol. 1, pp. 4, 8, 82; vol. 2, pp. 92, 135, 143, 264; Ingamells 1997, p. 30.

20. The 3rd Marquess bought one of the gems of the Dutch paintings collection, Caspar Netscher's *The Lace Maker*, 1662 (P237). He tried to sell it on two occasions, thankfully without success: Christie's, 4 July 1807, lot 86; Christie's, 12 March 1808, lot 90.

21. Waagen 1854, vol. 2, p. 154.

22. Ibid. Waagen was referring to collections formed since his last visit to England in 1834. 'Le plus grand collectionneur de l'Europe est, assurément Lord Hertford.' Bürger 1867, p. 537.

23. Ingamells 1981, p. 57.

24. Transcribed in Ingamells 1981. Hertford employed Mawson from around 1848 until 1862 to act on his behalf in salerooms, particularly in London.

25. Ibid., p. 63. The pair in question are cat. 3 and cat. 4; Lord Hertford fancied the latter. See cats 3 and 4 entry.

26. Ibid. Sir T. Bernard sale, Christie's, 31 March 1855 (L.22337). Lot 69 (cat. 3) was bought for £194.50 and lot 70 (cat. 4) for £204.15. The buyers' names were given as Edwards and King respectively.

27. Ingamells 1981, pp. 91, 95.

28. Ibid., p. 71.

29. Ibid., p. 94. G.T. Braine sale, 6 April 1857, Christie's, London (L.23505), lots 27, 28.

30. Ingamells 1981, pp. 122–23. That painting is now at the National Gallery, London: Canaletto, *Venice: A Regatta on the Grand Canal*, c.1735 (NG938).

31. Ingamells 1981, p. 129.

32. Ibid., p. 100. The 17th Earl of Shrewsbury's sale, Christie's, 6 July–8 August 1857 (L.23727), lots 194 ('A gondola race on the Grand Canal at Venice, with the Bucentaur and numerous figures. A work of brilliant quality') and 195 ('The companion picture – The termination of the fête').

33. Ingamells 1981, p. 122. Phillips, 26 July–30 August 1859 (L.25025), lot 93. Bought for £54.

34. On Wallace, see Higgott 2019.

35. Ibid., pp. 119–23.

36. 'I also am anxious to get the entailed things away from Manchester House which belong to me,' 5th Marquess to Wallace, 15 March 1871, WCA HWT/M5/01; 'on the subject of the entailed things at Manchester House … it is desirable on all accounts that something should

be settled if possible – The Will seems virtually proved & I should be glad to get into possession of the Deeds & other entailed articles which the Executors may feel justified in handing over to me at once,' 5th Marquess to Wallace, 28 April 1871 (copy at Warwickshire County Record Office [henceforth WCRO] CR114A/721/6).

37. 'Mr Wallace will authorise the Executors of the late Marquess of Hertford to give up all the articles and effects now at Manchester House marked "E" or in the inventory of 1834 … except … the six pictures by Canaletti,' Frederick Cadogan to the 5th Marquess, 30 June 1871, WCRO, CR114A/720/730; 'I accept the second alternative contained in the paper of the 30th June 1871 unconditionally,' 5th Marquess to the Executors of the 4th Marquess's will, 10 July 1871, WCA HWF/M5/01.

38. The other view was cat. 17. See pp. 126–29.

39. Letter in WCA HWF/M4/2/1/6.

40. Ibid. 'I told Mr Scott to ask you to try & get me tomorrow 2 Canalettis & I had mentioned £120 as a limit for the 2, but I will not mind your going up to £150 for them.' The sale was probably that held at Christie's, London, 3 May 1884 (L.43972). This was a multi-vendor sale, the title page of the sale booklet citing 'A fine series of works of Canaletti'. Lots 71 and 72 were two views of Florence by Canaletti, and were among a series of lots from various (unnamed) vendors. Lots 91–136 were 'Property of a Lady' and included lots 128–136, paintings by Canaletti. There is an annotation on the catalogue below these last, stating 'The Canaletti from 60–120 guineas, high price, considering the poor quality & condition of some.' The only other possible picture sale that took place on 3 May 1884 was in Paris (L.43974), but given that Wallace was writing to Davis from the Albion Hotel in Eastbourne about a sale taking place the next day, it seems more likely that he was referring to the London rather than the Paris sale.

41. Rue Drouot no. 5, Paris, 2–3 March 1857 (L.23405), lots 47 'Vue du Grand Canal' (View of the Grand Canal) and 48 'Vue de la douane' (View of the Dogana).

42. Narcisse-Vergilio Diaz, *Venus Disarming Cupid*, probably *c.*1855 (P266), Narcisse-Vergilio Diaz, *The Education of Cupid*, probably *c.*1855 (P268), Jacob van Ruisdael, *Sunrise in a Wood*, probably 1670s (P247), Nicolas Lancret, *The Little Dog Shaking Money and Gems*, *c.*1737–38 (P409), John-Louis-Ernest Meissonier, *A Sentinel: Time of Louis XIII*, 1851 (P287), Thomas Couture, *Harlequin and Pierrot*, *c.*1857 (P288). Higgott 2019, p. 72.

43. Archives de Paris, D.42E^{3}35. See cats 23 and 24 entry.

44. *A Gondola on the Lagoon near Mestre*, after 1780 (NG1454) and *Venice: Piazza San Marco*, *c.*1760 (NG210). There were 13 paintings by Canaletto at the National Gallery in 1900.

45. WCA HWF/INV/29-1.

46. Ingamells 1985, p. 440.

47. WCA HWF/M2/07.

48. The inventory exists in two versions: WCA HWF/INV/2, HWF/INV/5.

49. August 1846 list of loans to the French Embassy, the majority of which are no longer at the Wallace Collection, WCA HWF/M4/417.

50. 1842 inventory and valuation of Dorchester House, WCA HWF/INV/09. Listed under 'Entailed Pictures' as 'Canaletto – A Splendid View in Venice large – Ditto – A Ditto – large –'. No other pictures are listed in the Dining Room.

51. 1842 inventory of the China &c. removed after the death of the late Marquis of Hertford by order of his Executors from the Regent's Park Villa [St Dunstan's] to Dorchester House Park Lane, WCA HWF/M3/12.

52. *The Globe*, 26 May 1845, p. 1. Originally called Hertford Villa, the house was renamed St Dunstan's Villa in 1830, when an automaton clock was brought over from the Guild Church of St Dunstan-in-the-West on Fleet Street.

53. All six Canaletti are listed in the Manchester House 1843 inventory, WCA HWF/INV/12.

54. *Bell's Weekly Messenger*, 2 May 1846, p. 141. I am grateful to Alan Scollan for this reference.

55. *The Examiner*, 4 April 1868, p. 8. This was the first of the two rooms on the ground floor mentioned by the author. The other room contained Anthony van Dyck's portraits of Philip Le Roy and his wife, which we know from inventories (WCA HWF/INV/15) hung in the State Room (today's Front State Room) on the ground floor.

56. Mawson referred to the 'Canaletto Room' in a letter dated 15 July 1859. Ingamells 1981, p. 123.

57. *The Globe*, 26 February 1950.

58. *The Morning Post*, 1 January 1851, p. 3.

59. *The Builder*, 12 April 1851, p. 234.

60. Ibid., p. 227.

61. Waagen 1854, vol. 2, p. 154.

62. Ibid.

63. Ibid., p. 155.

64. On these occasions Waagen also saw Hertford's collection at 13 Berkeley Square, the contents of which were moved to Manchester House in December 1858, under the supervision of Richard Wallace. Higgott 2019, p. 77.

65. Waagen 1857, p. 80. Surprisingly, Waagen omitted the Bacino views in 1854.

66. Blanc 1857, p. 6.

67. Ibid.

68. He sent five works by Bartolomé Esteban Murillo, four by Anthony van Dyck and four by Rembrandt, as well as French and English eighteenth-century pictures.

69. WCA HWF/M4/5/14.

70. These were the brothers William and Philip Evans (active 1851–1907), who were carvers, gilders and picture restorers. They came from a family of frame-makers and worked out of 18 Silver Street, Golden Square, in London between 1801 and 1883; they moved to 36 Beak Street between 1884 and 1907. See https://www.npg.org.uk/collections/research/programmes/conservation/directory-of-british-framemakers/e (accessed 16 August 2023).

71. Bürger 1867.

72. 'À Paris, le noble lord a surtout recherché la satisfaction d'un gout qui lui était particulier,' *Le Voleur Illustré*, 5 April 1872, p. 219. The same author goes on to list paintings that Lord Hertford kept in Paris, which included works by Guardi.

73. Confusingly, the six core Canaletti were listed with both the entailed and unentailed property, WCA HWF/INV/15-16.

74. See p. 34.

75. WCA HWF/INV/19.

76. Ibid.

77. On the Bethnal Green exhibition, see Higgott 2019, pp. 278–88.

78. The pictures were spread across the North and East Galleries. Black 1874, pp. 18–22.

79. *The Northern Whig Belfast*, 6 July 1872, p. 6. The author got the number of pictures wrong.

80. *The Sheffield Daily Telegraph*, 26 October 1872, p. 3.

81. The official visitor figure was 2,282,238. Higgott 2019, pp. 287, 411, note 38.

82. There are three handwritten albums in the Wittelsbacher Ausgleichsfonds in Munich. Higgott 2019, pp. 219–61, 405–6, notes 22–24.

83. *Pall Mall Gazette*, 20 February 1897, p. 3. Yriarte described the room again three years later, albeit with some discrepancies: the same parlour is referred to as being on the right-hand side. He mentioned 27 rather than 40 views of Venice and omitted the idea of the four large Guardis hanging over the door. *Pall Mall Magazine*, 1900, pp. 4–18.

84. WCA HWF/INV/26-28.

85. Committee minutes, 12 and 19 May 1897, WCA.

86. Wallace Collection Trustee Minutes, 9 August 1897, WCA.

87. Wallace Collection Trustee Minutes, 12 January 1898, WCA.

88. The piece of furniture visible is the roll-top desk attributed to Jean-Henri Riesener (F277). In the early years of the museum, there were columns in place by the east and west walls in the centre of the Sixteenth-Century Room that were later removed, probably in the 1930s.

89. I am grateful to Alan Scollan for confirming these dates.

90. Spielmann 1900, p. 15. Gallery XII was split into today's Large and Small Drawing Rooms during building works in 1976–82.

91. *The Sketch*, 4 July 1900, p. 488.

92. *Whitstable Times and Herne Bay Herald*, 6 April 1901, p. 2.

93. Spielmann 1900, pp. 16, 84.

3. VENETIAN VIEWS BY PAINTERS IN CANALETTO'S CIRCLE
Charles Beddington

1. In Camp 1928, pp. 46–49, they are all catalogued as 'School of Canaletto' except for two superb Canaletti, cat. 3 and cat. 4, which are called 'Attributed to Bellotto', a tentative attribution credited to W.G. Constable.
2. Cat. 2 and cat. 1; cat. 6 and cat. 5.
3. Conway is recorded in Rheims in March 1737 on his way to Italy, in Rome in February 1738, in France in March 1739, in Genoa in November 1739, and back in London by March 1740. Ingamells 1997, p. 237.
4. Links 1977.
5. Constable 1962, C347, C348.
6. It is, in fact, the only painting illustrated in colour as 'Studio of Canaletto' in the best introduction to Canaletto's work in English, Links 1994, pls 2, 4.
7. That this is coeval with the execution of the painting was confirmed by the Hamilton Kerr Institute during the recent cleaning.
8. Constable 1962, C636.
9. For a summary of opinion in 1989, see Links 1989, pp. xiv–xix.
10. Tassini 1872, p. 680.
11. Catalogue of the Loveden Pryse sale, Christie's, London, 12 March 1859, lot 172.
12. Constable 1962, C259; Beddington 2010, p. 183, no. 25, illustrated p. 92.
13. Note in the Constable/Links Archive in the possession of the present author.
14. Kowalczyk 1996A, pp. 75–78, fig. 5.
15. See, for instance, Beddington 2010, p. 185, no. 42, illustrated p. 117.
16. *The Grand Canal Looking West with the Scalzi and San Simeone Piccolo, c.*1726–27, Royal Collection, RCIN 407267 (Constable 1962, C258; Razzall and Whitaker 2017, pp. 154–55, no. 59). Both Canaletto's views show the shed next to the church steps used by the workmen, which is also shown here.
17. Beddington 2022, *passim*.
18. Constable 1962, C107; Scarpa 2012, no. 34.
19. Constable 1962, C107(a).
20. Christie's, London, 10 July 1998, lot 81; Succi and Delneri 2001A, no. 41; Succi and Delneri 2001B, no. 41; Algranti 2002, no. 100; Pedrocco 2002, pp. 104–6, illustrated and with a detail on p. 70; Succi and Delneri 2008, no. 82.
21. Constable 1962, C191(aa), as 'A replica'; Whistler 2016, pp. 92–93, no. 16, illustrated, as 'After Canaletto'.
22. The pair is now split. The prototype of *The Entrance to the Grand Canal, Looking East* is now in the collection of the Fondo Ambiente Italiano at the Villa Necchi Campiglio, Milan (Constable 1962, C167; Scarpa 2012, no. 17).
23. The copy was sold at Christie's, London, 9 July 1999, lot 77 (with a note by the present writer relating it to the Molo view sold there

almost exactly a year previously); the original is Constable 1962, C156.
24. For the copy, see Constable 1962, C121(a), as 'a replica … doubtfully by Canaletto' and Scarpa 2012, no. 14; the protype is Constable 1962, C121.
25. 'è da compiangersi il nostro Francesco Tironi, che morto sia in troppo fresca età da qualche anno, poiché i Porti di Venezia e le Isole disegnati da lui, ed incisi poi dal nostro Antonio Santi [*sic*], ci fanno scorgere quant'oltre sarebbe arrivato' ['Our poor Francesco Tironi is much to be mourned, who died too young a few years ago, for the compositions of the Ports of Venice and the Islands, drawn by him and engraved by Antonio Sandi, show how much he would have achieved']. Moschini 1806–8, vol. 3 (1806), p. 78, note 1; quoted by Moretti 2008, pp. 206–7.
26. The *Ventiquattro Prospettive delle Isole della Laguna* in fact include views of the ports of Chioggia, Malamocco and the Lido, and of the *Murazzi* (sea walls). See Pignatti 1974; Succi 1983, pp. 344–47.
27. The painting was cleaned at the Hamilton Kerr Institute in 2018 and I am indebted for this information to Rupert Featherstone, who, however, points out that the ground is single, not double, and separated by a layer of glue size as would be typical of English practice.
28. Beddington 2021, pp. 56–61.
29. An article by the present writer on 'The Bateman Master' will be published imminently in the *Colnaghi Studies Journal*, vol. 15.

CATALOGUE

CATALOGUE 1–2
Lelia Packer

1. Waagen 1857, p. 80.
2. It has been suggested that cat. 1 depicts early afternoon. Constable 1962, C134.
3. Sweet 2012, p. 226.
4. Luca Carlevarijs (1663–1730), *The Bacino, Venice, with the Dogana and a Distant View of the Isola di San Giorgio, c.*1709, oil on canvas, 50.8 × 119.7 cm, The Metropolitan Museum of Art, New York, Robert Lehman Collection (inv. 1975.1.88).
5. Watson 1968, p. 52. Constable 1962, C134. In the latter catalogue, Constable changed his mind and considered cat. 2 to be entirely by Canaletto. Ingamells 1985, p. 229, agreed that cat. 1 has some studio involvement.
6. See p. 27.
7. Ingamells 1985, p. 225, dated them *c.*1735–44. Earlier, Watson 1968, p. 52, dated the pictures to 1735–40.
8. Constable 1962, C137.
9. Both National Gallery of Art, Washington, DC: Canaletto, *The Entrance to the Grand Canal from the Molo, Venice,* 1742/44, oil on canvas,

114.5 × 153.5 cm, inv. 1945.15.4; Canaletto, *The Square of St Mark's, Venice,* 1742/44, oil on canvas, 114.6 × 153 cm, inv. no. 1945.15.3.
10. *The Building News,* 5 July 1872.
11. First described in the 1834 Hertford House inventory as 'A Panorama View of Venice embracing the Doge's Palace St Mark's Place Custom House and the other principal Buildings from the Opposite side of the Adriatic enlivened by numerous vessels & figures – Canaletti – a splendid Picture of the Master' (cat. 2) and 'A View of ditto taken from the Custom House. The Companion to the preceding (£300 the pair)' (cat. 1). WCA HWF/INV/2 or HWF/INV/5.
12. See Black 1874, no. 256, 'Venice: Panoramic View taken from the Guidecca' (cat. 2), and no. 264, 'Venice: Church of S. Giorgio Maggiore and the Custom House' (cat. 1).
13. https://www.npg.org.uk/research/programmes/directory-of-british-picture-restorers/british-picture-restorers-1600-1950-h (accessed 8 November 2023).

CATALOGUE 3–4
Lelia Packer

1. Sweet 2012, p. 211.
2. The Grassi were admitted to the Venetian aristocracy in 1718.
3. This was probably a leaf from a sketchbook from which 15 other leaves exist. Constable 1962, C587.
4. The other version was painted around the same time and is in a US private collection.
5. Antonio Visentini (1688–1782) after Canaletto (1697–1768), *View of the Grand Canal and Palazzo Flangini in Venice, Prospectus ab Aedibus Flanginorum usque ad Bembos,* 1742, etching, 27.5 × 43.2 cm, plate 2 from *Prospectus Magni Canalis Venetiarum,* Rijksmuseum, Amsterdam (inv. BI-1962-1072-23).
6. Antonio Visentini borrowed the figural group in the Woburn painting in the foreground of *The Rialto Bridge from the North,* after *c.*1754, oil on canvas, 81.5 × 122 cm, Private Collection. This painting was recently published in Beddington 2022, pp. 70, 73, no. 19.
7. Antonio Visentini (1688–1782) after Canaletto (1697–1768), *View of the Grand Canal in Venice, Ab aedibus hinc Foscarorum, illinc Linorum, usque ad Templum Charitas,* 1742, etching, 27.3 × 43.2 cm, plate 2 from *Prospectus Magni Canalis Venetiarum,* Rijksmuseum, Amsterdam (inv. BI-1962-1072-7).
8. Watson 1968, pp. 54–55.
9. Technical report compiled by the Hamilton Kerr Institute in 2021 and stored in the object file at the Wallace Collection.
10. Oil on canvas, 78.5 × 47.2 cm, Royal Collection, RCIN 400532.

11. I am grateful to Charles Beddington for this suggestion. For more on the Countess's commission, see Beddington 2021, pp. 23, 32–33, note 39.

12. Letter transcribed in Beddington 2021, p. 33, note 39.

13. Canaletto, *Venice: The Mouth of the Grand Canal from the East*, 1734, oil on canvas, 47 × 78.4 cm; Canaletto, *The Molo with the Piazzetta and the Doge's Palace, from the Bacino*, 1734, oil on canvas, 47.1 × 77.7 cm. Christie's, London, 7 December 2023, lot 11.

14. One view in the Woburn series is comparable (although still distinct) to cat. 3: fig. 80 in this entry.

15. 4th Earl of Essex Sale, Christie's, 31 January to 1 February 1777 (L.2634). Beddington 2021, p. 33, note 39.

16. The buyers of Canaletti at the Essex sale were Lebrun, Turner, Doughty, Lloys, Crofts and Coppinger.

17. Ingamells 1981, p. 63. Letter dated 29 March 1855.

18. Sir Thomas Bernard was born in Lincoln. His father, Sir Francis Bernard, was appointed Governor of the province of New Jersey in 1857. Thomas moved to America with his family as a child. After studying at Harvard College, he returned to England. His first marriage in May 1782 to Margaret, daughter and co-heiress of Patrick Adair, assured him a considerable fortune. He soon retired from the law and devoted himself to ensuring the welfare of the poor. He was greatly involved with the Foundling Hospital and other institutions. His first wife died on 6 June 1813, and on 15 June 1815 he married Charlotte Matilda Hulse, youngest daughter of Sir Edward Hulse, Bt. For more on Thomas Bernard, see Baker 1819.

19. Listed as Canaletti, 'A view on the grand canal, at Venice, with gondolas and figures'. One of 11 paintings at the sale that formed 'the remaining portion of the collection of the late Sir Thomas Bernard, Bart.'.

20. Listed as Canaletti, 'A view on the grand canal – the companion'.

21. This is probably the agent William King who is described in 1853 as 'Mr King as Agent for the Marquis of Hertford' in connection with Hertford's purchase, through King, of two pieces of furniture (Wallace Collection F510 and F511) from the 2nd Marquess of Abercorn. Hughes 1996, vol. 1, p. 280.

22. See Black 1874, pp. 54–55. The paintings could be nos 270, 279, 287, 311 or 323, all attributed to Canaletto and described as 'Venice: View on the Grand Canal'.

CATALOGUE 5–6
Lelia Packer

1. Lassels 1670, p. 367.

2. Razzall and Whitaker 2017, pp. 284–87. Canaletto made other *capricci* inspired by Palladio's design, discussed by Links 1994, pp. 150–54.

3. Razzall and Whitaker 2017, p. 284.

4. Sweet 2012, p. 203.

5. In 1966 what remained of the damaged frescoes was removed and transferred to the Galleria Giorgio Franchetti at the Ca' d'Oro in Venice. On the frescoes, see Schulz 2001.

6. In folio 34 in the *Cagnola Sketchbook* Canaletto wrote 'Corpus Domini' above this tower. It may be that he was marking the area more generally rather than the tower itself or that he mislabelled it. See Nepi Scirè 1997, pp. 106–7. Constable 1962, C266, and Beddington 2021, p. 110, agree that this is the tower of Santa Croce.

7. Cowper 1864, p. 47.

8. Ingamells 1997, pp. 157–58.

9. Canaletto (1697–1768), *The Canale di Santa Chiara Looking North*, *c.*1722–23, oil on canvas, 46.7 × 77.9 cm, Royal Collection (RCIN 401403).

10. Constable 1962, C592; Baetjer and Links 1989, pp. 288–89.

11. Parker 1948, p. 42, no. 64; Constable 1962, C591.

12. Folios 34–39v. See Nepi Scirè 1997, pp. 96–107.

13. The fruit stand also appears in the Musée Cognacq-Jay and Woburn Abbey versions of this composition (figs 98 and 99).

14. Canaletto followed his colour annotations in his version of the composition at the Musée Cognacq-Jay (fig. 98).

15. Parker 1948, p. 32, no. 15; Constable 1962, C601.

16. Parker 1948, pp. 31–32, no. 14; Constable 1962, C600. A third drawing, today in the Royal Collection (Canaletto, *The Upper Reach of the Grand Canal, Looking South*, *c.*1734, pen, ink and pencil on paper, 19.9 × 27.1 cm, Royal Collection, RCIN 907476), includes the plain wall and corresponds to the composition at Woburn Abbey (fig. 99). Parker 1948, p. 31, no. 13; Constable 1962, C602.

17. Visentini based his etching on the Cognacq-Jay version of the composition (fig. 98), albeit with some variations: he replaced the featureless wall to the right of Santa Croce in the painting with walls of different heights and a small house in the print, as in cat. 6.

18. Canaletto (1697–1768), *The Grand Canal with the Rialto Bridge from the South*, 1730s, oil on canvas, 47 × 80 cm, Collection of the Duke of Bedford, Woburn Abbey. Another version of this composition is Canaletto, *Grand Canal: The Rialto Bridge from the South*, oil on copper, 45.5 × 62.5 cm, Viscount Coke and the Trustees of the Holkham Estate. See Constable 1962, C226; Baetjer and Links 1989, pp. 116–17, no. 21.

19. Another version of this view *c.*1730 is in the Mario Crespi Collection, Milan (oil on canvas, 50 × 80 cm). Constable 1962, C269.

20. Burollet 2004, pp. 81–83. Mentioned in Constable 1962, under C268 (cat. 6).

21. Antonio Visentini (1688–1782), *View of the Grand Canal from S. Chiara to S. Croce*, 1742, pen and ink on paper, 27.5 × 43.2 cm, plate 1 from *Prospectus Magni Canalis Venetiarum*, II, Rijksmuseum, Amsterdam (inv. BI-1962-1072-21)

22. Links 1969, pp. 13–14, believed the site to be as it appears in cat. 6.

23. The Convent of Santa Chiara was suppressed by Napoleon in 1806, after which the church was demolished. In 1819 it became a military hospital. Today, it serves as Police Headquarters. There is another painting similar to this view that was originally painted for Charles Spencer, 3rd Duke of Marlborough, the Duke of Bedford's brother-in-law, who may have seen it in his relative's collection and ordered himself a copy: Canaletto, *The Grand Canal, Looking South-East along the Fondamenta di Santa Chiara*, *c.*1736, oil on canvas, 47 × 77.7 cm, Private Collection, London. Constable 1962, C267.

24. WCA HWF/INV/2 or HWF/INV/5.

25. See Black 1874, pp. 54–55. Cat. 6 could be nos 270, 279, 287, 311 or 323. These are all paintings attributed to Canaletto and described as 'Venice: View on the Grand Canal'. Cat. 5 is no. 319, 'Venice: The Grand Canal and the Bridge of the Rialto'.

26. For example, Jan Hackaert, *The Wooded Banks of a River*, 1660s, oil on canvas, 62 × 46.3 cm, P245, and cat. 9.

27. https://www.npg.org.uk/collections/research/programmes/directory-of-british-picture-restorers/british-picture-restorers-1600-1950-p#PE (accessed 13 September 2023).

28. WCA HWF/M4/5/14.

CATALOGUE 7–8
Lelia Packer

1. Cook and Wedderburn 1903, p. 38.

2. Beddington 2010, pp. 159–60.

3. Sweet 2012, p. 281.

4. These were not cleared until 1889. Links 1977, p. xv.

5. Lassels 1670, pp. 401–2.

6. See cats 1 and 2 entry.

7. The poet Petrarch is believed to have lived along the Riva.

8. The assassin's house on the Riva was razed and it was decreed that no stone building should be constructed on the site. Jackson-Stops 1985, p. 248.

9. Identified by Links 1967, p. 409. Constable 1962, C112, thought that the dome was that of San Giorgio dei Greci and the further *campanile* possibly that of San Martino.

10. Lassels 1670, p. 402.

11. The church is formally known as the Chiesa del Santissimo Redentore, or Church of the Most Holy Redeemer.

12. For more on San Giorgio, see cats 1 and 2 entry.

13. Razzall and Whitaker 2017, pp. 136–49 on the paintings, esp. nos 54 and 55, and pp. 218–21 on the drawings, esp. nos 87 and 88.

14. C/L 574. It has been suggested that this ruled drawing was worked up in the studio. Baetjer and Links 1989, pp. 294–95. Other drawings from the same group are believed to have been done *in situ*. Razzall and Whitaker 2017, pp. 222, 225, no. 92.

15. Canaletto, *The Molo and Riva degli Schiavoni, Looking East*, 1729, pen and ink, 21 × 31.5 cm, Hessisches Landesmuseum, Darmstadt (C/L573).

16. Clayton 2005, p. 99; Constable 1962, C111.

17. This view was worked up more fully in two drawings at the Royal Collection from the mid-1730s. See Razzall and Whitaker 2017, nos 109, 110.

18. See 'Related Works'.

19. Two or three versions of cat. 7 passed through Smith's hands: C/L 113, C/L 115 and possibly C/L 111.

20. C/L 113 was used as the model for the view looking east to the Riva degli Schiavoni.

21. Ingamells 1985, p. 234; Constable 1962, C90, C112.

22. I thank Charles Beddington for his input in this dating.

23. C/L115 and C/L149; also catalogued in Baetjer and Links 1989, nos 18–19, pp. 112–14.

24. Passavant 1836, vol. 1, p. 227. The Dutch pictures were described as 'one of the richest and most choice collections of Dutch masters'. Passavant 1836, vol. 2, p. 71–72.

25. Ibid. For more on Wells, see 'Provenance'.

26. These were Berchem (P640), Van Dyck (P16), Murillo (P97), After Rembrandt (P55), Workshop of Velázquez (P4), Van de Velde the Younger (P143) and Wouwermans (P226). In May 1848 Hertford spent £8,515 at the Casimir Périer and William Wells sales altogether. Ingamells 1981, p. 21, note 3.

27. There is a note on page 184 in the Christie's 1848 Day Book that suggests that Wells used a Mr Westmacott as his agent. Westmacott brought pictures in and out of the auction house for Wells. Perhaps Hertford acquired the two Canaletti via Westmacott. A letter from Hertford to Mawson, London, May 1848, confirms that Hertford was in London. Ingamells 1981, p. 21. Wells's subsequent 1852 sale of British pictures unsurprisingly did not include the Canaletti. Christie's, London, 20 May 1852 (L.20847).

28. William Wells was a shipbuilder and art collector. He was a ship's captain for the East India Company and later owned Blackwell shipyard, which he sold in 1806. He served as a Trustee of the National Gallery between 1835 and 1847 and was a great patron of Edwin Landseer (1802–1873). Wells bequeathed one painting to the National Gallery (Guido Reni, *The Coronation of the Virgin*, c.1607, oil on copper, 66.6 × 48.8 cm, NG214); several other pictures from his collection ended up there, such as Rembrandt, *Portrait of Aechje Claesdr*, 1634, oil on oak, 71.1 × 55.9 cm, NG775. On Wells, see Robertson 1978, p. 296; Stourton and Sebag-Montefiore 2012, p. 180.

29. Wells lent the paintings to the British Institution in June 1838. They are listed in the accompanying catalogue under no. 137, 'The Doge's Palace at Venice' (cat. 7), and no. 142, 'St Mark's Place, at Venice' (cat. 8), accessible here: https://babel.hathitrust.org/cgi/pt?id=gri.ark:/13960t04x84f4s&view=1up&seq=583&q1=william%20wells%20canaletto (accessed 28 August 2023).

30. Listed as 'View of the Doge's Palace and Quay of St Mark, looking towards the prisons with gondolas and numerous figures – 36.5 in by 22 in'.

31. Listed as 'The Library of St Mark; and the Church of Sta. Maria della Salute, with figures on the quay – the companion'.

32. Sold to 'W.W.' in the auctioneer's catalogue at Christie's Archive. In the Index of Christie's 1848 Daybook, Wells is listed on page 184. On that page Mr Westmacott, presumably Wells's agent, is listed as bringing pictures in on 26 April 1848. Pictures were then returned to 'W.W.' (probably William Wells) on 12 June 1848, which were likely to have included the present pair. Although Hertford bought seven paintings at the 1848 Wells sale (see note 26), he did not buy the present pair, which he must have acquired at a later point.

33. See Black 1874, p. 54. Cat. 7 is no. 284, 'Venice: The Doge's Palace and the Quay of the Sclavonians'; cat. 8 is no. 288, 'Venice: Piazzetta of S. Marco and the Entrance to the Grand Canal'.

34. Ingamells 1985, p. 234. On Vallance see pp. 65, 77, 103, 157.

CATALOGUE 9
Charles Beddington

1. Constable 1962, C349; exhibited in *Canaletto – Guardi: Les Deux Maîtres de Venise* at the Musée Jacquemart-André, Paris, 2012–13, see Kowalczyk and Sainte Fare Garnot 2012, pp. 156–57, no. 38, illustrated in colour.

2. Constable 1962, C347; Razzall and Whitaker 2017, pp. 178–81, no. 70; Dario Succi has stated that the regatta shown is that of 8 June 1734 (Succi 2015, p. 132, under no. 4).

3. Constable 1962, C348; Beddington 2021, no. 24, illustrated in colour.

4. Constable 1962, C350.

5. Sotheby's, London, 5 July 1967, lot 24; Constable 1962, C351.

6. Camp 1928, p. 47.

7. Ingamells 1979, p. 40.

8. Note in the Constable/Links Archive in the possession of the present author.

CATALOGUE 10
Charles Beddington

1. For more on the subject, see Tamassia Mazzarotto 1961, pp. 31–39; Muir 1981, pp. 160–71.

2. Watson 1968, p. 53.

3. For the drawing, see Constable 1962, C636; or most recently Robison 2014, no. 85, illustrated. For the print, see, for instance, Succi 1983, pp. 90–91, no. 63, illustrated.

4. Magani and Fabiani, 2009, fig. 1 (as Pietro Antonio Novelli(?)).

5. Exhibited in *Francesco Guardi 1712–1793* at the Museo Correr, Venice, 2012–13, see Craievich and Pedrocco 2012, no. 77, p. 217.

CATALOGUE 11
Charles Beddington

1. Constable 1962, C259; Beddington 2010, p. 183, no. 25, illustrated p. 92.

2. *The Grand Canal Looking West with the Scalzi and San Simeone Piccolo*, c.1726–27, Royal Collection, RCIN 407267. Constable 1962, C258; Razzall and Whitaker 2017, pp. 154–55, no. 59.

3. Sir Claude Phillips in the first edition of the Wallace Collection picture catalogue; Phillips 1901A, p. 106.

4. Camp 1928, p. 48.

5. Kowalczyk 1996A, pp. 75–76, figs 5–6.

6. See Beddington 2014.

7. Hedley 2002, pp. 5, 7. The present writer must take some blame for Hedley's rejection of the attribution to Bellotto, although not for the reasons that she gives.

CATALOGUE 12–15
Charles Beddington

1. Ingamells 1985, p. 432.

2. Camp 1928, all as his 'Group A'.

3. Constable 1962, C203, C161, C153; Razzall and Whitaker 2017, nos 65, 69.

4. Constable 1962, C184.

5. Beddington 2022, pp. 84–5, nos 6, 12.

6. Cat. 14 and cat. 15 have chalk numbers on the relining canvas 'I – 24' [which is the appropriate lot number in the 1848 sale] and 'I – 2?' [illegible]. There are no such numbers on the relining canvases of cat. 12 or cat. 13.

CATALOGUE 16
Charles Beddington

1. Constable 1962, C107(a).
2. Constable 1962, C107.
3. Christie's, London, 10 July 1998, lot 81; Succi and Delneri 2001A, no. 39; Succi and Delneri 2001B, no. 41; Algranti 2002, no. 100; Pedrocco 2002, pp. 104–6, illustrated and with a detail on p. 70; Succi and Delneri 2008, no. 82.
4. On the stretcher is the stamp of the London liner James Spender (*c.*1815–1876), for whom see https://www.npg.org.uk/collections/research/programmes/directory-of-british-picture-restorers/british-picture-restorers-1600-1950-s.php (accessed 27 October 2023).

CATALOGUE 17
Charles Beddington

1. Cited by Redford 1996, p. 61.
2. Lane 1973, p. 417.
3. J. Moore, *A View of Society and Manners in Italy*, London, 1781, p. 58, quoted by Redford 1996, p. 62.
4. Constable 1962, C634. Another of the compositions is related to that of *The Festival of Giovedì Grasso in the Piazzetta* (cat. 10).
5. Watson 1968, p. 344.
6. 'è da compiangersi il nostro Francesco Tironi, che morto sia in troppo fresca età da qualche anno, poiché i Porti di Venezia e le Isole disegnati da lui, ed incisi poi dal nostro Antonio Santi [*sic*], ci fanno scorgere quant'oltre sarebbe arrivato' ['Our poor Francesco Tironi is much to be mourned, who died too young a few years ago, for the compositions of the Ports of Venice and the Islands, drawn by him and engraved by Antonio Sandi, show how much he would have achieved']. Moschini 1806–8, vol. 3 (1806), p. 78, note 1; quoted by Moretti 2008, pp. 206–7.
7. The *Ventiquattro Prospettive delle Isole della Laguna* in fact include views of the ports of Chioggia, Malamocco and the Lido, and of the *Murazzi* (sea walls). See Pignatti 1974; Succi 1983, pp. 344–47.
8. Shaw and Knox 1987, pp. 216–18, nos 178–79, both illustrated.
9. Stock 1980, pp. 73–74, no. 113, illustrated.
10. See Kostioukovitch 1995, p. 221, no. 193, illustrated.
11. See, for instance, Morassi 1959, p. 75, no. 115, illustrated, and Sotheby's, New York, 26 January 2000, lot 110 ($25,300).
12. Ward-Jackson 1980, pp. 180–82, nos 1185–90, all illustrated. An unpublished variant of the right section of the first of these was sold from the estate of Madame Carlo Broglio at the Palais Galliera, Paris, 20 March 1974, lot 2, as by Canaletto, and was subsequently with Agnew's, London, *Master Drawings and Prints*, 11 March–25 April 1975, no. 17, with the same attribution.

13. Bean and Stampfle 1971, p. 115, no. 298, illustrated.
14. A *Molo and the Riva degli Schiavoni, Looking East* was sold at Sotheby's, New York, 8 January 1991, lot 213 ($16,500).
15. Voss 1927–28, p. 270; Voss 1966, pp. 100–4.
16. Dario Succi has proposed that the painter who headed this prolific workshop may be Apollonio Domenichini (1715–*c.*1770).
17. Bonhams, London, 3 December 2008, lot 49; Galleria Cesare Lampronti, Rome, *Cento Capolavori di Pittura dal XVI al XVIII Secolo*, 22 October–22 November 2009, nos 62–63. The initials are not mentioned in either catalogue.
18. *Catalogo di quadri raccolti dal fu signor Maffeo Pinelli ed ora posti in vendita in Venezia*, p. 106: 'Tironi Francesco – Bella Veduta dell'Isola di San Giorgio Maggiore di Venezia. In tela, alt. p[iedi] 1 onc. 8 – l[argo] p. 2. onc. 4 [= 58 × 81 cm] – Quadro simile, Veduta di Venezia dalla parte della Pescaria di S. Marco. In tela, di grandezza simile, e in ambedue sta scritto F.T' (quoted by Moretti 2008). Maffeo Pinelli (1735–1785) was a printer.
19. Sotheby's, London, 23 March 1973, lot 52, as Giovanni Migliara; and Succi 2004, fig. 23.
20. Private Collection, Italy.

CATALOGUE 18
Charles Beddington

1. Watson 1968, p. 54.
2. Constable 1962, C27; Beddington 2021, no. 4.
3. Little is known, for instance, of the interior decoration of Fonthill Splendens, the great mansion in Wiltshire he built in *c.*1755–*c.*1770, which was demolished in 1807.

CATALOGUE 19–22
Lelia Packer

1. 'quatres fameux pendants de la collection de Morny, qui sont peut-être les quatre plus beaux que le maître ait jamais peints' (four famous pendants from the Morny collection, that are probably the four most beautiful [works] that the master ever painted): Yriarte 1878, p. 178.
2. Beddington 2010, p. 165.
3. See below for more on Le Zitelle in the discussion of cat. 22.
4. At the end of the nineteenth century, the neo-Gothic Palazzo Genovese was built on the site, today the home of the five-star hotel, Sina Centurion Palace.
5. On the Rialto Bridge and the surrounding buildings, see cat. 5 entry.
6. On the Dogana, see cat. 8 entry.
7. On Guardi's treatment of the Dogana, see Morassi 1973, vol. 1, pp. 244–45.

8. For example, see cat. 1 or cat. 8.
9. Another drawing depicting the Rialto from a similar viewpoint but slightly closer up is in the Musée Départemental des Vosges (inv. MO536_D.1920.78).
10. Also see 'Technical Notes', p. 151.
11. Guardi may have used a slightly darker paint to sketch the forms of the church interior, perhaps a combination of lead white and earth colours.
12. See the *View of the Cannaregio, Venice, c.*1775–80, oil on canvas, 50 x× 76.8 cm, National Gallery of Art, Washington, DC (inv. 1939.1.113), which was painted over a decorative design.
13. Hedley 2002, p. 15.
14. See 'Provenance'.
15. No. 508: 'Guardi quatre tableaux pendants vues de Venise (8000)'. WCA HWF/INV/19.
16. Ingamells 1985, p. 286, considered them a set of four.
17. Those findings are summarised in Hedley 2002.
18. Technical report in the picture dossier at the Wallace Collection.
19. See Technical Notes on p. 151.
20. See 'Collecting History' and 'Provenance'.
21. Charles Beddington shares this belief and I am grateful to him for his input on this matter.
22. See the discussion on Guardi's painterly handling on p. 139.
23. Morassi 1973, vol. 1, pp. 389–93, nos 418–35.
24. See, for example, Francesco Guardi, *The Grand Canal, Venice, c.*1760, oil on canvas, 73 × 119.4 cm, Art Institute of Chicago (inv. 1951.21). Also see cat. 13 entry, Visentini after Canaletto.
25. De Grazia and Garberson 1996, p. 133.
26. Morassi 1973, vol. 1, pp. 399–406, lists 14 variants that include the Salute (nos 472–96) and 17 that do not (nos 497–513).
27. For example, Francesco Guardi, *Venice: The Punta della Dogana with S. Maria della Salute, c.*1770, oil on canvas, 56.2 × 75.9 cm, National Gallery, London (NG2098).
28. For example, the pendant pair by the Workshop of Francesco Guardi, *Venice: The Rialto*, oil on wood, 18.1 × 32.1 cm, Metropolitan Museum of Art, New York (inv. 1982.60.15) and *Venice: The Dogana and Santa Maria della Salute*, 18.1 × 32.1 cm, Metropolitan Museum of Art, New York (inv. 1982.60.14).
29. Rossi Bortolatto 1974, pp. 98, 104, 113, dated cats 19 and 22 to the 1760s, and considered cat. 21 to be later, from the 1780s, due to the slightly darker tonality. Kultzen 1967, p. 270, dated cat. 20 to the early 1770s. Morassi 1973, vol. 1, pp. 408, 405, dated cat. 21 to *c.*1770–80 and cat. 22 to Guardi's mature period. Hedley 2002, pp. 17, 21, dated cats 21 and 22 to *c.*1770 and cats 19 and 20 to the 1780s.
30. Watson 1968, p. 140, dated cat. 19 and the other three paintings in the series to 1775–80 based on the hair fashion of this figure.

31. On Morny as an art collector, see Emlein 2008; Granger 2005, pp. 221–22. The fifth painting was described as a view of the Piazza San Marco. Lagrange 1863, p. 386. This is consistent with how it is listed in the 1865 sale catalogue of Morny's collection: 'La Place Saint-Marc. Toile. Haut. 68 cent.; larg. 91 cent.'. Paris, 31 May 1865 (L.28564), lot 120, bought by Lord Orford for 5,100 francs.

32. Francesco Guardi, *View of the Piazza San Marco*, oil on canvas, 69.5 × 97 cm, Rothschild Collection, Paris. Morassi 1973, vol. 1, pp. 370–71, no. 318.

33. 'un de collectionneurs les plus magnifiques qui soient en Europe … [Sa collection] serait digne d'être comprise au musée du Louvre'. Lacroix 1862, p. 124.

34. Their collecting practices were compared by Emlein 2008, p. 86.

35. All five paintings are listed as measuring 60 × 91 cm in the 1865 sale catalogue of Morny's collection.

36. 'emmenant aussi avec lui son expert conservateur. M. M., pour qu'il l'aidât á découvrir, soit á Pétersbourg, soit á Moscou, quelque chef-d'oeuvre'. Vernier 1861, p. 12.

37. 'Quand il revint á Paris … il rapporta … une bonne partie des toiles superbes qui orne sa nouvelle galerie. De ce nombre étaient … le Guardi'. Ibid. 'après avoire jeté un coup d'oeil sur deux Guardi étonnants (et il y en a quatre dans la galerie)'. Vernier 1861, p. 11. The author must have missed the fifth Guardi in Morny's collection.

38. Lagrange 1863, p. 386.

39. 'les cinq *Vues de Venise* de la galerie de Morny … ce n'est pas de Venise qu'elles y sont venues; c'est de la Russie' ('the five views of Venice in the Morny collection did not come from Venice but from Russia'). Ibid.

40. Son of Peter III and Catherine the Great, Paul reigned between 1796 and 1801. For more on his visit to Venice, see Pask 1992, pp. 48–51.

41. See Morassi 1973, vol. 1, pp. 182–83, 357–58, nos 255–61. One of the festivities, for example, was a concert performed on 20 January by the orphan girls at the Filarmonici Hall. This event was recorded by Guardi in *Venetian Gala Concert*, 1782, oil on canvas, 67.7 × 90.5 cm, Alte Pinakothek, Munich (inv. 8574). On 22 January a ball and gala dinner were given in their honour at the San Benedetto Theatre, which was also recorded in a painting by Guardi, *The Interior of the Teatro San Benedetto, Venice, with the 1782 Ball in Honour of the 'Conti del Nord'*, 1782, oil on canvas, 67 × 91.5 cm, Private Collection, previously Christie's, New York, The Ann and Gordon Getty Collection, 21 October 2022, lot 125.

42. They all measure around 67/68 × 90/92 cm.

43. Numbers began to be added from the late eighteenth century and seals from 1797. I thank Irina Artemieva for her assistance on this matter.

44. On Wallace's stay and acquisitions in Russia, see Higgott 2019, pp. 100–3.

45. 'quatre surtout sont sans rivals'. Lagrange 1863, p. 386.

46. Hertford paid 25,000 francs for cat. 21, 20,000 francs each for cats 19 and 22, and 18,000 francs for cat. 20. Lord Orford bought the view of the Piazza for 5,100 francs.

47. Lot 98: Jean-Honoré Fragonard, *Les hasards heureux de l'escarpolette* (*The Swing*), c.1767–68, oil on canvas, 81× 64.2 cm, Wallace Collection, London (P430). Most of the pictures he bought were French, including three *fêtes galantes*: Pater lots 113 and 107, now P420 (*The Pleasures of the Ball*, c.1730–36, oil on canvas, 54.8 × 64.1 cm) and P424 (*Fête Galante by a Fountain*, early 1720s, oil on canvas, 52.7 × 64.4 cm); and Watteau lot 112, now P416 (*Rendez-Vous de Chasse*, c.1717–18, oil on canvas, 124.5 × 189 cm).

48. See the prices paid for each of the pictures in note 46.

49. This was on 6–10 and 12 June. Among the objects acquired were OA1381 (lot 149), OA1430 (lot 151) and possibly OA1394 (lot 146). I thank Suzanne Higgott for this information. The sculpture is S26 (lot 445) and the snuffbox is G80 (lot 382).

50. Archives de Paris D.42E³ 47. On Laneuville and Hertford, see Higgott 2019, pp. 26–27, 64.

51. The paintings are listed as four pendant views of Venice hanging in a room described as 'une petite pièce éclairée par une croisée'. 1871 inventory of 2 rue Laffitte, WCA HWF/INV/19.

52. *Pall Mall Gazette*, 20 February 1897, p. 3.

53. Listed as 'L'Église de San-Giorgio-Maggiore', Toile. Haut. 68 cent; larg. 91 cent.'.

54. Listed as 'La Salute', Toile. Haut. 68 cent; larg. 91 cent.'.

55. Listed as 'Le Pont du Rialto', Toile. Haut. 68 cent; larg. 91 cent.'.

56. Listed as 'La Dogana', Toile. Haut. 68 cent; larg. 91 cent.'.

57. See Black 1874, p. 65. Cat. 19 is no. 282, 'Church of S. Giorgio Maggiore, Venice'; cat. 20 is no. 278, 'Church of the Madonna della Salute, Venice'; cat. 21 is no. 272, 'Bridge of the Rialto, Venice'; cat. 22 is no. 281, 'Mouth of the Grand Canal, Venice'.

58. All listed in Morassi 1973, vol. 1, pp. 403–6, nos 497–513.

59. The off-white upper layer is composed of two layers.

60. Frederick Haines & Sons were picture restorers active in London between 1878 and 1916. See https://www.npg.org.uk/collections/research/programmes/directory-of-british-picture-restorers/british-picture-restorers-1600-1950-h (accessed 29 August 2023).

61. Frank Morrell (1882–1964) was a picture liner with a studio at 5 & 6 Portland Mews, Poland St, Soho, London. See https://www.npg.org.uk/collections/research/programmes/directory-of-british-picture-restorers/british-picture-restorers-1600-1950-m (accessed 29 August 2023).

62. Auguste Prosper Momper (1813–1888), better known as Momper Aîné, was a liner active in Paris between 1843 and 1888. He trained with François Toussaint Hacquin and specialised in a process of doubling canvases that he invented, which involved removing the original canvas and replacing it with two new layers of material. See Volle et al. 2020, pp. 632–33.

CATALOGUE 23–24
Lelia Packer

1. A pair of the same subject by Guardi was sold at Christie's London, 3 July 2012, lot 52.

2. See cat. 19 entry for an in-depth discussion of the subject.

3. See cats 20 and 22 entry on the landmarks depicted.

4. See cat. 19 entry.

5. Morassi catalogued 19 versions of cat. 23. Morassi 1973, vol. 1, pp. 389–93, nos 418–35. See cat. 19 entry. Morassi 1973, vol. 1, pp. 399–403, lists 14 variants of cat. 24 (nos 472–96). See also cat. 22 entry.

6. Ingamells 1985, p. 295, dated the pair to c.1780, after the *campanile* of San Giorgio Maggiore collapsed.

7. Christie & Manson, London, 12–13 May 1848 (L.19021). See pp. 100, 103.

8. Lot 12, 'Guardi, The Church of St. Georgio Maggiore at Venice' and lot 13, 'Guardi, The Dogana – the companion'. Christie's Archive confirmed that lot 12 was bought for 36 guineas and lot 13 for 31 guineas.

9. Rue Drouot no. 5, Paris, 2–3 March 1857 (L.23405), See pp. 31–32.

10. Lot 47, 'Vue du Grand Canal' and lot 48, 'Vue de la douane'.

11. See Chapter 2, note 42.

12. Higgott 2019, p. 72.

13. Five paintings by Guardi are listed in that inventory: nos 420, 'vue d'Italie'; 508, 'quatre vues pendants' (cats 19, 20, 21, 22); 995, 'la place St Mark'.

14. See 'Exhibitions'.

15. See Black 1874, p. 65. Cat. 23 is no. 277, 'Church of S. Giorgio Maggiore, and the Lido, Venice'; cat. 24 is no. 271, 'Custom House and Church of Salute, Venice'.

16. Published in Beddington 2010, p. 146.

17. Previously sold at Christie's, New York, 28 January 2015, lot 21.

18. Previously sold at Christie's, London, 11 December 2002, lot 123.

19. I am grateful to Erma Hermens at the Hamilton Kerr Institute for assisting me in identifying the composition of the ground.

20. On Vallance, see pp. 65, 77, 103, 157.

1. The arch is comparable to that in a painting by Guardi at the National Gallery (fig. 161).
2. On the Doge's Palace, see cats 7 and 8 entry.
3. On the Lyons picture, see Lavergne-Durey and Buijs 1993, p. 218; Morassi 1973, vol. I, p. 458, no. 799. Levey 1971, p. 132, note 12, first suggested the possibility of a *terzetto*.
4. Suggested by Levey 1971, p. 131. For the paintings previously with the Earl of Normanton, see Morassi 1973, vol. I, p. 454, no. 776; Millar 1955, no. 21.
5. Other comparable drawings by Guardi with the arch of the Torre dell'Orologio are at the Courtauld Gallery, London (inv. D.1978.PG.136) and the Hermitage Museum, St Petersburg (inv. OP-10505). In the latter, he employed a groin vault rather than a barrel vault.
6. Watson 1968, p. 141, considered cat. 25 as probably a fairly late work of the 1780s and cat. 26 as being painted in 1780 or a little later based on the women's hairstyles. Levey 1971, p. 132, considered both paintings late, probably post-1780. Morassi 1973, vol. I, p. 461, considered cat. 25 a late work. According to Ingamells 1985, p. 289, both paintings are late works due to Guardi's execution and the costumes depicted. Duffy and Hedley 2004, p. 190, also considered them works of the late 1780s due to the costumes and fluid painting technique.
7. Ingamells 1981, p. 36, no. 20.
8. See Black 1874, p. 65. Cat. 25 is no. 274, 'Arcade of S. Giorgio Maggiore, Venice'; cat. 26 is no. 275, 'Arcade of the Ducal Palace, Venice'.

1. This corresponds to the lot number (93) from the 1859 sale at which the picture was acquired by the 4th Marquess of Hertford. See 'Provenance'.
2. There are two additional comparable drawings by Guardi at the Metropolitan Museum of Art, New York, with and without the staircase: *Architectural Capriccio: Courtyard of a Palace*, pen and brown ink, brush and brown wash, over red chalk on paper, 27.1 × 18.8 cm (inv. 37.165.71) and *Architectural Capriccio: Courtyard of a Palace* [recto], *Saint Aloysius Holding a Crucifix* [verso], pen and brown ink, brush and brown wash, nstaover red chalk on paper [recto], graphite [verso], 27.9 × 20.3 cm (inv. 37.165.80).
3. The same view of the Dining Room, with a slightly different arrangement of pictures but including the present work by Guardi, was depicted in a watercolour attributed to Harriet Rushout Bowles (1809–1852) from *c.*1843, today at the Cheltenham Trust and Cheltenham Borough Council.
4. *Hours in the Picture Gallery of Thirlestane House*, 1846, p. 50, no. CCL.
5. Lots 78, 80, 170, 183, 462, 463 466, 467, 482, 486, 931, 1771, 1849. Baron of Northwick's sale, 26 July–30 August 1859 (L.25025).
6. Letter from Mawson to Hertford, 15 July 1859. Ingamells 1981, p. 122. In the same letter, Mawson also advised Hertford to purchase a Canaletto: 'Lot 170 by Canaletto a superb picture & out to be secured for the Canaletto room as it is first rate.' This is now NG938 at the National Gallery, London (Canaletto,

Venice: A Regatta on the Grand Canal, *c.*1735, oil on canvas, 117.2 × 186.7 cm). Mawson had overlooked that Hertford already owned a Regatta view in cat. 9, which he had inherited from his great-grandfather.
7. 1890 inventory of Hertford House, WCA HWF/INV/23.
8. Listed in ibid.
9. Listed as 'F. Guardi, A Venetian Scene, with Figures'.
10. See Black 1874, p. 65. Cat. 27 is no. 276, 'Courtyard of the Ducal Palace, Venice'.
11. Simon Bobak suggested that the painting was relined between 1850 and 1870. This information is recorded in the Hamilton Kerr Institute technical report of 2018, and accessible in the picture dossier at the Wallace Collection. However, the lining canvas still bears the lot number (93) from the 1859 sale at which the picture was acquired by Lord Hertford. It is therefore likely that it was relined prior to 1859.

BIBLIOGRAPHY

ALGRANTI 2002
Algranti, Gilberto, ed., *Titian to Tiepolo: Three Centuries of Italian Art* (exh. cat., National Gallery of Australia, Canberra; Melbourne Museum), Milan: Skira, 2002

BAETJER AND LINKS 1989
Baetjer, Katharine, and J.G. Links, *Canaletto* (exh. cat., Metropolitan Museum of Art, New York, 1989–90), New York: Metropolitan Museum of Art, 1989

BAKER 1819
Baker, James, *The Life of Sir Thomas Bernard, Baronet*, London: John Murray, 1819

BEAN AND STAMPFLE 1971
Bean, Jacob, and Felice Stampfle, *Drawings from New York Collections, vol. 3, The Eighteenth Century in Italy* (exh. cat., The Metropolitan Museum of Art, New York, 1971), New York: The Metropolitan Museum of Art and The Pierpont Morgan Library, 1971

BEDDINGTON 2006
Beddington, Charles, ed., *Canaletto in England: A Venetian Artist Abroad, 1746–1755* (exh. cat., Yale Center for British Art, New Haven, 2006; Dulwich Picture Gallery, London, 2007), New Haven and London: Yale University Press, 2006

BEDDINGTON 2010
Beddington, Charles, *Venice: Canaletto and his Rivals* (exh. cat., National Gallery, London, 2010–11; National Gallery of Art, Washington, 2011), London: National Gallery, 2010

BEDDINGTON 2014
Beddington, Charles, *Bernardo Bellotto and his Circle in Italy & a Masterpiece by Francesco Guardi* (exh. cat., Charles Beddington Ltd, London, 2014), London: Charles Beddington Ltd, 2014

BEDDINGTON 2021
Beddington, Charles, *Canaletto: Painting Venice, The Woburn Series*, London: Pallas Athene, 2021

BEDDINGTON 2022
Beddington, Charles, 'Antonio Visentini as a view painter', *Colnaghi Studies Journal*, vol. 10 (March 2022), pp. 64–89

BETTAGNO 1993
Bettagno, Alessandro, *Francesco Guardi, vedute capricci feste* (exh. cat., Fondazione Giorgio Cini, Venice, 1993), Milan: Electa, 1993

BINION 1976
Binion, Alice, *Antonio and Francesco Guardi: Their Life and Milieu, with a Catalogue of their Figure Drawings*, New York: Garland, 1976

BLACK 1874
Black, Charles Christopher, *Catalogue of the Collection of Paintings, Porcelain, Bronzes, Decorative Furniture, and Other Works of Art, Lent for the Exhibition in the Bethnal Green Branch of the South Kensington Museum by Sir Richard Wallace Bart. June 1872*, London: HMSO, 1874

BLACK 1996
Black, Jeremy, 'Italy and the Grand Tour: the British experience in the eighteenth century', *Annali d'Italianistica, vol. 14, L'Odeporica/Hodoeporics: On Travel Literature* (1996), pp. 532–41

BLANC 1857
Blanc, Charles, *Les Trésors de l'Art à Manchester*, Paris: Pagnerre, 1857

BOMFORD AND FINALDI 1998
Bomford, David, and Gabriele Finaldi, *Venice through Canaletto's Eyes* (exh. cat., National Gallery, London, 1998; York City Art Gallery, 1998–99; Glynn Vivian Art Gallery, Swansea, 1999), London: National Gallery, 1998

BOWRON 2001
Bowron, Edgar Peters, *Bernardo Bellotto and the Capitals of Europe* (exh. cat., Museo Correr, Venice, 2001; Museum of Fine Arts, Houston, 2001), New Haven and London: Yale University Press, 2001

BOWRON 2016
Bowron, Edgar Peters, *Pompeo Batoni: A Complete Catalogue of his Paintings*, 2 vols, New Haven and London: Yale University Press in association with the Museum of Fine Arts, Houston, and the Paul Mellon Centre for Studies in British Art, 2016

BOWRON AND KERBER 2007
Bowron, Edgar Peters, and Peter Björn Kerber, *Pompeo Batoni: Prince of Painters in Eighteenth-Century Rome* (exh. cat., Museum of Fine Arts, Houston, 2007–8; National Gallery, London, 2008), New Haven and London: Yale University Press, 2007

BÜRGER 1867
Bürger, William, 'Les Collections Particulières', *Paris Guide*, vol. 1 (1867), pp. 536–50

BUROLLET 2004
Burollet, Thérèse, *Les Peintures, Musée Cognacq-Jay*, Paris: Paris-musées, 2004

CAMESASCA 1974
Camesasca, Ettore, *L'opera completa del Bellotto*, Milan: Rizzoli, 1974

CAMP 1928
Camp, Samuel James, *Wallace Collection Catalogues: Pictures and Drawings*, London: HMSO, 1928

CLAYTON 2005
Clayton, Martin, *Canaletto in Venice* (exh. cat., The Queen's Gallery, Buckingham Palace, London, 2005–6; The Queen's Gallery, Palace of Holyroodhouse, Edinburgh, 2006), London: Royal Collection Trust, 2005

CONSTABLE 1962
Constable, W.G., *Canaletto: Giovanni Antonio Canal 1697–1768*, 2 vols, London: Oxford University Press, 1962

CONSTABLE 1976
Constable, W.G., *Canaletto, Giovanni Antonio Canal 1697–1768*, 2 vols, 2nd edn, revised by J.G. Links, Oxford: Clarendon Press, 1976

CONSTABLE 1989
Constable, W.G., *Canaletto Giovanni Antonio Canal 1697–1768*, 2 vols, 2nd revised edn, by J.G. Links, Oxford: Clarendon Press, 1989

COOK AND WEDDERBURN 1903
Cook, Edward Tyas, and Alexander Wedderburn, eds, *The Works of John Ruskin, vol. 9, The Stones of Venice*, London: George Allen, 1903

COWPER 1864
Cowper, Mary, *Diary of Mary Countess Cowper, Lady of the Bedchamber to the Princess of Wales 1714–20*, London: John Murray, 1864

CRAIEVICH AND PEDROCCO 2012
Craievich, Alberto, and Filippo Pedrocco, eds, *Francesco Guardi, 1712–1793* (exh. cat., Museo Correr, Venice, 2012–13), Milan: Skira, 2012

DE GRAZIA AND GARBERSON 1996
De Grazia, Diane, and Eric Garberson, *National Gallery of Art, Washington: Italian Paintings of the Seventeenth and Eighteenth Centuries*, New York and Oxford: Oxford University Press, 1996

DUFFY AND HEDLEY 2004
Duffy, Stephen, and Jo Hedley, *The Wallace Collection's Pictures, A Complete Catalogue*, London: Unicorn Press and Lindsay Fine Art, 2004

EMLEIN 2008
Emlein, Robin, 'Le duc de Morny, collectionneur du Second Empire', *Histoire de l'Art. Musées, collections, collectionneurs*, no. 62 (2008), pp. 79–88

FRITSCHE 1936
Fritzsche, Hellmuth Allwill, *Bernardo Bellotto genannt Canaletto*, Burg bei Magdeburg: August Hopfer Verlag, 1936

GRANGER 2005
Granger, Catherine, *L'Empereur et les Arts: la Liste Civile de Napoléon III*, Paris: Ecole des Chartes, 2005

HASKELL 1960
Haskell, Francis, 'Francesco Guardi as vedutista and some of his patrons', *Journal of the Warburg and Courtauld Institutes*, vol. 23, no. 3/4 (July–December 1960), pp. 256–76

HASKELL 1980
Haskell, Francis, *Patrons and Painters: Art and Society in Baroque Italy*, New Haven and London: Yale University Press, 1980

HEDLEY 2002
Hedley, Joanne, *Visions of Venice: The Conservation of Five Venetian View Paintings at the Wallace Collection*, Newnham, Northamptonshire: Hellidon Press, 2002

HIGGOTT 2019
Higgott, Suzanne, *The Most Fortunate Man of his Day: Sir Richard Wallace, Connoisseur, Collector and Philanthropist* (2018), London: Trustees of the Wallace Collection, reprinted 2019

HUGHES 1996
Hughes, Peter, *The Wallace Collection Catalogue of Furniture*, 3 vols, London: Trustees of the Wallace Collection, 1996

HUGHES 2014
Hughes, Peter, *The Founders of the Wallace Collection*, London: Trustees of the Wallace Collection, 2014, 5th edn

INGAMELLS 1979
Ingamells, John, *Summary Illustrated Catalogue of Pictures*, London: Trustees of the Wallace Collection, 1979

INGAMELLS 1981
Ingamells, John, ed., *The Hertford Mawson Letters, the 4th Marquess of Hertford to his Agent Samuel Mawson*, London: Trustees of the Wallace Collection, 1981

INGAMELLS 1985
Ingamells, John, *The Wallace Collection Catalogue of Pictures I: British, German, Italian, Spanish*, London: Trustees of the Wallace Collection, 1985

INGAMELLS 1997
Ingamells, John. *A Dictionary of British and Irish Travellers in Italy, 1701–1800: Compiled from the Brinsley Ford Archive*, New Haven and London: Yale University Press, 1997

JACKSON-STOPS 1985
Jackson-Stops, Gervase, ed., *The Treasure Houses of Britain: Five Hundred Years of Private Patronage and Art Collecting* (exh. cat., National Gallery of Art, Washington, 1985–86), New Haven and London: Yale University Press, 1985

KERBER 2017
Kerber, Peter Björn, *Eyewitness Views: Making History in Eighteenth-Century Europe* (exh. cat., J. Paul Getty Center, Los Angeles, 2017; Minneapolis Institute of Art, 2017; Cleveland Museum of Art, 2018), Los Angeles: Getty Publications, 2017

KOSTIOUKOVITCH 1995
Kostioukovitch, Elena, ed., *Five Centuries of European Drawings: The Former Collection of Franz Koenigs* (exh. cat., Pushkin State Museum of Fine Arts, Moscow, 1995–96), Milan: Leonardo Arte, 1995

KOWALCZYK 1996A
Kowalczyk, Bożena Anna, 'Il Bellotto veneziano: "grande intendimento ricercasi"', *Arte Veneta*, vol. 48 (1996), pp. 70–89

KOWALCZYK 1996B
Kowalczyk, Bożena Anna, *Il Bellotto italiano*, unpublished doctoral thesis, Università degli Studi di Venezia, Venice, 1996

KOWALCZYK AND SAINTE FARE GARNOT 2012
Kowalczyk, Bożena Anna, and Nicolas Sainte Fare Garnot, *Canaletto – Guardi: Les Deux Maitres de Venise* (exh. cat., Musée Jacquemart-André, Paris, 2012–13), Brussels: Mercatorfonds, 2012

KOZAKIEWICZ 1972
Kozakiewicz, Stefan, *Bernardo Bellotto*, 2 vols, Recklinghausen and London: Verlag Aurel Bongers and Paul Elek, 1972

KULTZEN 1967
Kultzen, Rolf, 'Ein neuer Guardi für die Alte Pinakothek', *Pantheon*, vol. 25 (1967), pp. 270–75

LACROIX 1862
Lacroix, Paul, 'Cabinet de M. le comte de Morny', in *Annuaire des artistes et des amateurs*, Paris: Jules Renouard, 1862, pp. 124–28

LAGRANGE 1863
Lagrange, Léon, 'La Galerie de M. le Duc de Morny', *Gazette des Beaux-Arts*, vol. 14 (1863), pp. 385–401

LANE 1973
Lane, Frederic, *Venice. A Maritime Republic*, Baltimore and London: Johns Hopkins University Press, 1973

LASSELS 1670
Lassels, Richard, *The Voyage of Italy … in Two Parts: With the Characters of the People, and the Description of the Chief Towns, Churches, Monasteries, Tombes, Libraries, Pallaces, Villas, Gardens, Pictures, Statues, and Antiquities*, Paris, 1670

LAVERGNE-DUREY AND BUIJS 1993
Lavergne-Durey, Valérie, and Hans Buijs, *Catalogue sommaire illustré des peintures du musée des Beaux-Arts de Lyon, I. Écoles étrangères XIII–XIX siècles*, Lyons and Paris: Musée des Beaux-Arts de Lyon and Réunion des Musées Nationaux, 1993

LEVEY 1971
Levey, Michael, *National Gallery Catalogues: The Seventeenth and Eighteenth Century Italian Schools*, London: National Gallery, 1971

LINKS 1967
Links, J.G., 'A missing Canaletto found', *The Burlington Magazine*, vol. 109, no. 772 (July 1967), pp. 403–9

LINKS 1969
Links, J.G., 'Some notes on Visentini's drawings for *Prospectus Magni Canalis Venetiarum* in the Correr Library', *Bollettino dei Musei Civici Veneziani*, no. 4 (1969), pp. 3–19

LINKS 1977
Links, J.G., *Canaletto and his Patrons*, London: Paul Elek, 1977

LINKS 1981
Links, J.G., *Canaletto: The Complete Paintings*, London: Granada, 1981

LINKS 1982
Links, J.G., *Canaletto*, London: Phaidon, 1982

LINKS 1989
Links, J.G., 'Canaletto, 1975–1988: a review', in Constable 1989, vol. 1, pp. xiv–xix

LINKS 1994
Links, J.G., *Canaletto* (1982), Oxford: Phaidon, 1994, 2nd edn

LINKS 1998
Links, J.G., *A Supplement to W.G. Constable's Canaletto: Giovanni Antonio Canal, 1697–1768*, London: Pallas Athene Arts, 1998

MAGANI AND FABIANI 2009
Magani, Fabrizio, and Rossella Fabiani, eds, *Uno sguardo su Venezia. Canaletto a Miramare* (exh. cat., Museo Storico del Castello di Miramare, Trieste, 2009), Milan: Silvana, 2009

MAHON 1968
Mahon, Denis, 'When did Francesco Guardi become a "vedutista"?', *The Burlington Magazine*, vol. 110, no. 779 (February 1968), pp. 69–73

MARIETTE 1851–53
Mariette, Pierre-Jean, *Abecedario*, vol. 1, Paris: J.B. Dumoulin, 1851–53

MARTINEAU AND ROBISON 1994
Martineau, Jane, and Andrew Robison, eds, *The Glory of Venice: Art in the Eighteenth Century* (exh. cat., Royal Academy of Arts, London, 1994; National Gallery of Art, Washington, 1995), New Haven and London: Yale University Press, 1994

MILLAR 1955
Millar, Oliver, *Pictures from Hampshire Houses* (exh. cat., Winchester College; Southampton Art Gallery, 1955), Winchester: Wykeham Press, 1955

MORASSI 1959
Morassi, Antonio, *Disegni Veneti del Settecento nella collezione Paul Wallraf* (exh. cat., Fondazione Giorgio Cini, Venice, 1959), Vicenza: Neri Pozza, 1959

MORASSI 1973
Morassi, Antonio, *Guardi: l'opera completa di Antonio e Francesco Guardi*, 2 vols, Venice: Alfieri, 1973, reprinted 1993

MORETTI 2008
Moretti, Lino, 'Francesco Tironi', in Giuseppe Pavanello and Alberto Craievich, eds, *Canaletto: Venezia e i suoi splendori* (exh. cat., Casa dei Carraresi, Treviso, 2008–9), Venice: Marsilio, 2008, pp. 206–7

MOSCHINI 1806–8
Moschini, Gianantonio, *Della letteratura veneziana del secolo XVIII fino a nostri giorni*, 4 vols, Venice: Palese, 1806–8

MUIR 1981
Muir, Edward, *Civic Ritual in Renaissance Venice*, Princeton: Princeton University Press, 1981

MURARO 1960
Muraro, Michelangelo, 'The Guardi problem and the statues of the Venetian guilds', *The Burlington Magazine*, vol. 102, no. 691 (October 1960), pp. 420–29

NEPI SCIRÈ 1997
Nepi Scirè, Giovanna, *Canaletto's Sketchbook*, 2 vols, Venice: Canal & Stamperia, 1997

PARKER 1948
Parker, Karl Theodore, *The Drawings of Antonio Canaletto in the Collection of his Majesty the King at Windsor Castle*, Oxford: Phaidon, 1948

PASK 1992
Pask, Kelly, 'Francesco Guardi and the Conti del Nord: a new drawing', *The J. Paul Getty Museum Journal*, vol. 20 (1992), pp. 45–52

PASSAVANT 1836
Passavant, Johann David, *Tour of a German Artist in England with Notices of Private Galleries and Remarks on the State of Art*, 2 vols, London: Saunders and Otley, 1836 (English translation, first published in German in 1833)

PEDROCCO 2002
Pedrocco, Filippo, *Visions of Venice: Paintings of the 18th Century*, London and New York: Tauris Parke, 2002

PHILLIPS 1901A
Phillips, Claude, *The Wallace Collection*, London, 1901

PHILLIPS 1901B
Phillips, Claude, 'The Wallace Collection. By the Keeper of the Collection. The Italian Pictures – II', *The Art Journal* (1901), pp. 102–6

PIGNATTI 1974
Pignatti, Terisio, *Ventiquattro isole della Laguna disegnate da Francesco Tironi e incise da Antonio Sandi*, Venice: Cassa di Risparmio di Venezia, 1974

PROBLEMI GUARDESCHI 1967
Problemi guardeschi. Atti del Convegno di studi promosso dalla Mostra dei Guardi, Venezia, 13–14 settembre 1965, Venice: Alfieri, 1967

PUPPI 1968
Puppi, Lionello, *L'opera completa del Canaletto*, Milan: Rizzoli, 1968

PUPPI 1970
Puppi, Lionello, *The Complete Paintings of Canaletto*, London: Weidenfeld & Nicolson, 1970

RAIKES 1858
Raikes, Thomas, *A Portion of the Journal Kept by Thomas Raikes, Esq., from 1831 to 1847*, 2 vols, London: Longman, Brown, Green, Longmans and Roberts, 1858

RAZZALL AND WHITAKER 2017
Razzall, Rosie, and Lucy Whitaker, *Canaletto & the Art of Venice* (exh. cat., The Queen's Gallery, Buckingham Palace, London, 2017; The Queen's Gallery, Palace of Holyroodhouse, Edinburgh, 2018; National Gallery of Ireland, Dublin, 2018–19), London: Royal Collection Trust, 2017

REDFORD 1996
Redford, Bruce, *Venice & the Grand Tour*, New Haven and London: Yale University Press, 1996

ROBERTSON 1978
Robertson, David Allan, *Sir Charles Eastlake and the Victorian Art World*, Princeton: Princeton University Press, 1978

ROBISON 2014
Robison, Andrew, *La poesia della Luce: disegni veneziani dalla National Gallery di Washington* (exh. cat., Museo Correr, Venice, 2014–15), Venice: Marsilio 2015

ROSAND 2001
Rosand, David, *Myths of Venice: The Figuration of a State*, Chapel Hill: University of North Carolina Press, 2001

ROSSI BORTOLATTO 1974
Rossi Bortolatto, Luigina, *L'opera completa di Francesco Guardi*, Milan: Rizzoli, 1974

RUSSELL 1996
Russell, Francis, 'Guardi and the English tourist', *The Burlington Magazine*, vol. 138, no. 1114 (January 1996), pp. 4–11

SCARPA 2012
Scarpa, Annalisa, ed., *Canaletto à Venise* (exh. cat., Musée Maillol, Paris, 2012–13), Paris: Gallimard, 2012

SCHULZ 2001
Schulz, Juergen, 'Titian at the Fondaco dei Tedeschi', *The Burlington Magazine*, vol. 143, no. 1182 (September 2001), pp. 567–69

SCHUMACHER 2014
Schumacher, Andreas, ed., *Canaletto: Bernardo Bellotto Paints Europe* (exh. cat., Alte Pinakothek, Munich, 2014–15), Munich: Hirmer Verlag, 2014

SHAW 1951
Shaw, J. Byam, *The Drawings of Francesco Guardi*, London: Faber and Faber, 1951

SHAW AND KNOX 1987
Shaw, James Byam, and George Knox, *The Robert Lehman Collection, vol. 6, Italian Eighteenth-Century Drawings*, New York: The Metropolitan Museum of Art, 1987

SIMONSON 1904
Simonson, George, *Francesco Guardi, 1712–1793*, London: Methuen & Co., 1904

SPIELMANN 1900
Spielmann, Marion Harry, *The Wallace Collection in Hertford House*, London: Cassell, 1900

STOCK 1980
Stock, Julien, *Disegni veneti di collezioni inglesi* (exh. cat., Fondazione Giorgio Cini, Venice, 1980), Vicenza: Neri Pozza, 1980

STOURTON AND SEBAG-MONTEFIORE 2012
Stourton, James, and Charles Sebag-Montefiore, *The British as Art Collectors: From the Tudors to the Present*, London: Scala, 2012

SUCCI 1983
Succi, Dario, *Da Carlevarijs ai Tiepolo: Incisori veneti e friulani del Settecento* (exh. cat., Palazzo Attems, Gorizia; Museo Correr, Venice, 1983), Venice: Albrizzi, 1983

SUCCI 2004
Succi, Dario, *Francesco Tironi. Ultimo vedutista del Settecento Veneziano*, Mariano del Friuli: Edizione della Laguna, 2004

SUCCI 2016
Succi, Dario, *Michele Marieschi: Opera Completa*, Treviso: Zel Edizioni, 2016

SUCCI 2021
Succi, Dario, *Francesco Guardi*, 2 vols, Milan: Editoriale Giorgio Mondadori, 2021

SUCCI AND DELNERI 2001A
Succi, Dario, and Annalia Delneri, eds, *Canaletto: Una Venècia Imaginària* (exh. cat., Centre de Cultura Contemporània de Barcelona, 2001), Barcelona: Centre de Cultura Contemporània and Institut d'Edicions de la Diputació de Barcelona, 2001

SUCCI AND DELNERI 2001B
Succi, Dario, and Annalia Delneri, eds, *Canaletto: Una Venècia Imaginària* (exh. cat., Museo Thyssen-Bornemisza, Madrid, 2001), Madrid: Museo Thyssen-Bornemisza, 2001

SUCCI AND DELNERI 2008
Succi, Dario, and Annalia Delneri, eds, *Le Meraviglie di Venezia: Dipinti del '700 in collezioni private* (exh. cat., Palazzo della Torre, Gorizia, 2008), Venice: Marsilio, 2008

SWEET 2012
Sweet, Rosemary, *Cities and the Grand Tour: The British in Italy c. 1690–1820*, Cambridge: Cambridge University Press, 2012

TAMASSIA MAZZAROTTO 1961
Tamassia Mazzarotto, Bianca, *Le Feste Veneziane: i giochi popolari, le cerimonie religiose e di governo*, Florence: Sansoni, 1961

TASSINI 1872
Tassini, Giuseppe, *Curiosità Veneziane*, Venice: Grimaldo, 1872, 2nd edn

TORRINI 2012
Torrini, Annalisa Perissa, *Canaletto: il Quaderno Veneziano*, Venice: Marsilio, 2012

TREVES ET AL. 2021
Treves, Letizia, Lucy Chiswell, Stephen Lloyd and Hannah Williamson, *Bellotto: The Königstein Views Reunited* (exh. cat., National Gallery, London, 2021), London: National Gallery, 2021

VERNIER 1861
Vernier, Valery, 'La galerie de M. le comte de Morny', *L'Artiste*, vol. 12 (1861), pp. 11–13

VIVIAN 1971
Vivian, Frances, *Il console Smith mercante e collezionista*, Vicenza: Neri Pozza, 1971

VOLLE ET AL. 2020
Volle, Nathalie, Béatrice Lauwick, Isabelle Cabillic, Natalie Coural, Laëtitia Desserrières and Gaëlle Pichon-Meunier, *Dictionnaire historique des restaurateurs, Tableaux et oeuvres sur papier, Paris 1750–1950*, Paris: Mare & Martin/Musée du Louvre, 2020

VOSS 1927–28
Voss, Hermann, 'Francesco Tironi. Ein Vergessener venezianischer Vedutenmaler', *Zeitschrift für Bildende Kunst*, vol. 61 (1927–28), pp. 266–70

VOSS 1966
Voss, Hermann, 'Francesco Guardi und Francesco Tironi', *Pantheon*, vol. 24 (1966), pp. 100–4

WAAGEN 1854
Waagen, Gustav, *Treasures of Art in Great Britain*, 3 vols, London: John Murray, 1854

WAAGEN 1857
Waagen, Gustav, *Galleries and Cabinets of Art in Great Britain*, London: John Murray, 1857

WARD-JACKSON 1980
Ward-Jackson, Peter, *Victoria and Albert Museum Catalogue. Italian Drawings, Volume Two: 17th–18th Century*, London: HMSO, 1980

WATSON 1948
Watson, Francis John Bagott, 'Pietro Gradenigo's *Notatori* and *Annali*', *The Burlington Magazine*, vol. 90, no. 544 (July 1948), pp. 187–89

WATSON 1949
Watson, Francis John Bagott, *Canaletto*, London and New York: Paul Elek, 1949

WATSON 1966
Watson, Francis John Bagott, 'The Guardi family of painters', *Journal of the Royal Society for the Encouragement of the Arts, Manufacturers, and Commerce*, vol. 114, no. 5116 (March 1966), pp. 266–89

WATSON 1968
Watson, Francis John Bagott, *Wallace Collection Catalogues, Pictures and Drawings*, London: Wallace Collection, 1968, 16th edn

WHISTLER 2016
Whistler, Catherine, *Baroque & Later Paintings in the Ashmolean Museum*, Oxford: Modern Art Press, 2016

WILSON 2006
Wilson, Bronwen, 'Venice, print and the early modern icon', *Urban History*, vol. 35, no. 1 (2006), pp. 39–64

WILTON AND BIGNAMINI 1996
Wilton, Andrew, and Ilaria Bignamini, eds, *Grand Tour: The Lure of Italy in the Eighteenth Century* (exh. cat., Tate Gallery, London, 1996–97; Palazzo delle esposizione, Rome, 1997), London: Tate Gallery Publishing, 1996

YRIARTE 1878
Yriarte, Charles, *Venise: Histoire, Art, Industrie, La Ville, La Vie*, Paris: J. Rothschild, 1878

ZANETTI 1771
Zanetti, Anton Maria, *Della Pittura Veneziana*, Book V, Venice: Albrizzi, 1771

ACKNOWLEDGEMENTS

This book is the culmination of a multi-year conservation and research project that involved several talented and hard-working individuals to whom I am sincerely indebted. Christoph Vogtherr, formerly Director of the Wallace Collection and currently General Director of the Prussian Palaces and Gardens, Berlin, Germany, initiated the conservation project in early 2016, determined to restore all 27 of the Wallace Collection's *vedute*. Lucy Davis, then Curator of Old Master Paintings and currently Curator of Flemish and British Paintings, Miniatures and Works on Paper, judiciously led the project in its early stages. When the current Director, Xavier Bray, arrived at the museum in late 2016, he embraced the project wholeheartedly and has been committed to its completion ever since.

Upon my arrival at the Wallace Collection in 2017, I began leading the *vedute* conservation project and carried out research on the paintings. I want especially to thank Charles Beddington, who advised on the project and who graciously assisted with questions relating to attribution, dating, provenance and much more. Charles is the foremost expert on Canaletto and I have been extremely fortunate to benefit from his unparalleled knowledge of the artist and his studio. I thank Charles for his substantial and insightful contributions to this book, and for his kindness and good humour throughout.

For the technical findings in this book, I owe special thanks to many talented individuals at the Hamilton Kerr Institute (HKI), with whom we partnered on this project. Special thanks are due to Rupert Featherstone (now retired) for overseeing the project at the HKI and for diligently cleaning a number of the pictures himself. I am grateful also to Mary Kempski for her supervision of students working on the pictures and to Erma Hermens, the HKI's present Director, for ensuring the successful completion of the project. I thank all those at the HKI who restored the paintings with great care, namely Christine Braybrook, Jae Youn Chung, Anna Don, Rowan Frame, Jénnifer González Corujo, Kamila Aleksandra Gora, Molly Hughes-Hallett, Emma Jansson, Sophie Lamb, Joanna Neville, Ellen Nigro, Maria Carolina Peña Mariño, Elisabeth Petrina and Adele Wright. I am also grateful to Sara Harrop for her diligent administration of the project at the HKI.

This project and book would not have been possible without the generous support of several corporations, charities and individuals. Everything was externally funded and to that end I am extremely indebted to the Wallace Collection's talented, hard-working and committed Development Department, especially Sarah Harmer, Marine Farcy, Eva Cappon, Lauren Turner and James Smith.

The project was a collaborative endeavour and there are many others to thank for their generous contributions. At the Wallace Collection these include numerous colleagues, some of whom are now at other institutions. The Collection Care team was often on hand to take down, pack and rehang pictures as they were taken to or returned from the HKI. I thank Jürgen Huber, Stephen Craig, Will Flawn, Jon Slight, David Edge and Rosa Bacile, as well as Curatorial Assistants Isabelle Kent and Natalia Munoz-Rojas, for their assistance. I am grateful to Yuriko Jackall for covering the administration of the project while I was on maternity leave and for supporting me in her then role as Head of the Curatorial Department. Suzanne Higgott provided invaluable advice and assistance with numerous provenance and collection-related queries. I thank Suzanne sincerely for her patience and for her insightful feedback on the second essay in this book. I enjoyed sharing my discoveries about the locations of the paintings within Hertford House with Alan Scollan, whose knowledge of and enthusiasm for the history of the building is infectious. I also thank Melanie Newlands for her unwavering support and careful oversight and Sophie Caie for assisting with the book in the final stages.

Several external colleagues have generously shared their knowledge with me. I am grateful to Irina Artemieva, Edgar Peters Bowron, Grant Lewis, Lynda McLeod and Philip Temple for their assistance. I would also like to say a special thank you to Linda Schofield and Adrian Hunt, and to Beth Holmes, Claire Young and Oliver Craske at Scala, who produced this beautiful book, and to Maria Ranauro for her effective and efficient picture research. Last but not least, I want to thank my family for travelling to Venice with me over the years through these beautiful paintings. Ana, Maia, Emma and Adam, I love you more than I can say.

Lelia Packer

ACKNOWLEDGEMENTS

I am immensely grateful to Xavier Bray for inviting me to contribute to this publication about a group of paintings which has long been of particular interest to me. I gave a talk at the Wallace Collection on the attributional problems posed by its Venetian views as long ago as 2002 and I can say with confidence that I know a lot more about them now than I did then. It is extraordinary that the significance of the 1st Marquess of Hertford as a patron of Canaletto seems to have hitherto gone unnoticed.

My foremost debt is to J.G. Links, who bequeathed to me in 1997 his huge Canaletto archive and library and the mantle of passing judgement on Canaletto attributions. A most wonderful man, he gave excellent advice which was often far from the realms of art, notably, in this context, that one should always be very wary of anybody who claims to know all the answers.

It has been a particular pleasure to collaborate with the remarkable Lelia Packer, who has put an enormous amount of effort into this project and has held the ship on course with a very steady hand.

My thanks to all at Scala and to Maria Ranauro for making this book so beautiful.

Hugo Chapman, Alberto Craievich, Leopold Deliss, Edoardo Roberti and Francis Russell have all given friendship and help in different ways.

Above all I am grateful for the unwavering support of my wife Marina, to whom I owe everything.

Charles Beddington

PICTURE CREDITS

p. 4: iStock/BardoczPeter

pp. 10, 17 (below), 72, 73 (above right and below right): J. Paul Getty Museum, Los Angeles

p. 11: Sala Regia, Apostolic Palace, Vatican City

pp. 12, 13 (above), 29 (above left and right), 41, 62 (both), 76, 81 (both), 83, 85 (both), 87 (above), 97 (below), 98 (below), 106 (below), 141 (below), 166: Royal Collection Trust © His Majesty King Charles III, 2024

p. 14: Ca' Rezzonico, Venice. Photo Scala, Florence

p. 15: Manchester Art Gallery. Photo © Manchester Art Gallery/Bridgeman Images

pp. 16, 80: Gallerie dell'Accademia, Venice. Photo Scala, Florence

p. 17 (above): Museo Nacional del Prado, Madrid. Image © Photo MNP/Scala, Florence

p. 18 (above): Metropolitan Museum of Art, New York. Gift of David and Elizabeth Tunick, 1991

p. 18 (below): Museo Thyssen-Bornemisza, Madrid. Photo Scala, Florence

pp. 19, 49 (above), 87 (below), 102 (both): Rijksmuseum, Amsterdam

pp. 20, 69 (below), 70, 71 (above), 84 (both), 98 (above): Gallerie dell'Accademia, Venice. © G.A.VE – Archivio fotografico – su concessione del Ministero della Cultura

p. 21: Musée du Louvre, Paris. Photo © RMN-Grand Palais (musée du Louvre)/Gérard Blot

p. 22: Kunsthalle, Hamburg. Photo Scala, Florence/bpk, Bildagentur für Kunst, Kultur und Geschichte, Berlin

p. 23: Tate, London. Photo © Tate

p. 24: Ca' Rezzonico, Venice. Cameraphoto/Scala, Florence

pp. 25, 167 (left): Metropolitan Museum of Art, New York. Rogers Fund, 1937

p. 28 (above): Collection of Lord and Lady Hertford, Ragley Hall, Warwickshire. Reproduced with permission of Lord and Lady Hertford

pp. 29 (below), 30, 32, 35, 36 (right): Hertford House Historic Collection, The Wallace Collection, London

p. 33: Architectural Association Inc.

p. 34: Photo © Look and Learn/Bridgeman Images

p. 36 (left): Wallace Collection Archives, London

p. 37: Getty Research Institute, Los Angeles

pp. 40 (below), 53 (below), 75, 90 (below), 106 (above), 132: Collection of the Duke of Bedford, Woburn Abbey

pp. 43, 110 (below): National Gallery of Art, Washington, DC. Wolfgang Ratjen Collection, Paul Mellon Fund

pp. 45, 114: National Gallery, London. Bequeathed by Lord Farnborough, 1838. Photo © The National Gallery, London/Scala, Florence

p. 46: From the Castle Howard Collection. Reproduced by kind permission of the Howard family

p. 48: Palazzo Contarini Fasan, Venice

pp. 49 (below), 127 (below), 161 (right): British Museum, London. © The Trustees of the British Museum

pp. 50 (below), 124 (above): Pinacoteca di Brera, Milan

pp. 51 (above), 124 (below), 154 (above left): Ashmolean Museum, Oxford

pp. 52 (below), 127 (above): Metropolitan Museum of Art, New York. The Elisha Whittelsey Collection, The Elisha Whittlesey Fund, 1961

p. 60 (above and centre): Photographs by Lelia Packer

p. 63: Städel Museum, Frankfurt am Main

p. 64 (above): Museum of Fine Arts, Boston. Abbott Lawrence Fund, Seth K. Sweetser Fund, and Charles Edward French Fund. Photograph © 2024, Museum of Fine Arts, Boston

p. 69 (above): Galleria Nazionale d'Arte Antica, Trieste. Su concessione del MiC – Soprintendenza ABAP del FVG

p. 74: Minneapolis Institute of Art, Bequest of Miss Tessie Jones in memory of Herschel V. Jones

p. 82: Metropolitan Museum of Art, New York. Robert Lehman Collection, 1975

p. 88 (above): Galleria Nazionale d'Arte Antica, Palazzo Corsini, Rome. Photo Scala, Florence

p. 88 (below): Musée Jacquemart-André, Paris. Photo © Photo Josse/Bridgeman Images

p. 89: National Gallery of Victoria, Melbourne. Felton Bequest, 1919

p. 90 (above): Musee Cognacq-Jay, Paris. Bridgeman Images

pp. 95, 156 (below): Birmingham Museum & Art Gallery. Photo by Birmingham Museums Trust, licensed under CC0

p. 101 (above): Tatton Park, Cheshire, UK. National Trust Photographic Library/Bridgeman Images

p. 101 (below): National Gallery, London. Wynn Ellis Bequest, 1876. Photo © The National Gallery, London/Scala, Florence

p. 128: Private Collection

p. 140 (above): Borys Voznytskyi Lviv National Art Gallery, Ukraine

p. 140 (below): Collection Museum Boijmans Van Beuningen, Rotterdam. Loan Stichting Museum Boijmans Van Beuningen, 1940, former collection Koenigs. Photo Studio Tromp

p. 141 (above): Musée du Louvre, Paris. Photo © RMN-Grand Palais (musée du Louvre)/Sylvie Chan-Liat

p. 141 (centre): Kupferstich-Kabinett, Staatliche Kunstsammlungen Dresden. Photo Herbert Boswank

p. 143: Royal Museums of Fine Arts of Belgium, Brussels. Photo J. Geleyns

p. 145 (above): Musée du Louvre, Paris. Photo © RMN-Grand Palais (musée du Louvre)/Michel Urtado

p. 146: Toledo Museum of Art. Purchased with funds from the Libbey Endowment, Gift of Edward Drummond Libbey

p. 147: Norton Simon Museum, Pasadena. The Norton Simon Foundation

p. 148: National Gallery of Art, Washington, DC. Widener Collection

p. 156 (above): Private Collection. Courtesy Simon Dickinson Ltd & Galerie Sanct Lucas

p. 160: Musée des Beaux-Arts de Lyon. Image © Lyon MBA – Photo Martial Couderette

pp. 161 (left), 168: National Gallery, London. Salting Bequest, 1910. Photo © The National Gallery, London/Scala, Florence

p. 163 (left): Alte Pinakothek, Munich. Bayerische Staatsgemäldesammlungen – Alte Pinakothek München

p. 163 (right): Museu Calouste Gulbenkian, Lisbon

p. 169: Yale Center for British Art, Paul Mellon Collection, New Haven, CT

INDEX

First published in 2025 by
Scala Arts & Heritage Publishers Ltd
43 Great Ormond Street
London WC1N 3HZ, UK
www.scalapublishers.com
An imprint of B. T. Batsford Holdings Ltd

In association with
The Wallace Collection
Hertford House
Manchester Square
London W1U 3BN
www.wallacecollection.org

ISBN 978-1-78551-320-6

Project manager and copy editor: Linda Schofield
Designer: Adrian Hunt
Indexer: Nicola King

Printed in China

10 9 8 7 6 5 4 3 2

Scala is represented in UK and Europe by
Abrams & Chronicle Books, 1st Floor, 22–24 Ely Place, London
EC1N 6TE and 57 rue Gaston Tessier, 75166 Paris, France.
www.abramsandchronicle.co.uk
info@abramsandchronicle.co.uk

Note
Throughout the book, C numbers refer to the monograph on
Canaletto by W.G. Constable, first published in 1962.

Front cover: Giovanni Antonio Canal,
Il Canaletto, *The Bacino di San Marco
from the Canale della Giudecca* (cat. 1)

Back cover: Francesco Guardi, *The Grand
Canal with the Rialto Bridge* (cat. 21)

Inside front cover: Giovanni Antonio
Canal, Il Canaletto, *The Grand Canal
from the Palazzo Dolfin-Manin to the
Rialto Bridge* (cat. 5)

Inside back cover: Francesco Guardi, *San
Giorgio Maggiore with the Giudecca and
Le Zitelle* (cat. 19)

Frontispiece: Giovanni Antonio Canal,
Il Canaletto, *The Molo and the Riva degli
Schiavoni, Looking East* (cat. 7)

Pages 8–9: Giovanni Antonio Canal,
Il Canaletto, *The Grand Canal, Looking
South-East along the Fondamenta di
Santa Chiara* (detail) (cat. 6)

Pages 54–55: Giovanni Antonio Canal,
Il Canaletto, *The Molo with Santa Maria
della Salute* (detail) (cat. 8)

Pages 170–71: Francesco Guardi,
Santa Maria della Salute and the Dogana
(detail) (cat. 20)